MW01200135

The Siege of Vicksburg

THE SIEGE OF VICKSBURG

Climax of the Campaign to Open the
Mississippi River, May 23–July 4, 1863

TIMOTHY B. SMITH

7-22-21

To Bryan,

You are in my prayers, Brother!
God Bless,

University Press of Kansas

Published by the University Press of Kansas (Lawrence, Kansas 66045), which was
organized by the Kansas Board of Regents and is operated and funded by Emporia
State University, Fort Hays State University, Kansas State University, Pittsburg State
University, the University of Kansas, and Wichita State University

Library of Congress Cataloging-in-Publication Data

Names: Smith, Timothy B., 1974– author.
Title: The Siege of Vicksburg : climax of the campaign to open the
Mississippi River, May 23–July 4, 1863 / Timothy B. Smith.
Other titles: Climax of the campaign to open the Mississippi River, May 23–July 4, 1863
Description: Lawrence : University Press of Kansas, 2021 |
Series: Modern war studies | Includes bibliographical references and index.
Identifiers: LCCN 2020044314
ISBN 9780700632251 (cloth)
ISBN 9780700632268 (epub)
Subjects: LCSH: Vicksburg (Miss.)—History—Siege, 1863. | Mississippi—History—
Civil War, 1861–1865—Campaigns. | United States—History—Civil War, 1861–1865—
Campaigns. | Strategy—History—19th century.
Classification: LCC E475.27 .S694 2021 | DDC 973.7/344—dc23
LC record available at https://lccn.loc.gov/2020044314.

British Library Cataloguing-in-Publication Data is available.

Printed in the United States of America

10 9 8 7 6 5 4 3 2 1

In memory of my father

CONTENTS

MAPS

ILLUSTRATIONS

Gallery follows page 279.

PREFACE

As informal siege efforts commenced at daylight on May 23, 1863, nothing but impatience, disgust, and irritation existed for almost all connected with the Vicksburg operations. Over and above the terrible loss of life the day before in the Army of the Tennessee's grand assaults on fortress Vicksburg, nothing was going according to plan for anyone.[1]

Lieutenant General John C. Pemberton and his Confederate army inside Vicksburg were perhaps the worst off, despite having just fended off two days of assaults on May 19 and 22. Still, they were shut up inside Vicksburg, with little hope of getting out of the trap by themselves. Pemberton himself was discouraged, but his and the army's morale was growing with their defense. Still, many in the army were completely unhappy with their commander, a Pennsylvania Yankee at that, feeling like it was just a matter of time before they would be sold out, perhaps literally. In the meantime, the army and civilians alike would face increasing shortages of everything from food to military resources to patience.[2]

If Pemberton's situation inside Vicksburg was critical, so also was the only possible relief for him outside the defenses: the small but growing army under General Joseph E. Johnston. But nothing suited him either. Johnston was similarly perturbed that Pemberton had disobeyed his orders (but obeyed President Jefferson Davis's) and withdrew inside Vicksburg. Johnston had ordered him to get out of the trap, but Pemberton would not listen and now was ensnared, and the unwelcome task, and legacy, of relieving Vicksburg now fell on his shoulders.[3]

The feeling was no better in Richmond as a sick and horrified Jefferson Davis watched the events unfold at Vicksburg. Davis was agitated that so many defeats had come about in the previous few days and worried that Johnston might not give his all in trying to save Pemberton and his garrison. The

negative messages from Johnston and continuous calls for more troops did
not help the already negative feelings Davis harbored for him. On top of
that, Davis had personal worries as well. He had immense property holdings
around Vicksburg, and his brother Joseph was somewhere in the midst of all
the confusion.[4]

It would seem that the Federals had a better outlook, but a similar angst
settled on many on the Union side as well. The common soldiers had just been
through a massive assault that had netted nothing but death and destruction.
Some blamed their commanders such as Major Generals Ulysses S. Grant and
William T. Sherman. They, in turn, blamed corps commander Major General
John A. McClernand for the debacle. Despite being in a secure place with Pemberton hemmed in and a sure line of communication and supply, Grant still
worried about a possible breakout and the chance of trouble from the rear.[5]

Grant also had to worry about the mood in Washington. Having just come
off the disaster at Chancellorsville and the inactivity in Tennessee, President
Abraham Lincoln and his administration officials were in no mood for delay,
which is what a siege portended. They let it be known, through army general
in chief Henry Halleck, exactly how impatient they were with operations in
Mississippi. Grant, it seemed, was on a pretty short leash.[6]

Consequently, almost everyone was in some way disgusted as the siege
at Vicksburg began in earnest. Yet, almost everyone realized exactly what
was at stake. "If we can hold Vicksburg I am in hopes this will be the last
year of the war," wrote one Mississippian, "[but] if we lose Vicksburg it
will take a long time for us to gain our independence." Federal determination was as adamant if not more. "We must take this town. There is no other
alternative," wrote one Ohioan. Another Federal argued that "there is one
thing certain . . . the fate of the Rebellion all hangs on the Success or defeat
of our army at Vixburgh." Many tied the campaign's success to the Mississippi River. One Union colonel wrote that "the capture of Vicksburg will open
the Mississippi and strike the death blow to the rebellion." One even argued
Vicksburg's importance compared to that of the Confederate capital: "Richmond is worth scarce the naming compared with Vicksburg." One Ohioan,
Thomas D. White, wrote to his mother that "the capture of Vicksburg and
the opening of the river is of more consequence than the conquering of every
acre of old Va."[7]

If both sides saw the importance of the siege and the fate of the Mississippi River, the trans-Mississippi, and perhaps the Confederacy itself, there
was one looming difference as all embarked on the siege. Almost to a man,

the Federals had vast confidence in their commander on the ground while the Confederates showed no such assurance. "The army looks upon Gen. Grant with all the confidence and veneration that attended Washington," one Federal wrote. "His fame is established, his old canal schemes forgotten, and his position as the first general of the day must be acknowledged." He added: "And if he is not ruined by being transferred to the Army of the Potomac we think he will take us entirely around what is left of the Southern Confederacy by way of Mobile, Savannah & Charleston and take Richmond from the rear before the Grand Army of the Potomac again ventures across the Rappahannock." Another wrote that "the career of Gen Grants army since the 28th of April has bin one of the longest and most brilliant in the history of the war *by far*, and we intend to add one more, and the crowning Star to the already long list of victorys."[8]

Sadly, a Confederate around the same time lamented how "somehow this part of the army is the most unfortunate in its generals. Gen. [Martin L.] Smith, who was in command here until Pemberton came, was the most deficient officer of his rank in the service; and to tell you the truth, I do not believe Pemberton is much better." The fact that both were Northerners by birth may have had something to do with his bias.[9]

While historians have argued over the siege and the larger campaign and its importance in the Civil War, amazingly, that siege has not received its share of attention from historians. And although a few older books such as A. A. Hoehling's *Vicksburg: 47 Days of Siege* have appeared, there has been no major academic work on the siege itself. Most treatment comes in the form of a chapter or two in larger campaign studies. As such, the siege is often portrayed as a whimper at the end of the exciting land campaign leading to Vicksburg. Others have examined various aspects of the operation, such as Mike Ballard on Grant during the siege and Justin Solonick on the Union engineering work during that phase of the campaign. But no stand-alone treatment of the siege itself has ever been written, and because of that there is still a looming gap in Vicksburg historiography that needs to be filled.[10]

The basic argument is not necessarily a new one. Historians from Ed Bearss to Ballard to Terry Winschel have thoroughly covered the importance of Vicksburg. They have studied everything from the encapsulation of Ulysses S. Grant as Lincoln's man to the opening of the Mississippi River, the splitting of the Confederacy, the ending of supplies shipped from the trans-Mississippi, the removal of a large Confederate army from the scene, and the large ramifications of morale and commitment to the Southern cause of independence. Certainly, the larger campaign, brilliant in execution to the point that it is still used by modern military officers as a case study, contributed to all of the above, but it was the climax of the campaign—the siege itself—that put an emphatic exclamation point on the campaign and finally netted all those results. While the siege would not have been possible without the earlier efforts of the campaign, so the earlier gains in the campaign would not have netted much of anything without the final blow brought about by the siege. Often tacked on as a predestined or foregone conclusion, the siege operations in and of themselves have a lot to offer to our understanding of the campaign and war itself in terms of the extent of the operations, the complexity of the strategy and tactics, the grueling nature of the day-by-day participation, and the effect on all involved. Only by understanding the siege in vivid detail, in all its complexities, can we fully understand the larger Vicksburg Campaign itself.[11]

Many people have aided me in writing this book. The staff at the various archives were extremely helpful in my research. The University of Tennessee at Martin, my academic home, provided a generous faculty research grant to perform that research. Several historians read the manuscript for me and provided critical feedback. John Marszalek did his usual wonderful work on the prose and Terry Winschel provided many useful corrections and contextual thoughts in the narrative. The reader for the University Press of Kansas was likewise helpful. The staff at the press, including Joyce Harrison, Kelly Chrisman Jacques, and Mike Kehoe, were all a joy to work with again, and copy editor Jon Howard did his usual wonderful polishing of the manuscript.

My family means more to me than any other earthly possession, and Kelly, Mary Kate, and Leah Grace make life worthwhile. I have dedicated this book to the memory of my dad, who passed away earlier this year. He preached the Gospel of Jesus Christ for fifty years and was my biggest influence. I miss him dearly but am satisfied that he is now enjoying his Heavenly home with my mother, his bride of fifty-seven years.

PROLOGUE
"No Greater Topographical Puzzle"

———

John C. Pemberton and Ulysses S. Grant had never experienced anything like it in their military careers, but then neither had anyone else. Sieges were uncommon events, and these two young military officers were front and center during the first real one in US military history since the famed blockade at Yorktown in 1781. But they were learning from the foremost military figure in America in the nineteenth century, Winfield Scott. The stage was the Mexican War siege of Vera Cruz in 1847, and Pemberton and Grant were ironically on the same side, in fact serving in the same division, Grant as a quartermaster and Pemberton as a staff officer for division commander Major General William J. Worth. They were nevertheless "un-notables"; the generation's "stars" were the engineers, men like Robert E. Lee and George B. McClellan. Still, their participation in this rarity only foreshadowed a much more famous and perhaps higher-stakes siege sixteen years later, when they would not be on the same side. At Vicksburg in 1863, Grant would besiege Pemberton and his Confederates in one of the truly consequential actions of the American Civil War.[1]

Sieges were common since the beginning of recorded history, if not in the lore of the republic. The scriptures frequently told of sieges, and the past was replete with examples from ancient and even more modern times. Yet in 1863 sieges had been an uncommon occurrence in American military history. The most famous example was Washington's victory over the British at Yorktown during the American Revolution, as well as the siege at Vera Cruz many years later. Another example, before Texas joined the nation, was the Alamo, as was, to a certain extent, New Orleans in the War of 1812. Despite having observers in the Crimea to view the most famous example of the siege at Sevastopol, American military authorities had little to go on in terms of historical examples when the Civil War broke out in 1861.[2]

That said, the engineering of siege warfare was taught at the nation's primary military (and engineering) school, West Point. As much as Thomas Jefferson feared a standing army of regulars, he nevertheless wanted an engineering-rich military to help expand the nation. He therefore made sure the curriculum of the United States Military Academy at West Point was filled with engineering studies. All cadets took engineering courses, and the top of the graduating classes became commissioned engineers, illustrating the premium put on that trade. Professors Sylvanus Thayer and Claude Crozet, but most predominantly Dennis Hart Mahan, studied the teachings of the foremost siege expert, Sebastien Le Prestre de Vauban, and taught an entire generation of American military officers how to utilize the principles of engineering, including siege warfare, even if few had ever done it in reality and the forecast was not that much brighter for the future. Mahan even published his Americanized ideas as well as translations, most notably in *A Complete Treatise on Field Fortification* (1836).[3]

As a result, when the Civil War erupted and numerous sieges began, military commanders on both sides dusted off their knowledge learned long ago and did the best they could. Making the unknown worse, sieges did not always fit into neat categories as presented in lectures or on calculation tables issued for guidance. For instance, many "sieges" in the Civil War were really not anything of the kind. In the basic definition, a siege takes place when an army is hemmed in, most of the time by some type of water feature on one side and an enemy army on the other, or completely surrounded by the enemy forces with no way of escape. Mahan described it as "the operation of cutting off all communication with a work, and attacking by regular approaches." Consequently, the "sieges" during the Peninsula Campaign in Virginia in May 1862, at Corinth also in May 1862, Atlanta in August 1864, and even Petersburg in 1864 and 1865 did not meet the strict definition. Smaller examples such as Jackson, Mississippi, in July 1863 and Knoxville, Tennessee, in November 1863 were similar. In fact, in each case, the rear was open and the besieged forces actually withdrew and escaped, presaging more the type of trench warfare common during World War I. When the parameters were a little more in line with the definition, such as at Fort Donelson in February 1862 and Chattanooga in October and November 1863, these were more traditional siege-like events, but for various reasons there was no siege activity such as approaches or parallels. Port Hudson in the summer of 1863 was much closer, but obviously Vicksburg stands as the quintessential siege of the Civil War. It was the highest form of historic siege and, one historian argues, was the climax of Vaubanian siege warfare, the others starting to point ahead to more modern styles.[4]

Because Vicksburg was a traditional siege, it included most of the trappings, terms, and tools of historic siege warfare taught at West Point. The basic idea was to hem in the enemy either by completely surrounding him or using some type of physical barriers such as rivers or seas. Once that was done, the land side was cut off by what was scientifically called a line of circumvallation, which was a fortified line parallel with the enemy's, containing forts and batteries as well as simple trenches termed "rifle pits" in the Civil War. Once the line of circumvallation was in place, and possibly another similar line in the rear termed a line of countervallation to keep out an enemy force seeking to lift the siege, the besieging army would then attempt to move toward the enemy lines of defense. This was done by using trenches called "approaches" or "saps." These approaches were never dug straight ahead, because that would give the enemy the ability to fire down the line of advance. Rather, the approaches were normally dug in zig-zag fashion to protect the men moving through the covered approaches. Also providing cover were periodic parallels dug out perpendicularly from the approach, offering both soldiers with small arms in the trenches as well as artillery in forts the ability to cover those digging farther ahead as well as to pulverize the enemy's fortifications.[5]

Once the approaches reached the enemy lines and parallels emerged right up against the enemy works, and in some cases around salients (called "crowning" a work), the next step was discretionary. A commander could easily fill his closest parallels with troops and assault over the top from point-blank range. Or engineers could mine under the enemy's forts and blow them up with powder. The blast, combined perhaps with an infantry assault at the same time, would hopefully end the siege.[6]

It obviously took a lot of digging before these final-stage options could happen, and on such a large scale it could not be done haphazardly. The work had to be organized, and that required a lot of resources to make all the digging safe and stable even if there was good soil to work with. Three major manufactured items helped siege warfare along immensely, mainly in terms of safety and cover: gabions, fascines, and sap rollers. All had to be

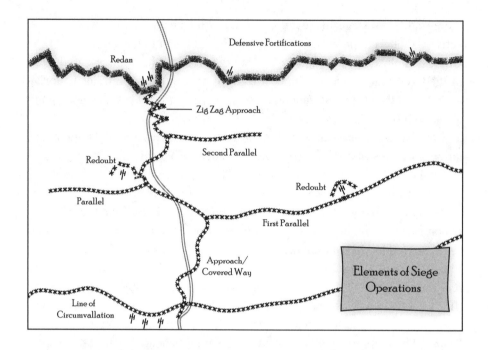

built from whatever raw materials were available in the area, and they were needed in great abundance. Illustrating the raw needs, one Iowan at Vicksburg described how "we are making gabions at the rate of 40 a day." Engineer Stewart R. Tresilian of Major General John A. Logan's Union division later noted the requirements of his division alone: his pioneers "obtained and used 370 wagon loads of lumber, built three magazines, put in platforms for all the heavy batteries, made 1,200 fascines, 650 gabions, 4 sap rollers, and kept in repair all the broken trails and gun-carriages of the division."[7]

Gabions were the staple of earthen fortifications. They were hollow, round, "basket like cylinders" with no top or bottom, used to shore up walls or trenches or build ramparts. When stacked atop each other and filled with dirt, gabions became a formidable wall that would not cave in. A Minnesota artilleryman gave a good explanation of gabions, describing them as "made of stakes, with grapevines, young cane or flexible bushes woven through them, so as to form a hollow cylinder something like a large willow basket without the bottom, only much longer. The stakes are left projecting at one end some distance beyond the wicker work, and when the gabion is put in its place these projecting ends are driven into the ground and the gabion is filled with dirt."

He also described the situation upon their arrival and the solution: "When we first came into the work the embrasures were not lined with gabions, and the consequence was that in one day's firing we blew out the embrasures so wide that a two horse wagon could have been driven through one of them." Of course, material had to be found close by to make gabions, mostly substances for weaving through stakes to make the walls of the cylinder. Engineers first experimented with the native vines in the area but found they were too large and "inconveniently heavy," making the prepared gabions impossible to use. Captain Henry C. Freeman, through experimentation with cane, found that "crushing the joints with a mallet" would break the cane into long strips, which proved perfect for the wicker work. The abundance of cane made this a perfect solution, the very light cane being easily woven between the stakes but the whole being very strong, "a good and very neat gabion." Cave-ins still resulted, and when the gabion production could not keep up with demand, the Federals shored up their approaches with everything from cotton bales to empty barrels filled with dirt. But it was the gabion that held the army's fortifications together, especially "when better work was required."[8]

A second staple of earthen engineering was the fascine, long bundles of sticks wound together to make walls or revetments. The same Minnesota artilleryman gave a good description of them: "Bundles of canes 15 feet long and a foot through, and tied around with wire from the Rebel telegraph line. These fascines are laid, one on top of the other, and each one is fastened down securely with stakes driven through it and through the ones below into the ground. The fascines are to prevent the earth from falling down into the fort, which the concussion of the guns would soon make it do if unsupported." Engineer Frederick E. Prime explained that "cane was largely used, it being found in abundance and making excellent and light work."[9]

Perhaps the most important tool for the digging and particularly advancing Federals was the sap roller, or what Federals called a "bullet-stopper." It was a large cylinder similar in form to a gabion but much bigger. The idea was to push the sap roller in front of working parties so that they would be covered as they dug toward the enemy fortifications. Consequently, sap rollers had to be much larger and "impervious to Minie balls," but at the same time they had to be movable, at least by rolling, even on the rough terrain around Vicksburg. Lieutenant Peter Hains of the XIII Corps developed a way to make a hollow sap roller by placing two barrels end to end and weaving cane around gabions set against the barrels. Thus, these sap rollers had a hollow middle but gabions to stop bullets. This formula produced light and easily usable sap rollers, although many other variations existed as well.[10]

Thousands of gabions and fascines and a score or more of larger sap rollers were needed. "The 'pioneers' of the corps were at once sent to the cane-brakes, swamps, and lowlands in the rear," noted engineer Andrew Hickenlooper. Fortunately, ample cane was available, and many men quickly became proficient at creating these staples of siege engineering. In most cases, the various pioneer companies were tasked with creating them, although others joined in frequently too. "Men who had never heard of a gabion or fascine . . . were taught in an hour to make them acceptably of cane and grapevines," noted one Federal.[11]

The Union engineering effort at Vicksburg was made easier by the thin and loose but very stable loess soil found in the area. Federal chief engineer Frederick Prime described it as "fine soil, which, when cut vertically, will remain so for years." Engineer Hickenlooper explained that it "consisted of a peculiarly tenacious clay, easily cut, self supporting, and not in the least affected by exposure to the atmosphere, thus rendering bracing and sheathing unnecessary." The Federals—and Confederate workers earlier, for that matter—thus found the soil easy to work and stable when dug, requiring little if any shoring up of vertical walls even when wet. Thus, less stabilization was needed than normal, although interference such as cannon blasts, marching feet, rain, and explosions could indeed upset the stable earth at times, when it was best to utilize the standard old forms of siege warfare that had been performed for centuries.[12]

Engineers to oversee these specialized operations were obviously in high premium. Although skilled training was not required in all military activity, both sides needed expert engineers. Added to the tougher scientific equation was the geography over which the Vicksburg operations took place, Federal chief engineer Prime describing the area as "an intricate net-work of ravines and ridges, the latter everywhere sharp, and the former only having level bottoms when their streams become of some size. . . . [T]he sides of the smaller and newer ravines were often so steep that their ascent was difficult to a footman unless he aided himself with his hands." No one would want to trust their lives to infrastructure that uneducated builders had constructed or to surgical procedures that uneducated practitioners performed. The same prevailed in siege warfare.[13]

The Confederate fortifications defending Vicksburg were a case in point.

Had they been erected and maintained by novices, they certainly would have lacked some of the defensive stoutness displayed in the assaults on May 19 and 22 and later during the siege itself. Had they been constructed on the wrong ridgelines, with unacceptable angles, too low or too narrow parapets, or of inadequate amounts or types of material, they would have been much weaker and perhaps fatally flawed.[14]

The task of building Vicksburg's defenses fell to Captain Samuel H. Lockett, West Point class of 1859. He had entered the military academy from his native state of Alabama. Lockett was smart, quick, and talented, as evidenced by his graduating second in his class and subsequent admission into the vaunted engineers. He nevertheless soon left the army that had trained him and joined the Confederacy when his native Alabama seceded. Lockett easily obtained a commission as a much-needed engineer and soon found himself on several high-ranking generals' staffs, most notably Braxton Bragg's, where he played a major role in the Battle of Shiloh. With Vicksburg's need for defenses in the summer of 1862, as exemplified by the Union arrival there that summer, Bragg sent Lockett to the river city on June 20. There he reported to Vicksburg's commander, Major General Martin L. Smith. Smith was ecstatic, labeling Lockett as "the accomplished engineer officer." He added: "I have to speak in terms of unqualified praise, both as regards skill in his profession and qualities as a soldier. The services of such an officer are so important and indispensable as to have all the effect of a positive increase of force in determining the issue of a contest." Lockett also quickly came to love Vicksburg's beauty, writing to his wife that "no point on the river is more picturesque than Vicksburg."[15]

The Confederate fortifications that would in 1863 be the main defenses holding the enemy out of the city actually emerged in the fall of 1862. "It became my duty to plan, locate, and lay out that line of defense," Lockett explained, and he began to analyze the area surrounding the city and quickly saw it was going to be a herculean task just to find the best places for the fortifications. "A month was spent in reconnoitering, surveying, and studying the complicated and irregular site to be fortified," he reported, adding that "no greater topographical puzzle was ever presented to an engineer." As he tramped across the heavily wooded landscape, traversing huge ravines and ridges, he surmised that "at first it seemed impossible to find anything like a general line of commanding ground surrounding the city; but careful study gradually worked out the problem."[16]

Lockett eventually built a series of fortifications that, once erected, were strong but in the ensuing months of disuse soon became ragged and washed, with erosion and other factors making them less than satisfactory. Lockett himself admitted how "not having been occupied they [the major earthworks] were now much washed and weakened by the winter's rains. The rifle pits connecting the main works had suffered in the same way, while on many parts of the line these pits had never been finished." In fact, when the Confederate army finally inhabited them in mid-May, many complaints emerged about their condition. Missourian Theodore Fisher noted that "the fortifications of Vicksburg are not as good as we expected to find them, though [we] are confident we can hold the place. The natural fortifications are very strong, but our engineers have not improved them as much as they should have done." A Mississippian similarly described his section of the works as "a very inferior ditch about four feet wide and as many deep." With plenty of labor, the earthworks soon became much stronger, becoming as good as when they were first erected and in many places even better with additional work being performed.[17]

Lockett's fortifications defending Vicksburg against siege operations consisted of three general types of works. One, the most important, were the large forts. Nine of them existed on the seven- or eight-mile line of defense, all but one on a major road or thoroughfare. For instance, Fort Hill on the extreme Confederate left flank on the Mississippi River commanded the Valley Road as it entered the city from the north. It also kept a menacing eye on the river itself, although it contained no heavy artillery as it was too high up the bluffs to depress the cannons. On the Graveyard Road sat the Stockade Redan, while farther along the lines at the Jackson Road entrance to the city lay two major forts, the 3rd Louisiana Redan (known to the Federals as "Fort Hill") and the Great Redoubt (known as the "Black Fort"). The 2nd Texas Lunette and the Railroad Redoubt (known as "Fort Pulaski" and "Fort Beauregard," respectively) covered the parallel Baldwin's Ferry Road and the Southern Railroad of Mississippi farther south, while the Salient Work on the Hall's Ferry Road and South Fort on the Warrenton Road on the extreme right flank covered those routes into Vicksburg. Only Square Fort between the Railroad Redoubt and the Salient Work did not sit on a road, but it did command a major angle in the works.[18]

These massive forts, with differing technical terms such as "lunettes," "redans," and "redoubts," stood high and tall along these roadways, blocking any easy entrance into the city. Built to mammoth proportions by Lockett, they were often ten or fifteen feet high and just as thick, with most having deep and wide ditches fronting them. Artillery and infantry manning them made these forts almost impossible to assault, although these very forts were mainly the focus of the Federal attacks on May 19 and 22, most notably those in the center along the main roads leading westward into the city. The Stockade Redan, 3rd Louisiana Redan, Great Redoubt, 2nd Texas Lunette, and Railroad Redoubt received the majority of the assaults on those days, and in large part because of the strength of these forts they held strong.[19]

A secondary level of fortifications consisted of actual forts, but not as large as the nine major ones. These sat on the lines between the major forts and covered ravines, hollows, or salients that could easily be utilized by an advancing enemy. Often having artillery embrasures for added firepower, these smaller and more numerous fortifications were substantial in themselves. They helped strengthen the entire line along the vast reaches between the major forts.[20]

Finally, the areas between the major and minor forts in most places contained simple trenches or rifle pits, one engineer describing them originally as "4 feet wide by 3 feet deep." These consisted of one line of works that included a parapet eventually high enough to cover a standing man, often with a headlog above to allow defenders to fire without exposing too much of themselves over the top. These at times could also contain embrasures for artillery or bombproofs, and few were like any other, the Confederates adapting them to the needs of any given position. Unfortunately, as late as the assaults on May 19 and 22, some stretches of the Confederate line did not even have these simple trenches, most notably around Glass Bayou on Brigadier General Louis Herbert's front and at Stout's Bayou on the south end of the line.[21]

Lockett had created the fortifications according to the accepted method taught by Vauban and Mahan, but unfortunately there were a couple of issues that by 1863 dated that method. One did not take into consideration the differing types of soil, and the fine Vicksburg loess, easy for digging, was also easily penetrable with cannon fire, making the fortifications that much weaker and that much easier to tear down with artillery. Second, the old method had been created before the more powerful rifled artillery emerged. Still, smoothbore cannons did a lot of damage to the works too.[22]

These fortifications nevertheless stood in the way of the besieging Federals, and they were well-nigh impregnable to assault, as Grant found out on May 19 and 22. That is why he turned to siege operations, although he quickly found that the Confederate fortifications were resilient against approaches as well, although it took an inordinate amount of work to keep them strong. The main extent of Lockett's engineering work after the siege began was to repair earthworks damaged by Union fire, to build additional support fortifications such as traverses and covered ways (the need for which became evident only during the siege itself), and some counter-building and counter-mining to combat Union efforts. Otherwise, Lockett's work had mainly been done beforehand—and he had done his job well. These fortifications and their attendant terrain and Confederate defenders repelled two assaults and held well during the siege itself.[23]

To take down these formidable Confederate defenses, Grant primarily depended on his West Point–trained engineers utilizing the age-old methods of Vaubanian siege warfare. The army's chief engineer, Captain Frederick E. Prime (West Point class of 1850), as well as Grant's staff engineer Lieutenant Colonel James H. Wilson, and later Captain Cyrus B. Comstock, who arrived during the siege (June 15) and took over for the ill Prime, all worked to make sure the engineering efforts went forward quickly. Fortunately, all the other West Point graduates had training in engineering as well and lent their considerable knowledge to the effort too, even though that was not their primary duty. Grant, in fact, ordered that "all officers who had graduated at West Point, where they had necessarily to study military engineering, should in addition to their other duties assist in the work." Grant acknowledged how "practical experience was gained and would enable any division of this army hereafter to conduct a siege with considerable skill in the absence of regular engineer officers." Prime agreed, writing that "officers and men had to learn to be engineers while the siege was going on." The navy helped as well. Amid the lack of a full compliment of engineers, Grant asked Rear Admiral David Dixon Porter, "have you an engineer Officer or two you can spare for a few days? I am much in need of such Officers." Porter responded by sending three men "who, I think are good and competent engineers." He only asked that Grant provide everything they needed as he was sending them without any equipment whatsoever "save their necessary instruments." Grant agreed and sent them down to the southern end of the line, telling commanders there to provide "horses, men and subsistence." Porter especially recommended one in particular "in case you should want any blowing up of the works done " as that engineer "has been engaged in that kind of business for some years, and that is his duty in the Squadron."[24]

Normally, anyone would want to do things by the book, especially when these young cadets now commanding great armies had been taught by the great Mahan and others, but reality did not always allow it, especially so at Vicksburg. Grant faced multiple issues in besieging the city. He had a shortage of engineers, did not have correct resources to do the job, and confronted awful terrain on which to do it. As a result, the siege operations at Vicksburg had to be modified from the book, and adaptation and improvisation were essential if they were to do the best with what they had. Conversely, inside the works, there were no manuals on how to survive against a siege, either for military forces or civilians trapped inside surrounded cities.[25]

The resulting story of that improvisation and defense against it is fascinating.

1

"The Great Problem"

Before May 17

Ulysses S. Grant was in uncharted territory. He had been around: studied at West Point, fought in Mexico, served in the army in the West. He was as well traveled as most any other army officer, and more so than most other Americans. But what he saw here at what was described as the "world renown city of Vicksburg" was unlike anything he had ever run up against militarily. "I am very well but much perplexed," he wrote to his wife, Julia, in early 1863 amid the torturous ambling to reach and capture Vicksburg, but it was just not happening—reaching much less capturing. "Heretofore I have had nothing to do but fight the enemy. This time I have to overcome obstacles to reach him," he grumbled.[1]

For many long months, Federal operations against Vicksburg had moved forward only to be repulsed, turned away, or abandoned. Union generals and naval officers had tried their best to crack this tough nut of Vicksburg in active operations for many of those months, many directed by the commander who would become the North's premier general, Ulysses S. Grant. Even Abraham Lincoln pushed for success at Vicksburg, including his famous statement that "Vicksburg is the key . . . the war can never be brought to a close until that key is in our pocket." That nothing ever succeeded was not so much a reflection on Grant or the many thousands of soldiers he led, or on the naval forces, or even Lincoln, but more of an indication of just how defensible Vicksburg really was.[2]

Set atop three-hundred-foot-high bluffs overlooking the Mississippi River at a hairpin turn in the "Father of Waters," Vicksburg was a naturally difficult area to reach, especially so in wartime when defenses blocked all reasonable

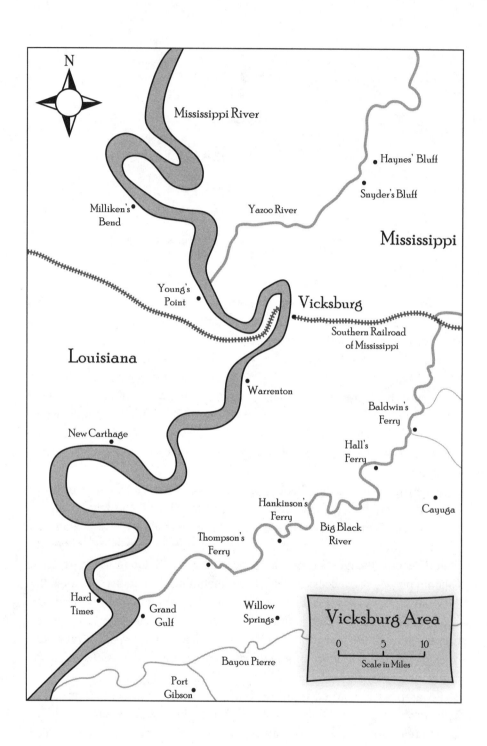

N

Mississippi River

Haynes' Bluff

Snyder's Bluff

Milliken's
Bend

Yazoo River

Mississippi

Young's
Point

Vicksburg

Southern Railroad
of Mississippi

Louisiana

Warrenton

Baldwin's
Ferry

New Carthage

Hall's
Ferry

Hankinson's
Ferry

Cayuga

Big Black
River

Thompson's
Ferry

Hard
Times

Grand
Gulf

Willow
Springs

Vicksburg Area

0   5   10

Scale in Miles

Bayou Pierre

Port
Gibson

paths. The mighty river was indeed blocked, although one Confederate admitted it was "not as grand a stream as I expected to see but nevertheless tis the noblest stream I ever saw." But it had not always been so defended. The easiest way throughout human history to reach the Vicksburg bluffs was by the river so long as the visitor had some type of floating vessel to utilize. One Indianan now waging war against the city could not help but connect with the past, speaking of "the mighty river on which De Soto, Hennepin, and La Crosse had gazed with glad surprise." Indeed, before the war, Vicksburg welcomed hordes of boats and travelers by river, they bringing with them business for the city's hotels, restaurants, banks, and other establishments. These same boats also took away from Vicksburg its chief trade commodity: cotton. Long the major port in Mississippi, Vicksburg was the chief trade center of the state in antebellum times and even after the war as well.[3]

An equally important way to reach Vicksburg emerged in the late 1850s as railroads began to appear all over the South. In this case, it was the Southern Railroad of Mississippi that ran westward from Meridian through the state capital at Jackson and on to its terminus on the river at Vicksburg. During its time in operation before the war, the railroad had become one of the major lines in the state, the only one in fact that ran the breadth of the entire state within Mississippi's boundaries. As such, it carried an immense amount of people and supplies. That it crossed two north-south trunk lines at Meridian and Jackson also added to its importance, as did the link with the river itself at Vicksburg, the only one in the state. Unfortunately, by the time war came to Mississippi, the line was in terrible shape. One of Lieutenant General John C. Pemberton's staff officers, Robert W. Memminger, described it as "in a miserable and even dangerous condition. Accidents occurred almost daily, engines being broken up, and there being a lamentable scarcity of any species of cars."[4]

Obviously, there were also overland routes leading into and out of Vicksburg, offering regular travel by wagon or horse. In all, some six different roads ran like spokes out from the city center, although it was only half a wheel, as the Mississippi River blocked any roads running in westward directions. These roads, while useful, were nevertheless not in any way improved or macadamized as in larger cities back east, but they nevertheless provided an adequate transportation system in and out of the city.[5]

While Vicksburg was comparatively easy to access in peacetime, such was not the case in war. Trying to move large bodies of men in armies with their wagons, cannons, and supplies was quite a different proposition. Accordingly, a few fortifications placed at important positions could delay and even block many of these routes, making first the task of even approaching Vicksburg monumental, and then, second, the hope of actually capturing the city even more problematic. Heavy artillery batteries positioned along Vicksburg's waterfront and the river both north and south of the city blocked most travel on the river itself, especially for unarmed merchant vessels or transports. Earthen fortifications to the north along the Walnut Hills near the path of the Yazoo River blocked any land advance from the north out of the vast Mississippi Delta. The Big Black River to the south and east blocked advance from those directions, it being unfordable most of the time and crossable only at ferries, which the Confederates were well aware of and blocked with additional fortifications.[6]

As a result, Vicksburg lay inside a cocoon of safety, shielded by the Mississippi River to the west, the Delta to the north, and the Big Black River to the east and south. One or more of these major water features would have to be breached, tamed, or conquered for Union forces to even approach Vicksburg, and that did not even factor in the actual capture of the city, which was itself ringed with fortifications along the half-circle to the north, east, and south, especially on each major thoroughfare's entrance into the city. In actuality, just reaching Vicksburg was problematic enough, but then taking it would prove just as difficult.[7]

That was the long, hard lesson Federal commanders learned through ten difficult months of just trying to reach the city. Worrying about how to actually capture it would be a concern for another day.

Despite some arming of the Vicksburg bluffs as early as January 1861 and a few shots at a passing steamer, the first organized Federals to lay eyes on the Confederate citadel of Vicksburg were naval personnel. Because the Mississippi River had played, and still was playing, such a huge role in American history and now military affairs out west, the great river provided the quickest, easiest, and safest route of travel for Union gunboats and their following transports and supply vessels. In fact, because of the geography and terrain of the Mississippi Valley, the first approach toward Vicksburg by river was relatively easy and uncomplicated.[8]

Naval assets from both upriver and downriver first reached the Vicksburg vicinity around the same time, in the summer of 1862. From the north, Flag

Officers Andrew H. Foote and Charles Davis led the famed City-class iron-clads as well as others converted to that service in the first wave of Federals penetrating southward. The ironclads fought and maneuvered their way southward along the Kentucky, Tennessee, Missouri, and Arkansas shorelines, meeting resistance in the form of earthen fortifications at such areas as Columbus, Kentucky, Island No. 10, and the various fortifications that Tennessee governor Isham G. Harris had established in his state, most famously Fort Pillow. None of these ever gave any real threat, however, not to anyone's great surprise. Confederate general P. G. T. Beauregard in fact wrote that they would be "but temporary barriers to the enemy's gunboats and great resources." Meanwhile, the big events were happening to the east in the Tennessee Valley, where Ulysses S. Grant's army, eventually reinforced by others, turned these positions and made them untenable. The cost of this success was staggering, of course, including heavy casualties at Fort Donelson and especially Shiloh. The eventual capture of Corinth, Mississippi—the goal of the entire operation on the Tennessee River—outflanked Memphis while the Union navy took possession of the city in early June 1862, clearing the river path to Vicksburg from the north.[9]

The other major Confederate tool of resistance besides earthen fortifications was a paltry navy on the river, and it came out to fight at various times, such as at the surprise at Plum Point Bend and then again at Memphis, where much of it was destroyed on June 6. The Confederacy had never had a thriving shipbuilding operation of note that produced huge results, and the effect was the Confederate high command's dependence on fixed earthen and masonry fortifications, which could be, and were, easily turned by these flanking land armies.[10]

The operations on the northern stretches of the Mississippi River and the capture of Memphis were turning points in the Union river advance from the north. Once Memphis fell, it was the last position on the Mississippi River that sat on high ground until many miles southward, where another line of hills butted up against the river: the Walnut Hills or, as one Federal argued, they should be named "Poplar Hills . . . as the principal timber is poplar." Thus, because of the existence of the wide Mississippi Delta, extending at points a hundred miles inland, no advantageous high ground existed between Memphis and Vicksburg on which Confederates could make a stand. Beauregard said as much, writing an engineer that "there are no points sufficiently high on the river between Memphis and Vicksburg which could be fortified for the defense of the Mississippi." As a result, the Federal navy had easy going southward all the way to the Vicksburg vicinity. That said, it was one thing to get near the high ground on which Vicksburg sat, but it was altogether another to actually get troops on that high ground to approach the place, not to mention actually taking it.[11]

But the northern advance was not all there was. Federals from the south also approached Vicksburg by midsummer. Flag Officer David G. Farragut had entered the river at its mouth with his oceangoing vessels, including his flagship USS *Hartford*, but like those from the north he soon faced Confederates blocking the way with land fortifications. This time it was masonry forts built decades earlier, after the War of 1812 and the obvious success of fortifications such as at Fort McHenry in Baltimore Harbor. Forts Jackson and Saint Philip sat on either side of the river miles below New Orleans, but after heavy bombardment that seemed to do little damage, Farragut decided to take his chances and run the batteries. "I witnessed this daring exploit," Major General Benjamin Butler wrote, "from a point about 800 yards from Fort Jackson and unwittingly under its fire, and the sublimity of the scene can never be exceeded." Farragut passed the forts in late April, and the result, much like when the Federals broke through at Memphis to the north, was that Farragut entered an empty shell. The Confederates had manned the outer defense, but once Farragut passed that, there was little to nothing to block his way thereafter, even though there was defensible high ground at many places along the southern stretch of the river.[12]

Accordingly, Farragut and eventually an infantry contingent under Brigadier General Thomas Williams moved northward, picking off Confederate river city after river city. First, New Orleans surrendered on April 25, Confederate commander Major General Mansfield Lovell wisely evacuating both to get his meager amount of troops out as well as to spare the city the destruction of a bombardment and assault. Then the Federals moved onward, capturing Baton Rouge on May 12, acquiring the state capital of Louisiana. Next came Natchez, Mississippi. Finally, by mid-May and then fully in June 1862, Farragut was knocking on Vicksburg's door, running what defensive batteries there were at Vicksburg at the time and taking station north of the city with Davis's flotilla. It was still a tough passage, one Louisianan declaring that Farragut found "Jordan a rough road to travel."[13]

Matters bogged down as the Federals found it was one thing to concentrate rapidly in the vicinity of Vicksburg by river, but quite another to actually begin operations against the city itself. Even with naval forces bombarding

Vicksburg and infantry units accompanying them looking for any opportunity to land and capture the place, it soon became apparent that it was not going to happen any time soon. Farragut himself reported that "the forts can be passed and we have done it, and can do it again as often as may be required of us. It will not, however, be an easy matter for us to do more than silence the batteries for a time, as long as the enemy has a large force behind the hills to prevent our landing and holding the place." After a call for Vicksburg to surrender that produced a tart response from one Confederate officer—"Mississippians don't know, and refuse to learn, how to surrender to an enemy"—Williams rightly realized that it would take far more troops than he had at the time to maneuver to a point where they could gain the high and dry ground east of Vicksburg, which was the only direction from which the city could be reasonably approached. He therefore merely put his emphasis on digging a canal across the base of the hairpin turn, making a vain effort to divert the river's course so that it would bypass Vicksburg. Farragut likewise realized that he could do no more and requested permission to return southward to the Gulf of Mexico, where his blue-water vessels would be of much more service. It was granted.[14]

The result was the first attempt to approach Vicksburg, in mid-1862 no less, but nothing came of it besides a heavy bombardment that one excited Louisianan described as "the greatest Bombardment . . . recorded in history for the length of time it lasted." He related that it was rough but "only killed five or six of our men, one Lady and one mule." Farragut and his infantry support returned southward while the ironclads (eventually under a new admiral on the river, David Dixon Porter) remained north of Vicksburg, occupying the river all the way to the city's environs. The Union failure in 1862 was obvious, but it was only the first of several major thrusts that would attempt to gain a position to capture Vicksburg. If there was a valuable lesson in this lack of success, it was that the Federals could easily use the river as their supply and staging area, and they would continue to hold on to this lifeline for the remainder of the campaign and even thereafter.[15]

The fall of New Orleans and the breaking of the Confederate defense line at Forts Jackson and Saint Philip caused a wave of concern over the Confederacy. New Orleans was the South's largest city, a haven of culture, and the chief financial center of the new nation. Its loss was devastating, and how it was done was perhaps even more so. Barely a shot was fired in anger over the city, the fight for possession having been made at the river forts far below. When the Federals arrived, in fact, Confederate commander Mansfield Lovell had evacuated his post without a fight, allowing the civilian government of the city to do the surrendering. "To this demand [for surrender]," Lovell wrote, "I returned an unqualified refusal, declaring that I would not surrender the city or any portion of my command." But then he added, "Feeling unwilling to subject the city to bombardment, and recognizing the utter impossibility of removing the women and children, I should withdraw my troops and turn it over to the civil authorities." Perhaps, many thought, there should at least have been a fight put forward for such a grand prize.[16]

There was no fight, however, and pitifully few defenses. In fact, there was initially nothing to halt the Federal push north of New Orleans really until Corinth, where P. G. T. Beauregard was holding out against forces from the north. Obviously, a defensive line facing both directions was not feasible, so a Confederate stand had to be made farther south, and the best locale was along the most able transportation artery running east and west. The Southern Railroad of Mississippi running from Meridian to Vicksburg and through Jackson was the next best line to hold for forces falling back northward from the heavy incursions from the south; it was ironically also the next best line to hold for Confederates falling back southward from Federal incursions from the north. One Confederate told Beauregard that fortifying Vicksburg was "for the double purpose of protecting the river and giving you a *point-d'appui* for the left of your line in case you are compelled to occupy a position in rear of your present one." Eventually, as all could see, the war in Mississippi would wind up around the Meridian–Jackson–Vicksburg line, with Vicksburg rising to be the linchpin.[17]

Realization of the geography sent a flurry of activity throughout Mississippi, one Confederate noting that "the occupation of Vicksburg was the immediate result of the fall of New Orleans." Lovell fell back with his meager forces (most of his original troops had earlier been shipped north to participate in the Shiloh concentration) to the Jackson–Vicksburg line, leaving everything between New Orleans and Jackson on the railroad largely defenseless and everything between New Orleans and Vicksburg on the river the same way. The Confederacy north of Forts Jackson and Saint Philip, as Grant had found when he punctured the eggshell of defense to the north at Forts Henry and Donelson, was hollow and defenseless once past the initial outer crust.[18]

This Vicksburg defense obviously had to be established even as Beauregard was holding out at Corinth. Now in command since General Albert Sidney Johnston perished instead of conquered at Shiloh and went to a grave in the soon-to-be-occupied New Orleans, Beauregard ordered defenses along the lower line, particularly at Vicksburg. "If at all fortified," Lovell informed Beauregard, "[Vicksburg] will be able (with the troops I shall send there), to hold its own against any force they will be likely to send for some time to come." A few heavy artillery batteries soon went up along the river itself at Vicksburg; Confederate engineers "proceeded at once to prepare for the approach of the enemy, then known to have passed Baton Rouge with a formidable fleet, having in view to open the river." It was enough to concern but not stop the Federal vessels, as Farragut showed by passing them easily. The land defense was more problematic. One Confederate described how the few troops available were mainly "disposed for disputing inch by inch the approach by land." Still, the meager defenses were concerning enough, along with the paltry infantry forces there as well as a new commander, Major General Earl Van Dorn, to cause the Federals to turn away and decide to come back later, with more help next time.[19]

Knowing they would indeed come again, real fortification of Vicksburg then began, with Beauregard sending the competent engineer Samuel H. Lockett to the area to lay out the fortifications. They were "pushed forward night and day with all possible vigor," one Confederate wrote, and put "us in a condition to dispute with a fair prospect of success a farther advance." Lockett toiled throughout the fall season to lay out the fortifications and then build them. Eventually, these defenses around Vicksburg consisted of four cordons. One consisted of the river batteries, which were strengthened and added to, eventually making truly formidable batteries both above and below the city and along the Vicksburg waterfront. These heavy guns, while they might not stop any passage if it was conducted right, could nevertheless discourage such activity and would certainly be heard from in any event. As an additional advantage, they obviously discouraged any Federal advance or assault from the west along Vicksburg's river-facing front, which was in actuality such a monstrous gamble that it was never even considered.[20]

The Achilles' heel of stationary river defenses—as illustrated perfectly earlier in the actions at Columbus, Island, No. 10, and most definitely at Fort Donelson—was their ability to be turned by a land force. Accordingly, Lockett also laid out a second cordon of defenses outside the actual riverside gun emplacements at Vicksburg. The Walnut Hills extended above the city, although they angled to the northeast with the beginning of the Yazoo River and Delta just north of Vicksburg. To keep Federals from landing troops to the north or south of the city, Lockett built fortifications southward toward Warrenton and northward along the hills to Snyder's and Haynes' Bluffs that butted against the Yazoo River, where heavy artillery also stopped any travel on that waterway. Essentially, these fortifications shielded Vicksburg far below the city as well as, more important, above it, the direction that most thought would be the main threat. Lockett's defenses stopped Yazoo River traffic with the big guns and shielded the approaches to Vicksburg and the high ground east of the city between the Mississippi and the big guns along the Yazoo.[21]

Eventually, lesser works—the third cordon—emerged to the east along the Big Black River, shielding the crossing points, although these were less durable than the others, constructed somewhat as an afterthought. Still, various fords and ferries such as Hankinson's, Baldwin's, and Hall's south of the railroad and Bridgeport and Messenger's to the north received some fortification, while the major position to be fortified was along the railroad and the Jackson Road crossing of the Big Black River just west of Edwards Station.[22]

If all that was not enough, Lockett also oversaw a fourth, inner cordon of defenses that would be literally the last ditch. If the river defenses, the outer works along the Delta and Yazoo River, and the Big Black River defenses were not able to keep the Federals from approaching Vicksburg, then an inner line of fortifications would stop them from entering the city itself. Eventually, an eight-mile-long system of fortifications established a ring around the northern, eastern, and southern sectors of the city, the Mississippi River shielding everything else to the west. Lockett took advantage of the rough terrain in doing so, one Confederate writing, "why it is just one hill piled up against another." If the Federals were able to penetrate through the outer layers and approaches to the city, these works would stop them closer in, with heavy redans, redoubts, and lunettes on the major roads and railroad coming into the city. This would be where the Confederates would make their last stand and hopefully defeat the all-out Federal attempt to capture Confederate Vicksburg.[23]

While the summer and fall of 1862 was one of major defense establishment for the Confederates, it was also one of the most chaotic periods in all the war for the Federals. Commanders frequently switched positions, including western commanders Major Generals Henry W. Halleck moving to Washington and John Pope to Virginia. Newer officers rose to the top in the West, including Major General Nathaniel Banks and of course Ulysses S. Grant, who retained his basic district command when Halleck left and became a department commander comparable to Halleck only in October. Confederate invasions of Northern territory across the board in Maryland and Kentucky and an abortive invasion in West Tennessee only added to the chaos, with Halleck realizing he could not oversee it all from Washington and loosening up on his subordinates such as Grant, giving him full departmental command. Grant took quick advantage. "This was a great relief," he later wrote, "after the two and a half months of continued defense over a large district of country, and where nearly every citizen was an enemy ready to give information of our every move."[24]

Almost immediately after his new authority was issued, Grant began formulating further movement southward toward Vicksburg, which by this time all saw as the main culprit of Confederate defense on the river. Now with the decision-making process firmly in his hands, Grant outlined a by-the-book campaign to gain that all-important high ground east of Vicksburg. Once there, having approached Vicksburg, he could then worry about how to take it. "I go forward with the advance," he wrote. "Will push on . . . , opening railroad and telegraph as we advance."[25]

The book said to move along a secure line of communication, working forward only when the supply line was ready and extended with the army. Conveniently, there was such a line of supply, the Mississippi Central Railroad running southward out of Tennessee through Holly Springs, Oxford, Grenada, and on down to Canton, where it in name only became another railroad, the New Orleans, Jackson, and Great Northern Railroad that moved on to Jackson and eventually New Orleans. It logically ran just east of the Delta, the engineers laying out the line's right-of-way wisely preferring to cross the many rivers and creeks feeding into the marshy Delta rather than try to trudge through the murky Delta itself. Grant thus began moving his forces southward out of Tennessee to Holly Springs and thence to Oxford, repairing the railroad as he went. The young upstart with his first real autonomous command, with high-level direction coming only from Halleck in Washington, wanted to do things by the book and impress his brainy superior, who had actually written the book, *Elements of Military Art and Science*, in 1846.[26]

By early December, however, Grant had more to worry about than lines of supply and even the Confederates. A growing menace in his rear was emerging in the figure of one of his least favorite subordinates, Major General John A. McClernand, an Illinois politician-general who had the ear of President Abraham Lincoln. McClernand had talked the president and Secretary of War Edwin M. Stanton into allowing him to recruit his own army to take Vicksburg. Unwisely given the go-ahead, McClernand did wonders recruiting in Illinois, Indiana, and Iowa but made his mistake by sending all those new regiments southward to Memphis to await his arrival to lead them to Vicksburg. For his part, Grant realized that "two commanders on the same field are always one too many." The new regiments now being in Grant's department and with a scheming Halleck behind him, Grant took many of those new troops and sent them on southward to Vicksburg under one of his favorite subordinates, Major General William T. Sherman. Now, the movement toward Vicksburg was a two-pronged affair, but each with secure supply lines on the river and railroad.[27]

Knowing the hurry needed and perhaps fueled by the fast one they were pulling on McClernand, whom Sherman disliked about as much as Grant did, Sherman started with his three divisions southward from Memphis and picked up one more at Helena, Arkansas, on the way downriver. "The preparations [and departure] were necessarily hasty in the extreme," he admitted. Knowing a direct assault could not be made up the Vicksburg bluffs, Sherman logically planned to move south on the Mississippi River to the mouth of the Yazoo, then up that stream far enough to outflank Vicksburg's big guns. He did so but soon suffered the effects of Lockett's fortifications. He could not travel far up the Yazoo River for fear of tangling with the big Confederate guns at Snyder's and Haynes' Bluffs. He also was wary of mines (then called torpedoes) in the river, which had already claimed one of the big City-class ironclads, the USS *Cairo*, earlier in December. Sherman therefore opted to land his divisions closer to Vicksburg and ascend the hills to that all-important high, dry ground east of Vicksburg. Unknown to him, Lockett's fortifications, full of Confederates troops with more arriving by the day, were waiting for him.[28]

Disaster soon struck this by-the-book Federal plan in a couple of different ways. The Confederates sent cavalry raids deep toward Grant's rear, one under Earl Van Dorn to sack Holly Springs, Grant's forward supply base, and another under Brigadier General Nathan Bedford Forrest to break the Mobile and Ohio Railroad, which was the supply line to that forward base. Van Dorn made a lightning raid to the depot and captured or destroyed its defenders and stockpiles, then made a clean getaway back to Grenada after a short foray up into Tennessee. Forrest wrought havoc on the Mobile and Ohio Railroad crossings of the Obion River branches in northwest Tennessee and also made a getaway, although he was caught and barely escaped with his life and command at Parker's Crossroads. With his supplies destroyed and the avenues of replenishing them broken, Grant momentarily panicked and called off his part of the offensive, eventually returning to Tennessee. One shocked Iowa foot soldier scribbled in his diary "the whole Division commenced moving *Northward*." Yet Grant gained a valuable lesson in that his troops, without adequate rations, found they could live off the land at least partially. The same Iowan declared from his camp he could "hear hogs squeal and chickens squall in all directions." Grant remembered as much and filed it away for future use: "Our loss of supplies was great at Holly Springs, but it was more than compensated for by those taken from the country and by the lesson taught." The idea of doing things strictly by the book was beginning to have less appeal to Grant the more he saw of the real war. Nevertheless, Grant's prong was done for; if Vicksburg would be taken this year—1862—it would have to be done by Sherman.[29]

That prong of the advance was having as many, and actually more, troubles if casualties were the barometer. Sherman easily moved to the Vicksburg vicinity, as everyone else had, and then moved up the Yazoo River that drained the Mississippi Delta and ran close to the line of the Walnut Hills, on which Vicksburg sat. Sherman disembarked his four divisions near Chickasaw Bayou and moved them forward through the wet lowlands made worse by terrible weather. He attacked the Confederate defenses on December 29 but was easily repulsed with "great slaughter," one Georgian in the Confederate defenses reported. Sherman himself summed up matter-of-factly: "I reached Vicksburg at the time appointed, landed, assaulted, and failed. Re-embarked my command unopposed." It was obvious that Sherman could not reach that high, dry ground east of Vicksburg by this route without massive amounts of troops, and even then it was doubtful. The Confederate works were far enough from the Yazoo River to mitigate gunboat support but utilized the high ground of the hills nearer to Vicksburg as the base of defense.[30]

Accordingly, the route to approach Vicksburg from the north was most certainly blocked, as Sherman found out so bloodily. And this came on top of the repulse Grant endured in trying to gain that same high ground east of

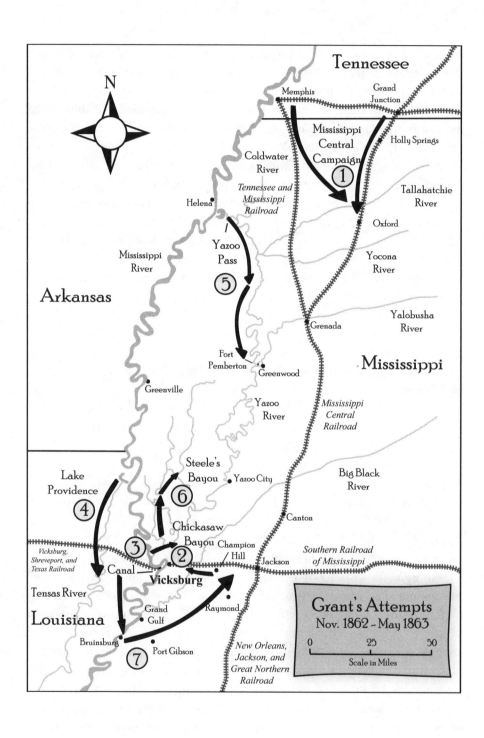

N

Tennessee

Memphis
Grand
Junction

Mississippi
Central
Campaign
①

Holly Springs

Coldwater
River

Tallahatchie
River

Tennessee and
Mississippi
Railroad

Helena

Oxford

Yazoo
Pass
⑤

Yocona
River

Mississippi
River

Arkansas

Yalobusha
River

Grenada

Mississippi

Fort
Pemberton
Greenwood

Greenville

Yazoo
River

Mississippi
Central
Railroad

Steele's
Bayou

Yazoo City

Big Black
River

Lake
Providence
④

⑥

Canton

Chickasaw
Bayou
②

Champion
/ Hill

Vicksburg,
Shreveport, and
Texas Railroad

③

Jackson

Southern Railroad
of Mississippi

Canal

Vicksburg

Tensas River

Louisiana

Grand
Gulf

Raymond

Bruinsburg

Port Gibson

⑦

New Orleans,
Jackson, and
Great Northern
Railroad

Grant's Attempts
Nov. 1862 – May 1863

0   25   50

Scale in Miles

Vicksburg via the central portion of Mississippi. Even with the railroad line of supply, it just seemed far too distant to be done. The direct approach from the north (by two routes)—a second major thrust to maneuver the army to Vicksburg—had ended in an unqualified defeat. The army thus settled into a period of winter lethargy, one Ohioan admitting that "a large part of our occupation was holding courts martial and sitting for photographs."[31]

As the new year switched over and the clock ticked on into the seventh month of Federals confronting Vicksburg, Ulysses S. Grant faced a myriad of problems. They were not all military in nature, although they all manifested themselves on the military scene. One involved John A. McClernand, who had been hoodwinked and his army swept out from under him. But he was aware of it now and was on scene, waving his orders with Lincoln's endorsement in front of anyone who would listen. "Either through the intention of the General-in-Chief [Halleck] or a strange occurrence of accidents, the authority of the President and yourself," he wrote the secretary of war, "as evidenced by your acts, has been set at naught, and I have been deprived of the command that had been committed to me." Perceiving himself as commander of the river expedition to capture Vicksburg, McClernand soon set out down the river from Memphis fully intent on taking over Sherman's contingent that had, in his view, left too early without its proper commander. Once McClernand arrived near Vicksburg, he wasted no time in putting Sherman in his place and taking command, even sending his force on what Grant described as "a wild-goose chase to the Post of Arkansas." Halleck decisively wrote the next day allowing Grant "to relieve General McClernand from command of the expedition against Vicksburg, giving it to the next in rank or taking it yourself." Grant's assistant adjutant general, John A. Rawlins, actually made out the order relieving McClernand, but Grant chose not to use it now. He nevertheless had what he wanted.[32]

At this time, Grant was still withdrawing from his overland campaign in central Mississippi, and he had a major decision to make. He had willingly made his advance a two-pronged attack when he could command one and his trusted subordinate Sherman the other, but now that McClernand, who outranked Sherman, commanded the other, Grant could not abide it. The only choice was to make the advance on Vicksburg a one-pronged attack so that he could himself command the whole, McClernand included. Grant later sheepishly admitted that McClernand's arrival and assertiveness "probably resulted in my ultimately taking command in person."[33]

Another problem was purely political. The movement down the river, which was of Grant's own making by sending Sherman, put the stalled army much farther south than he had wanted without a victory. To bring it back up to Memphis would be seen as a major defeat, if Chickasaw Bayou and Holly Springs were not already enough. Grant could not retreat, conceding how "it was my judgment at the time that to make a backward movement as long as that from Vicksburg to Memphis, would be interpreted, by many of those yet full of hope for the preservation of the Union, as a defeat, and that the draft would be resisted, desertions ensue and the power to capture and punish deserters lost. There was nothing left to be done but to go forward to a decisive victory." Tactical defeats were one thing, but wholesale strategic withdrawals were tantamount to admitting failure on a large scale and seeking a way to begin anew. Grant could not take the risk of moving a large chunk of the army back northward without politicians and newspapermen calling for his head. "The problem then became," Grant admitted, "how to secure a landing on high ground east of the Mississippi without an apparent retreat."[34]

A third problem, this one of geography, limited what Grant could do near Vicksburg as well. As the new year turned and winter descended in full force, the Mississippi River began to rise and with it the tributaries as well as every bayou, creek, and marsh in the Delta. Grant described how "this is a terrible place at this stage of water. The river is higher than the land and it takes all the efforts of the troops to keep the water out." For months, the region around Vicksburg—excepting the coveted high ground to its east—would be inundated and saturated with water. If Grant was going to stay put because of political and media reasons, he could not hope to make any active land campaign for months, which in and of itself could bring chastisement down on his head and add much more time to the ticking clock of Vicksburg that was now already passing seven months. Something had to develop wherein Grant could use the high water for his purposes, not as a detriment.[35]

Accordingly, Grant began a months-long series of waterborne operations amid the flooded Mississippi Delta and the similar flat land on the west side of the river, where his tiring army camped on whatever dry ground they could find, mostly levees. One Confederate described the view from Vicksburg itself, describing "myriads of Yankee tents gleaming in the . . . sun shine." The first endeavor was the logical continuance of the canal Thomas Williams's troops had begun back in the summer of 1862 across the base of the hairpin turn. If the river could be diverted—which it had done on its own numerous times before as testified by the many oxbow lakes that dotted the river's course—it would leave Vicksburg high and dry. Plus, President Lincoln was very interested in this effort: Halleck wrote to "direct your attention particularly to the canal proposed across the point. The President attaches much importance to this." Grant similarly later described how "Mr. Lincoln had navigated the Mississippi in his younger days and understood well its tendency to change its channel, in places, from time to time. He set much store accordingly by this canal."[36]

Grant's men worked long and tedious hours on the digging, but the cantankerous nature of the river and the continually rising water left it a doomed project. McClernand reported that "the water flows 3 feet deep in the canal, but gives no evidence of diverting the channel of the river." Sherman and Grant both were high on the prospects at first but quickly soured on the project as the water continually filled the canal and the water even ran backward through it. Soon enough, the project was given up as useless, although some work continued, if for no other reason than to give the bored and exercise-lacking soldiers something to do. Grant later reported that "the task was much more Herculean than it at first appeared, and was made much more so by the almost continuous rains that fell during the whole of the time this work was prosecuted. The river, too, continued to rise and made a large expenditure of labor necessary to keep the water out of our camps and the canal."[37]

Scrapping the canal was not that difficult of a decision, as Grant soon had a more promising project to keep his attention. Lake Providence was a large oxbow lake west of the river and north of Vicksburg, and the various bayous that ran from it all connected with each other and several of the rivers and streams west of the Mississippi. Engineers charted a path by which, if the levee was breached and water allowed into Lake Providence, a way could be forged through the bayous and rivers all the way to the Red River far south of Vicksburg. It was a roundabout project to say the least, but if successful it would provide Grant what he needed: a way to bypass Vicksburg. Sherman thought it was worth the effort: "I have hastily read the reports of the Lake Providence scheme. It is admirable and most worthy a determined prosecution. Cover up the design all you can, and it will fulfill all the conditions of the great problem." Sherman also added that "this little affair of ours here on Vicksburg point [the canal] is labor lost."[38]

The Lake Providence route was found to be promising as work continued apace, including breaking the levee and removing stumps in many of the shallow bayous. The work took more time than expected, however, and by the time the Mississippi River began to fall in late March and April, so too did the water in the route. The falling water created a couple of ramifications, making the path through less usable by water but actually opening up additional land roads to be used in ferrying material southward. Still, "I let the work go on," Grant later wrote, "believing employment was better than idleness for the men." Also, Grant was by this time turning his eye toward additional projects east of the river.[39]

Like the Lake Providence scheme, engineers found a way through the Mississippi Delta if the levee was cut near Helena, Arkansas, but on the Mississippi side. Doing so would flood Moon Lake and Yazoo Pass, which would offer access first to the Coldwater River, which flowed into the Tallahatchie River, which combined with the Yalobusha River at Greenwood to form the Yazoo River. While Federal forces could not ascend the Yazoo past the big guns at Snyder's and Haynes' Bluffs and could not ascend the hills toward Vicksburg below those points on the river because of the Confederate fortifications, moving through the upper reaches of the Delta down the Yazoo could put Grant's troops exactly where he wanted: on the high ground east of Vicksburg. As Grant described it, success "would enable us to get high ground above Haynes' Bluff, and would turn all the enemy's river batteries." It was certainly worth a try and Grant believed it to have a good chance of success, but the Confederates managed to fortify perhaps the only high point of ground sticking out of the water along the route at Greenwood, where they established Fort Pemberton and stopped the movement well short of its goal. The soggy Federals eventually had to turn around and admit defeat. Grant was not deterred, however; he had yet another project going by that time.[40]

Steele's Bayou ran into the Yazoo River well below the Confederate guns blocking it, nearer to Chickasaw Bayou. Porter soon told Grant of a route by which a flotilla and transports could move up the bayou and through several smaller ones to the Sunflower River, which flowed into the Yazoo north of the guns at Snyder's and Haynes' Bluffs. Taking this route could put the Federals on the Yazoo north and east of the guns blocking the river—the same idea as the Yazoo Pass operation but much shorter and beginning in the general area of operations, not so much farther north. Grant described it as "with a view of effecting a landing with troops on high ground on the east bank of the

Yazoo, from which to act against Haynes' Bluff," or in other words "to get all our forces in one place, and . . . [a] firm foothold . . . secured on the side with the enemy." Yet this plan brought only failure as well—and almost disaster. Admiral Porter and the Union ironclads quickly became bogged down when Confederates cut trees in front of them and then behind and were saved only when Union infantry, almost at a run all night, came to their rescue, providing more time for the vessels to slowly back their way out the way they had come in. It was a near disaster, and Porter, who had recommended the project, wanted no more of it or any of these roundabout projects.[41]

Neither did Grant, and he soon decided to go back to the book and the old, normal way of doing things. All of these major efforts, and some smaller ones, came to naught, but by April they had chewed up enough time for the river to begin to fall to levels where armies could operate. They had also kept the soldiers busy and exercising, even if none of the efforts provided any breakthrough. It had been worth a chance, however, these halfhearted yet high-potential efforts having little risk (Steele's Bayou notwithstanding) and great reward if any of them proved successful. None did, and Grant soon decided he would have to assault up the steep bluffs as Sherman had, though with his entire army in one grand fight to win or lose. He even went to scout the best areas himself but came away once more with the determination that it simply could not be done. "With present high water," he reported, "the extent of ground upon which troops could land at Haynes' Bluff is so limited that the place is impregnable." To Porter, he wrote, "after the reconnaissance of yesterday, I am satisfied that an attack upon Haynes' Bluff would be attended with immense sacrifice of life, if not with defeat." There had to be another way, and as the Union's third major effort (through the bayous) to reach Vicksburg faltered in the soggy bayous and creeks on both sides of the Mississippi River, Grant had to come up with something better. Politicians and newspapermen alike were on his case more than ever. His own future—and certainly the campaign's and perhaps the Union's—rested on it.[42]

If Grant had in the past been careful to do things by the book, firmly under the eye of the book's writer Halleck as he was, certain situations demanded more out-of-the-box thinking. Certainly, diverting rivers for flooding large swaths of geography was not frequently taught at military schools. Now, the ultimate need to go against the book came in mid-April 1863. "It was time,

therefore, to go beyond military logic," Bruce Catton argued. Grant had tried
to move overland and down the river, but geography, terrain, and Confederate defenses had stopped him. He had tried to move through the water-
logged bayous since then—certainly a form of going against the book—but
that had not worked either. Giving up hope for a finesse solution, Grant even
decided to launch the dreaded frontal assault up the Walnut Hills, but he was
so convinced following a personal inspection that it would be suicidal that he
changed his mind once more.[43]

Now, the only thing left to do, with nowhere else to go but onward because
of the political and media pressure he was under, was to move the army south
of Vicksburg, cross the river there, and fight his way to the high ground east of
Vicksburg. Grant had thought this could be a last resort all along, stating that
he kept the plan in the back of his mind "the whole winter [because it] could
not be undertaken until the waters receded. . . . I did not therefore communicate this plan, even to an officer of my staff, until it was necessary to make
preparations for the start." Now that the river was falling in April, it was time
to move.[44]

There were certainly problems with such a plan. First, moving the army
southward past Vicksburg brought a logistical nightmare, and that did not
even count what would happen once Grant crossed the river. Supplies would
have to be either gathered along the march or brought over an extremely
long and perilous route, with that line of supply stretching longer as the army
moved farther. Second, the navy would be required to ferry the army across
the river south of Vicksburg, which meant it would have to run past the heavy
Vicksburg batteries, now much more powerful than when Farragut had done
so in June 1862. Fortunately, Porter could use the current to aid him, but this
meant that, after steaming south of the city, there was no coming back up if
the plan failed; the current would be too strong to allow a quick movement
past the batteries going northward. Third, once in Mississippi, assuming all
else went well, Grant would be on his own with no hope of support if a setback occurred. If defeated, the army as well as Grant's career and even his
life could be in jeopardy. Many, even Sherman, railed against the idea, Grant
later writing about his argument at that time: "I was putting myself in a position voluntarily which an enemy would be glad to maneuver a year—or a
long time—to get me in." But there was no other option. Grant ordered the
operation knowing full well he was going against the book.[45]

For his part, Admiral Porter was willing but fully warned Grant of the potential consequences. "I am ready to co-operate with you in the matter of landing troops on the other side, but you must recollect that, when these gunboats once go below, we give up all hopes of ever getting them up again." he lectured. "If it is your intention to occupy Grand Gulf in force, it will be necessary to have vessels there to protect the troops or quiet the fortifications now there. If I do send vessels below, it will be the best vessels I have, and there will be nothing left to attack Haynes' Bluff, in case it should be deemed necessary to try it." With that warning, Porter then made two runs past the Vicksburg guns, once on April 16 and then again on the twenty-second, using the cover of night to aid his passage. While many of the ironclads and other transports moved south of the city, Grant had the army strung out along the meandering roadways now drying out as the river receded from its high stages. Soon, the leading elements of the army arrived at Hard Times, ready to cross, and an impatient Grant could not get it done fast enough. The crossing finally came on April 30, aided in no small degree by the diversion that was the famous Grierson's Raid that traversed the entire state from north to south and focused Confederate attention eastward instead of westward toward this new operation. Grant put several divisions ashore that day and the next and moved on to the high ground before he met any resistance.[46]

For the next seventeen days, Grant led a whirlwind campaign that was one of the most masterful in history. Meeting the Confederates southwest of Port Gibson on May 1, he easily pushed them back with heavier numbers despite hard fighting. Federals soon secured the town and the crossings of one of the major impediments to reaching Vicksburg, Bayou Pierre. Once across that hurdle, which outflanked Grand Gulf, Grant stopped to consolidate. He occupied Grand Gulf and made it his supply depot for the march inland. He also waited for the rest of the army to arrive, most notably Sherman's corps, which had been diverting attention north of Vicksburg. Finally, with much of the army assembled — major portions of all three corps — Grant moved forward. "Everything here looks highly favorable at present," Grant wrote one of his subordinate commanders back at Memphis, "the only thing now delaying us is the ferriage of wagons and supplies across the river to Grand Gulf. . . . Rations now are the only delay."[47]

Success was not as simple as marching up to Vicksburg and demanding surrender, however. First, Grant had to deal with more problems in his rear, namely orders to hold on at Grand Gulf and send troops southward to aid in the reduction of Port Hudson before moving on to Vicksburg. Grant decided the momentum he had was more important and—again going against the book and his direct orders—he dove off northward to gain Vicksburg once and for all. In fact, he calculated how much time he had with the lag in communications back across the river and up to Cairo and thence to Washington and back. "I remember how anxiously I counted the time I had to spare before that response could come," Grant later admitted, but he figured he had a little over a week. "You can do a great deal in eight days," he asserted.[48]

Moving north also required an additional decision, as marching directly across the Big Black River, the second major impediment he had to cross, would put him in a narrow area where he could undertake little maneuvering. Rather, he chose to march northeastward east of the Big Black River to the Southern Railroad of Mississippi, using the river as a shield against Pemberton, who would probably not be foolish enough to come out from behind its protection to fight. "It was my intention here to hug the Big Black River as closely as possible" all the way to the railroad, Grant explained. Once astride it, he would have Vicksburg's supply and communication route cut.[49]

Even that did not go strictly according to plan; Confederates from the northeast in the state capital at Jackson came out to fight, meeting Grant's right flank under XVII Corps commander Major General James B. McPherson at Raymond on May 12. Despite a hard fight, the Federals easily prevailed, but the strength of the test alerted Grant to the gathering enemy forces at Jackson. He accordingly changed his plan. Once astride the railroad, he would first march east toward Jackson instead of west toward Vicksburg. Grant first cut the railroad near Clinton, thereby severing Vicksburg "from Communication with the balance of mankind," as one of Grant's brigade commanders, Colonel James Slack, explained. Leaving McClernand's corps to shield the rear, Sherman and McPherson moved east and took the Mississippi state capital on May 14 and wrecked it as a supply or support center for enemy operations against his army while it moved on Vicksburg. "I therefore determined to make sure of that place and leave no enemy in my rear," Grant explained, and then asserted his next move: to "work from there westward." Grant thus moved toward Vicksburg, thinking the climactic battle was coming nearer and nearer.[50]

And come it did—on May 16 at Champion Hill. John C. Pemberton had unwisely moved out from not only Vicksburg's defenses but also the defensive ring of the Big Black River and met Grant in battle, only to be shattered and forced to retreat in chaos. "I am of the opinion that the battle of Vicksburg has been fought," Grant wrote to Sherman. One of Pemberton's divisions was cut off entirely, and Pemberton had no choice but to make a stand at the Big Black River to wait for it to arrive. Only Federals appeared the next day, and Pemberton took yet another major thrashing at the railroad bridge on May 17. By that time, Pemberton's morale was nearly gone, as was that of his soldiers. All fled dejectedly westward into Vicksburg.[51]

After crossing the Big Black River, Grant was finally on the ground that had taken the Federals ten months to reach: the high ground east of Vicksburg. It seemed Grant was right; he had done the unthinkable and prevailed at least this far. And much of it depended on his soldiers and their confidence in him, even if they did not like the plan itself. One put it bluntly: "I am a Grant admirer," L. S. Willard wrote to his brother, "he has not the Military jenious of Napaleon, but he has the cause at Heart[.] He is not fighting for General Grant but for the purpose of putting down the rebellion and restoring our Country to its former peacefull condition. God grant him success."[52]

2

"We Have Done Very Little, but Made a Great Noise in Doing It"
May 18–22

William T. Sherman was an insightful person, sometimes too much for his own good. Everybody has opinions, and Sherman's were good in most cases. His problem was knowing when he should speak those opinions and insights and when he should not. A case in point occurred earlier in the war when he deduced that this fight was going to be much more drawn-out and costly than anyone else was predicting. He turned out to be right, of course, but saying it so boldly at that particular time cost him his command amid rumors he was insane.[1]

A similar insight had occurred when Grant began his roundabout march southward through Louisiana to outflank Vicksburg to the south, crossing the river and fighting his way northward toward Jackson, Vicksburg, and most importantly the railroad that connected the two. Sherman saw it as a ludicrous proposition and railed against it both in staff meetings as well as privately to Grant himself, in word and by letter. Grant remembered Sherman telling him that "the line of the Yalabusha [should] be the base from which to operate against the points where the Mississippi Central crosses the Big Black, above Canton, and, lastly, where the Vicksburg and Jackson Railroad crosses the same river. The capture of Vicksburg would result." Significantly, however, Sherman did not take his concerns to the press or outside the chain of command. He had learned that lesson well. Despite his opposition, Sherman supported Grant to the hilt. Upon embarking on the attempt, he admitted, "I confess I don't like this roundabout project, but we must support Grant in whatever he undertakes."[2]

In truth, Sherman was probably right again, at least militarily, although Grant had that inner sense politically that Sherman seemed to sometimes be tone-deaf to, the war-ending negotiations for surrender in North Carolina being another example. Grant realized that the smart military move was perhaps going back to Memphis and doing it by the book, but that would reap huge political problems and perhaps cost Grant his command. "I thought that war anyhow was a risk," Grant admitted, "that it made little difference to the country what was done with me. I might be killed or die from fever." Grant being the commander, he did it his way.[3]

It worked. By May 18, when most of the Army of the Tennessee vaulted over the Big Black River on four newly constructed bridges, Grant was poised to finish a task he had set out to accomplish seven months before and others had attempted even earlier. Capturing Vicksburg had basically boiled down to a two-phase project: to reach the city, and then to capture it. Grant and others had found it extremely difficult to get within even striking distance of Vicksburg, it taking these long months of failed attempt after attempt to do so. But Grant was here now and proved as much by soon capturing the high ground overlooking the Yazoo River at Haynes' and Snyder's bluffs as well as the Chickasaw Bayou area where Sherman had been repulsed back in December. "My first anxiety was to secure a base of supplies on the Yazoo River above Vicksburg," Grant later wrote. Gaining that area short of Vicksburg proper nevertheless assured Grant a clear and unfettered supply line with the North that could bring in all the supplies, food, and ammunition his army would need to capture the city. One Illinoisan in the army wisely summed up that "these works [Haynes' Bluff] were the key to Vicksburg—from the right by coming in from the back door, both lock and key on the front door were comparatively useless therefore were immediately abandoned leaving thirteen miles of splendid works for military defense in our possession."[4]

What made Sherman different in the midst of this process was his almost complete loyalty to Grant and his willingness to admit when he was wrong. That loyalty, which many argue was solidified at Shiloh, actually took a little longer to cement as Sherman had hedged his bets even after Shiloh, staying friendly with both Grant and Halleck in perhaps an effort to delay and see which one was going to come out on top. Ultimately, Grant did of course, but not before Sherman kept close to Halleck just in case Grant flamed out and Halleck was the star he should hitch his wagon to. Nevertheless, by the Vicksburg Campaign, the Grant and Sherman relationship had solidly congealed, and by the time the two rode to the bluffs overlooking Chickasaw Bayou and the area of his earlier defeat—which now symbolized the achievement of the first phase of the Vicksburg operations (getting into position to capture the city)—Sherman was more than willing to give Grant the credit and admit he had been wrong. Perhaps Sherman's way would have turned the trick, certainly militarily, but it was unknown whether political factors would have tripped up that attempt. Doing it Grant's way, he achieved the result while keeping the political problems below the surface.[5]

Sherman said as much to Grant, illustrating the twofold nature of the Vicksburg operations. As the two viewed the Yazoo River bottom and the Delta from that coveted high ground as the army encircled Vicksburg, Grant noted: "Sherman had the pleasure of looking down from the spot coveted so much by him the December before on the ground where his command had lain so helpless for offensive action." Grant continued, stating, "he turned to me, saying that up to this minute he had felt no positive assurance of success. This, however, he said was the end of one of the greatest campaigns in history and I ought to make a report of it at once. Vicksburg was not yet captured, and there was no telling what might happen before it was taken; but whether captured or not, this was a complete and successful campaign." Such was evidence that the Union high command saw the capture of Vicksburg as a two-pronged operation: getting into a position to take it, and then taking it. The first was now accomplished. A lower-level Federal said it more succinctly: "General U. S. Grant our commander has been trying for a long time to occupy the position we now hold."[6]

Now, the focus became actually taking the city. But a strong line of Confederate fortifications and thousands of Confederate troops stood in the way before that could happen.

The Federals began encircling Vicksburg on May 18, one year to the date after Farragut had arrived at the city in 1862. But merely reaching Vicksburg, as complicated and time-consuming as it had been, was only the first step. Now confronting the Confederate fortifications ringing the city, Grant had to take it. Not wanting to waste any time and believing the Confederates would not put up much of a fight given the beatings they had taken recently, Grant wanted to quickly finish the campaign once and for all. He wrote that he would "either have Vicksburg or Haynes' Bluff to-morrow night." Little did he know that Confederate morale was on the upswing, especially given that two full divisions of troops had not been involved in the debacles of the past few days and stood ready for a fight. Pemberton wisely put these two divisions, Major Generals John H. Forney's and Martin L. Smith's, on the most dangerous fronts.[7]

Even as Grant was taking outlying areas and planning his next moves, his army was continually approaching Vicksburg, ultimately using three different roads. Sherman moved north and occupied the Graveyard Road entrance to the city at the Stockade Redan, with one division moving toward the river to the right to cut off that route of Confederate escape. McPherson moved from behind Sherman when he went north and approached along the Jackson Road toward the Great Redoubt and 3rd Louisiana Redan. His divisions also extended farther northward across Glass Bayou as well as southward. McClernand had made a turn and moved southward down to the Baldwin's Ferry Road and the railroad, approaching the 2nd Texas Lunette and Railroad Redoubt as well as extending farther southward toward Square Fort. By noon the next day on May 19, after some heated skirmishing the afternoon before and that morning, all three corps were sidling up to the Confederate works. Quite a view it was when they came into eyesight. One Ohioan described how "as the column climbed up out of the ravine it turned a curve in the road near a large white house. . . . Rounding this curve, the great line of defenses was suddenly disclosed. For three miles to the right and left, along the whole front, the sharp cut crest of the Rebel fortifications formed the horizon line. Instinctively the men wheeling into view of the scene, began to cheer." Another wrote that "we [soon] came within sight of its extensive fortifications. Numerous flags floating over the works proved that the persisting leaders of the enemy would try a last attempt to rally their men to fight again, and to save, if possible, the stronghold of rebeldom on the Mississippi River."[8]

Grant had to decide how to go about the second phase of the operation: capturing the city. He basically had two options. One was to lay siege, the time-honored and by-the-book way of doing things. But that would require lengthy preparation and perhaps even lengthier execution. But delay brought all kinds of concerns, from politics to malaria to yellow fever. The second option was to make a quick strike and break through by assault. Grant thought that option portended the most success in the shortest time frame. He firmly believed that he had the Confederates in a bind and that they would not put up much resistance. Engineer Frederick Prime asserted that "our own troops, buoyant with success, were eager for an assault, and would not work well if the slow process of a siege was undertaken." Grant added that "the troops themselves were impatient to possess Vicksburg, and would not have worked in the trenches with the same zeal, believing it unnecessary." He even wrote that the enemy "would not make much effort to hold Vicksburg." Perhaps it would take only a little nudge to force the Vicksburg defenses to implode and end this campaign once and for all. Accordingly, he ordered all three corps to attack at 2:00 P.M. that afternoon. It was a hurried and ill-planned attempt—the orders only going out at 11:16 that morning—but it was worth a try. "Push forward carefully, and gain as close position as possible to the enemy's works, until 2 P.M.; at that hour they will fire three volleys of artillery from all the pieces in position. This will be the signal for a general charge of all the army corps along the whole line," Grant ordered. One Iowan in Sherman's corps knew what it meant: "It is a beautiful morning. We expect to see hard fighting before night."[9]

Unfortunately, few of the commanders made any appreciable assault at 2:00 P.M. McClernand claimed to be too far away to launch an infantry attack, and he spent the rest of the afternoon slowly moving his forces forward. That said, there were periods of heavy fighting as the Federals advanced hilltop by hilltop amid heavy artillery fire and, the closer they approached, small arms as well. McClernand even lost one of his brigade commanders, Brigadier General Albert L. Lee, to a nasty wound in the face—"the ball entering my right cheek and passing out at the back of my neck." As he was being taken to the rear he nevertheless shouted to the 120th Ohio "stick it to them boys." Still, McClernand never approached close enough to make any real attacks, and as a result there was no success on his lines other than continually gaining a closer position. He did take stock of what he faced, however: "The enemy's defenses consist of an extended line of rifle-pits occupied by infantry, covered by a multitude of strong works occupied by artillery, so arranged as to command not only the approaches by the ravines and ridges in front, but each other."[10]

McPherson was not any more aggressive. Although a portion of Brigadier General Thomas Ransom's brigade north of Glass Bayou advanced disjointedly into heavy fire, the severe terrain broke up the effort. "To our surprise the rebs were not where we expected," one Illinoisan admitted, "and we were obliged to go down a hill and up another." None of the brigades of John Logan's or Brigadier General Isaac Quinby's divisions made anything even approaching an assault along the Jackson Road or south of it. Only Logan himself seemed to be itching for a fight, one Iowan describing how he "was in full uniform, his long black hair swept his shoulders, his eyes flashed fire, he seemed the incarnation of the reckless, fearless soldier. He must have thought cannonballs would not hurt him. For five minutes, perhaps, I stood in a little dip in the ground, comparatively protected, while he rode up and down under a storm of cannonballs, calling at the top of his warrior's voice." Nevertheless, McPherson, too, spent his time that afternoon positioning his corps and reconnoitering the approaches to the Confederate fortifications rather than assaulting.[11]

Sherman had led the march westward and so was farther ahead of the rest. But even then, Frederick Steele's division spreading out westward north of Mint Spring Bayou did not attack but like all the others took positions and crept toward the Confederate defenses. Still, Sherman was buoyant that "we had compassed the enemy to the north of Vicksburg, our right resting on the Mississippi River, with a plain view of our fleets at the mouth of the Yazoo and Young's Point, Vicksburg in plain sight." Yet he noted "nothing separated us from the enemy but a space of about 400 yards of very difficult ground, cut up by almost impracticable ravines, and his line of intrenchments." Another of Sherman's divisions remained in reserve along the Graveyard Road, and only Major General Frank Blair's division at the Stockade Redan itself managed to be in position in time to launch an actual assault at 2:00 P.M. While no other division did so on May 19, Blair assaulted with a ferocity that made up for the others.[12]

If Grant and Sherman had to pin all their hopes to one division, it may not have been Blair's by choice, at least earlier on when the politician-general first came to the army. "Frank Blair is a 'disturbing element.' I wish he was in Congress or a Bar Room, anywhere but our Army," Sherman had barked. Grant felt a similar way toward the politician turned general who had a brother in Lincoln's cabinet, but he did not blurt it out quite so vehemently, and fortunately so because it turned out Blair made a pretty good general. Grant later admitted: "I dreaded his coming; I knew from experience that it was more difficult to command two generals desiring to be leaders than it was to command one army officered intelligently and with subordination." He continued: "It affords me the greatest pleasure to record now my agreeable disappointment in respect to his character. There was no man braver than he, nor was there any who obeyed all orders of his superior in rank with more unquestioning alacrity. He was one man as a soldier, another as a politician."[13]

Blair spread his division in a crescent around the Stockade Redan on the Graveyard Road, which was where the Confederate lines turned from eastward-facing to northward-facing at an almost ninety-degree angle. The Confederates across the way watched in awe, one Mississippian declaring how "in grim silence, with guns ready for instant use, we awaited the shock." Then the assault began, Blair later reporting how "at 2 P.M. the signal was given for an assault, and my whole division dashed forward." Unfortunately, Sherman noted, "the ground to the right and left of the road was so impracticable, cut up in deep chasms, filled with standing and fallen timber, that the line was slow and irregular in reaching the trenches." And that did not take into account the defenders, among whom ran whispers of "A charge! A charge!" A Mississippian described how "we could plainly hear when the order was given to advance; the flags were seen mounting up the hill, and soon the long, glittering line of bayonets came in sight, as with martial tread this tremendous war machine marched to the attack."[14]

Blair's right brigade under Brigadier General Hugh Ewing, originally from the eastern theater, crossed Mint Spring Bayou heading south against a lunette held by the 27th Louisiana of Martin L. Smith's Confederate division. Ewing himself led the way and barked that "it would be a short job, and that we would be inside of the works, in less than ten minutes after receiving the order to move." One Ohioan declared that "when we gained the foot of the hill we sprang up its sides with a wild Yankee yell." Another added how "the men rushed with enthusiastic cheers over and through the brushwood and fallen timber up the hillsides, and into the ditch they poured in a determined mass." The left of the brigade made the most progress, the 47th Ohio and 4th West Virginia planting their flags on the lunette's parapets and Ewing himself describing how "the colors of the regiments waved near them [the Confederate lines] until evening."[15]

To Ewing's left, Colonel Giles Smith's brigade faced the stockade between the Louisianans and the main Stockade Redan and advanced at an angle, more southwestward than anything. Smith described how "the ground over which I had to move to reach the enemy's intrenchments was a succession of deep ravines and precipitous hills." Most of the regiments bogged down in the chaos as casualties multiplied. Captain John J. Kellogg wrote of a lieutenant "in his shirt sleeves and wore a white shirt; he and I went side by side several steps, when he lunged forward upon the ground, and in the quick glance I gave him I saw a circle of red forming on his shirt back." Confederate Brigadier General

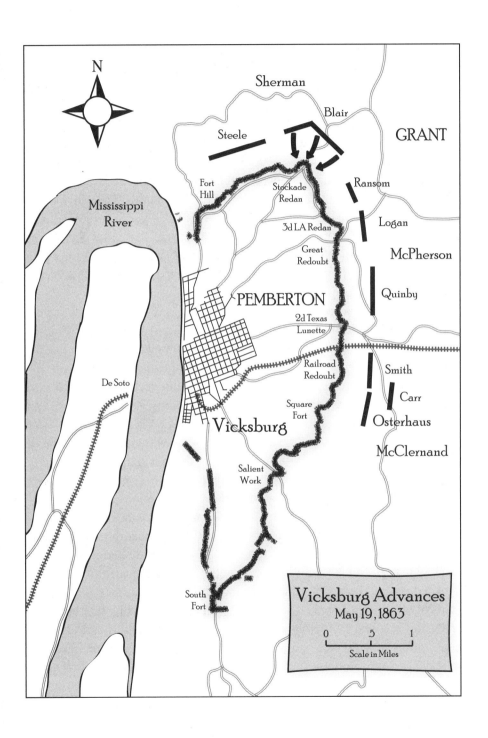

N

Sherman

Blair

GRANT

Steele

Ransom

Fort
Hill

Stockade
Redan

Logan

Mississippi
River

3d LA Redan

McPherson

Great
Redoubt

PEMBERTON

Quinby

2d Texas
Lunette

Railroad
Redoubt

Smith

De Soto

Carr

Square
Fort

Osterhaus

Vicksburg

McClernand

Salient
Work

Vicksburg Advances
May 19, 1863

South
Fort

0   5   1

Scale in Miles

Francis Shoup wrote that "our fire staggered him," and Kellogg admitted that most "had to pick his own way forward as best he could."[16]

To Giles Smith's left, on the left of the division, was Colonel Thomas Kilby Smith's brigade moving astride the Graveyard Road, advancing almost westward toward the Mississippians of John H. Forney's Confederate division. The high ridge on which the road ran split the brigade, Smith choosing to send two of his regiments forward on the right under Colonel Benjamin J. Spooner of the 83rd Indiana, "in whose ability and dauntless courage I repose fullest confidence," Smith reported. He ordered Spooner to "press forward as rapidly as possible, and in such order as he could best get over the ground." Spooner moved north of the road through the ravine that Giles Smith was trudging through while Smith himself led the other three regiments through a different ravine south of the road. No one dared exposing themselves on the road itself and its open high ground.[17]

Each brigade, starting with Ewing on the right, advanced through terrible fire from the 27th Louisiana, 36th Mississippi, and Missourians of Colonel Francis Cockrell's brigade of Major General John Bowen's division that arrived and fed themselves into the trenches alongside the original Confederates. One Mississippian described how "a thousand deadly guns are aimed and the whole lines are lighted up with a continuous flash of firearms and even the hill seems to be a burning smoking volcano." Brigade commander Francis Shoup explained that "he finally made a rush, with the intention of carrying our line, but was met by a terrific fire in front and flank, and fled in utter confusion, leaving many dead." Southern artillery blasted the attackers as well, and high casualties emerged as the various Union regiments struggled to move through the choked ravines full of abatis, cane, and fallen timber strung together with telegraph wire. Mississippian George Clarke of the 36th Mississippi described how "at the proper time our batteries opened on them with grape, canister, and shrapnel shells, which told fearfully upon their crowded ranks." Later, he added that "when they had reached within fifty yards of our lines we opened upon them with musketry, using the 'buck and ball' cartridge with murderous effect." He explained that "this cartridge was made with a round ounce ball, to which three large buckshot were fastened, so that when fired from the musket they scattered, giving a man four chances to hit every time he fired."[18]

Because of the heavy fire, only portions of each Union brigade managed to reach the fortifications and take a position in the ditches in front of the Confederate works. There they found the ditches even more difficult to cross, just as the Confederate engineers who constructed them planned. Nevertheless, the right two of Ewing's regiments, the 47th Ohio and 4th West Virginia, planted their flags on the parapets, although one of the bearers in the Ohio regiment soon left it and returned to the rear. Colonel Augustus C. Parry, suffering from an accidental bayonet wound already, "cursed him, called him a coward, and threatened to cut his head off with his sword." The 13th US Regulars and the 116th Illinois of Giles Smith's brigade also planted their colors, the assault costing the life of Captain Edward Washington of the Regulars, a great-grandnephew of George Washington himself. Even the two right regiments of Kilby Smith's brigade, the 83rd Indiana and 127th Illinois, were able to plant their colors alongside the Regulars, Spooner telling his Indianans, "this is the day of all days you are expected to show your valor and to show Jeff Davis that Indiana soldiers are not cowards," a clear reference to Davis's disparaging remarks about Indianans in the Mexican War. An Indianan also remembered Spooner barking that "if anyone should fall in battle or get wounded we were not even to turn him over or give him a drink of water until the battle was over." Casualties had unfortunately been severe, Smith reporting the "loss had been fearful, falling upon their best line and non-commissioned officers. Captain after captain had been shot dead; field officers were falling; still there was no flinching."[19]

The advance was not nearly as strong or successful south of the Graveyard Road, where Kilby Smith described how "a reconnaissance of the ground over which I should pass had developed the fact that it would be impossible to advance my whole brigade in line of battle, the hills and knobs being exceedingly precipitous, intersected by ravines in three directions, the bottom treacherous, filled with sink holes, concealed by dried grass and cane; the whole covered by abatis of fallen timber from a dense forest cut six months or more ago, affording spikes and *cheveaux de frise* most difficult to surmount." On top of that, the Confederate earthworks consisted of "an embankment some 18 feet high." None of the left of Smith's brigade made it to the parapets in any strength, one member of the 55th Illinois writing that the men went to ground "within fifty paces of the east curtain of the bastion at the Graveyard Road" and that "our colors waved for hours within pistol shot of the line of defense and were riddled with bullets." Nevertheless, the fighting here

provided the setting for the famous episode in which the boy Orion P. Howe
volunteered to get more ammunition and even though wounded still reported
the need to Sherman, even the size—"calibre 54!"[20]

Consequently, portions of Blair's Federals reached the fortifications, and
now was the time to break the enemy lines and capture Vicksburg. But those
who made it to the ditches were too few and the defenses still too strong
to permit farther advance. One of Ewing's soldiers recounted how "vainly
they strove time and again to climb the parapet. What a scathing fire swept
its crest. It could not be stood, and from each effort the brave men recoiled
into the ditch; but they maintained the struggle therein." One of Spooner's
Indianans added that "when we got to the fort we could not climb it the fort
is 15 feet high and a big ditch on this side 5 feet deep & 7 wide." And there
was nothing else to turn the tide. Sherman would not send in Brigadier General James Tuttle's reserve troops, and so the soldiers of Blair's division that
had made it into the ditches were stuck. Those who could and were still in
the open scampered away to safety, but those huddling in the ditches under
some cover were not about to leave their relatively safe havens and recross
the deadly zone under Confederate fire. They were stuck, but even those safe
positions soon became less so as the Mississippians and Louisianans learned
they could toss lit cannonballs over the parapets and do extensive damage to
the enemy below.[21]

Nothing changed for the rest of the day as Blair's troops, who had made
it to the enemy lines, prayed for a speedy nightfall. Only then did they attempt to make it back to their own lines, still a hazardous proposition as the
Confederates shot at anything that made a noise and even lit up the area with
bonfires. "The whole scene was brilliantly lighted by the flames," one Federal
wrote, although an Illinoisan declared that "this proved more dangerous to
them than to us."[22]

Grant had his answer. "The resistance offered was quite unexpected," recalled one Federal. A quick punch against a demoralized and beaten enemy,
Grant thought, would end the Confederate resistance. Unknown to him, these
Confederates defending the Stockade Redan area were not defeated Confederates from Champion Hill and Big Black River Bridge. Rather, they were
mostly from Smith and Forney's divisions, which had been left behind at
Vicksburg and its surrounding areas west of the Big Black when Pemberton marched east of the river to disaster. A smart Pemberton had placed his
freshest troops at the position he figured would be the most assailable. He

guessed right, and Grant happened to assault perhaps the strongest portion of the Confederate lines on May 19, certainly the strongest with the freshest troops defending it.[23]

It was a defeat, no question, to the tune of 942 casualties army-wide (157 killed, 777 wounded, and eight missing). Sherman admitted that "the rebel parapets were strongly manned, and the enemy fought hard and well." Most of the losses came in Blair's division, Hugh Ewing perhaps saying it best in his diary entry for May 19: "We charge—others not." But the defeat was not so convincing to Grant. Only one of his eight full divisions on the field had attacked, and Grant was not satisfied that an assault would fail if properly planned and handled. Thus, instead of turning immediately to siege operations, Grant wanted to be certain an assault would not work before going to such drastic lengths. He planned to do it again, only this time with the whole army participating. Perhaps the campaign could still be ended in a matter of days. He was certainly willing to give it one more try.[24]

Realizing that more planning was needed, Grant opted to take a couple of days and get his supplies in order and army well in hand before he tried again. He opened up a much shorter and safer supply route along the Yazoo River, and rations and ammunition soon flowed freely to the famished army. Then, on May 22, Grant was ready to try again. An army-wide assault was to take place at 10:00 A.M. Meanwhile, the Confederates watched and waited, not knowing when or where the next assault would come, although one explained "we could plainly see that another attack would be made on our works." Confederate brigade commander Stephen D. Lee explained that "the preparation was rather demonstrative than otherwise" and that "the nervous tension of all within Confederate limits . . . was kept to the highest pitch."[25]

Grant planned well—everything from the tactics used to the supplies provided to the necessary tools made beforehand, such as planks and ladders to scale the ditches and the tall parapets. Bringing his corps commanders together more than once, he went over the plan to attack either in columns or more preferably by the flank. His orders read that the troops should go forward in "columns of platoons, or by a flank if the ground over which they may have to pass will not admit of a greater front." They should also move "at quick time, with bayonets fixed, and march immediately upon the enemy without firing a gun until the outer works are carried. The troops will go light,

carrying with them only their ammunition, canteens, and one day's rations."
Given that Blair's wide linear formations had ground down in the ravines
on May 19, Grant wanted narrower, pinpoint assaults this time, hoping to
puncture the enemy lines at specific points rather than across the width of the
defenses. Each corps would advance on multiple fronts, but only at limited
areas on those fronts. In order to coordinate it all, Grant had his commanders
set their watches by his own. The assault would follow hours of bombardment, but he wanted all to go forward at 10:00 A.M.[26]

All three Union corps did assault, at varying degrees, at that time. In Sherman's corps, the main attack came once again at the Stockade Redan, but despite the different tactics this time Blair got no farther than on May 19. Blair
sent Ewing's brigade forward along the Graveyard Road, led by a 150-man
"'Volunteer Storming Party,' or Forlorn hope" carrying planks and ladders to
cross the ditches and parapets. "For a distance of about eighty rods," one Illinoisan wrote, "there was nothing to protect us, and as we were the only Union
troops moving at the time we got all the fire." He described the road being
"swept by a perfect hurricane of shot and shell. There was a constant whiz
of bullets, and it didn't seem as if a man of us could reach that fort without
being shot full of holes. And not many of us did." Much of the forlorn hope
was shot down, but some made it to the ditch in front of the redan despite the
volleys of the 36th Mississippi and even more Missouri regiments packed in
during the three-day break.[27]

"The forlorn hope carried my brigade flag and planted it on the rampart,"
a proud Hugh Ewing wrote in his diary. But when the head of Ewing's brigade popped out of a roadcut on the Graveyard Road, it almost immediately
ground down, with the lead 30th Ohio taking numerous casualties and the
following 37th Ohio plowing right into the dead and dying. No more movement was possible in the clogged roadway, and only a few Ohioans made it to
the ditches, but they planted their flag near where the forlorn hope had placed
Ewing's headquarters banner. With nothing else to do, Blair sent the rest of
Ewing's regiments and both of the Smiths' to the left down into the same ravines that some of those troops had trudged through three days before. It was
turning into May 19 again, the lead elements stopped at the ditches and the
rest of the division fanning out hopelessly in the ravines.[28]

Sherman's troops were also supposed to make an assault across Mint
Spring Bayou farther to the west, but Frederick Steele had a difficult time
getting his brigades in line and ready to go. "We had to pass through a narrow

contracted ravine under a most galling fire from eight pieces of the enemy's artillery," one Federal explained. "The distance we had to go through this ravine before we could again seek shelter was about twenty rods and to get through with little loss of life as possible we were ordered to take a single company through at a time and run rapidly through on single file. Thus company after company passed through until the entire regiment was all over the perilous position with the loss of only two men, one killed instantly by a shell and the other mortally wounded." An Iowan in Woods's brigade told a similar tale: "We had to run two or three places where the secesh could see us run the Blockade the boys call it. One place was awful hard to pass running down a steap hill." As a result, Steele was not able to launch an attack by the 10:00 A.M. deadline, and Blair was the only XV Corps attempt that morning, much like on May 19. And it took less time than previously, the realization that Blair's assault had failed coming within minutes this time. Unfortunately, unlike the previous assault that came later in the afternoon on May 19, these Federals stuck in the ditches on May 22 had much longer to await nightfall and a relatively safe chance to return to their own lines.[29]

Down the line to the south, McPherson's troops were having no better time of it. Unlike Sherman's XV Corps, McPherson's XVII Corps troops managed to launch two different assaults at 10:00 A.M., although they both came from Logan's division. Thomas Ransom's brigade north of Glass Bayou, the lone brigade from Brigadier General John McArthur's division on the line, only maneuvered that morning and did not advance. Likewise, all of Quinby's division south of the Jackson Road remained sheltered behind ridges and did not assault, although there was some advance and maneuvering. That left the fiery Illinois politician-general John Logan, much like the politician-general Blair under Sherman, to handle the assaulting in the corps.[30]

One advance came on the Jackson Road itself, where Brigadier General John E. Smith's brigade moved by the flank and quickly figured out this was a waste of time. "There was about 5,000 [Confederates] raised up out of the rifle pits and fired on us," one of his troops explained, and "we got behind trees, stumps, and logs." The 23rd Indiana led the pinprick attack, falling off into the ravines north of the road once they came near the Confederate lines. The following 20th Illinois could not make any more headway and filed off into the ravines south of the road, confronting the Louisianans in the redan at short range. It was "a rush for the base of the fort on a dead run amid a shower of lead that was hurled down upon us," an Illinoisan explained. It

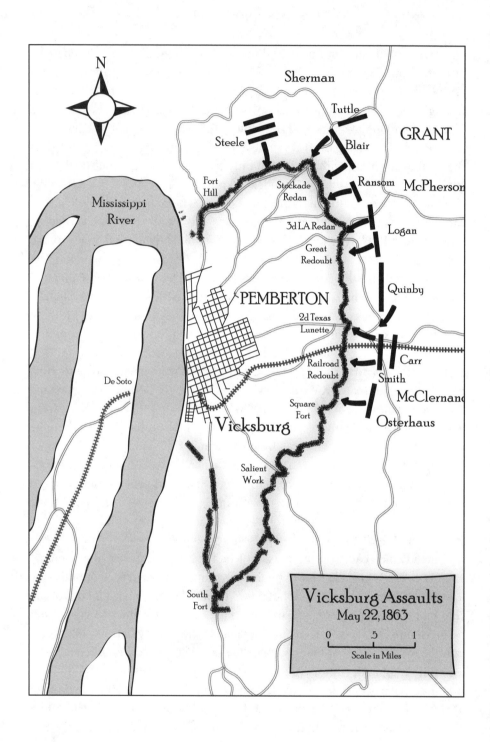

N

Sherman

Tuttle

GRANT

Steele

Blair

Ransom

McPherson

Fort
Hill

Stockade
Redan

3d LA Redan

Logan

Great
Redoubt

Mississippi
River

PEMBERTON

Quinby

2d Texas
Lunette

Carr

Railroad
Redoubt

Smith

De Soto

McClernand

Square
Fort

Osterhaus

Vicksburg

Salient
Work

South
Fort

Vicksburg Assaults
May 22, 1863

0   .5   1

Scale in Miles

took less time than even on Sherman's front to figure out this was not working, and Smith's attack similarly fizzled without even coming very near the Confederate lines.[31]

Not so with Logan's other assault, where Brigadier General John D. Stevenson's brigade to the south made an all-out assault against the Great Redoubt. Stevenson divided his brigade into two columns and advanced to the ditch in front of the redoubt, the 7th Missouri and 81st Illinois on the right taking the brunt of the punishment as the left column halted farther out. "From the moment our company passed over the ridge immediately in front of the line of Confederate works," one of Stevenson's soldiers described, "we advanced without cover, as all timber had been cut down and the face of the ridge and ravine at the foot and the ascending slope, thence to the Confederate works, was cleared of logs and brush, thus making us the fairest target possible for our Southern brothers to shoot at, and you can imagine that they made it so interesting for us that we had no time to look up the other Companies or regiments." Colonel James J. Dollins of the Illinois regiment fell in the fighting, but those who reached the parapets with their scaling ladders found they were too short to reach the top. A retreat brought most out, although numerous Federals also remained tucked away in the ditches until nightfall. They also had a miserable several hours to await the cover of night.[32]

McPherson managed two assaults, one feeble in comparison, while Sherman managed only the one advance. McClernand's XIII Corps to the south, however, undertook three major assaults. One Indianan wrote that "every experienced soldier knew what this calm portended, and with every nerve strung up to high tension, awaited the signal to do or die." Two of McClernand's attacks actually made it to the ditches in front of the Confederate works. He had counseled "concentration of our forces against one or two points, and not the dispersion of them into a multitude of columns," but then launched his entire corps at the Confederates. It was by far the strongest showing among the three corps.[33]

On the far left, Brigadier General Peter Osterhaus launched his assault in three columns, taking advantage of the lay of the land and the finger-like projections of high ground extending from the Confederate lines. "There was a minute or two of ominous silence, broken only by cheers here and there, as the men climbed up out of the ravines and rushed across the exposed ground to the ditch. Then, all in a moment, the Rebels' parapet became a fringe of gray and steel, from which streamed a livid sheet of fire," one Federal wrote.

Ahead of them was a hearty Alabama brigade under Brigadier General Stephen D. Lee, and they let out a fierce fire of small arms and artillery on the advancing enemy. The two rightmost advances accordingly bogged down before they reached the Confederate lines and heavy enemy fire. Osterhaus's leftmost column took a heavier fire as it crossed a tall ridge in front of Square Fort; casualties were heavy there. The single present brigade of Brigadier General Alvin Hovey's division supported this advance but did not enter action, his other brigade still back at the Big Black River to guard the rear.[34]

Similarly on the corps' right, Brigadier Generals Eugene Carr and Andrew Jackson Smith combined two brigades on the 2nd Texas Lunette on the Baldwin's Ferry Road. Brigadier Generals William Benton's and Stephen Burbridge's brigades found difficult going as they advanced on either side of the road, bogging down under the heavy fire. Here, too, only a few made it to the ditches in front of the lunette, but were stopped there, only one color-bearer making it over the parapet and into the fort. He was quickly seized, the blood of a previous bearer still on the flag. "We charged the forts with our bayonets," a Federal described, "but when we reached the forts we found a ditch twelve feet wide and seven deep which we had to cross, as well as a wall 10 feet high. It was impossible to climb it."[35]

McClernand's best success came in the center, on Carr's and Smith's left, where Brigadier General Michael Lawler's and Colonel William Landram's brigades assaulted the Railroad Redoubt south of the rail line. A defending Alabamian described how "I sprang to my feet and looked in the direction of the enemy, when they seemed to be springing from the bowels of the earth a long line of indigo, a magnificent line in each direction, and they kept for a while the alignment as if on dress parade, but moving at double quick." Little more success occurred here as elsewhere, however, but there was a slight penetration into the detached tip of the redoubt, where some hand-to-hand fighting occurred and a few Confederate prisoners were marched out. Several units such as the 21st and 22nd Iowa and 77th Illinois managed to plant their flags on the parapets, although one bearer "carried the flag on the fort that day, and when he planted the flag on the fort his body was riddled with bullets and he lay dead under his flag." The bottom line was that this assault stalled as well, with the issue inside the narrow tip still up in the air and probably going to whichever side managed to funnel in reinforcements first. Both sides called for them, but it was several miserable hours before any new movement took place.[36]

As a result, Grant's major attempt to breach the Confederate lines with his 10:00 A.M. joint assault came to nothing. On all fronts, the Federals were stopped, the only place where a breach was even remotely seen being at the Railroad Redoubt. A disgusted Grant quickly realized that assault was not going to work, and perhaps thoughts of siege were already entering his head. That would be a long and drawn-out headache, but before he could dwell long on that subject another, more pressing headache emerged. If Grant was disgusted before, it was about to get far worse.

Grant watched the morning assaults from the high ground along the Jackson Road, where he could see all of McPherson's troops as well as Sherman's up to the Graveyard Road and McClernand's down past the railroad. "I had taken a commanding position near McPherson's front, and from which I could see all the advancing columns from his corps, and a part of each of Sherman's and McClernand's," he explained. Others saw him there: "Generals Grant, Wilson, and Logan, with their staffs and several others, were on a small eminence," one officer reported. "Gen. Grant was quietly smoking, but all the rest were excited, looking through their glasses in order to see Gen. Sherman come up." Once he appeared, yells of "There he is!!" were abundant. There were spots Grant could not see because of foliage or the amazingly rough terrain, some guns near the lines even rolling back off the steep hills. One Federal described how "the hill was so steep, that they went down with fearful velocity, sometimes one side up and sometimes the other with but little damage to the gun carriages."[37]

Still, Grant could see most areas—and it was evident from his position that his hopes were not fulfilled. Saddened, he rode northward to Sherman's position near the Stockade Redan, but once there he began to receive a series of messages from McClernand telling him he had achieved success and that he needed the rest of the army to restart their assaults to support him and to send him reinforcements. "We are hotly engaged with the enemy," McClernand wrote. "We have part possession of two forts, and the Stars and Stripes are floating over them. A vigorous push ought to be made all along the line." Grant snapped in response: "I don't believe a word of it." Sherman retorted that "a major-general would at such a critical moment not make a mere buncombe communication." He later explained, "I reasoned with him," referring to Grant, arguing that "this note was official, and must be credited."

Grant ultimately agreed and ordered McPherson and Sherman to restart their advances and for McPherson to send Quinby's division southward to McClernand. It was the closet division to McClernand's and was not yet engaged.[38]

The gauntlet was thus thrown down, and Grant ordered the afternoon attacks. If they succeeded, McClernand would be the hero of the day. If they failed, McClernand would be the goat. McClernand had made his statement, so now Grant wanted results from the large forces he put into action once more and, though left unstated, from the many more lives that would be lost as a result. McClernand had better come through.[39]

Sherman restarted his assaults and this time actually managed to place a greater portion of the XV Corps into action than he had that morning. In all, Sherman made three separate advances in the afternoon. One came on Steele's line, where all three of his brigades had concentrated on Brigadier General John M. Thayer's brigade front. It had taken nearly all day to get into position, but by late afternoon—around 4:00 P.M.—Thayer led the way up the steep hillside south of Mint Spring Bayou. There, his Iowans met a vicious fire from the Louisianans and Mississippians of Martin L. Smith's division and were turned back, but not before several made it all the way into the ditches in front of the Confederate works and planted their flags on the parapets. "You never heard such a fire in your life," one Federal wrote; "the rebels made a crossfire on our men and slaughter them awfully." An Ohioan remaining to the right to cover the space when the brigades were pulled out of line watched and declared "we could see our men moving steadily up towards the works in the face of a most murderous fire of artillery and small arms until they were stopped by the stockades in front of the enemy's breastworks." There the surge ended, with one Iowan reporting that "Gen Thayer cryed over it."[40]

On the Graveyard Road itself, Sherman tried another advance by the flank, this time Tuttle's leading brigade under Brigadier General Joseph "Fighting Joe" Mower. "Have you a brigade that can carry that point," Sherman demanded of Tuttle, who responded: "I have one that can do it if it can be done." Sherman barked in reply, "then send them in." The famed "Eagle Brigade" went headlong down the road, just as the forlorn hope had done, and with the same results, the leading 11th Missouri being cut up and the rest of the regiments dashing to each side for the cover of the ravines. "As the head of the column emerged from the cover of the timber and passed an open space leading to the work," one soldier described, "it was met and literally melted down by a terrific fire of musketry and artillery, the latter double-shotted with canister and grape. From my position, within range, along the whole line of defenses a fire was concentrated upon this point, where the column must pass." One of the earlier attackers recalled that "about 30 of the Eleventh Missouri, with their colonel, major, and 2 lieutenants, succeeded in reaching us with their colors, which they planted alongside of ours." But they could go no farther.[41]

On Sherman's left, some of Blair's division who had taken refuge in the ravines now advanced once more. Ewing's and Kilby Smith's brigades remained stationary, but Giles Smith led his troops in an assault coordinated with Ransom's brigade of McPherson's corps on their left. Both climbed their way up the steep ravines and some into the ditches in front of the Confederate fortifications, but there was no success here either. Giles Smith explained the predicament: "I again advanced, but met so severe a fire from my front and left by both musketry and artillery that I found it absolutely necessary to order the brigade to fall back behind the crest of the hill, which was done slowly and in good order." The only results besides more casualties were that more flags now flew from the Confederate parapets and more Federals huddled scared to death in the ditches in front of them, awaiting nightfall. In reality, at no time did Sherman ever have a good chance of breaking the Confederate line.[42]

McPherson did no better. Ransom could not break the line in his front, even when coordinated with Smith's brigade of Sherman's corps. In actuality, Ransom, the only XVII Corps unit north of the substantial Glass Bayou, had been operating more as a part of Sherman's corps anyway. Nevertheless, those who could among the brigade filtered back to safety after the doomed advance, Ransom himself standing atop a stump and watching his men withdraw. When warned not to expose himself so, he retorted "silence!" To Ransom's left, Logan also sent another advance down the Jackson Road, this time the 45th Illinois "Lead Mine" regiment supported by the borrowed 20th Ohio. Neither made any headway, the Ohioans never even assaulting and the Illinoisans having to take cover on the left of the road near where the 20th Illinois still held the line from the morning assault. "The order was given to advance, and they were soon exposed to the fire of the whole of the rebel line, killing and wounding many at the head of the column," one Federal explained. The killed including the commander of the 45th Illinois, Major Luther H. Cowan. It took mere minutes for this attempt to wind down as well.[43]

Conversely, Quinby's division made up for their lack of action in the morning, but not on their original front. The entire division moved on Grant's order from its location south of Logan in midafternoon, moving southward to reinforce McClernand—presumably where the most success had been achieved. When the division arrived, however, McClernand inexplicably placed the three brigades everywhere but where the only success had taken place. The reserve brigade under Colonel Samuel Holmes reinforced Osterhaus, far to the south, who already had an idle brigade as its own reserve. The other two brigades under Colonels John Sanborn and George Boomer went into action at the 2nd Texas Lunette, both brigades hitting the Confederate earthworks north of the railroad. A Confederate described how "our men, as before, reserve their fire until they approach near, and then pour forth a perfect storm of Buck and Ball, so that the enemy fall by hundreds. They fill up the broken ranks and press on but they stagger before the deadly fire." Neither assault was successful, although more flags joined those already on the parapets in front of Sanborn's brigade. Boomer's troops did not make it that far, Boomer himself being killed in the advance and the movement failing at that point. "Colonel Boomer's last words were to let the rifle-pits alone," one Federal noted, while another declared that he stated, "Tell Col. [Holden] Putnam (of the 93rd Ills—our next senior Colonel) not to go over that hill."[44]

Amazingly, not a single reinforcing regiment went to the small breakthrough area at the Railroad Redoubt, and any chance at success, slim as it was to begin with, quickly evaporated. In fact, the Confederates pushed in reinforcements before McClernand did, and by that time the one remaining wounded Federal occupying the inside of the tip of the redoubt soon evacuated, Sergeant Joseph E. Griffith coming out of the Railroad Redoubt with a Confederate lieutenant and thirteen privates. The Confederate brigade commander in the area, Stephen D. Lee, tried to send some of his Alabamans in to clear out the enemy, and one attempt tried but failed while others refused to even try it. Lee turned late in the day to the Texans of Waul's Legion, and a small band moved forward and cleared the area and many of the enemy in the vicinity. Lawler noted that "all the [afternoon] efforts of the enemy to dislodge or drive us back were unavailing." Then he admitted, "At sunset, however, a determined rush was made by the rebels to regain possession of their work, which, in consequence of the exhaustion of the men holding it, was successful." Waul described how "with promptness and alacrity they moved to the assault, retook the fort, drove the enemy through the breach they entered, tore down the stand of colors still floating over the parapet, and sent them to the colonel commanding the Legion, who immediately transmitted it, with a note, to General Lee." Consequently, no more success occurred here on McClernand's front than anywhere else.[45]

Once the reports came in, Grant was livid that McClernand had misled him. Newspaper correspondent Sylvanus Cadwallader told his story at headquarters, reporting that "I was within plain view of the rebel earthworks—that McClernand never gained a footing inside them. . . . I was questioned closely concerning it." He later added: "[I] shall never forget the fearful burst of indignation from [John] Rawlins, and the grim glowering look of disappointment and disgust which settled down on Grant's usually placid countenance, when he was convinced of McClernand's duplicity, and realized its cost in dead and wounded." Others described how "most of the corps and division commanders were assembled. McClernand was spoken of in no complimentary terms." Sherman himself went so far as to term McClernand "a dirty dog." It soon became clear that McClernand had not achieved any real success, much less holding two of the enemy's forts as he stated in one of his dispatches. Restarting the assaults in the afternoon had been for nothing, and McClernand, according to Grant, was the culprit. McClernand had declared success and called for help, and then he did not come through. His days were numbered.[46]

Grant suffered a total of 502 killed, 2,550 wounded, and 147 missing on May 22, compared to the smaller 500 total casualties for the Confederates. It had been a trying day—"as loud yesterday as at Shiloh," Illinoisan William Reid declared to his diary. Also suffering was any idea of taking Vicksburg by storm, at least from the present position of the lines hundred of yards from the Confederate fortifications. The grand total of casualties in all the assaults amounted to a staggering 659 killed, 3,327 wounded, and 155 missing—more than 4,000 in all. Colonel David Grier of the 77th Illinois wrote home that "nothing will ever induce me again to take either myself or men into such a charge for it is nothing more nor less than downright murder to go into such a place." There was just too much ground to cover, allowing the enemy too much time to pour fire into the charging columns. If an assault was to be successful, it would have to begin from much closer forward, and the only way to do that was for the Federals to dig their way ahead. And that sounded a lot like siege warfare. But it seemed to be the only choice now that two different assaults had failed, one a quick strike hoping to benefit from the chaos of the

Confederate retreat into Vicksburg, the other a well-organized, near-total effort. Neither had worked. It seemed Vicksburg was impregnable to assault.[47]

The fighting in many areas continued until dark, especially at the Railroad Redoubt, where the Confederate counterattack that retook the full earthworks came around dusk. The confrontation of opposing soldiers mere feet from each other but shielded by a rampart of earth, as well as the sharpshooting along the remainder of the lines, continued well into the night. In fact, most Federals who had reached the Confederate entrenchments did not withdraw until well after dark, that being the nearest time it could safely be done, and even then Confederates shot at any sounds they could detect and again lit fires to illuminate the area. As a result, some Federals did not reach their own lines and especially their camps for many more hours. There was also fear that the fighting would restart during the night. "An attack was looked for last night on our left where the charge was made yesterday evening," Louisianan Louis Guion explained. "Every precaution was adopted to secure ourselves against surprise but no attack was made."[48]

Then as dawn neared on May 23 it came relatively quietly—a surprise to almost everyone. "I think we made them willing to behave themselves," one Alabamian wrote. "'Tis the holy sabbath and only an occasional shot is heard," one Illinoisan similarly wrote home. But the effect of the fighting would soon be plainly evident. The sheer amount of ordnance thrown from each side was huge, as the battlefield was littered in many areas, especially before the great Confederate forts, with equipment, spent projectiles, and the debris of battle. The effect of those projectiles was also plainly evident in many ways, one being the torn-up Confederate earthworks. While a lot of effort had been spent during the night to repair the breaches and damage, some shot-torn areas of the fortifications were still discernable.[49]

The major effect of all that flying ordnance was most evident in the human toll. While the Federals had struggled, especially after dark, to remove as many of their wounded as possible, it was not altogether feasible, especially where the terrain was harshest and where the Confederates were most vigilant and responsive. Those who could be moved went to hospitals in the rear and eventually northward on riverboats, they being in competition with Confederate prisoners also being ferried northward. Most of the Confederates who were killed or wounded were quickly removed in a much simpler process:

taking them rearward was much safer because the fortifications that sat on the heights of the ridges covered the movement.[50]

No such cover existed for the Union casualties. Obviously, the dead were beyond help, although any decent human would want a proper burial for his comrades in the Union army. Officers received special treatment, one Wisconsin artilleryman describing an ambulance nearby "waiting for the remains of Colonel Dollins of the 81st Illinois and Colonel Boomer, commander of the 3rd Brigade." Burying the dead brought additional danger, one group of Missourians burying their captain learning that lesson the hard way: "We were fired upon and had to hurry to get out of the way in order not to wake up as a corpse with him." Many a letter thus emanated from Vicksburg relating the deaths of sons or husbands.[51]

The wounded provided more concern, as the groans and screams of hundreds and perhaps thousands rose throughout the night. Those fortunate enough to be carried to a hospital faced their own struggle, one Federal reporting he saw "a pile . . . of legs and arms thrown from the amputating table in a shed nearby, where the wounded were being cared for." Those left in no-man's-land had it worse, and it would only get more pitiful when day broke following hours without water or care and piled on top of each other in the grueling heat. Worse, any Federals who wiggled were just as likely as not— unless they were under some type of cover—to arouse a shot from a watching Confederate sharpshooter.[52]

Those captured also faced their own trials, the Federals being taken to the city jail, which one Illinoisan described: "We were marched through a heavy iron gate, large enough to drive a team of horses through, into an enclosure made by a brick wall about fourteen or fifteen feet high, at the jail and near the Court House." The prisoners received their food through openings in the wall, and the same Illinoisan recognized the Mississippi River water and cornbread, but the meat was different. He asked what it was and learned it was mule meat—"but I never tasted any turkey in my life that tasted any better than it did," he confessed. These prisoners were later paroled and rowed across the river to be traded to the Federals, complete with the Union navy firing on them before the flag of truce became evident. All in all, one Union prisoner admitted that "the Confederates treated us very kindly, which convinced us that they were good citizens in time of peace and brave soldiers in time of war."[53]

Yet little had changed amid all the chaos, one Federal writing, "since

arriving here we have done very little, but made a great noise in doing it."
And that was a recipe for continued disaster, one side firm in its commitment
to hold, the other just as firm in its commitment to capture the city. "General
Grant is bound to have Vicksburg," wrote Henry Eells, "and from all we can
hear the rebels are just about as much bound he shall not. Which will conquer
of course time will show." Certainly, little seemingly had changed in the past
five days as Ulysses S. Grant's Federals nearly surrounded and then assaulted
fortress Vicksburg, and little seemed on the cusp of change now. The major
difference was that Grant had thousands fewer men to take whatever next step
there was and, perhaps more important, many fewer officers to work through,
several field officers and George Boomer having been killed or wounded
in the assaults. In fact, the feeling was already trickling down through both
armies that nothing was likely to change for the foreseeable future. One Illinoisan declared that "this taking Vicksburg is a big joke. My opinion expressed on arriving here was we will take the place in three days or failing to
will *not* under three months." Even Grant himself wrote a subordinate that
"the taking of Vicksburg is going to occupy time, contrary to my expectations
when I first arrived near it."[54]

Others expressed disbelief as well. One Federal who arrived later, looking for his brother's body, remarked that "it is a pity that effort [assault] was
made, and I was disposed, in my anguish, to complain that the general made
it, but the feeling was *so* prevalent among our officers, and men, that after so
many victories, and demoralizing the enemy by several hours bombardment,
they could take the strong hold. They tried it, and terrible failure was the
result." The only question now: How long would this continue? One Federal
succinctly wrote in his diary "what is to be done now I cannot say." But there
was an indication as the unwanted word "siege" began to creep into the ver-
nacular around Vicksburg.[55]

3

"I Think We Will Siege Them Out"

May 23–25

Dawn on May 23 brought to all who had been involved in the torrential fighting the day before a feeling of renewal. While there were still sharpshooters who made exposing any part of the body dangerous, the firing was comparatively limited and the break was welcome. One Louisianan described the respite, writing in his diary that "the fire from the enemy is not So Severe as usual this morning." This new day thus offered a seemingly fresh start even if that carnage from the day before was evident and very discernable. A light rain that came early in the morning also helped bring a newness to everything, as if the old was washed away and a new type of operation was now beginning.[1]

Still, many on both sides no doubt gasped when the first views came with the daylight on May 23. The scene told all that needed to be known as both sides got their first looks at the carnage after the fact, when a broader perspective of the whole could be obtained rather than a focused attention on their own little worlds. Much like the first glimpses the morning after a late-night hurricane or in a tornado-devastated region, this first one illustrated to everyone who could stomach it just how high the stakes were. And those feelings remained throughout the day as the fates of so many became known. One Illinoisan described the casualties in his company but declared that by evening none were unaccounted for, except that "a slight shade of uncertainty hangs over Mitchell's fate."[2]

There was also one other aspect plainly visible that morning that added to the feelings of waste, fear, and dread. Still fluttering over the city of Vicksburg on the courthouse—visible from many sections of the Union line—and at numerous positions along the Confederate fortifications themselves floated Confederate flags, telling all that the major assaults the day before had not been successful and that Vicksburg had held out. "Enemy stubborn as bull-dogs," one Illinoisan declared in his diary. Yet also plainly visible across the no-man's-land to the east and north floated just as many, and perhaps more, US flags, equally telling the determination of those who bore them of their untarnished desire to capture Vicksburg. They were indeed undaunted, division commander Alvin Hovey well describing the mind-set: "After the bloody repulse of the 22nd, our feelings can [be] better imagined than described, for over one month we had been acting on the offensive and in every engagement so far we had been successful." He also described the reality facing the Federals: "But now our further progress toward the grand goal of our labors was barricaded. We had attempted to carry their works by storm and had signally failed. This check upon us acted like a charm, for instead of discouraging us it only made us the more curious to see what the Rebs had inside, for well we knew that the eyes of the world were looking on us."[3]

No one was perhaps more surprised that Vicksburg was still holding out when the sun rose on May 23 than John C. Pemberton himself. He had been in and out of the pits of despair over the last week, especially after the major defeats at Champion Hill and Big Black River Bridge. The deepest pit came on the afternoon and night of May 17, when the nearly broken army fled westward into Vicksburg's defenses. As he rode with engineer Samuel Lockett, Pemberton confessed "just thirty years ago I began my military career by receiving my appointment to a cadetship at the U.S. Military Academy, and to-day—the same date—that career is ended in disaster and disgrace." Lockett tried to reassure him, but Pemberton simply dismissed it that, Lockett remembered, "my youth and hopes were the parents of my judgment." He added, "He himself did not believe our troops would stand the first shock of the attack."[4]

A good night's sleep combined with a delayed Federal follow-up did wonders for Pemberton as well as his soldiers and the general public in Vicksburg. The deflection of the May 19 and 22 assaults revived spirits as well, as did the arrival of numerous stands of colors Pemberton's troops had captured during the fighting. More important, the delayed Federal advance and defeated assaults gave time to sort things out momentarily, and a feeling of confidence and higher morale began to ooze back into the Confederates defending Vicksburg, Pemberton included. That the city had a heavy ring of fortifications surrounding it was much of the culprit, as were the two comparatively fresh divisions of troops who had not been in the trouncing at the battles on May 16 and 17.[5]

That said, there were still a million and one things for Pemberton and his Confederates to work on and decide as May 23 began a new chapter in the Vicksburg fighting. There had been some ten months of operations for the Federals just to approach Vicksburg, and then five days of actual assaults and preparations for assaults, which proved the taking of the city was going to be potentially as difficult as approaching it. By the end of May 22, all on both sides could see that assault would not work, and a new phase would be needed: logically, siege operations. That hearkened back to lengthy time frames, much like the effort to approach the city but this time with limited resources and no open line of supply. Most Confederates realized by this point they were mere "caged birds." Another wished, "Oh! for aid to get out of this bull pen."[6]

Pemberton's confidence was nevertheless growing, despite knowing time was his major cause of concern. The men's morale soared as well, one Mississippian writing in his diary on May 23, "Boys all cheerful and eager for the Yanks to charge." Yet if a siege went into weeks or months, food and provisions became the major factors inside a bottled-up Vicksburg. Also, siege operations by definition led to the enemy gaining ground closer to the fortifications under siege, which brought back into the picture the possibility of new assaults from much closer jumping-off points. Although that would take time, it would eventually happen. Thus, Pemberton knew that the longer he defended Vicksburg the less likely were his chances of success. The overarching hope was that relief could come from a gathering Confederate force outside Vicksburg—and that was needed sooner rather than later.[7]

That timeline of sorts was already in the works on May 23, even though Pemberton did not fully know it as yet. In Richmond, President Jefferson Davis wrote the epilogue, almost, to Vicksburg, telling Pemberton, who would not receive the note until much later: "I made every effort to re-enforce you promptly, which I am grieved was not successful." Davis's only hope likewise lay in relief from the outside, which he hoped "will join you with enough force to break up the investment and defeat the enemy." Still, the obvious sentiment was that Pemberton and the others in Mississippi were now on their own: "Sympathizing with you for the reverses sustained, I pray Got may yet give success to you and the brave troops under your command."[8]

Pemberton had much more tangible issues to deal with in these first few days of the siege than whether or not Davis's prayer would deliver what was shaping up to be a needed miracle. One concern was the continuing Union encirclement that if not completely airtight as yet would no doubt soon be; the skirmishing was already picking back up later on May 23, although Pemberton noted that "the sharpshooters of the enemy were more cautious, and he was evidently staggered by the severe repulse of the day previous." Then there were the Union gunboats and mortar boats on the river firing into the town, which Pemberton described as "heavy and incessant." To add more pain to the already afflicted, the bombardment caused problems at the various hospitals, one surgeon informing Pemberton of his patients, how "men in their condition, whose nerves are already shattered by wounds, bear this very badly, and I shall have great mortality among my amputations and serious operations." Some patients were outright killed in the hospitals by the bombardment, one Confederate writing that there were so many incoming shells that "bombs from over the Mississippi rumbled the bass, so we had a full concert."[9]

Even so, there was not a whole lot Pemberton could do but keep his troops in the basic positions they were already in. He depended on his four major division commanders to hold the lines, the leftmost along the north-facing works south of Mint Spring Bayou under Major General Martin L. Smith. He commanded three brigades under Brigadier Generals Francis A. Shoup, William E. Baldwin, and John C. Vaughn, the latter commanding very circumspect East Tennessee conscripts with a couple of equally green if not quite as circumspect Mississippi State Troops regiments made up of men "mostly passed the meridian of life." The two firm brigades held the right and center of the line and had seen action repelling the assaults, while the Tennesseans and Mississippians were wisely placed in perhaps the most defensible location along the lines to the west.[10]

The Confederate line turned ninety degrees at the Graveyard Road and its defending bastion, the Stockade Redan, named for a palisade wall across the road itself. There also was where Smith's right met a new division of two brigades under Major General John H. Forney. These two brigades under Brigadier Generals Louis Hébert and John C. Moore had held the major portion of the lines during the assaults and had turned back heavy attacks against the

Stockade Redan on the Graveyard Road, the 3rd Louisiana Redan and Great Redoubt on the Jackson Road, and the 2nd Texas Lunette on the Baldwin's Ferry Road. Since this was the most contested area of the works, Pemberton also allowed Major General John S. Bowen's trans-Mississippi division of two brigades under Colonel Francis Cockrell and Brigadier General Martin Green to support them where needed, and they provided wonderful aid, often taking position in the trenches themselves during the assaults. These were some of the crack troops of the army, they having made the dramatic assault at Champion Hill where one of Bowen's soldiers explained that his general was "the greatest man I had ever seen. . . . It appeared to me that there was a halo of glory around his head and face." That glory did not last as the Federals drove Bowen back and treated the division even harsher the next day at Big Black River Bridge. These were nevertheless still solid troops.[11]

The fourth division, under Major General Carter L. Stevenson, held the right of the line from the Baldwin's Ferry Road and the railroad southward to the Mississippi River. This division of four brigades under Brigadier Generals Stephen D. Lee, Alfred Cumming, and Seth Barton and Colonel Alexander W. Reynolds held the least-assaulted areas of the works, only the extreme left at the Railroad Redoubt and Square Fort being attacked on May 22. The rest of the line southward to the Salient Work and South Fort, and then up the high ground along the river, were not attacked per se and actually had few Federals even confronting it at this point. Vicksburg was yet to be completely encircled because of a lack of sufficient Federal numbers, so Pemberton could still get messages and potentially supplies in and out for the time being. Still, the line there had to be covered.[12]

Each of these divisions had been engaged in the assaults and were veterans by this point, although their condition holed up inside fortifications would quickly become a concern. More problematic immediately was the condition of Pemberton's works after the pummeling they had taken for five days now, especially in relation to the major assault the day before. The division commanders were loudly seeking any tools they could find, prompting Pemberton's staff to remind them that "the supply of spades and shovels is very limited," although Pemberton assured that "Major Lockett will be ordered to furnish as many as can possibly be procured." The division commanders also requested that the limited number of engineers come to the lines to see what needed to be done in the form of new earthworks, traverses, sandbag loopholes, and emplacements. They also needed laborers in the form of slaves,

Forney sending a small squad to round up any "unemployed" slaves: "Many can doubtless [be] collected in the ravines."[13]

Many of the lower-level commanders took it upon themselves to refashion their works within the larger directions from army headquarters. Pemberton himself remained above the minutia and details of individual work, giving larger contextual guidance and keeping the army on alert. In fact, Pemberton believed another assault was soon forthcoming. He sent word to his division commanders that the Federals were repositioning to enfilade the line and "will probably make a heavy assault," especially along the Graveyard Road where the major salient in the line was located, a ninety-degree or more angle in the lines. Even with Bowen's troops in general reserve, Pemberton felt the need to alert Stevenson on the less threatened right to be ready to send rein-forcements to the more threatened left at any time.[14]

Work developed at a feverous pitch even during the night of May 22 to get the fortifications resealed for whatever was coming. Messages ran quickly about needs here or there, requests for spare cannon carriages for cannons that had been put out of service during the day and for newer works to be erected to make a better defense. There was also a definite desire to utilize any and all personnel they could, Carter Stevenson arguing that if they were going to feed personnel they needed to be put where they could do the most good. He advised Pemberton that "we are issuing to more men than we have" and put the disparity in numbers at the feet of civilian workers employed by the quartermaster. Stevenson noted that they "could render better service in the trenches" and that "all stragglers or absentees from that duty shall be placed in the chain-gang, to work on the fortifications."[15]

Interestingly, after all the hype about another assault, May 23 turned out to be anything but heated. "All seems to be quiet in my front," Stevenson informed Pemberton on that day; "there has been very little firing on my part of the line today." Yet the telltale signs of what they were in for were unmis-takable. Samuel Lockett noted that the Federals "soon had possession of a line of hills on the main roads, not exceeding 350 yards distance from our salient points. These hills they crowned with heavy batteries and connected as rapidly as possible with their second parallel." These were the unmistakable signs of a siege.[16]

As bad as that thought was, the delay due to the additional work in the Federal lines on May 23 gave the Confederates in the trenches time to work as much as they could during the day and certainly during another night. Efforts went forward to reorganize the lines, potentially even planning a counterattack against some of the early Union approach work, as well as rounding up more slaves that were "unemployed for work on the fortifications." Some of the Confederates took advantage of another unassailed night and scouted ahead of their lines, picking up ammunition and weapons, Lee describing those in his front as being "all beautiful Enfields"; the 2nd Texas reported collecting eighty-three stands or arms. Lee also had his men again working on their fortifications, including efforts to "thicken the earth on the redan and redoubt on the interior, to render them more secure against their artillery, as at present they are by no means proof against it. I have [also] had pits sunk in all of them to render the men more secure." Pemberton even recommended Lee strengthen his forts by using the nearby railroad, which by this time was inoperable. He recommended "laying railroad iron, particularly in front of the guns. The iron you can procure, if necessary, by tearing up the railway." Cotton bales were also a usable commodity found in abundance.[17]

The extra time gifted to Vicksburg's defending Confederates was appreciated, but it was plain that the Federals were working just as hard on their side on May 24 and 25. Many Confederate commanders picked up on a major movement of Federals to the right, down near the Hall's Ferry Road. Forney reported from his headquarters ("on the Jackson Road, Stone House to the left about 600 yds in rear of the entrenchments") that they were "moving from his front toward our right — infantry, artillery, and wagons." Pemberton sent his commanders alerts concerning the threat and asking that the division commanders keep in touch on the issue and to "keep . . . him [Pemberton] informed from time to time." He even notified Smith on the far left to be ready to send "two of your best Louisiana regiments" to Stevenson's support this time, a direct reversal of the earlier orders when a renewed assault seemed imminent along the Graveyard Road.[18]

The work of rebuilding and defending of course could not go on without some type of cover, which led to additional need for clarification from Pemberton amid this new phase of the fighting. The various commands had been told to hold their fire to save ammunition, which would not last forever if this went on too long. Pemberton even had to council Colonel Edward Higgins, who commanded the river batteries, to stop firing on the enemy boats in the river, "it being regarded as a useless expenditure of ammunition." Intercepted signals from the Union navy also gave indication of preparations they were taking to keep from being hit or captured by Confederates.[19]

Yet there was a difference between skirmishing with the enemy as a time-killer and firing as sharpshooters for specific purposes. Some of the lower-level commanders such as Stephen D. Lee asked for clarification of the orders to save ammunition, arguing that "I consider it absolutely necessary to impede the progress of the enemy's work as much as possible, particularly as they are there within 200 yards of my pits. I consider this necessary not only to impeded them, but I do not like to see the enemy working within such short distance of our men without an effort to stop them. . . . Our not firing certainly emboldens the enemy." To get around the lack of ammunition, Confederates also shot anything they could. One Federal described in his diary how the enemy "shot a piece of railroad iron seventeen inches long over our heads today. It landed in the sutler's camp a half mile in the rear, where after bounding over a big tent it tore up the turf three or four rods like a plow."[20]

Pemberton certainly agreed to Lee's and others' resistance, writing that "the sharpshooting referred to is not in opposition to the spirit of his order, but meets his views on the subject. Sharpshooting is necessary, but not skirmishing." To John C. Moore, Pemberton similarly advised that "the order on this subject prohibits skirmishing, not the use of sharpshooters. They are deemed very necessary for a proper defense of the lines." Also deemed necessary were spies and scouts sent out between the lines and on the river. Pemberton advised such activity as the siege began in earnest, especially when the movement to the right was detected: "Send out a trusty and intelligent spy to watch and report the movement (if any) of the enemy."[21]

One last effort also had to be made, given the circumstances, and Pemberton issued a statement to his troops addressing his status and his intentions: "You have heard that I was incompetent and a traitor—that it was my intention to sell Vicksburg," Pemberton explained. "Follow me, and you will see the cost at which I will sell Vicksburg. When the last pound of beef and bacon and flour, the last grain of corn, the last cow and horse and dog shall be consumed, and the last man shall perish in the trenches, then and then only will I sell Vicksburg."[22]

If John C. Pemberton was relieved and just a little bit surprised that Vicksburg still held out after the mass assaults of the Union Army of the Tennessee, Ulysses S. Grant was just as perturbed. He had been convinced that the Confederates would not put up much of a fight, beaten and dejected as they were, and so he tried the hasty attack on May 19 that failed and then the more coordinated and massive assault on May 22. It failed, too, and Grant was now becoming convinced that assaults would not take Vicksburg, at least not in the present position his army held. "I feel that my force is abundantly strong to hold the enemy where he is," he informed Nathaniel Banks to the south, "or to whip him if he should come out." Then, he added, "the place is so strongly fortified, however, that it cannot be taken without either a great sacrifice of life, or by regular siege. I have determined to adopt the latter course, and save my men." An Ohioan said it more bluntly, writing to his parents that "we do not intend to charge again upon the dirt piles, and the men know it."[23]

The only option left was thus to do it the old-fashioned siege way by moving their lines closer to the Confederate works, which would allow for a couple of possibilities: either making a quick assault from close in before the Confederates could respond, or burrowing under the Confederate works with mines and then blowing them up—that is, unless Pemberton surrendered due to a lack of supplies before any military action took place. That is what Grant preferred, "to 'out-camp the enemy,' as it were." One of his Missourians noted, "It seems our generals have concluded to thrash the enemy with his tools, roughing up the ground." Edmund Newsome of the 81st Illinois similarly reported in his diary that Grant "says that he has 35,000 prisoners in Vicksburg, who are boarding themselves, and at no expense to the Government. He is satisfied if they are." A Confederate agreed, writing that "we can hear any quantity of gv [grapevine] news here, more apparently than before we were in this guard house. The Yanks holler across the lines and tell us we are in a guard house, which to my opinion, is near true."[24]

Either possibility—mining or more assaulting—meant the Federals would have to dig their way toward the Confederate lines, and that meant a lot of time would be wasted despite what everyone knew would be the probable outcome. "The enemy are now undoubtedly in our grasp," Grant informed Henry Halleck on May 24. "The fall of Vicksburg, and the capture of most of the garrison, can only be a question of time." And at least one aspect of the assaults' failure ironically worked to aid in the siege efforts, at least as Grant saw it: "The troops being now fully awake to the necessity of this, worked diligently and cheerfully." Charles Dana, a former newspaperman and now a War Department official sent to Grant's army to observe and report back to Washington (and commissioned a major to protect him if captured), echoed Grant in his reports to Secretary of War Edwin M. Stanton, writing that "there is no doubt of the final result" but adding "our army is in the best of spirits, though impatient at the delays." Even the sometimes bellicose Sherman was upbeat, writing that "we were in splendid condition for a siege, while our enemy was shut up in a close fort, with a large civil population of men, women, and children to feed, in addition to his combatant force. If we could prevent sallies, or relief from the outside, the fate of the garrison of Vicksburg was merely a question of time." Additionally, slowing down the process would also let the soldiers who had been marching and fighting hard for nearly a month now get some rest. One Indianan admitted: "I never saw men any nearer run down than we was when we got back here."[25]

Even if a siege would take time, Grant was going to start the process and thereby finish it as soon as he could, even the night of May 22. The various corps retained the positions they held that night and the next day, Sherman's corps on the north and northeast of the Confederate lines, Frederick Steele's division returning to its former position holding the line on the ridge north of Mint Spring Bayou from the Mississippi River nearly to the Graveyard Road and the Stockade Redan. Frank Blair's bloodied division retained its position south of the Graveyard Road facing west, while James Tuttle's reserve brigades took station on the front line north of the road, between Blair and Steele. McPherson's corps continued the line southward, Ransom's brigade the only corps asset north of Glass Bayou, "Dirty John" Logan's division south of Glass Bayou and astride the Jackson Road, and Isaac F. Quinby's three brigades farther south down toward the Baldwin's Ferry Road. There, McClernand's XIII Corps divisions under Eugene Carr, Andrew Jackson Smith, and Peter Osterhaus, with one brigade of Alvin Hovey's division present, were a jumbled mess of brigades from the railroad southward to Square Fort. Little force fronted the Confederate line farther south, only one brigade of John McArthur's division down on the Warrenton Road. Fortunately, the bloodied Army of the Tennessee still had confidence in their commander, one writing "Grant has no doubtedly done more toward putting down this cursed rebellion than any other man."[26]

It was not the perfect line, but it was tenable. It was also relatively close to the Confederates already. One Indianan noted "we could distinctly hear at night the barking of dogs in the city—the town clock striking—carriages rolling over the streets & such sounds." Thus, there were a couple of major issues Grant began to work on even that night, one of which was defensive in nature and the other offensive. Defensively, his own lines were a mess due to the assaults of the day and the disorganization they entailed. The problem was most noticeable on McPherson's left, where Isaac F. Quinby's division of three brigades was supposed to cover the line. Instead, due to calls during the day from John McClernand for reinforcements, Grant had sent Quinby's division southward, it being the nearest to the XIII Corps and the supposed breakthrough.[27]

Now as dark shrouded the field, Quinby's division was still to the south, leaving a gaping hole between Quinby and the rest of McPherson's troops farther north along the Jackson Road, only skirmishers of the 18th Wisconsin covering the gap. McClernand was worried about the opening and a possible attack on either his or McPherson's flank during the night. He thus corresponded with both Grant and McPherson about it, telling McPherson there was "a wide gap between our right and your left" and begging that he extend his left to meet McClernand's troops. McClernand throughout the night became quite agitated over the gap, at one point even writing McPherson an ultimatum of sorts: "I have extended my right as much as possible. You will decide whether you will extend your line, infantry or pickets, so as to substantially connect with mine until morning." McPherson also worried about a night attack, and Grant ultimately sent Quinby's three brigades back to their original position, but that did not satisfy McClernand who continued to pepper his commander about "mass[ing] a strong force upon some one or two points of his defenses."[28]

The idea of restarting the assaults even according to McClernand's ideas was out of the question by this point, despite one Wisconsin soldier declaring that he was "ready to go in again any day." Grant's made that clear in his other major action of the night, beginning the work of excavating and engineering a decisive result at Vicksburg, which one Federal colonel noted the men began "cheerfully and deliberately." An Ohioan added, "It is given up by all that it is impossible to take the place by storm and a regular siege is now commenced."[29]

The idea of digging instead of making more assaults was so logical that almost all could see it, and one Federal noted "the work of starving the Rebels at Vicksburg has commenced." Another wrote back home: "I think we will siege them out." Many so thought that the attacks had ended that they sent letters home telling of their safety up to that point. Sherman admitted that "the enemy and his works are stronger than we estimated" and informed Grant "we have had a hard day's work, and all are exhausted." He nevertheless also started thinking of engineering options even then, reverting to his training at West Point, and concocted an idea that "from Ewing's position a sap may be made to reach the right bastion, and it may be we can undermine and blow it up." But he readily admitted that "my men are too exhausted to do all this tonight," and Sherman simply ordered his troops to begin digging a line of earthworks: "I have ordered all to construct breastworks, and have a thousand picks and shovels for that purpose." More specific directions soon came, including orders to "construct in their front a rifle-pit or breast height of logs, and lay a covered road to their rear, to be constructed as soon as tools can be procured." Sherman also reported that "strong working parties are kept employed in opening roads to the rear and preparing covered roads to the front."[30]

McClernand and McPherson similarly ordered their troops to hold what they had gained and to dig a line of earthworks ringing the city and its Confederate defenses. One of McClernand's staff officers said it best: "Bayonets to the rear, shovels to the front." On the Jackson Road, Engineer Stewart R. Tresilian reported that "within the two following days I had the whole line intrenched on the right and left of the white [Shirley] house." McClernand told his troops to "spare no pains; during the night will make rifle-pits and intrench batteries in the most eligible positions." Yet McClernand still had some faint idea of another assault, he informing his officers that "orders from the general commanding the department are awaited, and will probably control the operations of to-morrow."[31]

Those orders indeed came the next day, on May 23. They were not what McClernand had hoped if indeed he wanted to assault again. Rather, Grant simply issued orders that "any further assault on the enemy's works will for the present cease. Hold all the ground you have acquired; get your batteries in position, and commence regular approaches toward the city." More formal orders went out on May 25, Grant informing the army in a special order that "corps commanders will immediately commence the work of reducing the enemy by regular approaches. It is desirable that no more loss of life shall be sustained in the reduction of Vicksburg and the capture of the garrison. Every advantage will be taken of the natural inequalities of the ground to gain positions from which to start mines, trenches, or advanced batteries." He also informed the army that engineer Captain Frederick E. Prime of his staff would oversee the work, adding that "he will be obeyed and respected accordingly." One low-level Federal realized what it all meant and described how "the siege was [soon] conducted in a better manner."[32]

The first and foremost effort in a siege, taught to every West Point student so that Grant, Sherman, and McPherson all knew the formula while McClernand was not as versed, was what engineers technically called a "line of circumvallation." Pemberton, of course, was also aware of what the first step would be ("completing and strengthening his line of circumvallation"). This was a line of troops preferably behind earthworks that was used to hem in the enemy. In this case at Vicksburg, the line was needed only on the north, south, and east sides, the Mississippi River and the navy taking care of the western approaches. This line could be anywhere from hundreds to just a few yards from the enemy position, and it logically paralleled the enemy line. It would provide cover for the besieging troops as well as allow for additional work to progress toward the enemy lines. It also could be defensive in nature to repel any breakout attempt by the besieged. The line of circumvallation was in direct opposition to a line of countervallation, which was a similar line to the rear but facing the opposite direction, protecting against a relief effort from the outside.[33]

In this case at Vicksburg, several factors controlled the building and manning of this initial line, which one Confederate described as "a long trench near to our breast-works." One positive aid was that many of the Federal troops had already begun building trenches when they arrived, even before formal siege operations commenced. Accordingly, many of the regiments and particularly artillery batteries had earthen protection by May 22, and this conveniently formed the basis of as complete a line of circumvallation as could be attained. Other trenches quickly took shape to connect these, one Iowan describing how "there was a heavy detail last night engaged in digging a rifle pit a half mile long. I was one of the detail, each man had to dig a space in front of him 4 or 5 feet long and 4 or 5 feet deep, throwing the dirt toward the enemy." Regiments who had a large number of coal miners in them, such as the 4th West Virginia, especially pushed forward these fortifications. With such manpower, it was not long until Grant's forces, even on the nonengineer McClernand's lines, had a working line of circumvallation on the positions originally occupied by their corps. Unfortunately, the steep terrain was so odd that continuous parallels as described in the textbooks could not be dug. Siege efforts nevertheless hit a much faster pace in the immediate days after the assaults. Henry Seaman of the 13th Illinois described in his diary how "spades, picks and shovels are coming up from the Yazoo landing and are going to the front. This looks like a protracted siege."[34]

Sherman proved to be the foremost corps commander in terms of starting the approaches, surprisingly so because McPherson was a trained West Point engineer. Sherman directed the effort from his headquarters on a spur of a ridge back near Grant's command post, where he kept the colors of the 13th US Infantry that had been hit so hard in the assault on May 19 in front of his tent, "the staff ¼ cut away by a ball," he informed his wife Ellen. He went out every day to inspect the work and "direct the fire of the guns." That of course troubled Ellen, who particularly worried over his spiritual condition and hoped a newly arrived priest from Notre Dame might convert him to Catholicism. Sherman was not interested.[35]

Sherman's corps engineer Captain William L. B. Jenney remembered that on May 23 he "received orders to report with all the pioneer force at the head-quarters of the Fifteenth Army Corps, to assist in the siege of Vicksburg." Soon, the first approaches went forward on Sherman's front, they being begun as early as that day. Sherman informed his corps that "the works of the enemy being too strong to be carried by assault, must be reduced by a system of regular approaches." He went on to say "each division commander will call in his pioneer corps, and proceed to make a good covered road from his base toward some salient of the work in his front, taking every advantage of the natural ravines characteristic of this country. Where these valleys do not fulfill the object, the regular 'sap' must be made." Sherman ordered that "on this species of work soldiers may properly be employed, and negro labor, when organized," adding that "sickness, also, will not be pleaded as an excuse. Sick soldiers must stay in their regimental camps or at the hospitals. If well enough to wander about, they can work on a road, or in loading wagons."[36]

Frank Blair's division took the lead on the approaches, two immediately going forward from Hugh Ewing's brigade and Giles A. Smith's position. The division had taken up the line where it left off on the night of May 22, holding the area south of the Graveyard Road while James Tuttle's reserve division moved into line north of the road, rounding around the salient to the west to connect with Frederick Steele's division. Ewing's approach began at the Union lines and started westward along the Graveyard Road under the command of Ewing's staff officer Lieutenant Emmett Headington. Workers from the brigade dug a covered roadway several feet deep and wide toward the Confederate lines, covered at the front with a sap roller that shielded them from enemy fire while they dug. The approach passed a single large oak tree that stood between the lines, known thenceforward as the "lone tree," lending its name also to a forward battery established there later. The tedious work took time, obviously, but each day that passed continually brought a Federal force nearer to the Confederate works. Those digging made an average of twenty or twenty-five feet per day, mostly working under the cover of night.[37]

A second approach also began from Blair's division on May 23, this time from Giles Smith's brigade. Located about two hundred yards south of Ewing's effort, it began a little closer to the Confederate works because of the presence of a large ravine parallel to the Confederate lines that afforded cover at the jumping-off point. The approach ran westward as men from Smith's brigade continually dug, another sap roller shielding them here as well. The target was the Confederate redan south of the Stockade Redan (termed "Green's Redan" later in the siege), and the digging was first under Lieutenant Emmett Headington and Clemens C. Chaffee, but eventually it fell to Captain William Kossak.[38]

Sherman quickly realized that he had perhaps been a little hasty in putting his engineering personnel all on the front lines. There was still plenty of work to be done in the rear, and he thus sent "detachments from the two companies, with the negro force from that of the Second Division," back to the rear to work on the roads. These included both the roads back to Chickasaw Bayou as well as lateral communication roads behind the corps, connecting the divisions and brigades. In particular, more bridges across Chickasaw Bayou took form, a second one two hundred and fifty feet long on the main route near the pontoon bridge leading to Johnson's Landing and a third farther to the west near the mouth, "where it was but a small creek." These new structures provided much more access to the landing depots, "from which the entire army received its supplies," Engineer Jenney explained. The workers also replaced the original pontoon bridge across the bayou with a permanent one, leaving the pontoon train available for future use despite the fact that in the heavy use already it was "so much injured that about one half of it was rendered worthless."[39]

McPherson's corps was also active in this initial burst of moving forward, the engineer having a clear hand in the work from his headquarters back on the Jackson Road several hundred yards behind Logan's divisional headquarters farther to the front. All dug the initial trenches parallel with the

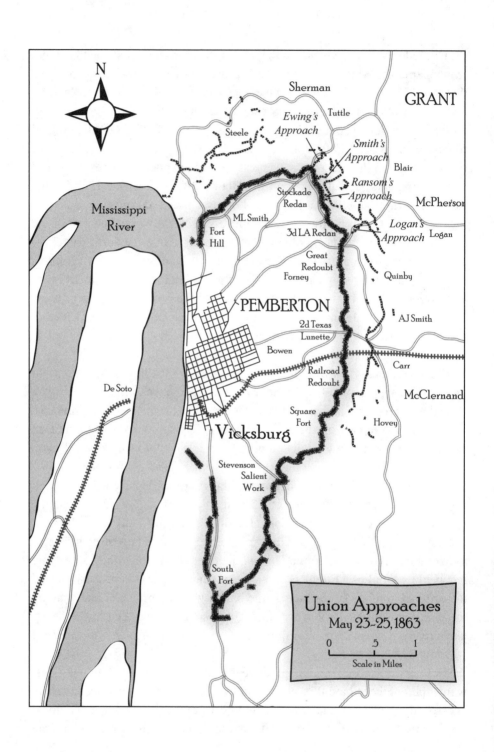

N

GRANT

Sherman

Tuttle

Ewing's Approach

Steele

Smith's Approach

Blair

Ransom's Approach

McPherson

Mississippi River

Stockade Redan

ML Smith

Fort Hill

3d LA Redan

Logan's Approach

Logan

Great Redoubt

Forney

Quinby

PEMBERTON

2d Texas Lunette

AJ Smith

Bowen

De Soto

Railroad Redoubt

Carr

McClernand

Square Fort

Hovey

Vicksburg

Stevenson Salient Work

South Fort

Union Approaches
May 23–25, 1863

0   .5   1

Scale in Miles

Confederate lines, George Carrington of the 8th Illinois describing how he and his comrades dug all night on May 24: "As the lines advance each man carries a spade or shovel. Then halt and go to digging a hole and the quicker the better. Throw the dirt in front until the hole is deep enough to protect the digger. Then turn and dig to the right. By morning a rifle pit will be excavated as long as the line. Lay down the spade and take the musket, because the surprised enemy will immediately open fire." Obviously, the engineer turned corps commander McPherson was also interested in starting approaches from those forward earthworks. Thus, another approach took form on May 23 as well, this time in Ransom's brigade of McPherson's corps, although because Ransom was the only XVII Corps brigade north of Glass Bayou he had acted more in concert with Sherman's troops during the assaults than McPherson's. It seemed that, in beginning the digging process forward, Ransom likewise took his cues from Sherman and his troops more than McPherson, although other troops of McArthur's soon-to-be united division—Colonel William Hall's brigade being ordered to move up from the Warrenton Road duty— would hopefully provide details for the work on this approach as well.[40]

Indeed, the early start alongside Sherman's troops seemed to be more the work of Ransom himself than McPherson, Ransom giving his "immediate and personal attention" to the effort. This approach began in the same ravine that Smith's emanated from, although farther south. Unfortunately, the area where Ransom's troops worked led to a "re-entrant" area of the Confederate works, meaning that the Confederate lines stuck out on both sides from the ravine where the approach lay, allowing the Confederates to fire from both flanks into the workers who were normally covered by a sap in front but needed additional cover here. Engineer Prime described the work on this approach as "difficult," but there were high hopes. The lay of the land allowed Union artillery to command the area immediately in rear of the Confederate lines the approach led to, meaning an assault issuing from this particular advance could be well covered against counterattacking Confederate infantry. Prime further explained that "it would have been difficult for him [Pemberton] to mass troops to resist an assault [here]." The work on this approach fell to Captain Albert M. Powell of the artillery, although Ransom was heavily involved at all times.[41]

McPherson soon joined in the siege efforts himself, dividing the engineering efforts up with Captain Powell overseeing those on Ransom's front, Captain Frank C. Sands on Quinby's line, and corps engineer Captain Andrew

Hickenlooper taking over Logan's work: "I have taken personal charge of central approach along Jackson Road," Hickenlooper wrote, and his would become the major effort of the corps. In fact, Logan's approach would become a multidirectional monstrosity that continually approached the 3rd Louisiana Redan, never running straight but "in a zig-zag way," one surgeon described, "like an old fashioned rail fence."[42]

Hickenlooper started this major approach in front of Logan's division on May 25, working hundreds of men a day and surveying the ground as he went. Logan held the Jackson Road sector, and McPherson started the approach from an artillery battery just southeast of the famed Shirley "White House." A civil engineer before the war who started service as an artillery commander, Hickenlooper took charge of the work, which steadily over the next few days moved forward along the high ridge on which the Jackson Road ran, zigging and zagging with the lay of the land to provide cover for the workers and infantry moving through the roadway at a mammoth seven feet deep and eight feet wide, "with beam and parapet," Hickenlooper noted. Sap rollers at the entrance of the approach likewise covered these workers, and one Illinoisan who was scolded for having a rusty musket retorted that he "had the brightest shovel . . . of any man on the job."[43]

Hickenlooper gave a detailed account of the establishment of this approach on his front. During the assaults, the troops had used the covering hills to advantage to approach and be shielded from the Confederate works, "supplemented by the construction of parapets at exposed points." But this line needed to be within sight and shot of the enemy and thus needed to be covered. The best time to do such initial work without much protection was at night, and Hickenlooper had a force of a hundred and fifty men ready at five-foot intervals, "each equipped with a gabion, pick, and shovel." When other troops made a demonstration against the Confederate pickets out in front of their fortifications, the workers rushed forward to where the new line would be, set their gabion, and went to work behind it, soon fashioning a meek line of cover joining with each neighbor five feet in either direction. By daylight it was done, and a relief of another hundred and fifty men came in and "was engaged in deepening and widening the sap thus commenced." The next night another section of the sap was similarly dug.[44]

There was even a premature effort at mining on Logan's front. The centuries-old effort at digging under an enemy and then blowing up their fortifications was a staple of siege operations, but it had to be done in the right way, not on the fly. Unfortunately, that was how this initial, naive attempt was done on May 24. Samuel Lockett reported how "some of the enemy's sappers crept up a ravine to within 40 yards of the work on the Jackson road and started a sap, apparently with the intention of mining." The Louisianans defending the redan responded with hand-thrown grenades and, Pemberton reported, "were soon driven off by the use of hand-grenades." A supporting Missourian also described how the battery commander made a trough and rolled cannonballs down on the digging Federals, who ceased their work soon enough.[45]

Unlike Sherman's and McPherson's efforts, non–West Pointer McClernand's work lagged behind, due in part to the lack of tools as well as the methodical exploration of the ground. Engineer Peter Hains of XIII Corps explained that "I immediately had as accurate a survey of the ground in front made as was possible with the assistance at hand." With the knowledge gained, Hains decided three points of advance were best, one for each division, directed toward the major bastions in each of their fronts, the 2nd Texas Lunette, the Railroad Redoubt, and Square Fort. Yet at this stage all that occurred was planning, although work soon began in the rear at a depot in a ravine a thousand yards back to make all the needed siege tools such as gabions, fascines, and sap rollers. Much of the blame for the delay, at least according to Sherman, was McClernand himself, who was no trained engineer from West Point. He later related privately to his wife: "I rode away round to McClernand's lines the day before yesterday, and found that he was digging his ditches and parallels further back from the enemy than where I began the first day."[46]

Across the efforts of all three corps, the approaches themselves were large affairs, as they were actually dug-out roadways several feet deep and wide. The idea was that they needed to be wide enough for either a column of four men to march forward or for a wagon and a team of horses to be able to fit, especially with artillery. Pushing men or wagons through the approaches of course required that they be deep enough to cover them, or at least all but the very tops of the wagons but certainly the men and horses. These approaches were eventually six to eight feet deep, making the process quite laborious and resulting in a huge amount of dirt moved back through the already excavated approach or either piled up on the sides of the approaches fronting the enemy. The latter was a win-win for the workers, because every clod of dirt placed in front of the approach had a double impact: it removed that much dirt in digging down and raised the height of the outside wall that much as well.[47]

Of course, the problem spot was the head of the sap, where the digging was being done behind the sap roller. If needed, the sap was stabilized with gabions and fascines or other materials such as cotton bales. Confederate defenders obviously focused their attention on the sappers, trying many ways to blow up or burn the sap rollers so there would be no cover for those doing the digging. As a result, the sappers tended to dig deeper than necessary right off the bat, alleviating the need for much revetment. The closer the approaches came to the Confederate works, the more intense the danger became, especially when the Confederates began to hurl hand grenades at the sappers. "Indeed," noted Prime, "when the enemy's grenades were most annoying, it was impossible to keep detailed working parties at their posts, and it was necessary to depend on the pioneers . . . for this dangerous work."[48]

Doing the digging was actually a myriad of groups. At times, pioneer companies did much of the work, at least for those brigades or divisions fortunate enough to have them attached and that were not detailed for other duties elsewhere. At times there were also blacks from the local area who were either put into the army or paid as workers; Prime described them as "paid $10 per month, in accordance with law, and proved to be very efficient laborers when under good supervision." That said, there were times when they also flatly refused to work because of the danger.[49]

However, the vast majority of digging was completed by the soldiers themselves. The various divisions from which the approaches emanated had the task of providing manpower, and the different brigades and regiments within them alternated their time providing details to do the work. There were also guards needed for the working parties, and all of this was over and above the details needed to man the trenches and parallels to provide cover in the form of sharpshooting. While there were thousands of troops with Grant at Vicksburg, the calls on them were so high that there was rarely any free time for the soldiers in the ranks. One Iowan said it well when he recalled how "our time during the progress of the siege was spent either on fatigue duty digging rifle pits or building earthworks for the protection of siege guns; supporting batteries; on picket duty, and occupying rifle pits. These various duties were constant; immediately upon being relieved from one we were called upon to perform another."[50]

The amount of work required not surprisingly provided some problems, especially when it came to soldiers doing the digging. Prime reported the soldiers' effort, "as is usual in such cases, was very light in comparison with that done by the same number of pioneers or negroes." He went on to explain that "without the stimulus of danger or pecuniary reward, troops of the line will not work efficiently, especially at night, after the novelty of the labor has worn off. The amount of night work done by a given detail depends very much on the discipline of the command from which it is taken and on the energy of its officers. Under average circumstances, such details do not in a given time accomplish half the work of which they are capable."[51]

With the digging started in earnest on Sherman's and McPherson's fronts, the other major action Grant embarked on in addition to starting siege operations was calling in more troops to allow those siege efforts to produce good effects. If a siege was going to be successful, the surrounding lines had to be airtight, and right now they were not. McClernand's left extended only down to opposite Square Fort, and only one brigade of McArthur's division of McPherson's corps initially held the Warrenton Road and Hall's Ferry Road areas. Pemberton could get messages and small supplies in and out easily in that area. To close the noose firmly, Grant needed more troops and thus began to call them in.[52]

Grant had three corps with him at Vicksburg, but he had another—the XVI Corps under Major General Stephen A. Hurlbut—in the rear at Memphis, Corinth, and other locales in northern Mississippi and West Tennessee. Hurlbut had fought with Grant at Shiloh in the famous Peach Orchard but seemed content with his rearward locale, he being more a politician and socialite than a warrior. Nevertheless, he watched as Grant made history, helping when he could, such as coordinating the famous Grierson's Raid and keeping the enemy in northern Mississippi occupied. He told Grant "we in the rear, and the country behind us, are watching with unspeakable pride the glorious track of the Army of the Tennessee. Every sort of congratulation for the glory already won, and the crowning victory to come."[53]

That victory would come a lot sooner if Grant had as many of Hurlbut's XVI Corps troops as possible, and he quickly called on him to send supplies, commanders, and troops. "General Grant has sent for heavy supply of ammunition," Hurlbut explained to his chief of ordnance, and he began to send down general officers such as the now recovered Major General Edward O. C. Ord (wounded at Davis Bridge in October last year) as well as Brigadier General Nathan Kimball, at Grant's request. Grant also told Hurlbut to "contract everything on the line from Memphis to Corinth, and keep your cavalry well out south of there. By this means you ought to be able to send here quite a large force."[54]

The flow of goods and men soon became a flood. Ordnance officer Stephen C. Lyford began the flow of ammunition from the department depot at Memphis's Fort Pickering, as well as keeping corps depots on steamboats at Chickasaw Bayou and Warrenton. The latter were mainly held as reserve ammunition, but a steady stream of steamboats continually brought down huge amounts of ammunition and goods. Eventually, the corps supplies ran out while more was on the way; Federal artillery shot so much that it reached "extreme difficulty" in providing enough ammunition, but one large depot eventually emerged at Chickasaw Bayou. Carriages for siege weapons, mostly captured at Island No. 10 in 1862, were also brought down, but they were in varying states of disrepair. Stragglers from the army that "are at nearly every house for seven or eight miles to our rear" also came in, as well as mules and former slaves, the mules corralled near Chickasaw Bayou and the contrabands (as former slaves were known) encamped near that landing.[55]

Reinforcements also soon began moving from all across the board, although Hurlbut's XVI Corps was the primary provider. In fact, one whole division of that corps was already nearby, Brigadier General Jacob Lauman's division of three brigades under Colonels Isaac Pugh, Cyrus Hall, and George E. Bryant. This division—Hurlbut's own at Shiloh—was mainly made up of veterans of that battle and were solid, although Grant had little faith in Lauman himself. Charles Dana reported that he "got his promotion by bravery on the field and Iowa political influence" and rated him as "totally unfit to command—a very good man but a very poor general." A slight stroke a couple of months earlier did not help. Still, the division had left Memphis on May 17, a terribly bitter surprise to all. One Illinoisan explained that he had received a letter at Memphis while "snugly ensconced in a [quiet] camp with never an idea that when I answered it I should do so in a cane brake in Mississippi." Another of Lauman's soldiers described the trip down on a "rickety old boat," and the division endured Confederate guerrilla fire en route along the river, Lauman reporting "9 men seriously and 5 slightly [wounded] of the Third Iowa." The Iowans had a section of an Illinois battery on board and turned one of the guns on the Confederates, "which was used with good effect on the battery on shore," Colonel Aaron Brown of the 3rd Iowa reported. The division was at Snyder's Bluff by May 20 despite a foray into the wilds of the Mississippi Delta north of Greenville chasing the enemy culprits as well as a roundabout movement around Vicksburg, which included guarding thousands of Confederate prisoners on the night of May 20.[56]

Grant soon ordered the division inland: "Start tomorrow morning with your command," he wrote to Lauman on May 23, telling him to march across the rear of the army to McClernand's left, where he would take over for McArthur's weak command. The division thus made a circuitous route all around Vicksburg, one Illinoisan declaring that their final leg of the march "made the circuit clear around the place for us and not dead yet." The men did, however, see the carnage from the assaults in the form of many hospitals filled with wounded. Worse, the route taken was along terribly hot and dusty roads. With his three brigades and three artillery batteries as well, Lauman nevertheless took a position in between the Hall's Ferry Road and Warrenton Road, but it was a wide gap to fill and the surrounding of Vicksburg was still not complete even with Lauman on site. A gap of a mile or so existed between Lauman and Hovey's division of McClernand's corps to the right, and a smaller one on the left near the river also existed. Certainly, an entire division helped on this weak left flank, but Grant needed even more.[57]

Perhaps the best thing Lauman's division provided was the effect on Pemberton and his Confederates watching from the Vicksburg fortifications. It was this movement to the south that the Confederate high command noted so adamantly. Pemberton certainly took notice, writing that "the enemy appeared in force to-day on the Warrenton and Hall's Ferry roads." Lockett also described the development, including the fact that the Federals "commenced establishing batteries in Gett's field." Most concerning, however, was that "their line of circumvallation was by this completed," or so it appeared to the watching Confederates. It was an ominous development.[58]

Another factor that weighed heavily on both sides' minds in the initial days after the assaults was not even technically a part of the newborn siege, but it was nevertheless very much a cog in how things were done both inside and outside Vicksburg. Joseph E. Johnston and his forces massing to the east near Jackson were perhaps the proverbial straw that would break the camel's back either way. In fact, Sherman later claimed that Grant admitted "he was about the only general on that side whom he feared." If Johnston could somehow amass enough troops to relieve Vicksburg, raise the siege, or cause Grant to break off his operations, then Vicksburg might be held or at the least the army inside saved. If, however, Grant was able to render Johnston a nonfactor in the siege operations, then it was truly only a matter of time until Pemberton capitulated. There was no other factor on the horizon save Johnston that could change the dynamics of the Vicksburg siege.[59]

How and why Johnston was even in Mississippi was an outgrowth of the extreme alarm felt for Vicksburg back in Richmond. Jefferson Davis had wanted to send part of Robert E. Lee's Army of Northern Virginia to Mississippi to help confront Grant; when that proved impracticable, he discussed sending part of it to Tennessee to threaten there, hoping such a move would cause Federal commanders to shift troops away from Vicksburg. In the end, Davis and his administration followed another plan: Robert E. Lee was ordered to once again invade the North, which would of course ultimately conclude in the Battle of Gettysburg in July.[60]

Even with Lee's northern movement, Davis still wanted more help for Vicksburg and ordered his western departmental commander, Joseph E. Johnston, to Mississippi amid the crisis unfolding there. By the time anything was in motion, however, Grant had crossed the river and was fighting his way northeastward toward the railroad and the state capital at Jackson prior to turning west to Vicksburg. Johnston left his easternmost western theater army in Tennessee, under the command of General Braxton Bragg, and dutifully moved to Mississippi to see to his westernmost western theater army under Pemberton. But he was not happy about it.[61]

Johnston brought far too much Johnston and far too little troops with him to make any difference initially. He, in fact, arrived in Jackson the day before Grant attacked the capital, there issuing the famous words "I am too late." In the chaos, Johnston could only retreat and spew words of wisdom to Pemberton to evacuate Vicksburg (and the same to Major General Franklin Gardner at Port Hudson), which was exactly the opposite of what Pemberton was hearing from Davis. Caught between two feuding superiors, Pemberton obeyed the higher-ranking one and slinked back into Vicksburg, only to be caught between two far more important factors that could determine life or death: the Mississippi River and Grant's Army of the Tennessee.[62]

Johnston accordingly began to plan a relief of Vicksburg from his headquarters at Canton, just north of Jackson. He informed Pemberton as much, and Pemberton had the news spread along the Vicksburg lines to boost morale. Johnston then began to assemble troops from almost all compass points, with his two present brigades under Brigadier Generals John Gregg and William H. T. Walker at Canton to the north, reinforcements coming in from the east along the railroad at Forest and other places, and additional reinforcements moving up from Port Hudson to the south. During the assaults, in fact, Brigadier General States Rights Gist's brigade from P. G. T. Beauregard's department in South Carolina arrived, Gist none too happy because he had just gotten married three days prior to leaving. Brigadier Generals Matthew D. Ector's and Evander McNair's brigades from Bragg's army in Tennessee, along with Brigadier General Samuel B. Maxey's from Port Hudson, also arrived near Jackson by May 23. Once the Federals left Jackson in near ruins and went to Vicksburg, many of these troops reoccupied the state capital but found it a wreck, especially in terms of military support ability.[63]

Yet Johnston exhibited from the start a lethargic attitude. His "I am too late" missive was enlightening, and he immediately began to offer excuses and requirements for not acting. Even before the May assaults were done, he requested two major generals to command divisions in his new army. Once the siege itself began, Johnston was adamant that Richmond not expect much out of him: "We have tremendous odds against us," he told Jefferson Davis, adding perhaps the key stroke of the campaign was that "the enemy gunboats have possession of the Yazoo," thereby establishing a secure line of supply. In Johnston's mind, Grant's taking Snyder's and Haynes' Bluffs even prior to the assaults was the final nail in Vicksburg's coffin. Later, he lectured that "from the present condition of affairs, I fear that confidence dooms you to disappointment." Johnston had seemingly made up his mind already that Vicksburg was doomed.[64]

Johnston nevertheless began to organize his "Army of Relief," as it became known, for operations against Grant's rear at Vicksburg. There were many problems, the biggest of which was the lack of troops and fighting material. At one point, Johnston even ordered the removal of guns from Fort Pemberton at Greenwood to bring them closer to his active area, although he noted that they should be remounted there soon "against the June rise." More problematic was the lack of troops, but Davis himself began to order in all sorts of forces, including an entire division under Major General John C. Breckinridge from Bragg's army in Tennessee, along with assorted other brigades. A grateful Davis wrote to Bragg that "your answer is in the spirit of patriotism manifested by you," although there was more to it than that. Bragg and Breckinridge had never seen eye to eye and were at "loggerheards," whereupon Bragg shifted the duty of choosing which troops to send with Breckinridge, whose Kentuckians did not want to go to Mississippi. The wise politician Breckinridge left it to a vote of his boys, and they decided to accompany him, fearing "outsiders" would see a rift if not. Breckinridge's three brigades, some 5,200 men, soon moved by three trains, all in a row.[65]

Adding to Johnston's numbers were other troops, including one of Pemberton's original divisions under Major General William W. Loring, cut off at the fight at Champion Hill. The division had gotten away, although it had lost a large number of soldiers in the process and much of its armament, especially artillery; the division's baggage also went into Vicksburg with the army's wagon train, so the troops were without much of their equipment. Loring eventually arrived at Jackson, which one Mississippian described as "looking very desolate . . . the feds had bin there & had burned down about half of the city." The troops were not much better, one explaining that "I was nearly worn out[;] my feet was blistered in several places." Still, the concentration of troops was occurring, albeit slowly, States Rights Gist describing his movement from South Carolina to Jackson as slow due to the "want of railroad transportation between Montgomery and Jackson, a large amount of the available transportation being employed in the removal of stores of the State and Confederate States from Jackson." Nevertheless, Johnston brought in fresh troops that, one of Loring's soldiers admitted, "was not so badly whipped as we were."[66]

Over the course of the first few days of the siege, these troops continually rolled into the Jackson area, although not fast enough for Johnston: "Troops are coming very slowly," he complained to Davis. He reiterated his desire for major generals, even asking if the wounded Richard Ewell of Robert E. Lee's army had been assigned. Of course, he was now commanding one of Lee's corps in the Army of Northern Virginia. Johnston also sent word of Grant's repulse at Vicksburg, which he said "gives me confidence in Pemberton's tenacity," Davis responding that "I concur in your reliance on the tenacity with which General Pemberton will defend his position." Itching for the battlefield again, Davis added that "if my strength permitted, I would go to you."[67]

In order to relieve Pemberton, Johnston also began to communicate with him inside Vicksburg. Such was still possible at this point because Vicksburg was by no means shut up airtight, the right of the Confederate lines to the south having little to no cover. Thus, couriers, as well as a few meager supplies, could still slip in and out. For instance, when Pemberton informed

Johnston that his most salient need at the time was percussion caps, Johnston began shipping them to Pemberton by courier, some of which made it through. At the same time, Pemberton was able to provide Johnston with word of what was going on inside Vicksburg, including the repulse of the earlier assaults. Pemberton was quick to point out the obvious to Johnston nevertheless, writing that "the men are encouraged by the report that you are near with a large army, and are in good spirits." Certainly, all looked to Johnston for help, one Mississippian confiding to his diary: "Will our government suffer us to be captured? Would it not be better to give up some other point and save Vicksburg?"[68]

As encouraged as the Confederates holed up inside Vicksburg were about Johnston, just the opposite effect was already brewing on the Union side. "I hear a great deal of the enemy bringing a large force from the east to effect a raising of the siege," Grant informed Washington on May 24. "The greatest danger now to be apprehended," he wrote to Nathaniel Banks down near Port Hudson, "is that the enemy may collect a force outside and attempt to rescue the garrison." Grant knew Johnston was out there and took great pains to make sure he was not a major factor. In fact, that was much of the reason why he had swiveled to the east instead of the west once he reached the railroad near Clinton in mid-May: to make sure Johnston was run out of the area and that Jackson was neutralized as a base that could be utilized for a relief effort. He wrote to Halleck as much on May 24: "The rail-road is effectually destroyed at Jackson so that it will take thirty days to repair it. This will leave a march of fifty miles over which the enemy will have to subsist an army and bring their Ordnance stores with teams." In fact, Grant reported on May 25 that "I can manage the force in Vicksburg and an attacking force on the rear of 30,000."[69]

Still, Grant wanted to know exactly where Johnston and other Confederates were and accordingly sent out various probes to find out. One force went from Haynes' Bluff across the Yazoo River into the Delta to break up Confederates in that area and to capture the stock they were gathering. Another under Major James Grant Wilson of the 15th Illinois Cavalry, sent out as early as May 21, checked the area between the Yazoo and Big Black Rivers all the way to Birdsong Ferry, reporting a Confederate presence at Brownsville and the main force nearer to Canton. The 4th Iowa Cavalry also scouted the area, fighting some skirmishes especially on May 24, when one trooper noted they had to retreat "but did it in good order." As a result of the knowledge gained,

Grant sent out a major cavalry force under Colonel Amory K. Johnson on May 25 to make sure of everything and to burn the nearest bridge over the Big Black River. Such a movement left Haynes' Bluff unguarded temporarily, especially with Lauman's movement south, and Grant contemplated sending a force from his Vicksburg lines there to cover it: "I am willing to weaken our force here rather than to leave it unoccupied," he wrote to Sherman.[70]

Grant did just that in the biggest move toward the rear to date. He sent Peter Osterhaus and one brigade of his division (Colonel James Keigwin's), along with some of his cavalry, rearward to the most logical place where the Confederates would cross the Big Black River, at the railroad bridge along the Jackson Road corridor. The brigade had to run from their positions on the Vicksburg lines across the bare hill to their rear but was soon on the way. Colonel James Slack's brigade of Hovey's division was still at the bridge, they returning to the army when Osterhaus made his move eastward on May 24. The move was obviously aimed at placing a higher-level officer than a brigade commander on site, and Osterhaus, as described by one of his colonels, was regarded as "a careful, brave and discreet General who is always sent with his fighting Division to the most difficult places." Osterhaus was supposed to find cavalry to aid him but could locate only fifty men of the 6th Missouri Cavalry and noted, "I am inclined to infer that the colonel will not join me soon, nor the balance of his command either." Still, it was not bad duty. Colonel Marcus Spiegel of the 120th Ohio wrote to his wife, "I feel relieved; I was almost tired of hearing the incessant roar of the hundreds of Cannons and Mortars, the rattling of musketry, which latter never ceased for a minute."[71]

Once arrived at the river, Keigwin's troops found little to do besides major efforts to fortify the western bank of the river, and contrabands performed much of that work. Diaries spoke of endless drill, picketing, and boredom. "We have a good time here," one Illinoisan wrote, "nothing to do but to stand picket and have plenty of grub and nice spring water to use." There were plenty of reviews by Osterhaus himself, and bathing was a luxury in the river. Eventually, one of the regiments was mounted, the 118th Illinois making frequent scouts out to the east, the only delay being waiting on saddles. And the only Confederate threat was miniscule, as it turned out: Colonel Hylan B. Lyon's command of Kentuckians who had escaped from inside Vicksburg earlier; one historian termed them simply "a nuisance."[72]

As a result of his scouting and prying, Grant continually saw the need for and sought additional resources, continuing the call for troops from Hurlbut in Memphis as well as from Banks farther south, especially Colonel Benjamin Grierson's two cavalry regiments fresh off their diversionary raid through Mississippi. But he put a positive face on this rearward threat early in the siege, writing Admiral Porter on May 23 that Johnston's Confederates, "who have been threatening me," have taken position on the Mississippi Central Railroad and that "there is but about 8,000 of them, much demoralized." Another couple of thousand were near Yazoo City, he learned, asking if they were a threat to Porter's gunboats on the Yazoo and contemplating sending infantry to clear them out if so. To Hurlbut he admitted, "From this force no serious danger is apprehended, but they may re-enforce it until it becomes formidable." Obviously, Grant did not want to take his eye off the prize at this point, adding in his message to Porter: "I do not like to detach any troops until this job here is closed up."[73]

The effort to relieve Vicksburg was thus complex to say the least, especially with a vigilant Grant already watching his rear with growing concern. But Johnston was probably not the right man for the job of relieving Vicksburg. It would take a bold leader willing to take a gamble for it to work—and Johnston was not that bold leader. Planning and careful precision were his forte, which in some cases and against some opponents worked. A case in point was Johnston's methodical defense of northern Georgia against Sherman later in 1864. Here at Vicksburg, however, a crisis was at hand, and it was questionable whether Johnston would ever get to the required ready stage he desired with the forces in the pipeline headed for Mississippi. And the opponent in this case was perhaps the biggest factor. While Ulysses S. Grant was the enemy army commander, Johnston and Pemberton faced an even greater threat: time. Accordingly, Johnston's queries to Pemberton on May 25 as to "which do you think the best route? How and where is the enemy encamped? What is your force?" must have seemed to Pemberton to be incomprehensible.[74]

Still, Johnston was on site and working, and it seemed to have an effect. One Confederate general caught up in the concentration, States Rights Gist, related how the situation was abominable, especially confidence in the Vicksburg commander. "Pemberton, of course, is censured by everyone," adding later that "it is said that the troops were badly handled by Pemberton, and other hard things are said about him." Yet things were looking up, and Gist himself showed optimism that "if troops are sent us in time, we can yet save

Vicksburg." He continued, reporting "the people, I regret to say, are somewhat desponding, but the presence of Johnston is rapidly restoring confidence."[75]

It was at this point not clear whether Johnston would be successful against Ulysses S. Grant or actually the greater opponent: time. Grant was already predicting that "one week is as long as I think the enemy can possibly hold out." But then, he had been notoriously wrong before—including on April 6, 1862.[76]

Even with all the major efforts both inside Vicksburg and out, and even back to the rear toward the Big Black River, by May 25 there was nevertheless one situation that began to consume everyone's attention. The first Union assaults had occurred on May 19, and then came the general attack on May 22, and both actions left thousands of dead and wounded, the injured continually "groaning from pain and calling for help." It was a delicate situation to be sure, and one that localized commanders sough to solve. On Francis Shoup's front west of the Stockade Redan, Jared Young Sanders described how at midnight on May 24 there was an "*informal* truce, for their dead was stinking & we hallowed to them to come over and bury their dead, both parties promising '*not to shoot.*'" Sanders talked freely with a lieutenant of the 9th Iowa, who told him some of the news from up North, including about the Copperhead movement. It was an ugly sight, however, as Sanders described how "the dead burst as they were moved." It made him think "what an awful thing is war—how callous & heartless it makes us. We begin to see the dead & dying with almost no emotion, & we soon—forget them.—Oh! may God soon give us victory & peace."[77]

Isolated incidents of care occurred elsewhere as well in the days after the assaults, such as in front of the Great Redoubt where a miserable Missourian lay wounded for days. One Illinoisan remembered how a few men from his siege works scampered ahead and took the poor fellow back to Union lines. It was a question of which was more astounding: that the Federals risked their lives to get their comrade, or that "our Southern brothers watched the affair and no shot was fired." Members of the 5th Iowa similarly did what they could and buried a comrade where they laid in line of battle: they even "placed a very respectable board at the head of his grave, on which his name, company and regiment, and date of death were engraved." Black servants were also known to go between the lines to find their employers, and, conversely, Confederates on Francis Shoup's front risked their lives to bring in a Federal captain who was terribly wounded. The dying officer gave the men his money, asking that it be sent to his wife, which it was. Others could be more hard-hearted. One Iowan described in his diary how on May 23 they "buried all the dead we could get, 23 I think, but probably left as many more on the hill, which the enemy would not permit us to take off. We asked to be either permitted to take them off, or have them do it, but got no satisfaction." He added, "They will be a stench to their nostrils by to-morrow."[78]

These early efforts were only on isolated spots, especially where less action had taken place on May 22 than elsewhere and so there were fewer wounded and dead bodies. By May 25, all understood that something had to be done at the major assault areas, although rumors circulated that Grant had asked for a truce to bury the dead and care for the wounded as early as May 23 but Pemberton denied it. No evidence exists that such occurred. By May 25 it was different. The major attack was three days ago by now (May 25)—an eternity for those wounded who had not been fortunate enough to be evacuated. And some in front of the Stockade Redan had been there three additional days, from their May 19 attack. Stephen D. Lee notified his division commander on May 24, two days after the main assault, that "many of the enemy's wounded are still in my front, and seem to be suffering very much." Many lay there for days without help, groaning and crying for aid, although gradually, perhaps mercifully, the noises slowly lessened as many of the more horribly wounded succumbed to death following the lack of assistance. Ephraim Anderson described one poor Federal in front of the Stockade Redan who "was seen repeatedly raising both his arms and legs for nearly two days, when he became still—was dead."[79]

Worse perhaps was the condition of the dead. Most of the bodies lay closer to the Confederate works than the Union lines, with some filling the ditches immediately on the other side of the Confederate parapets. As a result of the hot late-May weather, these bodies quickly became foul and the odor became almost unbearable. For that reason, the impetus for doing something about it actually began with the Confederates. In fact, Colonel Claudius W. Sears of the 46th Mississippi noted that his men began "to tote their carcasses down to the picket lines at night."[80]

The odor soon became intolerable. A Missourian noted that "the enemy's dead . . . were almost stinking us out of the works." A Mississippian similarly explained that "these bodies had become so offensive that our troops could hardly remain in the trenches along those points where the slaughter had been greatest." The views were not much better, one Confederate describing how "the reeking bodies lay all blackened and swollen, and some with arms extended as if pleading to heaven for the burial that was denied them by man." A Louisianan described "the fowls of the air and wild beasts preying on them."[81]

Grant seemed little inclined to do anything about it for security's sake, but messages about the awful situation began to run through the Confederate high command as early as May 24, when Martin L. Smith, division commander on the north side of Vicksburg, alerted Pemberton that "the enemy's dead are becoming very offensive along portions of my front, and it is respectfully suggested, in case a truce is asked to bury them, whether it may not be well to grant it, under such instructions as will prevent an examination of our works."[82]

With no request from Grant as yet, Pemberton queried some of his officers "whether the stench arising from the bodies outside of the intrenchments renders it necessary that a flag of truce be sent on this subject." Smith, surprisingly, responded, "I do not think the stench arising from the dead bodies outside the intrenchments renders a flag of truce necessary." Apparently, he wanted Grant to make the first move, not Pemberton. Carter Stevenson responded that "the stench from the dead Federals is sufficient to warrant a flag of truce" and also added that "it may enlighten us as to the movements of the enemy." Pemberton sided with Stevenson and alerted the division commanders that he would send the flag to Grant and that he wanted all firing stopped during this time "unless it is continued by the enemy."[83]

Pemberton sent Grant a message, the third draft he worked on, carried by a courier who approached the Union lines near Logan's division. The sudden appearance of a white flag prompted some to think a surrender was near. After some trouble finding officers who would meet the bearer, Logan himself met the Confederate and kept him there for over an hour while a runner took the message to Grant's headquarters. In the meantime, Logan "ordered out a keg of whiskey & from what I can learn they had a big drunk in the meantime." The note went to Grant, Pemberton cajoling that "two days having elapsed since your dead and wounded have been lying in our front, and as yet no disposition on your part of a desire to remove them being exhibited: in the name of humanity I have the honor to propose a cessation of hostilities for 2 ½ hours, that you may be enabled to remove your dead and dying men." Pemberton even gave Grant another option, saying that if he could not do this—if he would only promise to cease firing—the Confederate general would have his men bury the dead. Grant quickly responded that he would agree to the truce, although he noted that it would take some time to get word back to Pemberton, for him to send the orders to all his army, and for Grant to notify all his commanders. Grant thus proposed a late cessation, starting at 6:00 P.M. "From that hour for two & a half hours all hostilities shall cease on our side," Grant wrote. Probably the cooler time of day for digging graves was a factor as well.[84]

This was a new and novel occurrence to all. One Confederate declared that it was all done without the knowledge of the troops in the trenches: "A flag of truce was sent in by us, the purport of which We Know nothing." It was new for Grant as well. He had not been in this position before; at most battles, the field was left in one side's hands or the other. At Fort Donelson, Grant had retaken the field on February 15 and held it until the surrender. At Shiloh, Grant had also held the field and denied the Confederates a request to send "a mounted party to the battlefield of Shiloh." Similarly at Iuka, Corinth, Port Gibson, Raymond, Champion Hill, and Big Black River Bridge, Grant had held the field and detailed troops to care for the wounded and bury the dead. Only at Belmont had Grant been made to yield the field. But here, where neither side held the battlefield as yet, there was no clear party responsible for the act. In fact, this was a first in terms of there being a no-man's-land between lines still locked in combat, making the situation even worse.[85]

Perhaps because of the novelty of the situation, neither side had done anything about it for days. But once the process started, all wanted it done right. Neither side wanted to be deemed as breaking the truce or taking advantage of it. Pemberton informed his division commanders sternly that "by agreement entered into by flag of truce with the enemy, all hostilities will cease from 6 to 8:30 P.M., to enable the enemy to bury their dead." Grant also sent out his orders for the operation, and Sherman threatened his subordinates that "all commanders will respect the truce with absolute fidelity, and avail themselves of the opportunity to bring in and bury the dead. Surgeons will be sent with stimulants."[86]

The hour for the "suspension of hostilities" soon neared, but many were logically nervous about it. Forney wanted more information during the negotiation process, asking that Pemberton's headquarters "notify me if the 'flag' is received and of how long duration the 'truce' will be." He also alerted headquarters that he had given orders, just in case there was some trickery, for his men to "fire if the enemy advances in column or makes any demonstration of attack." Still, the risk had to be taken, Samuel Lockett testifying that "the dead had become offensive and the living were suffering fearful agonies."[87]

Then all fell quiet. One Mississippi chaplain described how "presently the firing began to cease on the center of the line and gradually extended from right to left until quiet reigned along the whole line. . . . The stillness seemed unnatural but was very welcome." Illinoisan John Griffin agreed that "all at once the noise ceased. Conjectures were many and some even cherished the hope that the place had either surrendered or was going to do so." Many others thought the same.[88]

Then something odd occurred as the Confederate began to mount their fortifications to watch the show. "The butternuts crowded on top of their earthworks and seemed anxious to make as great a display as possible," Federal George Remley explained. They were not the only ones, as the trusting Federals quickly followed their lead. An Illinoisan related how "we were all surprised at seeing the rebels all appearing above their breastworks, [and] our men equally anxious to know what was going on also showed themselves." A Mississippian described how Yankees came out "as numerous as the ants from a freshly stirred up nest."[89]

It was an odd occurrence to say the least in the "bright evening sunshine." But it was only going to get odder. Many of the watching Confederates could not help themselves and dove off their own fortifications to help the Union work parties. "As most of these dead, or a goodly number at least, were so near our works that there was a detail made up from our ranks to move the dead out a certain distance from our works," recalled one Mississippian. That said, the amount of aid the Confederates gave was different on various parts of the line. Lieutenant William T. Rigby of the 24th Iowa described in his diary that the Confederates all stayed in their own lines on his front, allowing the Iowans to come all the way up and gather their dead. "But of course," he noted, "[we] were not allowed in the works." One of Confederate brigade commander John C. Moore's staff officers described how "we were permitted to stand on our brest works, some mingled with the enemy but soon [were] debared from that privilege, but not from talking."[90]

The Confederates did what they could to help nevertheless, although motives were questioned, as would be expected. Lockett asserted simply that during the time "both parties were engaged in performing funeral rites and acts of mercy to the dead and wounded Federal soldiers." Charles Dana was not so sure and reported that Pemberton "probably also hoped to gain information." Lockett admitted as much, adding: "Naturally, the officers of both armies took advantage of the truce to use their eyes to the best possible advantage." Several Confederates also picked up lost Union battle flags on the ground close to their works.[91]

As the horrible task of cleaning up the wreckage of May 22 began, the wounded were the first priority. Amazingly—three days after the major assaults and an astounding six days after the limited action in front of the Stockade Redan on May 19—there were still some alive.

A watching Mississippian described how "among them were found living men, who had fallen, perhaps on Wednesday and certainly not later than Friday before, who had lain there without a drop of water or the particle of shade." Another described one unfortunate Union soldier: "One poor fellow was picked up . . . who had been wounded two days before; what must have been his sufferings!"[92]

Henry Reynolds of the 36th Mississippi at the Stockade Redan related how he left the earthworks and wandered among the Federal dead and wounded. He came upon a wounded Union soldier lying beside a tree trunk to try to get out of the hot sun and "seeing my canteen hanging by my side he began to beg for water." Reynolds knelt beside him and watched as the pitiful situation played out: "His lips were parched, his feverish eyes followed the canteen. He was weak from loss of blood. When I raised his head with one arm I touched the canteen to his lips and he took a deep draught and begged for more." Reynolds admitted "it was pitiful but our time was limited and many yet to be moved out, so I had him carried out and moved on." He added, many years later, "I often wonder whether he lived or whether his was the face of hundreds of others—there to fill an unmarked grave. But how was I ever to know? He wore the blue—I the gray." Sadly, many of the wounded who were recovered soon died anyway.[93]

The major reason for the truce of course was to bury the dead, and that was a ghastly task given the heat, length of time they had been there, and types of wounds they had endured. It was so bad some did not even participate, such as Federal Joseph Stockton who admitted that "I did not go in the field having no relish for such sights." One participant described how "they were an awful sight, bloated & black and alive with worms & maggots almost ready to fall to pieces." Some were so bad they could not be moved and the Confederates buried them where they were: "When we got to them such a horrible sight as met the eye is difficult to describe. They were covered with flies and literally eaten up by maggots. We buried them as best we could in the short time we had to do it in." Illinoisan George Carrington described how some of the dead "had lain so long in the hot sun their bodies had turned black and fingers like bird claws."[94]

The process of burying the dead was also different on varying parts of the line. Most of the Federals were carried back to the rear and buried in a line. Many could not be moved, however, and were simply buried where they were. "They dig ditches near the dead and then roll the putrid bodies in—sometimes with a blanket for the winding sheet—sometimes with nothing but the clothing in which they fell," a Mississippi chaplain explained. "A little earth is thrown over them and they are left unmarked, unknown, to sleep until awakened by the last trump—which we all shall hear on the great Judgment Day."[95]

Nicholas Miller of the 8th Indiana described burying the only casualty in his company, a sergeant. "He was as black as a negro. We dug in the ground as long as we could stand it and then some other man would take his turn until we got a hole deep enough to cover him up, then took sticks and pushed him in and threw a little dirt over him and left him." Stephen D. Lee similarly described how the two sides "met on the line and chatted, and performed this sad duty. The bodies of the gallant soldiers from Iowa and Illinois in the ditch of the railroad fort were so decomposed that dirt was thrown on them in the ditch. The wounded left in the ditch had died. They could not be moved. This was the case nearly everywhere on the field, and they had to be buried generally where they fell." Sadly, there was also some stealing from the dead reported.[96]

Perhaps the sad duty got to the grizzled soldiers, because after the horrific tasks were completed something even more odd occurred. Union brigade commander James Slack wrote to his wife how "they very soon began to hollow at each other & very soon began to visit [and] shake hands and talk, trade knives, exchange papers, &c." From the other side, one Mississippian described how when all the work was done "we, the common soldiers of both armies, met on halfway ground and had a friendly chat. Old acquaintances were hunted up, and the broken ties of friendship and consanguinity were reunited." One Mississippian declared "it was impossible to keep them apart, and they met as old friends and not as enemies."[97]

The visiting took many different forms. One Texan described how the two sides "talked and gossiped as though they were the best of friends and nothing had happened. Our men were invited over for coffee." The comradeship was even deeper when kinfolks were found. Iowan Myron Knight related that "there was a good many boys of our division who found brothers, cousins and other relatives in the Rebel army some of which they kept.—Was also one Rebel major." Another described how "when the bugles gave the signal that the truce was ended, I saw two pairs of brothers clasp hands in farewell, and go in opposite directions." In front of the Stockade Redan, both sides quickly figured out that Missourians were facing Missourians.[98]

Not surprisingly, the discussions at times turned to the war and the sad reality of the situation, punctuated by the reason they were even meeting together. The common soldiers also proposed solutions. Some of the 14th Wisconsin met Confederates, probably Mississippians, in a ravine between the lines and "we had a long talk over matters and things in general," recalled Federal James Newton. "They agreed with us perfectly on one thing, if the settlement of this war was left to the Enlisted man of both sides we would soon go home."[99]

While a sincere bond emerged between the two sides, fears of someone taking advantage of the situation were also very real, and officers especially took care to make sure some security was still maintained on both sides. Orders went out in some Union units to "remain in their positions that Rebs might not gain information, but a few on both sides violated these orders and mingled with each other." Even that was uneven. An Iowan described how "strange as it may seem, our men were permitted to go up to and examine their works, and they came down and passed their remarks on our tunnels, and trenches. It was emphatically a dutch mix." Most took more care, however, a Mississippian writing that "the enemy are not allowed to come up to our works but are kept back at a distance sufficient to prevent them from over-looking our fortifications."[100]

There was also some actual news shared, which quickly went up the chains of command; one Confederate officer reported that "some of the enemy's men told some of our men yesterday during the truce that the movement of the enemy yesterday was not troops changing positions from left to right, but infantry (about 3,000) moving down the line from Snyder's." Confederates who were tired of their entrapment and took this opportunity to desert also reported news from inside Vicksburg, mainly short supplies. "A great many of the rebs stayed with us and would not go back," an Indianan wrote to his wife. Perhaps making sure these deserters were not believed, Confederate officers "loudly declared that they had provisions for six months." Others simply innocently took the opportunity to look over the ground they had assaulted across on May 22.[101]

At times, the Confederates wandered too close for comfort to the Federal lines and camps. McClernand informed Grant about one Confederate commissary who went all the way into Union lines. "Stupidity, on the part of the Major, induced him to bring the officer to Genl Lawlers Hd Qrs, to obtain an interview with Col [Daniel W.] Lindsey, and having seen our defenses; I deem it unsafe to permit his return," McClernand informed Grant. He recommended sending the officer north to Kentucky, where he was from. In a separate incident, one of McClernand's staff officers described how several Confederates went all the way to McClernand's headquarters. "He drove them back," the officer wrote, and the Confederates ran and hid, only later coming out and giving themselves up. Ironically, one Federal colonel reported how McClernand rode "all along the lines examining our own and the enemy's works."[102]

The primary way both sides took advantage of the truce was in looking over no-man's-land. Obviously, that was the most critical area, whether for Union engineering efforts or Confederate attempts to repel assaults. Thus, while little actual engineering was done, with chief engineer of the XVII Corps Andrew Hickenlooper explaining how the "flag of truce [was] in [effect], in consequence of which we did very little work," there was ample opportunity to take in all they could see. Hickenlooper added that the truce did give "the chief engineer a much needed opportunity of closely inspecting the ground to be passed over, of fixing the salient points in his mind, and of determining upon the general direction of the various sections of the sap." Hickenlooper clearly saw that the high point of ground between the white house and the 3rd Louisiana Redan was important, and he determined even then, once the sap reached that area, to create a battery there to cover the farther progress of the approach. Specifically, Hickenlooper noticed "a particular and sharp bend in the direction of the ridge over which we would have to lead our sap, and which it would be of great advantage for me to be able to find and identify after dark some future time." He nonchalantly picked up a musket with a bayonet and stuck it in the ground as a marker, but he was just as quickly confronted by a Confederate officer on the parapet who ordered him to remove it. Hickenlooper argued that it was merely a broken musket, but the Confederate threatened to shoot and brought up several soldiers to aid him. Hickenlooper concluded "prudence was the better part of valor."[103]

One of Hickenlooper's counterparts did not have such luxury, by an odd occurrence. Samuel Lockett also planned to take the truce as an opportunity to reconnoiter, but he was diverted. "On this occasion I met General Sherman for the first time," he related. While he stood on the parapet of one of the forts, a Federal orderly approached and stated that General Sherman wished to speak to him. Lockett followed the orderly to a group of Federal officers when Sherman advanced and introduced himself, saying, "I saw that you were an officer by your insignia of rank, and have asked you to meet me, to put into your hands some letters entrusted to me by Northern friends of some of your officers and men. I thought this would be a good opportunity to deliver this mail before it got too old." The young Lockett replied with some cocky banter: "Yes, General, it would have been very old, indeed, if you had kept it until you brought it into Vicksburg yourself." Sherman could banter as well, responding, "so you think, then, I am a very slow mail route," to which Lockett humorously cajoled, "Well, rather, when you have to travel by regular approaches, parallels, and zigzags." Sherman retorted, "Yes, that is a slow way of getting into a place, but it is a very sure way, and I was determined to deliver those letters sooner or later."[104]

Sherman then got the best of Lockett, whether either of them knew it immediately. Lockett had wanted to examine the ground, but Sherman asked him to sit with him on a nearby log, "and thus the rest of the time of the truce was spent in pleasant conversation." Lockett remembered that there was some talk of the positions, Sherman complementing the Confederate defenses: "You have an admirable position for defense here, and you have taken excellent advantage of the ground." Lockett no doubt swelled with pride, although Sherman probably had no idea Lockett was the one who had laid out the defenses, but the Alabamian responded, "Yes, General, but it is equally as well adapted to offensive operations, and your engineers have not been slow to discover it." Whether Sherman knew he had Pemberton's chief engineer on his hook is not known, and obviously Lockett did not know he would be tethered for the rest of the precious two and a half hours. Whether it was a purposeful act on Sherman's part is also not known, but it sufficed to keep Pemberton's chief engineer busy the whole time. "Intentionally or not," Lockett later mused, "his civility certainly prevented me from seeing many other points in our front that I as chief engineer was very anxious to examine."[105]

Whether simply visiting or more clandestinely seeking any gain they could, soldiers of both sides soon parted as the end of the truce neared. "The truce ended, the sharp-shooters immediately began their work and kept it up until darkness prevented accuracy of aim," an amazed Lockett recalled. But the truce had broken some of the ice, Lockett adding that once night fell the pickets took position in front of both lines "so near to each other that they whiled away the long hours of the night-watch with social chat."[106]

Random acts of nonsense occurred even as the two sides parted, however. One Louisianan described a shot being fired during the truce when he wrote of a welcomed "few hours of rest & free breathing," or so he thought. Toward the end when all the Confederates had scampered back to their fortifications, one Louisianan stood atop the works and a Union sharpshooter "took a deliberate fire at me." He explained that "the ball passed harmlessly by," but he added that "it was an infamous act," especially with many Federals still between the lines. A fellow Confederate yelled out "if ye do that again we will fire into ye & it will take all day tomorrow to bury ye're carcasses!"[107]

Mostly it was an amicable separation, however. Kind parting words were spoken as the two sides left each other, although few minds were changed on the issues. When one Federal told a Louisiana captain, "Good day, Captain; I trust we shall meet soon again in the Union of old," he responded that "I cannot return your sentiment. The only Union which you and I will enjoy, I hope, will be in kingdom come. Good-bye, sir." Another Federal similarly left his meetings with the firm conviction that "they seem disposed to fight it out."[108]

The siege thus began again, although reluctantly for both sides who had enjoyed a bit of humanity within all the madness. "It has been a period of recreation to us all. We have been permitted to come from the ditches and walk about and relieved from the continuous firing of the sharpshooters and cannon," one Confederate admitted. Another added, "It was with seeming reluctance that the firing was resumed; and even next day it seemed less vicious than before."[109]

Still, it was a war they were in, and a cannon shot signaled the end of the truce. "We were enemies again," one recalled. "Separate now, ye brothers and relations and old friends and resume the miserable work of killing each other," quipped a Mississippian. A Michigander perhaps described it best, observing that "when the armistice was over both sides withdrew with a cheer and commenced the work of slaughter as usual."[110]

4

"My Men Are in Good Spirits, Awaiting Your Arrival"

May 26–31

If the first couple of days after the May 22 assault consumed both sides in getting their bearings and setting up more lengthy siege operations, the last week in May saw those operations come in full force. The assaults had been a vivid shock to the armies. Those on the Confederate side who saw the majority of the action—Smith's and Forney's divisions—had mainly been in garrison duties for months, and most, although not all, had not seen battle in that time, really since Corinth in October the previous year. The Federals received a shock as well, most thinking the harshly handled Confederates would just give up. That had not been the case. Frankly, neither side thought this day would come, when Vicksburg would hold solid and the Federals would have to start digging in earnest. But it was here, a new phase of the campaign, and as one Federal explained to his wife, "the eyes of the north are directed at this point." The temporary armistice on May 25 seemingly marked the change, creating a clear break with what had happened heretofore. One Federal described it well when he related that they were now "adhering to the policy of keeping up a close Siege without attacking them in their fortifications."[1]

As the calendar swept on through what was left of May toward the coming of June, almost all elements of the full-fledged siege became present. Inside fortress Vicksburg, John Pemberton and his thirty thousand troops, along with an unknown number of civilians, huddled as best they could to live another day, although because of sickness only a little over half of the troops were effective enough to actually fill the trenches. Out in those trenches, the heat was miserable, the food poor, and the rest fleeting. "If this is May's warmth," one Missourian wrote in his diary, "what will July's heat do else than fry us a live." Worse, the almost constant firing of Federal sharpshooters and artillerymen combined with the frightening bombs being dropped on Vicksburg from the Federal naval and mortar boats created a feeling of never knowing exactly when one's end might come. Many hid out in caves for protection, although if a cannonball landed exactly on the right spot, those caves could be just as dangerous as being on the outside.[2]

Pemberton himself was by now fretting, worried about the stock of food, stock of supplies, and stock of energy for his men. Supplies were already starting to run low in some cases, such as percussion caps needed to fire small-arm muskets. Pemberton had his staff keep a close watch on inventory and turn all excess caps over to the ordnance department. The only thing seemingly keeping morale up and hope for a way out of this trap was the almost universal thought that relief was coming, mainly from Joseph E. Johnston. Unknown in Vicksburg, Johnston was having almost as difficult a time organizing his force amid the broad expanses, dry weather, and lack of will to fight. Perhaps it was better those details were not known inside Vicksburg.[3]

The main culprit causing all this commotion was Ulysses S. Grant, and he was fast formulating an organization that would see to every need that came up during the siege. He was already ordering vast amounts of food and ordnance stores to be sent south to his army. He was also ordering additional troops to Vicksburg, knowing he had still not as yet, even with the arrival of Jacob Lauman's division, closed the gate to Vicksburg securely. More troops were also needed to secure the back door as well, Johnston lurking as he was to the east with an unknown but probably growing number of troops. That growing number was what concerned Grant the most, and in late May he began to put much more emphasis on securing his rear so that he could win the victory at Vicksburg.[4]

Those at the Union front at Vicksburg itself were likewise getting into their mid-siege routines. With food flowing, the digging was going well. Approaches were already begun by Sherman's and McPherson's corps, and others would be started this week. "Men in good spirits & prefer the spade & pick to charging," one Illinois officer wrote. Charles Dana reported Sherman working fast and steady and on May 26 informed Washington that the general "might tomorrow plant his guns within 50 yards of the fortifications and clear them out for an assault, but he has not yet got near enough to commence mining." Yet there was even this early a perceptible difference in the various corps' zeal, Dana reporting that "on McClernand's front, where the approaches are naturally most favorable to us and the enemy's line of works evidently much the weakest, nothing in the way of siege operations had been accomplished when I was there last evening." McClernand's corps engineer detailed the delay, writing that, after surveying the ground, he requested "the necessary intrenching tools" but that "the week elapsed before any considerable number of intrenching tools could be procured. In the mean time the most was made of the few that could be gathered together around camp and from the pioneers." The result was that the initial parallels on McClernand's front, much less approaches, were not begun until the end of May.[5]

The digging would not stop until Vicksburg was in Grant's hands—that is, when Lincoln's key was in his pocket. Other branches worked just as hard, the navy in the rivers supplying, patrolling, and shelling to great effect. All the while, the sharpshooters kept the enemy down, one writing in his diary, "We are still throwing lead at Rebs." It was truly a combined effort, and all of it was done with the continual realization that there was, barring some major unforeseen miracle, little doubt as to the outcome. Grant himself noted that "there is no doubt of the fall of this place ultimately, but how long it will take is a matter of doubt. I intend to lose no more men, but force the enemy from one position to another without exposing my troops."[6]

Even though just a matter of time, that was the worst part even now just a week or so into this new type of siege warfare. The waiting and waiting and waiting was already mind-numbing, and it would only get worse, but Grant had the advantage in most ways. "I think we can stand it as long as Pemberton can," one of his soldiers wrote home. That seemed to be Grant's ultimate strategy.[7]

One of the truly important but often overlooked aspects of the Vicksburg Campaign, and including the siege in large part, was the Union naval contribution. Ulysses S. Grant had never been one to disregard the afloat services, even from his days in 1861 with the amphibious movement to Belmont. Forts Henry and Donelson likewise solidified his respect for the naval arm, and the Federal forces thoroughly utilized the gunboats and vessels in the Shiloh operations as well, although the large majority of the big gunboats remained on the Mississippi River while the army gutted West Tennessee via the Tennessee River.[8]

Both combined once again as Grant made his foray to Vicksburg a one-pronged effort, it being on the Mississippi River itself. Transports, supply vessels, and gunboats were all needed in large numbers to do what Grant wanted to do, and he found a willing partner in Admiral David Dixon Porter. The relationship was a little different than Grant had been used to in his earlier river campaigns, mainly because the navy was no longer under the army's control, as it had been earlier in the war. Now, Porter was a completely autonomous officer who could do pretty much as he pleased, but fortunately for Grant and the Union itself he was open to whatever Grant suggested.[9]

A case in point was Porter's passage of the Vicksburg batteries twice in April, on which Grant's entire roundabout operation hinged. Without Porter's vessels below Vicksburg, Grant had no way to cross the river. Yet Porter was not a yes-man to Grant; while he agreed with sound military logic and often put his vessels in danger doing it, he drew the line at times and on other occasions talked frankly with Grant about what certain operations would mean in terms of future naval support. The passage of the batteries was a case in point. Porter candidly described to Grant that, once the boats moved below Vicksburg, there was no coming back.[10]

Grant depended on Porter greatly, especially in getting across the river initially in late April and then again when he approached Vicksburg. Grant's famished army needed a supply outlet soon, and he called on Porter to provide it on the Yazoo River. Grant also depended on Porter during the assaults as well, at which time the admiral had several of his gunboats shot up pretty badly in supporting Grant. The exasperation Grant felt even seeped into his communications with Porter, the two friends and comrades sharing curt messages in the immediate aftermath of the reversal. In telling Porter after the failed assaults "I now find the position of the enemy so strong that I shall be compelled to regularly besiege the city," Grant perhaps unwisely mentioned that he requested that Porter "give me all the assistance you can with the mortars and gunboats." He even reiterated, in the next paragraph, "let me beg that every gunboat and every mortar be brought to bear upon the city."[11]

Apparently, the prickly Porter took Grant's words as a condemnation of not doing enough to support the assaults. He fired back that "I am doing all with the mortars and gunboats that can be done," then explained all he had done in support of Grant, almost getting his boats shot out of the water. He ended with a terse "hope you will soon finish up this Vicksburg business, or these people may get relief." Perhaps realizing he had misspoken or Porter had taken his request the wrong way, Grant simply replied, "I am satisfied that you are doing all that can be done in aid of the reduction of Vicksburg."[12]

As the last week in May slowed down the efforts into the same old digging and bombarding day after day, Grant still depended on the navy, often asking Porter for aid in various matters where the situation could have gotten serious if not for the naval contribution. For instance, when Grant wanted to send troops northeastward to check on Johnston, he sent troops from Haynes' Bluff, they being nearest. Afraid to leave such a strategic point uncovered, Grant asked that Porter send the Mississippi Marine Brigade ashore to hold the place until additional troops could be dispatched. On another occasion, when transports were at a premium, he asked that the brigade be sent ashore so that their boats could be sent northward to Memphis to ferry troops southward to the army. Amid the forays northeastward to check on Johnston's relieving army, Grant also asked Porter to cover the movements with gunboats on occasion, giving any infantry or cavalry forces a big-gunned support nearby if they needed to withdraw to it on the Yazoo River for cover.[13]

The most significant and appreciated naval effort during the siege, however, was the bombardment support both flotillas provided. Porter had the gunboats that had run the river batteries south of Vicksburg, while he also had gunboats north of town as well. Mortar boats provided additional firepower, and Grant wanted the Confederates in Vicksburg harassed night and day. Sherman, in his no-nonsense manner, desired the mortars "come within easy range and drop shell by the thousand in the city." They did, one of Pemberton's staff officers, John C. Taylor, describing "seven shells being in the air at once, sometimes—an average of two a minute."[14]

The effort to draw supplies as well as close and pound the enemy nevertheless brought problems, including one major disaster on May 27. Both the gunboats north and south of Vicksburg moved toward the city and bombarded it, and Porter sent unmanned coal barges afloat in the river to supply the flotilla south of Vicksburg. One of the barges was captured, and Pemberton ordered that his men sink it, "it being found impracticable to unload it." Worse was the loss of a gunboat itself. Combined with a massive land and water bombardment, Grant and Sherman had requested Porter send down an ironclad to investigate the Confederate defenses north of town, but Dana described

Porter as "extremely cautious about exposing vessels." Unfortunately, Porter
and Lieutenant George M. Bache, commanding the newly arrived ironclad
USS *Cincinnati,* did not know Confederates still manned a powerful river
battery nearby. *Cincinnati* had already been sunk once before, at Plum Point
Bend back in May 1862, but was raised only to face the same fate yet again.[15]

Sherman had been requesting help for days, and Porter sent the *Cincinnati* that morning, laden with coverings of hay and wood. Bache quickly uncovered the powerful Confederate battery. Pemberton noted that the gunboat
"pushed boldly down the river, rounded the peninsula, and was soon hotly
engaged with our upper battery at short range." The effect was instant. "The
enemy fired rapidly, and from all their batteries," a dazed Lieutenant Bache
reported. Some bounced off, one Confederate admitted, like "an india rubber
ball," but a fatal shot hit the magazine and flooding began in earnest. Then,
the steering was shot away, and other balls peppered the gunboat, Bache
explaining that "the enemy fired with great accuracy, hitting us almost every
time." Plunging shot from the elevated batteries also did a lot of damage,
Bache reporting that "the shots went entirely through our protection—hay
wood, and iron." With so many shells hitting his vessel, Bache related how
"she commenced filling rapidly." Bache wheeled the stricken gunboat around
and made as much speed as he could northward out of range and to the right
bank of the river, where he hoped to ground the dying vessel.[16]

The vigilant Confederates had been ready, as were numerous civilians
watching from such high ground as the high hill known as Sky Parlor, one
Louisianan writing: "Soon we discovered from the smoke above that a boat
was advancing from that direction." The battery well down the bluffs fired
rapidly but could not tell what was happening, although "cheer after cheer
from the men above told us that some good had been done." A watching
Mississippian declared that "the waters all around tremble and no doubt the
fishes, terrified at the unusual noise and shock, retire from the field of combat." Indeed, a Louisianan reported that "the monster had become companion
to the fishes under the waters of the great Mississippi," although there was
some discussion as to which ironclad it was inside Vicksburg, the *Cincinnati*
or the USS *Baron De Kalb.* A Missourian in Sherman's lines nevertheless
picked up on the impact, including more shots from the Confederate artillery
facing them, writing that "they now seem to feel saucy again."[17]

The gunboat's pilot was killed in the shelling, but Bache himself managed
to steer the stricken vessel to the shore and even had time to send a plank to

the bank to remove the wounded. He also ordered a line tied to a tree, but still being in range of and under heavy Confederate fire, the men left and the boat slipped back into deeper water. The *Cincinnati* thus went down, only the top of the casemate and parts of her flagstaffs above the surface. One staff still carried the flag, however; it had been shot away initially, but Quartermaster Frank Bois ran amid the shot and nailed it back to the stump of the post, he being one of several who won the medal of honor that day. Others sadly did not live through the ordeal, the *Cincinnati* losing five killed, fourteen wounded, and fifteen missing, one of whom turned up at Vicksburg itself, he having drifted down on debris. When he landed at the city he retorted, "Wall, I started for Vicksburg, and, I'll swow, I've got here at last." Much of the crew's personal effects also floated off the vessel and on down to Vicksburg, where civilians and soldiers alike recovered what they could. The crew lost almost everything, one wise sailor only bringing off the "public money."[18]

Watching Federal officers were aghast. Porter himself had followed in a tug and saw Bache turn around. He soon found out the horror occurring onboard. The admiral simply reported, "They had moved none [of the big guns], and were pouring the shot and shell in her very rapidly." Sherman was likewise watching from his lines ashore, describing how the gunboat hove to and sped away, but not before firing a broadside at the enemy. He knew it was fatal when "her bow appeared down and her stern up."[19]

The sinking of the *Cincinnati* of course was a major boost of morale for the Confederates, Pemberton having a celebratory lunch with Vicksburg elites the next day. He issued congratulatory orders that stated "you manfully worked your guns of the upper batteries against his force, and by your skill, sank one of his vaunted champions of the river, the gunboat *Cincinnati*." He went on to say that the repulses of the Union navy both above and below "caused silence to reign around the shores of our beleaguered city," adding that "by your gallantry and heroism to-day you have added to the garland of Vicksburg victories another bright chaplet. May God speed you in your good work." A watching Confederate surgeon crowed that the "gunboats are now as much afraid of our batteries as we were once of them."[20]

The victorious Confederates were not finished, however. Pemberton tossed around the idea of attacking the mortars with some type of force, even asking his river-front commander, Colonel Edward Higgins, if there were any more gunboats north of Vicksburg and if "it would be a good opportunity to take the mortars across the river." That plan never came to fruition, but an additional attack on the *Cincinnati* did two nights later when Pemberton allowed a party of the 1st Missouri Cavalry to go to the stricken vessel to burn what was left, at least to the waterline. Lieutenant Harris Wilkerson led the effort with forty-seven men, "all the boats could possibly carry," and managed to further damage the vessel with fire and also brought back the colors that had been nailed to the broken flagpole. Pemberton again issued his thanks for their bravery, ordering that the regiment could keep the flag they had won so daringly.[21]

It was a setback for Porter to be sure, the *Cincinnati* being one of the only major Union gunboats left above Vicksburg. And it probably stung a little more after Porter's sharp words about aiding Grant in all he needed. Still, the loss embedded even more into the minds of those fighting ashore the importance and help of the naval arm. They were in this together. Perhaps Sherman said it best, writing Porter of his condolences and adding that the episode "will stimulate us to further efforts to break the line which terminates on the Mississippi in such formidable batteries."[22]

Matters on the front lines at Vicksburg itself began to fall into a constant rhythm as well, the shock of the assaults and their effect, as seen up close in the truce on May 25, now in the past. As the last week in May came and went, most soldiers of both sides settled down more and more into the daily tedium of siege, working on earthworks, situating camps, sharpshooting, and above all trying to stay alive. And it was all in the context of knowing it was a fight against the calendar: "It is only a question of time," one Illinoisan wrote home.[23]

John Pemberton and his Confederates were merely playing a waiting game, mainly for relief from the outside. Confederate morale inside Vicksburg—knowing they were in a no-win situation as far as their individual plight was concerned—seemed to hinge directly on Johnston's ability outside Vicksburg to gather a large enough force to grapple with Grant, whose force was itself growing. "My men are in good spirits, awaiting your arrival," Pemberton informed Johnston on May 29. The assumption was that Johnston would do something. That was, after all, the whole reason he was there, and why would not perhaps the most important piece of the western Confederacy, and perhaps in the entire South at this point, be the all-encompassing focus of relief?[24]

While stopping other commanders from sending out their own messengers, ordering that "any courier sent to Genl. Johnston should receive instructions from these Hd Qts.," Pemberton corresponded with Johnston throughout this last week in May but received neither aid nor any promise of such quickly. At one point, Pemberton wrote that "no other messengers from you since (18th). I have dispatched about 8 messengers." Johnston had received Pemberton's request for caps and sent them by couriers, but few arrived, most being captured by Lauman's division as those couriers tried to pick their way through the southern opening into Vicksburg. One large shipment carried by Lieutenant J. W. Gibson and four of his men met that fate, with some two hundred thousand caps falling into Federal hands, one of those captured having been taken by Lauman a few days earlier as well. Only a trickle thus came in, twenty thousand in one lot and eighteen thousand in another. Courier Lamar Fontaine eased down the Yazoo River in a log canoe with one of the shipments of caps.[25]

One Federal of the 15th Illinois provided detail of capturing the young Confederate courier a second time and said the episode "will be very memorable in the history of Co. I." About 3:00 A.M., the videttes detected a rustling in the cane along a road and threatened to fire, when out came "a tall rebel soldier, with a strange looking pack on his back." Another came out as well, and the Illinoisans soon dove into the cane and flushed out ten more, each with a pack of twenty-thousand caps. One tried to make a run for it but was shot in the arm, whereupon all surrendered. It was found their guide was a boy whom Lauman had let through the lines earlier because he was so young and had a pitiful story. This time was different, the boy being held but still unafraid; one Illinoisan described how "cocking one eye in a comical manner," he jeered: "Oh, I guess they won't hurt me much, coz I'se so little."[26]

Perhaps most disheartening to Pemberton was Johnston's continued stalling and request for direction. On May 29, he flatly told Pemberton, "I am too weak to save Vicksburg" and lectured him that "it will be impossible to extricate you, unless you co-operate, and we make mutually supporting movements. Communicate your plans and suggestions, if possible." That was certainly not a message full of confidence, Pemberton probably thinking that Johnston was the one with the higher rank and flexibility, so he should be the one to do the suggesting. Nevertheless, Pemberton responded unwisely: "I do not think you should move with less than 30,000 or 35,000, and then, if possible, toward Snyder's Mill, giving me notice of the time of your approach." In hindsight, that was probably not the best advice. All he gave an already unenthusiastic commander was cover for not acting.[27]

Other worries also infiltrated the Confederates' lines and various

headquarters as the hours turned into days and as the wait for Johnston continued. There was a near constant expectation of attack, whether a general or
isolated one, either of which could prove disastrous. Pemberton sent out word
on May 29 that "it is highly probable that there will be an attack along the
whole line of your intenchments and on the river to-night," and at other times
throughout the days he sent word of expected isolated attacks by Brigadier
General Alfred W. Ellet's Mississippi Marine Brigade on some of the river
batteries, causing the division commanders to send troops to reinforce them.[28]

Making matters worse, on the far right Carter Stevenson detected a new
and powerful force on his front along the Hall's Ferry Road and Warrenton Road areas: Jacob Lauman's recently arrived division of the XVI Corps.
There was some slight skirmishing in fact during the night on May 26, when
a few Confederate pickets somehow managed to get in the rear of their Union
counterparts. The Federals had openly described how an entire division was
"at the gin-house about three-fourths of a mile beyond our works" and that the
troops had just marched in from Haynes' Bluff. Stevenson put all his reserves
into line to defend the expected attack, but none came despite some skirmishing when Federals appeared "to see what we were doing." The Confederates managed to capture several of "our inquisitive friends," one Southerner
wrote. A Federal artilleryman reported that "the 46th Illinois, which had been
placed in picket just before dark, behaved in the most careless and unaccount-
able manner, some of them, right under the guns of the enemy, proceeded
to make fires and cook coffee, etc., and the consequence was that the rebels
came out and gobbled two entire companies—70 men." Others said it was a
much larger haul—more than a hundred, although several made their escape,
including Colonel William O. Jones, who "knocked his guard down and ran
for the canebreak." Nevertheless, a member of the 14th Illinois cajoled that
this turn in events the first night on the line made a "pretty good start for
the second brigade." Lieutenant Colonel William Camm of the 14th Illinois
blamed it on "carelessness or ignorance of the picket officers."[29]

The arrival of more Federals in this area also opened Confederate eyes to
one of the most defenseless portions of the line, the segment of high ground
defenses that ran from South Fort back along the line of bluffs northward
along the river to Vicksburg itself. There was little chance of attack up the
bluffs, but Stevenson worried about the low ground nearer the river being "a
narrow strip of open land along the river bank to the city, entirely practicable
for the movement of a column at night." Stevenson brought Pemberton's

attention to the issue and received a somewhat scathing note that news of the plight came "at rather a late hour" because Stevenson had held his position "over a week" and had reported he could maintain it even longer. Certainly, the arrival of Lauman's Federals changed Stevenson's mind.[30]

Pemberton nevertheless acted and sent one of Bowen's brigades to hold the line, which caused another dustup. Stevenson received orders for his troops to dig trenches along that portion of the line, but Stevenson balked at the idea, asking if it "be just to require my division, under the circumstances, to dig the trenches, when the troops to occupy them are in position." That brought another terse response from Pemberton that the trenches were on Stevenson's lines and that Bowen's troops were a temporary reserve that "cannot be expected to dig the trenches at every point to which it may be ordered." Pemberton also jumped on one of Stevenson's brigade commanders, Seth Barton, for "interfer[ing] with the disposition of guns as ordered by the general commanding." Pemberton had to stop other tampering with the guns as well, particularly on Colonel Ashbel Smith's 2nd Texas line.[31]

As for Bowen, the continual movement of his reserve troops persistently wore on him and his men. He adamantly complained when his troops were put in other areas of the line, three regiments aiding Forney's division and two elsewhere. Bowen asserted that the 6th Missouri "was assigned to a position in the trenches, which had become intolerable on account of dead animals near by and the filth of the troops who formerly occupied it." Bowen first wrote to Forney asking that the troops who had made such a mess "be made to police it, which he declined." He then complained to Pemberton, asking "is it not sufficient that when a general find a weak point or enfiladed trench that he withdraws his regiment and calls for one of mine to occupy it, without compelling my men to clean up the filth they leave behind them?" Bowen further complained of the use of his troops all over the line, some going to areas only to find there were already reserves there and others taking most dangerous positions. "We are in a different position from any other command here," Bowen asserted; "our men are constantly moving from place to place."[32]

Obviously, Pemberton's and his generals' patience was growing thin even this early, after only a week or so as a besieged army and its commander.

If Pemberton's nerves were fraying, that is exactly what Grant wanted. Knowing he had more time than anything else, the Union commander wanted to starve the Confederates of strength, food, and patience, and therefore he did not in any way consider new assaults like those Pemberton was bracing for inside Vicksburg. But it was a two-way street. Orders also went out from the various Union headquarters that Pemberton was the one planning to attack and cut his way out during the night. One deserter, among many others, reported that the plan was put into effect and that "the signal was actually given, but was not responded to by the men." Unknown to Grant, it was a mere fabrication by the soldiers, as Pemberton had concocted no such plan.[33]

Instead, Grant was content to gather more troops, secure his rear, dig, and harass the Confederates all he could. He ordered army-wide artillery barrages at times, for thirty minutes on the morning of May 31, for example, simply to harass the enemy and the inhabitants of Vicksburg: "Throw shell near to the parapets and well into the city also," he ordered. It worked, McClernand reporting on May 29 that "our firing this morning burned some buildings in the city,—as a very large smoke was seen in that direction." The constant firing did as Grant hoped, it being steady and strong. "At long intervals," wrote a medical inspector with Grant's army, "firing has been kept up since I arrived yesterday, while the pickax and spade have been constantly at work, day and night, for days." Grant ordered his corps commanders to get as much ordnance as possible, notifying them he had sent to Memphis for additional guns, mostly siege weaponry, and ammunition, the latter of which arrived on May 28. In the meantime, Admiral Porter provided some heavy guns.[34]

The digging continued as well, the four initial approaches on Ewing's, Smith's, Ransom's, and Logan's fronts continuing to make progress toward the Confederate lines at the Stockade Redan, 3rd Louisiana Redan, and in between. On the Jackson Road on Logan's approach, one Illinoisan described how the digging went "through Shirley's door yard" and was wide enough for cannon and limbers, "with occasional spaces to turn around in." In this last week of May, engineers also began three additional approaches, all of them again in Sherman's corps. On the extreme far right of Sherman's position in Steele's division, brigade commanders Colonels Francis Manter and Charles Woods began an approach across the deep and wide Mint Spring Bayou. Their intent was good, but the ground was not favorable in the least, the valley being the deepest and widest, and the adjacent ridges the steepest, here on the west side nearest where it emptied into the Mississippi River. It was for this reason that no assaults had taken place here on May 22 and why Pemberton put the most unreliable troops to guard this sector. Steele's brigade commanders found out as much when they began digging, the work going smoothly and quickly until, in the words of Chief Engineer Frederick Prime, "it met a deep ravine, precluding farther progress." Little more could be done on this far-right flank.[35]

Not so with Steele's other brigade, although it also faced the formidable Mint Spring Bayou. Brigadier General John M. Thayer's regiments faced the valley much farther upstream than did Woods's and Manter's, thus allowing for at least some semblance of activity with a chance of success. It had been for this very reason that the entire division had congregated on Thayer's front on May 22 and launched its assault here, just west of the Stockade Redan area. It was still a rough go, the Confederate works sitting atop the ridge that was nearly vertical, but this was the best place on Steele's entire front to both assault and approach with a sap, so it was done here. Captain Herman Klosterman, in charge of the pioneers attached to the division, led the effort at what the corps engineer Jenney described as "a long and somewhat difficult approach," which indeed found its own difficulties in the valley of Mint Spring Bayou. One was an intervening ridge in the valley between two forks that caused a dilemma if crossed. Approaching along the uphill northern side would be no trouble and even atop it could be defended with a sap, but coming down the southern side of the intermediate hill would expose the troops and workers to Confederate fire with nothing to shield them. Engineer Prime reported that, "as it was difficult to defile this approach, blinding was resorted to." Accordingly, Klosterman opted to tunnel through the ridge—quite the novelty at Vicksburg—and used fascines or bundles of sticks or cane to cover the trench as it moved forward in the valley of the bayou: "Fascines made of cane were used; these being placed across the trench, which was about 6 feet deep, formed a roof which hid the movements of our men, and, where well constructed, was impenetrable to musket balls." Fortunately, no artillery fire railed against it. The work on this approach progressed from its start date on May 30, the sap eventually reaching across Mint Spring Bayou and dividing into two different approaches, each covered by a sap roller at the front to protect the workers. The fearful Louisianans at the top of the ridge constructed a stockade wall to help stop the advance when it arrived.[36]

A third new approach also went forward beginning on May 30, this time on Brigadier General Ralph Buckland's front north of the Stockade Redan. A veteran of the fighting at Shiloh Church, Buckland was part of James Tuttle's division that had seen little action in the assaults. But when Frank Blair's

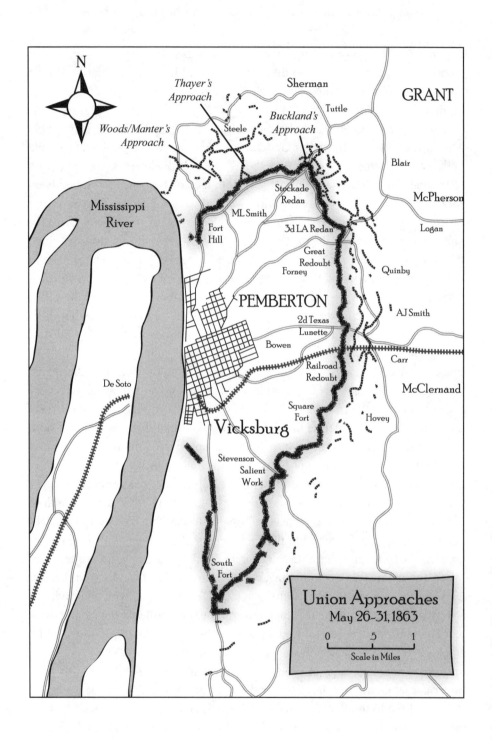

N

Thayer's
Approach

Sherman

Tuttle

GRANT

Buckland's
Approach

Woods/Manter's
Approach

Steele

Blair

McPherson

Mississippi
River

Stockade
Redan

ML Smith

Logan

Fort
Hill

3d LA Redan

Great
Redoubt

Forney

Quinby

PEMBERTON

2d Texas
Lunette

AJ Smith

Bowen

Railroad
Redoubt

Carr

De Soto

Square
Fort

McClernand

Hovey

Vicksburg

Stevenson
Salient
Work

South
Fort

Union Approaches
May 26–31, 1863

0   5   1

Scale in Miles

division went into permanent position for the siege south of the Grave-yard Road, Tuttle came forward from reserve and occupied the area north of the road, extending west as the Confederate line shifted from east-facing to north-facing. Captain William C. Young began Buckland's approach on May 30 and moved from the corps' artillery position on the tall ridges across from the Stockade Redan down the steep hill and across the valley, where the work moved uphill once more. As this approach moved closer and closer to Ewing's approach directly to the south, both aiming at the same basic area, a parallel trench eventually connected Buckland's and Ewing's approaches, although both continued forward on their own.[37]

The goal of all the digging in so many areas was twofold, these two being two of the three main possibilities for victory. If starving the enemy out would take too long, then perhaps these approaches could either position masses of troops close enough to the Confederate works for a quick assault before the enemy could react or could allow for mining under the enemy works and blowing them up, at which time massed infantry could storm through the gaps. Either way, the two possibilities not involving simply waiting and starv-ing out the enemy required large numbers of troops doing the dirty work.[38]

The key to waiting, digging, or assaulting was thus more troops, and Grant worked hard to have them shuttled to him from any source. He carried on a vast correspondence with Nathaniel Banks down at Port Hudson, who actu-ally outranked him, frequently requesting that Banks send him troops but always being met with Bank's own request that Grant send him part of the Army of the Tennessee. Each lectured the other on what was most important, each obviously seeing his own actions as dominant; Banks spewed that "if we hold Murfreesborough, Vicksburg, and Port Hudson at the same time, the enemy will beat us all in detail, and the campaign of the West will end like the campaigns of the East, in utter and disgraceful defeat before an inferior enemy." Banks then notified Grant that he did not have the transportation to move his men, so he requested Grant come to him. Grant responded, "Con-centration is essential to the success of the general campaign in the West, but Vicksburg is the vital point. Our situation is for the first time during the entire Western campaign what it should be." Obviously, there would be no help ar-riving from Banks.[39]

It seemed Grant had the upper hand, however, in that he had the support of Henry Halleck in Washington, and most of the reinforcements eventually sent to the Mississippi Valley went to him instead of Banks. And Grant knew what to do with them. Three critical areas existed where he needed troops, one being in his rear to take care of Johnston. The threat from the rear was ever growing in Grant's mind, and he even became willing to dispatch some of the frontline troops at Vicksburg to see to it. A second area was Haynes' Bluff, which was the general area from whence Grant's supplies emanated. He could not leave that position uncovered at all. Third was his left at Vicksburg, the area that still was not fully covered by troops, allowing Pemberton and Johnston to communicate.[40]

Fortunately, Grant was able to plug the southern gap at Vicksburg somewhat with the arrival and deployment of Lauman's division. The three brigades had made their way southward on May 24 and by the last week in May were deploying, getting their bearings, beginning the digging, and already meeting the enemy, as indicated by those captured by the Confederates. Lauman had first operated down along the Warrenton Road but soon took his more permanent position upon very detailed orders from Grant, who told Lauman on May 28, "You will immediately place your division in camp on the Hall's Ferry road, on the south side of the creek, near the large hospital, its left resting on the road, and right extending toward McClernand's left." Grant wanted a continuous line as far as there was a line, so he opted to put Lauman on McClernand's left down to the Hall's Ferry Road. Lauman did so on May 30. With additional troops on the way, Grant could later extend on farther to cover the final gap in the line. Still, Grant ordered that Lauman take special care to put out pickets front and back to prevent another surprise from either direction and to picket the gap to his left all the way to the river to keep "the enemy from communicating in any manner upon these roads." He also wanted Lauman to use "every means . . . in order to harass the rebels." Lauman did so, dealing with his flank and reporting Confederate raids in the area, but mostly through large batteries established along this new line. Not all were enthused with the progress, however, one 14th Illinois soldier writing that their encampment was "the worst camp that could be had in all Miss."[41]

While Lauman's arrival was certainly important, Grant wanted more. He was busy corresponding with those who might provide more help than Banks, or at least those who were under Grant's authority. That mainly consisted of Stephen A. Hurlbut and the XVI Corps at Memphis and Corinth. Hurlbut wrote to his own subordinates that "Vicksburg is going to be a siege. Grant demands more force from me." With Grant's call for more troops than just Lauman's, Hurlbut now organized another division of twelve regiments, four from the Hungarian Alexander Asboth's command around the Columbus, Kentucky, area in the rear and eight from Richard J. Oglesby's command at Jackson, Tennessee, and Corinth, Mississippi. These Hurlbut put under the command of Brigadier General Nathan Kimball, as Grant had requested. Of course, taking the equivalent of another division from Hurlbut caused him to abandon several posts in his area, but Grant deemed Vicksburg to be more important at this point. The only cause of delay was finding transportation to get the troops to Vicksburg, and Kimball left Memphis only on May 31.[42]

That did not stop Grant from calling for additional troops as well. As Hurlbut struggled to get boats to take Kimball's three brigades southward, Grant followed up with more orders on May 31: "Vicksburg is so strong by nature and so well fortified that a sufficient force cannot be brought to bear against it to carry it by storm against the present garrison. It must be taken by a regular siege or by starving out the garrison." He continued that he had plenty of troops if his rear was not threatened, but it was, so he needed even more. "I want your district stripped to the very lowest possible standard," Grant wrote to Hurlbut, adding that "you can be in no possible danger for the time it will be necessary to keep these troops away. All points in West Tennessee north of the Memphis and Charleston road, if necessary, can be abandoned entirely. Western Kentucky may be reduced to a small garrison at Columbus and Paducah." Specifically, Grant called for even yet another division, the four-brigade force under Brigadier General William "Sooy" Smith. "Add this to all other force you can spare," Grant ordered.[43]

No doubt Hurlbut took Grant's admonition with a grain of salt that he would be in no danger but began the process of sending the troops. He was also a little chagrined at just how he was supposed to get all those troops southward. But the commander had called, and Hurlbut did his best to get it done. The fate of Vicksburg perhaps hung in the balance.

One of the main reasons Grant wanted more troops was to cover his rear and keep track of Johnston to the east. He continually received reports of Confederates gathering from almost all compass points, with whole divisions coming from Braxton Bragg's army in Tennessee and others from more distant departments such as P. G. T. Beauregard's in South Carolina. It was all very disconcerting and was a growing factor in Grant's operations as May continually waned. Grant stated repeatedly that he could hold with what he had, but he also noted that, "with an additional force here, I could detach everything but about 25,000 men, and go with the balance and capture or disperse him [Johnston], leaving the State of Mississippi an easy prize to our armies." In either case, he had to have reinforcements to man both fronts he was overseeing in Mississippi.[44]

Johnston's strength was indeed growing by the day. "We was hurried through from Shelbyville [Tennessee] to this place as fast as possible," one of Bragg's Confederates wrote once he arrived at Canton. Jefferson Davis even sent Brigadier General Gabriel J. Rains to the area with his inventions ("our submarine and subterra shells") to work against the Union navy at Vicksburg. Yet these were not enough for Johnston. "When all the re-enforcements arrive shall have but 23,000," he complained to Davis. "Tell me if additional troops can be furnished." That inquiry touched off a debate between Johnston and Richmond over how many troops Johnston had requested and how many had been sent, Davis arguing that "the re-enforcements sent to you exceed by, say, 7,000 the estimate of your dispatch of 27th instant. We have withheld nothing which it was practicable to give. We cannot hope for numerical equality, and time will probably increase the disparity."[45]

That was certainly the case, but Johnston seemed to not be willing to do anything now but complain even more: "Unless you can promise more troops, we must try with that number. The odds against us will be very great." He then again requested another seven thousand troops and a major general, lecturing Davis, "I have to organize an army, and collect ammunition, provisions, and transportation." Davis shot back that "the Secretary of War reports the re-enforcement ordered to you as greater than the number you requested" and that "the troops sent to you were so fully organized that I suppose you will have little trouble as to organization." Separately, General Samuel Cooper in Richmond (the Confederacy's Adjutant and Inspector General) informed Johnston that no more troops would be forthcoming.[46]

Yet Johnston was not ready to do anything with his growing numbers, he showing little desire for offensive operations. In fact, Johnston seemed to be willing to let circumstances or others dictate what he would do—mainly Pemberton and Grant themselves. He frequently called on Pemberton for information and suggestions about plans, illustrating a less than take-hold mentality. More troublesome for any relief of Vicksburg, Johnston also seemed to be in a reactionary rather than offensive mind-set when it came to Grant.

Johnston took the Federal commander's continual probing of the Confederate area of concentration and operation as a reason to go on the defensive rather than an opportunity to go on the attack.[47]

A case in point was when Johnston detected some of the Union movements eastward, such as that by Colonel Johnson's cavalry along the ridge between the Yazoo and Big Black Rivers. It did not help when Pemberton informed him that troops were leaving the lines at Vicksburg: "I apprehend for a movement against you." Johnston informed William W. Loring at Jackson that a scout warned "some 15,000 of the enemy's troops are moving up between the Yazoo and Big Black." Johnston quickly began concentrating his force to meet them before they reached Canton and the Mississippi Central Railroad, including most of Loring's division from Jackson who had regained their strength somewhat with the addition of equipment so that "we began to feel lively again." Johnston sent trains to ferry them northward, but not all were fortunate enough to get rides, one 15th Mississippi soldier explaining that "we made a forced march by night and very dark one too, across Pearl River swamp to Canton." Fortunately, the people of Canton were glad to see them: "The citizens . . . cheered us all through the town," and as they made camp "no soldiers ever camped among kinder more hospitable people. The citizens of Canton were exceedingly kind to us."[48]

The defensive lethargy around Johnston's horde was well described by the famous British observer Arthur Fremantle, who sojourned with Johnston for a few days. He had made his way northward from Louisiana and happened to reach the Jackson area right around the major events of mid- and late May. He described seeing Loring's wandering division still escaping from Champion Hill, as well as other brigades concentrating around Jackson from every compass point. Once in Jackson, he stayed at the Bowman House, where he saw Ulysses S. Grant's name in the register, a result of his visit on the night of May 14.[49]

Fremantle met almost everyone associated with Johnston's force, from brigade commanders to those commanding the divisions such as States Rights Gist before W. H. T. Walker took command of most of it and moved to Yazoo City. He also met Loring and commented on the troops themselves, their equipment, and ability. He described the Georgians in detail: "The straggling of the Georgians was on the grandest scale conceivable; the men fell out by dozens, and seemed to suit their own convenience in that respect, without interference on the part of the officers. But I was told that these regiments had never done any marching before, having hitherto been quartered in forts and transported by railroad." Fremantle was also with the army on May 22, when a huge ruckus could be heard to the west as the Federals assaulted Vicksburg.[50]

The main attraction obviously was Johnston himself, and Fremantle spent a good deal of time with him before his departure eastward. "General Johnston received me with much kindness," Fremantle explained, "when I presented my letters of introduction, and stated my object in visiting the Confederate armies." He described Johnston as "rather below middle height, spare, soldierlike, and well set up." Fremantle was amazed at the simpleness of Johnston's headquarters, with only a frying pan and coffee pot. There was only one fork for general and staff, and it had a missing prong. The guest was nevertheless given the honor of using the fork at meals.[51]

Johnston talked freely of the campaign as well as historic operations, telling Fremantle that he regarded Marlborough as a better general than Wellington. The two spent several days together, moving by rail on occasion and at one point having to get off the train and gather firewood for fuel, which Johnston himself participated in to the point "to cause his 'Seven Pines' wound to give him pain." Yet when Fremantle inquired of the current campaign and when he might be able to move, Johnston informed him "that at present he was too weak to do any good, and he was unable to give me any definite idea as to when he might be strong enough to attack Grant." Fremantle wisely chose not to wait on Johnston and planned to move on to other parts of the Confederacy: "I still have so much to see." Fremantle realized, as Pemberton was learning, one could grow roots waiting on Joseph E. Johnston.[52]

Obviously, Johnston was in the mind-set of protecting what was still Confederate-held, especially Jackson and the north-south railroad that ran through it to the Confederate forces holding back Hurlbut's Federals in northern Mississippi and West Tennessee. Thus, he seemingly gave up any desire—if there was ever any true desire to begin with—to fight for Vicksburg. Such a decision doomed Pemberton and his garrison, of course, and was ironically completely wrong. Grant at the time had no plans to invade eastward into Mississippi, take Jackson, or order a movement southward from West Tennessee; Hurlbut's force, in fact, was dwindling fast, being ferried down to Vicksburg. Grant was simply desiring to cover his rear and concentrate on his main goal of capturing Vicksburg. That said, the way Grant went about it certainly led Johnston—and any other fair-minded observer for that matter—to conclude that a huge operation to the east was coming.[53]

By this time in the last week of May, the major reason Johnston thought such a Union offensive was in the offing was due to Grant's growing worry over his rear and the classic way Grant dealt with such issues: head-on and with force. Accordingly, Johnston began to detect more Union movement east and in growing numbers and strength until, by the time June rolled around, it seemed Grant was actively making plans for a further invasion rather than just hemming in Vicksburg.[54]

Grant already had troops out east of his line at Vicksburg, cavalry forces under Colonels Amory K. Johnson and Clark Wright riding all over the country and sending back plenty of information, at times also skirmishing with the enemy. Cavalry to the south along the Big Black River ferries encountered little opposition, one Illinois trooper declaring they "saw nothing of importance *save* a pretty girl." Others to the north of the railroad had a different story. They reported that civilians in the area declared Johnston had some forty-five thousand troops by this time, although Colonel Johnson made sure to note in reporting it that he did not believe such numbers. He also reported more accurate news that troops were congregating near Jackson under Loring, States Rights Gist from South Carolina, and others. He also included the obvious misinformation that "A. P. Hill" had come west with troops, though Hill was even then about to command a corps in Robert E. Lee's Army of Northern Virginia at Gettysburg.[55]

While Colonel Johnson's cavalry forces were fast-moving, they were also limited in strength. Grant's other major dispatch of troops early on, actually on May 24, had sent an entire brigade east from McClernand's corps under Peter J. Osterhaus. Grant had sent Osterhaus with one of his brigades under Colonel James Keigwin back to the Big Black River Bridge on the main Jackson Road as well as the railroad to watch that obvious crossing point. Osterhaus left Lindsey's brigade of his division back on the siege lines, temporarily attached to Alvin Hovey's division. Of course, this river crossing was where Grant himself had mostly crossed in heading to Vicksburg a couple of weeks earlier and seemed the logical point any Confederate effort to relieve Vicksburg would take. Osterhaus was a solid commander, and Grant trusted him implicitly.[56]

Now, as Osterhaus settled into his new command area in this last week of May, Grant gave him specific instructions over and above his task of defending the most logical route to Grant's rear. Osterhaus was to also play the destructor's role, tearing up the railroad as well as taking any "Confederate cotton, grain, and provisions in store." Most was to be destroyed, but Grant wanted the cotton brought into Osterhaus's lines. Eventually, on May 26, Grant also combined the two major commands back east by ordering Osterhaus to alert Johnson to work with him in destroying the railroad bridges toward Bolton and damaging the infrastructure as much as possible. "All Negroes, teams, and cattle should be brought in," Grant ordered, "and everything done to prevent an army coming this way supplying itself." Osterhaus and Colonel Clark Wright and his 6th Missouri Cavalry worked closely and performed this job flawlessly, Osterhaus reporting "almost every bushel of corn destroyed along the railroad line and the public road." In addition, numerous mules, horses, cattle, and cotton were brought into the Union lines. The infantry also foraged, one Illinoisan in Keigwin's brigade describing how some of them went foraging several miles out and "confiscated four loads of hay & fodder for the horses."[57]

Osterhaus's lone brigade under Keigwin continued to find this rearward duty to their liking, with little to no fighting and nice accommodations. "In the absence of tents we make sheds out of boards to protect us from the weather," one wrote, later elaborating how the boards kept the wind and rain out but the other three sides were open to provide "plenty of fresh air." A bed of soft cotton and his knapsack as a pillow, along with a cracker box for a cupboard where he kept his dishes and pans, rounded out his abode. He added, "We have plenty of grubb the plums black berries and dew berries are ripe and very abundant," as was beef, ham shoulders, sides of bacon, and fresh bread at times when flour was available. The troops also had plenty of time to write letters and do their other work, one writing to his wife that he had to stop his letter for a time "to attend to some of my domestic duties such as cooking washing dishes mending clothes and keeping things straight generally in my habitation."[58]

Osterhaus's strength and Johnson's mobility, in addition to orders for each corps commander to "picket all roads, respectively, in rear of their respective positions, by which their camps or the city of Vicksburg can be approached," gave Grant a certain calm about his rear. Still, there were continual reports of Confederates hovering to the east and "scouting around to see whom they may devour," one Illinoisan wrote home. As reports continued to drift in of Johnston's gathering numbers, Grant decided to make certain once and for all that his rear was covered. On May 26, he informed Colonel Johnson that "since ordering you to proceed north on the east side of the Big Black River, I have determined to send a large infantry and artillery force to clear out any force the enemy may have between the Black and the Yazoo Rivers." Johnson was to join the main expedition, which would include a whopping six brigades from Grant's army now digging its way to Vicksburg. Without any more assaults in mind, and with more troops that he could actually send forward in an assault anyway (as he found out on May 22), Grant decided he could spare several brigades to cover his rear, especially as more troops were soon to come in.[59]

The expedition was to head northeastward, to "clear out that quarter," Sherman noted. It would be concerned mainly with the corridor of land between the Yazoo and Big Black Rivers, an elongated slot of high ground sloping toward each river that would funnel any military movements to that area. To clean out the slot, Grant's expedition involved three brigades of Sherman's XV Corps and three of McPherson's XVII Corps. None came from McClernand's corps, as Osterhaus already had a portion of that corps on the rear defense work at Big Black River Bridge. Two of Sherman's brigades were to move via Haynes' Bluff toward the corridor, picking up a third that was garrisoning that place, while three of McPherson's from the front lines moved on the Oak Ridge Road toward the same area, both wings ordered to unite at Sulpher Springs. Having just settled in their camps, however, "none of them [were] very anxious to go," although an Illinoisan admitted "a little marching in the country will be quite a desirable change."[60]

The force contained six brigades of the two corps, one from each of the three divisions in each corps, one Indianan noting "so as not to weaken any particular corps." From Sherman's troops, Grant detailed Francis Manter's (Steele's division), Kilby Smith's (Blair's division), and Joseph Mower's (Tuttle's division), while out of McPherson's corps came Brigadier General Mortimer D. Leggett's (Logan's division), William Hall's (McArthur's division), and John B. Sanborn's (Quinby's division). One of Leggett's men wrote "our brigade was [the] one from Logan's division to go." In all, it was around ten thousand men. Commanding the whole was one of Sherman's division commanders, Frank Blair, who had made attacks on the Stockade Redan on both May 19 and May 22 and never went anywhere, unlike Grant, without a large staff and escort tailing along. The force left on the evening of May 26, most in an easy position to do so as they were on the north and northeast sections of the lines. The artillery was a different matter, Charles Affeld of the Chicago Light Artillery describing how "we commenced letting our guns down the hill into the ravine and after hard work succeeded in getting them all down and up to where the caissons are." Only Hall's brigade encountered any delay, it initially being deployed on the extreme southern end of the lines near the Warrenton Road. These troops joined the expedition on May 27, after Lauman's brigades arrived and took their tasks. The force's orders were to carry seven days' rations in wagons and 150 rounds of ammunition. Grant obviously meant business, and he told them to unite at Sulpher Springs and "move upon and drive out the enemy now collecting between the Black and Yazoo Rivers." An Indianan described it in more homespun rhetoric: "For the purpose of routing some Rebels that were said to be in the direction of Yazoo City."[61]

Having no command structure per se as each brigade hailed from a different division, Blair instituted a temporary division system in which John McArthur, who accompanied Hall's brigade as he had done now for the duration of the campaign, and Joseph Mower led three brigades each, from their own corps. The wings met at Sulpher Springs as ordered and Blair led them out into the slot, one Missourian in Mower's brigade remarking that they passed "the most beautiful springs I have yet witnessed." Others described the "splendid view of the [Yazoo] valley." Many foraged freely, one Illinoisan describing how he and a friend gained a hive of bees full of honey "in spite of the guards." On other occasions the fare was easier gained but still organized, "the guard letting but 2 men in at a time" at one plantation storehouse. Sheep were a favorite meal for many: "I caught a sheep on the way which we skinned," one Federal explained.[62]

Yet the force knew little of what was going on, a Missourian writing that "we have no idea whither we are marching or for what purpose." They logically expected a big fight any time now, especially as they moved farther and farther away from Vicksburg toward whatever Confederate force was out there. Only the mileposts along the road indicated how far the column was from both Vicksburg and Yazoo City. Grant had little better idea, complaining once the operation began that Blair did not report quite as often as he desired, Grant writing him on May 29 how "not hearing from you since you left I have become somewhat uneasy lest the enemy should get some portion of his force

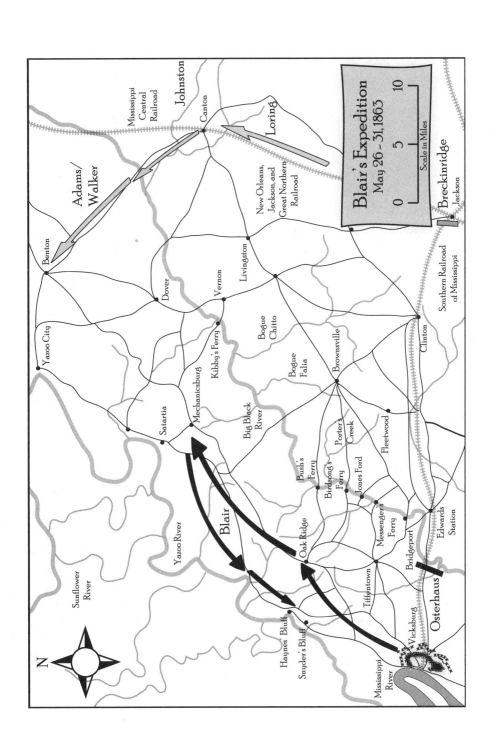

Blair's Expedition
May 26 – 31, 1863

Scale in Miles
0   5   10

in your rear." Blair had actually written on May 28, but his message had not yet reached Grant when he sent the scolding note. Blair had reported that he was out in the corridor between the rivers, the brigades camping on the luscious plantations in the area, but that he had not yet decided what course to pursue. Colonel Johnson, within eight miles of Mechanicsburg, was forwarding reports of inflated enemy numbers, and Blair consulted his division and brigade commanders about whether to push on farther or not. He informed Grant that if he pushed on and ran into trouble, he would head for the Yazoo River, where he hoped Grant would send a gunboat and transports to get them back safely. If he did not push on, he would simply march back to the army. Upon receiving Grant's note, Blair reported again, giving the big picture that Johnston was at Canton organizing an army but that there was apparently little Confederate force between the rivers, Canton being east of the Big Black. "Col Johnson has scoured the country pretty thoroughly," he assured Grant.[63]

The brigades were nevertheless up early each day intent on catching Johnston, one Illinoisan writing in his diary that "the early bird catches the worm." Johnston never showed, and the Illinoisan added later that "we tried the truth of that adage this morning, but failed to make the catch." That said, there was some skirmishing at times with small bands of Confederates, one officer in charge of the advance ordering his small battalion: "Battalion, run, shoot and yell—march!" There was plenty of extracurricular activity as well; members of the 15th Iowa attended a slave wedding and dance.[64]

Blair eventually decided to push on. William Hall's brigade held the advance and moved forward behind the skirmishing troopers of the 4th Iowa Cavalry, eventually through Mechanicsburg. As the Confederates made a firmer stand just outside the hamlet, Hall deployed three of his Iowa regiments and kept the fourth in reserve, pushing up the hill toward the enemy. A few shots broke some Confederates who retreated but, as a disgusted Hall reported, continually deployed "as soon as a regiment was thrown into line of battle to attack them." About two miles back, the Confederates "made a more decided stand than they had before done," and Hall brought up artillery, which once more scattered the enemy. Hall camped on the skirmish ground that night while the rest of the troops followed in the rear, one of Mower's Federals bragging that they "took undisputed possession of the town." One of the Iowans merely reported, "We met the enemy and flirted with him awhile."[65]

Reaching all the way to Mechanicsburg and Satartia, one Federal describing the latter on the Yazoo River itself as "a little hamlet of perhaps a dozen houses without inhabitants save a few women and children," Blair's expedition sent shock waves through the Confederate high command. The force was a mere fifteen miles from Yazoo City and not that much more from Canton itself. Confederate cavalry watched the movement closely and reported back to the high command that there were two divisions in the slot, "destroying all the provisions, corn, meat, &c., in the valley." Confederate cavalry at the front were harassing them as best they could "and will probably harass them some to-day," wrote Lieutenant W. S. Wise. Word quickly spread of the two divisions marching on the Valley Road between the rivers, although there was some confusion among the Confederate generals as to which road was actually referred to. Nevertheless, larger Confederate units soon gathered near Benton in the slot, troops under Brigadier General John Adams and W. H. T. Walker. One Tennessean in Walker's command noted they crossed the Big Black River on a "floating bridge" but did not encounter the enemy, rather moving on to garrison Yazoo City itself. It was a good thing, because the slot between the rivers could be inhospitable, and he related that "the weather [was] verry warm and dry it was with much dificulty that we marched." In fact, two men died from the heat and others were prostrated: "The water that we had to drink from big black to yazoo city was verry bad."[66]

Ironically, Colonel Johnson and Blair conversely detected these Confederate movements and alarmingly referred them to Grant. With reports of large Confederate numbers only increasing as the days went by, Grant now became even more concerned. He lectured the seemingly indecisive Blair to "take no risks whatever, either of a defeat or of being cut off." He told him that if he believed there was a major Confederate force in front of him to return, leaving Mower's brigade at Haynes' Bluff and possibly McArthur with Hall's brigade as well if needed. Blair was to make sure to destroy everything valuable to an approaching army, however, even sending out Engineer Andrew Hickenlooper from McPherson's corps with a detail of pioneers and men to do the work. With their aid, Blair began marching his force back amid a heavy rain, which one Federal admitted "laid the dust and rendered our situation much more agreeable, though our clothing was saturated." Still, Grant hinted that it might be time to get really serious about the rear: it may be "advisable to send out an army large enough to clean out Joe Johnston and his party." But this was a delicate matter, and Grant ordered Osterhaus at the Big Black River crossing to burn what was left of the railroad bridge and any others he could reach east of the river: "Pile the ties up, and lay the rails across them and burn them up." To the corps commanders on the siege lines, Grant also renewed his orders to cover the roads to their rear, this time with more obstructions: "Take immediate steps to obstruct and render impassable for troops all roads leading into the rear of their respective commands and into Vicksburg," the only exceptions being the Jackson Road and the supply roads that led to the Yazoo River.[67]

Grant was obviously becoming more concerned at the prospect that Johnston could soon be a factor. What he had dismissed only a few days ago as an almost impossibility now seemed increasingly possible. In fact, by May 31 Grant had become so skittish that he was seeing possibilities that perhaps were not even there. He had worried over the Big Black River crossing, and now the slot between the rivers took his attention as well. In a note to Hurlbut, he added another doleful possibility: "It is now certain that Joe Johnston has already collected a force from 20,000 to 25,000 strong at Jackson and Canton, and is using every effort to increase it to 40,000. With this, he will undoubtedly attack Haynes' Bluff, and compel me to abandon the investment of the city, if not reinforced before he can get here."[68]

It was only eight days into the siege—the end of May—and Grant was already becoming anxious from the waiting, watching, digging, and, perhaps most important, boredom.

If Grant was becoming miserable because of his situation, he needed only to look at another group caught in the growing maelstrom. Those less covered and more inexperienced set of civilians inside Vicksburg were also beginning to suffer in the early days of the siege. In fact, their lot was more pitiable than that of the soldiers, simply because they had not signed up for this but were subjected to it simply by the choice of where they lived. They became mostly innocent bystanders, caught in perhaps the most horrid of events in this horrid Civil War. Some felt pity for them, such as Ohioan John N. Bell, who remarked in his diary, "This is horrible but is only one of the many terrible results of besieging a city." Others had less sympathy; Illinoisan Samuel Irwin added in his diary that the Confederate "citizens are coming to grief—tired of their evil deeds now since it has overtaken them."[69]

Inside Vicksburg was nothing but pure misery. The decreasing food supply even this early, constant bombardment from all directions, compounding numbers of dead and wounded in their midst, and even the horrible sights, smells, and tastes of war soon overcame their idyllic antebellum civilization. One dentist described the new situation they found themselves in: "Shot shell and minie balls are passing over and around us in all directions. The whurur of the paret shell is frightful. The whize of the mine ball has an undescribable affect When you heer on[e] you know it has passe[d] you, but you have a dread of the next one." Emma Balfour shuddered at just how dangerous it was on city streets amid the bombardment, although many claimed it was fairly easy to watch and make sure all mortar shells went over their heads: "As soon as a shell gets over your head you are safe for even if it approaches near, the pieces fall forward and do not touch you."[70]

Times of intense bombardment were most dreaded, such as in late May when "the enemy opened a terrific fire from the rear, and for four hours a storm of shot and shell was rained upon the city, seriously damaging many buildings, killing and wounding a large number of soldiers and citizens." One little girl explained how "the fiery shower of shells goes on day and night," adding, "there are three intervals when the shelling stops, either for the guns to cool or for the gunners' meals, I suppose,—about eight in the morning, the same in the evening, and at noon." Civilian casualties began to accumulate as the town became more and more shot up from Federal batteries and mortars encircling Vicksburg. And nothing was off-limits to Federal fire, which admittedly from such long range could not be perfectly directed anyway, although the same dentist in the city noted that most of the mortar shells fell "back of Cherry St." One observer even saw a piano with three bullet holes in it.[71]

To make a safe refuge for women and children especially, Vicksburg civilians began to inhabit caves that had been dug for this specific purpose. May 1863 was not the first time the city had come under Federal fire, obviously, and the local people realized—as far back as a year before when Farragut's naval vessels first took Vicksburg under fire—that caves could protect them. By the time the siege began, many had caves already dug, and they now moved into them. "The caves were plainly becoming a necessity," described Mary Loughborough, and those who could not dig their own or have it done had the option of renting. One family paid fifteen dollars for two caves.[72]

The particular loess soil around Vicksburg that so aided siege fortification work had the same effect on the inhabitants and their caves inside Vicksburg. It was easily cut; one noted "you may cut with a spade as you cut a cheese with a knife." Some caves were small affairs, just one room, some two, although a few were more elaborate. "I saw where two rooms were cut out, for a single family," one observer wrote, "with a door-way in the clay wall separating them. Some of these were carpeted and furnished with considerable elaboration." Young William Lord described another with a central gallery and chambers like prongs extending from it where different families lived. The largest cave, it was said, belonged to the Thrift family and was a hundred feet in length with four large chambers. The family lived in one, the servants in another. In a third the cows and hogs lived, and in the fourth was kept provisions for man and beast. Most ceilings were arched for strength, while the floors were planked and the walls covered with paper or carpets. Unfortunately, the caves and even cellars where others took refuge were so damp that "the bedding has to be carried out and laid in the sun every day, with the forecast that it may be demolished at any moment." Beds were elevated on barrels, although the stoves normally sat just outside the entrance because there was no ventilation for the smoke. That said, few cooked, most preferring to subsist on stored items. If cooking was done, the servants could easily flee into the caves when the horrible sound of approaching cannonballs gave warning of danger.[73]

Obviously, there was danger even in the caves. One girl later told of a bullet bouncing around in her cave and landing in a pan of water, while a shell also entered at a different time and knocked a bunch of rags into the molasses, something a family under such circumstances could hardly spare. Cave-ins also resulted, causing many to brace their caverns, including arching the ceilings and doing all they could to make them safe, but it was a trade-off. Mary Loughborough explained that "the supports of the bracing [took] up much room in our confined quarters."[74]

The constant bombardment, as well as the whole concept of living underground like animals, affected everyone; it had a way of leveling the field and casting down classes. Many of even the most affluent families were humbled by their surroundings, one Federal who could see into Vicksburg describing the indignity when the bombardment slackened: "I could see the citizens and their families crawling out of their holes from under the hills like turkeys out of a mill pond after a rain." Little William Lord, only a boy during the siege, later explained, "in caves of this description a common danger abolished the unwritten law of caste. The families of planters, overseers, slave-dealers, tradespeople, and professional men dwelt side by side, in peace if not in harmony." Another noted the same thing, writing that just being a Confederate soldier helped make acquaintances: "A man's being a good soldier became a sufficient reason of itself to recommend him to the notice and acquaintance of a lady, and the gatherings that occurred about the caves and in the parlors of their well born dames of Vicksburg presented a mixture that under other circumstances would not have been allowed."[75]

Much of the horror fell on the women and children remaining inside Vicksburg, although they tried to maintain some semblance of normal life. One Northern reporter described "two sisters who prided themselves upon their expertness in getting out of the way of shells, as if it were quite a ladylike accomplishment." Some showed more fear, which under the circumstances was not uncommon or particularly noteworthy. "There was great commotion in the city," one Louisianan described; "the women and children and even men ran for their rat holes thinking that there would be a general attack in front and indeed this was the opinion of officers and men."[76]

Many of the women and children in Vicksburg were wives and children of soldiers, mostly officers, who came to be with their men and became trapped as a result. Many of them worked just as hard as the defenders in the army. One woman cared for her husband and several others by making periodic trips with supplies to their artillery camp until her horse became lame. Then she would catch anything she could until they moved camps and she ambled upon brigade commander Seth Barton's headquarters. The general would not allow her to go farther but called for her husband, who came and received the goods. There was a lot of firing at that moment, and the husband said it was only because one of them had snuck down in the ravine in between the lines to get water from a spring. They normally did it at night, but a shell had broken their supply of water that day and they needed more. The same woman believed some people in town were hoarding flour and extorting people at high prices, which she reported to General Pemberton's headquarters.[77]

The poorest situations involved the children who were subjected to many sights and fears that no child should ever have to face. One observer told of a little one who cautioned her mother as the bombardment increased and they ran to shelter: "Yun, mamma, yun. Ankees soot ou; . . . tum on twick." Another told of a woman trying to capture her young son on the streets, who would not be corralled. She caught him as a mortar shell came upon them, only for him to slip through her grasp. The shell exploded right where he would have been, maiming her arm but saving the child's life. Unfortunately, there were several times when the bombardment, certainly not targeting specific women and children but absolutely targeting the city itself, killed these almost defenseless civilians. However, there were also births in the caves during the siege—at least two. One bore the name Lee Rogers but the other child received his name because of the circumstances of his birth: William Siege Green.[78]

That said, the women caring for the children tried to make life as smooth as possible amid the worst possible circumstances. Emma Balfour noted that the enemy thought they could wear out the women and children and that Pemberton would act in their care, "but they little know the spirit of the women and children if they expect this." In fact, one citizen got up a petition for Pemberton to ask Grant to let them leave, which he said he would do if everyone signed it, but few would. Conversely, many tried to make life seem as normal as possible, one child later remembering making taffy. Singing and music also enlivened the long, weary days and nights. Unfortunately, even the children's pets paid the price of being in Vicksburg, one girl admitting, "I think all the dogs and cats must be killed or starved, we don't see any more pitiful animals prowling around." Theodosia McKinstry's dog Bulger was smart enough to stay alive, keeping near their cave: "He ran no risks; he stayed in and near the cave as if he understood the whole situation." Still, she later admitted, "what we could have given him to eat in the last lean days I haven't the slightest idea."[79]

With such large-scale military maneuvers going on, more than just Vicksburg's citizens were affected. Those outside the lines, in rear of the Union army and in areas where the Federals still watched, were also involved. In Vicksburg, the civilians were within friendly lines. Outside, the civilians were subject to the enemy. One woman who lived a mere mile from Grant's headquarters reflected that "our home was surrounded by Yankee's both day and night. . . . We were utterly in their power and in a constant state of uneasiness for fear we would be killed."[80]

Perhaps the worst possible place to be was between the opposing lines. Most houses had been burned by this point to keep the enemy from using them as cover, but the famed Shirley House on the Jackson Road, known to almost all as the "White House," still stood and actually contained Mrs.

Shirley and her son Quincy as recently as just a couple days prior. She and some servants had endured the first assault within the chimney of their house, but McPherson himself had personally urged her to leave, which she did. She lived out part of the siege in a cave and later moved to more structural quarters farther to the rear.[81]

Many fled rather than remain and take a chance on being mistreated. Frank Blair's force found a deserted landscape when it marched to Mechanicsville. One Iowan noted, "We burned some fine plantation houses and other improvements. I saw only one residence left standing, and that was where the family had the courage to remain at home." An Illinoisan on Blair's trek remarked, "It is [as] difficult to find a free born white man here as it would be to find a white man in the unexplored regions of Central Africa."[82]

Those who refused to leave felt the consequences, although most of their homes survived. One old woman outside the Federal lines displayed her hardheadedness when told to evacuate. "My dear grand mother took her knitting and sat on the front gallery," her granddaughter explained, "and said, 'come on gentlemen — I will die where I have lived.'" She remained, as did the family, although the house was soon filled with wounded and sick, and "right busy was every member of the family obeying orders from the surgeon and administering to the needs of the suffering." One Federal described the appreciated care he received from the local civilians who remained: "[T]he people treat me with the greatest kindness. The old lady of the house has nursed me like a mother during my sickness. She is very kind."[83]

Still, most houses were plundered at some point, though not all Federals were involved. "I have not the heart to do it," wrote Parson Rumsey, "but there are plenty to do it." One lady told of a Federal who called the mistress of a farm near Mount Alban to the fence to tell her how carefully he had dug up her dishes: "I want you to see how nice I have dug up your china. I have not broken a piece." She was milking a cow at the time but went with him, he beaming, "Haven't I done it nicely?" Then he scolded her: "Now, ma'am, as I have no use for such fine china, you had better take it and if you want to save it, keep it in your house in future." He even carried it piece by piece in for her and carefully stowed it away in a closet. Other Mississippians likewise tried to hide as much as they could, burying silver and other valuables under houses and in fields. One woman, "to keep some meat where we could get it to eat, . . . put two mattresses on a bed and placed a layer of bacon, hams between them." Sometimes the greed became a morbid obsession among Federals, however. Another Mississippi woman told of different groups of Federals digging up a baby's grave three different times in search of valuables.[84]

Sometimes the Mississippi civilians, particularly women, fought back, often too much for their own good. "The girls here is the spunkiest ones I have seen in Dixie," related one Federal. A woman told of the Federals taking her honey, she barking at them, "I hope the bees will sting you to death." Ida Barlow Trotter similarly told of a young cousin, Elizabeth Read, who was "not so patient and spent her time doing all she could to aggravate the Yankee's and kept the older members of the family in a constant state of uneasiness for fear they would kill us or burn the house as a result of our cousin['s] attacks upon the enemy with her tongue." At one point a captain was jawing back at her, and she referenced a beautiful diamond ring on his finger, which she loudly presumed he had stolen from some Southerner. He held out his finger and said she could have it if she could get it off his finger. She retorted, "Give me your knife." He foolishly did, and she immediately slashed his finger, he bellowing, "Why I believe you would kill me if you could."[85]

If plunder and shame were not enough, these Mississippians also had to deal with a rearrangement of the racial hierarchy. Ruffin Thomson explained how "the whole course of the Yankee army through our country presents a scene of waste and desolation," although he was fortunate and lost only his horse Shakespeare and his mule Babe. More concerning to him was that "a great number of negroes went over to the Yankees," but he noted that because "the negroes are made soldiers of, and put to work upon the fortifications[,] they are badly fed and worked hard. Many of them on this account are returning to their homes, perfectly disgusted with Yankee masters." Thomson hoped for the best but prepared for the worst: "My fears and hopes commingle. If the enemy succeed I shall pack up what I can take with me and leave the country." This early in the siege it was only a trickle, but the rearrangement of the white/black relationship would burst forth in full as the days and weeks passed.[86]

While not in any way under the same stress as Confederates inside Vicksburg or just behind the Union lines, there was another breed of civilians in the area as well: Northern visitors. "The investment of Vicksburg and opening of water communications northward was the signal for a large influx of civilians," one observer noted. Grant added that many visitors arrived: "Some came to gratify curiosity; some to see sons or brothers who had passed through the terrible ordeal." Humorously, many brought poultry, but it was not well accepted by the army that had feasted mostly on fowl they could catch or kill for much of the campaign. "But the intention was good," Grant admitted.[87]

Sometimes, the visitors were high-level officials. Grant explained that Richard Yates, governor of Illinois, came with his state officials, and "I naturally wanted to show them what there was of most interest." Governor Edward Salomon of Wisconsin also visited, as did an entourage from Iowa, including Governor Samuel J. Kirkwood, Adjutant General Nathaniel B. Baker, and former governor and current Iowa supreme court justice Ralph P. Lowe, who touched off a cannon. Baker thought he would like to get in on the action "to tell the folks at home" and scrambled out to a covered trench, where he fired a musket through the hole below a headlog. As usual, Confederates bullets replied, one hitting a tree about ten feet over Baker's head. He immediately fell flat and snuck out on all fours, telling those with him: "I tell you, boys, that was close, wasn't it?" One of the laughing Iowans was sure "the story of his 'close call in trenches at Vicksburg' was often told by the Adjutant General of Iowa to his admiring friends at home." Congressman James F. Wilson of Iowa also visited during the siege.[88]

These visitors created quite a stir among the troops, especially the big-name politicians. One 4th Iowa Cavalry trooper went to meet his governor: "Our object was to see the Governor of Iowa & talk some about who we should have for our Pol—found him in a Grove & very talkative, talked plain too." Governor Salomon of Wisconsin visited with his state's troops, one of his soldiers writing that "the boys enjoyed seeing him."[89]

Yet, some visitors such as Adjutant General Baker were obviously not fighting material, one 15th Illinois soldier describing one who "invariably dodged after the ball had passed; was as likely to run from as to shelter." An Iowan quoted Poor Richard that "fish and visitors stink in three days," although he said it was more like three minutes during the siege. One Federal even described the arrival of a German who wanted to know what the sound of bullets were, singing around his ears. They told him, whereupon he remarked, "Oh, I tot dy ver leetle pirds." Some of these martinets could be in the army as well, although there were quite a few visitors from the reinforcements eventually on the rear line who managed to get away and play the tourist and take in the sites of the siege, including the trenches. One officer did so, writing to his wife that he could see "the spires" of Vicksburg. Unlike these legitimate soldiers, others were clearly not soldier material, being termed a "dude" officer. One such well-dressed colonel on McPherson's staff wanted to sharp-shoot one day and was given a specially loaded musket, with two charges of powder in a fouled and therefore very tight barrel. It kicked incredibly hard, knocking the colonel to his seat and bruising his shoulder no doubt. He added, "Your gun, Sergeant, recoils considerable," to which the unassuming sergeant who feigned knowing nothing replied, "Does it?"[90]

Fred Grant, the general's thirteen-year-old son who accompanied him during the campaign, told of a similar humorous episode. "Being with the skirmish line of the Eighth Missouri," he explained, "I saw an excited little group of soldiers at one point, and made haste to ascertain the cause." It seems a group of "Northern visitors" were there, and some wanted souvenirs. "A shot through his hat was thought to be a good idea," Fred recalled of one of the civilians, and the Missourians played right along, telling the man the "'Johnnies' were anxious to send North as many souvenirs of their skill as possible." They told him simply to hold the hat above the works "and he would be immediately accommodated." Obviously, the Missourians meant to hold it up on a ramrod, but the overzealous civilian stuck it up with his hand and "got the bullet not only through his hat, but also through his hand." Fred remembered that "our boys consoled themselves with the thought that he got a real souvenir, instead of the make-believe one he sought."[91]

Any number of other types of civilians showed up as well. What one Federal described as "Yankee school teachers or 'Marms' as they were called" arrived to teach the contrabands. "Sutlers are beginning to get around," another noted, "but the less a man patronizes them the better, if he wants to keep out of the hospital." Sanitary and Christian commission "agents arrived with immense quantities of provisions, clothing and hospital supplies from all the northern cities and states having troops in that department," newspaperman Sylvanus Cadwallader reported. One sanitary commission worker, Mrs. Jane Hoge, came, and she just happened to be the mother of the colonel of the 113th Illinois, George B. Hoge. She gathered all off-duty men and gave them a speech; it is not known whether the colonel was proud or embarrassed. In addition to Cadwallader, there were many other newspaper correspondents as well who stayed mainly on boats at Chickasaw Bayou. Cadwallader was the only one who stayed at Grant's headquarters and often had the scoop as a result. Most, as opposed to the war-weary Cadwallader, in his words "visited the lines occasionally; and wrote glowing accounts of the progress of the siege on marble-top tables in the ladies' cabin of some palatial Mississippi River steamboat."[92]

Perhaps most interesting were visitors from Chicago. "The Lombard Brothers of Chicago (Julius and Frank)" were singers who visited hospitals and headquarters "to give free concerts to enliven the monotony of camp life, and to cheer and inspire the troops by their excellent singing. The lines and Camps were made vocal at night for several weeks, and the uproarious encoring and applauding which was always given them, proved how heartily and deeply the soldiers appreciated the entertainment." The brothers sang ballads and opera, but the "home songs" were most popular and "were better than rations or medicine to many a poor homesick private."[93]

The siege's effect on the civilians in the area is not often analyzed but was of extreme importance. And it had a bearing on military matters as well, as morale on the home front was always an important barometer. In this case, especially with the civilians inside Vicksburg, it was crucial because of proximity and the fact that Pemberton was essentially responsible not only for his army but also for the citizens of Vicksburg. Thus morale became a factor even this early in the siege, and one Vicksburg woman freely admitted her conflicting thoughts. After a heavy bombardment and some talk of surrender, to which other ladies responded heatedly in the negative, she admitted, "But after the experience of the night, I really could not tell what I wanted, or what my opinions were."[94]

Not surprisingly, Emma Balfour summed up most civilians' feelings, as well as those of the military personnel inside Vicksburg. Joseph E. Johnston seemed to be the only hope at this point for the doomed city and its beleaguered garrison. Even this early, hopes began to be cast firmly on relief from the outside: "Oh!," she wrote in late May, "how we all look to him as our savior."[95]

5

"WE HEAR NOTHING BUT THE CRACK OF GUNS SMELL NOTHING BUT POWDER"

June 1–2

If the nerve center of the Union operations at Vicksburg was Ulysses S. Grant's headquarters, then the heartbeat of the effort was the Chickasaw Bayou landing on the Yazoo River. It was there that the lifeblood of the army—food, ammunition, supplies, equipment, and even reinforcements—was pumped out to the various parts of the force encircling Vicksburg and elsewhere as well. As such, it was a busy place; one Federal counted one hundred and sixteen steamers at the landing at one time "and teams for nearly every regt in the field here." That many vessels in the little Yazoo River made for quite a traffic jam, and although the flatland between the river and the Walnut Hills was more expansive, it was still a mass of moving men, horses, and wagons as well. That Chickasaw Bayou, Thompson Lake, and any number of other little bodies of water cut through and across this expanse made the logistics even more tricky on top of the sheer mass of humanity, animals, and equipment already there. As a result, it was normally bedlam around the landings, one Federal describing it as "one Grand circus all the while."[1]

By the time the siege was going good and steamboats had started bringing in their hordes of supplies, all manner of almost anything imaginable could be found near Chickasaw Bayou, especially at the main depot at Lake's Landing. There were corals for horses and mules, feeding lots, and parking areas for wagons. There were repair shops for the artillery and wagons that had been damaged in battle or broken down. There were cargo areas for food and equipment, including on some of the numerous steamboats used primarily for storage. Also at the landing areas were hospitals as well as hospital boats in the river. On top of that, there were pens for guarding prisoners. Guards innumerable abounded around it all, and it soon took on a city-like feel.[2]

The one main reason for the depot's existence, however, was to supply the army, much like the human heart supplies the body through its flow of blood. Thus, wagon teams came and went at all hours of the day and night, rumbling along beside camps, hospitals, and prisons and keeping all awake no matter what time of day. Each regiment sent its own quartermaster or commissary team to the landing for supplies, normally two teams per regiment, which quickly added up. Massive amounts of supplies thus went out, as much as seventy-five wagons filled only with ammunition per day just for the XV Corps. Others came to the shops to get their personal needs filled, one Iowan reporting getting fitted out with a brand-new uniform and other items. Also there was what Henry Seaman of the 13th Illinois described as "a large collection of sutler tents well filled with all kinds of trash—to sell to the soldiers at extravagant prices."[3]

The trick was, of course, getting the goods from the landing to the army, and the road network thus became critical. Grant had originally put in new supply roads even during the assaults in late May, and these were expanded as the siege wore on. Problems arose because of distance, with Sherman's corps on the north side of the lines needing a lot less effort than McClernand's regiments miles farther out. Bridges were key in getting across the water features before the roads rose out of the Yazoo River valley, but the roads even to the army needed guarding as well, Grant putting the shot-up battalion of 13th US Infantry on duty to guard roads in the rear. Weather played a role in the supply efforts as well; the roads turned to mud pits when heavy rains came, and getting up the steep hills to the high ground could be taxing even during dry weather. One Illinoisan saw a large siege piece being hauled to the army by eleven yoke of oxen, and another explained the difficulties: "The heavy cannons and caissons had to be pulled up this steep bluff. They got ropes and it took hundreds of men to pull them up. It was well on in the day before we got all off."[4]

Yet Chickasaw Bayou offered one other curiosity found nowhere else amid the army's deployment and operational area. It was also the scene of a former battle, and many a soldier who had business going to and from the landing—and even some who did not but were pure tourists—went to the battlefield made so bloody in December 1862 when Sherman first tried to reach

Vicksburg by that route. All knew of the area's significance whether they had been engaged there or not. One mentioned the supply area was "on the very battle-ground where our troops under Gen Sherman fought so hard last January [December]." Another marveled at how "the enemy had the strongest natural position in the west if not in the whole south, to protect them. I never saw anything near its equal."[5]

Seeing the Chickasaw Bayou battlefield became that much more special to those who had actually been engaged in the battle. Sherman himself remarked that "we have good bridges where Morgan Smith was and where [George W.] Morgan crossed." One Indianan reflected that "the ground looked very natural except the timber in which the battle was fought was slashed to prevent another attack." An Ohioan "rode past the scene of last December's operations. Saw where I worked all night of Dec. 29 in throwing up fortifications." Others viewed initials in trees where they had been. Not surprisingly, where there was a major battle, there were also burials, and some even went to the battlefield and dug up bodies buried in December and sent them home.[6]

The Chickasaw Bayou area was thus a haven, a distribution point, a focal point of life for the Army of the Tennessee. But its entire existence was because of the city just up the bluffs now ringed with troops either trying to capture or to defend Vicksburg. There, Confederate flags waved proudly over the works. The Union flags were just as noticeable, one Federal writing that "the old flag is waving in a few steps of me and although many holes in its broad stripes show it has been often struck by Rebel shells & bullets yet it waves none the less proudly." Illinoisan Albert Chipman similarly reflected that "Vixburg or the rebs in there still holds on to their doomed City with an iron grasp, and tenacity that is worthy of a better cause." Then he added, in large part because of the supply resources provided at Chickasaw Bayou, "but the chord grows tighter every day."[7]

By the time June rolled around, siege life at Vicksburg had settled into a certain monotony and routine. Soldiers of both sides had grown accustomed to their strictly regulated lives, with most of their time being spent either on the front lines or in their camps to the rear. For the Confederate soldier— less so for the Federals—the two could not always be split, as the Southern camps were often, because of space limitations and geography, right behind the lines. And, because of the fear of another assault at the time and place of the enemy's choosing, these Confederates had to stay alert and on guard at all times, even at night. Finally, because there were far fewer of them to go around than in the Union army, Confederates were required to stay on the front lines longer than their Northern counterparts. Accordingly, many Confederate soldiers spent much of the siege on the front lines, not fighting, skirmishing, or sharpshooting at all times by any means but certainly manning the defenses in case any of those activities were needed. Thus, most of any given Confederate's life during the siege was spent on the front lines, waiting and dodging the heavy enemy fire. One Confederate could only think that "if a deaf man could see this whole party make a dive once in a while into holes in the Bank he would no doubt be highly amused."[8]

Life on the front Confederate line was anything but easy, and that difficulty started early each day. Night provided some relief, allowing the soldiers at least to stand erect and walk around a little with less possibility of being picked off by some enemy sharpshooter. But that freedom came to an end early each day, well before daylight. "The command was daily aroused and under arms at 3:30 A.M., to guard against surprise," Confederate brigade commander William E. Baldwin explained. Fellow brigade commander Stephen D. Lee added that "an hour before day every morning the whole force were aroused, ready to repel any assault."[9]

Once the infantrymen filled the trenches and the artillerymen manned their pieces, normally little of anything major occurred on their side, and the hours began to run together. Brigade commander Louis Hébert described his men being cramped up "in pits and holes not large enough to allow them to extend their limbs." Orders had gone out not to fire unless it was necessary, although after some request for clarification word came that sharpshooting was permitted, but not needless skirmishing. In fact, orders came not to return fire "unless the enemy came within 200 yards of our works." One Mississippian took exception, as "they saw their comrades being shot down every day, while they were not permitted to fire a gun!" Even officers were indignant at the restrictions, division commander Martin L. Smith later writing, "I am inclined to think caution in this respect was pushed rather to an extreme, and that a little more firing would have proved beneficial." Stephen D. Lee agreed, protesting that "both ammunition and provisions were husbanded too much."[10]

Morale suffered from the lack of fighting while still holding the lines. "We are often forbidden to fire," one Confederate noted, "and ordered to cease, when firing." That the Federals shot all they wanted was also an issue, with the same Confederate describing how "some are killed and wounded every day, but we cannot say how many." Hébert described his troops "at every instance under a fire they were forbidden to return." Most deaths in these front lines were from Union sharpshooters—"minie balls do the most execution." Comparatively, the naval and artillery fire was less dangerous to the men, it falling mostly between the fortifications and the town, although the land artillery did a lot of damage to the works which had to be repaired every night.[11]

Confederate artillery did not fire a lot either, for much the same reason but also because such a demonstration quickly brought Federal artillery fire that would do much more damage than the good resulting from one Confederate shot, often including damaging the gun so that it was useless in the future. Division commander John H. Forney later wrote that "the artillery, though well served, was of but little advantage to us during the siege. The enemy concentrated a heavy fire, dismounting or disabling gun after gun. To this fire we could make but a feeble response. Ammunition was scarce, and orders forbade its use except against advancing columns of infantry or batteries being planted. The proportionate loss of officers and men of the artillery was unusually great." It was especially dangerous to load and fire the pieces, the cannoneers being easy targets for Union sharpshooters. Accordingly, little was done with the artillery except for the pieces being loaded under cover of night and shot in the morning one time. Two guns damaged with broken trunions on Smith's line were simply "kept loaded with grape, and, in case of an assault, will be fired at least once more." Of course, the lack of Confederate artillery fire did not keep the Federals from banging away. It was not uncommon for Confederates to describe "right smart of sharpshooting and cannonading during the day."[12]

To help ensure against another assault, Confederates on the front lines prepared additional firepower over and above small arms but far safer to maintain and operate than cannons. Brigade commander Francis Shoup "organized my artillerists into a hand-grenade and thunder-barrel corps, since our guns are of no service." Any number and type of weapons resulted, with some inspiration from enemy grenades thrown into their own lines, one Confederate describing one as "a curious Yankee hand grenade": egg-shaped with a percussion cap on one end and a five- or six-inch wooden arrow on the other to keep it straight in flight. Larger types included "thunder barrels," which were filled with powder and shells that would be rolled onto the attackers when they assaulted next. The barrels would first explode, then the "scattered shells will explode among the Yankees," a Louisianan explained. It was the concept of a huge shotgun with buckshot, even more so than canister rounds.[13]

That said, to prepare for the inevitable assault, Confederates on the front line continually worked to build new batteries so additional guns could be mounted or moved to new positions when the old ones were discovered. Most of these new guns on the land side came by bringing some of the smaller cannons in the river batteries to the line in rear of Vicksburg. Eleven guns were moved on June 11, with some of Colonel Edward Higgins's river battery cannoneers manning them on the landside. Others arrived later as well, including a mortar that did good service behind John C. Moore's line. Some of these forts were never completed, however, due to "the working party being driven off by the enemy's sharpshooters."[14]

Ordnance was nevertheless the key issue, and Pemberton had his men collect "all the ammunition scattered in front of our trenches, and to have the cartridge boxes of the enemy's dead emptied of their contents, it being important to add in any way to our limited supply of ammunition." Most important were percussion caps (and to a lesser degree friction primers), "of which latter we stood greatly in need, having one million more of cartridges than caps, without which latter, of course, the former could be of no possible value." Pemberton also had "unexploded Parrott shells scattered around the city sent to Paxton's Foundry and recapped."[15]

Many ingenious ways were continually attempted to get more caps and primers into Vicksburg, Johnston sending all he could with each courier. Fortunately, some percussion caps arrived by couriers on May 28 and 29, eighteen thousand by the first and twenty thousand by the latter. Pemberton also noted in his diary that another courier later arrived with two hundred thousand caps. Engineer Samuel Lockett noted that these came by way of men who "floated down the river on logs." Others would leave Vicksburg in small boats going south on the river and thence to Jackson, returning by putting in the river north of Vicksburg and floating down on planks or logs. Of course, many of these couriers were captured, "from which they know that we are short of that important article," one Louisianan surmised. One of the Confederates captured had apparently broken his parole from when he had been taken earlier, and although his final fate was never determined, one Indianan noted that "he is to be shot for breaking his parol[e]."[16]

Making it harder on the continuously alert Confederates manning the lines were occasional moves as Pemberton authorized some troop movements within the trenches themselves. Bowen had been arguing since the assaults that being the reserve was grinding on the troops and asked for a place on the lines. Pemberton allowed Bowen to place Martin Green's brigade in the trenches, but he kept Cockrell's Missourians in reserve. On the night of June 2, Green's trans-Mississippians took a portion of the lines from the Stockade Redan down to Glass Bayou, allowing Louis Hébert to move his Mississippians farther to the right, the 36th, 38th, and 7th Mississippi Battalion moving from the left of the brigade to the right, past the Great Redoubt. Forney noted that "my line was contracted by closing in to the right, in consequence of its close investment and the reduction of its numbers by casualties," although one 38th Mississippi soldier added to his diary "the men very much dissatisfied with the change." Another Mississippian elaborated why: "Somebody had been in our second position before us as we found it fully occupied by a most energetic type of 'war bugs' or 'gray backs' with whom we soon established most intimate relations." The Arkansans and Missourians of Green's brigade thus took over the defense of the east face of the Stockade Redan and the small redan to its south, which quickly became known as "Green's Redan." Yet Green was not satisfied with the fortifications he assumed either, writing three days later that "our works are in better condition than they were when we came here. They still need work." As with all others, he needed more tools "so as to get them completed." Colonel Thomas P. Dockery of the 19th Arkansas was also upset, writing that the sector he assumed "was one of the most exposed positions on the line, the enemy's guns enfilading the works."[17]

Other troops shifted as well to cover weak spots or reinforce problem areas, especially some places on Forney's front where there were no troops at all. Having no reserves for the division, Forney wanted more regiments: "There is a space along there now unoccupied by troops." Others of Bowen's regiments temporarily went into line as early as May 27, one regiment into the trenches between the 3rd Louisiana Redan and the Great Redoubt and two others in reserve in "Magazine ravine" behind the line between the Jackson and Baldwin's Ferry Roads. Small-scale shifting, not on the brigade level, also led to additional problems. One Tennessean left a dog named "'Bob Hatton,' named for General Bob Hatton, of Tennessee" (who was killed earlier in the war at Seven Pines). Another lost his horse, who "is strayed or killed. I think killed as I can't find her any where in these lines. As dead horses are hawled to the Miss River and she having been gone 8 days, may now be landed at Port Hudson." That was not so facetious; Federals in Warrenton described dead horses and mules from Vicksburg floating past.[18]

Even getting food to the front lines was quite a job. Cooks prepared what food there was for the common soldier behind the lines and then took it to the trenches late in the day. Some of these "cookyards" were as much as three-quarters of a mile in the rear in ravines or hollows, and often the terrain in between was swept with enemy fire, making the transition to the front line dangerous. But the result was worth the wait. "Often I have seen men so hungry that when the rations came, they would eat the last morsel allotted them at once, and not leave even a crust to stay the pangs of hunger till another twenty-four hours had passed," admitted one Mississippian.[19]

Just because the food arrived on the lines did not mean it made it into the soldier's stomachs. The continual Federal barrage made eating difficult. "We had," one Mississippian recalled, "sometimes to eat a good deal of sand in our peas, knocked into them by bullets and shells from the enemy's lines." William Pitt Chambers described how he and a couple of others put all their grub together on a plate, it being molasses, a little meat, and the hated pea bread. Just as they prepared to eat, a shell hit their works and penetrated through, throwing boards used as shade and dirt all over the men. Their food was ruined, they scratching the dirt covered meat and molasses from the ground: "Our 'pea bread' was intact, however, barring the 'grit' that adhered to it." Yet priorities were established: he declared, "I think it made men madder, when playing cards in the trenches, to have their cards covered with dirt by a cannon ball, than anything else. It seemed to me that they could 'cuss' with more vigor then than under any other circumstances."[20]

The net result of all the moving and constant manning of trenches was weariness, even this early in the siege. "General Moore reports his men much worn in the trenches, and recommends that a portion of them be withdrawn during the day to a short distance from the trenches for rest," his division commander Forney endorsed, but added: "I would concur in this recommendation were it not that the enemy is so close at hand." Division commander Carter Stevenson described the "sleepless nights and days, under all the hardships incident to their position. Confined, without a moment's relief from the very day of their entrance into the fortifications . . . to the narrow trenches; exposed without shelter to the broiling sun and drenching rain; subsisting on rations barely sufficient for the support of life; engaged from the earliest dawn till dark, and often during the night, in one ceaseless conflict with the enemy."[21]

The tiring duty on the front lines also included labor on the earthworks. Samuel Lockett's engineers built siege fortifications much like the Federals, and these Confederates manning the lines could look out "sand-bag loop holes . . . along the whole line to protect our sharpshooters. These sand bags were made from tent-flies and old tents turned over to me by the quartermaster's department, and from the same source I obtained a supply of material during the whole siege," he explained. Yet, these fortifications were no match for the constant Federal abuse, many Confederates finding that artillery rounds would go through most of them. Colonel Ashbel Smith of the 2nd Texas experimented and found "16 feet of earth was thus seen to be about the measure of the penetration of the enemy's 6-pounder and 12-pounder elongated shot." Smith ordered two more feet of dirt added to the parapet, which stopped most shells. The troops were still subjected to the shells' effects, however, "sometimes strewing clods of earth over our men." Brigade commander John C. Moore recommended using cotton bales to add strength.[22]

Other housekeeping work to make the front lines safer and more livable took place as well, Stephen D. Lee explaining that "everywhere the trenches were made more comfortable, and made wider, traverses were constructed to prevent the artillery from being enfiladed, as also in the rifle pits, wherever found necessary." He provided other details on how this was accomplished: "Head logs and sand bags were used along the rifle pits to protect the heads of the men in the trenches, and arrangements made to shade the men with their blankets overhead, from the sun. Openings were made to the rear for convenience in getting back of the trenches, and to let water run off in case of rain."[23]

But much of the front line work meant rebuilding what had been torn down. Many of the works quickly began to show heavy erosion due to the continual Union bombardment, and Confederate engineers were fully tasked with rebuilding, mostly at night, and "thickening the parapets, which had begun to show the effects of the enemy's continual battering." A particularly large breach in the 3rd Louisiana Redan had to be "filled up and repaired with sand-bags." One Mississippian noted the futility of this type of work, however, explaining "they were worked all night building a parapet or mounting a gun that dared not fire a shot, only to see their work demolished before the day was an hour old!" Such a process was not lost on the Federals either, one writing that "our artillery does not seem to do them much damage either only to knock down their breastworks and they can build them up as fast as we can knock them down." Still the incoming fire came, heavier and heavier, often wounding men in the trenches. Lockett noted on occasion how "the artillery fire of the enemy was unusually severe, and several of our works were considerably damaged, especially the works on General Lee's front, and on the Graveyard and Jackson roads."[24]

The continual battering even led Lockett to begin new fortifications immediately in rear of some of the major forts. "The stockade redan and the stockade on its left beginning to suffer a good deal from the enemy's artillery, a new line of rifle-pits was started in front of the stockade, and the ditch of the redan was prepared for riflemen, to give a double line at this point," he reported. Later, more work was added: "[A] new series of rifle-pits was begun, running along a couple of spurs in the rear, so as to envelop the stockade and its redan, as a precaution against the contingency of the enemy's carrying this point by assault, or rendering it untenable by his mining operations." On the Jackson Road, "this work had also become considerably battered by this time, and the old parapets were nearly gone. A new one was accordingly made a few feet in rear of the first, and the main body of the work was still preserved entire, and our men protected from the enemy's fire." Eventually, Lockett ordered "retrenchments . . . in rear of all the threatened points, to provide against the possibility of the enemy's being successful in their attempts." Yet this safeguard occurred only at the major forts from the Stockade Redan southward to Square Fort. The smaller earthworks between them were not as badly mauled, Lockett noting that they were "easily kept in repair by fatigue parties working at night."[25]

The result was an increasing worry about the Confederates' ability to defend their lines. John C. Moore reported that "I hope that I am not an alarmist, yet I cannot help feeling uneasy about the right of my line." And all the while, the enemy artillery was getting closer and thereby that much more powerful, Lieutenant Colonel Samuel D. Russell of the 3rd Louisiana reporting "one of the enemy's works in his front (Jackson road) is assuming the shape of a formidable redoubt." It was all very disconcerting—but especially for those tiring men who had no relief on the miserable front lines of the Confederate works at Vicksburg.[26]

Life on the front lines of the Union army was much different. There was not the constant alert felt by the Confederates, although there was some initial concern about a breakout attempt by Pemberton's troops. Most soon realized that if anyone made offensive moves it would be the Federals. Thus, they could pick the time and place and would have plenty of alert beforehand. And there were many more Federals than Confederates, allowing commanders to swap companies and regiments out to get them rest, sustenance, and cleansing in the rearward camps.

"We had not been many days in the rear of Vicksburg before we settled into regular habits," one Federal explained. "The men were detailed in reliefs for work in the trenches, and being relieved at fixed hours everybody seemed to lead a systematic life." Another declared that "our duties here have taken a fixed routine and day after day goes by without bringing anything to us new or strange." A routine quickly emerged in the 46th Indiana, for example, where two companies were on duty per day. Others had picket duty every other day. In the 76th Ohio, one soldier explained "our company is divided off into five reliefs who occupy the rifle pits two hours at a time for the purpose of making 'secesh' hug their holes on the adjoining hills. This they do pretty effectually." Since commanders were able to shift troops in and out, Confederate Stephen D. Lee later postulated that the average Union regiment spent about a quarter of the time in the trenches, unlike the Confederates who spent the entire siege there. Unfortunately, at times the schedule went afoul, such as when one soldier explained how "our Capt. was to call us before day break to come out, but overslept himself."[27]

Still, the amount of work needed—which increased as the siege wore on— left the men less and less time for recreation. Many worked even when not in the trenches per se. "The command has been constantly on duty," Union general John E. Smith wrote, "when not in the rifle-pits, throwing up works to be used for attack or defense, as occasion might require." Others had to spend the night in the trenches, and Charles Dana reported that "one night in riding through the trenches I must have passed twenty thousand men asleep on their guns. I still can see the grotesque positions into which they had curled themselves."[28]

While there was plenty of duty, most commanders tried to fashion a system by which the soldiers would serve a period on duty, whether that be picket, guard, skirmishing, or digging, and then have ample off hours to recuperate. It worked some of the time, many soldiers describing off-duty times, but on other occasions it did not. Colonel John McNulta of the 94th Illinois explained that "six companies were on duty every third day, and 75 men on fatigue twelve hours out of each thirty-six, . . . and in addition to which was detail for making gabions, camp guards, and fatigue parties for digging rifle-pits and shelter for the pickets and reserves, and other duties that were very laborious."[29]

Colonel George W. Clark of the 34th Iowa described how "one half my men who were able for duty were on duty all the time, and not unfrequently I was compelled, in order to fill the details, to send men who had just been relieved, thus keeping the same men out in the ditches forty-eight hours without rest." He added that his men "behaved well on picket, and worked faithfully on fatigue. Unaccustomed as they were to such duty and such a climate, and having to use water of inferior quality, I think they have exhibited powers of endurance seldom surpassed by men under any circumstances." Nevertheless, some suffered from sunstroke or were "overcome by heat and heavy duty." Lieutenant Colonel Daniel Kent commented that the work "was continued and unremitting (well named fatigue duty)."[30]

It was all very tiring even for the better off Federals. Many worked all night, as that was the safest time to be out and about, but it made for bad sleeping conditions during the day: "If we sleep at all which is nearly impossible for me it is so warm in the daytime." As the workload grew, so did the grumbling, aided by continual boredom due to the monotonous work. Dana later observed how "apathy grew in our ranks." He added how "the heat of the weather, the unexpected length of the siege, the absence of any thorough organization of the engineer department, and the general belief of our officers and men that the town must presently fall into our hands without any special effort or sacrifice, all conspires to produce comparative inactivity and inefficiency on our part."[31]

Working with the artillery added another degree of difficulty with the additional weight, fortification needs, and horses if applicable, some of the larger guns not being field pieces borne by teams. Still, they had to be initially pulled into place by draft animals. Such was the case with several guns eventually taken off the gunboat *Cincinnati*. When the water fell, a team went and tried to retrieve the guns for use on land, but watchful Confederates fired at them. One Federal reported, "we had a 'Lookout' posted on the stern who, every time he saw the flash of the guns, yelled 'lookout' or 'Lie down,' and then such skeedaddling to get on the safe side of the boat or in the rifle pits which we had dug on the shore, you never saw." The ball soon whizzed by and work resumed.[32]

Other artillery batteries dealt with a myriad of change, danger, and action. Some change proved positive, such as when the Chicago Light Artillery received new guns to replace their old Parrots; the men were very excited about their new Napoleons. Others performed odd duties, such as when a field battery was placed across the Mississippi River on De Soto Point, where "we are placed here in case the enemy should attempt to cross in skiffs (which deserters report) they are building for the purpose," one cannoneer explained. The infantry was often tapped to help build fortifications for the guns, terming it "planting a battery," which George Carrington took as humorous, writing in his diary that "at this time of year some people plant corn." Of course, the limited incoming artillery fire also had to be dodged, especially from the guns that soon became familiar to the men on the front lines, including cannons such as the famed Confederate gun "Whistling Dick"—named "from the shrill whistle of its shells as they sped through the air." They also named one "Crazy Jane," because it had its barrel shorn off and no one knew exactly which way the ball would go. There was so much cannonading (mainly Union), in fact, that one soldier thought it would have atmospheric repercussions, a common thought at the time. "Notwithstanding the great amount of cannonading," he wrote, "there has been very little rain for the last 6 weeks."[33]

Union soldiers tried to make life in the trenches the best they could, and there were as many individual experiences as there were individuals. One soldier described an encounter with John Logan, whom, he quoted, "didn't mind the shells but they were spoiling his tents and demoralizing his cooks." Samuel Byers remembered he was in the forward trenches when his colonel came "creeping along the trench to where I was." He had a package, inside of which was an officer's sash: Byers had been commissioned as regimental adjutant. Many amused themselves with the obligatory game of lifting a cap to see if it would be shot: "A favorite amusement of the soldiers was to place a cap on the end of a ramrod and to raise it just above the head-logs," one soldier wrote, "betting on the number of bullets which would pass through it within a given time." But it was not all fun and games. Division commander Alvin Hovey wrote how "the strain upon my forces was extreme. . . . [T]hey were under constant fire, casualties happening daily . . . in the rifle-pits, and yet, during all this long period, there was no murmur, no complaints. They were veterans and determined to succeed." And they were doing that little by little as the approaches continually advanced. "Should General Grant think it advisable to assault again," Dana reported to Washington, "we are now in position to do it with effect; but, unless Johnston becomes very pressing, he will rather trust to time and general compression."[34]

There was nevertheless constant danger in the midst of the work on the front lines, the soldiers always being within range of the Confederates and drawing closer every day. That danger came in several forms. Just getting to duty areas on the front lines through the maze of trenches was dangerous enough; soldiers had to run the gauntlet to reach the forward trenches before covered ways went in, one Illinoisan describing how they "have to 'turkey' in these places, that is double up and run half bent, letting them shoot at us." Despite the moratorium on Confederate fire, the enemy did manage some punch-back, including artillery at times. Charles Dana described in one missive to Washington that "the enemy yesterday laid aside his long-standing inactivity, and opened violently with both artillery and musketry. Two mortars placed at the left of our center, in a ravine near the railroad, in front of A. J. Smith, fired during the day some sixty shell at the trenches of Logan, in McPherson's center. These mortars are out of reach of our artillery and sharpshooters." The massive amount of work was also dangerous, one Illinoisan telling of a death from the "falling in of some dirt when they were making a magazine." As in the Confederate lines, even carrying the food to the soldiers on the front line was dangerous. One Wisconsin soldier told of carrying kettles of food to the trenches, where the hungry soldiers were watching them move forward. A bullet hit one of the kettles and his partner Sam, a third sergeant, ran to the rear. The Wisconsin soldier saved what was left and went on to the trenches in a hurry, noting that "Sam lost his stripes, and also the boys' respect, because he went the wrong way, although the danger was no less."[35]

Unfortunately, danger also lurked from the rear in the form of friendly fire from their own forces. There was quite a dread of artillery firing over infantry, as "rotten" shells that exploded early could do a lot of damage to the infantry who were huddled down. In fact, one Federal argued that they faced more danger from a "battery of regulars" on the ridge behind them who frequently shot a dud shell that often fell among the Illinoisans. One soldier had both arms shot off "by one of their shells bursting too soon." It became so bad that "our boys declare they will go up and spike their guns if they don't throw away that bad ammunition." The regulars thereafter started warning the Illinoisans before they fired: they "always send a man to tell us when they are going to shoot." One battery commander described another incident: "This most unfortunate accident has made us all feel very badly, while it could not in any wise be avoided. . . . These accidents have been frequent all along the line, but this fact does not make it less unpleasant to have them happen to us." One general even described how they "kill more of our own men than of the enemy," and Dana reported to Washington how "much of the ammunition supplied to this army is very bad. A board of survey just held here reports that the Parrott shells are uniformly defective from sand holes. Some of these are filled with putty; some are left undisguised. The small-arm ammunition from Indianapolis is rascally, the powder worthless and deficient in quantity." Almost as bad, an Iowan in McPherson's XVII Corps related that "occasionally Sherman's shells would come over Fort Hill in our midst causing an uneasy feeling."[36]

Casualties were steady but not overwhelming in the Union trenches. "We are still alive and well," one Ohioan wrote to his uncle, "but still we are in danger every minute for most any minute we can hear a musket ball whizzing to close to our ears for the sound to be pleasant." As enumerated by Abram Vanauken, who was diligent about keeping notes in his diary, only one or two or three casualties per day occurred in his regiment, and that was when the unit was on picket duty. There were few if any injuries when not on duty.[37]

Death was nevertheless a real possibility on the front lines, and even though common, it was very personal when it came. William T. Rigby described the death of "one of my best friends." He said a few words and another offered a prayer at the simple ceremony at his burial, but the real grief came later as he had to deal with all his friend's personal effects. Similarly, Ohioan John W. Griffith noted in his diary, "My bunk-mate shot through the head and I fear mortally wounded." He lingered a few days, Griffith going to check on him often in the hospital. He later described another wounded man: "I was so near him that the blood flew upon me when the ball struck him."[38]

The result of the continual death was yet another duty: burial parties. "He was buried the best he could be under the circumstances," one soldier wrote to his sister. "He was buried with the clothes he had on with his blanket wrapped around him. I have no doubt but that looks like a hard way to you of burying a man but there is hundreds that in the army that are buried with out even a blanket around them."[39]

One last danger also lurked in front of the Federals on the front line, but not from the Confederates actively fighting them. Rather, it came from those Confederates who came forward seeking to give themselves up, mostly at night. Obviously, the pickets in front of the lines of troops initially met them, and there was always uncertainty about what they were up to and the danger of exposing themselves while dealing with them. Yet Confederate deserters were common, and the numbers grew as the siege progressed. "All the indications point to the speedy surrender of this place," Dana wrote to Washington. "Deserters who came out yesterday say that the Tennessee and Georgia regiments have determined to stack their arms within three days and refuse to continue the defense on the ground that it is useless, and that it is impossible to fight on the rations they receive." An Illinoisan described how "deserters come to our lines every night. They represent a most deplorable state of things within." Another declared deserters arrived "every day in large numbers."[40]

And there apparently would have been more had the Federals lessened their fire. One Illinoisan noted how two deserters came out and "ate a large quantity of provisions for breakfast at Logan's head-quarters." They told the Federals more would come "but that they are afraid that our men would shoot them, for they can't put up a hand or turn a rail to fix it, but it is instantly shot away by our bullets."[41]

It was a fine line. Grant would like for every Confederate to desert, but he could not lessen the sharpshooting and skirmishing of his own army on the chance that many more Southerners would cross the lines. The result was yet another major duty on the front lines for both sides: the constant sharpshooting and skirmishing that Vicksburg became known for.

S harpshooting and even heavier skirmishing and artillery fire became a hallmark of Vicksburg. "We hear nothing but the crack of guns smell nothing but powder," one Indianan wrote to his wife, another declaring that "it is fine sport to be in the rifle pits and pop every secesh that sticks his head up above the brest works." The receiving end was not as much fun, an Illinoisan countering that "there is no fun in being where the balls are flying like hail." The skirmishing mainly came a couple of hours at the beginning of the day and a couple at the end, with the hottest parts of the day less active. And it had a point. Grant wrote to Julia, "I have the town closely invested and our Rifle Pitts up so close to the enemy that they cannot show their heads without being shot at at short enough range to kill a squirrel. They dare not show a single gun on the whole line of their works." The Confederates, who were the recipients of the heavy Federal fire but also meted out their own at times, agreed, brigade commander Alfred Cumming relating that "an almost unremitting fire of sharpshooters was kept up during all hours of daylight during the whole time, varied by occasional brisk cannonading." Pemberton himself described "the habitual sharpshooting and artillery fire."[42]

The basic confrontation at Vicksburg came through sharpshooting, which was much heavier on the Union side than among the Confederate ranks, mainly because of their limited ammunition. Grant told the 15th Illinois "he had plenty of ammunition and not to be afraid to use it." In fact, one Iowan declared that almost anyone in the Union army who wanted to was allowed to take a gun and go sharp-shoot, whether they were officially on duty or not. Even artillerymen would borrow rifles when not on duty and sharp-shoot: "[I] find it quite an exciting amusement," one admitted. That said, not all were so inclined: "Many of the men consider the sharp shooting fun and many when not otherwise engaged will take their pockets full of ammunition & go to skirmish line, but I am not very venturesome & prefer to stay where I am safe unless sent out to the front on duty."[43]

Those on duty were expected to keep up a steady fire—at least forty rounds daily. Members of the 124th Illinois put pads on their shoulders because of the heavy firing. One explained how he had fired as many as "60 or 70 rounds," and one claimed taking as many as a hundred and eighty shots. Some Federals shot so much that their guns became too hot, at which point they would sit back and read the paper while waiting for them to cool. Some trenches had seats in the rear and shades over them "to keep the hot sun off our heads."[44]

Most of the sharpshooting was close in, especially as the lines drew nearer over the course of the siege. When anyone showed any part of their bodies, death or at least a terrible wound was almost instant. One Iowan called the sharpshooters "the body snatchers," and another admitted, "I got many a splendid shot at the d____m rascals when they would bob their heads up to look over their breastworks." Union brigade commander John D. Stevenson reported that "no rebel dare show himself outside the works or carelessly expose his person within, unless he subjected himself to a fire that caused his instant disappearance." Confederate brigade commander William E. Baldwin agreed, noting "the greater portion of our losses during the siege was caused by the fire of small-arms."[45]

The sharpshooting was almost constant, with the Confederates taking part much of the time even if in less volume and being at somewhat of a disadvantage. One Confederate described how their works were higher than the Federals. Some would think that would be an advantage, but as he explained, "The firing was done through port holes, and ours, being depicted against the sky, revealed the sharpshooters instantly." The time of day also made a lot of difference as to when each side did most of its firing. Confederates were at a disadvantage in the morning mainly looking eastward into the sun, whereas the Federals looking westward were worse off in the evening. Still, it went on nonetheless, Captain A. C. Roberds of the 23rd Alabama writing that "we did not waste our powder, but no Abolitionist could show his head without danger from ball or buckshot." A German in the 29th Missouri described how the firing sometimes sounded like "the axes at a large wood chopping," and Charles Dana reported to Washington that the "firing was quite active throughout the day yesterday along the whole line." Another confessed that even amid the lead balls flying around "we have got so used to them that we don't mind them much."[46]

Confederate brigade commander Stephen D. Lee gave a particular vivid description of the sharpshooting. "The fire from their small-arms commenced generally about half an hour before daylight, and continued until about dark in the evening," he explained. "There was no relief whatever to our men, who were confined . . . in their narrow trenches without any opportunity of moving about, as there was during the day a perfect rain of Minie balls, which prevented any one from showing the least portion of his body, while at night, in consequence of the proximity of the enemy, it was impossible for the men to leave their positions for any length of time."[47]

Sometimes, the bored soldiers took chances at longer shots. One Iowan described setting the gunsights "to 800 yards." This was especially the case when some units received better arms. The 81st Illinois exchanged their old Austrian muskets for Enfield rifles, and Edmund Newsome described how the boys were eager to try them out: "I shot about seventy rounds yesterday, and some of the boys exceeded that number." He added that "they could shoot much better than our old guns did, for we could put the bullet just where we wanted it to be." One Federal even loaded his Enfield with "eight revolver balls, I calculate to give it a sling and slay a whole regiment."[48]

In the open expanses, most watched what was happening. Accurate hits brought cheers from both sides while bad ones brought jeers and laughter. Often, the two sides held shooting matches, when a hat on a pole would be the target and the quality of the shooting brought cheers or jeers. Many witnessed the death of some who took great chances. Several Confederates climbed trees, but "we get these sharpshooters every time they climb up in trees," George Carrington of the 8th Illinois explained. "Never takes very long to locate them, a puff of smoke tells the tale. We never try that game on our side, but keep close to the ground."[49]

Given the distance at times, there was often a lack of certainty about the results. "I think I picked off one reble," a Federal wrote in unconvincing fashion. An Indianan noted that "I did not hit any one as I know of. I know I did hit a horse at nine hundred yards. I fired twenty to thirty rounds before I got him. You see that killing a horse is as good as a man for we don't let them bury them and they stink them out as lead and iron won't drive them out." Some knew they had done poorly, as in the case of one who admitted to his officer, "Sir, I ain't had no kind of luck today. I ain't killed a feler." Yet close calls could be almost as frightening as getting hit. An Indianan, although unhurt, had a piece of tobacco shot out of his hand while lifting it to his mouth. An Iowan similarly described how "the dodging and ducking of the boys to avoid them are very comical and unnecessary. We tell each other so, but, nevertheless, we all duck."[50]

While sharpshooting was the main ingredient in a soldier's day, at times the fighting could reach slightly larger proportions. One Illinoisan described how things could quickly escalate when "somebody shoots at it & then somebody else shoots at that somebody & then the piquet-fighting gets loud and in earnest though it is very seldom that anybody gets hurt." Add in occasional artillery and it soon could get really heated: "Once in a while we give them a shell to keep them alive." At times it could get loud; a cavalryman noted that "the firing of the small arms makes me think of a 100 or so of woodchoppers in the forest falling trees, and the reports of the cannon just like that when the tree falls to the ground. This noise continues day and night."[51]

The sound made others think a real battle was occurring, even if few were being hit. One Illinoisan wrote to his wife of "the same rattle & crash of musketry & booming of cannon from morning until night & from night until morning till one gets heart-sick of so much noise and confusion." He added, "Yet after all there is very little of the fighting that amounts to much except that which is done with the artillery as all the musketry fighting is at long range & it is seldom that a man gets injured and especially at our end of the line." Many Confederates, of course, would have disagreed.[52]

Some skirmishing was indeed small in scale, such as when Union soldier Carlos Colby described how "the men in the front rifle pits, formed themselves in two ranks, the front rank taking dead aim on the tops of the forts, while the rear rank raised a shout and ordered forward double quick, the instant the rebs showed themselves to see what was up, our men fired and dropped down out of sight, letting a shower of balls pass over them Such is the way in which we are continually harassing them." Others were unknowingly targeted when they were outmaneuvered during the night, as on the extreme Union right where some soldiers made a new trench during the night. The next morning "out came four or five rebs out of their tents and were putting on their cloths. Jo took deliberate aim and there was one rebel less to contend against." It worked the other way as well, as with Steele's men on the Indian mound they named "sugar loaf." Confederates snuck up on them one night and fired a volley. "Our party woke up from their sound sleep looking pretty wild. Our men were running in every direction." One who was "rattled pretty badly" ran all the way back to camp and reported everyone captured. It was over in thirty minutes and quiet again, an Iowan surmising that "they merely wished to bluff [us] off the mound for we were getting uncomfortably near."[53]

The most heated skirmishing took place down on the far Union left as new troops arrived and sought to stake their claim to this previously uncontested land. One Federal officer reported "a sharp little skirmish," although not all the efforts involved actual shooting. Colonel John McNulta of the 94th Illinois reported his men took a "very troublesome work of the enemy . . . known as the 'Cane Pit,'" explaining how "they worked their way between the enemy's forts and rifle-pits, and took one of the latter, with 4 prisoners, without firing a shot." Division commander Jacob Lauman especially seemed to get into more fracases than anyone, perhaps because the ground on his front was more slanted toward the ridges on which the enemy line sat. Perhaps also it was because his opponent, Alfred Cumming, was more alert and prickly than others. Lauman saw fairly large skirmishes in early June, his engineer, Captain Henry C. Freeman, writing that in an advance "the enemy were driven back, and the crest of the ridge gained on the left of the Hall's Ferry road. The enemy retired across the valley after a sharp skirmish in which some of our men were wounded." The 33rd Wisconsin and 3rd Iowa "rushed forward with a deafening cheer, under a heavy fire of musketry and artillery, and in less than fifteen minutes we had gained the crest and driven the enemy from their pits and into the works beyond," reported Colonel Aaron Brown of the 3rd Iowa. A few days later, Freeman reported, "an advance was made at dusk on the right, the enemy's advance guard driven into their works." Night skirmishing was especially common on this front, particularly later in the siege when Freeman described how "the enemy attacked our picket guard at the advanced post on Hall's Ferry road. Being in the line of fire of the musketry, work was suspended for two hours, until the firing ceased, the men being obliged to lie down for safety." One Illinoisan in Lauman's division chalked up the problems to "a disgraceful neglect on our Div. Comd and his picket officers who was reported drunk."[54]

The skirmishing and even sharpshooting, especially on the Union side, were not done with small arms only, however. Artillery often joined the fray, and the big guns made their voices known very quickly. One Federal described a concentrated artillery bombardment in late May, explaining how "the concussion was terrific, shaking the earth so that loose earth and gravel was sifted down the sides of the ravines." When huge siege guns arrived later, often pulled by multiple yoke of oxen, one soldier noted that "they are monsters, and their voices are very loud." And their fortifications were often very intricate—specially built, in fact. Those artillery units not fortunate enough to have dedicated forts in and of themselves nevertheless had parapets to cover them; the men buried ammunition chests to the rear to keep them safe.[55]

The artillery fire was almost constant. Union field and siege pieces fired mostly during the day, the naval mortars at night, but both could be heard at any time. Confederate brigade commander Colonel Alexander W. Reynolds wrote that "these guns continued to play upon my works incessantly throughout the siege, except at night and a few hours during the heat of the day." Fellow brigade commander William Baldwin noted "a constant fire of artillery was kept up with considerable briskness early in the morning and late in the evening, slackening and sometimes altogether ceasing during the seven or eight middle hours of the day, and kept up during the night at regular but longer intervals." A Federal agreed, writing that "there is an almost incessant roar of artillery day and night with an occasional interval to let the guns cool."[56]

Sometimes the targets were specific items, but mostly there was just generic firing at enemy works and the city itself. That said, batteries on McClernand's front were "used daily in trying to destroy the mill, where, it is said, the enemy grind all their corn." At times, hot shot was used as incendiary devices. McClernand's artillery also directed some of its fire toward a bridge across the railroad cut, it being the Confederates' only quick means of communication from one side to the other.[57]

Although Confederate artillery replied on occasion—some guns becoming famous, such as "Whistling Dick" that got everyone's attention (one Federal dug up one of its shells: 20 inches long and weighing 80 pounds)—Federal artillery so swamped the enemy cannoneers that it had little effect on the siege. "Once in a while they would get a gun loaded when we would get a blast," an Illinoisan wrote. "We would then lie down flat upon the ground and let the shot go over our heads." Another wrote of "the enemy contenting himself with occasionally running a gun into position, firing two or three rounds, and withdrawing it again as soon as our fire was concentrated on it." Small-arms fire from the sharpshooters also had an effect: "Our sharpshooters prevent their firing cannons at all, except in the morning they sometimes discharge the pieces they have loaded in the night." Some Confederate guns also burst, which normally put them out of commission indefinitely. William Pitt Chambers of the 46th Mississippi described one such episode: "I was looking on when the lanyard was pulled. The concussion was terrific, and as the smoke lifted I expected to see dead men all around; but strange to say not a man was hurt."[58]

The net effect of the lopsided Union fire was stark, mainly on the fortifications themselves. There were problems in the Federal artillery to be sure, such as when a large brass cannon caused some problems in Logan's division on the Jackson Road on June 1. It was not properly secured on a tall hill, and "when it was fired it run backward down the hill over Co 'H' [124th Illinois] running right over I or G shebangs smashing them all to pieces but nobody was hurt. The cannon stopped by the Colonels tent where it upset and fell into a ditch. It was soon in place again." Most of the damage, however, was suffered by the Confederate side, as would be expected from the heavy volume of Union fire. One chaplain declared "the top of our breastworks are in some places leveled with the ditches and our men become more exposed." Only at one point did Pemberton report that "the enemy breached our works on the Jackson Road and ran their sap close up to our parapet." A couple of days later he reported an intense barrage "in which the works in front of Hébert were nearly demolished." Others told of more localized damage, brigade commander Francis Shoup at the Stockade Redan explaining that "the stockade between the redan and lunette is perfectly riddled, but is still about as good as ever; it is of poplar timber. The enemy seems to take delight in firing at it."[59]

Casualties also resulted from artillery fire specifically. At one point a single shell wounded three in the 31st Louisiana, and Indianan James Vanderbilt wrote to his mother that "we often get to see a reb fly above their works." The 8th Wisconsin dealt with a Confederate sharpshooter in a tree with massive force, alerting a nearby battery to fire at him. The shell exploded at exactly the right time, and the Confederate was "torn to piece and we could see parts of him flying in different directions."[60]

Without the ability to fire directly from their lines, Confederates had to depend on indirect fire and soon brought a ten-inch mortar to the lines behind Forney's division near the Great Redoubt. Mortars, usually deployed on boats on the river, at times were used on land as well because they could be fired from cover, their tall, parabolic arch clearly visible to all as the shell made its way up and over the lines. Such a sight made one officer admit "I never appreciated the words of the glorious National Anthem until now—where it says—'and the bombs bursting in air.'"[61] This particular Confederate mortar did especially good service, as one Federal admitted it "was fatally brought to bear on the battery and exploded one shell between the two guns, killing 2 and badly wounding 4 men, but not interfering with the further work of battery." The 31st Illinois even had to move its camp because of it. Playing as it was on the Jackson Road area, Logan put a guard in place to warn everyone when a shell was incoming: "The guard had to call, 'look out she is coming' and it was so large a person could dodge it."[62]

"What a terrible fuss this mortar produces amongst the enemy," wrote Chaplain William L. Foster of the 35th Mississippi. The Federals responded, incensed at this "mortar in a hole some where," and a much heavier fire emanated from the Union artillery within range. One Federal described the vicious Union response, from both land and water. Federals on land shot off rockets to indicate to the navy where to throw the mortar shells, while the nearby army batteries pummeled the same area. "It was curious [to] see shells coming from east and west, and all dropping into the same ravine where the enemy's mortar was planted," one Federal wrote.[63] One of the Mississippians enduring this massive fire declared that "so severe was the fire that our breastworks were leveled to the ground in places and this regiment [40th Mississippi] forced to retire for a while from the ditches. Stop that old mortar was the command!" He continued: "The impudent thing was commanded to close its mouth and to remain as meek as a lamb. . . . Only now and then, at long intervals, and very slyly would our old mortar dare to open her mouth—though concealed deep in the valley below."[64]

Similarly, as might be expected with so many troops packed into such a small area, freer minds began to work, and therefore new and novel ways to sharp-shoot and fight soon appeared out of either necessity or boredom or both. Some of it was off-the-cuff, a momentary whim, such as random shots being taken even with small arms at Vicksburg itself, which could not possibly hit the city: "Some times we fired toward Vicksburg at an angle of forty-five degrees with the horizon, knowing that the bullets carried potential destruction over into the city."[65] At other times the novelty was much more deliberate. One Illinoisan told how they would take plows from the local plantations and have blacksmiths flatten and bore them out to the size of a musket to protect them from return fire. The Confederates did the same thing, although one being used in the Missouri brigade was ordered removed because it drew too much fire. Some Confederates made a wide, v-shaped shooting cove to give good range, and one Illinoisan fixed small traverses to protect himself from side fire and "stuck a row of little canes that were growing near along the top in order to hide my cap when looking over." Word also went around that the Federals lashed a musket aimed directly at a Confederate porthole so when a dark form appeared all that was needed was to pull the trigger. This, a Confederate noted, was done "with unfailing accuracy."[66]

This ingenuity could be used with artillery as well. One lieutenant in Lauman's division undertook placing a gun as a special challenge. He found an old farm wagon and braced it and hauled a captured Confederate 32-pound rifle up from Warrenton to the lines. He had located a damaged barbette as well and hauled it up, although many of the pieces were missing. One artilleryman explained that "there were no wheels for it and no chassis, but he went to work and rigged up a chassis to slide on the traverse circle and made the carriage to slide on the chassis." The artillery captain admitted "I had some serious doubts about it working," but the gun performed well.[67]

Confederate ingenuity also emerged, although it was more limited because of the lesser rate of fire and fewer options for resources and maneuver. Many found ways to respond to the Union approaches, such as how "a row of palisades had been placed some 20 yards in front of our trenches at this point, and a ditch excavated behind these to shelter an advanced line of sharpshooters as an additional obstacle." Also, "procuring a dozen hunting rifles, these in the hands of experienced marksmen rendered their approach very slow and cautious."[68]

Despite the need to save ammunition, there were times to fire, such as when Confederate brigade commander John C. Vaughn gave the permission "for the purpose of discharging the guns that were exposed to the rain during the previous day." When the 3rd Louisiana received new Enfields, there was a sudden increase in sharpshooting near the Jackson Road, as all wanted to test their new weapons. They still kept their old muskets with buckshot to help repel an assault, however.[69]

Sometimes, truly remarkable episodes occurred. As one Wisconsin soldier was returning from skirmishing on the front lines, for example, a Confederate bullet fell at his feet in the trench. He picked it up and remarked that "the 'Rebs' would regret throwing their shot around in that way." He went back on skirmish duty that afternoon and loaded his musket with the same bullet. He dropped a Confederate and "had the satisfaction of knowing that he had at least wounded a 'Reb' with one of their own bullets."[70] Similarly, Joseph Stockton in Ransom's brigade saw a very interesting sight in the skirmishing. The 14th Wisconsin had a company of Native Americans, and he reported to his diary, "I was much interested today in watching a number of Indians that belong to the 14th Wisconsin, acting as sharp-shooters." He described how "those Indians had fixed their heads with leaves in such a way that you could not tell them—they moved across on their bellies a little distance then kept quiet." An Illinoisan described how they made good skirmishers, but "they don't like to fight in line, do best on their own hook."[71]

Some soldiers became famous because of the cover they constructed. "Buffalo Bill" on the Confederate side formed a hole and did much damage before being located and killed. Probably the most famous of all sharpshooters was 2nd Lieutenant Henry C. Foster of the 23rd Indiana, who wore a raccoon-tail hat that earned him the nickname "Coonskin." He was "an unerring shot" and first made a "burrow" in the ground near where the forward battery on Logan's Approach eventually came to be; there he would stay for days, with provisions, while taking shots at the Confederates. Presumably once the battery took over the area, he decided to go up instead of down and began to construct a tower of crossties taken from the now-defunct Southern Railroad of Mississippi. He had learned the craft of log-cabin building as a youngster and put that knowledge to work in constructing a tower of the ties so high that at the top he could see into the Confederate works on the Jackson Road. Obviously, that meant trouble for the Louisianans, now with no place to hide, and Coonskin worked for days firing between the slits in the tower. The Louisianans found that musket balls did no damage against the timbers, as they simply embedded themselves into the wood. The use of artillery, which could have knocked the structure down, was also by that time a suicide operation due to skirmishers such as Coonskin and others manning the rifle pits along Logan's Approach.[72]

While Coonskin Foster became famous for his tower, others had similar ideas. A different version was undertaken by a member of the 8th Illinois, J. D. Lyons, who built a "look out" of twelve poles lined with hogshead staves doubled up as a frame with earth thrown up against it as it rose higher and higher. "None of the boys would help him," one Illinoisan remembered, but he labored for two weeks, the same Illinoisan adding that "the boys in the mean time hooted at him for building such a thing." He nevertheless soon "had a lookout sure enough," with a seat in one corner. He spied two Confederates eating breakfast one day and fired at them but elicited at least a dozen shots in response, some of which penetrated his double staves. "He wasn't long in getting down to the bottom," a comrade remembered, and no one else would risk manning it in the daytime. At night it offered "a fine place to watch the mortar shells and the night firing of artillery."[73]

Coonskin's much more substantial tower stood the test of time and became a notorious tourist attraction during the siege. Several called it an "observatory" or "a tower made of hewn timber built high." Some declared it was as high as forty feet, and a trip to the top offered a panoramic view so that "a man dare not raise his head above the breastworks. If he did he was apt to be killed." Many came to climb up in it, one Federal describing his trip up the tower: "I saw Vicksburg the other day, by climbing up in the 'look-out.' This was a high, wooden tower. It was a splendid view to see the city spread out, and the river shining beyond; but I couldn't stay long to enjoy it, because the enemy made a special target of this tower, and shot in at the port-holes whenever they saw them darkened with an optic." Grant even went up into Coonskin's invention, only to elicit a cussing from a soldier who was supposed to be guarding against such tourists but did not recognize that it was the general himself. Eventually, the tower became so popular that Coonskin started charging twenty-five cents to go up.[74]

At times, perhaps because of boredom, some soldiers took chances while sharpshooting or skirmishing. One exchange in mid-June resulted in an officer losing his sword and overcoat, whereupon another went out into the constant fire and found it. The officer paid the man a dollar "for his trouble" but had "a perfect whipped dog countenance." Another Federal described a comrade who leaped up on the embankment under fire to grab a small bird that was hurt. He got it, but "as he was showing it to us, it slipped out of his hand and fluttered out in front again with Larry close after it." Some grabbed at him and others scolded that it was "a fool-hardy exposure he had made of himself and that he might have been shot." Larry replied that "he was not born to be shot—he was born to be hung!"[75]

Confederates could be just as foolish. One officer mounted a parapet and taunted the enemy, whereupon an artilleryman fired a shot at him and it exploded perfectly: "It struck the fellow midway of the body and bursted him like a glass ball. I have never seen pieces of flesh fly in so many directions as I saw there."[76]

Sometimes the liquids the soldiers drank caused reckless behavior. A lot of skirmishing was over springs of water in the ravines between the lines. Both sides needed water and went in the night to get it, often leading to confrontations. Whiskey also caused problems. One Illinoisan became so drunk that he bellowed that he was "going to walk right up on top of Fort Hill." A guard stood over him, but he got loose and "he went bolding up to Fort Hill and climbed the fort," looking over when he got to the top. One of the Louisianans, William Tunnard, told his side of the affair, writing that "one of the enemy climbed up to the parapet of the Third Louisiana works, and boldly looked over, no doubt with the very laudable intention of having a good view of the affairs within the forbidden ground." A Confederate nearby shot him immediately, and Tunnard added that "the attempt was considered an unusually bold and fool-hardy one"—but he apparently did not know that it was a whiskey-related incident. The man's Federal comrades buried him, one thinking that if he had "let the accursed whisky alone he would have been living." The small group concluded that "whisky was a greater enemy than the men who opposed us with their muskets."[77]

Sadly, deaths such as this were constant because so many projectiles flew around Vicksburg. One Mississippian lamented how "somebody wounded; somebody dying—all the time. . . . Day by day some friend or comrade died, and 'who next?' was on every man's lips and in every man's heart." Many came to retrieve bodies as a result, although not all could because of the proximity of the burials to enemy lines. Many sad letters thus poured out of the armies notifying those at home of the deaths of loved ones.[78]

Total losses each day are not known, but the most dangerous place, as would be expected, was in the trenches, and casualties there each day were steady. A glimpse into reports from Forney's division for late May illustrated the small but constant rate: on May 23, the returns showed eight killed and thirty-two wounded. On May 24, two killed, ten wounded. May 26 tallied one killed and seven wounded. May 27 saw two killed, eight wounded. May 28, two killed and ten wounded, five of those wounded resulting from "a shot passing through the parapet and exploding an ammunition chest."[79]

Many particularly sad cases emerged. One US Regular soldier working a gun had spent twenty years in the service and his time was up the next day, but he took a bullet that night while walking his post. "Such is the fate of war," one Illinoisan mourned. A litter-bearer in the 46th Mississippi was similarly hit as he moved behind the lines. "I distinctly heard the ball strike the ground after passing through his body," William Pitt Chambers wrote, "when it ricocheted and went whizzing onward as though it had met no obstruction." Chambers was detailed to help carry him to the rear, and the group stopped by a spring to rest. The boy asked that someone pray for him as he lay in agony. "One of the little group at the spring, a stranger to me, responded," noted Chambers. "A few of us knelt down, with bursting shells and whistling bullets above our heads, and the stranger earnestly plead for mercy for the dying man before us." He died a couple days later. Another noted a casualty in the 38th Mississippi, writing that "he was shot by a sharpshooter in the left eye whilst looking over the parapet last night about 9 o'clock. His death has cast a gloom over our little company, and it will be long before we can realize that Aleck is no more."[80]

Oddities also occurred. At one point a single bullet killed two men in an Indiana regiment—both being shot through the head. Their comrades buried them "in 1 box." One Louisianan described a novel affair when a Confederate responded to a Union sharpshooter, writing that "the sharpshooter & himself both fired at the same time. He fell with his gun empty as soon as he pulled the trigger." Horribly, amid a cannon shell explosion, one Mississippian told how "a bit of warm, quivering flesh fell on a soldier's hand."[81]

Accordingly, most days and nights for these men on the front lines were filled with constant firing in one way or another, and most of it was random, individual, and seemingly unimportant except to those who happened to be hit. None of it necessarily changed the situation, although there was some bluffing and efforts to distract and dupe in a deadly cat-and-mouse game. Confederate brigade commander John C. Vaughn reported that "the 24-pounder siege gun and 3-inch rifle also opened, I having given orders to that effect, for the purpose of attracting the enemy's fire, and drawing it from the 32-pounder, that it might work undisturbed."[82]

Yet there was benefit mainly to the Union side amid all the sharpshooting and skirmishing. All the while, under the cover of this massive amount of fire, Union approaches continually crept forward, Confederate nerves continually wore thinner, and an appalled nation continually watched as the horrors of Vicksburg moved into another month.

6

"GRANT IS PRESSING, AND MUST BE SUPPLIED"

June 3–6

By the time the calendar reached June, the siege of Vicksburg was heating up in more ways than one. The assaults in May had been notorious for the warm conditions, but a lot of that had been exacerbated by physical activity that made the heat even more recognizable and problematic. Still, in reality, May and early June are sometimes comparatively cool in central Mississippi, nights even that far along being still somewhat chilly and enjoyable. One Illinoisan reported as late as June 18 that "the nights is very plesent it is so cold that you can sleep very comfortable under a woolen blanket." But as June rolled around, so did the oppressive daytime heat that Mississippi summers are known for: high temperatures, intense humidity, and frequent rain showers in the afternoons that cool things off for a while. But such rains result in an even more balmy and humid aftereffect that was not worth the original cooling produced by the short showers. Fortunately, the nights were still cool, as attested to by another Illinoisan who wrote to his wife that "the weather is quite hot in the day time but the nights are cold enough to get under a blanket. It appears to be a characteristic of the South to have hot days and cold nights." Of course, as July and August rolled around each year, day and night alike became almost unbearably hot and humid. "Laid still pretty much all day," one Illinois cavalryman explained to his diary amid the heat, "but it was so warm that one could not do anything else." Still, some found good aspects to it. "The air is more refreshing and the water better [here] than any place I bin in Dixie Land," one Illinoisan admitted.[1]

Also heating up were the siege operations, both in front of Vicksburg and in the rear. "Still it holds out with a courage and perseverance worthy a better cause," one exasperated Federal wrote in his diary. Yet by the first week in June, the full Federal effort was churning along, including bringing in reinforcements, digging their way forward toward the Confederate lines, and covering the rear against whatever Johnston was doing. "The approaches are gradually nearing the enemy's fortifications," one Federal reported on June 3, adding that "five days more should plant our batteries on their parapets." He added "we shell the town a little every day, and keep the enemy constantly on the alert." At the same time, the full Confederate effort to defend or relieve was also in full swing, likewise including gathering reinforcements for a relief effort, digging their own counter-efforts to the Union engineering work, or simply keeping the population and army fed.[2]

Grant was all the while thinking of his best options, even considering a renewed assault. Sherman's approaches were already nearing the Confederate lines, as were McPherson's. Charles Dana reported that "General Grant is considering the subject of a sudden attack in great force on the south, where there are no siege lines and where enemy expect nothing." He added that "from the drift of his remarks, however, I conclude he will not adopt the measure." Through all the decision-making process, the Federals continued their work, one writing that they were "still pecking away at the City all the time." Others frequently used the phrases "cracking away," "hammering away," or "whacking away."[3]

Through it all, nerves continued to fray, soldiers continued to dig, and the armies continued to gather around Vicksburg in what was shaping up to be the major effort of the summer in the West and perhaps the war. And it was all done in increasing monotonous misery, one Federal describing "a man in a ditch earth thrown up in front of him watching intently an opportunity to shoot any one who may be so daring to show himself, men six miles in a line just in this condition." Another simply wrote in his diary, "And still the siege goes on." These soldiers and civilians alike were enduring circumstances that they probably thought a week ago could get no worse. But it had.[4]

"The enemy is making gradual approaches upon our works by digging trenches and throwing up breastworks and traverses," Confederate division commander John H. Forney wrote around the change in months. "In this they are strongly supported by columns of infantry, and I do not see that it is practicable for us to attempt to stop them." A Federal across the way agreed, writing in his diary "it would appear as though the fighting in this quarter would be done with shovels and picks," to which he added "that will suit me very well." Consequently, at the core of the Vicksburg fighting was the engineering war, as one side tried to dig their way to Vicksburg and the other tried to keep them from reaching what one Illinoisan described as "our Vicksburg pen."[5]

The most concerted effort on the Confederate side in the first days of the siege, even into June, was to basically refashion the works from a temporary tactical defense line to one that was habitable for weeks. "We found them uncomfortable and very dangerous to go in or out during the day," one Confederate explained of the fortifications, "and as we had to have water and food it was the first difficulty to solve." Lockett had originally laid out the line for defense, for which it served well, but the works quickly became inadequate as the Confederate soldiers began to realize they had to live here too. For one thing, the trenches needed to be deeper, thicker, and stouter. Cover in areas that quickly became exposed also took form, such as additional walls, traverses, and fortifications. Logistical access was also needed, such as covered ways to the rear so that troops could come and go and food, supplies, and ammunition could be brought safely to the front. The Confederates lines were not only a defensive barrier by the time June came; they were also home to thousands of Confederate soldiers who had to man all sections continually because of the ability of Federal commanders to pick and choose where and when to launch an assault.[6]

Yet overzealous Confederates with little engineering training sometimes went too far, producing some comical episodes. On the far Confederate left, the militia boys of the 5th Mississippi State Troops, known as the "Minute Men," held the line at perhaps the most defensible position at Vicksburg. They were told to dig trenches despite being on the least concerning section of the lines. Engineer James T. Hogane described how "either from zeal or inexperience, [they] kept on night after night, adding depth to the rifle pits it defended, until, in the gloom of night if you wanted an officer you had to telegraph, by voice, to the far deep. After a few nights' work, I instructed the General to employ the energy of his men in filling up the caverns, hinting that, in the far bowels of the earth he might find it as hot as on the surface." Similarly, on John Vaughn's front was a 32-pound cannon that he intended to fire at a Union battery that opened up, but "the embrasure was too high to admit the gun being depressed enough."[7]

Additional work of course took place over time, with a heavy emphasis on providing rearward defenses as the siege wore on and Federal approaches neared. Lockett especially wanted new works across the rear of salients, redans, and other fortifications, otherwise known as "retrenchments." Francis Shoup urged this contingency often, and Lockett soon saw the wisdom of such a move, especially at the Stockade Redan "to command [the] redan should it fall." Other additions to the barriers out front such as stockades, brush, and "wire entanglements" also went in where they were available and could be emplaced.[8]

A good example of the extent of engineering work, as well as the danger, in the Confederate lines can be found in the various engineering reports submitted in this first week of June. The officers under Lockett (Captain Powhatan Robinson on Stevenson's front, Captain David Wintter on Forney and Smith's fronts, and Lieutenant William Flynn on the river front) provided details of the work on the various brigade lines. Work obviously included repairing damaged earthworks and guns as well as moving cannons, strengthening and extending existing earthworks, and building new embrasures, traverses, magazines, and approaches to the works. Also created were new portions of abatis and *chevaux de frise* (anti-assault devices utilizing long spikes). Slaves performed much of the physical effort, although at times Pemberton could not supply all that were requested. He alerted Louis Hébert on one occasion that none were available to be impressed and that "you will use your men to work in the trenches."[9]

The work took a dangerous turn on June 2, when a cave-in occurred. It resulted from a mortar blast in one of the caves being dug to house ammunition at the arsenal on the Baldwin's Ferry Road. The engineer commanding the digging reported that the cave fell in, "breaking the leg & seriously wounding the head of one negro, severely wounding two others, & one more slightly." Lockett noted that to make the caves "safe and serviceable [they] will have to be well lined and supported by strong timber." Of course, a lack of lumber was a major problem inside Vicksburg. Lockett recommended placing the ammunition in smaller caves spread out around the arsenal for the time being.[10]

Pemberton himself described the engineering effort: "It required the active and constant attention of our engineers to repair at night the damage inflicted upon our works during the day. . . . Orders were issued to prepare thunder barrels and petards for the defense of weak points, and every precaution was taken to check the enemy in his operations and to delay them as far as possible." And it was obvious across the lines, Sherman writing to his wife that "the enemy like beavers are digging as hard as we."[11]

Yet Pemberton had many more troubles than the chief one of blocking the enemy advance with adequate fortifications. By the first week in June, Pemberton was overseeing a worsening situation in which his soldiers were growing weaker due to declining activity, hope, and morale because of being bottled up and the lack of action on Johnston's part. Civilians were also beginning to despair.

Food inside the city was already becoming a problem, although there were stores for future use. Grumbling emerged because it was saved for later days and not utilized to the fullest now. John Bowen complained directly to Pemberton of "discontent" in his division and warned of "disease in a day or two." Pemberton shot back that he had very little extra to offer, even going so far as to state that "there is not one single barrel of flour over the hospital supply, nor had there been for some days past." A perhaps tiring Pemberton then scolded Bowen, writing that he had ridden the lines, as had his inspector general, and they heard "very little, if any, complaint . . . by other commands on this subject." Then he lectured: "a city besieged, and an army cut off from all means of generous supplies must be borne in mind both by officers and men, and a due and proper consideration given thereto, up to the eleventh hour, even, and certainly so in the initiatory stages of the fact. It is due to a patriotic and hopeful spirit that every forbearance, nay, cheerfulness, should prevail under the circumstances." He ended by emphasizing : "Every energy is being employed to serve the condition of our good soldiers and to facilitate the division commanders in the judicious admixture, economy and healthfulness of food."[12]

Bowen's reaction is not known, but it can be guessed at such a condescending tone. Still, it produced some results. Pemberton was obviously watching the food situation carefully, and on June 1 he ordered that "all Negroes not absolutely necessary for labor in the trenches or elsewhere shall be sent beyond the lines." Pemberton also authorized changes in the rations, such as allowing Carter Stevenson, whom he had tapped to oversee the commissary issues, to "increase it [salt ration] to the extent you may deem necessary and proper" and ordering that "one ounce of lard be issued as a ration to General Bowen's division and other troops that may desire it; a corresponding diminution being made in the beef ration in lieu therefore." He also ordered that "the full ration of rice and sugar may be issued, and if you find the ration of sugar insufficient it can be increased. Peas can be issued at the regulation allowance alternately with rice."[13]

Also continually worrisome was the ammunition supply. Pemberton had limited how much his troops could fire with both artillery and small arms ever since the assaults two weeks ago, and he had not let up much since. The only thing specifically allowed was sharpshooting, with obvious approval for firing if another assault took place. Types of ammunition also mattered, several of his commanders thinking they had done well in exchanging their old smoothbore muskets for captured rifled muskets such as British-made Enfields. Pemberton had to remind Bowen that "the amount of Minie cartridges on hand is so small that the Minie musket in the hands of our troops is utterly valueless. The practice of exchanging our own arms for those captured from the enemy must, therefore, be rigidly prohibited." However, powder was plenteous, and Pemberton ordered his division commanders to have their ordnance officers create "a number, say four dozen, 'thunder-barrels,' petards, &c., for defense of weak points on the line." These were similar to hand grenades but a little larger and could be used against the enemy assaulting the lines.[14]

And that went back to the major problem of Vicksburg: blocking the ceaseless Union efforts to reach the city. Time and patience seemed to already be running thin inside besieged Vicksburg even this early in the crisis.

A completely different mind-set emerged on the other side as Grant's engineers continued the process of approaching Vicksburg's defenses. Unlike the Confederates defending Vicksburg, the Union engineering effort only really began once the siege started. There was some digging going on during the assaults phase, but it was mostly defensive in nature and not siege or offensive-oriented. Now it was on full display. Unfortunately, as Grant elaborated in his report, "there was a great scarcity of engineer officers in the beginning."[15]

The lack of official engineers hampered the effort somewhat, and all who had any training in that area helped out. Even Sherman, trained at West Point, got in on the teaching. One day he rode upon a detail from John Sanborn's brigade who was tasked with making fifty gabions and fifty fascines. He asked if they knew what they were doing—and even if they knew what those terms were. The leader responded truthfully: "We have been in the service less than a year, and have not been engaged in any sieges, and do not feel very well posted in regard to these matters." Sherman immediately dismounted and barked "give me an ax." He began to cut small trees for stakes and grapevines for ties and soon had a gabion and fascine together. He did it all himself, no orderly doing the muscle work, and the leader of the detail remembered "in five or ten minutes, had at least a hundred men as well informed upon these matters as if they had been in the regular army for five years."[16]

Dana elaborated on the lack of engineers, writing on June 5 that "the siege works progress steadily, though there is a deplorable lack of engineer officers." Especially odious was the fact that "of the half dozen of those in this army, one very valuable, sent from Rocky Springs about May 5 with dispatches to General Banks, has been retained by him just as he has retained Grierson's cavalry." And it affected more than just Vicksburg. Dana reported also on June 5 that "the fortifications at Haynes' Bluff advance with exceeding slowness for want of both engineers and laborers." Grant had to send his personal staff officer, Lieutenant Colonel James H. Wilson, up there to superintend the fortification effort along the Yazoo River.[17]

Chief Engineer Prime also elaborated on the process and the problems with so few engineers, describing the whole as "very deficient, if we judge either from the practice of nations wiser in the art of war than ourselves or from results." The main problem was that where "thirty officers of engineers would have found full employment," there were "with the army two engineer officers doing engineer duty." As a result, he reported, "superintendence at any particular point was impossible, without neglecting the more important general superintendence of the whole line." Grant tried to gather more engineers but found it very difficult, so the only option was to use West Point or professionally trained civilian engineers to make up the gap, and these were "detailed, either from a list of additional aides-de-camp or from the line," and assigned to various corps and division headquarters. The only other source was the various pioneer companies attached throughout the army, but they were for work rather than thinking. The overall result was that, in Prime's opinion, "the rate of progress, of an approach or even its position, often depended on the energy and engineering skill of the division or brigade commander who furnished the working party for it." Basically, the Army of the Tennessee had to adapt, but then that is what it had been doing under its very adaptable commander for months now in its effort to capture Vicksburg.[18]

There was some humor in extending to all West Point graduates the collateral duties of engineers. Grant even called on his chief quartermaster,

Lieutenant Colonel Judson D. Bingham, and chief commissary, Lieutenant
Colonel Robert MacFeely, for their knowledge. The heavily rotund MacFeely,
whom Grant described as "a large man; weighs two hundred and twenty
pounds, and is not tall," responded lightheartedly that "there was nothing in
engineering that he was good for unless he would do for a sap-roller." Grant
thought it through and concluded "as soldiers require rations while working
in the ditches as well as when marching and fighting, and as we would be sure
to lose him if he was used as a sap-roller, I let him off."[19]

Still, the lack of engineers—"at no time more than three on engineer duty,"
Prime recalled—became a local problem quickly. Engineer Cyrus Comstock
explained that "the approaches and parallels were in some places badly located and much unnecessary work done." Prime echoed him, writing that
"only a general supervision was possible, and this gave to the siege one of its
peculiar characteristics, namely, that many times, at different places, the work
that should be done, and the way it should be done, depended on officers,
or even on men, without either theoretical or practical knowledge of siege
operations, and who had to rely upon their native good sense and ingenuity."
As a result, one veteran remembered that "every man in the investing line
became an army engineer day and night." Prime gave the examples of men
constructing a battery for the first time or "a sap-roller made by those who had
never heard the name" and admitted that "it was done, and, after a few trials,
was well done. But, while stating the power of adaptation to circumstances
and fertility of resources which our men possess in so high a degree, it must
be recollected that these powers were shown at the expense of time, and while
a relieving force was gathering in our rear."[20]

Thus the Union engineering effort went forward with the men adapting in
starts and fits. Some who started closer and moved faster far outpaced others, they finding the right spots to start from. One Ohioan described how "in
front of nearly every division was a natural covered approach, through some
defile, to within three or four hundred yards of the enemy's line—in some
cases these distances were less than one hundred yards." Engineers guided as
they could, one Indianan remembering that "engineers were laying out lines
of ditches and trenches, and picks and spades are brought up, and digging
ditches, rifle pits, and tunneling was the order of the day; and while sharpshooters were keeping the rebels down and picking off their artillery-men,
protecting us while we dug, and made tunnels toward the rebels forts." And
the farther they dug the more dangerous it became, one Illinoisan describing

how "they have to go with their arms in one hand and their spade in the other." Additional matters also sometimes took attention away from the main work. Many Federals, as they dug their way across no-man's-land, were especially anxious to see the ground over which they had assaulted on May 22. They soon approached and passed their various previous positions on the way to the Confederate fortifications, this time by siege approaches rather than assault.[21]

Work nevertheless continued, mostly at night, one Illinoisan declaring that "each morning presented some new parallel and newly made forts." It also occurred during the day, the sappers mostly on their knees and digging in zigs and zags, more parallel than straight toward the enemy lines but continually and gradually moving toward the enemy; one Illinoisan described how "it was made very crooked so that the Rebels could not rake it from any direction." The frequent turns of course allowed those moving in the trenches to be covered except where the zig turned to a zag, which could be covered by a large pile of dirt or other manmade objects. Still at times, one Indianan noted, "in passing through the zigzag trenches we were compelled to crawl past the low places." Yet it worked and progress continually came. Dana reported that by the beginning of June "Sherman has his parallels completed to within 80 yards of the rebel fortifications. He is able to carry artillery and wagons with horses under cover to that point." McPherson's were about the same distance.[22]

On other occasions, advances were made more by trickery. Oscar Stewart of the 15th Iowa of McArthur's division described how "on the night of the 5th of June, three hundred of us were detailed for a hazardous piece of work." They moved silently from the main line to a forward knoll fronting a deep ravine and the Confederate works. There, they were to dig a parallel, gaining huge amounts of territory by the cover of night. Once there, "we fixed bayonets, stuck our rifles in the ground inverted, and after the most stringent injunctions to silence, went to work with pick and spade." The Confederates did not hear them, but the detail was nervous they might, for "if the enemy had known or suspected we were there they could have swept us into eternity before we could get back to shelter." By daylight, there was a trench good enough for skirmishers to fill, and on subsequent nights more of the fortification took form, even holding artillery.[23]

Yet not all commands began approaches, and by this first week in June only Sherman's and McPherson's corps had begun a total of eight different saps toward the Confederate lines. None had as yet been begun on McClernand's front, he being less versed in the art of engineering, which needed technical and educated officers to lead the efforts. McClernand evidently spent the first week or two of the siege completing his line of circumvallation, and only later would approaches start forward from his divisions. Still, not all in even Sherman's corps were zealous, Dana reporting on June 3 that "those prosecuted with the least energy and the least intellectual effort are, I regret to say, those of General F. Steele. His inertia is surprising. His camps are also in very bad order and very dirty." Ironically, Steele was a West Pointer, a classmate of Grant's, but the lethargy may have come from the fact that Steele was sick during much of the siege.[24]

Despite the tedious and slow process, seven of the eight approaches started to date continually moved forward (Manter's and Woods's being the exception), and others would soon join them. The movement forward with the approaches correspondingly led to additional siege operations, including what in engineering were termed as "parallels." The whole idea of siege warfare was to move closer to the enemy under cover, and periodically as the approaches moved forward and gained appropriate terrain features such as ridges, engineers began to emplace parallels, which were essentially new lines of circumvallation closer to the Confederate works. These branched off the approaches at appropriate points a few hundred yards closer, allowing infantry and artillery to be moved that much nearer to the enemy and therefore fire that much more effectively. Obviously, it was to move these troops and artillery that the approaches themselves had to be wide and deep enough to accommodate them. Eventually, one Illinoisan declared, there were fortifications running in "every conceivable direction."[25]

Of vast importance was moving artillery batteries closer to the enemy fortifications, both to protect the lines and pummel the Confederates. Eventually, the Federals established some eighty-nine batteries made up of two hundred and twenty guns. As these moved forward with the parallels, the same old ramparts, revetments, and platforms took shape, utilizing whatever was available on site. Prime reported that in some batteries "they were well and neatly reveted with gabions and fascines, and furnished with substantial plank platforms, while in others reveting of rough boards, rails, or cotton bales was used, and the platforms were made of boards and timber from the nearest barn or cotton-gin house." The parapets in front were six to eight feet thick of earth, which proved adequate against weak Confederate counterbattery fire, but the embrasures where the guns poked through were the danger spots. Engineers devised various inventions such as "plank shutters" to protect the cannoneers from small arms fire. Attending bombproofs and magazines also went in.[26]

Between the batteries and along the parallels themselves were positions for armed troops to sharp-shoot. Prime described how "loop-holes were either formed in the parapet, made by using sand-bags, or in a timber laid along the parapet." While dangerous if under artillery fire, these timbers, often called "headlogs," were good enough to protect sharpshooters from small-arms fire. Artillery fire was different, and at times they would be rolled off the top, but most had skids leading to the rear bank of the trenches so it could roll harmlessly backward if dislodged.[27]

A glimpse into the heavy Union engineering work during the siege can similarly be had through the daily reports emanating from McClernand's corps engineer, Lieutenant Peter C. Hains, from this first week in June. Every day, he reported in writing of what went on the night before, when most of the work was done because it was safer and cooler. Although no approaches were going forward on McClernand's front this early, Hains reported that at any one time each division would have hundreds of men working on anything from covered ways to rifle pits to batteries and magazines. The basic flow of work was in layers, wherein one night's work on Hovey's division front, for example, garnered a small, three-foot-deep trench that was only eighteen inches wide. Hains explained that this was all that could be done in a night, but nevertheless the trench was "affording cover for men in passing though not sufficiently wide for men to pass each other rapidly." Obviously, on ensuing nights this trench was widened and deepened until regulation size.[28]

As the trenches and covered ways became regulation size, the parapets in front of them gained strength as well, and more and more artillery went into the line. Hains reported on June 5 how brigade commander Stephen Burbridge placed two guns behind defenses to "sweep the branches in [the] main ravine in a very effective manner." Some work was not so well done, however, and in that same report he explained how one of A. J. Smith's batteries, put there on the general's orders, had to be torn out and "rebuilt in the proper way." There was therefore some tension between the engineers who knew what they were doing and the generals who thought they knew best, although it seems that most of the initial work in McClernand's corps came in A. J. Smith's and Carr's divisions, both West Pointers with engineering training.[29]

Nevertheless, the work went on, one Illinoisan noting in his diary of "having got fascines and gabions, went to work, and made a very nice job." Once the fortifications became solid and the approaches neared the enemy lines close enough—and this had not yet happened anywhere this early in June—a new era of the siege operations would begin, which was actually the goal for digging forward in the first place. Once the approaches reached the close proximity of the Confederate lines, allowing infantry and artillery to take stations up next to the enemy works, two new possibilities emerged. The first was an all-out assault by the troops now in parallels right up next to the enemy works. An assault from cover only fifteen feet out was much more likely to succeed than had Grant's May 19 and 22 assaults from several hundred yards out.[30]

Second, once the approaches and parallels reached that close, the ability to start mining operations to dig under the Confederate fortifications and blow them up from underneath was also a possibility. Then, of course, infantry assaults from the covered parallels and approaches could surge through the opening blown in the enemy's lines, taking advantage of the chaos at the same time. Yet those operations—either assault from close parallels or mining activities—were still far in the future. Now, in early June, the Federals still had a lot of digging to do just to get to the point where they could dig closer parallels or start mining activities. That was all in the future, and for now they merely continued day in and day out, a never-ending process of digging and scratching their way ever closer to the Confederate lines. Illustrating the importance, one Illinoisan even wrote to his sister that "he [Grant] and Gen Logan has been seen to take a shovel and go with the boys and work but I don't suppose you will believe it yet it is so."[31]

By the first week in June, the Union siege machine was up and running, although not entirely at the rate Grant wanted. The army was well dug in along its line, and the approaches that had been begun by this point were working their way forward across the difficult terrain. But there was a problem developing: perhaps because of the dearth of engineering officers, only Sherman and McPherson had any approaches started at this point. There were no major approaches moving forward as yet on McClernand's lines, which was not only an engineering problem in that McClernand was the only non–West Point graduate of the three corps commanders; it was also a political problem. Grant had had his fair share of troubles with McClernand thus far in the campaign, the blame for the high casualties on May 22 being the largest issue laid at the politician's feet. When the siege tactics lagged behind on McClernand's front, it only added to the problems existing between the commanding general and his senior corps commander, although Grant made little if any written complaint in that regard.[32]

Still, Grant pushed amid the issues, often ordering a barrage at a certain time to quickly shell the Confederates. For instance, on June 2, he ordered all three corps commanders that "you will commence firing at 6.30 o'clock this evening. Fire ten minutes, stop twenty, and fire again for twenty minutes more." Despite a lack of ammunition, Pemberton responded with his own barrage on the morning of June 3, which the Federals responded to with more heavy fire. The constant skirmishing likewise kept the wearying Confederates on the lookout.[33]

More administrative duties also took Grant's attention, such as sending a surgeon with a note addressed to the "Commdg Officer Confederate Forces," so that he could get his wounded left behind at Raymond, Champion Hill, and Jackson to hospital boats and to hospitals up North. Similarly, Grant responded to a woman from Fifth Avenue in New York City who sent him a cigar case, telling her he would "continue to carry and, appreciate it, long after I could have done 'smoked' any number of cigars the Express Company are capable of transmitting." He labeled his letter "Close to Vicksburg" and added, "I wish I could have dated my letter 'Vicksburg.' I cannot yet. My forces are very near and so far as all the 'Pemberton' forces are concerned nothing can keep me from possessing town and troops."[34]

Continual word of potential breakout attempts also kept the Union forces on edge, McClernand even ordering his and his staff's horses to remain saddled at night just in case. Admiral Porter informed Grant that "we get about 15 deserters a day, who all tell the same story—shortness of food and intention to hold out ten or twenty days." Others brought word of potential breakout attempts, although Pemberton never seriously considered such a move apparently until nearer the end of the siege. One such rumor circulated in early June that there would be an attempt that night. Dana described how "we had an alarm on McClernand's front, and it was supposed that the enemy were about to attempt a sally." McPherson took the news as realistic and went so far as to order his troops "to sleep on their arms and to be turned out under arms at 2 A.M., and so remain until after sunrise." The artillery was also to be fully manned and ready "to stand to their guns at the same hour."[35]

While the boredom of siege warfare began to become laborious, Grant himself had plenty on his mind. Quite a few issues continually cropped up, some of them emergencies that needed attending to, others the product of boredom. One dealt with the slaves being sent out of Vicksburg under passes from Pemberton, which Jacob Lauman on the southern end of the line turned back with orders "not to pass any one out unless they deliver themselves prisoners of war; in other words, General Pemberton's passes are not good, or those of any rebel general." One Federal also noted to his sister that the Confederates tried to drive out their mules, but Grant would not allow even that. In fact, he ordered that they "shoot them whenever we can near their works so as to make it as unpleasant as possible for them."[36]

Grant's best friend Sherman also caused some trouble, perhaps from boredom. Sherman sent Grant a long missive in early June griping about the Federal policy of creating new regiments of recruits and conscripts rather than placing new troops in existing regiments. Sherman had a liking for the old regiments that had fought at Shiloh and elsewhere and argued that "it would be an outrage to consolidate these old, tired, and veteran regiments, and bring in the new and comparatively worthless bodies." Sherman asked that Grant "use your personal influence with President Lincoln to accomplish a result on which it may be the ultimate peace and security of our country depends." For his part, Grant probably wondered what personal influence he had with Lincoln, whom he had never even met and who had until recently been sending messages of disfavor with Grant's lack of conquering Vicksburg. Grant sent the note anyway.[37]

A more worrisome bit of news came when Sherman informed Grant that Admiral Porter was sick. He had come on land to view the lines with the idea of setting up a naval battery to help the army, as well as to visit Grant's headquarters. "I took the party forward to the trenches," Sherman explained, "the sun glaring hot, and the admiral got tired and overheated." Obviously he did not make it to Grant's headquarters, but he did affirm his support in the wake of the loss of the *Cincinnati*, Sherman quoting him as being "willing to lose all the boats if he could do any good." Porter also wanted to send a big gun battery inland and put the charge under Captain Thomas O. Selfridge, Jr., recently the commander of the ill-fated USS *Cairo* then lying at the bottom of the Yazoo River. Selfridge brought two 8-inch howitzers and placed them on Steele's front near the Mississippi River, although Sherman admitted "I don't think 8-inch howitzers can do any particular good at that point, but they will clear off that hill, and make the enemy suppose it is to be one of our main points of attack." Other naval batteries followed in the coming weeks as Grant and Sherman wanted to humor Porter in his desires to help, but they were perhaps more concerned about the admiral's health. Fortunately, he quickly recovered.[38]

Porter's presence was needed after all, and while there would be no more major advances such as that which got the *Cincinnati* holed and sunk, Porter would continue to do all he could. The mortars made life inside Vicksburg miserable until the Federals experienced a shortage of shells, but the supply was soon renewed. The navy's efforts also included trying its best to deprive the Confederates of food inside Vicksburg, and not just by stopping any traffic across or on the river. Porter quickly found where the Confederates kept their cattle for slaughter and fired on the herds to deprive the enemy of that source of food. "Our mortars have killed a great many cattle of all kinds," Porter informed Grant. Even in the downtime when ammunition was low for the mortars, the gunboats filled in and "keep shelling in direction of the cattle pens. All the cattle drivers (Mexicans) have deserted us." He added later: "I have just found out where they have moved their cattle to for safety, and am going to shell them with the gunboats."[39]

The biggest concern Grant had about his Vicksburg front was a lack of men, especially with seven brigades mainly under Blair (one under Osterhaus) pulled back to cover the rear. That left only nineteen of the original brigades confronting Vicksburg, along with Lauman's three new ones. Grant needed more troops to cover his rear and make the Vicksburg lines secure, especially on the southern face, where Lauman still did not have the entire stretch secured with properly manned fortifications; only pickets covered some of the area. And that sector seemed, as would be assumed, to be the most active, as Lauman's division continued to skirmish heavily, one firefight resulting in spooked battery horses of the 5th Ohio Battery, the same unit that defended the Hornet's Nest at Shiloh. One limber team ran wild and "fell into a pile into a deep ravine cut by rain water, and the harnesses had to be cut up very badly in order to extricate them." Obviously, it would take many additional brigades to fully cover the left all the way to the Mississippi River and thereby allow for a complete line of circumvallation to adequately hem in the Confederate army. Dana explained that "it is a mistake to say that the place is entirely invested. I made the complete circuit of the lines yesterday. The left is open in direction of Warrenton, so that the enemy have no difficulty in sending messages in and out. Our force is not large enough to occupy the whole line and keep the necessary reserve and outposts at dangerous and important points." He nevertheless added, "Still, the enemy cannot either escape by that route or receive supplies."[40]

From an engineering standpoint this gap was a big deal, but from a larger contextual military perspective it was less of an issue. Although any Confederates who went in or out of Vicksburg did so here, Grant did have some troops in the area, mostly skirmishers and pickets while more and more larger units filtered in. But any Confederate movement in this area was small in scale, and there was no real concern that Pemberton would lead the entire Confederate army out in this direction. If there was going to be a breakout attempt, it would most likely come with fighting around the northern areas for a couple of reasons. The first was that the north was the direction where Johnston lurked, and if Pemberton was going to make an attempt to break out, it would need to be on the north side so Johnston could aid and cover. If Pemberton broke out to the south, Johnston would be hard-pressed to help him out. Second and more important, if Pemberton broke out to the south, he would be quickly hemmed in between the Mississippi River and the Big Black River, which angled toward each other south of Vicksburg. Pemberton would be maneuvering in a continually constricting triangle of space, needing to get his army quickly over the few ferries on the Big Black River. It was a recipe for disaster. Grant knew this and consequently left his line open to the left rather than anywhere else, although giving stern warnings of possible breakout attempts early in the siege. Artillery even took station in ravines to guard exit points, one Federal cannoneer describing how they were there solely to guard the route and did not fire on the enemy lines and were consequently well protected. "We have nothing to do during the day but make ourselves as comfortable as possible," he noted, "but we have to sleep with one eye open at night."[41]

Still, Grant had to have more men if he was to cover everything properly. He wrote to Halleck himself about the issue back on May 29, describing the threat to the rear and the reported forty-five thousand Confederates heading toward him: "If Banks does not come to my assistance, I must be re-enforced from elsewhere. I will avoid a surprise, and I do the best I can with all the means at hand."[42]

Grant's note, delayed a couple of days in route, got the attention of Washington leaders, even Abraham Lincoln. At the same time, Charles Dana was also sounding the alarm: "Pardon me for again urging that re-enforcements be at once sent here from Tennessee, Kentucky, or Missouri in numbers sufficient to put our success beyond all peradventure. . . . Better retreat to Nashville than retreat from the hills of Vicksburg." The president himself wired on June 2, asking, "are you in communication with General Banks? Is he coming toward you or going farther off? Is there or has there been anything to hinder his coming directly to you by water from Alexandria?" Halleck also wrote, explaining, "I have sent dispatch after dispatch to General Banks to join you. Why he does not I cannot understand. His separate operation upon Port Hudson is in direct violation of his instructions." Nevertheless, Halleck promised that "I will do all I can to assist you."[43]

Fortunately, some reinforcements were already arriving. Grant had been able to call forward all the troops Hurlbut had at Memphis because Hurlbut was under his command in the Department of the Tennessee. It took no outside prodding or orders from Washington to make that happen. Accordingly, Lauman's three-brigade division was already on site, first down on the Warrenton Road and then moving up to its permanent position that linked with McClernand's left. Grant also had others on the way as well, having ordered Hurlbut to send down the three-brigade division under Nathan Kimball and, later, yet another four-brigade division southward under William "Sooy" Smith. But because of transportation issues, these would be delayed somewhat. Nevertheless, by June 3 Hurlbut informed Halleck that he had sent twenty-eight regiments in the two first divisions, and the same day he received the orders to send Smith, who left Memphis on June 5 and 6. One Indianan in this division was excited to actually get to a real front in the war, stating "the Vicksburg fight is a No. 1 affair and if a man is killed in that he gets his name in the papers although it will probably be spelled wrong." What Hurlbut had left was paltry: "It is now not more than enough to strongly hold my line and make those offensive movements which are the best defense." Hurlbut could only order black regiments to be armed and that "cavalry patrols must be kept moving far in front, so as to cover our line by distant patrols." He reminded his nervous commanders of the stakes: "Grant is pressing, and must be supplied."[44]

Fortunately, Kimball's three brigades arrived by June 4, after a mostly monotonous trip downriver. "We have left our comfortable quarters . . . and are now bound apparently for the scene of active operations," one Michigan soldier wrote. "It was a very sudden move." The men gathered what they could

take and "smashed things generally" among what was left. The only excitement the 25th Wisconsin had on their boat steaming southward was finding
a sutler's cache labeled "glass," which led them to believe it was whiskey.
Some of the troops stole the boxes but found it to be painkiller. The sutler was
angry and kept vigilant watch over the rest of his goods for three days and
nights, but on the fourth he was so tired he fell asleep. One member of the
regiment noted, "It was reported that the boys took the boots off his feet."[45]

The arriving troops soon disembarked on the Yazoo River bank, Leander
Stillwell writing "it was quite a relief to get on solid ground, and where we
could stretch our legs and stroll around a little." Kimball's arrival was a relief to Grant as well—or so Grant thought. Blair had not performed so well,
and Grant desired Kimball to take charge of the rear effort. After all, he was
a veteran, having been in many of the eastern battles such as Antietam. But
Kimball was not fully himself and was not that great even when well. He
brought with him a lingering and painful leg wound from a couple of canister
and shrapnel wounds in the right thigh area at Fredericksburg, the December previous. He had not recovered well but was here now, even though the
wound was still not fully healed.[46]

Illustrating where his major concern lay, Grant sent Kimball's troops to
the rear to stabilize that area in place of the brigades Frank Blair had taken
up the slot and that had fallen back to Snyder's Bluff after "an extremely
fatiguing and severe march." Indeed, even though Blair was back by this
point, his soldiers were not happy with him, mainly because of the rushed trip
back southward on May 30–31. One described how "there is about as much
order and regularity in marching troops on this expedition as there would be
in stampeding a mass of new recruits through an enemys country." It was so
bad that one Federal noted in his diary that Blair was "not well liked by the
soldiers [who] were put through beyond all reason." Yet there was some success in terms of rendering the slot unusable for the Confederates, if charred
ruins of the dwellings and destroyed fields along the path were any indication. And a horde of slaves followed along as well, seeking freedom, which
also demonstrated the success of the expedition. One slave woman declared
loudly: "Bress de Lord! Bres Almighty God! Our friends is come! Our friends
is come!"[47]

At Snyder's and Haynes' Bluffs, Blair's Federals received some much-
needed rest, and Sanborn's brigade, he reported, was "furnished . . . [with]
shoes, socks, and other articles greatly needed." Fortunately, Kimball's arrival

freed up Blair's troops to return to the Vicksburg lines, all but Mower's brigade doing so, Mower's troops staying in the slot for the time being despite
one Federal not knowing why: "We have toiled long and I fear but little has
been accomplished." Yet rather than send Blair's brigades back to their parent
divisions immediately, Grant—again displaying the ranks of the concerns on
his list—now saw an opportunity to use this major force to once and for all
shut the southern opening. He therefore ordered Blair to take the other five
brigades to Lauman's left: "Major General Blair will be charged with making
the investment of the south side of the city so perfect as to prevent the possible ingress or egress of couriers of the enemy, and will also commence and
push his approaches on their works with all possible dispatch."[48]

Oddly enough, Blair never made it to his assigned position, Dana reporting
that he was "called back about noon, the brigades returned to their original
divisions." Dana further explained why "this was a result of some new demonstrations of the enemy, thought to be indicative of a purpose to sally, and
also of General Grant's unwillingness to scatter his troops." One of Blair's
soldiers testified to the harsh marching and countermarching, writing, "I hope
they will get us into a permanent Camp for this continual marching is wearing
me out."[49]

What to do with Blair illustrated the greater problem: the need for more
troops almost everywhere. Grant could strip Hurlbut to the bare minimum
without any outside effort or approval, but if any reinforcements came from
any other place (different departments) it would require explicit orders from
Washington or the cooperation of distant commanders. Halleck realized as
much and began a full press of other western commanders to supply reinforcements for Grant. Success depended on how far Halleck was willing to
go to order troops away from any given commander's force, which in turn depended largely on the willingness of those commanders to send troops away
and their view of how many could be spared. As would be expected, the more
stubborn commanders, such as Major General William S. Rosecrans, were
unwilling to any degree, while a couple proved more than affable.[50]

Keeping his promise to aid Grant, Halleck sent a flurry of messages on
June 2 to Rosecrans in Middle Tennessee, Major General Ambrose Burnside
in Cincinnati, Major General John Schofield in Missouri, and others. To each
he explained that "Johnston is collecting a large force in General Grant's
rear." To Rosecrans he wrote that Bragg, confronting him, had sent some
troops to Vicksburg and added, bitingly, that "if you can do nothing yourself,

a portion of your troops must be sent to Grant's relief." Not surprisingly, just as Banks had done while actually calling for Grant to send him more troops ("a little additional strength would carry us through the enemy's works without delay"), Rosecrans refused to send any despite assuring Halleck that "my anxiety about General Grant equals your own." He begged off that he was starting an operation of his own, soon to be the Tullahoma Campaign. Obviously thinking it was more of Rosecrans's dallying—he had not done anything in the five months since Stones River—Halleck let it go without opening up a new argument.[51]

More willingness to cooperate came from Burnside and Schofield. Burnside responded to Halleck's query of "how many can you spare?" by stating that eight or ten thousand men could be sent if he did not cooperate with the advance Rosecrans was planning. Again thinking it was more covering for doing nothing from Rosecrans, Halleck ordered Burnside to send the men: "You will immediately dispatch 8,000 men to General Grant at Vicksburg." Wanting to go along, arguing that "I may be able to help Grant," Burnside asked about commanding the troops himself. Halleck cut that notion short, pointedly stating, "it would be obviously improper for you to leave your department to accompany a temporary detachment of less than one quarter of your effective force." Burnside also outranked Grant, which probably figured into Halleck's thinking. Nevertheless, Burnside started two full divisions of the IX Corps under the command of Major General John G. Parke. The only major issue was gaining transportation to send them, but that had not always been an issue. Because of the corps' operation both in the east as well as on the Carolina coast, and now heading to Vicksburg, one Michigan soldier labeled these troops the "Flying Corps" because of all its travels.[52]

John Schofield in Missouri also showed a willingness to help. Halleck ordered "if you can possibly spare some troops, send them immediately to General Grant." Schofield responded enthusiastically, writing on June 3, "I have concluded to send eight regiments and three batteries." He cautioned that "this leaves me very weak, but I will do it in view of the vast importance of Grant's success." Halleck was pleased, telling Schofield because of the need for haste to "send those nearest, and replace them from the interior. It is all-important that Grant have early assistance." The result was a division of two brigades under Major General Francis J. Herron, who received his orders to "report for duty to Maj. Genl. U. S. Grant." One of his brigade commanders, Brigadier General William Orme, celebrated the news and "the opportunity to take part in the grand struggle for opening the Mississippi & ending the rebellion."[53]

The net result was that by the first week in June a vast array of at least six new divisions—some seventeen brigades of varying sizes—were either arrived or were on the way to reinforce the original twenty-six brigades with which Grant had approached Vicksburg. Halleck gave Hurlbut in Memphis the option to retain a few of these passing down the river if he so needed them, but the vast majority went right on down the river. It was a massive reinforcement befitting the massive and crucial undertaking Grant was performing at Vicksburg.[54]

By the first week in June, Ulysses S. Grant had had enough of worrying about his rear. He had first sent small bodies of troops and then increasingly larger ones eastward as word of Johnston's growing strength continually came in. By the time the siege reached June and looked like it would not be over soon, certainly not in the week Grant had originally given it, he began to put even more attention on his rear in two ways. One was additional plans to cripple any Confederate movement to relieve Vicksburg, and the other was to go himself and see to the situation. "Joe Johnston is still threatening us on the other side of the Big Black," Grant informed Hurlbut on June 3; "what his force is now is hard to tell, but all the loose characters in the country seem to be joining his standard, besides troops coming over the railroad daily. I have a strong position front and rear, and expect to worry him out, if he should come."[55]

Johnston was indeed gaining strength. John C. Breckinridge's division of about 5,600 men including artillery arrived in the Jackson area around June 1 after a harrowing train trip through Chattanooga, Atlanta, Montgomery (where the troops were issued whiskey), Demopolis, Alabama, and Meridian, Mississippi. The division had left Middle Tennessee on May 24 under "confidential" orders, taking with them three days' rations, which some of the Kentuckians acknowledged "made us all fear that we were to go back to Mississippi." Their train trip was harrowing, the soldiers riding "in Cattle cars & flat cars & freight cars." Johnny Green of the Orphan Brigade wrote that "railroad travel was at this time tedious & hazardous," and at one point while going around a curve in a rain-soaked area "the rails spread & our whole train rolled over & over down a thirty foot embankment." At another point,

according to John Jackman of the 9th Kentucky, "the train ran away with the
engineer while coming down the mountain," and with such a steep grade it
took only four and a half minutes to run seven miles. Later on the trip, the
gun-shy troops were stopped on their train in the dead of night only to hear
another barreling down on them. All jumped overboard into a miry swamp
"with mud & water . . . up to our middle." Fortunately, the tracks at this point
were doubled, although the Kentuckians did not know it, and the other train
passed safely. Despite these minor mishaps, the men made it as near to Jackson as they could, the rails having been torn up by Sherman in mid-May.
Johnston gave Breckinridge command of the Jackson sector, Breckinridge
corresponding with Governor John J. Pettus for slaves to work on the earthworks plus militia to allow for the most men in the regular ranks. They took
over the city itself—at least what was left of it after Grant's treatment in
May—Breckinridge careful to post heavy guards "lest there be among us
enemies in disguise." With Breckinridge's arrival in Jackson, Johnston called
William Loring northward from Jackson in response to all of Grant's activity
up the slot.[56]

Breckinridge's division camped wherever it could, one Kentuckian notifying home that "I am writing in the Senate Chamber of the capitol—do you not
expect a burst of eloquence on that account." He described the "elaborately
furnished chamber with its marble columns its beautiful ceiling in stucco and
its massive candelabra." He also described a "cabinet of curiosities," mostly
geological in nature but including a French musket and bayonet from the
early 1700s. The 19th Louisiana of Brigadier General Daniel W. Adams's
brigade—not quite home but overjoyed to be that much closer—became provost guard for the city.[57]

More troops also arrived, including a division of cavalry under Brigadier
General William H. "Red" Jackson from Bragg as well, another brigade from
South Carolina under Brigadier General Nathan G. Evans, and even some
from recruiting efforts by Mississippi militia officers such as Major General
Samuel Gholson, the men being enlisted for six months. Yet there were many
problems, some big and some small. Breckinridge, a native Kentuckian who
knew a thing or two about horses, worried about his animals shipped from
Tennessee, saying that "unless his own horses are ordered down here, he will
get none worth sending." Desertion was a bigger problem than the horses,
with many slaves leaving ("encouraged to run off by their masters") and even
soldiers, one a lieutenant who was described as having "had charges against

him for disobedience"—"he is a Yankee; gone to his brethren." Perhaps worst of all, there were still pitifully too few troops in Johnston's mind to hold Jackson and Yazoo City, much less attack Grant; one of Johnston's division commanders noted that it would take so many men to defend Yazoo City that "the only thing I see under the circumstances is to have a small garrison, and trust to the enemy's not attacking." Still, plans continued about how best to raise the siege and relieve Pemberton, one of Johnston's division commanders at Yazoo City, W. H. T. Walker, despite sickness advising that they could "pierce the enemy's center and fall upon his left, whilst Pemberton marched out on his right." That Walker's troops at Yazoo City could hear the continuous bombardment at Vicksburg when the wind was right made the need for action all the more real. Another Confederate advised his wife from Jackson that "[we] are looking for a big fight between here and Vicksburg."[58]

Perhaps unknown to all involved, the crisis of the Vicksburg siege had already arrived by this point in early June. By this time Johnston had all the reinforcements he was going to receive, and his window of opportunity was about to close. In late May his force had stood at 22,500, but by June 3 it was up to 31,000 and 78 cannons. Combined with Pemberton's 29,000 in Vicksburg (not all effective for either Johnston or Pemberton), that put Confederate numbers at more than 60,000 while Grant's still hovered around 56,000 in the first week of June. Yet massive Federal reinforcements were on the way, which would soon act in, as historian Edwin C. Bearss noted, "redressing the manpower balance in favor of the Union." Richmond realized as much, Secretary of War James A. Seddon writing Johnston on June 5 that no more troops could be spared and that "you must rely on what you have." The situation could not be plainer to Johnston.[59]

Yet the main problem was Johnston himself, despite word arriving that the Federals had been blunted in their assaults, one Tennessean even writing that "the news reached us today that the yanks made another sever attack on Vixeburg on last Friday and they got a severe whipping as usual." Nevertheless, Johnston had pretty much made up his mind that nothing could be done, especially in terms of saving Vicksburg. He would continue to explain saving the garrison was perhaps possible, but not the city: "My only plan is to relieve Vicksburg," he informed Secretary of War Seddon. But even when his numbers reached the largest possible level they would, and Grant's rearward forces were still comparatively smaller prior to the great infusion of troops Halleck was even then working on, Johnston did nothing. His window of opportunity was slim, and it would close within a week or so, Jefferson Davis himself perceptively admonishing that "we cannot hope for numerical equality, and time will probably increase the disparity." If Johnston was going to help Pemberton, then he had to move immediately. And he knew it; scouts farther north frequently reported the many transports seen moving down the river from Memphis. Perhaps to help bolster his case with the president, with whom Johnston was not that popular, Mississippi governor John J. Pettus also wrote begging for more reinforcements. Davis simply replied that "to furnish the re-enforcements sent to Mississippi we have drawn from other points more heavily than was considered altogether safe."[60]

Instead of acting against Grant, Johnston chose to continue to bicker with Richmond, particularly Davis. "The Secretary of War is greatly mistaken in his numbers," Johnston wrote on June 1, requesting the secretary himself the next day to "tell me if it is your intention to make up the number you gave the President as my force, or if I may expect more troops. With the present force we cannot succeed without great blunders by the enemy." Then he came up with another excuse. He had requested major generals and Davis sent him Samuel G. French from the Department of Southern Virginia. Johnston countered that "it has been suggested to me that the troops in this department are very hostile to officers of Northern birth, and on that account Major General French's [born in New Jersey] arrival will weaken instead of strengthening us. I beg you to consider that all the general officers of Northern birth are on duty in this department." In a lecturing tone, he concluded, "There is now a want of major generals. It is important to avoid any cause of further discontent." An incredulous Davis had the War Department look up where Northern-born generals were posted, retorting that, "surprised by your remark as to the general officers of Northern birth, I turned to the register, and find that a large majority of the number are elsewhere than in the Department of Mississippi and Eastern Louisiana." Regarding French specifically, Davis replied that "he is a citizen of Mississippi; was a wealthy planter until the Yankees robbed him, and, before the Confederate States had an army, was the chief of ordnance and artillery in the force Mississippi raised to maintain her right of secession."[61]

French arrived in Mississippi on June 10 but promptly asked for and received a leave of absence to go to his Deer Creek plantation up in the Delta to see his family. French had not been home since the war began, and he later tellingly noted that "the service was not pressing" at the time, which sheds ample light on Johnston's lethargy. French went home and saw his mother, sister, and seven-year-old daughter before returning and taking command of his division on June 24.[62]

Still, amazingly, Grant was the one worrying the most. Phantom Confederates and some real ones (or at least reports of them), including Loring's movement northward toward Yazoo City to camps on Cypress Creek near Benton, seemed to be appearing everywhere along his rear defenses. For instance, down along the southern end of the Vicksburg siege lines on McClernand's corps front, reports of Confederates crossing at Baldwin's Ferry arrived in early June. Grant ordered McClernand to investigate, and McClernand sent Colonel John J. Mudd with cavalry, but he found that "no enemies are in the neighborhood." It was not altogether unexpected, as it would be foolish for the Confederates to operate that far south anyway. The real areas of concern were still the main crossing point of the Big Black River and the slot between it and the Yazoo River farther north.[63]

Grant could get few solid answers there, however. By the first days of June, Frank Blair was back within the closer confines of the Federal operational area, he stopping at Drumgould's Bluff just south of Snyder's and Haynes' Bluffs to inform Grant of what he had done. There was little more that the large contingent of infantry could do, and so most were sent back to the army, the brigades first going as a group to the very southern extent of the line in an effort to shut off Vicksburg once and for all. Left at Haynes' Bluff to protect the supply points to the west along the Yazoo River was Mower's brigade of Tuttle's division of Sherman's corps.[64]

Before leaving, however, Blair gave Grant another option to take the fight to Johnston. Grant had sent Blair an additional regiment of horse soldiers, the 5th Illinois Cavalry, which was strong and well-armed. Once added to Colonel Johnson's troops already patrolling the slot area, it made a strong force of twelve hundred troopers, a number larger than most of Grierson's raiders on their famous trek. Johnson came up with the idea of moving up the slot with infantry support, Mower's brigade going as far as Mechanicsburg, and then making a dash to the Mississippi Central Railroad bridge over the Big Black River just north of Canton. If Amory Johnson could destroy that bridge, it would severely hamper Johnston's efforts at relieving Vicksburg. For one thing, it would put the Confederates on the defensive rather than the offensive, as if Johnston needed any nudging, but for another it would also break the rail connection between Jackson and Canton, where much of Johnston's force was, with north Mississippi, where more of the force was as well as many of the supplies that would be needed to support Johnston. "I think this plan is judicious and feasible," Blair wrote to Grant.[65]

Grant jumped on the idea, agreeing to anything that would protect the rear. He gave Blair permission to order the move "in exact accordance with the plan within proposed." Grant also coordinated with the navy for its support in supplying the forward units as well as protecting them in case of trouble. He notified Admiral Porter that Blair "has clearly ascertained the fact that Joe Johnston is collecting an army at and around Canton, Miss.," and he was sending infantry to Mechanicsburg, which Grant described as the "key point to the whole neck of land." Grant asked that Porter send a gunboat and supply vessels to Satartia on the Yazoo, just three miles west of Mechanicsburg, to supply and cover the infantry while the cavalry made its run to the railroad.[66]

Although there was some confusion about the naval vessels getting the correct orders from Porter, the venture went forward on June 3, Mower moving by boat to Satartia and thence overland toward Mechanicsburg. "The stream is narrow but very deep," one of Mower's Federals wrote, "so that steamers can not run rapidly through it." Fortunately, gone were the barricades the Confederates had erected earlier made of rafts and chains: "Their timber rafts are lieing on the banks of the river as a memento to their folly," one Federal wrote home. The navy met only small amounts of Confederates at Satartia (just "a few scattering rebel Cavalry"), and upon landing Mower located two artillery pieces on the bluffs that fired of all things cut-up railroad iron. One 8th Wisconsin soldier in Mower's "Eagle Brigade" (named for the regimental mascot "Old Abe," a bald eagle) reported that these bits of fodder "when crashing along through the timber made a fearful noise." The guns were quickly captured and the march inland began to Mechanicsburg, not much bigger than Satartia, having only one current resident—"a German Jew . . . too much frightened to know anything." Mower was to watch all ferries on both rivers, as well as the front, for any collection of Confederates. Grant also notified Osterhaus at the Big Black River Bridge of the actions, asking him to also keep cavalry well out front. He did, and there was some lively skirmishing with the 8th Kentucky (Mounted), some of it with cavalry patrols and even some with his advance pickets east of the railroad bridge. Yet nothing of major import was afoot on Osterhaus's front, despite the report of a captured slave who informed Osterhaus that he had heard that Johnston would "re-enforce Pemberton and give us a severe 'whopping.'"[67]

Grant's concern over the rear eased further as Kimball's provisional division from Hurlbut's corps arrived right in the middle of the operation, Johnston's window of opportunity decidedly beginning to close shut. Grant ordered Kimball to move on up the Yazoo River to Satartia and then to Mechanicsburg as well, where he told him Mower would be, but as Kimball was senior he was to take command when they joined. Kimball had with him three brigades of troops from the XVI Corps, under Colonels Adolph Engelmann, Jonathan Richmond, and Milton Montgomery. Many were Shiloh veterans, so this was nothing new to them. A relieved Grant reported to Washington that "I am now placing all my spare force on the narrowest part of land between the two rivers," and he divulged plans to "make a waste of all the country I can between the two rivers."[68]

Kimball's troops went into action, Grant ordering one brigade (Montgomery's) to Haynes' Bluff to garrison that place while Mower was away. Richmond's brigade, which had arrived on June 4, as well as Engelmann's brigade moved on up the Yazoo to help with the plan, Engelmann writing to his sister that the transport simply stopped at Haynes' Bluff and unloaded "in great haste" before continuing on up the river: "Just as the last piece of baggage was to be carried ashore we received orders to proceed." On the way, the 61st Illinois learned of a feature known as "Alligator Bend," where they were promised to see some of the creatures. They did, and many took potshots at them before Kimball "sent word mighty quick from the headquarters boat to 'Stop that firing!'—and we stopped." It was not before a myth was shattered: Leander Stillwell noted how he had once read that the alligator's hide was so tough it could stop a bullet. These were not. "The boys would aim at a point just behind the fore-shoulder, the ball would strike the mark with a loud 'whack,' a jet of blood would spurt high in the air, the alligator would give a convulsive flounce,—and disappear."[69]

Kimball arrived at Satartia by 11:00 A.M. on June 4 with two of the brigades, and he immediately set out for Mechanicsburg. He found Mower still near Satartia and pushed on with both commands. Just before reaching the small village, however, he met Confederates of the 20th Mississippi for another skirmish. These veterans of Fort Donelson had been recently mounted in response to Benjamin Grierson's famous raid in April, and one officer noted that they had "done more fighting in six weeks than most of the cavalry in this state have done since the war." Now, the Mississippians skirmished with the enemy all the way back to Mechanicsburg, where, Kimball reported,

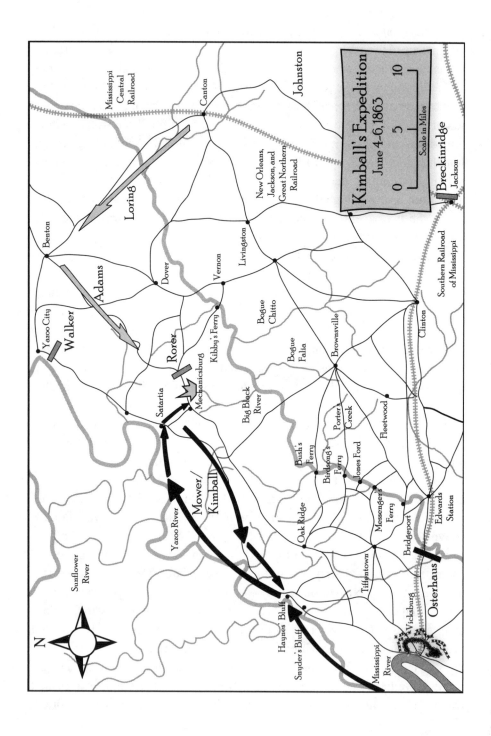

Kimball's Expedition
June 4-6, 1863

0   5   10
Scale in Miles

N

Mississippi Central Railroad

Canton

Johnston

New Orleans, Jackson, and Great Northern Railroad

Loring

Benton

Adams

Dover

Vernon

Livingston

Breckinridge

Jackson

Southern Railroad of Mississippi

Walker

Yazoo City

Rorer

Satartia

Mechanicsburg

Kibby's Ferry

Bogue Chitto

Bogue Falia

Brownsville

Clinton

Big Black River

Porter's Creek

Fleetwood

Mower/ Kimball

Yazoo River

Bush's Ferry

Birdsong's Ferry

Jones Ford

Oak Ridge

Messenger's Ferry

Edwards Station

Sunflower River

Tiffentown

Bridgeport

Osterhaus

Vicksburg

Haynes' Bluff

Snyder's Bluff

Mississippi River

they met him "drawn up in line of battle." Kimball deployed a brigade and drove them away, sending Johnson's cavalry after them, the 5th Illinois Cavalry leading. He then moved into and secured Mechanicsburg, which Engelmann reported was "almost entirely burned."[70]

The Confederates told a different story. There were four companies of the mounted 20th Mississippi under Major William Rorer, who, one officer reported, "commenced skirmishing with them at Bear Creek bridge about daylight, ambushed them seven times, and checked their progress so that they did not reach Mechanicsburg until about 2:00 P.M." Brigadier General John Adams soon arrived with more troops, including an artillery battery that played on the head of the enemy, and skirmishing continued into the afternoon, mainly by the 8th Wisconsin.[71]

With Kimball's arrival, he took firm command, and Grant communicated his desires through him. Grant told Kimball exactly what he had been telling the others: to watch the fords, particularly on the Big Black River, and obstruct the roads, at the same time taking all cattle and provisions in the area, including wagons, horses, and mules from the local civilians. "It is important," Grant wrote, "that the country be left so that it cannot subsist an army passing over it." To support the division, a gunboat and supply boat were to be kept at Satartia at all times. At the same time, Porter sent a flotilla up the Yazoo to near Greenwood before it was stopped by obstructions in the river. Unfortunately for the Federals, the Confederates either destroyed all their own boats or took them to safety farther up the river, causing Porter to lament to Grant: "I was in hopes of presenting you with some fine transports."[72]

By June 4, Kimball was firmly in control at Mechanicsburg, but matters deteriorated quickly. It certainly did so for one member of the 11th Missouri of Mower's brigade who was forced to straddle a rail and had a sign tied around his head and mouth that labeled him a coward. He had remained at Satartia as the regiment moved out to Mechanicsburg, but the problem was chronic. One observant Illinoisan noted that "he has been 2 years in the regiment and never fired a musket." Grant was also having problems, much larger in scope if not in pain, mainly second thoughts about implementing Blair's earlier plan of sending the cavalry ahead. "I have just received information that a portion of Joe Johnston's force has gone into Yazoo City," he informed Kimball, worrying that if a Union cavalry force went to the railroad it could easily be cut off in the rear and destroyed. "I do not want to run any great risk of having any portion of the army cut off or defeated. If, therefore, your

judgment is against reaching Big Black River Bridge with security, and getting back again, you need not attempt it." Showing his growing concern,
Grant wrote again the next day, ordering: "I will renew my instructions not to
run any risk of having your forces cut off from the main body. If Mechanicsburg is not safely tenable fall back to Oak Ridge Post Office or Hain's Bluff
as necessity may dictate."[73]

Just such a need arose as a growingly startled and jumpy Kimball sweated
through the next few hours. He was fresh on the scene and unsupported. And
reports he was receiving were not good. He notified Grant that "the whole
[Confederate] force on this side of the Black River is 20,000 Infantry & Cavalry and twenty-five guns." One of his troops noted that "we were assured we
were surrounded by 15,000 Rebs" and that "the Potomac Genl. K" was very
much frightened. Kimball later sent another startling message raising the total
in Johnston's force to more than forty thousand, adding he thought that it was
high time he return to Oak Ridge or even Haynes' Bluff. A staff officer with
Kimball explained that "the General learned that an effort was being made
by a large force of rebels to cut us off from communication with Vicksburg."
One of his soldiers was spooked enough as well, Michigander Samuel Eells
telling of larger numbers of Confederates and that "it was evident we could
not assume the offensive but might be glad to get off with whole skins."
Charles Dana ascribed another issue to the retreat as well, writing that "the
reason for Kimball's movement appears to be an extraordinary fall in the
Yazoo, which caused him to fear that his supplies might become insecure at
Satartia." There was a rock ledge in the river at Satartia, and if the water level
fell too low it would trap Porter's vessels above it.[74]

The news certainly shocked Grant, who agreed with the withdrawal, of
course having approved it earlier if needed, but he told Kimball to "look on
Hain's Bluff as the point where you are to make a stand against all odds."
After plundering and burning Mechanicsburg thoroughly (one Union soldier
writing that the houses "made very pretty bonfires in the night"), Kimball
withdrew overland in a forced march on June 6 while the boats removed all
stores and prisoners. The same rough treatment developed for houses and
farms on the trip southward, made worse by the bad mood among the troops.
Many described the march through a huge cornfield that stretched for miles
along the bank of the river as one of the worst in all their service, brigade
commander Engelmann telling his wife that he "marched to Haines Bluff in

a fierce heat and in frightful dust, arriving here that evening, nearly dead." In fact, Kimball's troops did not think much of any of this new duty, having been domiciled in garrison tasks for more than a year now. One wrote in his diary, "I am once more living the life of a soldier and gradually forgetting the civilization I have just left." Kimball's staff surgeon warned that too many would die of sunstroke if the march continued, but Kimball callously replied "it would be better to lose five hundred from the heat, than fifteen hundred from a fruitless fight." One Illinoisan resorted to putting hickory leaves in his cap and wetting them occasionally to keep his head cool. Another Illinoisan was not so spooked and asked why the haste, "as if for life or death when nothing is ahead of us or in our rear to occasion so unnecessary haste." To the brigade at Haynes' Bluff, Kimball ordered a quick defensive perimeter established, using troops and contrabands to dig fortifications.[75]

Grant was obviously worried over the prospects of doing something, but he was just as worried about the prospects of doing nothing. "I am exceedingly anxious to learn the probable force of the enemy on the West side of the Black River," he wrote to Kimball. "Keep me constantly informed of all you may be able to learn," he lectured the general, who at one point dropped out of sight so much that staff officer Wilson spent a good amount of time out "hunting for Kimball." By this time, most of the troops were back at Haynes' Bluff and comfortable with "good spring water, [but] very little shade, great heat, [although] my tent is on a hill where I get any breeze and it is comparatively cool." But being so far away at Vicksburg itself was excruciating to Grant when it seemed that by the first week in June things had settled down around Vicksburg and the main area of concern was the slot. As a result, Grant decided to go there himself, by boat to Satartia, to take a look with his own eyes. "I am going up to Mechanicsburg," he informed his corps commanders on June 6, unknowingly the same day Kimball began his retreat. "Cannot be back before to-morrow night. Make all advance possible in approaches during my absence. Communications signaled to Haynes' Bluff will reach me." It was a decision that would come back to haunt Grant.[76]

The basic story was that Grant boarded a navy vessel and went up the Yazoo River to Satartia on the evening of June 6, his thirteen-year-old son Fred along for the ride. Kimball had withdrawn back to the Oak Ridge area, so when the boat arrived there were few Federals around. By that time, Grant was in his cabin sleeping, some said from "illness" and others from one drink too many. The next morning, Grant came out perfectly normal, thinking the boat had tied up at Satartia. In reality, it had returned to Haynes' Bluff because of concern for Grant's safety since Kimball had left the area.[77]

Over the decades after the Civil War, the story took on a life of its own, with several writing larger-than-life accounts (significantly now that Grant was dead) about what had happened. Charles Dana made himself out to be central to the affair, while newspaper correspondent Sylvanus Cadwallader concocted a wild story of a drunken Grant riding through Federal camps hooping and hollering. Historians have thoroughly dissected the accounts and the affair, few of which added up to contemporary sources, and have concluded that, although Grant perhaps had something to drink on the trip, he slept it off on the boat and was no worse for the wear.[78]

Grant had been sick for a few days with dysentery, and one of Sherman's surgeons recommended wine to ease his hurting. The realization that Grant was taking a little medicinal ration caused his staff officer and sometimes-guardian John Rawlins to write the famous letter dated June 6, stating that "the great solicitude I feel for the safety of this army leads me to mention what I had hoped never again to do—the subject of your drinking." The timing of the letter—June 6—has been labeled by some historians as proof of Grant's binge on that day, although it is clear Rawlins delivered the letter before Grant left on the trip.[79]

While there is question, especially by recent historians, whether Grant was even an alcoholic because of his ability to leave it alone for months at a time, there is no evidence that Grant or the army was ever in danger in the episode or that it was anything other than a little too much to drink for a general who was feeling ill and was on a boring steamboat trip amid what had become a boring siege at Vicksburg. Dana described how "it was a dull period in the campaign. The siege of Vicksburg was progressing with regularity." In fact, as Grant could not hold his liquor, he probably had only one drink. He became loopy, with staff officer James H. Wilson noting in his diary: "Genl. G. intoxicated." Wilson admitted later that Grant "fell sick, and thinking a drink of spirits would do him good, took one with the usual unhappy results." And it apparently happened more than once, Sherman later writing that "we all knew at the time that Genl Grant would occasionally drink too much." He even told the famed story of Lincoln's response to a minister who called for Grant's removal because of drinking: "Do you know where Grant buys his whiskey? I would like to present some to other generals not so successful."

Sherman also related that "he always encouraged me to talk to him frankly on this & other things and I always noticed that he could with an hours sleep wake up perfectly sober and bright—and when anything was pending he was invariably abstinent of drink."[80]

More significant, what the episode does show—in addition to perhaps the boredom Grant was beginning to feel in these siege operations now some three weeks old—was that Grant was concerned about more than just his siege lines. The threat that Joseph E. Johnston posed to the rear was real. The fear grew on Grant so much that, by June 6, he felt the need to go himself to the slot to take a personal look. Part of the concern may have been from the lack of finding someone whom he could trust to take care of that sector, first Blair and then Kimball having been a little spooked. Dana had little regard for Kimball, writing that "he is not so bad a commander as Lauman, but he is bad enough." His soldiers had no better thoughts, at least those of Mower's brigade attached to Kimball for a while: "This march has cost many a man his life. Gen Kimball is at fault." An Illinoisan declared, "It is said that Gen. Kimball left Mechanicsburg out of fear, and without orders so criminally marched the troops because he was afraid of being gobbled, which fear none but his staff and he shared." He added that "the boys call it a regular Potomac management of troops and think if Kimball is a specimen of Eastern generals there can be no wondering at the constant failure." Grant obviously had still not found someone who could take care of the situation in the rear, allowing him to worry mostly about capturing Vicksburg. The rear would continue to weigh heavy on Grant.[81]

Yet the debacle of the Yazoo/Big Black slot operations produced some good fruit, even if no one realized it at the time. Grant showed just enough force in the area, despite it being scared and marched hard, to convince the Confederate high command that they were the ones about to be attacked. Both Walker and Loring sent reports of the Union movements to Johnston, and the already defeatist-minded Johnston did not need much help in fully giving up on relief operations and going heavily on the defensive. Thus, Grant's unco-ordinated and miserable showing up the slot had nevertheless produced fear in Johnston's mind.[82]

More important, it did so at the absolute most critical time. If Johnston was going to do anything it had to be now, when numbers were at parity or perhaps even a little better. Even a delay of a few days would end that oppor-tunity. The argument can be made that even with the window of opportunity still open, Johnston had little chance to break the siege or relieve the garrison, but there was absolutely no chance if he did not act immediately. Thus, Johnston was during the first week of June in much the same position that the other Johnston in the Civil War west, Albert Sidney Johnston, faced during those fateful first few days of April 1862. If he and Beauregard did not attack Grant's forces at Pittsburg Landing, Major General Don Carlos Buell's Union army would soon arrive and Grant and Buell together would march on Corinth with overpowering numbers. Albert Sidney Johnston's window of opportunity at parity or better was slim there as well, but he acted, resulting in the Battle of Shiloh. Johnston had known it was a gamble; he argued that he must roll the "iron dice of battle." He also asserted that it was do-or-die time, that he had to "conquer or perish." Obviously, he perished on the fields of Shiloh.[83]

In much the same position, Joseph E. Johnston was not so willing to roll those iron dice of battle.

7

"THE MENTAL STRAIN BECAME AWFUL UNDER SUCH CONDITIONS"

June 7–9

"This is a day of rumors," one Louisianan noted in his diary on June 7. Word had come about of trans-Mississippi Confederates under Kirby Smith driving Nathaniel Banks back to New Orleans. News also arrived that Confederates had taken Helena on the Mississippi River. Other rumors floated in as well, some regarding Lee in Virginia: "[Jubal] Early's Div stormed and captured Winchester." Down to the south there was word that "25 charges" failed against Port Hudson.[1]

If there ever was a rumor mill, it was at Vicksburg. Almost every day some new tale cropped up, mostly falsehoods but with enough reality to make hearers wonder. One Federal warned his family not to trust anything: "Do not believe every thing that you hear until it is confirmed, for there is many rumors that go like the wind that has not the least particle of truth in them." It became so bad, in fact, that one Ohioan finally concluded that "all news is contraband." Another soldier figured out the obvious: "If we were to take rumors we would have had Vicksburg long ago."[2]

The rumors, as told in diaries, letters, and even newspapers, ran the gamut of reality and sometimes hilarity and illustrated just how quickly falsehoods could spread. One rumor insisted that Pemberton had resigned on June 1. Others noted that Grant asked Pemberton to send all women and children out of Vicksburg but that Pemberton had refused. A very large number of rumors floated around about alleged Confederate breakout attempts taking place at night, prompting James McPherson to order his corps to "endeavor to give him a warm reception." Word in the Union lines was that "Vicksburg would have been surrendered before this if it had not been for the earnest desire & urgent appeals of the women who still remain there, to fight us off to the very last." One Federal wrote home and used this rumor as an appeal for women's patriotic efforts in the North.[3]

Other major rumors revolved around what was happening back on the rear line. Constant alerts of one side beating the other continually floated around, while back on that rear line the rumors of Vicksburg's daily surrender made the rounds. One Federal cited his confusion: "Some of the prisoners say that Johnston whipped them on the other side of Big Black, but others say they whipped us."[4]

The larger war was also ripe for rumors. One insisted that Robert E. Lee had won a major victory and that he was at the doorsteps of Washington. Several newspapers repeated the story that Lee "had whipped Hooker in Va. and was on Arlington Heights and was threatening to shell the Capitol." None referenced whether Lee visited his home while there. Other rumors were as absurd as having New Orleans retaken by the Confederates.[5]

While many of the rumors concerned military actions, others revolved around personalities. Many told of arriving reinforcements on both sides, which were true enough. But some said Rosecrans himself was nearing, followed by Bragg and his army. Others noted Hurlbut was nearby with his corps and that Banks had actually come north from Louisiana. Other officer-related rumors had McClernand under arrest as early as May 24, presumably for his actions during the assault two days before.[6]

By far, the most rumors swirled around the deaths of officers. Grant was frequently killed off, as was Sherman. Lower-level Federals also died in the rumors, officers such as Osterhaus and Lawler being mentioned as mortally wounded; division commanders Eugene Carr and Frederick Steele were outright killed. The problem was that many believed these rumors, such as one Illinoisan in Logan's division. He noted a rumor of the death of his brigade commander, John D. Stevenson, and remarked in his diary that "the loss will be deeply felt as he was well liked."[7]

The most unfounded rumors dealt with purported events inside Vicksburg. Federals who had never been in the city could only speculate about the mysterious happenings inside the Confederate lines. Still, one declared that Pemberton's wife and child had been killed in the bombardment, even though they had actually traveled to Alabama before the Union army arrived. More remarkable was the notice that Jefferson Davis himself was inside Vicksburg, "as he came here to view the works."[8]

Rumors about Vicksburg from outside swirled as well. One Confederate soldier in Virginia noted in mid-June the "glorious news this morning from Vicksburg. Grant has been driven off twenty two miles by Gen Johnson and you may know he has saved Pemberton this time."[9]

At times, the rumors simply bordered on the absurd. One Tennessean repeated the rumor, perhaps hoping for the best, that "an English fleet of boats have come over to our aid." Taking the prize for the best rumor was one that circulated inside Vicksburg: "The ghost of Gen. Andrew Jackson has been seen near Vicksburg Court House twice since the new moon." Wishful thinking once more, as it would probably have taken the likes of "Old Hickory" himself to save Vicksburg, and Pemberton and Johnston together hardly measured up.[10]

"The history of one day is pretty much the history of all," grumbled Confederate division commander Martin L. Smith as the siege moved on into the second week of June. Others agreed, with numerous variations of the same explanation appearing in many letters, diaries, and reports. "This week passes away without any particular variation," wrote a Mississippi chaplain. "Day or night there was little variation and almost no cessation," added another. Brigade commander John C. Moore characterized it as "the history of each day was generally but that of the proceeding." A Louisianan expressed how "the history of one day of this Siege is about the Counterpart of the next." By this second week in June, even the engineering had taken on a feeling of repetition: dig, rest, dig, rest, dig. The food began to be bland. The weather was hot and dry. Even the rumors began to repeat one another. "And so the days wore on;—each one almost a repetition of the one that preceded it."[11]

The boredom and misery of the siege was very apparent in the camp or off-duty life of the average Confederate soldier trapped inside this miserable bastion. Even when not specifically on the front lines, their day never really ended, being on guard constantly to repel any advance or attack. Daytime was the worst because of the need for cover as well as the brutal heat and sun. One Louisianan confided in his diary how "we went into the trenches exposed fully to the Sun which was very hot. It Seemed that I could hardly Stand the heat but did, and now write this in the ditch in the Evening when it is cooler."

Other weather effects such as rains and storms likewise caught these soldiers with no place to go.[12]

Most Confederates, whether in the trenches or not, tried to find at least some type of cover. Many fashioned shelters, whether boards to cover them in the rain or blankets stretched across poles to shield them from the sun. Some dug holes. One Mississippian described his: "Being somewhat luxurious in my taste I had excavated a sort of open grave in one of these cross ditches, and covered it with poles, sunk below the natural surface, and upon these earth was thrown as a protection against the hot sun." Another wrote "the weather is growing so hot, that it fairly makes me dizzy to remain in the sun long, particularly on these dusty, white looking roads where I have to breathe nothing but dust which fills my ears, eyes, nose, hair & everything."[13]

The rains were often welcomed as breaks from the sun and heat, but in other ways they merely added to the misery if they fell in torrents, enough to alter the ground and trenches. Colonel Ashbel Smith of the 2nd Texas described some of the heavier rains: "There were several showers of rain, two of which were drenching. The loamy soil of this region was rendered a mire. The men in the trenches were over shoe in mud. With only a single blanket, they were obliged to bivouac in the mud." Smith added, "My chief apprehension was lest the enemy should make an assault when our guns were wet."[14]

The smells were horrendous as well. "Truly we are surrounded by a wall of fire," one Louisianan wrote, "the atmosphere is smoky and filled with the sulphureous smell of gunpowder. They are plowing up the land with their deadly missiles & sowing it with gunpowder." The sounds were not much better, he adding that "sometimes the powder falls around us, & sounds like a shower of rain among the trees." One Mississippian declared the troops "heard no sound from one sunrise till the next save the crack of the rifle, the boom of cannon, the screech of the shells and the 'whizz' of bullets."[15]

Boredom quickly set in. In addition to the obligatory raising of a cap on a ramrod and having it shot, one Mississippian described a dangerous game the soldiers played. There was a certain place in the lines where they were shielded from sharpshooters from the front but were in view of a battery at a much longer distance away on the flank. The men would intentionally show themselves, and the Federal battery would always "launch a cannon ball at us." Most of the time the ball would pass harmlessly overhead, although sometimes it would hit the parapet and sprinkle dirt all over the men. "This was a dangerous pastime, but it was exciting, and also exhilarating," the Mississippian admitted. Eventually the fun came to an end: "Our officers soon ordered us to leave off this practice, as it drew the enemy's fire."[16]

Boredom often gave way to short tempers. On one occasion, George Clarke laughed at the face made by a comrade when he was nonthreateningly hit on the shin by a spent ball. The man "drew his face into such ludicrous contortions, that I could not restrain my laughter," Clarke admitted. The man's brother saw all this and "got very angry at me for laughing" at his kin's misfortune: "He proceeded to give, what would, in these days, be called a genteel 'cussing.'"[17]

The camps themselves were situated to the rear in any place that could be found, and even "the city grave yard was filled with camps," one Confederate morbidly noted. Most camps were below ridgelines where more, but not total, cover could be obtained. There, the men also dug "like gophers in the piney woods, for nearly all of them had holes in the ground to get into when not on duty." Lounging in camp when not required to be on the front lines was common, as officers soon realized troops could not keep up their stamina if on alert constantly. Shifts would take their turns in the trenches, allowing the others at least some break, although the men were really never out from under constant alert. Conversely, on some parts of the line it was the direct opposite. "We had very little to do," Simeon Martin of the 46th Mississippi explained. "We would sleep in the trenches, but as soon as daylight appeared would return to our refuge and stay there the remainder of the day, engaged in such occupations as came to hand, mostly playing cards or drafts."[18]

Any number of hobbies or games wiled away the time. Some whittled little oddities out of wood or lead bullets. Others read novels and other works, including Charles Dickens and Marion Harland. One reported reading the adventures of Hernán Cortés against the Aztecs. Boredom also fostered trickery. Engineer James T. Hogane told of just sitting down to a wonderful meal prepared by another engineer's wife, when several of his comrades told him a Union mortar shell had clipped off one of his mule's ears. Hogane obviously went to see, and he found the mule's ear had been tied down with string. When he returned, of course, he found "my share of the sweet potato pie eaten up."[19]

The elements were almost as hazardous as the enemy, most notably the filthy nature of the trenches and camps. Bugs and lice were common. "Boys, here is a big one," someone would call out upon discovering a particularly robust insect. Mosquitoes were also terrible, one Tennessean writing, "I dreaded the mosquitoes more than the Yankees. I would press my old hat tightly over my face, wrap my blanket around my head, stick my hands under my semblance of a coat, yet the mosquitoes would so bite me as to make me look in the morning as if I had chicken pox." The common soldiers had little extra covering in terms of clothing, which wore out as the weeks moved along, "often half fed and illy-clothed, exposed to the burning sun and soaking rains." One Louisianan was overjoyed when "I got me two pairs of drawers but could afford no undershirts & my old ones are all to pieces."[20]

In such miserable conditions day in and day out—not to mention the constant fire from small arms and artillery from the enemy—death, wounds, and sickness were unfortunately very common. Burials were sad but frequent affairs, with little time for major formalities. In fact, one Confederate told of digging a grave in between shots of small arms and cannons and then hiding in the grave itself to escape the fire.[21]

The almost constant bombardment was certainly unappealing and produced deaths. Engineer Henry Ginder wrote home that he had a very close call. "Last night I was on foot returning from the scene of my labors," he explained. He could hear a shell coming in but did not see it. The sound told him it was coming nearer and nearer, and "I thought it would light on my head, when splosh! It went into the earth a few feet to my left, throwing the dirt in my face with such force as to sting me for some time afterwards." It was indeed a close call, Ginder adding that "the Lord kept it from exploding before it reached the earth, otherwise it would have singed the hair off my head & blown me to pieces in the bargain." Still, the shells damaged several magazines Ginder had been working on and they caved in. He had to condemn one and move it away after a fifty-foot slide "which would have buried me & all my niggers if we hadn't been working somewhere else at the time." Others described similar close experiences, one writing that "a Minnie ball has just struck the cane mattress on which I am lying opposite my shoulder."[22]

Not surprisingly with this number of people grouped so closely together, accidents were also common and resulted in some deaths. "We are in constant danger from accidental shots," one Confederate wrote. "This is quite a school for patience." A 7th Mississippi Battalion soldier was killed by accident as he was on picket, while seven men in the 38th Mississippi succumbed to friendly fire during the siege. Filth in the camps was also an issue, at one point Pemberton seeking a quantity of "disinfecting agents" so that Bowen could "purify the woods in rear of his command."[23]

At times, the accidental deaths were strange. Two of John C. Moore's staff were killed when a shell exploded while they were attempting to get the powder. On another occasion, a group of soldiers behind the line was just sitting down to supper when a shell burst in their midst. One Mississippian reflected that it "show[ed] how little we know at what moment the summons of death may come and the uncertainty of life." There were even several accounts of errant shells killing previously wounded or sick soldiers in the hospitals.[24]

The family loss, when multiplied, was also odd. One account described how two siblings, the Williams brothers, were killed at almost the exact time and same way in the 38th Mississippi. Another particularly sad event occurred when the same bullet killed two men who were brothers-in-law. Others reported similar odd ways of receiving casualties, one engineering soldier being struck by lightning during one of the storms "but not seriously hurt." A staff officer even described crossing a rude bridge with a team when "one of the mules in crossing made a push; threw up the plank which struck me in side of the head & threw me some distance." Obviously, deaths from these freak accidents, and even some unexplained causes, were more common than wanted. One described how an artilleryman "went to bed & was found dead by his comrades." Another clerk in one of the brigade offices died in late June, "killed by explosion of shell he was fooling with." He was trying to open it when it exploded and set off another too. A courier nearby was also badly wounded.[25]

With so much death and destruction, there was no wonder the soldier's minds often turned to religion. Many soldiers' letters and diaries describe reading the Bible, although the soldiers could not routinely gather for worship as they were in the trenches. Still, one Louisianan noted, "I have just opened my Bible and my eye fell on the 5th verse 30th Psalm: 'for his anger endureth but a moment, in his favour is life: weeping may endure for a night, but joy cometh in the morning.'" Prayers for deliverance were also common, an example being an Alabamian's prayer: "Oh, that God would interpose in our behalf as a nation and give us the power to drive the invader from our soil and that speedily and that peace on honorable terms, sweet peace, might overshadow us."[26]

Sundays were days of rest and worship for most of the farm and small-town boys now making up the Confederate army. As such, the lack of almost any observance of that day struck many of them as odd. One wrote how Sunday, May 31, was "a most beautiful, bright, Sunday morning—What a pity that such a beautiful day cannot be enjoyed by both Yankees & us but they must convert it into a day of strife." Fortunately, that particular morning was comparatively quiet. Another described Sunday, June 7, as also quiet. "'Tis Sabbath day again," wrote one Mississippian, "God's holy day and all is more quiet than usual, this morning. It appears that the enemy was disposed to keep the Sabbath holy; would that we would follow their example in this respect, but we may have a warm time before night."[27]

The constant death and subsequent turn toward religion fostered repentance in many soldiers, fearful of entering eternity at any moment. A Mississippian confided to his father how "this siege and events incident thereto have brought me to see the danger of my condition and made me resolve to try to turn from my heretofore sinful course and follow the teaching of the Bible." Another described how some of the soldiers received New Testaments "supplied us by some good Christian people." He added, "I had observed that shells and minie balls exerted a fine missionary influence on most of us; and that language was less strenuous, and that Bible study and devotional exercises were much more common under these conditions." This Mississippian was reading one of Paul's letters one day when a shell hit his "lair." He was almost buried alive, having to dig his way out, "clearing my eyes and mouth of dirt." He admitted, "I confess to being somewhat demoralized. In fact, some of the boys insinuated that I was badly scared." Obviously, the chance of facing eternity with sins on his account did not appeal to him.[28]

There were still times when religious services did take place, however. A Georgian described how his religious association in the 42nd Georgia "set apart all or a portion of the hour between sundown and dark of each day to supplicate Almighty God that he will pardon our sins, receive us graciously and deliver us from the hands of our cruel enemies, and that we solicit all Christians and soldiers throughout this beleaguered army to enter with us in prayer at that time." Other forms of worship also took place, such as preaching in the hospitals. One Texan even marked Whitsuntide, or the days after Pentecost. Even the Federals reported on the religious practices in the Confederate lines, one Illinoisan explaining that "they had a real Methodist prayer-meeting, with psalms and such things; could hear them perfectly."[29]

Perhaps the most basic daily challenge for these Confederates—besides staying alive in the miserable surroundings—rested on obtaining sustenance for strength. As might be expected, the most basic need was water. The human body can exist much longer without food than it can without water, so obtaining healthy liquids became a matter of daily survival. Unfortunately, the best practices were not always adhered to; wells were carefully guarded and at times off-limits to soldiers. And inexplicably, by order of Pemberton himself on several occasions, dead horses and mules were taken to the Mississippi River and dumped. As a result, as Texan Ashbel Smith noted, "the water next to the bank teemed with maggots, so as to be unfit for any use. The cisterns in the neighborhood being exhausted or forbidden, my men were soon reduced to the sipe water got from shallow wells dug in the hollows immediately in our rear. This was indifferent in quality and barely sufficient for our scanty cooking and drink. Sentinels were placed over the wells, that none might be wasted for purposes of cleanliness." Of course, in the heat of summer, many springs and wells soon dried up.[30]

Much of the available water was totally unfit for use. One Texan wrote that "the air was contaminated by the many dead animals that lie around. The water is also uncertain." Some hauled water in barrels from the river, despite the dead animals thrown into it, and it was kept only for drinking, but one Tennessean noted that "under the southern summer sun it soon became tepid and unpalatable." One Vicksburg lady wrote of her "cistern I had to give up to the soldiers, who swarm about like hungry animals seeking something to devour. Poor fellows! My heart bleeds for them." With so little water, bathing was a luxury to say the least. The same Tennessean added that "our dirty hands and faces were strangers to water for many long days." Some took advantage of any ponds or pools of water behind the lines as "a bathing place," and at times Pemberton even ordered whole units relieved temporarily "for the purpose of cleansing themselves."[31]

Food also became scarcer and scarcer as the siege wore on. A lot of dissatisfaction in the ranks came from poor rations, although it had long been an issue in Vicksburg even before the siege; one Louisianan in a letter to his wife mentioned in March 1863: "I cant tell you how bad wee fair but bad anuff to eat all the rats wee can git. This looks hard, but they eat very well." Pemberton did the best he could, weighing the use of rations against the need to hold a reserve. "The meat ration having been reduced one-half," he explained, "that of sugar, rice, and beans was largely increased. It was important above all things that every encouragement should be given to the troops. With this object in view, I ordered the impressments of chewing tobacco and its issue to the troops. This had a very beneficial influence." Later, it became worse, Pemberton writing that "about this time our provisions, particularly of meat, having become almost exhausted, General Stevenson was instructed to im-press all cattle in the city, and the chief commissary directed to sell only one ration per diem to any officer. He was also instructed to issue for bread equal portions of rice and flour, four ounces of each."[32]

The daily fare was indeed small for the troops, one Missourian writing of being "in our safety holes, impatiently awaiting our small rations." One gave an amount, stating that "five ounces of musty corn-meal and pea flower were normally issued daily. In point of fact, this allowance did not exceed three ounces." Another nevertheless admitted that "scant rations were received with more pleasure than the most abundant heretofore."[33]

An examination of the daily rations over the course of the siege illustrates the declining nourishment given to the soldiers. On June 10, soldiers reported the daily ration as a quarter-pound of bacon and a third-pound of meal. By the following week, on June 18, one soldier described how "to-day our rations of corn meal gave out, and we now draw, instead of ¾ lb of meal per man, ¼ lb of wheat flour ¼ lb rice flour and 1 oz of peas as breadstuff, and ¼ lb of bacon meat rations." Four days later one soldier described receiving only four ounces of flour, three ounces of rice, four ounces of beans and "some sugar and salt . . . , also tobacco." By June 26, "rations [were] cut down from 8 small biscuits, enough peas for one meal, & a quarter Pound of bacon, to 4 biscuits rice, about 2 inches square boiled, a small amount of peas & bacon." Two days later saw four ounces of pork, four ounces of flour, six ounces of sugar, one and a half ounces of rice, five ounces of peas, and one ounce of lard.[34]

"Rations are short & we eat two meals per day at 9 in morning & at 3 in evening—stylish in a ditch!," one Louisianan joked. A Missourian put it more plainly, writing: "I would draw my rations for a day in a pint cup. They were cooked, and a day's rations did not fill the cup much over half full." Another complained that "we get one-quarter pound of bacon, 9 ounces meal, made of ground peas and corn, sometimes a cupful of beans and a little sugar or molasses, as rations." As a result, there was much sickness, a Confederate judging that a full one-quarter of the garrison was sick with diarrhea and the rest terribly weak. "Don't think we could march 5 miles in a day in regular marching order," he confessed.[35]

As the flour ration dwindled inside Vicksburg, officers came up with a sub-stitute they hoped would satisfy the army's needs; one Missourian declared that it "grew out of the fertile brain of some official." Pea bread was made of small peas normally used as forage for animals. When ground, this became a meal, but the bread that resulted was hard as a rock on the outside and doughy on the inside. The longer it baked, the harder it became on the outside but doughier on the inside. The soldiers had a field day complaining, of course, as this mixture of peas, beans, and rice to make flour was inedible. "The soldiers could not eat the mixture," one Louisianan explained. "O! how our stomachs loathed that pea bread." One Mississippian called it a "villainous invention of General Pemberton's, and even this was measured out in ounces." A woman who tried it described the taste as "peculiar and disagreeable," and it was discontinued after only a day or two.[36]

More worrisome was the dwindling meat rations, which began to run out in late June. Without the customary beef or swine, Confederates in Vicksburg turned for meat to beasts of burden such as horses and mules. When Colonel Thomas Dockery's horse died, it "afforded a choice meal to a great many of the brigade." The camel mascot of the 43rd Mississippi, "Old Douglas," also provided good protein when killed. Most of the new fare was mule meat, however, begun opportunely anytime a mule wandered too near the Federal lines and was shot. Confederates were quick to slice off the choicest parts and eat well for a while. "I was as hollow as a gourd, and when my back began to cave in I thought it about time to eat anything I could get," one famished Confederate admitted.[37]

Many described mule meat as good, and on occasion there was even a bidding war for it, one Mississippian paying as high as a dollar for a mule tongue. One noted that it was "equal to the best venison . . . the flesh tender and nutritious and, under the *peculiar circumstances*, a most desirable description of food." However, another Mississippian just could not eat the mule meat. "I tried to eat some of it," he explained, "but could never get it to the swallowing point. . . . [T]he more I chewed the bigger it got, and I finally had to give it up."[38]

One Mississippian talked of experimentation with both pea bread and mule meat: "when the siege began, we were receiving one third of a ration of meat, and about two thirds of a ration of meal. This was soon greatly reduced. In lieu of the cornmeal, we had cow peas ground and made into bread. This bread after being baked was about the color of an Indian, and a few hours after being baked would, on being broken, show a substance resembling spiders webs, which would stretch a foot or more before finally breaking." He explained: "For a time we had fresh beef instead of bacon, and for a few days at one time we had rice bread issued to us. Then the bread ceased altogether. Our ration then consisted of about one teacup full of boiled peas and a small bit, perhaps about two, ounces of bacon." He also mentioned eating mule meat, adding "curl the lip in derision if ye will," but he declared that nothing was ever better to hungry soldiers. "The flesh of the mule seemed of coarser grain, but more tender than that of the ox, and had a decidedly 'horsey' flavor. To starving men, however, it was very good."[39]

To help augment the paltry daily rations, soldiers found what they could elsewhere. Sassafras "grew all over the hills," one Missourian noted, and tea was consumed. Fruit also grew during the summer, although less in the city than in the country. Worrying that it would not be there when ripe, many were reduced to eating "all the unripe, half-grown peaches, the green berries growing on the briars, all were carefully gathered and simmered in a little sugar and water, and used for food. Every eatable vegetable around the works was hunted up for food."[40]

The common soldier had to make do. "I see men to-day boiling wild pea vines for greens and wishing for mule beef," one Louisianan noted. Another wrote in his diary, "I had to-day for dinner Mule Beef, Poke Salad, and rice Soup." The next line was "very sick this evening." Men of the 36th Mississippi daily watched a pear tree in their rear for the fruit to become ripe, all hoping to get some of the pears before other soldiers cleaned them out. Fearing they would be late, one soldier climbed into the tree and shook them loose or dropped them down while another gathered them on the ground. Just as the picking began, the Federals noticed the commotion and sent a shell through the tree, cutting off several branches and sending a shower of green pears to the ground. "It would have amused anyone to have seen my comrade come tearing down through the limbs of the tree," one of the Mississippians explained. "He did not climb down, but just simply turned loose and fell down." That did not stop the two from hurriedly gathering as many pears as they could.[41]

As the situation became worse, drastic measures had to be devised. Pemberton noted "the experiment of using mule meat as a substitute was tried, it being issued only to those who desired to use it." He happily added, "I am gratified to say it was found by both officers and men not only nutritious, but very palatable, and every way preferable to poor beef." Other items were also mentioned less frequently, such as one soldier describing a liquor ration only occasionally, although the commissary reported early on that there was not "a sufficient quantity on hand for one drink to the troops present." Pemberton's staff, in fact, kept a constant inventory of how much liquor was inside Vicksburg, at times even confiscating it from private hands. Later it was earmarked for the medical department. Some did not partake even when offered, one soldier writing that "I never drank my portion. Doubtless it went to some other fellow, and probably he was the worse for it. At any rate, I endured the hardship of trench life just as well, if not better, than the men who drank their liquor rations."[42]

The nadir of the food situation came with the oft-cited consumption of less-than-desirable items. Samuel Lockett mentioned eating "young shoots of cane," but one Mississippian declared "I have strong reason to believe that a dog had been eaten in a La. Reg't." There was plenty of jesting about "Tomcat wienerwurst" and the question of "what's become of Fido?," although Vicksburg *Daily Citizen* editor James Swords printed that "we have not as yet learned of any one experimenting with the flesh of the canine species." Mule meat was common, but horses seemed to be "a great luxury." Most famously, several mentioned eating rats; they were of course not an issued item but rather what any individual Confederate managed to catch in the first place and consume in the second place. Some have ventured that they were talking about muskrats, but Colonel Winchester Hall of the 26th Louisiana noted "the privates of the regiment successfully undertook a decrease in the rodent population." James L. Power noted rats were being sold at the market, and elaborated that "there is no reason in the books why rats should not make a good dish. They are as cleanly in their habits as rabbits and squirrels, and infinitely more so than hogs. What [is] more filthy than a hog?" Yet, he added, "I don't consider myself an exception, for I don't intend to—eat *rats*." Pemberton staff officer John C. Taylor wrote in his diary on June 30 that "some of our garrison have taken considerable gusto to eating mules, horses, rats etc—the last named have been sold for the last week $2 ½ apiece and are in great demand."[43]

A Louisianan wrote in his diary that he had "a hearty breakfast on fried rats, whose flesh," he added, was "fully equal to that of squirrels." He later added "traps were set for rats, which were consumed in such numbers that, ere the termination of the siege, they actually became a scarcity." Even the Federals mentioned the rats, one writing of how bad it must be getting as they were running out of Vicksburg across Union lines: "If their rats are coming, the Rebels must also be soon tamed."[44]

While the common soldier floundered with smaller and smaller portions, officers fared better. Brigade commander Francis Shoup told of how he had a kitchen at his headquarters with a wood stove brought out from town. There, his "colored artist" produced fine pancakes and all other assortments of good food. Engineers and officers in town also fared better. The wounded Colonel Winchester Hall of the 26th Louisiana explained how "I was the recipient every day, for several days, of a newly laid egg, kindly sent to me by Mrs. Bond, the wife of Captain Bond of the heavy artillery." He also noted that "a pond was found by my boys stocked with crawfish, which furnished our table with a toothsome dish, until the supply was exhausted." A Louisiana engineer similarly reported, "we live with a man who has a vegetable garden & keeps our table pretty well supplied," although he explained that "we are economical, take only two meals a day, at 8 A.M., & 4 P.M." Even that did not last long, however, because he later complained that "our vegetables are disappearing fast, being stolen by our soldiers. The worst of it is, that, as they come at night, they cannot tell whether anything is ripe & they take them green, so they do no good to them or us."[45]

Word of the dire food situation inside Vicksburg quickly made its way outside the lines, and Federals enjoyed joking with the Confederates about it: "A courteous inquiry was often made as to whether it was true that General Pemberton had been superseded in the command of Vicksburg by General Starvation." The joke began as early as May 29 when Grant of all people toured the lines and stated to his soldiers, according to one Indianan, "that he was not the commanding general at this point." When asked who was in his place, Grant replied, "General Starvation." Conversely, one Federal noted that it was actually the Confederates on his front who made the joke, telling them they had better "look out as they had a new general."[46]

Even the Confederates themselves had a laugh at their predicament, one making out a menu at the "Hotel de Vicksburg." It had an assortment of goodies, mostly of the mule variety: mule tail soup, mule sirloin roast, mule rump stuffed with rice, mule head stuffed "a la reb," mule ears "fricasseed a la gotch," "mule liver, hashed, a la explosion," mule salad, mule hoof soused, mule brains "a la omelette," "mule tounge, cold a la bray," and mule foot jelly.[47]

All jokes aside, conditions dwindled as the siege wore on against this "pen of imprisoned humanity." The net result was that the constant duty and dwindling resources left the Confederate army weaker and weaker by the day. One soldier lamented the "long confinements in narrow trenches, without exercise and without relief, being constantly under fire and necessarily on the alert." Samuel Lockett admitted that "we were so short-handed that no man within the lines had ever been off duty more than a small part of each day."[48]

The physical stress was apparent. One chaplain described how "our hungry men could be seen walking the streets in search of something to eat." Another noted how the hot sun added to the misery: "Day after day they must endure its sultry beams, with only an outspread blanket to keep off the rays, which also excludes the air." Sickness obviously followed: "All gradually emaciated and became weak, and toward the close of the siege many were found with swollen ankles and symptoms of incipient scurvy."[49]

The mental strain was perhaps worse, the troops being on "incessant alert." A constant watch had to be kept, and at places on the line where the enemy could not be seen, officers kept station and signaled the main forts of enemy movements. At the same time, many were required to man the trenches continually. "We have had no reliefs in the trenches until the last few days, and now they are put on because the men are getting so weak," described one Confederate. He also noted that, as far as he knew, few would be willing to try to cut their way out: "It might be that half would try, if ordered, but I doubt it." Stephen D. Lee noted that "the object seemed to be to worry out and exhaust the Confederates by constant vigil, and strain of the nervous system by continuous alarm." Another Mississippian added how "the mental strain became awful under such conditions."[50]

Not unexpectedly, desertions increased. Some Confederates argued that "we came out because we are starving." Others were convinced that Vicksburg would surrender soon, and one who deserted admitted "more would come over, but the Federal pickets fire too much for us. A great many are expecting that the place will be surrendered in a few days, and would prefer to be taken prisoners than to run the risk of deserting." One Federal declared that a lieutenant and as many as 120 men deserted on one particular night. They came to the ravine between the lines and waited for daybreak to surrender. The lieutenant had been in charge of the relieving pickets and simply marched them on into the ravine.[51]

There was quite a show when these deserters arrived in the Union camps. One Illinoisan was amused over several Confederates who were brought in as prisoners with loaded guns still being carried at their side. "I think they must have been quite willing to be taken," he surmised. Beyond being questioned about conditions inside Vicksburg, they were given plenty to eat. One Federal remembered, "the way they rolled down the victuals was a sight to see." One deserter went so far as to join the Union army; John G. Jones of the 23rd Wisconsin told of a Confederate who deserted and found his brother in the 17th Ohio Battery. "He is now in our uniform," and even more traitorous, "he belonged to the Battery which we are attacking, and he is shelling their magazine and guns. He also shows us their weak spots."[52]

The constant pressure on the soldiers led to a gradual loss of the will to fight. There was a general feeling of despondency, one Confederate remarking, "We think that Vicksburg can hold out two weeks yet, if the men don't get tired before that time." The result was a growing dejectedness by the time the first couple of weeks of June came about, and it only grew after that. "All I am acquainted with are getting very dissatisfied, officers now as well as men," wrote one dejected Confederate. "Our only dependence is in General Johnston, and we are losing faith in him." Another dejectedly noted that June 8 was the two-week deadline Johnston was supposedly to have set, and still there was no sign of him. As for their commander, he remarked that "we don't like General Pemberton at all, and think General Grant is too sharp for him." That he was a Pennsylvanian obviously did not help.[53]

What little hope of relief there was continually faded as time went on. "The enemy had then constructed in my front, and for 1 ½ miles in depth, a tremendous hornet's nest of lines and works, bristling with cannon and bayonets and crammed with soldiers," one colonel wrote. Thoughts thus turned inward, and many a dejected Confederate began to think of home and family. Many wrote home, although they knew full well the letters might be captured. "I write without any painstaking," one declared, "for I may be writing for the Yankees." That said, there was an effort by Absalom Grimes and Robert Louden to establish a clandestine mail service for the soldiers trapped inside Vicksburg.[54]

With time for the mind to wander, many Confederates wondered what had become of those at home. "They have passed my home," one Confederate worried, "and I cried to hear the condition in which I fear they have left my wife and children." Others could only remember better times. One poor Confederate wrote in his diary on May 31 that "this is the birthday of my child Lizzie May Killgore—daughter Lizzie." He added, "To-day she is Two years old. God grant that her next birthday may be a quiet one and that I may be permitted to be with my family in peace." Another reflected on a special day to him: "On this day I was married. On that day our first child was born & on the same day we had an Angle born in Heaven." A Texan similarly found brigade commander John C. Moore "rather sad, his thoughts were of his wife & children" way off in Kentucky where she had to scrape by teaching music. He was especially concerned that he could not send money, Confederate currency being no good there.[55]

Still, duty called and most Confederates responded. No more fitting epitaph could be found than one officer who wrote how many of

> the men bore with unrepining cheerfulness and undaunted spirit the fatigues of almost continual position under arms, of frequent working parties by night and day, the broiling of the midday sun in summer with no shelter, the chilling night dews, the cramped inaction at all times in the trenches, short rations, at times drenched with rain and bivouacking in the mud, together with the discomforts inseparable from their having no change of clothing and an insufficient supply of water for cleanliness, tired, ragged, dirty, barefoot, hungry, covered with vermin, with a scanty supply of ammunition, almost hand to hand with the enemy, and beleaguered on every side, with no prospect and little hope of relief.[56]

Such was daily life for the Confederate soldier inside Fortress Vicksburg.

Ulysses S. Grant intended to keep life in those enemy camps just as hard on these Confederates as he could. The skirmishing that constantly took place kept the Confederates on edge and on the defensive, as did the heavy barrage of artillery that continually rained down from both field pieces and naval guns. And then there was always in the back of all minds the possibility of a renewed assault, especially with the various approaches continually nearing the Confederate fortifications. As the Federals drew ever closer, the logical assumption was that they would use that proximity eventually to make a sprint at the Confederate works. That Grant had ample food and ammunition by this point flowing in from the Yazoo River landings made the disparity between the two sides almost endless.

The Federal war machine doing such annoyance to the Vicksburg defenders was rolling full steam by this point in the siege. Most soldiers agreed that surrender was only a matter of time and that the result was not in doubt. Of course, the uncertainty of Johnston looming in the rear and even potential

Confederate breakout attempts always concerned the Federal high command, Sherman admitting to a friend that "we hardly know what Johnston is doing in the interior." But as far as the siege itself went, there was no doubt for most what the end result would be. That said, there were a few more nervous than warranted, such as Frank Blair. The politician general had seen perhaps more of the effort than anyone else besides Grant himself, having made attacks on both days of the assaults on May 19 and 22 and then commanding the initial rearward defense up the Yazoo/Big Black slot. Then, he had moved toward the extreme south end of the lines to try and bottle up the last remaining opening in the siege lines. He had seen the width and breadth of the operations, and perhaps because he was not trained in the military art per se, he took a somewhat different view of it than Grant. In fact, he wrote to his brother Montgomery Blair, Lincoln's postmaster general, on June 8: "Tell the President to re-enforce this army, as there is great peril. General Banks declines to co-operate with General Grant."[57]

What caused Blair to pull these political strings is not known. There is slight chance Grant would have asked him to send such a note, making the situation out as far worse than it actually was, as that was never Grant's way of doing things. Rather, Blair no doubt was freelancing from his own viewpoint. And as obvious in his near panic while up the slot, Blair could be overwhelmed by fear at times. Conversely, the fact was that, by this time, Grant had huge numbers of reinforcements already arrived or on the way from numerous commands. He accordingly saw no such imminent peril, and there was consequently no such panic.[58]

All the while, the three corps commanders continually sealed their respective sectors, ever tightening the noose around Vicksburg. As an example, General Sherman sent out elaborate orders on June 9 about how to make the lines airtight. "To prevent communication between the enemy, now closely invested in Vicksburg," he wrote, "and their friends and adherents without, the following rules must be observed." He went on to stipulate the sector each division was to control: Steele from the Mississippi River to Thayer's position at "Abbott's Valley," Tuttle from there to the Graveyard Road and "Washington Knoll," and Blair southward to McPherson's line at what he described as "Ransom's Hill." Sherman, of course, used the names of his officers killed in the assaults on May 19 and 22 in the first two cases, Colonel Charles Abbott of the 30th Iowa killed on Thayer's front and Captain Edward C. Washington of the United States Regulars killed at the Stockade Redan.[59]

In these sectors, the commanders were to see that "a continuous chain of sentinels must extend from the Mississippi River to the main Jackson road, along our front trenches." These sentinels, working in shifts, were to skirmish and sharp-shoot continually, but the main goal was that "no human being must pass into or out of Vicksburg, unless on strictly military duty, or as prisoners." In fact, he ordered that soldiers wandering around be arrested and even that officers without passes be turned away as well. Sherman kept his harshest treatment for "soldiers or citizens (not regular sutlers within the proper limits of their regiments) found peddling," he ordering that they "be put under guard, and set to work on roads or trenches, and their wares turned into the hospital or distributed among the soldiers on duty." To keep the men in the camps and trenches, he also ordered that roll be called three times a day and officers held responsible if they did not keep order: "He cannot shift his responsibility to an orderly sergeant." Sherman then tried to inspire the troops, writing that "the magnificent task assigned to this army should inspire every officer and soldier to sacrifice everything of comfort, ease, or pleasure to the one sole object, 'success,' now apparently within our grasp. A little more hard work, great vigilance, and a short struggle, and Vicksburg is ours."[60]

The engineering activities were likewise coming along well, even now on the southern sectors of the line. Sherman and McPherson were well on their way prior to this, Charles Dana reporting on June 10 that Sherman's approaches, though conducted through the most difficult ground, were nearest of all. "His sap was within 50 feet of the rebels' front at 9 P.M. yesterday. McPherson is at about 80 yards or more. Both Sherman and McPherson have abandoned the idea of mining, and intend to crown the enemy's parapet with their artillery." Conversely, the digging on the left had been delayed, obviously on the extreme left by the lack of troops in that area first and then by the shuffling of others in and out. Blair's brigades fresh off their Yazoo River jaunt moved through temporarily, and others were on the way, but the constant on the left was Jacob Lauman's division of the XVI Corps. Yet by the second week in June little had been done there in terms of engineering and nothing in terms of approaches. Grant wanted efforts begun, and on June 8 he assigned three new officers to Lauman to aid in "the survey of the enemy's works and our approaches from your extreme left, and work toward General McClernand, until they connect with the surveys now in progress." In the larger context, Grant was also having trouble with Lauman's overall military

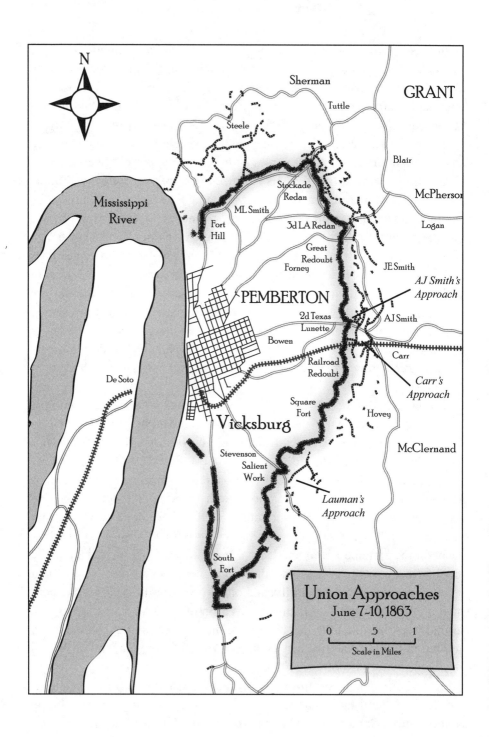

N

Sherman

Tuttle

GRANT

Steele

Blair

McPherson

Stockade
Redan

ML Smith

Logan

Mississippi
River

Fort
Hill

3d LA Redan

Great
Redoubt

JE Smith

*AJ Smith's
Approach*

Forney

AJ Smith

PEMBERTON

2d Texas
Lunette

Bowen

Carr

Railroad
Redoubt

*Carr's
Approach*

De Soto

Square
Fort

Hovey

Vicksburg

McClernand

Stevenson

Salient
Work

*Lauman's
Approach*

South
Fort

Union Approaches
June 7–10, 1863

0   .5   1

Scale in Miles

ability, writing to him on June 8 to "move your left Brigade to the right, so as to leave one Regiment, on the left of Hall's Ferry road. As you now have your troops disposed, there is great danger of having them picked up in detail."[61]

Lauman soon began approaches, although the confusion of his several moves caused delays and restarts. Lauman himself was not the best taskmaster, his troops calling him "Grannie Lauman." When the division moved several times, once back to its original spot, Lieutenant Colonel William Camm of the 14th Illinois noted in his diary, "We are under a set of old grandmothers." Lots of engineering work initially went on behind the lines, building roads connecting the division with McClernand's troops to the right and advancing not by approaches but ridge to ridge by force. After engineering surveys of this new ground with only a "2-inch pocket compass," Engineer Henry C. Freeman explained, including using triangulation to pinpoint the enemy's position, Lauman then began an approach "which runs out from the enemy's line 300 yards east of the Hall's Ferry road." Prime reported that "a good deal of work had been expended on it, when it was decided to abandon it for an approach along the Hall's Ferry road, ravines there giving cover within 300 yards of the enemy's line." This second approach was a "zigzag" trench that went toward the Salient Work, which Prime described as "very salient, and, therefore, weak." Because of this weakness, the Confederates were especially watchful, often making "sorties" outside the lines to keep the Federals from accomplishing their aims. Captain Freeman had charge of Lauman's efforts.[62]

By this time, McClernand was also getting started on the approaches. Grant was continually tiring of the politician general, and not just from the campaign itself but also since he had reached Vicksburg. Grant squarely laid the numerous casualties on May 22 to McClernand's false claim of success, and throughout the siege McClernand continued to try to influence Grant by stating his unsolicited opinions and desires. For example, McClernand wrote to Grant on June 7 that, if reinforcements were not forthcoming quickly, enough to seal the rear, then "is it not expedient to mass our forces on some point of the Vicksburg works, and try to force it? This is an important question; but probably is the alternative to waiting, and being attacked by the enemy in the rear." McClernand even offered his opinion as to where the success would be most easily gained—on the far right, Steele's front, where the gunboats could aid in the attack. Obviously, McClernand had never been to that area or viewed the vast valley of Mint Spring Bayou.[63]

Grant was no doubt peeved at McClernand's suggestions, but he was most desirous that McClernand work on his siege lines, particularly approaches toward the Confederate works. To date, in this second week in June, Mc-Clernand had yet to even begin approaches despite the fact that Sherman, McPherson, and Lauman had all done so. Finally, around June 10, McClernand started two approaches from his lines, those on A. J. Smith's and Carr's fronts. The one on Smith's front followed the Baldwin's Ferry Road almost exactly, except for one position where Chief Engineer Frederick Prime described "injudiciously leaving it in one place to avoid hard digging." Corps engineer Hains explained that "the ground along the road was so hard that to approach by boyas there would be a difficult piece of work, especially as we have no sappers and depend entirely on the troops of the line for every shovel full of dirt thrown up." He also described it as "almost like rock." Later, Hains wrote that "the ground is very hard, and complaints already begin to be made of being worked hard. The weather is very warm. This retards the work more than anything else. The men cannot work at all during the middle of the day." This approach nevertheless ran toward the 2nd Texas Lunette, which had been stormed by these very troops on May 22.[64]

On Carr's front, the approach followed the Southern Railroad of Mississippi through a deep cut for about a hundred yards, then moved southward toward the Railroad Redoubt. When closer in, workers began a parallel, "from which the salient might have been stormed," Prime noted. Carr's work was mainly a system of zig-zag trenches, twenty-five feet per zig or zag. That afforded frontal protection most of the way, but where it turned was dangerous, one Iowan explaining that "two or three points in the zig-zag line were not as well protected as others, and the Confederates had the range at these points to perfection. It was a great scramble to get through in places and escape the shower of bullets." In many cases, the work was also slowed because of the existence of barriers, in this case the railroad itself, which caused delay in that "the hardness of the earth together with the difficulty of tearing up the track have hitherto rendered progress on this part of the work slow and laborious." Buildings or where former buildings had stood, in this case mere burned chimneys, also factored into the work. Nevertheless, hundreds of soldiers working in each division, along with a solid number of former slaves, could do a lot of work in a night.[65]

By June 10, then, Grant had some nine approaches (Wood's/Manter's having been abandoned) moving forward with sap rollers at their heads to protect those digging. Left in rear was a deep and wide roadway leading back to the main lines, as well as in some cases new parallels closer to the Confederate fortifications. The Federals were continually inching their way closer and closer to Vicksburg.

That continual forward movement worried John C. Pemberton the most as he oversaw the defense effort from his headquarters nerve center in a plush neighborhood of the city rather than on the front lines or out in the field. Pemberton kept his headquarters in downtown Vicksburg at an ornate mansion on Crawford Street owned by the Willis family. He had originally stationed himself farther out toward the lines but was far too close to enemy fire, so he moved into the Willis House on May 21. The Greek Revival mansion had been built in the mid-1830s like many of the plantation owners' city dwellings, and Mrs. Willis still lived there, although by 1863 her son formally owned the house.[66]

Pemberton's headquarters sat near other socialites and well-to-do families in Vicksburg, in fact just down from the Balfours, where news of Sherman's advance in December 1862 had famously interrupted the Christmas ball. William Balfour was a Vicksburg doctor, and his outspoken wife, Emma, was a frequent social acquaintance of Pemberton and his staff who seemed, like many of the generals even with headquarters out in the field, to socialize a lot. Stephen D. Lee was a frequent guest at the Balfours.[67]

Pemberton's wife and children had left Vicksburg for Alabama when it became dangerous, and Pemberton missed them dearly. Biographer Michael Ballard has surmised that the reason Pemberton enjoyed Emma Balfour's and her husband's company so much, besides being nearby, was because she had an "upbeat, strong voice . . . similar to Pattie's." Emma Balfour frequently laughed at Pemberton "for being gloomy," so when a courier from Johnston arrived with hopes of help, he specifically sent word to her of the news. Balfour noted, "I think he is inclined to be rather despondent and very persistent hopefulness cheers him."[68]

Pemberton needed cheering given the almost hopeless situation he was in. His army was trapped by a bigger force, it was being pummeled night and day by Union artillery, his supplies were running out, and his only hope was a decisive effort by Joseph E. Johnston. Consequently, as the days of the siege wore on, Pemberton became more and more despondent, first taking

Johnston's messages of attempting to help at face value but over time realizing that there was little hope of Johnston ever doing anything. His messages, Pemberton noted, eventually made it "painfully apparent" that Vicksburg was doomed.[69]

Pemberton was also worried about the constant danger even at the Willis House. It was actually hit by a shell on May 23 and then by two on May 30, killing two horses on the street in front of the house; Pemberton and his staff took to a nearby cave for safety. As the bombardment became worse and the need for additional hospital space grew, Pemberton ordered that he and Stevenson, who also had headquarters there, move so that the structures could be used for hospitals. He ordered on June 17 that "the house now used as offices by himself and Genl. Stevenson shall be taken for hospitals" and that his staff find alternate quarters. There is no record of Pemberton actually moving out, however, or of the house on Crawford Street being used as a hospital, so he may have changed his mind shortly thereafter. Nevertheless, he did order several days later that two more "dug-outs" be made, so he and his staff conceivably spent some of their time underground during the most intense bombardments.[70]

Meanwhile, Pemberton's supplies and resources inside Vicksburg became critical, and he kept a constant and worried eye on their levels. Water was a big issue, and the policy of throwing dead animals into the river was, amazingly, continued so that the river became filthy. There were many cisterns in the city, but one Confederate complained directly to Pemberton that officers had taken them over and "from which the private soldier is driven, as if he were a mere dog." Pemberton took up for the civilians in Vicksburg, never declaring martial law, stating that if the soldiers drank it all "no citizen would have sufficient water for his family." He added—perhaps showing his loss of reality—that the Mississippi River "has always been considered excellent water." Pemberton also became involved in a dispute when "Mrs. Cisco's" cow was killed for beef at the city hospital, ordering restitution be given her.[71]

Food was also critical, and it became more and more obvious as the days went by. Pemberton's experiment with the pea bread did not work, and ultimately mule meat became an option. But the number of mules and horses, and even cattle, inside Vicksburg was a mixed blessing, as they had to be fed until killed and eaten. Pemberton devised a plan to drive them outside his lines to be rid of the food-consumers, but one Federal remarked how "several times have the rebels essayed to drive large droves of horses, mules, cattle

&c. into our lines, but each time they have been driven back by our shells. They don't want to feed them and yet don't want them to die in the town—so says Rumor."[72]

Ammunition was also critical. Pemberton had his troops early on in the siege raid the dead and wounded Federals to gather all ammunition and caps they could, "paying particular attention to the percussion caps." There was a foundry in Vicksburg—A. M. Paxton's Foundry—which continued to work most of the siege, as plenty of coal was on hand; Pemberton even provided rations for its workers. Many shells fired into Vicksburg were gathered and taken to the foundry to be recast into shells for the Confederate army, although artillery fire from the Confederate works grew less and less as the siege wore on. Ultimately, with Union guns set up across the river, the foundry near the riverbank and near the railroad depot was soon out of action. Even getting the ammunition to the front became a constant and tiring issue, Pemberton ordering the ordnance department to keep two sets of horses for each wagon, "one to graze in the day, the other at night."[73]

Manpower was also a concern for Pemberton, especially with large numbers of his army in the hospitals. Morale began to fade and dissolution turned to despair, prompting some Confederates to desert. Many made their way across the lines on land, giving themselves up to whomever would take them, and it even occurred on the river as well. Colonel Edward Higgins kept out picket boats on the river, and some of the men deserted, prompting Higgins to have to change the signals used to communicate. Pemberton ordered that the "River Police" arrest anyone trying to take "possession of a boat."[74]

It was a deteriorating situation to say the least, but Pemberton did the best he could, juggling water, food, and ammunition stores, weighing using what was needed against what should be held in reserve for worse times. There was obviously no need to have large stores left in reserve at the end, but using up what was available too fast might bring on the end too soon. Not knowing when the end would come made the consumption of supplies a moving target. It was a fine line to walk to be sure, and Pemberton did the best he could.[75]

Fortunately, Pemberton had help, his four division commanders and their brigade commanders often being tapped for advice by a general who was so unsure of himself that he was renowned for calling councils of war. In addition, Pemberton had his personal and army staff, on which Carter Stevenson also served; Stevenson supervised the "subsistence of the troops."

Pemberton's chief of staff, Major R. W. Memminger, was a solid sounding board, and his main scribes served as assistant adjutant generals, including Captain William H. McCardle and 2nd Lieutenant F. M. Stafford. Chiefs of various departments such as Major L. Mims (quartermaster), Major Samuel Lockett (engineering), Major Theo Johnston (subsistence), Major George L. Gillespie (commissary), and Surgeon E. H. Bryan (medical) all led their departments faithfully. Brigadier General Thomas H. Taylor served as inspector general, and Colonel Louis M. Montgomery, on his way to his station in the trans-Mississippi but cut off at Vicksburg, served as a volunteer aide. Former cabinet official Jacob Thompson also served on the staff. These staff officers kept a firm grip on what was happening on the front lines and in the city and informed their commander of the goings-on. Pemberton also utilized larger entities. He used a portion of the 7th Tennessee Cavalry as couriers inside Vicksburg, and bands also often played at his headquarters on Crawford Street, much to his delight. Pemberton rode out to the lines on occasion, at times reviewing the troops with the division commanders. He also watched the naval action from the high bluffs along the river.[76]

Pemberton wielded a firm hand when needed, such as placing officers under arrest and holding courts-martial. He even held one artillery captain under arrest, but he, as well as others, was finally released, Pemberton needing all the troops he could muster. At one point Pemberton even ordered the release of a surgeon, writing that "the demand for the services of all the Surgeons is so great at present that none can be dispensed with." Ultimately, Pemberton even went so far as to impress Vicksburg citizens into service as teamsters, thereby releasing soldiers for the front lines. He also attempted to solidify the morale of his troops by sending out memos congratulating certain ones on occasion. More often than not, however, doing so he created more problems than he solved when others took offense at not being included or for the wordage. Division commander John Forney, for instance, complained, "I am confident that it is not necessary to mention my troops . . . to ensure their doing their duty." Often, Pemberton had to recall his original memos before any more damage could be done. He soon found it much better to send out army-wide memos of hope when he received word of Johnston's preparations to the east. Louis Montgomery on his staff worked in the newspaper editing industry beforehand, and he proved helpful.[77]

John C. Pemberton thus oversaw a declining situation from his palatial

Crawford Street headquarters. Unfortunately, the overall situation was not befitting such a grand mansion, and the developing results were not either.

One of the wishes Pemberton had at his downtown headquarters was for outside help. That seemed as time went on to become a fainter and fainter hope. Johnston showed little desire to help, but there was some movement, ironically, across the Mississippi River. The problem was that, in the Confederate military departmental system, the trans-Mississippi was a separate department outside the jurisdictions where Pemberton and Johnston were in command. Thus, any relief would have to be coordinated from Richmond. Even if that happened, there were pitifully too few troops in that department across the river to do much of any good. But unlike Johnston—east of the river where his actions really mattered—Confederates west of the river—who could achieve but little even if successful—actually tried to help, even fighting a battle as the second week of June rolled around.[78]

Action west of the Mississippi River was exactly what Ulysses S. Grant did not desire. As if all the issues that Grant let bother him were not enough, another major headache exploded in Louisiana on June 7. Grant had been heavily dependent on the Louisiana countryside during his initial operations, because all supplies had to move down the western side of the river and then across at Grand Gulf and then up to the army. This was the case until he opened up a new supply line at Chickasaw Bayou. Now that the line of communication was on the Yazoo River, the Louisiana side became much less important, but it still served major military purposes such as guarding the river, hospitals, and other necessities such as leased farms growing cotton for the government. There was little to do there initially, one Federal at Milliken's Bend writing to his wife that Vicksburg "is about fifteen miles from here and we can just hear enough of the guns to excite us." When the Confederates suddenly appeared and attacked one of the Union instillations, however, it was only another headache for Grant.[79]

Grant had left the area west of the Mississippi River under the command of Brigadier General Jeremiah C. Sullivan, and that was where most of the newly recruited African American regiments were stationed. In a day of rampant racism even within the Union and its armies, segregation and white supremacy were very much alive. One Indianan referred to the black troops as the "Wooley Brigade." In fact, these troops "of African descent" were segregated under their own commander, Brigadier General John P. Hawkins. A change in command soon occurred, however. Dana reported that Sullivan "has been relieved of command there for inertia," later describing him as "heavy, jovial, and lazy." Sullivan's replacement was Brigadier General Elias Dennis, whom Dana touted as "a hard headed, hard-working, conscientious man, who never knows when he is beaten, and consequently is very hard to beat."[80]

There had been some warning of a potential Confederate attack earlier, Sullivan worrying over "rumors of an attack on this place [Milliken's Bend]" as early as June 2. Sullivan assured Grant that he had ample force to hold all stations on the western bank of the river but could not move out and meet the enemy before they arrived. Obviously, naval gunboats in the river provided another layer of protection as well. Over the next week, Confederates showed up elsewhere, on June 3 with a minor attack at the Perkins Plantation on the river south of Vicksburg. The gunboat *Carondelet* fired into the Confederates and drove them back. Another foray near James's Plantation saw the Union commander there burn all his stores prematurely. Warnings continued to arrive, even as late as June 7, when a colonel at Grand Gulf warned Grant that Confederates were moving "up [the] Tensas, and that they intend to attack Milliken's Bend." He estimated the force at six to ten thousand strong.[81]

Confederates were indeed on the move, in part because of high-level planning between Johnston and Pemberton and the trans-Mississippi Confederate commander, Lieutenant General E. Kirby Smith. The latter ordered Major General Richard Taylor to aid Pemberton by attacking Grant's communications "between Young's Point and New Carthage." Taylor himself was opposing Nathaniel Banks farther south and was thus surprised to learn that "this line of transit had ceased to be of importance to the enemy," but he sent troops against it nevertheless. The job of attacking Grant's lines of communication fell to Major General John G. Walker and his Texas division.[82]

Walker moved forward through Richmond (Louisiana) and on June 6, after meeting a Federal reconnaissance, sent a brigade eastward to Young's Point and another northward toward Milliken's Bend, a third remaining in reserve miles to the rear. The brigade moving toward the Young's Point defenses, under Brigadier General James M. Hawes, approached on June 7 but was late, Taylor describing him as having "consumed seventeen hours in marching 19 miles over a good road without impediments." Hawes was delayed in finding a bridge over a river, but arriving late, he admitted that "I could not carry the camp and destroy the stores there without a useless sacrifice of life, [so] I determined to retire by the road I came."[83]

The main attack came at Milliken's Bend, where Brigadier General Henry E. McCullough's brigade of about fifteen hundred troops attacked through hedgerows against the Federals behind entrenchments and levees. He approached about daylight and moved forward over the morning hours until the heat of the day became oppressive, one soldier describing it as "95 degrees in the shade." The Confederates found the going tough, McCullough describing how "we encountered a thick hedge, which could not be passed except through a few gaps or breaches that had been made for gates and pass-ways." McCullough eventually attacked the Federals behind the levee and drove them to the river, but the gunboats *Choctaw* and later the *Lexington* stopped the advance, and McCullough's troops fled with 44 killed, 130 wounded, and 10 missing. McCullough blamed their actions on the men being "possessed of a dread of gunboats such as pervaded our people at the commencement of the war." The results were not kind for Hawes or McCullough. Hawes was cashiered, and Taylor described McCullough poorly: he "appears to have shown great personal bravery, but no capacity for handling masses."[84]

Part of the defending force of a thousand Federals were African American regiments, which McCullough admitted fought "with considerable obstinacy." Another Confederate described how they fought "with tiger like ferocity." Also there was the 23rd Iowa of Michael Lawler's brigade back at the entrenchments, which had been guarding prisoners of late. These infantry regiments held for a time, the white troops veterans of Big Black River Bridge while the blacks had no training in their arms, which were inferior. Both broke and fled under the repeated Confederate volleys and a flank attack. Still, they fought hand-to-hand for a time, the Confederates yelling "no quarter" and Colonel Kilby Smith—now out of brigade command and acting as Grant's roving eyes—declaring that the Confederates carried "a black flag bearing a death's head and cross-bones." Eventually, the naval gunboats stopped the Confederate advance, Dennis writing that the Southerners "immediately disappeared behind the levee." The action, especially the gunboats' big guns, could be heard all the way inside Vicksburg.[85]

The performance of the black troops received a lot of attention. "The darkies pitched in and gave the rebs a good thrashing," one Illinoisan reported. Another Federal wrote home that "the darkeys drove the rebs like a covey of quail." Dana added that "the negro troops at first gave way, but hearing that those of their number who were captured were killed, they rallied with great fury and routed the enemy." Grant himself gave praise to the black soldiers, writing the army's adjutant general Lorenzo Thomas that "in this battle most of the troops engaged were Africans, who had but little experience in the use of fire-arms. Their conduct is said, however, to have been most gallant, and I doubt not but with good officers they will make good troops." Admiral Porter, who sent the gunboats and followed in the *Black Hawk,* noted that the enemy "nearly gobbled up the whole party." The Confederates, he said, "commenced driving the negro regiments, and killed all they captured. This infuriated the Negroes, who turned on the rebels and slaughtered them like sheep." He added that the Confederates "got nothing but hard knocks."[86]

The affair, of course, became a heated racial incident, Porter describing how he saw "the dead negroes lined [up] in the ditch inside of the parapet, or levee, and were mostly shot on the top of the head." Another Federal labeled it "butchery." Others in the main army heard the commotion, one Missourian writing "reason not yet known." But once it became news, he added that "it gives me pleasure to hear the darkies had done so well." Even those who were racist in nature against the blacks admitted their good fighting: "The force was saved by the Gun Boats, but the fact remains that the blacks did fight, & well," one admitted. Yet it portended to him more trouble, because "if the blacks at Milliken's Bend did as represented[,] . . . they will soon in this climate become the Masters & uproot the whites." Others were just flat-out opposed to emancipation and abolition, although one admitted that he did not blame the blacks for fighting for their freedom. He did note, however, that he had no sympathy for the whites who served as officers in the black regiments: "I Dont care if the secesh get hold of them and hitches mules to them and pull them apart. But perhaps I am too wicked in this."[87]

Many others echoed the same about the contrabands' fighting ability and the racism they faced. One Wisconsin soldier managed to talk to a wounded former slave of the 9th Louisiana and reported that "I have made inquiries, and all agree that the Negroes fought bravely, and used the bayonet freely." He asked one if he had shot many times during the fighting, to which he replied "yes suh, I shot right smart, and I punched with my bayonet too." The white man asked in an astonished voice if he had killed a Confederate with his bayonet, to which the black man added "ho, yes suh, I'm sure I killed him for I put it clear plumb through him, and he just light over on his back, and I know he is done gone dead sure." Others were terribly prejudiced. One newly arrived Massachusetts officer admitted to his wife, "Unfortunately I must say that they are exceedingly dirty and one can hardly travel among their tents for the stench."[88]

Grant was shaken by the news and quickly ordered his mobile brigade at Haynes' Bluff under Joseph Mower west of the river to support Dennis, the brigade forming a line of battle on the levee in the days afterward as rumors of more attacks came in. The move was so quick that the brigade and the Chicago Light Artillery were awakened in the night and prepared to move. One of Mower's soldiers had just celebrated being back from Mechanicsburg, writing "how refreshing the breeze upon these hills, but how soon we must [be] away again." And the trip was no better; he described the "soldiers and cattle piled up together." Grant made sure Dennis realized the brigade was "merely for temporary service," but he added that if more troops were needed in the meantime he would gladly send them. Grant wanted the area west of the river secured, talking of "driv[ing] the enemy beyond the Tensas River" and even that "our troops should push on to Monroe." More Confederates lingered all the while, disrupting the work on the leased plantations and capturing slaves. A smaller force also attacked at Lake Providence on June 9, Union brigade commander Brigadier General Hugh T. Reid describing how, by putting "on a bold front, I made the rebels believe the other day that I had four full regiments by drawing my forces up in one rank and dividing the six companies of the Eighth Louisiana into two battalions, which showed quite an extended front."[89]

Grant wanted no further conflict on the other side of the river, and because of "present danger of attack upon your command" he ultimately ordered protection of the public stores at Young's Point, Milliken's Bend, and Lake Providence. He also gave specific information about how to handle the troops where most of the black regiments were located. While reminding Dennis to send Mower back "as soon as the emergency ceases," Grant told Dennis to keep "the black troops . . . as much to themselves as possible, and required to fortify." He later elaborated that "Negro troops should be kept aloof from white troops, especially in their camps, as much as possible. Wherever the movements of the enemy require a concentration of your forces, bring them together without regard to color."[90]

The area west of the river soon settled down again, the troops going into camps and watching for more signs of activity. Times became so calm, in fact, that the 11th Missouri of Mower's brigade took time to drum out a coward from camp. "The boys said he was a coward and they did not want him in the regiment," an amazed Wisconsin soldier in the brigade reported to his diary, and they drummed him out on a rail with the fifes and drums playing "The Rouge's March." They took him a mile out and left him in a swamp. Still, Mower's Federals had to be watchful, as intelligence soon confirmed that it was John G. Walker's Confederate division that had attacked, with some seven or eight thousand troops. Yet only minor skirmishing, including a Union foray into the inland areas to Richmond under Joseph Mower and Alfred Ellet's Marine Brigade—which Dana ironically described as "a very useless as well as a very costly institution"—took place thereafter. Little fighting occurred, although Richmond itself ceased to exist. Once back, one of Mower's Missourians noted he caught up on his letter-writing, "yet it is not labor when compared with the long weary march through the hot sultry days of summer in a climate like this."[91]

Still, Dennis and his subordinates watched carefully, including Hugh T. Reid, who begged for "a good regiment or two of white men, with some artillery." Reid was confident nevertheless, writing that he could hold at Lake Providence until Vicksburg fell: "All Southwestern rebeldom will submit, I think, when that is done."[92]

8

"THE MOST MISERABLE PLACE WE HAVE EVER BEEN IN"

June 10–11

The Siege of Vicksburg was an inherently individual experience for all involved in it. Despite being surrounded by thousands of soldiers and civilians on each side, each human being caught up in the process had at least in some ways to face their days and nights as best they could alone, with their individual well-being at heart. Certainly, soldiers held their comradeship in high esteem, and civilians cared for friends and family members, but in terms of the basic necessitates of life each had to care for themselves for food, clothing, and shelter. The loneliness brought about by being away from home, suffering immensely, or continually being under the threat of death or maiming only added to the individualism felt during the siege of Vicksburg. Perhaps that is why so many confided their inner thoughts to diaries or journals and in letters to loved ones they were missing back home. These letters and diaries reflected inner thoughts and even at times larger happenings, but mostly—certainly from lower-level ranks—only with very limited scopes. "I have no knowledge of what is going on in this siege," admitted Indianan Louis Knobe, "as no man has but little opportunity of seeing any more of the proceedings that is going on only as far as his own brigade extends consequently I only endeavor to take a slight sketch of the progress and proceedings in our front as far as the lines of the 1st Brigade." Thus, rarely do these contemporary accounts from the lower ranks give the larger picture.[1]

That said, some specific times and events were shared by the larger whole as a group, even if bearing them was done on an individual level. There were a certain few events that transcended rank, space, side, gender, wealth, civilian or military status, or any other circumstance. For instance, almost everyone who left accounts—from the lowliest privates to the highest generals as well as the civilians inside and around Vicksburg—described in some way the assaults on the city. Most also described in some fashion the sinking of the *Cincinnati* on May 27. Other overarching events that gained almost comprehensive coverage included a massive fire inside Vicksburg, the truce to bury the dead on May 25, as well as major bombardments on particular days and even the continual shelling of the city by the mortar boats. Concerning the latter, numerous accounts described in similar fashion the rising of the shells in the dark nighttime sky, the parabolic flight path, the explosion, and the eventual low booming of the detonation.[2]

One such event that caught up almost everyone, except perhaps those inside cover in Vicksburg, was a massive weather front that moved through the area beginning on June 10 and continuing on June 11. This storm system that brought heavy rains on that Wednesday and more of the same early on Thursday affected everyone caught outdoors, and that meant practically everyone in both armies as well as civilians to a lesser extent in caves and even within frame structures. Even the naval personnel were affected. Storms came through fairly often during the weeks of the Vicksburg siege, with rain falling in fairly large amounts on May 23 and 29–30 and June 21 and 23, but the June 10–11 storm was by far more extended than anything these soldiers had seen recently.[3]

The skies gave evidence of what was coming to those who could get a look at the vast panorama west of Vicksburg. Situated as they were high on the bluffs overlooking the Mississippi River, anyone could look out over the valley and the vast Delta flatland in Louisiana and see storm systems coming from the west. Thunder and lightning the closer it came also gave warning. "Early this AM by the deep mutterings of the thunder we knew the storm was not far away & everybody was busy fixing up their traps to keep them dry," remembered one Federal. A Confederate described "heavy lightening last night in northeast—and this morning a very heavy rain." Some even noted how there had been lightning for several weeks but that it had not rained as yet.[4]

The storm itself was not long in arriving with heavy wind and torrential rain, and it had its dreaded effect on the defending Confederates inside Vicksburg. "A hard rain is suspending firing," one Louisianan wrote. "Our pits a perfect mudhole—awful time! Looks like it would rain for a week." The monsoon indeed came, although it slackened in the afternoon before another round moved through around dark on June 10. There was not much to do in response, one writing how he "covered over head & ears & took a soldier's unquiet rest." At least one Confederate was ready when more rains came. He and his comrades covered "12 feet of pits with wood covered with dirt. Have my bed inside of the ditch."[5]

The sudden downpour of heavy rain completely overpowered the defenses of Vicksburg, something the Federal armies had not yet been able to do. "The drainage to our ditches not being good," Alabamian Elbert Willett wrote in his diary, "the ditch overflowed." A Mississippian described how "it is very muddy and disagreeable in the trenches," and another added how "it rained so hard that many of the cooks' helpers had to swim. Blankets, knapsacks, clothing, and everything that was on the ground was floating." Perhaps of most concern were the already pummeled and loose fortifications. Certainly, the undisturbed loess soil kept its structure even when dug out or cut into, but the fortifications at Vicksburg were by definition moved earth and had been subjected now to weeks of bombardment and trampling, causing it to erode quickly. "Many of the intrenchments caved in," wrote one Texan, and "others were full of water." Still, the Confederates manned their works, fearful of an enemy advance during the storm. One Confederate admitted that "a wetter, dirtier, muddier, lot of rebels were never seen," adding "but we kept our powder dry."[6]

The storm was no respecter of rank either. One Confederate colonel slept too long and was caught up in the flash flood of rushing waters through his camp. One of his men described, no doubt with some glee, how the colonel bobbed "through all barriers, enveloping him completely in mud, water, sand, and sediment." He described how the colonel "sprang from the ground in a towering rage, and could scarcely be persuaded that he was not the victim of a practical joke."[7]

If the storms did not respect rank, neither did they respect side. Many Federals seemed to be amazed at the ferocity of the storms and the rain they produced. Certainly, these Northern boys had seen their share of storms and hard rains on the plains and open extents of the upper Midwest, but many reflected on the monumental proportions here at Vicksburg. One Iowan was amazed at the thunder, writing how "'heaven's dread artillery' put ours to shame." Indianan George Rogers described how "it poured down in torrents reminding us of the days of Noah." Wisconsin native H. H. Bennett explained that it was "the most rain fall in the time I think that any of us ever saw."[8]

Many tried to take cover, an Indianan noting he "spent the evening in the Cotton gin," but most had to simply endure it. "I get drove out of my (shanty) by the hard rain," explained one Illinoisan, "also my self drowndedin' wet." Others were similarly caught while moving camps or having just resettled into new sites. The established camps suffered greatly as well, most being situated in ravines sheltered from Confederate fire but therefore susceptible to flash-flooding. A Union artilleryman in Lauman's division described how the little creek at their camp in the ravine, dry most of the time, caused "a most unlooked for and sudden flood." The creek "overflowed its banks and covered the whole hollow." He noted the "3d Iowa boys were routed out first, some of them without their clothes." Sutlers lost their goods, and a lot of equipment, including medical supplies, was carried downstream but later located.[9]

Others attested to similar experiences in their own camps as the floodwaters washed away everything loose, including kettles, pans, and other items. Unfortunately, the water did not recede as quickly and kept the camps flooded. Brigade commander James Slack noted the water was around a foot deep in his tent: "I had to wade out." One soldier reported water two feet deep in the camp of the 48th Indiana. Cave-ins also occurred in the Union camps, one in the 8th Illinois nearly covering three men. "One little Dutchman" brought a laugh when he commented dryly, "T'was a mity coot ting' that wan of 'em had 'is 'ed out so's he could holler."[10]

Those in the rear were not immune either, the weather front covering a large area. The heavy rainfall damaged some of the works at Haynes' Bluff. One Federal in Kimball's division in the rear described the "grand retreat from Dress Parade caused by a rain storm, great confusion of Officers, for fear they would get their uniforms wet." The 4th Iowa Cavalry was out scouting all day, one noting "boys done some swearing over it." The heavy rains came right as portions of Mower's troops, who remained in the rear and then moved across the Mississippi River, were making their camps. Johnston's Confederates suffered also, as hail was reported on his front.[11]

Still, the torrential rains did not stop all progress, although Charles Dana reported to Washington that "the siege works have been checked for twenty-four hours by violent storms, but were resumed yesterday." One Federal noted "sharp Shooters working away lively between showers." And there was some good that came of it. While miserable in the midst of the storm, others found positive benefits such as laying the dust, cooling the weather, and providing fresh water, one Federal officer even going so far to say it "was enjoyed by all." The rains also filled the cisterns and wells, and the cold front brought much cooler temperatures for the next week or so. "A heavy rain in the morning and at night making it more cool and pleasant," one Confederate jotted in his diary, and many others wrote similar tidings. Another noted as much as a week later that "since the rain the weather has not been so unbearably warm as before." One Illinoisan humorously predicted snow was coming.[12]

Despite the good effects, it was a miserable time that affected everyone the same, regardless of rank, side, or wealth. And for many, it added a bit of depression to those already individually confronting their own issues such as isolation or homesickness. One Federal wrote how he "took shelter under our blankets. Did not work. Pretty tiresome setting in the rain waiting for it to stop." Another Illinoisan admitted "its rather inclined to be a lonely day."[13]

D espite the same overall issues of environment and psyche, individual life in the Union camps was very different than in the Confederate works. "It is hard perhaps for a person to understand *what* we are *doing* here, but every day brings some new advantage to us," reported an upbeat Illinoisan. An Indianan added that they were sure of victory and that made all the difference: "This army don't know what defeat means."[14]

Still, these besieging Federals faced many of the same challenges their Confederate counterparts did, and in some cases such as the heat, it was worse on them simply because they were not as used to it, being from higher latitudes. One described how his regiment was camped in "one of the little narrow gulches . . . being down in those deep ravines the sun pours down on us powerful hot." He concluded that this was "the most miserable place we have ever been in." Attendant to the heat and dryness, of course, was the dust, which one said was "one to four inches deep." Another put it into larger context, coming as they were off a tiring campaign, writing how "this past month has been the hardest I have seen since I have been in the service. The intolerable heat and dust has almost made me sick."[15]

Many of the Federals used hyperbole to express their feelings on the weather. One declared it was "about 300 [degrees] in the shade." He later stated, "I am on the verge of melting down and running off in gravy." Another agreed that "the weather is very warm and we almost melt laying here on the hillside." Missourian Richard Burt made a play on words about the heat: "It is very hot here in more ways than one—the bullets cannon balls and shells not only make warm times, but old Sol comes down so heavy on us that we have to keep in the shade as much as possible." He reported much firing in the mornings and evenings, but less in the heat of the day. John Merrilees used no exaggeration, simply writing how "the weather is so hot that a man feels languid and good for nothing—no appetite, no life, no ambition."[16]

Some gave actual numbers, Colonel Marcus Spiegel of the 120th Ohio writing home, "I do not like this hot weather here quite as well as I might. The heat is never under 88 degrees and often as high as 92 in the shade." And that was only in early June. Another later wrote that "weather is hot; thermometer at 95 degrees. The springs from which we get water are becoming bad. They are full of lime from destroyed shells." The highest temperature mentioned was "103° in the shade." Fortunately, regulations were dispensed with in many ways, one writing home wanting shirts with pockets: "I have heard tell of pockets in shirts and now I would like to have one or two in my shirts for it is too hot to ware a coat."[17]

Unlike the Confederates who were forced to live mostly in the trenches or very close nearby, the Federals had the luxury of placing their camps far to the rear behind ridges and in covered ravines for protection. But these were not always the best spots, as the bottoms could be hot and also susceptible to flooding, such as on June 10–11; one Federal wished they could "camp on the hills where we could have purer air." Yet camping on the ridgetops would put the men in the line of fire, so the slopes of the ridges were the best spots—preferably on the slope closest to the Confederates so arching shells or bullets would not hit them. There, balls passed mostly overhead, unless one hit the earthworks and spent its force, bringing it into camp. Some of these still had force enough to kill, one Illinoisan describing how "one came bouncing along past me this morning." He noted that there were few casualties in such a covered position and that "most of these seem to happen through sheer carelessness on the part of the men who are struck."[18]

The Federals mostly placed their camps on the sides of the hills, which in and of itself took some digging to create level areas tucked into the slopes. "We are reposing on a hillside 75 yards behind the Peoria Battery (Davidson's) each soldier sitting or lying in a little dugout nich," one Illinoisan explained. Another declared that "when I first came here I had to tie myself fast when I laid myself down to sleep to keep from rolling down hill but now

I have a hole dug into the ground." Once a level area took form, the men built any type of shelter or arbor they could, often terming them "shebangs" or "brush quarters" on the sides of hills—"making shades out of cane," one Illinoisan wrote. Another explained that "we dig in the hillside and put some cane over it." One described his as "our coops which are made about like a shed for a dog house. Cane leaves for head and roof of about 3 ft. high."[19]

Sometimes the units gained especially good campsites, such as the 15th Illinois in late May. "An hour's march brought us into a man's vegetable garden, where we pitched our tents, much to the injury of the green stuff." Even better, he noted, was that "the men found Irish potatoes as large as hen's eggs here." They also found Confederate uniforms hidden in cottonseed, and he related that "Rebel clothes are cheap in camp today." Another told how "our food and water are wholesome and we have a good dry atmosphere. The camp rules for cleanliness are pretty well enforced but the air does not stir quite as much as it ought to for purity in the camp. . . . We make our quarters in the middle and on the west sides of the ravines." Division commander Alvin Hovey described the ease after the men made "Shady Arbors" and "shebangs of green cane." Those off duty could thus "recline at our ease in the Shade" and listen to the sharpshooting and bombardment. "We would listen to them with a smile of grim satisfaction knowing at the time that each one of the messengers were writing a small history of its own in the reduction of Vicksburg."[20]

The absence of personal items made the camping situation more difficult at first. When Grant left his camps around Young's Point and Milliken's Bend in March and April, the troops took only what they could carry. Consequently, tents, cooking utensils, knapsacks, and other personal items needed in camp were left behind. They arrived only in a trickle. Knapsacks left behind arrived for the 93rd Illinois on June 4. Others arrived about the same time, most straggling in from late May onward. Tents came up throughout June, one Wisconsin soldier writing that once theirs finally arrived in mid-June they had been forty-three days without them.[21]

One of the more unfortunate soldiers wrote that "we have not received our knapsacks yet, so you may imagine how we feel, after rolling around in the dirt for a month without a change of clothing." One Iowa unit waited until June 19 to get their knapsacks. Some put a positive spin on things, however, writing that "we have not seen our tents for a long time and have got use to living without them and don't miss them now." Still, when they did come up it was a joyous time: "[Now] we are well fixed for comfortable living."[22]

New clothing was also issued on occasion, although not everyone received what they needed at the time they needed it. One Federal bemoaned the fact that he was barefooted because "no shoes or boots ever comes here large enough for me, or at least I have been unable to find any so far but thank God I can soldier barefooted in this climate as well as our old revolutionary soldiers did during the memorable war in a northern climate." He added: "I think I can face the music eleven months more and then fight copper heads three years more in Ill. I had rather shoot one of them any time than a dozen good honest secesh soldiers down here in Dixie."[23]

The arrival of clean clothes rivaled the ability to take a bath in popularity: "A good bath today which was enjoyed," one Illinoisan admitted. Most got the chance at some point to go to the rear and clean up: "We retired as before nearly two miles to the rear to bathe and wash clothes." Many washed in the Mississippi or Yazoo Rivers, one Illinois artilleryman, Charles Affeld, explaining that "a good wash makes one feel 50% better." Calvin Ainsworth of the 25th Iowa, positioned near Mint Spring Bayou, described how "there is a small stream of water on one of the side hills that falls about 15 feet on a solid rock floor." He added that "we get under it and have a fine bath." One Illinoisan when he got a break noted that "last night is the first time that I slept with my pants off for nearly 3 months."[24]

Other morale-boosters also arrived throughout the siege, such as Captain Allen C. Waterhouse's Illinois Battery giving up their Parrott rifles for brand-new Napoleons. New flags arrived for the 23rd Wisconsin: "They have the picture of the badger and the eagle." The colonel of the 4th West Virginia was not so excited when Illinoisans presented him with his regiment's flag lost in the May 22 assaults. The 113th Illinois found the flag as they steadily progressed forward and retrieved it under fire, later taking it to the Virginia colonel's tent when off-duty. John Kellogg gave a short speech that he thought included "well chosen remarks" but ended with "take back your flag colonel, and next time when you are in battle hang on to it." The colonel snatched the flag away and "turning very red in the face . . . and without thanking us even, vanished into the bowels of his tent." The Illinoisans decided they would leave it out there next time.[25]

While the common soldiers made the best of their camping situations, the generals' headquarters were much better stocked. One of McClernand's staff officers wrote of his: "My tent is reasonably well furnished. I have a carpet and a rocking chair (both doubtless plundered from some Secesh house), a bed and another chair, and what more can a man, fighting, bleeding and dying for his country, desire[?]" He added later, "Our table is passable only for a Major General—reasonably good for a Lieut. Colonel." Similarly, a brigade commander improved his camping arrangements with a rocking chair taken from a nearby home, as well as a cow that gave nice milk every day: "We have captured a very nice cow that gives us three or four quarts at a milking." Another noted he and his comrades had three cows they were milking, providing enough milk to give away to friends as well.[26]

Union camp life during the siege seemed to be laid back, perhaps a tenor gleaned from the army commander himself. Following Grant's example, many officers eased up on regulations and did not require full dress. One brigadier general wrote that "I wear, no collar, a loose linen coat & my old white hat—This is my regular dress; and no one could guess that I was an officer by seeing me riding along or in the discharge of my ordinary duties." Still there were troubles, such as one Federal who declared they had no tents throughout the siege and dug a well in rear but had to guard it constantly because "other men would take it all from us." John J. Kellogg told of building for half a day a "cane palace," only to have it wrecked by a Confederate shell.[27]

While few Confederates had any off-duty time, Federals opposite them managed to find some, but not a lot given the needs of digging, sharpshooting, guarding, and sundry other tasks. Yet these Northerners managed to wile away their time in many different ways, some odd in themselves. One Illinoisan described how "I have made a curious collection of bombshell fragments, grape and battered bullets which the rebs have been so long flinging over our heads." There was also entertainment often in camp, such as the singing brothers from Chicago. One Illinoisan described watching "a slight of hand performance at which I saw seemingly whole rings put together so that two men pulled on them with all their might and did not move them." He also mentioned a "magic paper and its copper trick."[28]

Others mentioned reading quite a lot, some the Bible and others more secular books. "Marion is reading some works on Physiology," one Federal wrote to his wife. Another who lost most of his books in the campaigning lamented to the point that "I would rather have lost my money than those books." Illinois artilleryman Charles Affeld had quite a collection of books that his transportation enabled him to carry, including Shakespeare and Washington Irving's five-volume biography of George Washington. Illinoisan Bela T. St. John described reading *The Last of the Mohicans*. Brigade commander

Mortimer Leggett read *Don Quixote*, and according to his son who tagged along much like Fred Grant, he "appears to enjoy it pretty well for every once in a time, he commences to laugh, puts his feet up on the trunk, laughs again, and takes them down, thereby impressing upon his mind more firmly." Also, newspapers and magazines such as *The Atlantic* were readily consumed. Most papers cost twenty-five cents.[29]

Others found additional ways to spend their time, one even recording his regiment's action in poem and another practicing his shorthand in his spare time. Some had photos taken, one Grant look-alike explaining to his wife of the similarity: "Looks and acts like an old farmer." He added, "I passed it off to a good many yesterday for a first rate picture of Gen. Grant." Charles W. Beal of the 11th Illinois adopted a dog and named him Pemberton.[30]

Those on the rear Union lines seemed to have more spare time than soldiers on the lines at Vicksburg itself. Colonel Marcus Spiegel back at the Big Black River enjoyed showing pictures of his children to other officers, including his fellow German division commander Peter Osterhaus. He even had time to return back to the Vicksburg lines on a visit but stated, "I must confess that the place looks no nearer taken than it did when we left." Lieutenant Colonel Oran Perry of the 69th Indiana wiled away his days playing on a piano. One of his soldiers wrote in his diary, "He is pretty good at playing for he has a large nice Piano which General Osterhaus gave him." It had been taken from a "large fine mansion" whose secession inhabitants had left. An Illinois cavalryman with Osterhaus similarly reported a lot of laying around in camp, although some of the time was spent shoeing horses.[31]

Just like inside Vicksburg, the most critical need was good water, and campsites both at Vicksburg and in the rear were normally chosen based on its availability. The 16th Iowa camped originally in one place, but "this camp proved unhealthy, and on the 12th we were moved about a mile farther back to better quarters," one soldier explained. An Iowan described how his regiment "leveled the side hill to form sleeping places and built shades of canes from the brakes near by," all just to be near water.[32]

Sometimes water could not be had nearby, a few regiments having to carry it over a mile. Others had to nearly fight for it, the closest spring being between the contending lines. The 12th Iowa's water came from one such spring: "The approach to the water was within range and in plain view of the enemy's sharpshooters, and any one going for water in daylight had to run the gauntlet of their fire. Drinking water was therefore at a premium, and was sold in camp at 25 cents a canteen." When it came to it, some dug their own wells; in the 81st Illinois, each company dug their own, most "about eight feet deep." Still others had to beg and accept anything they could find, including water that "horses refused to drink."[33]

Dana described the water situation on May 26: "It is an incomparable position as regards the health and comfort of our men. These high, wooded hills afford pure air and shade, the deep ravines abound in springs of excellent water, and if they should fail it can easily be brought from the Mississippi." He changed his tune later as the full summer came on, on June 16 writing that "the days here are hot, thermometer sometimes rising to ninety at noon, but the nights are very cool. Showers have laid the dust for a week past. The army has hitherto got water from springs in the ravines, but this source is running out. Some brigades are digging wells; others haul water from distance." Ohioan Osborn Oldroyd agreed, writing that, as it got drier in the summer, water became more limited. He told of how "water is becoming very scarce, for the branches which we have to depend upon have now stopped running, and all we can get is the water left in the sink holes in the creek bottom."[34]

Food was another major need, but clearly the Federals ate much better than their Confederate counterparts. Obviously, that was because Grant had a solid and secure supply line north by water, delivering boatloads of food and provisions to the Chickasaw Bayou landings throughout the siege. Army fare was also augmented from sutlers and goodies sent in boxes from home.[35]

Union soldiers related a smorgasbord of food they had, much of it such as hardtack and meat issued by commissaries, but the real luxuries were the local natural fruit and wildlife. Soldiers gathered wild plums and blackberries, one explaining that he "had Plum Sauce and Blackberries and sugar for Supper." Another related how he had "black berries, bakers bread and condensed milk for tea and coffee. Too good for a soldier." There were so many blackberries that some made a business out of selling them.[36]

Others fished, one catching a forty-eight-pounder. Many caught and ate catfish, and extras were sold, one that weighed fifteen pounds bringing a dollar and a quarter. Other natural foods were sought out as well. Ohioan John Griffith explained how he "cut a large tree" for bees. In the end, he got very little honey and concluded that it "didn't pay." Beef from the commissary or caught from the local civilians was also routinely slaughtered. One Wisconsin soldier described how "my boys killed a fine steer this evening. He was captured by some of them while on picket, he came along without the countersign and on trial was condemned as a spy and according to the law of nations his life was forfeited on the gallows but the boys were merciful & shot him." Oxen were also slaughtered and eaten. In all, an Illinoisan admitted he was "getting fat again, since we have stopped marching." Another wrote to his family, "No doubt our fare is better than you have at home."[37]

Some units hired contrabands to cook, one Illinoisan admitting "the boys are getting tired of doing cooking." The commissary in the 45th Illinois had the great idea to cook all rations in the rear and send them to the front. A "regimental mess" soon emerged, with the paid servants doing the cooking and transporting the victuals in what became known as the "black brigade." It caught on so well that Logan ordered it copied in every regiment in the division.[38]

That said, there were occasional gaps in the provisions, and some grumbled about a lack of food, especially on the outlying lines. A major need was vegetables, one surgeon predicting "they will all die with the scurvy. There are now several slight cases." One artilleryman had a confirmed case, it starting with "a very sore mouth," the doctor telling him to eat more vegetables. Drawing such sustenance was rare, but troops did so on occasion. Unfortunately, the major crops in the area were not necessarily of the vegetable variety, with the exception of corn.[39]

Still, the Union camps were dangerous places, and a soldier could certainly be killed in the relative safety of his camp. A member of the 81st Illinois took a bullet "in camp while eating his dinner," one of his comrades lamented. He died later in a Memphis hospital and was "the first man in Co. 'B' that was killed by a bullet." One Federal described the physics of how the camps were dangerous, writing that "there was one Rebel gun that would sometimes send a shot whose force would be so nearly spent as to drop at about the same degree as the slope of the hill." He added that "this gun beheaded two in our camp." Shells constantly went through tents, one even through brigade commander John D. Stevenson's, and some died as a result. One shell hit in front of an Ohioan's tent, and "when it bursted it nearly buried the tent with dirt." Another hit a meal group, but oddly none were injured. Some of the determined fire came from "Whistling Dick," and as the fire slowed over the weeks the same Ohioan mused that the Confederates were running out of ammunition: "I guess Whistling Dick has run out of fodder." Perhaps the most famed casualty of this kind was Captain Samuel De Golyer of the 8th Michigan Battery. A Confederate bullet hit him in the thigh as he lounged in his tent reading a newspaper; he died a couple of months later. One Iowan nevertheless declared "it was safer in camp than in the ravine below, where the bullets deflected to the ground."[40] An Iowan told of one such dangerous shot that came through camp: It "went through the Colonel's tent, hit the corner of a cracker box and passed out under the colonel's horse. A sick nigger in the tent came out on all fours, he was too frightened to stand up, he looked wild, and he was the whitest black nigger I ever saw. A dog bounded after him yelping from fright and the colonel's horse was trying to see how high he could kick with both feet. When I got through laughing I got behind a rock."[41]

Danger in the camps did not only come from the enemy in front of these Federals or the lack of good food and water out in the wilderness of Mississippi, but also from the local environment. "The variety of bugs here would astonish you," one brigade commander wrote home to his wife; "at night my tent is full of all kinds of bugs, insects, spiders &c." Another wrote home, "I can hardly write a single word without having to stop and knock a bug off of my face or neck. There is as many as a hundred in the tent now flying around." An Iowan declared that each soldier had a thousand comrades, "five hundred mosquitoes, three hundred gray-backs, one hundred and one ants, and the other ninety-nine just 'plain bugs.'"[42]

Some were vicious little creatures despite not being potentially fatal. One Federal especially noted that "I am covered all over my body with large red lumps occasioned by the bite of some kind of bug—said to be the 'jigger.' The bumps itch me very much & make me feel very uncomfortably." He added, "We are all suffering from its depredations." These chiggers, or red bugs, were indeed pesky and painful but harmless; one Illinoisan described them as "a minute little red insect and inflict a sting worse than the bite of a mosquito. They are decidedly an institution hereabouts."[43]

Lice was also one of the major opponents. One Iowan declared that the trenches were "regular flea-holes in hot weather." Much of it was a result of dirtiness due to a lack of changing clothes; brigade commander John E. Smith wrote to his wife, "I wish the job was over so that I could get clean clothes. I had no chance to change my clothing but once in 27 days, think of that." Another wrote, "We felt pretty dirty and lousy too, as we had not had a clean stitch of anything to put on for more than six weeks, and we were covered with graybacks, as we had not had any chance to clean up for the last two and a half months, not even to pick them off." He continued: "Sometimes we were not able to get water enough to wash our faces for two weeks at a time, and other times some of our trench did not have outlets and when it rained we had to take our caps and bail the water out with them so we could stay in them[.] We were a miserable looking set, I doubt if our own Mothers would have recognized us if they saw us then."[44]

One Federal almost died as a result of the invasive bugs. This soldier, "whose extreme sense of modesty probably wouldn't allow him to make an inspection of his nether garment 'before folks,'" tried to get to a place where he could not be seen, only to be in view of Confederates, who allowed him to continue until he killed a lice and stood up in satisfaction. Bullets peppered the area, and he sprinted toward the Federal lines. One watching noted that "instead of being shot through a vital part as he deserved, [he] escap[ed] with just the loss of the nail and point of his little finger!"[45]

Mosquitoes were also a nuisance that literally pained the Federals, who had a lot of fun describing them. An Iowan declared that you could "swing a pint-cup and catch a quart." One referred to "birds called mosquitoes. They are so thick that we can stir them with a stick." Another described mosquitoes "with bills as long as a knitting needle." One even vaulted the fight against them up to common warfare: "We were attacked about six o'clock by a strong force not of Rebels but of Mosquitoes for a time we thought we were defeated but a smudge of smoke both in front and rear soon drove them off but not until we were badly bitten by them."[46] Richard A. Hall took his hyperbole to extremes in describing the mosquitoes. He declared to his parents that they were "big as bats," and he described one that "came into My tent & Attacked me. he grabed me By the throat & Began to knaw me, I got up jumpt at my revolver And shot him through the head But did not fase him. So he Esscaped carrying with him my Boots, hat, & 5.000 doll. In Green Backs."[47]

Larger critters were also a danger, and these were life-threatening if not respected. Northern boys were amazed at the alligators in the Yazoo River. One Michigan soldier had his arm bitten while swimming, and another claimed that garfish nearly bit another's arm off. An arriving Massachusetts officer was told alligators had killed three men, but that might have just been hazing a just-arrived rookie. Still, many a soldier wrote home that the Yazoo River's name in Indian meant "river of death."[48]

Worse for the Federals on land, although just as much an obsession as the alligators, were the snakes. One Northerner described rattlesnakes and "another kind called copper head here." While copperheads and water moccasins were plentiful, the rattlesnakes seemed to be the main amazement for these Federals, who quickly learned to tell how old a snake was by counting the rattles. One Federal noted that one of the boys killed a rattlesnake "with the rattles making him 17 years old."[49] New Englanders who eventually reinforced Grant were especially enthralled with the snakes, finding them as they did amid their tents and under their blankets and knapsacks when returning to camp. A Massachusetts man wrote home that "the day before yesterday one of the boys brought one [rattlesnake] alive. He was very handsome indeed, but not the style of beauty that suits me."[50] One Federal summed it all up: "The mosquitos are in their glory—fleas sport with us—and the lice are getting so fat that we are going to brand them US like our horses. With all these little companions and a good allowance of goats, lizards, spiders, centipedes and alligators we have quite enough excitement in this outer line till Johnston comes."[51]

Other critters were harmless, and the soldiers actually enjoyed them. "We have the largest and most beautiful butterflies I ever saw," one wrote to his wife, and "our fire flies are about three times the size of the ones we have at home. The lizards are also very pretty little fellows and are very harmless." The lizards—or what one Federal called a "chameleon"—were indeed much less frightful, he describing how one "visited me regularly every day in my tent and perched himself on a camp stool, throwing out his pink film [under his neck] and winking his beautiful little bead-like eyes." Another Federal acquired two young mockingbirds and sent them home: "Take good care of them, for they will make nice pets." The Northerners were also fascinated with what one described as a "chuck-will's widow," similar to the whippoorwill.[52]

The natural environment was also impressive, and sometimes dangerous, as soldiers soon found quicksand to contend with. Poison ivy was also plentiful and terrible: "I have come in for a small share and am in a dancing way today with my hands," one Federal admitted. Yet most Federals, especially the New Englanders, were completely enthralled with two types of harmless growths in trees, one being Spanish moss. Illinoisan Leander Stillwell described it as "a most fantastic looking thing. It grew on nearly all the trees, was of a grayish-white color, with long, pendulous stems. The lightest puff of air would set it in motion, and on a starlight night, or when the moon was on the wane and there was a light breeze, it presented a most ghostly and uncanny appearance." The Federals quickly found it was wonderful for making soft beds.[53]

By far, the most commented on natural phenomenon was the Magnolia, which one called the "queen of the forest." Another described the "the noble Magnolia, the pride of the South, it is a splendid looking tree, grows very large, and bears a large white blossom as large as a plate when full spread." Yet another wrote of "a very large white flower and they sent the air for a good ways around very nicely." Many wanted to send them home in letters, and one Illinoisan noted how "the Magnolia Trees grow spontaneous. The Hills are spotted with them all in bloom they look so nice one would be worth lots of money in Illinois."[54] One Federal combined his admiration of both the moss and the Magnolia at the same time: "The stately magnolia with its large white blossom perfuming the air pleased the eye, while the long heavy bunches of moss trailing and waving from all the tree branches was both a novel and beautiful sight to us. The vines and creeping plants with which this country abounds were here to be seen in more than ordinary profusion."[55]

Perhaps the beauty of the environment of Mississippi led many to reflect on the Creator and other religious aspects. Certainly, the increased chance of death did. Religion was observed in the Union camps, although not always on a Sunday. In fact, Sunday was inspection day in the Union regiments. "The officers passed through our quarters at 10 A.M., finding our guns and accoutrements bright and clean," one Federal explained. He admitted on another Sunday to his diary that "if such a thing should take us by surprise some time, our beds might be found not made, and things in general upside down." Another on the skirmish line complained how it was a "poor way to spend the Holy Sabbath but cannot help it." One chaplain confessed, "War knows no Sabbath," while another admitted that "*some* respect is being paid to the Sabbath." A Missourian wrote on a Sunday, "All quiet today, is it showing respect to the Lord's day?"[56]

Services actually took place when they could be organized. One Confederate wrote he could "hear the enemy singing hymns in their camps," and this was on a Thursday. He took exception, writing, "what incongruity, an invading horde burning & devastating the land with unrelenting vigor at the same time having the sacred name of God upon their lips." Another Confederate in conversation with Union pickets, one Federal explained, said "we paid no respect for the Sabbath. He was right." Still, these religious services were not at terribly frequent intervals. One Iowan declared the first sermon his regiment had in nearly six months came on June 21, from John 14:2. The chaplains nevertheless did their best, those of "Sooy" Smith's division at Haynes' Bluff meeting together and working out a preaching rotation. Given the ethnic mix, some preaching was in both English and German. Of course, the chaplains ministered in other ways as well, a Federal writing of one being "faithful to the sick and wounded so that the men are getting confidence in him." There was almost always preaching in the hospitals.[57]

At times, people other than chaplains organized or directed services. A devoted Catholic, brigade commander Hugh Ewing held Mass often at his headquarters. One Illinoisan similarly noted that "last Sunday there was a preacher from Chicago, but preaching does but very little good for there is but few attends." Even the contrabands in the area took part, one Federal describing how at the meetings "one good old darkey present spoke out in meeting and praised God." The Northerners also watched and were amazed at black religious services: "Our darkies had their religious services & became quite warm and fervent in them."[58]

Others exhibited their religion in life, one Federal writing of the loss felt by the death of his lieutenant: he was "liked by the boys He was a nice man & not ashamed to own his Lord." Another assured his wife that he put his trust in Jesus: "My trust is in God and I need not fear for he has promised us that all things shall work together for good to those that love him and I know that I love my Savior." Another scribbled in his diary, "I am afraid that I am straying from My Savior. Oh blessed Jesus help me trust in thee. Keep me in the true path and in the shadow of thy wing." One even told his wife, "I am made though often to shudder at the wicked acts of some of the boys who are in our army[.] I desire the prayers of some Christians that I may not be overcome by temptation."[59] Such wickedness rampant in the army exemplified the need for religion. One Federal wrote how "I have seen so much wickedness of all kinds and heard so much profane language used that I have become utterly disgusted at the way a great many carry on here." He added, "It has become such a source of disgust to me that my desires have changed, things I used to love I am learning fast to hate."[60]

The availability of money certainly brought the possibility of evil, and that mostly came with the arrival of the monthly pay. The paymaster appeared at Vicksburg on June 11, but "General Grant has ordered him back to Memphis for the present," perhaps fearing the evil influence large amounts of money would have on the bored army. Sherman requested that Grant change the order so he could pay his corps "and any others whose commanders may desire it." Grant relented, and the paymasters soon filtered out through the army. "This made the men feel good & put us all in good humor with Uncle Sam," explained Joseph Stockton. The 17th Illinois had the good fortune of not only getting paid but also missing picket duty so they could do so. Another added, "Tis said Grant is to pay us off next time in the court house at Vburg. We shall see. I hope so soon."[61]

Leander Stillwell of the 61st Illinois described their paymaster, Major C. L. Berney, who was "a fine old German, of remarkably kind and benevolent appearance, and looked more like a venerable Catholic priest than a military man. After he had paid off the regiment, his escort loaded his money chest and his personal stuff into an ambulance, and he was soon ready to go to some other regiment."[62]

Although one Federal admitted "greenbacks create no great excitement here now," that was not the normal sentiment. The suddenly rich soldiers had three basic options of what to do with their money. One was to send some home to their families, although that was a chancy prospect as the mails were not always reliable. There was, however, a company specializing in sending money and packages home, the "Adams Express Company," which "could be relied upon to carry money safely," one Iowan explained.[63]

A second option was to spend the money at the local sutler, but while many items could be bought there, so too could things less needed and more destructive, such as alcohol. "We have been payed today and the boys are feasting on the good things which the hustler sells," William Murray wrote in his diary. "We have plenty of whiskey meat bread and hard work to do here digging trenches and throwing up breast works," one Illinois soldier wrote to his father. Whiskey was mainly available at the sutlers, although it was sometimes issued in barrels "*for the health* of the men," one noted. Beer was also available to buy. One Illinoisan noted that after being paid "the boys threw in 50 cts apiece for beer and went over for it. It took some time to get . . . [it] but not long to drink the beer." It sold for twenty-five cents a pint. And the alcohol did not just make it to the lower ranks. Rumor went around that Logan was "stupidly drunk . . . every night."[64]

A third option brought vice—namely gambling. There was lots of card-playing, but one Federal assured his wife, "I am proud to say that I never have and hope never will have any inclination to try such a game." Not all were so self-controlled. "The day after we were paid there were a good many of the boys to be found who had not a cent left of their two months pay. Every cent of it was gambled away. On the other hand there was some of the boys who had made hundreds of Dollars gambling. The orders are very strict against it

but that's all the good it does." Another noted there was a "large gambling resort broke up by guards no one arrested." Poker was common, as were games
called "Chuck Luck" ("this was a game to lose money," one Iowan admitted) and "Seven-up." Some gambling even went on in the trenches while on
duty.[65]

The arrival of so much money also produced the desire to steal—and not
just greenbacks. Theft was common even among comrades. One Indianan
sent to the landing at Chickasaw Bayou admitted taking an officer's coat from
camp, it later proving to be a captain's: "I was not long in removing the bars
and made a nice dress coat for a Corporal out of it." Another took more than
a hundred dollars from a sleeping soldier, only to be caught. He admitted to it
when personal papers of the man were found with the money, including notice of his sister's death. Another had his boots stolen while he was climbing
up a tree to spy on the Confederates.[66]

Other crimes included one officer arrested when he did not respond to a
summons to appear at headquarters. He told the man sent after him, for a third
time, "that if the Gen. wanted to see him he must come where he was." No
surprise, he quickly found himself under arrest. At other times nerves frayed
because of the boredom or alcohol or both. In certain cases, race played a role.
There was lots of animosity between whites and contrabands and even black
soldiers. Similarly, one German Ohioan described a fight he had with a member of his regiment whom he said over time became "lazier and lazier and
meaner." He added, "What can one expect from a nasty crazy Jew: to lie was
his highest art, typical for Jews. They do anything to get out of doing work."[67]

While making the best out of their transplanted situation way down here
in the wilds of Mississippi, most Federal soldiers thought of home in their
spare time, just as the home front was keenly keeping an eye on the army's
movements. The best way to fill the idle hours as well as keep a connection
with home was to write letters, and thousands and thousands emanated from
Vicksburg from all ranks and languages, some of the ethnic soldiers even
writing to their parents in Germany. Because of quick and constant movements and then several days of assaults and operations in late May, many had
not had a chance to write during the overland campaign but made up for it
when matters slowed down. "You must remember that our communication
with the North has been, for a long time, almost entirely cut off and until
recently we had no chance to send letters to the river," one Federal wrote to
his family.[68]

Most wrote about their health, their friends, and the actions they had been involved in. "My health is good yet and in full spirit & not ded yet," one summed up to his family. Others showed concern about those at home, one Illinoisan writing that "you will be spared any excessive anxiety on our account knowing as we all do that even a sparrow shall not fall without our Father's knowledge and sanction, and while in the earnest performance of our duty surely we may ask his protection anywhere." Another explained to his sister that "you will see from my letters as you get them that we have been sent right to the very place you hoped we had not been sent." He assured her that "I do not expose myself only when I am called out on duty. Am very careful when I go so I may not be seen by the enemy."[69]

Many had requests for those at home, such as sending pictures of loved ones. One Illinoisan was concerned about the corn crop, writing to his wife: "My dear the removing of sprouts from among the corn is not only important to the growth of the corn but is considerable work." He recommended hiring a local well-digger but cautioned that "if he boards with you (I mean eating only) do not have him sit down with you or your daughters. It will be enough to have him eat with the boys." Many soldiers also sent goods and trinkets from Vicksburg in their letters. One wrote how, while writing his letter, "a bullet from a rebel sharpshooter cut off this leaf, which fell upon my paper, and I send it to you." Many others took their chances with the regular mail and sent money home.[70]

Others had no desire to correspond, having little time or inclination to write home or dwell in diaries. Others were so busy they forgot some of the most personal of matters. John Griffith related in his diary that he "forgot to mention that yesterday was my birth-day. Passed over without myself knowing it." Another had a better excuse. One Federal who had his thumb blown off by an accidental musket discharge had his friend write his letter to his sweetheart, but it was worth it: "He received a nice one in reply."[71]

The opposite effect was receiving letters, which were some of the most joyous times in the army. Most would respond to mail call when the deliverer would stand on a log and call each name. Unfortunately, the ratio of letters sent out from Vicksburg and those arriving at the army was drastically in the outgoing favor. Rumors stated that Grant had stopped all letters, which he did not. That said, most soon realized it took a lot longer for the letters to get home than for home-front letters to arrive at the army.[72] "A letter in these unsettled times is an inestimable blessing which but few can appreciate with out long and constant experience in such a life as ours," wrote one Illinoisan. Another explained that "it does a soldier and a loving husbands heart good to read, and I hope you will not weary in writing and sending these joy inspiring missives." Another added "your letters I prize higher than anything else that I can get here." Of course, the depression felt when no letter came day after day could be deep, and many wrote chiding their family for not writing more. One admonished that he wanted "big long letters and good many of them." Another cajoled, "Oh can it be that they have all forgotten me."[73]

Even better was when the letters contained personal items. One wrote home of his joy in receiving a letter with a surprise—"the golden lock of hair of little Viola I was proud to find in your letter[.] O the sweet Viola how happy I should be to see her tottering over the floor." An Illinoisan similarly wrote of the joy he had when he received a picture of his wife and children. He got several letters that day and a lot of news, "but the best part was the likeness of you and the children. . . . The glass got broken on the trip, but not so as to spoil it." Perhaps best was when boxes of goodies arrived, one Federal writing home that "our box was distributed right on the battlefield." Of course, the exact opposite feeling of pain emerged when letters arrived with bad news. The worst was when news of the deaths of loved ones arrived, such as when one Ohioan received news of his father's passing.[74]

One particular issue the soldiers often wrote (and wanted to hear) about was the burgeoning Copperhead movement up North. Not surprisingly, these soldiers in the ranks were almost wholeheartedly against the Copperheads and made forceful statements about them in their letters, although one Ohioan actually wrote: "I have not fully made up my mind yet what I will do. I do not like old Val [Vallandigham] but perhaps he will make a good governor." One Illinoisan was more in the majority, he being disgruntled at a friend who had apparently turned since he had been away. "All of the letters that I used to get from him were Union but the last that was Secesh," he complained to his aunt. "If he cannot do better I shall not spend money in writing to him." Another noted, about an acquaintance, "if they would shoot him it would be a fine thing for he is only a holerin to hide the cecesh in him and to make them think he is a union man. They better hang him and be done with him."[75]

When word filtered down to Vicksburg about the Copperhead movement, which one soldier labeled as "disastrous in the extreme to the *Union cause*," many perhaps jokingly offered their services up North. When one company heard of Copperheads organizing in their home town, one wrote "I and Co, 'L' would like to know who their drillmaster is." An Ohioan similarly wrote home that "there is a report come from some source that the people at home were having quite a lively time with the Copperheads but there is surely enough loyal men in the North to crush them. If not just send down for the old 32d [Ohio] & we will haste to the rescue." Later in the same letter, he counseled to "shoot a few of them if you had the chance and possessed a gun for if any of the young men of the North are too cowardly . . . they had better give their Briches up to the ladies for I am sure there is more Patriotism in them than in the . . . stay at home cowards." One declared flatly: "I had rather shoot a Copperhead than a Rebel for I think they are a good deal worse."[76]

Other politics also entered the letters over and above the Copperheads, such as when the question of a postmaster position back in Illinois came up. One soldier told his wife to pick someone and he would see his division commander Frank Blair about it. "The Post Master General at Washington, D.C. will do any thing Frank P. Blair requests; and Frank P. Blair is our General. He commands our Division of the Army. He will do it for me in a moment," he asserted.[77]

Of course, much of the talk of and news from home made many soldiers homesick. One ill Illinoisan was especially lonely, his small son sending tiny flowers in his mother's letters, and he admitted he "often looks at them little hands marked off on his letter with the pencil." An Illinoisan wrote of a comrade who had the flux "pretty bad, [and] he had the blues with it badly which makes it hard on him." Another constantly looked at his watch and thought of what those at home were doing at that specific time.[78] Nights made homesickness worse. An Illinoisan related that he would "gaze at the stars and wonder what they were doing at home." One wrote to his two little daughters that "you must both be good girls and do as your good mama tells you and love one another and be kind and love your little brother Walter." The common bond of religion also brought thoughts of home and family as well. One Illinoisan wrote home on a Sunday morning how "at this hour (10 ½ A.M.) I imagine that you or at least some of you are on the way to church." Another thought of home and how even at that moment "church bells at the North are calling good people to worship, and to hear words of cheer and comfort to the soul."[79]

Sadly, most of the noises heard in the Union camps around Vicksburg were anything but calls for words of cheer and comfort. They were instead the drastic sounds of war and death.

The civilians trapped inside Vicksburg never had even the thought of such a chance to relax. "We are utterly cut off from the world, surrounded by a circle of fire," wrote Dora Miller in her diary. While certainly not all, even some of the Federals felt for those trapped amid the fighting sides. Some reported they could see Vicksburg's courthouse and church spires and watched shells go into the city and burst. One Federal declared, "I can't pity the rebels themselves but it does seem too bad for the women and children in the city." He continued: "I can distinctly hear the shells crash through the houses. Indeed some of the boys went so far as to say they could hear the screams of the women and children, but their ears must have been better than mine." Another could only think about what each individual shell entailed. "There are women and tender children where those shells fall," one Federal admitted, "but war is war."[80]

About all those women and children, and most men not of military age, could do was hunker down and endure it. That meant staying in their caves when the worst bombardments took place. One journal writer described the caves where "on the first appearance of danger they would betake themselves like rats when Tom goes mousing." It was clear that everyone needed to be under shelter, and partly for that reason some soldiers helped the civilians, a staff officer joking of his brigade inspector general "who might strictly be termed a gentleman, very politely gave up to the crowd . . . his cave, bunk & Bedding." He added, humorously, "there was a very fine looking young lady in it too."[81]

Yet the caves continued to be second-best, the people much preferring to be in their regular homes. That was just not possible most of the time, as they had to be either in the caves or close enough to get in them when the heavy shelling started. And they had to endure additional problems in the caves, such as the huge rainfall on June 10, which obviously had an impact on the subterranean holes. Many caves flooded. Mary Loughborough described how "a perfect spout of muddy water burst through the embankments" and that "I and the servant sat, disconsolately, with our skirts drawn around, and our feet on little blocks of wood to keep them out of the mud, with rueful faces." With all the trouble, some just flatly refused to go inside the caves. Emma Balfour declined to stay in hers, although her house shook under the concussion of the shells.[82]

Life became no better as the siege rolled along. In fact, it grew worse with the dwindling supply of food and the growing nervousness of the situation. One colonel, Claudius W. Sears of the 46th Mississippi, even declared the "town more dangerous than the lines." A chaplain described how "there is confusion and bustle amongst the citizens of Vicksburg. There is hurrying to and fro with the women and innocent children." Children being children, they were hard to keep corralled and occupied. One chaplain noted the families in a nearby cave with several children who "could with difficulty keep them within." Prices also soared. By the time the siege was in full swing, costs in Vicksburg had climbed incredibly high. "At the meat market in Vicksburg a hambone sells for $5.00," one Texan reported, "2 or 3 lbs. of cornmeal for $5.00 to $8.00. The last beef was gotten today [June 22]. The troops had mutton for 4 days."[83]

Sadly, the children were especially affected. Some issues were small in context, although a big deal to a child. One little girl had her pet pony taken, and "I was only a little girl but I went and told the general about it and sat on the general's lap." Dora Miller admitted, "I am so tired of corn-bread, which I never liked, that I eat it with tears in my eyes." Some, however, miraculously had fond memories later on of certain parts of life in wartime Vicksburg. One boy remembered his "gnome-like life was the Arabian Nights made real. Ali Baba's forty thieves and the genni of the ring and lamp lurked in the unexplored regions of the dimly lighted caves; and the sound of a guitar here, a hymn there, and a negro melody somewhere else, all coming to us from among swaying Oriental draperies, sent me off at night to fairyland on the magic carpet of Bagdad." He added nevertheless that it soon wore off, and "squalling infants, family quarrels, and the noise of general discord were heard at intervals with equal distinctness."[84]

Sadly, there were many more serious issues for the women and children than just ponies and crying infants. The worst possible situation was when death came. Numerous sources spoke of women and children being injured or killed in the bombardment. One shell hit a little girl holding the hand of an adult as they walked down the street. On another occasion, Mary Loughborough described hearing "the most heartrending screams and moans." A shell had struck a cave and decapitated a young child that had just been put to bed in safety, the mother thought. She recalled how "I sat near the square of moonlight, silent and sorrowful, hearing the sobs and cries—hearing the moans of a mother for her dead child." Word of these horrific instances filtered into Pemberton's headquarters, but there was little he could do.[85]

It *was* heartrending, and it certainly had an impact on the children who were not hurt but who were always afraid. One child exclaimed fright of the "mortar tell." Others did not know what to make of it all. One Confederate complained to a Federal while meeting between the lines that "yesterday a bomb fell on a little baby, & killed it, sir, killed it." The Federal reflected for a moment and could only respond, "Well, I should think it highly probable that it would."[86]

Physical damage to property also grew as the siege entered mid-June, some of it from the citizens' own side. The 27th Louisiana tore down a building owned by Mrs. Coffee "to use the lumber as firewood." They stated their colonel had given them permission and that they would return later and take the entire building. Similarly, soldiers of Bowen's division tore up two bridges on the Graveyard Road for firewood, despite orders not to do so. Many citizens had gardens and became increasingly indignant at hungry Confederate soldiers prowling around for food. One citizen, William Porterfield, even shot several, killing one and wounding the others. Vicksburg dentist Rowland Chambers made a vocation out of watching his garden every night because so many onions, cabbage, peaches, and other items had been taken. Hungry Confederates also stole one of his turkeys and even his peacock, in response to which Chambers scribbled in his diary: "I hope it will choke him to death." Chambers also shot at some of the thieves, wounding one. Even the *Daily Citizen* editor James Swords mentioned the "lax discipline of some of our company officers."[87]

Most of the destruction came from the enemy, not surprisingly, as the shelling continued unabated throughout the siege from both land batteries as well as the mortars. Troops on Federal division commander Alvin Hovey's front built "furnaces to heat shot for the 24 pdrs.," later adding that "furnaces were completed and hot shot thrown into the city." Grant also asked Porter "can you furnish me with some Sulpher, Nitre and Meal powder. If so I can burn such of Vicksburg as may be desirable." Porter replied that he had none, but there was some at Chickasaw Bayou. He added, "I am firing incendiary shells and burn a house now and then." Of particular interest was burning the

Confederate mills that produced food. One report indicated that "Hovey's artillery have destroyed one of their mills and injured the remaining one."[88]

With all the shot and shell landing inside Vicksburg, it was no surprise that fires raged on occasion. Little could be done about the houses and personal items in the path of these shells, but Confederate officials could move the highly volatile ammunition stores that, if hit, would only make the situation worse in broadening the destruction as well as depriving the army of its use. Orders went out for "scattering out ammunition, which was much exposed to the enemy's fire at the depot magazine." New magazines sprouted in a ravine out near the Baldwin's Ferry Road, on which toiled an engineer and "a working force of 25 negroes from the jail-gang."[89]

Many feared a large fire in town, and several did occur, including one on May 26 when "a little after 8 a fire broke out in a frame house back of Brown and Johnson's." A much larger fire emerged on the night of June 1. "A large fire broke out in the city," one officer reported, "close upon the magazine of the Whig Office battery, which was at one time in great danger." The ammunition was removed, and many of the river battery crews fought the fires. Edward Higgins noted that "all the men of my command that could be spared from the guns were ordered out immediately to assist in arresting the progress of the conflagration." Higgins's men also served double duty in other ways: "They formed a portion of the city guard, discharged the duties of firemen in case of fire, policed the river, &c., and the reliefs were almost nightly under arms as infantry in the trenches." On this night, they were primarily firefighters.[90]

"Last night about 12 large fire in Vicksburg which burned nearly a square," one Louisianan marveled. A Vicksburg citizen noted that the fire started at "J. A. Peale and Co.," a store on Washington Street, while another said a shell hitting a house caused it. The fire raged from Brown and Johnson's to Crutcher's Corner and burned "many goods and stores—loss very heavy," one observer reported. Another described it as "the Square opposite to the Post Office on Washington Street," while dentist Rowland Chambers wrote how the "fire broke out in Wadworths store and burnt the whole block except Crutchers, Sweets and Freds houses." A large crowd gathered to watch the flames and try to put them out, but it was no use. A saddened woman watching described the flames as "casting lurid lights over the devoted city."[91]

The conflagration was so large that many soldiers reported on it from the front lines. "It was a magnificent spectacle from our lines, but a sad one," William Pitt Chambers of the 46th Mississippi reported in his diary. Even the Federals saw it, one Illinoisan in Ransom's brigade writing in his diary of "a large fire in Vicksburg last night." A Wisconsin soldier wrote to his father that "I could distinctly hear the firebells ringing the alarms." Yet there was no rest for the weary, as he added how "our batteries were instantly turned in the direction of the fire and shot and shell rained thick and fast on that portion of the city, which, without a doubt, effectively prevented the gathering of a very large crowd to put out the fire. It was still burning at noon of the next day." One of Pemberton's staff officers, John C. Taylor, corroborated the Union shots concentrating on the fire and facetiously declared that it "led us to *congratulate* ourselves on being so fortunate as to participate in the gaieties and festivities of a beleaguered city."[92]

Enemy fire also damaged other structures, apparently the ones with the highest spires receiving targeting. The courthouse was hit, and there were injuries in the Catholic church when a shell hit it during Mass on June 28. Most still held services nevertheless. Rector Lord rang his steeple bell at the Christ Church many Sundays after parishioners requested they start back, and services were held other days of the week as well. Few attended because they wanted no part of the bombardment, but one civilian noted that "still, the church-bell reminded us that it was the Sabbath day." One Illinoisan across the river even noted he heard the courthouse bell plainly on the night of June 25.[93]

Caught as they were, the citizens of Vicksburg mainly just waited and hoped, although a few took matters into their own hands. Federals detected a woman riding horseback right behind the Confederate lines one day near Mint Spring Bayou. Captain Allen Waterhouse looked through his field glasses and determined it was a trick—she was simply "'a weak invention of the enemy' to work on our feelings." Waterhouse sent a shot over her and she "got out of range in a *hurry*." Some civilians actually got out of Vicksburg by trying to cross the river and were taken by the Federals. Others simply found small joys in the most horrific of such horrific surroundings, such as collecting shells that had fallen on their fair city. One Louisianan described how "there is no house or yard where people cannot gather all sorts & sizes & shapes of missiles; some use them for ornaments to their gateposts." Emma Balfour related that "I have quite a collection of shells which have fallen around us and if this goes on much longer, I can build a pyramid." One little girl vividly remembered years later how hot the shells were and how she had to let them cool off before collecting them.[94]

Those outside the lines were also affected more as the siege wore on, especially with the continual influx of Union reinforcements in the rear area and their spread outward. Still, the plight of those in the rear of Vicksburg was not as adverse as inside the city. In fact, relations on the rear lines could be civilized and friendly on occasion. For instance, three Ohioans gained leave to visit relatives in the area, namely an uncle. The three "went out on the commons and gathered up a mule for each of us, rigged up bridles and used our blankets for saddles." Once at the home some ten miles to the north, they found that the uncle had died in 1861, but his stepdaughter and her husband were living there. They "appeared glad to see us" and gave them what food they had, including corn bread and pickled pork, despite being "in sore straits as regards food supplies." Others utilized a barber who had been put out of Vicksburg because he was German, but mostly because "he and his family (a large one) were too much Union and ate too much of their scanty rations." Illinoisan William Reid noted the "Union soldiers patronize the fugitive largely," although at lesser prices than inside Vicksburg.[95]

One Indianan on the rear defense in particular cared for those who were being hurt in the mess of war. He noted that "we have no service to do and it is thought that they cannot bring a very considerable force to attack us," but he added that "if the rebs do come up on us I pity the poor children they would be as likely to be hurt as any one." One lady asked him to "advise her when the danger was approaching that she had no where to go & that if a fight should take place that she thought that she was in as much danger as any one in the south." He went on to reflect that the people of Mississippi "are feeling the effects of this war, it is in their own country[.] I find more Union people here than I expected to find."[96]

Most of the time the relations were not so friendly. "The people seem to be in high glee, and sanguine that the rebels will soon be in number strong enough to raise the siege," division commander Osterhaus reported in early June. One pro-Confederate woman really got on Sherman's wrong side, and she barked for him to imprison her. He barked back, one observer explained, asking "how she would like Ship Island, but there it ended."[97]

Many civilians made no secret of their aid to the Confederacy. Women openly cared for Confederate wounded and wrote letters upon their deaths: "I was one of several ladies who visited the hospital daily to render what service we could to our poor wounded soldiers," Sarah Bigelow wrote a mourning mother, "and all that we could do was done to make them more comfortable." She added comforting assurance that "when asked if he [the woman's son] knew he had but little time left on earth, he replied 'his trust was in Jesus.' . . . Tearful eyes and sorrowing hearts surrounded his dying bed, and all regretted that one so young and gifted must so soon be a martyr for his country's cause." Citizens also commonly gave information to aid Johnston: "A citizen, who is well known and lives near that place, says they have a division that has been badly cut up at Vicksburg." A Federal officer similarly ordered that "there is a citizen living about four miles from your Headquarters, who I understand is scouting about the country very suspiciously. He rides a very fine brown stallion, and may be known by the Provost Marshal 13th Corps. Arrest him and have the horse kept by some one of your staff until it is determined what should be done with him."[98]

Ruin came on most. "Not a house remains," one Federal on the rear line reported, "all have been burned. It is a rule here I am told. There are no mistakes made. All are rebels. We confiscate everything and drive the people off before us farther into Dixie." Describing the territory between the Big Black and Yazoo Rivers, one Confederate cavalry officer probing the area was aghast that "some who were once worth a million are now worth nothing and if they go to their friends are compelled to subsist on charity as they go along." One Federal described the process, writing that "I prevailed upon a wealthy planter near the battle ground of Champion Hill to make me a present of two pairs of linen pants—they belonged to one of his four sons who were in the rebel army at that place and I thought they would never want them again." Plunder of unoccupied houses and mansions was common as well. One Federal noted "a fine piano standing open in the parlor" of one house.[99]

While white civilians with loyalties to both sides, both inside and outside Vicksburg, pretty much knew their place and circumstances, the African Americans caught up in the siege operations were in a completely upside-down world and at times had difficult choices as to what to do and where to go. William N. Brown of the mounted 20th Mississippi reported: "I find the Negroes immediately in the neighborhood of Edwards Depot and Big Black greatly demoralized, doing nothing, and in some instances very insolent."[100]

Not all were lethargic, however, and many outside of Vicksburg took the opportunity for freedom by making their way to the Federal lines; others sought every opportunity to hand back a little grief to their owners. "Negroes raising a good deal of cane," one Illinoisan related, and "are getting ahead of their masters. [Masters] came to us to get us to come whip them—no go." Many went to the Federal armies to gain freedom and became cooks for the officers. One Indianan wrote of his cook being "the best negro that I ever saw" and wrote home that "he was a poor cook [but] could wash and sew equal to a woman." This particular contraband had been free up North and accompanied a white man to the South, where the man sold him for $1,000: "He has been here 19 years in servitude." Another Indianan feigned concern for the masters who lost laborers, writing home that "I do not know what will become of them. The Negroes is not at work for them now but is fighting against their masters."[101]

Most slaves inside Vicksburg had no such opportunity for freedom unless they escaped, which was not likely. One did, however, and went into the Union lines bent on revenge. He showed the Federals the Confederate lines and specifically where "his master was burrowed in a cave and insisted upon our stirring him out with a shot." The shot raised a lot of dust over the area and sent men scampering, whereupon the slave "clapped his hands with delight and said he wished it had taken his captain's head off." The Federal surmised that "although the man had been born and brought up on his master's plantation he showed very little affection or sympathy on this occasion."[102]

In the midst of such fighting, injuries and death obviously occurred among the black population. Some inside Vicksburg became casualties as a result of the very Union bombardments working to set them free. One slave became trapped in a cave-in. Workers unearthed him, but he had been dead a while. One white woman pitifully remembered how "his wife and relations were distressed beyond measure, and filled the air with their cries and groans." Other blacks perished as a result of the exploding shells, and one child died while playing with an unexploded projectile. A Tennessean similarly described how "a negro boy had his head shot off with a cannon ball in sight of us in the morning and two others wounded. He was in a house near the breast works."[103]

Those contrabands outside also faced their own problems. One Federal described a slave who showed up at camp who had "sores on his legs with maggots in." An Indianan told of another pitiful episode when "last night a young wench was delivered of a young wooley head, which she very quietly disposed of by throwing it into the sinks for safe keeping. The boys fished it out and after examining it till their curiosities were satisfied the[y] hit it a kick and sent it back headlong into the sink, where it now remains."[104]

Even when they made it to Union lines, contrabands often faced racism even there, or at the least unnerving and at times cruel tricks. One Illinoisan admitted that "the colored population I must confess have got into my good graces more than I ever expected of them. Before the war I knew very little about them but have slowly arrived at the conclusion that they are superior to the Irish and far more likely to make useful citizens. Of course I refer to the well known *lower class*. The Protestant Irish are many of them superior to the Scotch and English."[105]

The Federals could also be quite mean to the gullible contrabands, some of whom were officers' servants. Colonel Charles Woods, commanding one of Sherman's brigades, had a servant named John who was especially afraid of the Minié balls singing around camp. "His head seemed to be on a pivot," one Federal remembered, "all the time dodging the balls as they came singing overhead or spattered the dirt from our works." The officers soon realized they could heighten John's nervousness when they loudly "started the story that the Rebels were using explosive bullets." Many claimed such existed, although Confederates denied it even after the war. Nevertheless, the poor man was thereafter very afraid one would hit him and "blow him up." That led to a cruel "exhibition" at Wood's headquarters, where they rigged up several friction primers under tables and behind furniture; when they purposefully continued the conversation loudly about the explosive bullets and then clandestinely pulled the lanyards and the pop occurred right under John, he "jumped to the other side of the table. Another went off right under him and he hopped nearly through the top of the tent. This was followed by one or two more explosions, when he made for the door and another went off right at his heels accelerating his motion to a high degree of speed."[106]

Blacks could also be used as pawns for jokes on other Federals, such as a little Irishman named Jerry Ring. He was amusing from the start for his skittishness, especially deep in the night when the hoot owls were bellowing. He was also an avowed racist who hated blacks. One night a "negro wench" came into camp all "tired and hungry, having escaped from a plantation and walked a long way." She was fed and then "it occurred to Quartermaster Wright that Jerry Ring's tent would be a good place for her." Jerry was already asleep and snoring very loudly, but the protesting slave was assured it was merely a little boy. She climbed in and snuggled up to Jerry, and the wait was on for the reactions the next morning. The jokesters threw back the tent fly and huddled in the nearby bushes to get the full reactions, and when he awakened, "such a drawing down of his mouth and such a look of indignation it was amusing to see. He jumped out of the tent and looked around, fearing that someone would discover his suspicious situation." One added that when he was caught "it was really pitiful to hear Jerry's protestations of innocence." He also added that "after this, whenever Jerry bragged about the Democrats and his hatred of the negro, we reminded him of this little occurrence."[107]

White, black, Southern, Northern—it did not matter; all had been caught up in this terrible tragedy that was the Siege of Vicksburg. And the home front was not totally exempt. While folks back home tracking the operations either through sound closer to Vicksburg or newspapers farther off were not susceptible to bullets and camp sickness, they had the duty of worrying over loved ones and their respective nations. One Federal reminded his mother, perhaps not with the best theology, not to worry: "The Lord has promised the Saints those who have relatives in the army that if they are faithful in the discharge of their duties toward him that their friends and relatives will be protected and brought back to them." Similarly, a mother who received good news wrote to her son: "I was so glad to hear from you once more and also glad to learn that you was not at Vicksburgh[.] I had been worrying about it thought you was at Vicksburgh and they were fighting so long and the weather so hot I thought you would all die in a pile but I have learned since that your regiment was not at Vicksburgh."[108]

Yet not all good news emanated from the Mississippi River bastion. As more and more newspaper reports and letters from soldiers returned home both North and South, with them went word of killed and wounded, sick and maimed. Such was the true sadness of Vicksburg.[109]

9

"Can't Our Government Send Us Relief?"

June 12–15

"This morning the sun rose beautifully and clear," wrote Missourian Theodore Fisher on June 14. "The birds are warbling their morning melodies and all nature seems to be happy. Man alone is arrayed against each other." Certainly by mid-June man was arrayed against one another—for weeks now—and the effects were building. Confederates both inside and watching from far away worried more than ever about Vicksburg. The mood was getting especially serious inside the city, where one chaplain admitted how "towards the end of this [second] week such hardships and exposure and the scanty diet began to tell upon our garrison." Many dreaded one of two fates that were appearing to be more and more likely: "Don't know whether we will be surrendered or cut our way out." Ultimately, Pemberton gave orders "to arm teamsters and all other unarmed men connected with the several brigades." One Confederate wrote "perhaps the lieutenant general has suddenly rallied from his lethargy and intends to do something." More likely, Pemberton was grasping at the last straws he had, trying any way he could to keep his lines around Vicksburg intact.[1]

Many railed against Richmond. Chaplain William Foster asked rhetorically: "Can't our government send us relief? Shall Vicksburg fall for the want of energy on the part our government? Will all the blood shed be spilled in vain? For the first time, dark doubts would cross my mind." He informed his wife that many men "considered the place as lost, though they were willing to lie in the trenches another month if it would save the place." A Louisianan looked at the situation in context: "I am almost sorry to hear of Lee's progress Northward; for it looks as if the importance of Vicksburg were not understood. What is Phalada [Philadelphia] to us if the Miss. Be lost[?] Our existence, almost, as a nation, depends on holding this place. Why not then remain on the defensive & send troops hither, instead of employing them on useless expeditions, which are only raids on a grand scale, having no decisive results."[2]

By far, any hopes Vicksburg's defenders or civilians still had rested on Joe Johnston. Numerous Confederates expressed their anticipation for Johnston: "Our only hope was from without and Johnston's name was no doubt reported thousands of times every passing hour," Chaplain Foster explained. "We are still hoping that General Johnston will come and deliver us," a Texan confided in his diary. A Mississippian declared, "We will try very hard to hold Vicksburg until he arrives." Even one Mississippi civilian lady wrote hopingly that "I can imagine how the soldiers and citizens in Vicksburg will feel when they hear firing in Grant's rear."[3]

Yet as the calendar moved on into mid-June, that hope began to wane. "We were repeatedly informed that he was coming!" wrote one Mississippian, and "that dispatches had been received from him stating that he had gained important victories, and that the siege would surely be raised in two or three days at the farthest. This was repeated so often and the men were so often disappointed that they naturally became skeptical and despondent." At times, firing was heard to the east and "how high rose the hopes of our men! And how eagerly we listened for a renewal of the fight on the morrow!" But, he added, "we heard it no more, and in a day or two the men were as despondent as ever." He concluded, "They saw nothing before but death or a prison after weeks of gnawing, debilitating hunger." Obviously, Pemberton had been using Johnston's messages of a quick relief to keep up Confederate morale inside Vicksburg, but that ruse was beginning to be useless. "So many false reports have been circulated that our men are slow to credit any. It is now near the middle of June and no relief. The sanguine still hope, while the desponding give up all hope," explained Chaplain Foster.[4]

The slow decline of will to resist illustrated the loss of confidence in Johnston's relief. A Mississippian, W. R. McRory, confided his inner thoughts to his diary often over the course of the siege: first, it was "Johnston, we want to see you. Why don't you come?" Later, he asked, "will not Johnston come to our assistance? He is our only earthly hope. Come soon." By mid-June he noted "some of our men desponding," but he was willing to try to cut their way out: "I for one will go, if any attempt it. I had rather risk my life in trying to go out of here than in a Northern prison." News of some potential move-ment on June 21 rallied his morale, but three days later he was still watching, and "nearly every person is looking eagerly for Johnston. I expect him this week." By late June, he scribbled, "he must come soon if he saves us. . . . A great many have despaired of Johnston coming. But I still have strong hope." By the next day he wrote of "no news from Johnston. I must own I am begin-ning to despair of his coming." By July 2, he confessed "I own I am getting out of hope myself," adding that rumors of Johnston taking Snyder's Bluff had purposefully been let loose, some by brigade commander Louis Hébert himself.[5]

While few if any high-level officers let it be known that all hope was lost, that hope even waned among staff officers to the generals. J. H. Pepper of Brigadier General John C. Moore's staff related in mid-to late June, "He will be up in due time, yet,—no danger of his appearance too soon, if sufficient force. For my patience, as well as many others, are almost worried out." An engineer added, "I shant never have believed that we would have been left so long without assistance." He later discussed "what makes Johnston act so slowly; he wishes to run no risks, but make a sure thing of it by making all due preparations." Even one of Pemberton's staff officers, John C. Taylor, groaned in despair in his diary, "nothing from outside world." He added, "Come Joe! Come quickly!"[6]

Desperation soon arrived for many. One Confederate noted that with the lack of ability to respond to the enemy's fire, with less and less food, and with Johnston no where to be seen, "in our regiment (I knew nothing of the sentiment prevailing in any other) a willingness to capitulate, soon became quite prevalent." A Louisianan admitted that "no news from Johnston and hope deferred makes the heart Sick." One Texan even described how "several of our men out of pure desperation climbed up a hill and cried 'Hurrah for Johnson.'" He noted how "a bullet came flying and drove them down the hill. Their haste was cooled."[7]

For their part, the Federals could not figure it out any more than Vicks-burg's garrison, one Union soldier writing how Johnston was rumored in rear but "things are entirely to[o] quiet out that way to suit me. . . . I expect we will wake up a hornet's nest some of these mornings." One Union soldier asked a local lady "where is Johnston," but she snapped back that the North-erners "ought to know better than we did." Still, Grant and company were confident if Johnston did ever move. One Illinoisan welcomed Johnston and a fight, saying "we rather wish he would come so we could do both jobs at

once." Grant himself argued on June 15 that "if Johnstone should come here
he must do it with a larger Army than the Confederacy have now at any one
place. This is what I think but do not say it boastingly nor do I want it repeated
or shown."[8]

Consequently, by mid-June much of the confidence Vicksburg had placed
in Johnston was practically gone. Even Pemberton himself was beginning to
see the end nearing, writing Johnston on June 15 that "we are living on greatly
reduced rations, but I think sufficient for twenty days yet." One civilian even
went so far as to admit "it is the Lord who enables us to hold out." By the
looks of things, it would also be the Lord who would save Vicksburg if it was
saved, certainly if by the hands of Joe Johnston. That would take a miracle.[9]

The mastermind behind the overall Union operations causing so much concern inside Vicksburg was of course Ulysses S. Grant. Wherever he was became a beehive of activity, and although he traveled greatly in many of the
areas under his command—mostly the siege lines around Vicksburg and the
rear defenses—the central position where he wielded his authority was from
his headquarters behind the lines on the northeast section of the siege works.
The site at John R. Gee's place "was well chosen on a pleasant elevation,"
Sylvanus Cadwallader wrote, "in the edge of a strip of timber which afforded
protection from the glaring, burning mid-day sun, made drainage and sanitary
conditions easily secured, and was also near to a brook of running water kept
from pollution." There, on a small ridge between two creeks, Grant governed
the Vicksburg siege and all its attending aspects. If the Chickasaw Bayou
landings were the heartbeat of the operations, pumping goods and supplies all
over, then Grant's headquarters was the nerve center, the brain.[10]

It was a good life at Union headquarters: "On the whole story very comfortable. We never lacked an abundance of provisions. There was good water,
enough even for the bath, and we suffered very little from excessive heat."
Dana recalled how "every night I sleep with one side of the tent wide open
and the walls put up all around to get plenty of air. Sometimes I wake up in
the night and think it is raining, the wind roars so in the tops of the great oak
forest on the hillside where we are encamped, and I think it is thundering till
I look out and see the golden moonlight in all its glory, and listen again and
know that it is only the thunder of General Sherman's great guns, that neither
rest nor let others rest by night or by day."[11]

Grant also had a more structural dining room and kitchen, which an industrious sergeant built him out of cane and lattice work. Grant enjoyed his meals there, but he had to draw the line at too much comfort. He and the sergeant became well acquainted, and the sergeant sought permission to go out into the country and find Grant some suitable tables and dining utensils for his new kitchen. Grant agreed, but when the sergeant returned with a grand assortment of fine utensils, the general became suspicious, especially when the sergeant was less than forthcoming about where he obtained them, mumbling only that he got them "out in the country." Finally, the sergeant admitted that he had taken the items from a country church, and Grant made him take them back. "Those things are sacred," he counseled, "and I will not permit them to be used for any profane or common purpose."[12]

Grant clearly ran things around headquarters, although Dana described him as "a social, friendly man, too, fond of a pleasant joke and also ready with one; but liking above all a long chat of an evening, and ready to sit up with you all night, talking in the cool breeze in front of his tent." Grant enjoyed the fun around headquarters, even though he was almost never the one creating it. He once enjoyed watching a group of soldiers trying to get a large cache of honey from a tree near headquarters. One particular bald-headed soldier went in and was driven back by the angry bees, those watching advising him and others to "flank them, charge them from the rear, surround them, and so on." The main man was soon whipped and began his retreat, one noting "his one purpose seemed to be to hit the air." The same observer added that "no one seemed to enjoy it more than the general, who laughed heartily and who never saw the soldier afterwards that he did not smile."[13]

Fortunately, Grant remained extremely healthy throughout the siege, with only one episode of sickness, which he described to Julia later as "an attack of Dysentery which now has entirely left me." Unfortunately, that issue caught up with him when he apparently drank that glass of alcohol to settle his stomach on the trip to Satartia on June 6, with the bad results attending.[14]

Second to Grant in dominance at headquarters was his friend and adjutant, John Rawlins, who Dana described very differently: "He had a very able mind, clear, strong, and not subject to hysterics." Yet, "he bossed everything at Grant's headquarters" with a "rough style of conversation" that made him "one of the most profane men I ever knew." At times, the dominant role was somewhat blurry, Dana writing that "I have heard him curse at Grant when, according to his judgment, the general was doing something that he thought he had better not do." Others such as Engineer James H. Wilson were an integral part of the operation as well, Wilson performing a number of jobs such as relaying messages, interrogating deserters and prisoners coming into Union lines, and of course his engineering duties.[15]

Obviously, Grant did not stay at headquarters all the time but moved about the entire area on his horses such as Kangaroo or the one given him from the Confederate president's plantation, which Grant named "Jeff Davis." Some of his staff accompanied him on these trips, at least those not needed at headquarters, as well as Dana and newspaper correspondent Cadwallader. Also along on many of the rides was his escort, Company A, 4th Illinois Cavalry under Captain Embury D. Osband, "the proprietor of a cigar and tobacco stand under the Tremont House, Chicago." This company had been Grant's escort since Belmont and was "in every engagement I have been in since that time [and] rendered valuable service, attracting general attention for their exemplary conduct, soldierly bearing, and promptness." Grant often toured the front lines in his plain dress, at times causing some to misunderstand who he was. One soldier shouted to him, "Say! You old bastard, you better keep down from there or you will get shot." The man was mortified to later learn he had been talking to the army commander. Division commander Alvin Hovey also scolded Grant to get down, telling him "I'm only a general of a division and it's easy to fill my place, but with you, sir, it's different."[16]

One Federal claimed Grant himself would move up to the front line and talk with the Union and Confederate soldiers meeting in front of the Stockade Redan, he of course wearing no insignia and "forbidding salute or personal recognition." One Federal observed Grant and his frequent cohort Sherman: "The one taciturn, smoking slowly, his impassive face telling no tales of any workings of the mind within,—the other nervously chewing a cigar and voluble, his restless eyes noting everything within the field of vision." An artilleryman similarly described how "Gens. Grant and Sherman were here this afternoon to see us fire and complimented us on our shots."[17]

On one of the trips, a mule driver did not recognize Grant and got into a lot of trouble. The general spied a man beating and cursing a team of mules, and he ordered him to stop. The man, supposing he was "a mere meddler," began cursing Grant, who was unrecognizable in his common uniform. Grant ordered the man arrested and brought to headquarters, where he had him tied up by his thumbs. He was soon released and brought to Grant's tent, where he received a severe reprimand. The man lavishly apologized for insulting

Grant, who responded with surprise: "That makes no difference. I could defend myself, but the mule could not."[18]

Many remarked on Grant's homespun style. One Wisconsin soldier declared Grant "puts on no style, is not afraid to talk to privates, many a second lieutenant would appear to outrank him in appearance and manners." Another noted, "You wouldn't know he is a General he looks like an old farmer," adding, "and so does Logan."[19]

Many soldiers reveled in having an up-close look at Grant. One Ohio artilleryman described him as "a smaller man than I had supposed from having always seen him on horseback; has gray eyes and whiskers cut short; is a little stoop shouldered; is very quiet in his manner and of unchangeable countenance; was smoking a cigar and had on a blouse and a low crowned hat." Most of the observation came when Grant went to the front lines. One Indianan admitted, "I used to tremble for General Grant when he would come into our rifle pits and take a squint at the enemy through the holes." Illinoisan Wilbur Crummer was overjoyed the rest of his life that Grant, moving through the trenches, had asked for water and there being none, Crummer gave him his canteen full of warm water. Grant drank a swig and "handed it back, thanking me for it, and passed on." A Minnesotan described a similar encounter. Grant went with the visiting governor of Wisconsin to a battery, where the guard "said sharply, 'no smoking allowed in the Battery.'" An amazed onlooker described how "Grant, who had two thirds of a Havana stuck between his teeth, instantly flung it through an embrasure, to the great delight of a crowd of high privates who, like myself, witnessed the incident." He added, "When the General went away the guard went and got the cigar and said he should send it home in a letter, and tell the folks that he ordered it out of General Grants mouth."[20]

Even civilians did not recognize Grant. On another occasion, as the general rode along with Engineer Wilson, they met two elderly women. The nondescript Grant was smoking as usual, and one of the women shouted "soldier, please give me a cigar!" Grant immediately reached in his pocket and handed her several of them and moved on, but Wilson lagged behind and informed the woman, who obviously had no idea who she was addressing, "madam, you had better make those cigars go as far as possible, for General Grant will not be coming this way every day to keep you supplied."[21]

Also along on the rides on numerous occasions was Grant's thirteen-year-old son, Fred. He had been with his father since March and saw everything there was to see of the campaign—and then some. The boy had a tendency to wander off and go his own way but always seemed to find his way back. Or, he found himself under the protection of Grant's thousands of babysitters. Sometimes Grant tried to leave him behind at critical points, but Fred always seemed to get loose. One such occasion occurred at Port Gibson, when Grant thought the boy was asleep back on a steamer on the river. Fred later recalled how "in after years he often told the story of my following him on the battlefield of Port Gibson with more interest and satisfaction than he manifested to me at that time." Now that Fred was witnessing a siege, it was harder for him to get loose, and the boy recalled that "I saw a great deal of my father's methods, his marvelous attention to detail, and his cool self-possession." One local lady, Emilie McKinley, mentioned Fred, describing him as "a good natured-looking boy—not smart. He ranks as a captain on his father's staff." One Union brigade commander described him as "quite a nice little soldier" who reminded him of his own little boy at home. Fred was sick during the latter part of the siege, explaining that "a wound in the leg which I had received early in the campaign [at Big Black River bridge] now began to trouble me very much, and under Dr. Hewitt's expressed fears of having to amputate my leg I remained much at headquarters." Grant sent him to a relative nearby on a leased plantation, but Fred was back by late June. Grant admitted to Julia that "he does not look very well but is not willing to go back until Vicksburg falls." Other family members also arrived, such as on June 29 when a message reached headquarters that "Gen Grants brother and five friends are here awaiting transportation to camp."[22]

Since Grant could not move around everywhere, certainly not at the same time, communication to and from the nerve center of headquarters was key to his control of the army. His forces were spread out all over the difficult terrain, and not just in front of Vicksburg, which itself required a considerable lengthy line of eight to ten miles. Grant also had units watching Johnston, the supply area around Chickasaw Bayou, the navy in the river, and the land forces in Louisiana. He was conducting a multifaceted campaign, and keeping track of all units and more importantly communicating with them in an efficient and timely manner was a challenge. Fortunately, there were several layers of communication available to Grant, the original and oldest simply being a messenger on horse, which he utilized on numerous occasions.[23]

Grant also employed his signal corps to communicate with the various forces under his command. Although one Confederate wrote in his diary "last night Saw what I suppose was a balloon," this department primarily utilized signal flags in semaphore, wagging and waving the code to produce whatever messages needed to be sent. Quite a lot of communication occurred by this manner during the assaults, and it only grew as Grant positioned his forces for the siege and then conducted them during it. But it was a bulky system, needing numbered "stations" every little bit on high ground that could be seen from the adjacent stations along the line. For long distances on harsh terrain, this could mean every ridgetop, so numerous stations needed to be manned constantly. And those in range often became targets for Confederate artillery. At night, the signalers used lanterns, and one Illinoisan who was fascinated by watching them described how "the movements of the lights looked curious and strange, something elf-like . . . they would make all sorts of gyrations, up, down, a circle, a half circle to the right, then one to the left, and so on."[24]

Captain J. W. De Ford first established the signal efforts at Vicksburg, although eventually resigning and giving way to Captain L. M. Rose, who himself became sick midway through the siege and turned the effort over to Captain J. M. McClintok. Several "lines" developed early on, perhaps most importantly between Snyder's Bluff and Admiral Porter's flagship *Black Hawk*. Army signal officers manned both stations, and thus Grant could communicate with Porter from land. Of course, Porter had his own naval system of signals that he used to disseminate messages to his squadrons. This particular line of communication was some four or five miles in length, Porter's flagship staying primarily in the Yazoo River for central command.[25]

Eventually, three major lines developed on land. One ran from Grant's headquarters to Haynes' Bluff, it being the primary way to communicate with the various commanders that came and went in Grant's growing concern for the rear. Captain Rose reported that this line "is of the greatest importance, as it is the only means of communication with the two divisions of our troops in that part of the country, stationed there to observe the movements of General Johnston's forces in our rear. The best officers I have are on this line, and it works to a charm." A second line ran to Young's Point and eventually took over the communication between army and navy. "It is the means of communication between the army and the navy," Rose reported, adding that "Admiral Porter is highly pleased with the corps." A third major line went to the Yazoo River landings, which Rose described as "the depot of supplies for the use of the medical, commissary, quartermaster's, and ordnance departments."[26]

There were also lines to the individual corps commanders. Grant's headquarters were on the northeast section of the lines and was only a ridge or so over from Sherman's at "Willis's woods." McPherson was close as well, in the rear of Logan's division. McClernand's headquarters were farther away, and Lauman and others were even farther. Captain De Ford established a line of stations to the far left early on but closed it down soon thereafter due to "the peculiar topography of the country [that] necessitated so many stations that, in the opinion of Captain De Ford, this line was nearly useless, as a courier could ride over the line in less time than a message could be transmitted in the usual manner." Captain Rose reinstituted the line when De Ford left the army.[27]

As the siege progressed, all manner of supplies became abundant at Vicksburg, including telegraph equipment run on acid batteries carried in wagons. "Telegraph instruments and an operator have been sent from here to you," Grant informed one general at Haynes' Bluff on June 10. Grant also soon had telegraphic communication to each corps headquarters as well as elsewhere to the various landings and toward the rear at Snyder's Bluff, that line becoming operational on June 8. Where telegraph line could not be strung, the original signal stations took up at the end of the telegraphic lines. Chief signal officer Captain O. H. Howard reported that "these lines were in constant use, transmitting messages of the first importance—the Chickasaw Landing and Haynes' Bluff lines until relieved by the telegraph," with others remaining for the duration. Cannibalizing equipment also caused some problems with the telegraph operation, including McClernand complaining in mid-June that someone—Sherman, he expected—had taken down his telegraph line to Osterhaus at the Big Black: "Please have it restored and further interference stopped," he barked. Sherman explained that "the Pioneer Companies have been in the habit of using Telegraph wire to tie Fascines."[28]

Grant also kept out a number of spies, including one named "Tuttle," who worked the back line of defenses, as well as "Bunker," whom Blair's force in May "captured." In addition, Grant had a larger network of scouts and spies out working on his behalf, the genius of Brigadier General Grenville Dodge in Corinth.[29]

As an added layer of security in these communications, many of the messages, especially to Washington, were written in ciphers, as were the enemy's. Grant captured many Confederate couriers and notes, some of them unreadable. "Having no one with me who has the ingenuity to translate it," he wrote,

"I send it to Washington, hoping that some one there may be able to make it out." They did, with a couple of possible translations only different in the minutest ways.[30]

Grant's communications also went to the home front, where he was a little late in letting Julia know of his whereabouts. He finally wrote on June 9, explaining, "I wrote to you by every courier I was sending back up to the Capture of Jackson. Having written to you to start for Vicksburg as soon as you heard the place was taken, and thinking that would be before another letter would reach you, I wrote no more." By early June, however, it was looking like Vicksburg was going to be tougher than he thought. Still, he told her again to start down when she got the letter, and if Vicksburg had not fallen by the time she arrived she could stay on a boat "with the prospect of my calling to see you occasionally." He later elaborated that "if you should come down before Vicksburg falls you would hardly see me until the place is taken however. My Hd Qrs. are six miles from the landing with the road always blocked with wagons bringing supplies for our immense army. My duties are such that I can scarcely leave."[31]

Julia would not arrive any time soon and later noted that "my summer was not a happy one," primarily because she was surrounded at her father's home near St. Louis by secessionists, her father included. Grant consequently kept writing over the course of the siege, giving his news and wanting to know about family affairs. "I have enjoyed most excellent health during the campaign," he wrote, "so has Fred. Fred . . . has enjoyed his campaign very much. He has kept a journal which I have never read but suppose he will read to you." Significantly, Grant did not mention Fred's wounding at Big Black River Bridge on May 17, which his mother probably would have reacted negatively to, especially at so far a distance. As for the other children, Grant had a pony waiting when they arrived—"the smallest horse I ever saw."[32]

Grant also saw to his personal needs. "I sent up to Memphis and got all the clothing I wanted except cravats," he wrote to Julia. "You may bring me two black ones and half a dozen light ones." Julia, fortunately, was taking care of the farm, land, money, as well as the children. She took over the home-front duties so that Grant could concentrate on Vicksburg with his customary bulldog grip.[33]

Grant wrote others as well, including his father, but explained that while many family members wrote to him, "as I have to do with nineteen twentieths of those received [I] have neglected to answer them." He nevertheless assured his father that the position he held was strong and that "Johnstone will have to come with a mighty host to drive me away.—I do not look upon the fall of Vicksburg as in the least doubtful." But then he turned introspective and admitted that it was not all he had hoped for: "If however I could have carried the place on the 22d of last month I could by this time have made a campaign that would have made the state of Mississippi almost safe for a solitary horseman to ride over." He continued: "As it is the enemy have a large Army in it and the season has so far advanced that water will be difficult to find for an Army marching besides the dust and heat that must be encountered. The fall of Vicksburg now will only result in the opening of the Miss, river and demoralization of the enemy. I intended more from it. I did my best however and looking back can see no blunder committed."[34]

John Pemberton had no such luxuries inside Vicksburg—even of corresponding with his wife and children—but rather continued to watch his situation deteriorate inside Grant's cage. By the second week in June, the Confederate defenders had settled well into the siege but with a very different set of contextual circumstances overshadowing them. Without any source of supply, Pemberton's troops were left to feed on what was inside Vicksburg itself at the time of the siege. Calculated observations continuously took place to determine how long the garrison and inhabitants could survive on different percentages of rations, although numerous deserters during these days told of "short rations and divided councils within, a great part of the soldiers and all the citizens desiring to surrender." More ominous was the ammunition factor, where some of the most needed items such as percussion caps could be readily brought in because they were so light; Charles Dana described how "they fired a good deal yesterday, having evidently received a new supply of caps." Heavy lead or iron ammunition was a different story, and there again the defenders had to basically utilize what was inside Vicksburg at the time of the Union army's arrival. Of course, just like food, the more they shot away the less would be left. Most troublesome was the confusion over the arrival of an altogether different kind of support, different from food or ammunition. That was soldiers, not so much in terms of more to defend Vicksburg, which would only add to the drain on food and ammunition supplies, but rather the arrival of Johnston's forces on the outside to pressure Grant into raising the siege or at least allowing Pemberton a fighting chance at a breakout attempt.[35]

The food situation, while not yet dire, was perhaps the biggest issue, it swiftly becoming a concern by mid-June. Carter Stevenson did the math and reported "we have 742 barrels of flour. If we make the ration of it half a pound, the breadstuff will be fifteen days." He also enumerated how much mutton, bacon, pork, lard, rice, beans, and beef was on hand, with unsurprisingly more rations of rice and beans than anything else, over two million of each. Unfortunately, some of the rice was damaged, but "I will grind it," Stevenson wrote, "and make it go as far as possible." He also noted "there is an abundance of sugar, which, when the bread has been consumed, can be substituted with rice."[36]

Connected to the sustenance issue was growing concern about the condition of the troops themselves. Because of the nature of the siege and the need for all troops to man the trenches at all times, unlike in the Federal army, the Confederates were growing increasingly tired. "Our men have no relief," Pemberton informed Johnston on June 15, "are becoming much fatigued, but are still in pretty good spirits." The continual firing by Federal naval and land batteries was especially tiresome, in that the noise was continuous and one never knew when a shell might land nearby.[37]

Also of major concern were the continually approaching Federals. Pemberton noted in his diary on June 13 that the enemy sap "is now within fifty feet of us on the Graveyard road." In the next few days he continually wrote that the enemy was "pushing his work rapidly forward," with a notation on June 17 that "the enemy saps are now very near to the salients of the line in front of Hébert, Shoup and Green." Growing more alarmed, he noted a few days later, "the enemy's saps on the Jackson and the Graveyard roads are now very near to our works."[38]

Despite the lack of resources, there was nevertheless the need to fight continuously, creating a fine line to walk. Pemberton had sent out orders for all unneeded firing to stop, which brought requests for explanation from some such as Stephen D. Lee. Apparently, Alfred Cumming took the orders as not to fire at all, prompting Pemberton to scold: "Brigadier General Cumming has strangely misconceived the order in relation to firing from the lines." He bluntly ordered that "the enemy are not to be allowed to show themselves within range with impunity, and certainly they are not to be permitted to strengthen their works or construct new ones without molestation, as the lieutenant-general learns has been the case in front of Brigadier General Cumming."[39]

Obviously, the food and manpower situation would become moot if Johnston did something to relieve Vicksburg before it became critical. Unfortunately for the Confederates, Pemberton and Johnston could never agree, as
their correspondence in mid-June showed perfectly. Part of the problem was
that it took so long for messages to move back and forth, the couriers having to bypass the growing Federal army besieging Vicksburg. Couriers now
also had to give wide berth to the growing Union presence back east of the
city and its besiegers. Johnston complained how "the slowness and difficulty
of communication rendered cooperation next to impossible." Indeed, it took
days for messages to arrive and responses to come back, by which time the
situation had usually changed so much to warrant the original plans, if any, to
be obsolete. But alas, there were hardly ever any original plans.[40]

Pemberton complained as early as June 7, "I am still without information
from you later than your dispatch of the 25th," adding that "I have sent out
couriers to you almost daily." Even when messengers arrived with percussion caps, they had no notes from Johnston: "Courier Walker arrived this
morning with caps. No message from you." On another occasion on June 14,
Pemberton wrote, "Last night Captain Sanders arrived with 200,000 caps but
brought no information as to your position or movements. . . . I am anxiously
expecting to hear from you, to arrange for co-operation." The captain and
his men had been two weeks in sneaking through bayous and swamps "subsisting as best they could on berries and craw fish," but they brought little
confidence from Johnston. Pemberton almost demanded when he returned
word: "When may I expect you to move, and in what direction?" Yet in messages that crossed in transport, Johnston was writing the very same day that
"we are nearly ready to move, but don't know the best route. Co-operation is
absolutely necessary. Tell us how to effect it, and by what route to approach."
Both Pemberton and Johnston wanted the other to take the lead and offer a
bold plan, to be the adult in the room, but neither indecisive general took the
initiative. All the while, Vicksburg floundered at the hands of much more
decisive Federal generals.[41]

Johnston was indeed working on his command from his headquarters at
times near Canton and at other times the Bowman House in Jackson, right
next to the statehouse. Federal scouts continually reported the effort and the
buildup that had by this time ceased, one writing that "every good man has
gone to Johnston, and that squads of poor militia are left behind gathering provisions and forage." The Confederates were indeed stripping northern Mississippi of food bound for Johnston, one commissary ordering subordinates to

"use all possible exertions in procuring a large quantity of bacon for the army at Jackson. . . . Urge the planters to send it forward as fast as possible." To another Johnston advised "20,000 more troops being sent to this department to be provided for. . . . It will be impossible to keep the army together unless we can feed them."[42]

Yet Johnston showed a nauseous paradox of offensive plans and defensive actions. There was admittedly some offensive preparation. He ordered W. H. T. Walker's division from Yazoo City southward to the Big Black "as preparations to move toward the enemy are nearly completed." Since it was farther from Yazoo City than it was from Jackson, where much of the rest of the army was, Johnston wanted Walker at a "distance . . . nearly equal to that from Jackson." He also planned for the coming moves in terms of who and what should go, including minutia that a commanding general probably should not concern himself with. Ammunition was rated at forty rounds per man with an additional sixty in the ordnance wagons. Orders regarding exactly how much transportation could be included also went out, such as one wagon for a major general's staff, one for a brigadier general's staff, one for each one hundred men, and so on. Johnston also required that there should be no leaves or furloughs granted except to those approved by himself.[43]

But there was plenty of hesitating and defensive actions even amid the preparations. A want of horses limited mobility ("to make a movement at anything like the time necessary, we will be forced to impress teams"), one of Johnston's staff officers even calling for the dismounting of several companies of cavalry. A shortage of harnesses and other equestrian items was felt as well. Similarly, earlier in June, Johnston had held up the process because "I have been waiting for [cavalry commander Brigadier General William H.] Jackson to get into position fairly, to dismount all the mounted infantry and send it back to its brigades, and take the best horses for cavalry service." Johnston also reorganized much of his army, sending brigade commanders back to original divisions with the dismounting of their commands and one even to Port Hudson. Perhaps most telling, Johnston's commands seemed to be starkly defensive in nature rather than offensive. "The enemy's scouts must not be permitted to show themselves east of the Big Black," he warned cavalry commander Jackson. Those defensive orders trickled down and infected the lower units as well, Jackson telling his subordinates to alert headquarters "of the first movements of the enemy" and that "the enemy's scouts are not permitted to show themselves east of the Big Black." Jackson also warned in a negative tone that there were at the railroad bridge "eight of the heaviest caliber field pieces in position on the west bank, guarded by the division of infantry commanded by General Osterhaus; also one at Bridge-port."[44]

One wonders if Johnston, much like when he arrived at Jackson on May 13 and quickly surmised "I am too late," simply decided nothing could be done and that he would do just enough to appear that he was working toward a so-lution but never really intending to do so. Reports of heavy Union reinforce-ments moving to Vicksburg from commanders nearer to Memphis may have also influenced his opinions, James Chalmers writing from Panola, "Three boat-loads of troops passed Memphis Wednesday night, going down." John-ston knew the window of opportunity was closing if not closed, but he con-tinued to spew excuses, such as "I have not at my [disposal] half the number of troops necessary," and "it is for the Government to decide between this State and Tennessee," a sentiment he had others, such as Governor Pettus and leading men of Mississippi, to also argue. Still, he knew he had better at least show some activity, especially with Confederates west of the river now acting and the news of efforts around Milliken's Bend soon arriving.[45]

Certainly, Johnston had little hope of doing anything. He sent Pemberton a telltale note on June 14, writing "all that we can attempt is, to save you and your garrison. To do this, exact co-operation is indispensable. By fighting the enemy simultaneously at the same point of his line, you may be extracted. Our joint forces cannot raise the siege of Vicksburg. My communications with the rear can best be preserved by operating north of railroad. Inform me as soon as possible what point will suit you best." Once again, Johnston—the ranking department commander—was deferring to Pemberton the subordi-nate. Trouble was, that subordinate had immense trouble making decisions.[46]

Apparently, the indecision at Vicksburg impacted the higher command of the Confederacy as well, Richmond even contemplating sending P. G. T. Beauregard from South Carolina eastward. For his part, Johnston requested Lieutenant General William J. Hardee's entire corps from the Army of Ten-nessee be sent to him if reinforcements from Rosecrans had been detached. Davis even asked Bragg in Tennessee if he knew if any of the reinforce-ments had gone from William Rosecrans's Army of the Cumberland and if so whether he could aid Vicksburg "by advance or detachment?" Of course, Bragg was about to face his own onslaught (the Tullahoma Campaign), and besides, none of the reinforcing troops had come from Rosecrans's army.[47]

Pemberton nevertheless kept somewhat of a positive tone, for the most part, although he pulled no punches in describing his situation to Johnston.

"The same men are constantly in the trenches, but are still in good spirits," he wrote earlier in June, and he elaborated on June 15: "The enemy has placed several heavy guns in position against our works, and is approaching them very nearly by sap. His fire is almost continuous." He added, significantly showing his mind-set, "I think your movement should be made as soon as possible. The enemy is receiving re-enforcements."[48]

The problem, of course, was that in all the talking past each other nothing was done in the critical window of opportunity that existed in the first week or so of June when Johnston had all his forces but only a minority of the rein-forcements Grant would get had arrived. By mid-June, those reinforcements were arriving, and Johnston knew it, and thus the Union rear was soon so heavily defended that Johnston, even if he wanted to, would be hard-pressed now to do anything militarily. The moment had passed—and it was with Johnston's knowledge. On June 15, he thus wrote to Secretary of War Sed-don, "the odds against me are much greater than those you express. I consider saving Vicksburg hopeless."[49]

Unfortunately for Pemberton's forces huddled inside Vicksburg and any hope of Johnston's relief efforts, those Union reinforcements were indeed on the way. And they could not arrive fast enough for Grant. He had so much to do and too few men, but the heavy influx of troops that Henry Halleck's early-June rash of work produced would soon be arriving. Then, he could fi-nally close off the pesky Confederate right down at the southern extremity of his lines. He could also make sure there were enough troops in the rear guard to make that area secure even if Johnston amassed an army as big as reports were indicating. It was a tense time of waiting, but soon these troops began to pour in, mostly in large numbers of brigades and divisions and others such as the 80th Ohio in smaller numbers who were then attached to existing bri-gades, one regiment informing the veterans of Vicksburg they "had never saw a Rebel with a gun on his shoulder yet." But with greater numbers of troops came greater responsibility, Halleck writing on June 12: "I hope you fully appreciate the importance of time in the reduction of Vicksburg. The large re-enforcements sent to you have opened Missouri and Kentucky to rebel raids. The siege should be pushed night and day with all possible dispatch."[50]

Many of the troops were from the ever-shrinking XVI Corps around Mem-phis and Corinth. Lauman's and Kimball's divisions were already on site, Lauman on McClernand's left and Kimball in the rear despite rumors of his arrest because of the harsh forced march from Mechanicsburg. One Illinoisan declared, "We all hope that it is true." Grant had ordered even more of Hurl- but's troops southward, including the division under Brigadier General Wil- liam "Sooy" Smith, who was regarded as a much better general than the other XVI Corps leaders Lauman and Kimball; Dana described him as "a man of brains, a hard worker, unpretending, quick, suggestive, he may also be a little crotchety." Yet it was a trickle of troops to say the least, due to a lack of transportation as well as chaos. "Smith's division is embarking in great confusion," Hurlbut informed Grant on June 8, "from the inefficiency of the quartermaster's department, but will be off to-day." Hurlbut also included reports on some of the others moving southward, all of which would have to pass by Memphis. Grant was impatient, writing, "I am looking every day for the arrival of Gen'l W. S. Smith."[51]

So many troops of the XVI Corps now being in or soon arriving at Vicks- burg presaged a bit of a command issue. Hurlbut himself commanded the corps at Memphis; being satisfied with city life and lacking a real desire for field operations, he was content staying there. And in actuality, he served a real purpose: keeping the Confederate northern flank occupied and holding the northern Mississippi and West Tennessee line. But now that there would be three entire divisions of XVI Corps troops at Vicksburg once Smith ar- rived, it seemed there was enough of the corps on site (certainly as much as the other corps had in terms of brigades and divisions) to warrant an overall commander. Accordingly, Grant assigned the XVI Corps troops at or soon to be at Vicksburg to another new general in the area, Major General Cadwal- lader C. C. Washburn.[52]

Washburn was an interesting choice. He was another one of the politician- generals in the army, having served numerous terms in congress prior to the war. He had served well nevertheless, involved primarily in the earlier Yazoo Pass operation. The most notable connection Grant had to Washburn, how- ever, was that his brother Elihu, also a sitting congressman but spelling his name with an *e* at the end, was Grant's sponsor and perhaps political guard- ian in Washington. Congressman Washburne was certainly responsible for Grant's promotion to general earlier in the war. Now, his brother took com- mand of the corps's troops at Vicksburg, Hurlbut retaining command of those nearer to Memphis. It was a confusing situation, with one Illinoisan writing home, "General Washburn is commanding something round here with Hd Qts at Haines Bluff just above us."[53]

At Haynes' Bluff, Washburn took command of the entire rear operations around the slot, including outranking Kimball, whom Grant was not nearly as pleased with as he had thought he would be. Dana described to Washington how "Kimball had retreated from there . . . in a semi-panic." His troops were likewise not fans, one writing that "he requested our boys not to make any noise nor whistle as the rebels were on the hills and would be apt to hear us. The boys in consequence made more noise than before." Grant also complained to Washburn that "directions were given General Kimball to station his Cavalry at Oak Ridge P. O. I find from Maj. Wilson of the Cavalry that no force is kept." Grant wanted cavalry out front to harass and drive the enemy, who should be "made to feel that it is not safe to venture too near Haines Bluff." Yet Washburn also had his moments, Dana reporting on June 15 that he "in some alarm, thinking he would soon be attacked, sent for a division of re-enforcements."[54]

Miscommunication within the brigades over command and details for work, along with a lack of adequate tools, also caused problems. Brigade commander Adolph Engelmann described to his sister the "very thorough calling down" he received because of one mix-up. The terrain was also problematic, one of Kimball's soldiers writing "this country is a very strange one. It is cut in all directions by deep gulleys and the hills are almost impassable." Of course, Osterhaus retained his own command and better ground to the south around the railroad bridge across the Big Black River, where he fortified his line and detected and reported rumors that Nathan Bedford Forrest and his cavalry were at Mechanicsburg. Colonel Marcus Spiegel of the 120th Ohio nevertheless reported to his wife on the good duty there, writing over the early weeks that the railroad bridge was "a very quiet place where we hear the cannonading of our folks at Vicksburg Day and night." Another wrote of the leisurely atmosphere, which Osterhaus himself had to confront; one day he slipped toward the picket lines and "arrested some of the pickets and sent them to camp for having their accouterments off." At times, however, matters turned more concerning. "We do not know how soon we may expect some fun here of our own," Spiegel wrote, "inasmuch as General Johnston is this afternoon positively reported to come this way." Within a week, he was reporting that "for three nights past our Regiment lay on its Arms every night and several times during each night drawn up in Battle line."[55]

Commanders were helpful, but Grant needed troops, and they could not arrive fast enough. He informed Admiral Porter that he expected "Sooy" Smith's boats to appear as early as June 9, but none had shown. "Their non-arrival

causes me much uneasiness lest they may be interrupted some place by a battery of the enemy," he admitted. Grant asked that, with some nineteen thousand
troops he knew of on the way, "until they all get here" could "a gunboat ply
about Island No. 65 and other dangerous points below it." He apologized that
"I am aware, admiral, that heavy drafts have been made on your fleet above
Vicksburg, but hope you will still be able to comply with the request made
herein." Porter did so, and many troops coming south on the river remarked
about the gunboat escorting them near Greenville. To perhaps illustrate again
his nervousness about the rear and the needed reinforcements, Grant added that
"all the forces coming to me now are being sent to Haynes' Bluff, and I need
not tell you how anxious I feel for the arrival of those I know to have started."[56]

Grant even sent a staff officer to Memphis "to assist in expediting movements of troops." Colonel William S. Hillyer reported to Hurlbut once he
arrived, but Hurlbut was not impressed. "I am not aware of any assistance
rendered by him, although his society was very agreeable when time was allowed to converse with him." Hurlbut added, "I am satisfied that his forte is
not in quartermaster's duty."[57]

Fortunately for Grant, the reinforcements soon began arriving in the
wilderness of Mississippi, where the scum on the water foretold of misery;
"there were lots of alligators and no end to mosquitoes," one Wisconsin soldier bemoaned. Feeding Washburn's force at Haynes' Bluff, of course, was
"Sooy" Smith's imminent arrival there, on June 12 despite many drunken
soldiers taking in the sites of Memphis and being left behind. The trip down
the river was also prone to problems, one Illinoisan writing that "the water
upset the digestive apparatus of a good many of the boys, as well as my own."
Worse, Lemuel Newell of the 99th Indiana fell off his transport at Helena
and drowned. One chaplain living in luxury in the ladies' cabin of a fine boat
wrote to his wife, "We are comfortable in the cabin, but the men are crowded
on deck and around with scarcely room enough to lie down." Despite also
taking some fire as the boats rounded into the Yazoo River and headed for
Snyder's Bluff, Smith's four brigades under Colonels John M. Loomis, Stephen G. Hicks, Joseph R. Cockerill, and William W. Sanford—some seven
thousand troops with four batteries of artillery (another was dropped off at
Helena to aid Benjamin Prentiss's defense there)—significantly beefed up the
force in the slot, allowing Grant to breath a little easier.[58]

These Northerners were not impressed with their new area of operations
to say the least, one Indianan writing that "we are in the rear of Vicksburg

amongst some of the awfulest hills in God's creation if it maybe could be God's creation but I don't think he had any hand in making this part of the world." Nevertheless, the area was soon scraped clear of all pigs, chickens, and cows, some of the men camping in fine peach orchards with clear springs nearby, as well as the former campsites of the Confederates. The 6th Iowa for a time took the 3rd Louisiana's old campsite, one Iowan remembering thankfully that "they had erected artistic and comfortable quarters, gathering about them many of those little conveniences which became actual luxuries to the soldier." They also went to work immediately fortifying Haynes' Bluff even to the south along the high ground adjacent to the Skillet Goliath Creek watershed, properly named Skillikalia Bayou but most often referred to contemporaneously as Skillet Goliath. Dana reported after a visit there on June 13 that they were "working upon the intrenchments with admirable zeal." Some of the old Confederate works were incorporated into the new line, but the fresh earthworks were much more formidable. Dana pronounced the fortifications able to contain twenty-five thousand men and that "it is a stronger defensive position even than Vicksburg."[59]

Even better was that more troops were on the way as well. Hurlbut informed Grant on June 8 that Major General Francis Herron's two brigades under Brigadier Generals William Vandever and William W. Orme were also headed southward. As part of the "Army of the Frontier" under Major General John Schofield, the two brigades had been at Rolla and Pilot Knob, Missouri, prior to receiving orders on June 2 to move. Those at Pilot Knob marched to the river and took steamboats southward, while the Rolla force took the railroad to St. Louis and thence moved southward by boat. All were aboard transports by June 4, and Vandever had reached Memphis by June 8, with Orme still to the north. The transports did all they could to muscle the troops southward, at times more than they should. One Iowan described to his parents how "the boat shakes so that I can hardly write and don't know whether you can read it or not." There was also a bit of a scuffle at Cairo among the 19th Iowa. While the boat was taking on coal, "the mate abused a negro and most shamefully; but speedily found that he was 'reckining without his host' and at once made it convenient to go ashore, where he remained." Once at Memphis, obviously, all effort was going along to get Smith's division of the XVI Corps on the way, but Hurlbut intended to send Herron's brigades on southward as soon as possible.[60]

Herron's two brigades, some five thousand in total, moved on southward on June 9 and arrived near Vicksburg four days later. "A tall, slim man with red side whiskers," as one Ohioan described him, Herron was a force within himself, Dana describing him as "a driving, energetic sort of young fellow, not deficient either in self-esteem or in common sense," and "the only consummate dandy I ever saw in the army." He added that "he was always handsomely dressed; I believe he never went out without patent-leather boots on, and you would see him in the middle of a battle—well, I can not say exactly that he went into battle with a lace pocket-handkerchief, but at all events he always displayed a clean white one." That was quite remarkable for a young twenty-five-year-old, although Dana explained, "but these little vanities appeared not to detract from his usefulness."[61]

Despite his worry about the Haynes' Bluff area, Grant suddenly decided that the open left flank of the siege lines was more important, especially with Smith's division having just beefed up the slot defense. Grant therefore sent Herron on southward across land to the Warrenton area, where the division crossed the river on June 15, "taking care, of course, that the garrison at Vicksburg shall see the whole of his march from Young's Point across to the point just below Vicksburg." Herron soon took a position on Lauman's left, where Dana reported "egress and ingress [now] absolutely impossible." Herron and Orme and their staffs rode inland to scout this new territory and meet up with Lauman, who would be on their right. The two met a couple of officers of the 53rd Illinois, who offered to show them the way to Lauman's headquarters. Once the introductions had been made, Herron's troops began the process of digging in as well, despite "a want of transportation" and difficulty "in collecting engineer tools." The troops now in the major theater seemed to take it all in stride, at least outwardly: "Everyone seems as unconcerned as though there was nothing going on," wrote one of Herron's soldiers. The Missouri troops nevertheless started their initial parallel, or the extension of the line of circumvallation on this southernmost area of the lines, some twelve hundred yards from the Confederate fortifications. Eventually, from this fortified line, approaches would be begun as well toward the Confederate works.[62]

The Confederates indeed took note: one admitted that "when the real investment began a cat could not have crept out of Vicksburg without being discovered." Concerning Herron specifically, division commander Carter Stevenson advised Pemberton that "General Barton reports that the enemy are crossing troops at Warrenton." Some minor fighting took place as a result, but Stevenson reported that his scouts described "the enemy's line complete and compact, and that it was impossible for them to get through it." Over the next several days, minor skirmishing continued as the Georgians of Barton's brigade, along with Colonel Alexander Reynolds's Tennesseans, felt out Herron's new forces and how hard they would push. At one point Barton admitted that they did not contest much ground as "the loss which must have ensued in forcing the point would have been out of proportion to the value gained."[63]

Then, there were other reinforcements on the way as well, including the five brigades in two divisions of the IX Corps Ambrose Burnside was sending down the Ohio. They were nearing Cairo and Memphis in waves by June 10 and would be sent on down as soon as possible. Warming to the idea of complete enclosure of Vicksburg, Grant also mentioned to McClernand that the rest then on the way, John G. Parke's IX Corps troops totaling some eight thousand in number, would also be sent to the southern extremities, although they still could be used in the slot as well. One Federal noted that all these reinforcements would "do away with all further apprehensions of the mischief that Johnston can do in rear."[64]

It was not just infantry and artillery that made its way to Vicksburg. Hurlbut worked to send all manner of large siege cannons down as well, including 32-pounders and carriages for 10-inch Columbiads. All in all, it was a massive array of firepower and force assembling around Vicksburg—but then Vicksburg was perhaps the most important place in the Confederacy at this point. It was worthy of a major buildup to ensure success, and Grant was grateful. "This increase in my force," he reported, "enabled me to make the investment most complete, and at the same time left me a large reserve to watch the movements of Johnston."[65]

It was indeed a staggering amount of troops concentrating on the Vicksburg area. And it was actually more than was needed at this point, as circumstances now sat idle with Johnston. "We do nothing particular but picket and fortification duty," Ephraim Dawes of the 53rd Ohio wrote home from near Haynes' Bluff. He added, "We are building a splendid line to protect us from any force coming from any direction." It was rather boring duty, but essential if matters changed even slightly. And those numbers would be especially welcomed if Johnston suddenly began his move.[66]

Even with that massive buildup, Ulysses S. Grant was still not satisfied—or content. Many of the reinforcements went to the rear areas to protect against any threat Johnston posed. And Johnston's numbers presumably grew by the day, while the Big Black River was falling almost as quickly, allowing, Oster-haus reported on June 14, a crossing at many more sites: "The present stage of the river is such that the greatest vigilance is necessary to protect against a sudden attack of the enemy's, it becomes fordable almost at any place." Thus as mid-June came, despite the reinforcements, Grant was still spiraling down into paranoia about his rear, so much so that he would begin to make major plans to guard against any problems there, even to the detriment of the siege operations if need be.[67]

Grant continually received updates about the Confederate buildup east of him, mainly from Hurlbut, in Memphis, who advised that some estimated Johnston's force at fifty thousand but more likely was only around thirty thousand. Still, more were "constantly arriving from Charleston, Savannah, and Tennessee," Grant thought. Hurlbut kept out a vast array of spies and scouts and detected much of the earlier movement toward Vicksburg. Gren-ville Dodge at Corinth kept a large spy network going as well, and others gave detailed information too. At one point, Hurlbut wrote of sending "my best spy from this place to pass down the entire line [Mississippi Central Railroad] and bring you all the information he can gather." Hurlbut assured Grant he was "a man of sharp observation and of capital judgment, and about as effective a scamp as the Nineteenth Illinois ever had on their rolls."[68]

Hurlbut's news was worrying, both about the Confederate buildup as well as his own paltry numbers and uneasiness about northern Mississippi and West Tennessee. He especially feared a Confederate attack on his lines near Memphis, but Grant reminded him that "they cannot send any large force against you without your cavalry being able to give timely notice of their approach." Grant assured Hurlbut that "should Johnston disappear from my flank," he would send troops after him or up by river, but in either case Hurl-but was going to be safe. And Johnston was probably not going after Hurlbut anyway: "It is now evident the enemy have brought large re-enforcements from Bragg's army, and I cannot think it is with any other design than to raise the siege of Vicksburg." At one point, Hurlbut even asked Grant about sending a raid to destroy the railroad below Grenada, most opportunely at the bridge over the Big Black north of Canton, "the highest and most important bridge on the route." Grant was not accommodating but rather ordered Hurl-but "to be prepared to reduce them [troops] to a much greater extent." Then Grant tipped his hand, adding that "the enemy is collecting a large force at

Canton, and some of it is now east of the Big Black River. We must be prepared for any emergency."[69]

Grant indeed had word that Johnston was on the move. Washburn reported that Confederate cavalry commander William H. "Red" Jackson had moved all the way to within two miles of Mechanicsburg with ten regiments of cavalry, obviously an overstatement, although he did have one brigade under Brigadier General George B. Cosby near Mechanicsburg in the slot and the other under Colonel Lawrence S. Ross east of the Big Black along the railroad and down to the lower ferries. Whatever the force, it was a move toward Grant's lines. And the movement was not just in the slot.[70]

Farther south, Osterhaus was also reporting movement, including an advance by the 8th Kentucky that had been mounted for cavalry operations across the Big Black at Macon's Ford, some seven miles north of Bridgeport. A prisoner taken in the skirmish on the Edwards Station Road informed Osterhaus that Johnston was soon to attack at Snyder's Bluff and Breckinridge would move toward Osterhaus's position at the railroad crossing. The report went through McClernand, who sent it on to Grant, McClernand asking for more cavalry. Grant obliged. McClernand also pried into Grant's affairs, asking: "Ought not communication to be opened between Osterhaus and Kimball, and each be ready to succor the other?" No doubt Grant thought McClernand viewed him as too much of an imbecile to think of that. McClernand also agitated Grant when he reported on the advance in a separate note, saying he had sent all his cavalry beforehand and that the crossing north of Bridgeport "is far to my right." He asked, "Can't McPherson and Sherman send reinforcements?" To further direct Grant, he added, "should not a mobile force be immediately thrown between Bridgeport and Oak Ridge Ferries?" Grant calmly replied that he had everything under control, with the force under Washburn at Haynes' Bluff watching the Macon's Ford crossing. He also noted he was sending Osterhaus the 2nd Illinois Cavalry, "as you request."[71]

Confirmation of major Confederate moves came in the next few days, including a report on June 12 from Colonel Clark Wright of the 6th Missouri Cavalry: "I have quite reliable information that Johnston is moving, via Yazoo City, with five divisions, or about 30,000 troops. His reinforcements are from Bragg's army." Worse news was that "the fords on the river are fordable this evening again." Washburn himself was loudly crying of Confederate advances as well. With so much activity, Grant finally decided he had to do something major. He thus took a bold step forward toward full security of his rear by establishing a contingency plan by which, if this episode or something more in the future developed into a full-scale advance by Johnston, he would have a plan in place to deal with it. The central part of it built on the reinforcements arriving even then, most notably Smith's division from Hurlbut, which when they took position at Haynes' Bluff gave Grant a steady garrison of nearly fifteen thousand men there, not counting Osterhaus's force farther south. And then there were the others coming in from Schofield and Burnside, Herron's division from Missouri slated to join the besieging lines and perhaps Parke's from Kentucky as well, although that could change.[72]

To augment this force in an emergency, Grant set up a contingency plan similar to that which he had utilized initially during the siege with Blair. Grant informed Sherman he would send two brigades of his corps (since one, Mower's, was already on detached duty across the river where the major pastime was "fishing and many meet with good success") and three of McPherson's to rush eastward and support Washburn and Osterhaus. If it became clear that more troops were needed, Grant even planned this force to be further strengthened "if it should become absolutely necessary, by taking all the troops to the left of McClernand." In perhaps the most profound part of the contingency plan, with both Kimball and Washburn having shown some panic during times that needed steady leadership, Grant told Sherman: "In case this has to be done, you will be detached temporarily from the command of your corps here, to take command at Haynes's Bluff whilst it may be besieged." That would put a corps commander, and Grant's favorite and most trustworthy one, in charge of a large amount of troops along the Big Black River and the slot to deal with Johnston. The senior division commander in Sherman's corps, Frederick Steele, would take command of the corps.[73]

McPherson soon received word of the plan, as did McClernand, who would hold a key position in the process. None of his brigades would be detailed for the support, given that he had one fewer to begin with (two brigades per his four divisions as compared to three brigades in the three divisions of the other corps), and one of those was already back at the Big Black River. Yet if it came to it, Grant informed McClernand, " I will have to entirely uncover on the south side of the city. This will necessarily involve an exposure of our left flank from the garrison of Vicksburg." Grant wanted McClernand to hold that left flank tightly. Lauman, who soon fell under McClernand's command, would remain unless it became desperate: "I do not want to give up the front occupied by Lauman unless it should become absolutely necessary to do so." Thinking of every possibility, Grant added that, in the event the Confederates attacked elsewhere, he wanted McClernand to hold the position while the rest of the army moved into Vicksburg and used the defenses in reverse to keep the Confederates out.[74]

The plan was not put into action at this point but simply devised, with the brigades on the siege lines to "be held in readiness to march to Haynes' Bluff at the shortest notice." By June 15, in fact, Grant informed Washburn at Haynes' Bluff that despite the activity it "does not look like an intention to attack Haynes' Bluff immediately, but a disposition to get and hold a footing on the ridge as near to it as possible, while they are collecting their forces for an attack. Their intention evidently is to come down suddenly when they do move, and for that reason they will endeavor to get a position as near us as possible."[75]

Sherman soon had his affairs in order nevertheless, moving Tuttle's remaining two brigades, Ralph Buckland's and Joseph Woods's, out of the line so that they could be ready to move, their front being covered by Blair's brigades extending to their right, namely Joseph Lightburn's taking over for Woods's brigade on the front line. Thinking this would be the perfect timing to rearrange other things, Sherman wrote back that he would be ready to move, but he requested that one of Lauman's Indiana regiments be sent to Wood's brigade to make the standard four regiments per brigade. The colonel, Walter Gresham, had requested the move and, Sherman noted, "is very anxious to come to my corps." He added also that "he is one of my Kentucky colonels," but Sherman stipulated that Lauman would have to approve before anything was done. Sherman also informed Grant that he would like to ride out and "reconnoiter the ground . . . before an enemy makes his appearance from the direction of Yazoo City, on the ridge back of Haynes'."[76]

It seemed the operations around Vicksburg were consequently coming to a climax, and the rear was less and less a concern because of the growing reinforcements. One Federal went so far as to say, "I predict that they will get worse whipped than they did at Champion's Hill and Big Black River Bridge if they come in rear." Still, it seemed very probable that Johnston would move soon if he was going to at all, and at the same time it appeared that the Confederate garrison inside Vicksburg could not hold out much longer. Admiral Porter, for example, notified the Navy Department in Washington that "the situation of affairs has altered very little. We are still closing on the enemy." While he noted Grant's "position is safe," he advised any more troops that could be scraped together should be sent southward. Then he made his prediction: "I think the town cannot hold out longer than 22d of June."[77]

The mastermind of the impressive Vicksburg Campaign, Major General Ulysses S. Grant overcame obstacles and adapted to reach Vicksburg and then to secure it. Waging a siege in front and a rearward defense behind, Grant overcame all obstacles and with the help of numerous reinforcements won the victory with Vicksburg's capitulation on July 4, 1863. (Library of Congress)

The ranking corps commander (XIII Corps) in the Army of the Tennessee, Major General John A. McClernand had been a thorn in Grant's side for the entire campaign but proved fairly able in his military command. That did not stop Grant from relieving him once the result of the siege was largely no longer in doubt. (Library of Congress)

Major General Edward O. C. Ord replaced McClernand as commander of the XIII Corps in mid-June. Ord seemed to be everything McClernand was not: a West Pointer and a Grant ally. Ord quickly brought the engineering aspects of the XIII Corps up to the level of the others, something the non–West Point trained McClernand had not done. (Library of Congress)

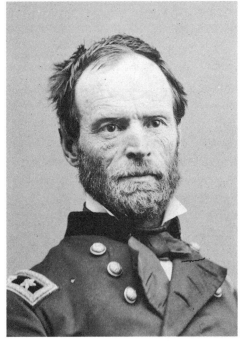

By far Grant's favorite subordinate, Major General William T. Sherman commanded the XV Corps. When the concern for the rear became especially alarming, Grant sent Sherman to take control there in an independent command. (Library of Congress)

As the ranking division commander in the XV Corps, Major General Frederick Steele took command of the corps when Sherman left to command the rearward defenses. Although sick much of the siege, Steele commanded ably. (Library of Congress)

Politician-general Major General Francis P. Blair, Jr., former member of Congress and brother of one of Abraham Lincoln's cabinet officers, led a division of Sherman's XV Corps. He also commanded the first foray to the rear of Vicksburg in what became a succession of commanders tapped to secure that area. (Library of Congress)

Another of Grant's favorite subordinates, Major General James B. McPherson commanded the XVII Corps. As the most inexperienced of the original three, McPherson was by the time of the surrender the senior corps commander on site at the siege. (Library of Congress)

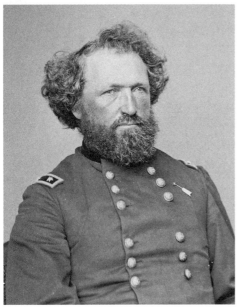

A brigade commander in the XVII Corps, Brigadier General Mortimer D. Leggett led the ill-fated assault on the crater produced by the mine blown at the 3rd Louisiana Redan. Leggett fell wounded in the attack. (Library of Congress)

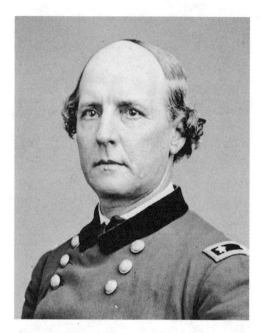

Many of Grant's reinforcements during the siege came from Major General Stephen A. Hurlbut's XVI Corps in northern Mississippi and West Tennessee. Hurlbut commanded the northern regions of Grant's department while Grant went after Vicksburg. (Library of Congress)

Brigadier General Jacob G. Lauman commanded a division of Hurlbut's XVI Corps near Memphis but moved southward to Vicksburg in mid-May. He took a position on the lines soon after the siege began, helping to block Confederate movements on the southern extremity of the siege lines. (Miller's *Photographic History*)

Another division commander of the XVI Corps, Brigadier General William "Sooy" Smith led his brigades southward to Grant's army at Vicksburg and helped hold the rear of the line around Haynes' Bluff. (Library of Congress)

A third division of Hurlbut's XVI Corps moved southward under Brigadier General Nathan Kimball, who briefly took command of the efforts to solidify Grant's rear while he continued the siege of Vicksburg. (Library of Congress)

Brother of Grant's guardian congressman, Major General Cadwallader C. Washburn was another political general and arrived at Haynes' Bluff to command the XVI Corps divisions there. He ultimately commanded a quasi-corps consisting of "Sooy" Smith's and Kimball's divisions. (Library of Congress)

Commander of the IX Corps, Major General John G. Parke brought two divisions of mostly eastern troops from Ambrose Burnside's department in Ohio. Parke added these troops to the rearward defense and by rank took command of the rearward effort until Sherman arrived to command the whole. (Library of Congress)

Major General Francis J. Herron was a young general but did well in his position on the extreme southern end of the Federal lines. He led his troops southward from Missouri, where John Schofield had responded positively to calls for reinforcements for Grant at Vicksburg. (Library of Congress)

Grant's naval soulmate was Rear Admiral David Dixon Porter, who managed the two parts of his flotilla at Vicksburg, one to the north and one to the south of the city. The navy, especially the mortars, continually bombarded Vicksburg and added a great deal to the successful capture of the city. (Library of Congress)

As the Confederate commander at Vicksburg, Lieutenant General John C. Pemberton was caught between two superiors who advised opposite strategies. Trapped inside the city for the siege, his only hope was relief from Joseph E. Johnston, but Pemberton and Johnston could not communicate well enough to work out a plan of relief. (Library of Congress)

Pemberton's senior division commander, Major General Carter L. Stevenson commanded the siege lines on the southern end of the Confederate fortifications. He also oversaw the logistical aspects of the siege. (Library of Congress)

Major General Martin L. Smith commanded one of Pemberton's divisions, manning the defense on the northern end of the Vicksburg lines. (Library of Congress)

Having primarily repelled the assaults on May 19 and 22, Major General John H. Forney and his division defended the main roads into the city of Vicksburg during the siege. His troops helped repel the attack when the mine blew on June 25 at the 3rd Louisiana Redan. (Library of Congress)

Sick for much of the siege, Major General John S. Bowen commanded Pemberton's reserve division, although many of the troops wound up on the siege lines anyway. Bowen played a major role in the surrender negotiations but barely survived the siege, dying just days later. (Library of Congress)

Brigadier General Martin E. Green commanded a brigade under John S. Bowen at Vicksburg, manning mostly the lines near the Stockade Redan. He died from a sharpshooter's bullet as he peered over the works late in the siege. He was the only general officer on either side to perish during the siege itself. (Miller's *Photographic History*)

Commanding the Confederate western theater as a whole, General Joseph E. Johnston was on site near Vicksburg at the direction of Confederate president Jefferson Davis. His purpose was to relieve Vicksburg, but Johnston made little effort in doing so, offering more excuses than help for the beleaguered Vicksburg garrison. (Library of Congress)

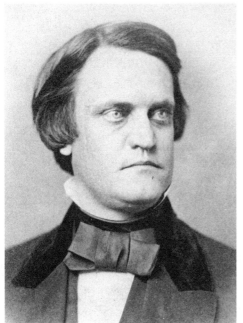

Former vice president of the United States, Major General John C. Breckinridge commanded a division under Johnston. His troops had been transferred from Braxton Bragg's army in Tennessee and manned the Jackson area, never engaging the Federals in battle. (Library of Congress)

Originally a part of Pemberton's army defending Vicksburg, Major General William W. Loring and his division became cut off at Champion Hill and marched eventually to Jackson. They became part of Johnston's army but were of little help in relieving Vicksburg. (Miller's *Photographic History*)

Major General William H. T. Walker originally commanded a brigade but took on division command as more and more Confederate troops assembled near Jackson. Yet these troops were never used to relieve Vicksburg, mainly because of the lethargy of their commander, Joseph E. Johnston. (Miller's *Photographic History*)

A Northerner by birth, Major General Samuel G. French was nevertheless loyal to his home state of Mississippi and the Confederacy. Jefferson Davis sent him west when Johnston called for more generals, where he took command of a division. (Miller's *Photographic History*)

Vicksburg, Mississippi, as seen from the Mississippi River. The Warren County Courthouse dominates the skyline. (Library of Congress)

Probably the most iconic photograph from Vicksburg, this view shows not only the Shirley House, known to the soldiers simply as the "White House," but also the campsites of John A. Logan's Union division. (Library of Congress)

One of the few photographs of the siege lines, this view shows Logan's approach toward the 3rd Louisiana Redan. The structure in center is Coonskin's Tower. (Library of Congress)

This drawing shows the crater created by the Union mine blown underneath the 3rd Louisiana Redan. The fight for possession of the mine took place on June 25. (Library of Congress)

Several Confederate guns gained nicknames during the siege. Probably the most famous was "Whistling Dick," so named because of its whistling projectile. (Library of Congress)

Many Vicksburg civilians survived the siege in caves dug into the steep hillsides around Vicksburg. This drawing illustrates well the struggles attendant to living underground. (Library of Congress)

10

"I SHOULD HAVE RELIEVED HIM LONG SINCE"

June 16–19

"Vicksburg is a mighty hot place right now," Benjamin Wiley wrote to his wife. Certainly the weather was warm in this Mississippi summer, but the fighting was also growing hotter and hotter. But the harsh conditions were not just on the front lines or in the camps. The results of what happened on those front lines and in those camps became more and more horrible as the siege went on, and it fell to the medical department of both armies to try to care for those wounded on the front lines and who became sick in the camps. There were plenty of both, and it was not limited just to humans. One chaplain relayed a pitiful scene where a captain had his horse shot: "He falls upon his haunches, pierced through with a piece of shell. His entrails protrude. He groans and moans with pitiful cry and tries in vain to rise."[1]

Obviously, care for human beings took top priority, as sad as the plight of the animals was. That duty fell to the various medical departments, and each faced its own issues. For Grant, he had sick and wounded piling up at the end of a long string of communication and supply, which meant everything needed to care for them had to be brought over long distances, and—perhaps worse—evacuation to general hospitals up North was just as lengthy.[2]

Yet Grant faced a larger issue right in the middle of the campaign, one sent from Washington, namely a change in his current department medical director, Surgeon Madison Mills. Grant protested: "I regret this order was ever issued. This Department has probably suffered more than any other from frequent changes in Medical Directors, and from incompetency of some of those serving as such. Surgeon Mills has brought up his department from a low standard to a very high one." He emphasized, "It will be manifest injustice to Surgeon Mills to order him before a Retiring Board, and a greater injustice to the service to have such Board retire him." Grant asked, at the least, for Mills to stay through the siege.[3]

Mills and the hierarchy of surgeons and other medical personnel worked to care for all through a system of hospitals set up on the division level and above, including on many of the steamboats in the various rivers around Vicksburg. Yet many soldiers had a stark fear of the hospitals: "I never wish to see another Army hospital or at least don't wish to be an inmate of one." An Iowan declared that many wounded and sick soldiers came back to the regiment when they could, "preferring the dangers of the enemy to the loneliness of the hospital." But there was much sickness in those camps too, he describing a lot of bowel trouble, declaring it was from "the incongruous and indigestible hard-tack fried in bacon-grease." He also said that the water was so bad that many had the "shaking ague." Others had chills and fever, joking that they "were so common that time had to be divided so that each could have room in the dog-tent to 'shake.'" One Iowan also related the procedure of the surgeon's call in the morning in the 22nd Iowa: "Half the regiment lines up at the 'surgeons call' every morning for their boluses of cayenne-pepper and bitter medicine with its dark brunette taste." Accordingly, most trusted their own, known regimental surgeons over those in the cramped, putrid larger hospitals.[4]

Some had to be sent on to the larger hospitals, however, and one Federal declared "there you find the horrors of war." Orders went out about where to do surgery, where to set up primary depots "established for temporary relief," and so on. There was also a dependence on alcohol at these hospitals, much of it confiscated from the army. "I understand some one is selling Ale at the Point," Grant wrote. "If so confiscate the entire stock in trade, turn it over to the Sanitary commission, arrest the parties and send them North by first boat." Wine and alcohol was soon prohibited, but the sutler of the 16th Ohio found forty-four cases of "Spark Catawba wine" on his hands, obtained by permission of Hurlbut before the crackdown. He sought a way to get rid of it and devised selling it to the medical corps, which he did. That said, soldiers still obtained alcohol, one Ohioan who had been left behind when his unit went to the rear to watch for Johnston noting in his diary that he "went out and got drunk."[5]

Some actually found the rearward hospitals comfortable. "I am very well satisfied here I have nothing to do only to eat and sleep and that is easy work," wrote Solomon Lynd to his father. Another explained that he was "a Convalescent Soldier, as all is called who are not able for duty. I have a very good time here have plenty of grub to eat that you know is what always suited me." Every effort at comfort was made, including cotton bales broken open and laid out so the men could lie on them. Yet there were so many patients that many sick at the hospitals had to be laid out on cots underneath the trees.[6]

Fortunately, the medical personnel had a lot of help, namely from nurses who came down to Vicksburg to aid the sick or wounded. These females had to be protected, however, one describing how they were often huddled about when fear of a night breakout attempt came, especially early in the siege. One recalled how "I left the tent for the Landing to remain till the following day, as the threatening of the rebel outbreak was so serious that it was considered unsafe for a woman to remain in the encampment during that night."[7]

One of those Sanitary Commission nurses described the Union hospitals. "I . . . was rejoiced to find them so clean comfortable and well supplied. They were situated on a clearing, on a pleasant green bluff, with sufficient trees for shade. There were three long rows of new hospital tents abreast with accommodations for several hundred men, provided with comfortable cots, mattresses, soft pillows, clean sheets and pillow-slips—even mosquito-bars admirably arranged on uprights." Still, the suffering was enormous, she adding that "the muttering of delirium, in which sharp, quick orders were given, companies called out, men sheered and led to battle, grated painfully on a strained ear and aching heart." The bugs did not help either, and the constant rattling of army wagons on the adjacent road was not at all beneficial to soldiers who needed quiet to rest.[8]

With the land hospitals full, many of the sick and wounded had to be kept on hospital boats. These ranged from those at the Chickasaw Bayou landing to others somewhere in the vicinity, such as at Milliken's Bend and Young's Point. Even with the additional space, these hospital boats soon filled, and many were then taken north. Hospital boats were not all bad either, one soldier declaring that the food was much better on the boats than in the land hospitals.[9]

Basically two types of patients received care in these hospitals. One was the large number of wounded, which grew as the siege progressed and the skirmishing and sharpshooting continued. Many of the wounded were kept in the division hospitals, hopefully so they could return to duty once their injuries healed. Unfortunately, some wounded from the assaults in May were still in the divisional hospitals in mid-June.[10]

Little could be done for extremely bad cases, most of which soon died. Amputees were out of the war for good and were sent north. Others with less serious wounds remained in these hospitals and suffered extreme boredom: "I do not feel very well from the affects of a ball that took me adrite on my head," Charles Vanamburg wrote to his father; "they came very near smashing my brains out but they held to high and they don me but little injury but I shall have a very soar head for some time but I hav nothing els to do but to take cair of my self until it gets well." James Palmer similarly scribbled in his diary: "I was wounded on the 17th of June 1863." He went on to note, "It was my birthday in the 29 year of my life I was wounded on the left side of my head by a piece of shell that exploded in the air over our heads my wound was not verry serious but gave me considerable pain for several days and nights. I staid in the Brigade hospital 3 days when I returned to my command in the ditches."[11]

Unfortunately, Grant had more wounded to worry about than just those produced at the siege. Having marched and fought his way inland for two weeks, fighting five battles in the process, he left wounded all along his trek, and their care added a degree of difficulty to the equation. Grant sent a surgeon to the rear to Edwards Station and Raymond "for the purpose of removing such wounded Federal soldiers as will bear transportation, and for taking supplies, medical stores, &c., for those whose condition requires them to remain where they are for a longer time." He and others had little hope of fairness, however, one Federal writing, "they will undoubtedly visit our hospitals in every direction, in order to swell their numbers of prisoners." Division commander Peter Osterhaus, guarding the Big Black River Bridge, noted "the large number of wounded at Champion's Hill expressed the desire to be removed into our lines."[12]

Still, the rearward Federals, even though prisoners, were treated well. One soldier in Raymond wrote, "May God bless the ladies of Raymond and surrounding country—I could write a volume about the kind treatment which the wounded soldiers receive from the hands of the ladies." Those who could also performed the morbid service of burying their dead there. Ultimately, Grant was able to get supplies through to them.[13]

However, sickness could be just as deadly too. Diseases ran the gamut, but most dealt with bowel issues. Brigade commander Adolph Engelmann wrote of his bout with diarrhea in great detail to his wife. He had begun the problem before leaving Bolivar, Tennessee, and tried some "bullion the doctor gave me," but it was ruined as attested to when he stuck his knife in the can and it squirted into his face, "having a very unpleasant flavor."[14]

Others had similar issues, including brigade commander James Slack, who described his bout with "this miserable diarrhea." One soldier had been sick since Yazoo Pass, where he and others drank bad water they termed "Death in the Pot." Many other issues existed with common names such as the "flux," "chills," and what many termed the "ague." "I came near shaking my toe nails off, with the ague," wrote Anoniram Withrow, "and did not feel like writing. I had a hard chill, but I guess I am as able to stand it as any one, there is one consolation about it, and that is it only comes every other day." One Ohioan blamed his family for his sickness: "You and Abbie has been writing to me so much about the chills that you have finally given them to me." Worse, there were some accounts of smallpox brought down among the reinforcements, but the cases were quickly quarantined and it did not spread.[15]

Some sickness was just a nuisance. A Michigander went to the hospital with chigger bites head to toe. "The itching is almost intolerable," he groaned. Others reported toothaches. One had a tooth pulled and "have got the swell head in consequence," which fortunately got him off duty the next day. Another described sitting up to write a letter "by a dim light with my mouth stuffed with tobacco to allay toothache (the surgeon will attend to it tomorrow) and my nerves all in a flutter."[16]

Of course, some of the wounds and sickness resulted in death, and that was a miserable duty to tend to. Only a few bodies were sent home, mostly officers such as brigade commander Colonel George Boomer, killed in the May 22 assault. One Illinoisan described sending a letter home with a comrade "who goes home with the body of our Captain who died yesterday he had the flux and was in the Hospital about a week." He would be particularly missed because "he was the only one of the three Commissioned officers that could do the writing that was necessary." Death made many think all the more about the afterlife: "He had gone to his eternal home where the weary are at rest and where there will be no rebellion, no wars, no bloodshed to trouble them in that happier land."[17]

An Iowan similarly wrote how "the hospitals were crowded with the victims of disease, and every day the burial parties performed their sad duties at the graves of newly departed comrades." Sadly, the number of deaths held steady, some in the most pitiful of ways. One Illinoisan told how some were injured worse in ambulance rides, even a few with nonfatal wounds being killed. Such resulted in the almost constant stream of sad letters emanating from Vicksburg beginning with doleful words: "It becomes my painful duty to inform you. . . ."[18]

Medical care inside Vicksburg under the Confederate medical director, Surgeon E. H. Bryan, was just as challenging, perhaps more so, although at least one Confederate described eating good on "beef heals & tails." Yet just getting the sick and wounded to the hospitals was a chore. Ambulances were everywhere, but the rides were hard on the wounded. Most ambulances did not have springs, making one Confederate note, "just to think of a wounded man with broken limbs and mangled body being borne on such a rough jolting vehicle as this. No wonder they groan under such circumstances." Housing such large numbers was also a problem, especially when others hung around as well, such as those described by the dentist Rowland Chambers: "They have three hospitals on the place and them full of sick wounded and shirks an[d] lofers of which the latter are well represented." The post surgeon advised Pemberton in late June that "wounded are arriving every day at our hospitals" and that there were no beds for them. Pemberton had stopped shipments of lumber to the hospitals for beds, but the surgeon insisted that "it is impossible to treat wounded men as their wounds require, upon the ground and floor." Pemberton turned to other means to acquire the lumber, even ordering his staff to locate "some frame houses unoccupied and of as small value as possible." These would be assayed for worth and then torn down for their lumber. Pemberton also offered the lumber of the "broken pontoons" for that purpose.[19]

Confederates distinguished between sickness and wounds in their hospitals, the two cases being separated into different localities. The suffering was the same. One chaplain told of the horror at the hospitals: "Every tent is filled with the wounded and dying. There they lay, poor, helpless sufferers; some groaning from excessive pain, others pale and silent through weakness and loss of blood." He added an additional nightmare: "Flies swarm around the wounded—more numerous where the wound is severest." He continued, saying "the whole air in the tents was contaminated. It sickened the heart and the body to pass amongst them." He described one particularly bad case of a soldier shot in the body who was tormented by flies and in his state pulled his bandages off. The result revealed an awful scene: "The vile worms crawl in and out of his body."[20]

Besides all this suffering, the mortar shells constantly burst all around the hospitals. Sometimes pieces flew so near the patients "as to unstring their nerves"; some wounded and sick were even killed. Surgeons were also wounded at their posts, one writing how "the wounded are killed in the hospitals, Surgeons wounded while attending to their duties." One mortar hit the City Hospital in the night, blowing up several rooms and medicine and injuring one surgeon "so badly as to require instant amputation." To replace the loss, "an entire outfit of drugs, and the use of a carpenter and brick mason for a couple of days," was required.[21]

Myriad problems abounded. Stephen D. Lee complained that his brigade hospital was so full that the sick and wounded were also at a "convalescent camp" at the Smedes House but had no medical furniture or equipment. The medical officials would not send any, and the post surgeon would not accept the sick and wounded because the brigade had its own hospital. Pemberton himself had ordered the post surgeon to furnish the Smedes House with needed equipment in early June, but he had not done so, and now Lee's sick and wounded received less care while Lee himself could get no clear answers. On another occasion, medical officials confiscated sixty-nine bottles of whiskey at one grocery and searched individual residences, but the 27th Louisiana somehow gained access and became drunk and thus not all of the whiskey made it to the hospitals.[22]

"The first ten days generally decides whether the wound will prove fatal or not," one hospital worker explained. "The weather was so warm that many died who might otherwise have recovered." One chaplain described the burial efforts, the dead laid to rest in their plain blankets in the nearby hollow. "Though no tear is then shed over the grave, yet far away hearts will bleed and tears will flow from the eyes of mothers and sisters and wives for those who lie sleeping in the valley—unnoticed, unhonored and unsung."[23]

Some Union wounded were also brought into Vicksburg and cared for at the hospitals. A citizen described how "one of them had a hole shot in the side of his head and his brains were running out of it." He described another extremely proud soldier: "One man was 68 years old sais he is fighting for the constitution and would rather die than live with ceches [secesh]." Those who lived faced prison, some in the city jail and others in the courthouse. One Ohioan, long after the war, remembered, "I recollect every brick and creeping creature in its infernal jail. It was the most densely inhabited spot in America."[24]

By the same token, some Confederates became prisoners outside Vicksburg, and they, like the Union soldiers at Raymond, wondered when they would be saved. "One week has passed," wrote a Confederate wounded at Champion Hill and taken into custody, "and no news from our army at V-g yet." Other Confederate prisoners faced uneven treatment at times. Two Confederates who tried to escape "not to rejoin their troops but to go home" were still ordered shot by the Union officer in charge. A more understanding officer allowed two other Confederates "to return home to tend their fields but they must return to prison when their work has been done."[25]

Such was the morbid reality behind the scenes of war where sick, wounded, and captured soldiers fought time, germs, and inefficiency to survive at the Siege of Vicksburg.

By mid-June, additional reinforcements were arriving to set Grant's mind more at ease, but there would never be enough troops to satisfy him. Still, the influx of two eastern divisions of IX Corps troops from Kentucky helped; "they arrived none too soon," Grant later admitted. Major General John G. Parke, an army engineer himself, led two divisions, one under Brigadier General Thomas Welsh, whom a Massachusetts officer told his wife was "a kind of an old granny, frightened at his own shadow." There was also the division under Brigadier General Robert B. Potter, or five brigades total in the corps. The troops initially moved southward by railroad to Cairo. "Where we are to go, I have no idea," one Massachusetts officer wrote to his wife upon the initial movement. Despite numerous accounts of drunkenness and men falling off the cars or being left behind at stations, most arrived safely. There were no passenger cars in the train on which the 36th Massachusetts traveled, and William F. Draper described to his wife how he rode on top of a freight car, where "dust and cinders were plenty and we had to lay close to the cars as there were numerous low bridges on the route." The people along the route were kind, however, one Michigan soldier declaring that "they gave us all the bread, butter, milk, cake, pies, &c that we could eat."[26]

Once at Cairo, the brigades boarded steamboats and slowly made their way southward, stopping at dark due to the low level of the river. "It is just one week to [the] day since we came aboard this boat at Cairo," Massachusetts soldier Robert Jameson wrote to his sister, but "it seems longer for we have had miserable accommodations and more miserable fare." Only the beautiful setting sun made the trip tolerable. The troops moved onward to Vicksburg nevertheless, coming under fire from guerrillas at times but eventually arriving at "Sherman's Landing" near Young's Point in Louisiana, according to Colonel Zenas R. Bliss of the 7th Rhode Island. One official added, "Parke [also] has two splendid batteries of siege guns, which will be useful to General Grant." Perhaps most useful of all, these were all veterans of eastern battles such as the Seven Days, Antietam, and Fredericksburg. One Massachusetts soldier recalled how the westerners came to look at them, thinking they were "recently-mustered troops . . . little knowing that they were actually deriding the sunburnt veterans of the Peninsula, and the heroes of Antietam."[27]

Many eyes were on the corps's route, including the soldiers themselves who bought maps and carefully traced their progress along the Mississippi River in this foreign territory: "Many of the regiment had provided themselves with little maps of the river, and with true Yankee curiosity, studied the various points of interest with the skill and style of veteran tourists." The calliopes on the steamboats also fascinated the New Englanders. Grant uneasily watched their progress throughout the trip, as did the Confederates when Bragg picked up on the movements across his front. Stephen Hurlbut at Memphis mostly kept Grant informed. "A portion of the Second Division, of Ninth Army Corps, arrived this afternoon," Hurlbut reported from Memphis on June 10, "the balance will be here in a few hours from Cairo." Parke became increasingly irritated at "granny" Welsh's slowness in moving southward, but the division soon caught up. Yet logistical problems emerged as they reached Memphis, where the Ohio River boats were swapped for Mississippi River steamers, the originals going back to their area of service. Hurlbut lamented that "everything is being pressed forward as fast as possible, but there is terrible scarcity of boats." Hurlbut laid some of the blame on Grant himself, adding that "it seems as if boats that go down to your parts never return. It is impossible to send anything down until some of the boats below are returned. Every boat from Saint Louis is in service. They should not be kept an hour after they are discharged of their cargoes."[28]

The commanding general originally intended for Parke's five brigades, once they arrived, to fully plug the gap in the southernmost siege lines, on the left of Herron's now-arrived division. Grant even tinkered with the idea of placing Lauman's, Herron's, and Parke's troops all under a new corps commander, the daily-expected Major General Edward O. C. Ord, who arrived by June 18. An Ohioan described him as "a tall man with gray mustache, and is brusque and unapproachable in his manner. I was not at all favorably impressed with him," he adding that "Gen. McClernand, on the contrary, is affable and gentlemanly." Grant even informed McPherson that Parke would go south "if nothing else occurs between this and the time of their arrival to change the present phase of affairs." He noted, however, that if something did happen, troops to defend the rear would come from those troops to the south.[29]

That is exactly what happened, even though a portion of Parke's troops had arrived and begun to move south of the city on the roads west of the river. The main culprit was the Confederate movement to the east that continually worried Grant, although he kept a watchful eye on that area, even sending his staff engineer James H. Wilson to Snyder's and Haynes' Bluffs to oversee the construction of fortifications there. With no letup in Confederate activity, Grant changed his mind about Parke. It was almost a split-second decision, in fact. Grant was in the midst of writing to McClernand on June 15, informing him of the Sherman contingency plan and the troops that would be put on his left, including Parke, who would "take position on the south side of the city, thus making the investment complete." Grant went so far as to describe how Parke's arrival would free up Herron to shift right, which would allow McClernand to concentrate his three divisions on two of the division fronts. Yet in a new paragraph in the same letter, Grant wrote, "after writing the foregoing, and after General Parke had moved one division of his command to opposite Warrenton, I had to change my plan and send him to Haynes' Bluff." He explained further that "from information received, the enemy has 12,000 infantry and artillery at Yazoo, with orders to move south, four thousand cavalry already between the Yazoo and Big Black River, and Loring ordered to cross. This made it necessary to send the extra force up the Yazoo River." Charles Dana elaborated the next day, writing that the decision to send Parke to Haynes' Bluff "is done on no new information, but after fuller consideration of that received yesterday morning." That information, of course, was Washburn's semi-panicked warning of an imminent attack. Grant had to cover his rear, and he evidently figured McClernand, Lauman, and Herron could make do on the south side of Vicksburg.[30]

Parke's divisions, after braving the guerrillas firing on them on the trip down and the roundabout moves south of Vicksburg, arrived at Snyder's

Bluff on their transports and disembarked on June 17, a day many of the soldiers in the Massachusetts regiments celebrated as Bunker Hill Day. The western troops took note, one writing that "it seemed odd to hear of such and such Mass. Regiment, Penn. And New York regiments." The 79th New York Highlanders even had with them what one termed as "a new 'institution' attached to the regiment—nothing less than a Scotch 'piper' from Michigan, who joined us on our way down here." One New Yorker described him as "has a full suit of the kilts and often so entertains us with his alleged *tunes* on the pipes, that we have several times threatened to 'fire him out' and not allow him to perform again till he learns how." The westerners of Grant's army wanted a good look at these spick-and-span easterners, one of whom reported that "crowds of soldiers came down to see the Eastern troops as they call us." Animosity began almost immediately. One New Englander reported that some of Grant's army "hooted us with 'Bull Run!' 'Fredericksburg!' and other insulting cries." He admitted, "Our boys, having come down there to help the Western army out of a tight place, were much surprised at such treatment, and they were not only surprised, but so indignant, too, that there would have been a fight of no small dimensions if our officers had not hurried the troops off to Milldale." Another later noted that "these Western troops are very jealous of any interference, and expect to do all the work and get all the credit of taking the place themselves," and he later added, "the Western men are very jealous of us and don't want to give us a chance. They call us the Yankee division." The New Englanders also took note of the westerners, a Minnesotan describing how "these troops are loaded down with baggage and wonder how we get along with so little, but admire our scant supply and say that if the Potomac army was stripped as ours is it would be more effective."[31]

Parke's arrival added five more brigades to Smith's four and Kimball's three already there, making a grand total of twelve brigades near Haynes' Bluff. One of Parke's Michigan soldiers concluded that "he [Grant] does not seem to need us," and the lack of work and main duties of cleaning and lying about camp did not help the feeling. While Grant was not that impressed with Kimball or Smith, and had placed Washburn in command of those XVI Corps troops, Parke ranked all of them and soon became the de facto commander in the rear, until of course any time the contingency plan was put in place and Sherman took command. In fact, Grant began to correspond about matters in the rear with Parke as early as June 18, filling him in as best he knew of the locations of Confederates divisions and their perceived intent. "No order has been published assigning you to the command of all the forces at Haynes' Bluff," he wrote, "but being isolated from the general command, and being the senior officer, you necessarily command the whole."[32]

Desiring to show his authority and organize what seemed to be a haphazard effort, Parke took firm control on June 19. "Owing to the immediate and close connection between the forces under your command and mine, and our being isolated from the main army," Parke wrote to Washburn, "I have the honor respectfully to inform you that by virtue of my seniority I assume command of the whole. You will please make your reports through these headquarters." Wanting to get to know the situation as best he could, Parke asked for reports on Washburn's strength, organization, and sketches showing his positions. Fortunately, too, some of the tension between the easterners and westerners began to subside, one Iowan born in New Hampshire finding among the 9th New Hampshire "one company who were nearly all from my native town." Sadder, he also found that the two cousins he was seeking had both been killed earlier in the war.[33]

Parke soon found that with the privilege of higher command came responsibility as well, especially after a visit from Grant himself on June 21. Grant ordered: "I want the work of intrenching your position pushed with all dispatch, ready to receive an attack." But there was also a hint of change in Grant's instructions to Parke. Grant had long been worried about the enemy marching toward his siege lines to raise the siege; he had always thought strictly on the defensive in regard to the rear. Yet with the arrival of more and more troops—now some twenty thousand strong not counting Osterhaus's brigade at the railroad bridge—it was perhaps enough to start thinking about offensive operations, especially if the six brigades from the siege lines were added in the contingency plan. In fact, Grant noted in his defensive instructions that the fortification of the Haynes' Bluff area would also "leave the troops free to move out should the enemy remain where he is." Later, he described how Breckinridge's division was too far away at Clinton to be a factor near the slot "on the first day of battle, should we march on them." It was a mere hint, but Grant was ever so slightly changing his outlook as his worries began to lessen. Still, he cautioned Parke, "report all that you learn promptly."[34]

For his part, Parke planned well but began complaining immediately. Although being new to the army and theater, he felt the necessity to inform headquarters of his need for wagons to support his troops. "Now, I am not importunate nor given to complaining," he wrote, "but it is manifest that with but twenty wagons I cannot keep my men supplied at any considerable distance from the river. . . . I must have at least 100 wagons here to-morrow." He also requested axes for obstructing roads and fortifications. Water was also an issue, one of his New Hampshire soldiers writing to his father that "the water in the Yazoo was not allowed to be used as it was poisonous."[35]

All the while, Parke continued fortifying the rough terrain. One of the eastern troops explained, "Our division has to move tomorrow about three miles farther on to the right, to a very rough and hilly piece of ground. The colonel says the roughest we have seen is a meadow compared to it." Nevertheless, Parke spaced his twelve brigades out southward from the "immense fortifications" at Haynes' Bluff toward Osterhaus at the railroad bridge. Thirteen Union brigades now manned the rear, with five more being held in readiness to aid them. At that very moment, there were only twenty-three brigades (not counting those five held in reserve and the others doled out across the Mississippi River) on the siege lines at Vicksburg.[36]

Yet, Parke was only a temporary fix to the command situation in the rear; the major effort at defending the rear—or, for that matter, even going on the attack—would be done if concrete information arrived of Confederate movements and Grant implemented his contingency plan whereby Sherman would bring the five brigades from the besieging army and take command himself of all eighteen brigades in the rear, some thirty-three thousand men. Grant was not quite ready to act on the plan as yet, despite increased skirmishing, including a fairly large affair on June 18 near Birdsong Ferry on the Big Black River. Still, Sherman was active. He wanted to know what he was facing, what the ground was like, and where the troops were. Consequently, on June 15 he left Steele in charge of the XV Corps operations on the siege lines and went to the rear to look things over. He took Grant's young engineer, James H. Wilson, with him, they riding up to Snyder's Bluff the night of June 15 and returning to the Vicksburg lines the next night.[37]

That next morning, June 16, Sherman and Wilson looked over the area. He found the works at Haynes' Bluff fine: "They appear to me well adapted to the end in view, and will enable the two divisions of Kimball and Smith to hold any force coming from the north or northeast." Then he reconnoitered the area to the south, taking with him Generals Washburn, Smith, and Kimball, Parke not yet having arrived, although he noted that, as he was leaving that afternoon around 4:00 P.M., "I saw steamboats coming, which I think

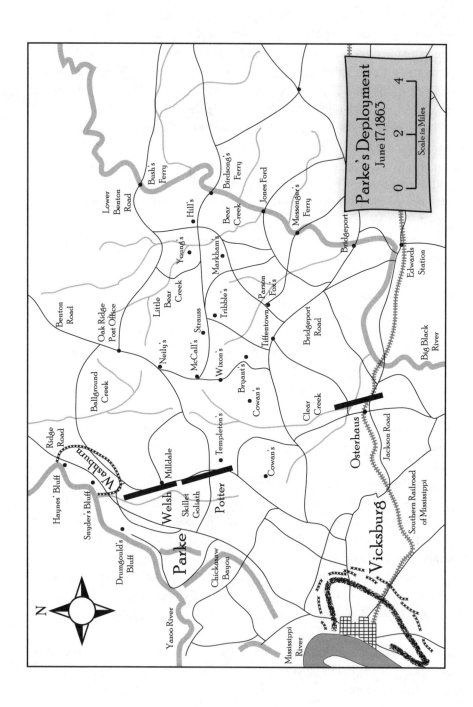

N

Parke's Deployment
June 17, 1863

Scale in Miles
0   2   4

Parke

Welsh

Potter

Osterhaus

Vicksburg

Haynes' Bluff
Snyder's Bluff
Drumgould's Bluff
Yazoo River
Chickasaw Bayou
Mississippi River

Ridge Road
Washburn
Milldale
Skillet Goliath
Templeton's

Benton Road
Oak Ridge Post Office
Ballground Creek
Neily's
McCall's
Strauss
Wixon's
Bryant's
Cowan's
Cowan's

Little Bear Creek
Markham's
Tribble's
Tiffentown
Parson Fox's

Young's
Hill's

Lower Benton Road
Bush's Ferry
Bear Creek
Birdsong's Ferry
Jones Ford
Messenger's Ferry
Bridgeport
Bridgeport Road
Clear Creek

Jackson Road
Edwards Station
Big Black River

Southern Railroad of Mississippi

contained his troops." Sherman recommended a line behind the Skillet Goliath Creek watershed, running southward from Snyder's Bluff to Milldale and on to Templeton's Plantation. Parke chose to make the line a little farther east. Nevertheless, Sherman was satisfied and ready to do whatever Grant requested. "As you know," he wrote, "my corps has done much labor, but I will do anything and everything in human power to achieve final success."[38]

Part of that success might actually be an offensive, to which Grant's mind more and more drifted. To finally clear out the slot once and for all, Grant continued to think of a possible offensive, especially if Sherman were dispatched to that area. Dana reported on June 18: "General Grant is ruminating the idea of an offensive movement suddenly and without impediments from Haynes' Bluff. Will threaten all the enemy's detachments in detail and take them separately, if possible."[39]

While Grant tinkered with the idea of offensive operations on the rear line, he was already doing so on the main lines at Vicksburg itself. These took form in more traditional siege efforts such as saps, approaches, and parallels. And these were quite extensive by this point in mid- to late June, one Illinoisan writing that "the Sap is a perfect labyrinth of a lane or walk, in which we got lost several times on our way from one position of the battery to another." He went on to describe how it "extends from one end of the works to the other, so that we can transport troops without the least danger of being shot or even seen, to their very works and from one end of the line to the other. It is up and down hill but seldom exposed."[40]

Sherman had begun his work as early as May 26 when Dana reported "Sherman has pushed the siege works in front of his center with great energy and admirable skill." Now, even though his attention was split between work here at Vicksburg and preparing for possible duty in the rear, Sherman kept the work going at full speed. It helped that new engineers also arrived on duty and continued the work already started. Woods's brigade no longer worked on its original sap; rather, he was to "continue as heretofore to push his work round by the right, along the Mississippi." Emphasis was now on "crowning the hills in front of Buckland's and Thayer's brigades." Quite a heated resistance emerged in Thayer's front as the approaches loomed nearer and nearer the Confederate lines. Engineer Frederick Prime reported that "this approach was sharply resisted by the enemy, who came outside of their line, and had to be driven from the ground they occupied before the work could be pushed forward." Problems also developed on Buckland's approach, where after much digging the sappers ran into "impracticable ground." They simply stopped the forward movement and began a parallel about forty yards out from the Confederate works, which was loop-holed for sharpshooters. Artillerymen also received orders to "advance their batteries as rapidly as the advanced works justify [and be] prepared to crown the enemy's works when the engineers report the work done." Even Admiral Porter realized the success Sherman was having, writing that he had his approaches much farther along than the others: "When the other generals are up with him," Porter wrote, "I presume that an assault will be made."[41]

By far, the most effort on Sherman's front went into Ewing's approach at the Stockade Redan. By mid-June, Sherman had reached "the ditch of their main fort at the salient." Company I of the 35th Missouri acted as sappers while details of fifty infantrymen from the division alternated into and out of the approach to aid in the work. The effort progressed rapidly, and Dana described Sherman as "now opening trenches parallel with the ditch along each flank of the work and crown of the glacis. . . . The curtains are each about 100 feet long." Sherman also placed artillery up close, some as near as within fifty yards of the Confederate line. Yet the Confederates in the redan were not idle, they resisting heartily; Engineer Prime reported that "it was pushed forward until the enemy annoyed the sappers very seriously with grenades and mines, the grenades being 6 or 12 pounder loaded shells, with short, lighted fuses." One Illinoisan admitted that "we found them to be bad roommates." Because of the trouble above ground, Prime explained "we then resorted to mining." The work here on "the most important one in Sherman's front" fell to Lieutenant Clemens C. Chaffee when Ewing's staff officer gave way, and later to Captain William Kossak on June 19 when Chaffee became ill.[42]

Upon arrival, Kossak took stock of what he had and found that the sap was within twenty feet of the Stockade Redan. Still, he noted "such obstructions in front of the sap roller as to make it impossible to move the roller one inch without having the party engaged in the moving killed outright." He made the sap roller into a parapet itself with added gabions and sandbags, and upon hearing "the dull, deep sound of tamping to the left, [indicating] that the enemy was mining to blow up the head of my sap," he began mining operations of his own. His intent was to dig "at right angles to the direction of the mines of the enemy, hoping to strike either their chambers or their powder-hole." He soon found he was way too deep and simply began countermines to mitigate the explosion if there was one.[43]

On McPherson's front, Engineer Andrew Hickenlooper, now back from his rearward duty, oversaw the XVII Corps advances once more, particularly on the Jackson Road, where his patented tandem of a "flying-sap by night and deepening and widening by day" continued to yield success. The engineer himself would crawl out at night and stick bayonets in the ground where he wanted the sap to run, tying white cord on them for the men to follow. Then, a squad of soldiers with a gabion each would spread out along the cord every four feet and start digging, first themselves a hole and then rearward to connect with the next man in line. Some questioned Hickenlooper's methods, but another officer noted that "General McPherson believed in Hickenlooper, and allowed him to construct the work in his own way." That was high praise from one of the United States military's most brilliant engineers, McPherson. The approach eventually wound its way from the Shirley House forward to an advanced battery, complete with a magazine, and from there onward toward the 3rd Louisiana Redan. This advanced battery, within a hundred yards of the fort and named for the chief engineer—"Battery Hickenlooper"—ultimately contained two 24-pound howitzers, two 30-pound Parrotts, and a 6-pounder, close enough to pummel the Confederate redan. But it was also close enough to be pummeled by return Confederate fire, and Hickenlooper himself described how "heavy rope shields, or aprons, were hung in front of the embrasures for protection of the gunners." Success was occurring elsewhere as well. Sappers on the right at Ransom's position "gained yesterday an important advantage by permanently occupying a fortification or spur of the ridge along whose crest the enemy's lines extend." All that occurred on Quinby's front, conversely, was the establishment of heavy batteries.[44]

The work did not stop just because it neared the Confederate lines. On Logan's front, Engineer Stewart Tresilian moved on forward the last hundred yards, brigade commander Mortimer D. Leggett right there in command of the operation. Hickenlooper was sick part of the time and had to correct some of the engineering, but Tresilian's approach continually moved forward so that in a few days the "sap yesterday debouched upon the rebels' salient at which he has been working." As there was no ditch in front of the 3rd Louisiana Redan, Dana presumed "McPherson will either dig down or mine." Help also came from the flank. On Ransom's front, he found a way on the night of June 19 to "push . . . his trenches so that at daylight his sharpshooters were able to take in reverse the whole right flank of the main rebel fort in his front, called Fort Hill. He soon drove out the enemy, killing and wounding many, and will be able to crown the rebel parapet with his artillery whenever the order is given." The artillery commander on Ransom's front was the one-armed Illinoisan John Wesley Powell, who had lost his limb at Shiloh but would go on to be the first white man to explore the Grand Canyon.[45]

Some problems occurred, however. Confederates with little more to do than devise new ways to fight destroyed several sap rollers. One novel sap roller on the Jackson Road approach consisted of what Confederate brigade commander Louis Hébert described as "cotton bales placed on a car, which car was moved along at will." Another called it "a land Monitor." It was, another Confederate described, "the platform of a freight railroad car, and the wheels apparently iron." A Union pioneer gave the accurate details: "Our Pioneer Corps constructed what was termed a dry-land Gun-boat. A frame about 8 or 10 feet square resting on two wooden axles, equipped with wooden wheels, the machine was propelled by levers which were run through holes in the axles by soldiers on the inside of the frame protected by bales of cotton being placed all around on top of frame." He noted, "I expect the rebels wondered what the thing was that was moving very slowly towards their works. The men moving it forward with the levers inside could not be seen by the enemy." But they made a loud noise in turning the axles, another Illinoisan remembering that "the noise made by turning of the axles was the signal for the Confederates to give it a volley." Hébert thought it would become necessary to send men out to burn it, the contraption having come to within seventy five yards of the redan, but fortunately for them, he said, Lieutenant Colonel Samuel D. Russell of the 3rd Louisiana "invented a safer and a much simpler course." On the night of June 8 he wrapped musket balls in turpentine and tow and fired them "with light charges" into the cotton bales. The cotton began to burn, one amazed Louisianan screaming, "I'll be d____d if that thing isn't on fire." The flames soon expanded to the car, while Confederate sharpshooters kept away anyone trying to extinguish it. More than twenty bales of cotton and the car were destroyed, the pioneer writing that "our gun-boat was soon reduced to ashes." Hickenlooper admitted the loss, "but through what agency was, at the time, a great mystery." On the night of June 17, the Louisianans fronting the approach managed to burn another sap roller. "The working party leaving it alongside cotton-bale," a disgusted but smarter Hickenlooper wrote, "the rebels threw over fire-balls, setting cotton on fire, which communicated to sap-roller before it could be removed."[46]

The nonengineer, non–West Pointer McClernand was still far behind at this point, although a few approaches had been begun on the XIII Corps front. "McClernand is pressing his approaches," Dana admitted, but despite the urging of Engineer Peter Hains he "is still much farther off than either of the others." Dana went on to complain that "the corps commanders and generals of divisions were not willing to follow his [Hains's] directions, either as to the manner of opening the lines of advance or the positions of the batteries to protect those lines." Still, by June 15, McClernand stated that some of his approaches were within thirty yards of the Confederate fortifications, and he reported daily of the developments, most of the major work occurring on A. J. Smith's front and some of it being done by "a party of negroes." In fact, Engineer Hains later described how a black regiment "is very necessary working by day in the trenches." Another effort on Carr's front was a "zig-zag approach, near the railroad," although McClernand reported "considerable opposition has been experienced, the enemy throwing out each night, a strong line of pickets, and at times opening a small gun on our working party." Mc-Clernand also reported "considerable difficulty is experienced at this point as the ground is somewhat marshy," but by June 19 Smith had reached the parapet of the 2nd Texas Lunette and was ready to begin mining.[47]

There were difficulties on McClernand's front as well, however, especially with sap rollers. The ground on Smith's front, utilizing a ravine part of the way, was such that a sap roller was not needed until later in June. Engineer Hains built three before he could get one to work. The first was too heavy to roll, the second too flimsy and "was crushed, of its own weight," but a third worked well, even taking occasional shots from artillery and small arms. Hains also decided to split the approach on Smith's front, one on each side of the Baldwin's Ferry Road, which required more workers and sap rollers. He complained of the details: "The want of sappers is now at this point more felt than heretofore. A different detail goes to work every day, who knows nothing of what is to be done, and much valuable time is lost in repeating instructions." Also causing issues was the lay of the land, up and down. At times, tunnels were used before the approach was once again pushed forward by use of sap roller; most of the time, the Federals would cover the approaches with fascines, making somewhat of a tunnel. This also worked well close in when the Confederates flung grenades at the sappers, the Federals covering their saps "with rails, thus making a sort of gallery."[48]

Resistance also emerged on McClernand's front, Engineer Prime describing how A. J. Smith's "progress was much impeded by the enemy's artillery fire, grenades, &c." Corps engineer Peter Hains brought in his own grenades from the navy but explained that "from their peculiar form could not be thrown any considerable distance. Even when the approaches were only 10 feet from the ditch, it required an extraordinarily powerful man to thrown one into the works." Prime added, "The enemy also attempted to blow up the sap-roller with a mine, but failed by underestimating the distance and using too feeble a charge." Yet he did admit that the Texans in the lunette succeeded "in burning one sap-roller by lodging a fire-ball against it."[49]

Actually, the Confederates burned two sap rollers in front of the 2nd Texas Lunette. Lieutenant William Allen of the 2nd Texas burned one: "He used turpentine fire balls. At first the enemy pulled away the balls as fast as they were thrown against the roller; but the officer threw over a loaded shell wrapped in cotton, saturated with turpentine, which exploded the moment the enemy seized it. After this the roller was soon burned." Colonel Ashbel Smith noted that the shell, an 18- pounder, was "bowled against the sap-roller." A Mississippi artilleryman burned the other sap roller, he shooting "a piece of fuse into it from a musket." That seemed to have stopped them, although a confused Confederate noted the Federals "have begun what appears to be a mound, at which he is working industriously."[50]

Engineer Hains described one of the burning sap rollers from his vantage point: "[The enemy] threw a fire-ball, which lodged under the edge of the sap-roller. They then threw hand-grenades into the fire made by the spreading of the inflammable fluid which it apparently contained; bursting, threw pieces all around it, tearing it considerably; at the same time they kept up an incessant fire of musketry on it. In about one half hour it was entirely destroyed, exposing to their view a portion of the trench." The same happened to the other roller in the divided approach. Eventually, Hains ordered the head of the saps closed with sandbags.[51]

McClernand thus lagged behind in his approaches, Dana noting on June 18 that the siege works of Sherman and McPherson are "slackened in order to give time for McClernand, Lauman, and Herron to bring theirs up." Engineer Hains was working as best he could, moving the approaches forward and building parallels on Smith's and Carr's front, they eventually joining near the railroad. Farther south, work also progressed, with one of Herron's brigade commanders, William Orme, making visits to the front lines to check on the progress at least twice a day. Dana went on to explain that, while the others caught up, the majority of the work on Sherman's and McPherson's lines consisted of "enlargement of covered ways and strengthening of the lines than of direct advances."[52]

There were of course other military efforts taking place in mid-June other than the approaches. Massive work went on at the rear line, where fortunately Parke brought with him more engineers and Dana explained how "two competent engineers absent on sick leave also returned yesterday, so that we shall no longer be deficient in that regard." Back on the Vicksburg lines, the artillery and naval bombardment was still intense and, often, choreographed to certain times and spaces. For example, McClernand issued orders that the large batteries such as 20-pounders and up would fire "eight guns per hour from each battery" between six in the morning and six in the evening. The smaller batteries were rated at five guns per hour. These shots were "to prevent the enemy from mounting additional guns or erecting additional works, if practicable, and also to throw as many projectiles into the enemy's intrenchments and camps as possible." The limitation was to make the ammunition, which was now flowing better than before, to last: "The strictest economy consistent with the end in view should be exercised in the expenditure of ammunition." Other orders from Grant's headquarters also limited the firing, one from June 15 stating to "fire your artillery as little as possible until you receive orders from here, it being desirable when there is artillery firing to have it all around the line, and continuous for certain periods of time."[53]

The result was incessant sharpshooting and skirmishing as the approaches continually neared the Confederate lines. Some of it had a special effect. On June 17, Colonel Isham W. Garrott of the 20th Alabama, commanding the Square Fort on Stephen D. Lee's front, fell to one of the crack shots of the Federal army. Pemberton lamented that the "most excellent and gallant officer, was killed early this morning by a ball through the head from one of the enemy's sharpshooters." Pemberton began calling the Square Fort "Fort Garrott," leading the historian Edwin C. Bearss to quip that you never want a fort named after you. Sadly, Garrott had recently been promoted to brigadier general, but word had not yet reached Vicksburg.[54]

Right in the middle of the monotonous and now smooth-running siege, a bombshell blew up on the night of June 18 and morning of June 19. This was no ordinary explosion of ordnance or even a planned blowing of a mine to create a hole through the Confederate works, but rather a major change in the Union command structure that affected the highest levels of the Army of the Tennessee and even higher up. It was now that Grant finally took care of what historian T. Harry Williams described as "the McClernand problem."[55]

It was a long time coming. Before the war, McClernand had been the successful, outspoken, opinionated politician from Illinois who was a personal friend of Lincoln's. By contrast, Grant was the unsuccessful, quiet, unassuming, dirt-poor farmer who was worlds away from politics and had never even met the president. So the relationship, once it began early in the war, was one of Grant's commonness compared to McClernand's elitism. The problem was that Grant outranked McClernand, who thought that he should command things. Grant gained that position by virtue of a West Point education that evened the playing field between the two during wartime. McClernand still operated on nonwartime presumptions, however; after all, he had been a congressman when Grant had resigned from the army due to drunkenness and thereafter failed in everything he tried, finally taking a small position in his father's leather-goods store in Galena, Illinois.[56]

War leveled the field, however. That became clear early on, and Grant rose quickly—much too quickly for McClernand, who chafed at this commoner giving him orders. The tense relationship simmered through the early war actions at Belmont, Forts Henry and Donelson, and Shiloh, where McClernand often loudly pushed his ideas and Grant just as quietly ignored them even while forming a not-so-positive opinion of this politician from Illinois. At one point Grant confided to Halleck: "I am sorry to say it, but I would regard it as particularly unfortunate to have either [John A.] McClernand or [Lew] Wallace sent to me. The latter I could manage if he had less rank, but the former is unmanageable and incompetent."[57]

When the campaigning shifted to the Vicksburg realm, however, the relationship broke open, courtesy of the politicians in Washington, Lincoln included. An unwise promise of command for McClernand if he raised the troops came in the fall of 1862, ordered by Secretary of War Edwin M. Stanton and endorsed by Lincoln himself. None of the chief military men in uniform were consulted, not even army general in chief Henry W. Halleck. McClernand began to raise the troops and send them southward, a worried Grant later acknowledging that "two commanders on the same field are always one too many." To remedy the growing calamity, a bit of trickery—covered politically by Halleck from Washington—saw Grant hijack the troops and send many with Sherman southward to the assault at Chickasaw Bayou.

As historian Michael B. Ballard noted, "If Grant could take Vicksburg, the McClernand problem would be solved."[58]

But Sherman failed, as did Grant in his bid to get behind Vicksburg via central Mississippi. Worse for them, McClernand showed up at Memphis demanding to know where his troops were and waving his papers, including Lincoln's endorsement, at everybody. He emphasized "the order of the Secretary of War recognizing the Mississippi expedition and assigning me to the command of it" and added "the President's endorsement thereon manifests the interest he feels in the expedition." McClernand wrote to Washington for backing, even to Lincoln himself. "I believe I have been superseded. Please inquire and let me know whether it is and shall be so," he told Stanton. He telegraphed Lincoln: "I believe I am superseded. Please advise me."[59]

Grant's horror was compounded when McClernand then pushed on southward to take command of what he deemed to be his army, he of course ranking Sherman and taking command when he arrived near Vicksburg. He promptly took the force Sherman had fought with up to Arkansas Post, which Grant described as "a wild-goose chase" and severely reprimanded him. McClernand responded haughtily, writing, "I take the responsibility of the expedition against Post Arkansas, and had anticipated your approval of the complete and signal success which crowned it rather than your condemnation. . . . I accept the consequences of the imputed guilt of using it profitably and successfully upon my own responsibility." He also added that "the officer who, in the present strait of the country, will not assume a proper responsibility to save it is unworthy of public trust."[60]

Obviously, Grant had to do something, and with backing from Halleck he put his foot down and assumed command of the whole in a one-prong advance toward Vicksburg. As Grant still outranked McClernand—even with Lincoln's endorsement on his orders—McClernand had no choice but to obey, even though he did so hesitantly and with loud remonstrations over the next few miserable winter months. Grant admitted that "his correspondence with me . . . was more in the nature of a reprimand than a protest. It was highly insubordinate, but I overlooked it, as I believed, for the good of the service."[61]

As an example, McClernand wrote to Grant on January 30:

> I understand that orders are being issued directly from your headquarters directly
> to army corps commanders, and not through me. As I am invested, by order of
> the Secretary of War, indorsed by the President, and by order of the President

communicated to you by the General-in-Chief, with command of all the forces operating on the Mississippi River, I claim that all orders affecting the conditions or operations of those forces should pass through these headquarters; otherwise I must lose a knowledge of current business and dangerous confusion ensue. If different views are entertained by you, then the question should be immediately referred to Washington, and one or the other, or both of us, relieved. One thing is certain, two generals cannot command this army, issuing independent and direct orders to subordinate officers, and the public service be promoted.[62]

Worse, McClernand also acted on his political connections. He wrote to Governor Richard Yates of Illinois but saved his biggest complaints for Abraham Lincoln himself:

I believe my success here is gall and wormwood to the clique of West Pointers who have been persecuting me for months. How can you expect success when men controlling the military destinies of the country are more chagrined at the success of your volunteer officers than the very enemy beaten by the latter in battle? Something must be done to take the hand of oppression off citizen soldiers whose zeal for their country has prompted them to take up arms, or all will be lost. Do not let me be clandestinely destroyed, or, what is worse, dishonored, without a hearing.

In a particularly low point, McClernand also advised Lincoln in March that Grant was "gloriously drunk and in bed sick all next day."[63]

Grant tried to ignore it all, even though many on his staff were already recommending relieving McClernand. Grant "was greatly annoyed by McClernand's insubordinate behavior," one of his staff officers later wrote, and some tried to get Grant to remove McClernand or either "give him such a rebuke that he could not effect to misunderstand his position as a subordinate." Grant calmly demurred, telling them, "No, I can't afford to quarrel with a man whom I have to command."[64]

Yet Grant was further forming his low opinion of McClernand. He informed Halleck: "I regard it as my duty to state that I found there was not sufficient confidence felt in General McClernand as a commander, either by the Army or Navy, to insure him success. Of course, all would co-operate to the best of their ability, but still with distrust." He later added: "I have not confidence in his ability as a soldier to conduct an expedition of the magnitude of this one successfully."[65]

Matters changed over the course of the winter and spring of 1863 as Washington finally made a decision on the command mess it had created out in the Mississippi Valley. In response to McClernand's letters, Stanton responded: "I think you need no new assurance of the sincere desire of the President and myself to oblige you in every particular consistent with the general interest of the service, and I trust that the source of events will be such as will enable the Government to desire the utmost advantage from your patriotism and military skill." Lincoln's reply was much clearer: "I have too many family controversies (so to speak) already on my hands, to voluntarily, or so long as I can avoid it, take up another. You are now doing well—well for the country, and well for yourself—much better than you could possibly be, if engaged in open war with Gen. Halleck. Allow me to beg, that for your sake, for my sake, & for the country's sake, you give your whole attention to the better work." Halleck also had the last laugh, finally writing Grant that he had permission "to relieve General McClernand from command of the expedition against Vicksburg, giving it to the next in rank or taking it yourself." Chief of staff John Rawlins actually made out the order, but Grant decided against it—for now. He evidently thought McClernand could still be of use if properly overseen.[66]

In truth, Grant felt he could not relieve McClernand at this point. One reason was the continued political backing of Stanton and Lincoln, even if they had backed off the idea of McClernand's sole command of the Vicksburg operations. Another was that Grant needed McClernand, especially after Grant began his do-or-die attempt to reach Vicksburg by going south of the city and crossing the Mississippi River there. Sherman was not a fan of the project, although he obeyed orders, and McPherson was still too inexperienced (and out of position, being farther north) to give major tasks to. Thus, McClernand became Grant's go-to leader as the army moved southward on the Louisiana side of the river, McClernand leading the way. McClernand also led the crossing at Bruinsburg, a most dangerous task. As the Army of the Tennessee moved northeastward, it was also McClernand who held the most dangerous and critical position: on the flank nearest the Confederates at Vicksburg. In perhaps the most dangerous part of the march, McClernand shielded the rear of the army against Pemberton while Sherman and McPherson marched to and captured Jackson. Grant needed a hard and experienced fighter through it all, and for the most part McClernand performed well.[67]

Still, the politician grated on Grant's nerves throughout the operations. Although Grant had even initially forbidden officers from carrying their own horses across the river, McClernand brought along his brand-new wife.

Charles Dana noted, "Though it is ordered that officers' horses and tents must be left behind, McClernand carries his bride along with him." The delay in crossing at Bruinsburg also taxed Grant's nerves. At one point he even wrote to McClernand "a very severe letter," although he did not send it. At another point at the Battle of Port Gibson, Grant had to stop McClernand and Governor Yates from giving speeches and move them onward.[68]

And McClernand could be almost insubordinate at times. At one point, he lectured Grant that "the political consequences of the impending campaign will be momentous." On another occasion, he charged favoritism against his corps in terms of transportation, writing "the officer in charge of transports has given preference to the Seventeenth Army Corps in everything." He added that "the baggage of that corps is being sent forward, to the exclusion of ammunition and provisions for the Thirteenth Army Corps; priority is given to forage over necessary supplies for the Thirteenth Army Corps."[69]

At times, Grant seemingly had all he could stand. In terms of the transportation issue, he countered: "I have passed one and a part of another of your divisions, and am satisfied that the transportation with them, to say nothing of the large number of mules mounted by soldiers, would carry the essential parts of five days' rations for the soldier, and Negroes now riding." He added directly: "You should take steps to make the means at hand available for bringing up the articles necessary for your corps. Equal facilities have been given each of the army corps in all respects, no special order having been given to favor any one, except to give the first 30 wagons to the Thirteenth Corps."[70]

Actual insubordination also took place. Upon receipt of one of Grant's orders, McClernand huffed, "I'll be _____ if I'll do it—I am tired of being dictated to—I won't stand it any longer, and you can go back and tell General Grant!" James H. Wilson was the staff officer who delivered the message and was so incensed that he shouted, "Although you are a major general, while I am only a lieutenant colonel, I will pull you off that horse and beat the boots off of you!" McClernand backed down and explained that he was only "expressing my intense vehemence on the subject matter, sir, and I beg your pardon." Wilson and McClernand had long been enemies—and now it was a growing feud.[71]

McClernand was thus a real problem, but Grant was actually appreciative of his fighting ability, later writing that McClernand performed his job in holding the rear "with much skill and without loss" while the rest of the army marched eastward to Jackson. Yet it was at Jackson where the entire relationship changed. While Halleck had allowed Grant to supersede McClernand in the overall command of the expedition months ago, now Halleck gave explicit orders that McClernand could also be removed from his corps command. When Grant was at Jackson, the Mississippi capital, on May 14, a message dated May 5 arrived from Halleck that gave Grant permission to relieve McClernand if he needed to: "General Grant has full and absolute authority to enforce his own commands, and to remove any person who, by ignorance, inaction, or any cause, interferes with or delays his operations. He has the full confidence of the Government, is expected to enforce his authority, and will be firmly and heartily supported; but he will be responsible for any failure to exert his powers. You may communicate this to him." The final sentence was as broad a hint as Grant needed.[72]

Still, it is telling that Grant did not relieve McClernand immediately, and McClernand fought at both Champion Hill and Big Black River Bridge thereafter. All the while, Grant declined to remove him even though he found fault in his effort at Champion Hill. The proverbial straw that broke the camel's back, however, occurred on May 22. McClernand had not assaulted as instructed on May 19 but had merely approached the Confederate fortifications. Yet neither had McPherson nor most of Sherman's troops, only one division actually making an attack. McClernand attacked with perhaps too much gusto on May 22, and the famous dispute where he alleged he had broken through and needed support from the other corps in terms of both additional troops and additional diversionary attacks in their sectors led Grant to renew the assaults in the afternoon. Grant blamed McClernand for the additional casualties: his "dispatches misled me as to the real state of facts, and caused much of this loss." Grant even wrote to Halleck that "he is entirely unfit for the position of corps commander, both on the march and on the battle-field. Looking after his corps gives me much more labor and infinitely more uneasiness than all the remainder of my department." It was apparently at this time that Grant decided he had to get rid of McClernand once and for all.[73]

Charles Dana informed Washington on May 24 that

yesterday morning he [Grant] had determined to relieve General McClernand, on account of his false dispatch of the day before . . . , but he changed his mind, concluding that it would be better on the whole to leave McClernand in his present command till the siege of Vicksburg is concluded, after which he will induce

> McClernand to ask for leave of absence. Meanwhile he (General Grant) will
> especially supervise all of McClernand's operations, and will place no reliance
> on his reports unless otherwise corroborated.

Dana then added "my own judgment is that McClernand has not the qualities necessary for a good commander, even of a regiment."[74]

Even then, Grant still needed McClernand, who began to entrench and conduct siege operations on his front in the weeks after May 22. In fact, although McClernand had been his same insufferable self, matters had decidedly cooled off. Grant was more worried about his rear and closing the gap at the extreme left than worrying about McClernand, although the lack of quick movement in digging approaches on McClernand's front was a matter of concern. That said, there were still some arguments—mainly McClernand complaining about his treatment in regard to the May 22 assaults. He wrote to Grant on June 4 of "what appears to be a systematic effort to destroy my usefulness and character as a commander." He also unwisely mentioned how it was reported that "I am responsible for your failure and losses." McClernand wanted Grant to make a declaration absolving him of fault. And then there were some conspiracy rumors as well, Dana reporting that "it appears that ten days ago he [McClernand] invited General M. K. Lawler to attend a meeting of officers from his corps, at which resolutions commendatory of himself (McClernand) were to be passed." Lawler refused, "on the ground that it would be a mutinous proceeding, and does not know whether such a meeting was held."[75]

Still, when Grant issued the order on June 18 for McClernand to be relieved, it seemingly came almost out of the blue. The ostensible reason was that McClernand had leaked a congratulatory order for his corps to the press without first getting it approved by the War Department. It was a decidedly minor offense, but Grant used it as the excuse for removing McClernand. Sherman and McPherson had both made a big deal out of it, likely salivating at the opportunity they saw in a breach of regulations. McClernand's ill-advised order was thus the perfect opportunity. The order was certainly egotistical, McClernand writing of defeating the enemy at Champion Hill "with the assistance of General McPherson's corps" and that during the assaults his men achieved "the first and largest success achieved anywhere along the whole of our army." Sherman, who sent Grant a copy found in the Memphis *Evening Bulletin* just as soon as he read it upon returning from his reconnaissance to Snyder's Bluff (it being brought to his attention by the politically savvy Frank Blair), called it "such a catalogue of nonsense—such an effusion of vain glory and hypocrisy," adding that "I know too well that the brave and intelligent soldiers and officers who compose that corps will not be humbugged by such stuff." Sherman also charged that the address in which McClernand was described as "the sagacious leader and bold hero" was not aimed at McClernand's soldiers but was "for ulterior political purposes." McPherson similarly sent Grant a copy the next day found in the Missouri *Democrat*, writing that "the whole tenor of the order is so ungenerous, and the insinuations and criminations against the other corps of your army are so manifestly at variance with the facts." He also concluded that it was written "more to influence public sentiment at the North and impress the public mind with the magnificent strategy, superior tactics, and brilliant deeds of the major-general commanding the Thirteenth Army Corps than to congratulate his troops." Almost gleefully, Sherman added: "I beg to call his attention to the requirements of General Orders, No. 151, of 1862, which actually forbids the publication of all official letters and reports, and requires the name of the writer to be laid before the President of the United States for dismissal."[76]

Grant decided now was the time but covered himself, writing McClernand and including a copy of the article: "I would respectfully ask if it is a true copy." McClernand was absent from headquarters at the time but later responded that it was a true copy and even worse that "I am prepared to maintain its statements," but added, perhaps knowing the trouble he was in, "I regret that my adjutant did not send you a copy promptly, as he ought, and I thought he had." Grant informed Washington: "I have found it necessary to relieve Major-General McClernand, particularly at this time, for his publication of a congratulatory address calculated to create dissention and ill-feeling in the army." He went on to explain, "I should have relieved him long since for general unfitness for his position." The astute Dana informed Washington that the congratulatory order was "the occasion of McClernand's removal, [but] it is not its cause."[77]

In actuality, Grant had likely made up his mind long before but certainly by May 22. Although one Indianan noted, "we may never know the truth of the McClernand—Grant hassle," clearly Grant had the upper hand. Yet he let McClernand linger until he was absolutely sure he did not need him anymore politically or militarily. Lincoln, after all, had appointed him for political reasons, but as astutely pointed out by McClernand biographer Richard Kiper,

"by June 1863 military considerations were at least equal to political calculations." The political considerations were indeed lessening, McClernand
having lost some favor with the administration; Grant was finally in a secure
political position: Vicksburg's fall was simply a matter of time. The military
concerns were also less troubling. By June 18, Grant had the siege well under
control, even reporting of "our position in front of Vicksburg having been
made as strong against a sortie from the enemy as his works were against an
assault." Yet it was significant, of course, that the removal was done only after
all the troops coming to Grant had arrived, Parke being the last. The removal
indicated just how secure Grant thought matters along the siege lines and in
the rear were by this point. He was relieving his senior corps commander and
planning any day now to send his second-ranking corps commander to the
rear, leaving only one (the most inexperienced) of the three original corps
commanders still on the siege lines. Grant believed that the siege portion of
the operations were all but done and that he no longer needed McClernand
militarily.[78]

Amazingly, McClernand apparently did not know that he was treading on
thin ice. In fact, several recent events may have led him to think he was well
regarded. On June 4, he had personally delivered to Grant a paper explaining
his actions during the May 22 assault. According to McClernand, Grant "remarked, in substance, that he had underrated the obstacles frustrating the assault upon Vicksburg's defenses, and that he would answer my note in writing
and, as I understood him, satisfactorily." Likewise, he either requested or was
glad to receive letters of confidence from some of his officers, brigade commanders Stephen Burbridge and William Landram writing on June 9 that they

> desire[d] to assure the Maj. Gen'l Commanding the Corps of our entire confi-
> dence in his ability as a Leader; and also to say that, in our opinion, the manage-
> ment of the troops under his command, during the most arduous, and trying, as
> well as the most honorable campaign of the war, has been such as to reflect the
> highest honor upon himself and command. Vigilant and untiring in the discharge
> of duty—cool and fearless upon the field, he has won for himself a fame as pure
> and undying as the glory of the cause in which we are engaged.

Most telling, Grant had just two days before enlarged McClernand's authority
by placing Lauman's division under his supervision.[79]

Despite such apparent support for McClernand, Grant issued the order to remove him late on June 18 and planned for it to be delivered the next day. James H. Wilson on Grant's staff, however, chose to ride to McClernand that very night and arouse him out of bed to deliver the order. He had hated McClernand since he was a boy in the town where McClernand resided and wished to relish the duty as soon as possible. He did so, dressed in full uniform and taking along a guard of soldiers. Rousing McClernand up from his sleep and waiting while the Illinoisan put on his full uniform, Wilson was soon ushered into McClernand's tent and happily handed him the note. McClernand threw it on the table without opening it, but Wilson stated his orders were to remain until he read it. When McClernand read it, he exclaimed: "Well, sir! I am relieved." Then, McClernand added, "Sir, we are both relieved." Grant was relieved as well; he wrote to Lorenzo Thomas that "a disposition and earnest desire on my part to do the most I could with the means at my command, without interference with the assignments to command which the President alone was authorized to make, made me tolerate General McClernand long after I thought the good of the service demanded his removal. It was only when almost the entire army under my command seemed to demand it that he was relieved."[80]

McClernand protested but perhaps realized his time had passed: "I might justly challenge your authority in the premises, but forbear to do so at present," he wrote to Grant. Still, he fired off a note to Lincoln: "I have been relieved for an omission of my adjutant. Hear me." One of Grant's staff officers noted that it was a wise choice for McClernand to leave quietly and not protest, "since Grant had all the bayonets." He also asserted, perhaps not all that accurately, that "the departure of McClernand was a relief to the whole army." For his part, McClernand was especially irate that Grant had "banish[ed] me from the Department of the Tennessee," the order stating for McClernand to "proceed to any point he may select in the State of Illinois." Grant had plenty of evidence, however, especially with Dana pumping Stanton full of stories of McClernand's "repeated disobedience of important orders, his general insubordinate disposition, and his palpable incompetence for the duties of the position." Dana also advised Stanton that he had learned from "private conversation" that "his relations with other corps commanders rendered it impossible that the chief command of this army should devolve upon him, as it would have done were General Grant disabled, without most pernicious consequences to the cause."[81]

McClernand knew when he had been outmaneuvered and left the army quickly after making, according to William T. Rigby, a "short but earnest speech to his staff claiming that he had always been in the front of the fight." He then left and returned to Springfield as his orders required. In fact, he left so quickly that some officers did not even have time to pay their respects. Staff officer Lieutenant Colonel Walter Scates wrote to McClernand on June 22 that Eugene Carr, one of his division commanders, had come by headquarters to say farewell but was too late. "He expressed many regrets at not seeing you," Scates explained, "and specifically requested me in the first communication to present his compliments and say that he should have called earlier had he known of your intention to start so early."[82]

Interestingly, there was little reaction within the army, although a slight few mentioned it as indicated by letters and diaries, mostly in support of Mc-Clernand. One Illinoisan wrote that "the report has just come into camp that Gen. McClernand has been relieved of his command, I hope it is not so, for he is liked by his Army." Another stated, "The removal of Gen. McClernand is generally regretted by all his corps. . . . Gen. McClernand was universally admired and his removal at this time is most unfortunate." Yet another wrote to his sister that "a jealousy between Grant & McClernand was the cause of this change," adding that "his removal just at the present time is generally considered illy advised & unnecessary as well as unjust.—Grant ought to be sensured for it." Others were not so kind, especially from Sherman's corps. One wrote that "Genl. McClernand was relieved of his command 2 days ago for good & sufficient reasons." He went on to add: He "is a Contemptible *Political* Maj. Genl. . . . I expect there will be great howling now in the Northern papers, as he is a *paper* man and the Democratic leader if Ill." Thomas Kilby Smith simply wrote: "McClernand . . . is at last superseded. We are most thankful." But he was also astute enough to realize "it will doubtless raise a good deal of a breeze." Still, the vast majority of writers never mentioned the affair at all in diary or letter.[83]

McClernand's replacement was a high-ranking general who had already arrived on June 18: the West Pointer Major General Edward O. C. Ord. The timing of McClernand's removal could certainly have also been based on Ord's arrival. Ord had been a major player earlier in the war until a bullet to the leg at Davis Bridge in October 1862 sidelined him for months. He was a West Point–trained officer, which meant he had much more education in terms of siege warfare and engineering than McClernand had. He was also a good friend of Sherman's and a Democrat like McClernand, so no charges of political motivation would be leveled. Grant had thought about combining Lauman and Herron on the far left under Ord's quasi–corps command, but with the decision to relieve McClernand, Ord was the perfect fit. He took command on June 19 and promptly began to get the engineering aspects up to speed with the other corps as well as introduce himself to his troops. Some were not enthused, such as Colonel Marcus Spiegel of the 120th Ohio, who was thinking of asking for a furlough but admitted to his wife that it would "be a little more trouble for me now, since General McClernand, who was a friend of mine, had been removed." Spiegel confessed that he knew little of Ord, but "he is said to be a very strict disciplinarian." Others were simply in the dark, one writing home, "of his successor, Gen. Ord, we know nothing." An Illinoisan quipped that "Grant considered him an extra-Ord-inary man."[84]

Ord arrived at headquarters just a few minutes after McClernand departed and set about quickly catching up. He took command, noting that "existing orders will continue in force unless otherwise directed," and met and discussed the operations with his division commanders as well as Lauman, who was attached: "I am directed by Maj. Genl. Ord Commdg to present his compliments and request your presence at these Head Quarters at your earliest convenience. He also desires that you would bring with you any drawings or maps showing the condition of your advanced works."[85]

Helping Ord was Captain Cyrus Comstock, who quickly began moving forward the zig-zag lines, particularly on Lauman's front. "Ord is working very hard to bring up the lines where McClernand left them behind, but it will take some time to remedy the disorder which that incompetent commander produced in every part of the corps he has left," Dana noted. He went on to later explain that "the trenches opened by McClernand are mere rifle pits 3 or 4 feet wide, and will neither allow the passage of artillery nor the assemblage of any considerable number of troops." The batteries had not been moved forward either and were "in the position they apparently held when the siege was opened. The rifle pits are also not systematically arranged for the defenses and strengthening of each other." Ord judged on June 22 that in about ten days he could have the "siege works in his front to the same general efficiency and safety as those of McPherson and Sherman."[86]

The McClernand affair was clear and convincing evidence that Grant was feeling much more confident by the latter half of June. If he would remove his ranking corps commander on the possible eve of also sending his second-ranking corps commander off the Vicksburg lines, he must have felt

Vicksburg was his. The thousands of reinforcements that had arrived by that time created this confidence, so that by June 20 he had both major portions of his operation well in hand, as well as the other smaller parts such as across the river in Louisiana. Grant could rest easier, but like so many times in his career he perhaps became a little too confident. The next week would show just how volatile the situation still was.

11

"JOHNSTON WILL ATTACK WITHIN FORTY-EIGHT HOURS"

June 20–22

Most Americans received word of the progress in the Vicksburg Campaign via newspapers. Many correspondents crowded around the army, mostly at the Chickasaw Bayou landing, although a few such as Sylvanus Cadwallader spent much of their time inland. Some wrote stories whether they were even there or not, one Federal describing reading in the newspapers that Vicksburg had fallen, which was news to him as bullets still sung around the Union lines. He surmised that "if some of their reporters were here, I think they would learn better." One newspaperman even made it into Vicksburg, Richard T. Colburn of the New York *World*. He had been captured when a barge he was on sank in the river, and the Confederates gobbled him up. He was kept in prison for a couple of days in the city jail before being released. The stories these correspondents wrote, whether accurate or not, tinted most of America's views of the operations, unless some families actually received letters from their loved ones in the army. Even then, however, the papers still probably gave a much more whole account than just what an individual soldier could see from his vantage point. Thus, newspapers from as far away as New York City almost daily tracked the siege.[1]

Closer to Vicksburg than these Northern papers, the Jackson *Mississippian* editorialized often: "All eyes are now eagerly turned towards Vicksburg. Tremendous firing has been heard there for the last two days and intelligence as to the result of it is looked for with intense anxiety." Of course, in a day before wire services and pool reporters, many newspapers also picked up each other's stories and printed them verbatim.[2]

News also flowed inside Vicksburg. Some people insisted that there were spies inside the city acting very strangely, but the exaggerated news was mostly the result of imaginations running wild. One who was perhaps a real spy was a purported editor named Armstrong of the Vicksburg *Whig*, who seemed to spend a lot of time around Louis Hébert's headquarters as well as John Forney's. He seemed to have some sinister motives, even telling a few ladies that he would be in Union lines by the next weekend. Forney took him into custody, writing that "if he is true to our cause I think he should now be in the trenches instead of going round collecting information."[3]

The main dispensator of news inside Vicksburg during the siege was editor James M. Swords's famed Vicksburg *Daily Citizen,* issued from an office on Crawford Street just down from Pemberton's headquarters. Swords was a Northerner by birth, originally from Portsmouth, Ohio, but he moved to Mississippi as a boy. He learned his craft working for a paper in Raymond, Mississippi, before starting the *Daily Citizen* in Vicksburg.[4]

Swords's paper was a one-sheet, four columned broadside that contained news from around the United States and the Confederacy, often reporting what other newspapers had written. His "News from the North" column contained updates on the Lincoln administration and the Copperhead movement. The news most important was from the Vicksburg siege, however, and he often carried stories such as the death of officers, Grant's reinforcements, and the state of the siege. There was also a lost-and-found section, such as when James Steele of the 1st Arkansas Cavalry Battalion lost his black pocketbook with $465 and some coins in it. Swords sold his paper for twenty-five cents, but the newsboys who carried them on the streets started charging double that, causing Swords to disclaim them, saying "we cannot control the trade or prices of newsboys." Some complained even at the lower price, one describing it as a "tiny sheet," adding that "tis, of course, but a rehash of speculations which amuses a half hour."[5]

Editor Swords took it upon himself to keep morale up and thus primarily published good news. He assured his readers that the army would defend as long as necessary: "The army at Vicksburg now stands among the veteran troops of the world," adding that "no other army has been placed in such a critical position in this war, and those who are compelled to endure the privations and hardships of a protracted siege against such immense odds, should be remembered by a grateful country, and their merits fully and liberally rewarded." He also often reminded those inside the city that Johnston was on the way: "The utmost confidence is felt that we can maintain our position until succor comes from outside," Swords editorialized. "The undaunted Johnston is at hand." In the June 18 issue, he penned, "Ho! For Johnston!—The most agreeable news now-a-days is to hear from Genl. Johnston. But we have nothing to record of his movements, except that we may look at any hour for his approach. We may repose the utmost confidence in his appearance within a very few days." He continued: "We have to say to our friends and the noble army here that relief is close at hand. Hold out a few days longer, and our lines will be opened, the enemy driven away, the siege raised, and Vicksburg again in communication with the balance of the Confederacy." Swords also called on the people to pray, he leading the way. One headline read: "O Lord how long shall the siege continue, how long shall it continue O Lord."[6]

Swords dealt with problems too, such as when a Union shell hit his office. He wrote that "as we were working on our edition on Tuesday afternoon a thirteen inch bombshell made a dash into our office, striking a short distance from the press, and going through the floor and into the lower room, thence into the ground, where it exploded, and sending its fragments upward again bulged up the floor and filled the office with dust, smoke and a suffocating stench of powder." No one was injured, but Swords could not help but opine that "the Yankees have no better sense than to throw bombshells at the printers while they are trying to circulate truth and intelligence among the people."[7]

An even bigger problem came when he ran out of paper. With nothing to print the news on, the paper would go out of business. Thus, Swords famously invested in all the wallpaper he could obtain in the city. He explained humorously that

> cut off from all outside resources, we are enabled to bring into play our own native genius to cater to the public taste in the most approved style. At a great expense and with the most untiring labor, we have succeeded in making our paper a pictorial sheet, to the great delight of our readers. Citizens will please save these illustrated papers until the war is over, when they can ornament the walls of their rooms with the most beautiful designs.—The soldiers also will be very glad to obtain the variegated papers for the embellishment of their tents. Thus we go.[8]

Most were not enthused. One civilian, Dora Miller, complained that it was originally "a foot and a half long and six inches wide." She added, "To-day the 'Citizen' is printed on wall paper; therefore has grown a little in size." One staff officer still described it as "our little paper." The wallpaper editions even made their way into Federal hands, where the novelty was also noticed. Federal brigade commander James Slack described reading an issue traded from Confederates as early as June 14 and explained to his wife that it was "printed on one side of some cheap wall paper." He added, "The whole thing worded very poor indeed." In all, Swords printed at least seven issues on wallpaper, maybe more, certainly on June 14, 16, 18, 20, 27, 30, and July 2.[9]

Swords obviously printed mostly what was known or desired inside Vicksburg. Only Johnston's missives swinging between promises of relief and declarations of inadequacy came from outside Federal lines, and of those only the promises made it into the paper. Just like everything else in isolated Vicksburg, it was internal news or nothing. One Federal had it just about right when he scribbled in his diary, "They can neither obtain ammunition, rations or news, but are completely cooped up in their den, and we are trying to smoke them out."[10]

Ulysses S. Grant wanted to do more than smoke them out. Flush off relieving McClernand and setting into place a contingency plan for covering the rear lines if need be, as well as welcoming thousands of newly arrived troops, Grant decided the time was right for an intense bombardment of the Confederate works. While there was no major consideration given to another assault as yet, Grant ordered that all be prepared to take advantage of anything this artillery bombardment might develop. On June 19, he thus issued orders that "a general cannonading" start the next morning at 4:00 A.M. "from all parts of the line on the city of Vicksburg." It should last six hours, until 10:00 A.M. The artillery was also to make sure they kept enough ammunition to support any advances by the infantry, which were ordered to be ready: "All the rifle-pits will be filled with as many men as can be accommodated in them . . . ready to take advantage of any signs the enemy may show of weariness, or to repel an attack should one be made." To make sure he was understood, Grant added, "It is not designed to assault the enemy's works, but to be prepared. Should corps commanders believe a favorable opportunity presents itself for possessing themselves of any portion of the lines of the enemy without a serious battle, they will avail themselves of it, telegraphing immediately to headquarters of other corps and to general headquarters what they are doing, and suggesting any assistance or co-operation they may require."[11]

There had, to be sure, been times of intense bombardment before, one Federal describing the shelling on May 29: "As fast as the men could load and fire." On that day, Pemberton also described how "the morning opened with a terrific fire from the artillery on the enemy's outer line, and for four hours shot and shell were literally rained upon the deserted city." It slacked during the day, but another two hours' worth came that evening "with increased violence," which caused few casualties but much damage: "Many buildings were seriously damaged," Pemberton admitted. One Minnesotan enjoyed the show, especially the night bombardment, writing that it was "one of the grandest sights I ever saw."[12]

Occasionally, there was less firing. Pemberton reported on May 30 that "with the exception of the mortar firing, which rarely ceases, great quiet prevailed along the entire line. The enemy seemed busily engaged in pushing forward his saps." There were even times when the mortars ceased for days at a time. Pemberton noted on June 6 that "the mortar fleet . . . has been silent for three days," and then again on June 23 for three days prior. Ammunition of course was the culprit. Others commented too. Confederate brigade commander John C. Vaughn over on the far Confederate left remarked surprisingly each time there was a falling-off of firing: "Everything unusually quiet along the line."[13]

That said, the firing never ceased for long. Pemberton noted a "furious fire" from the enemy's Parrott guns for four hours the next day after a lull, and on June 1 he reported, "the day opened with a rattling salute of Parrott shells and spherical case and wore on with the usual sharpshooting and battery firing." Even the "heavy drenching rain" on June 10 and 11 could not stop the mortars, which were "rapid, heavy and constant." The bombardments were not lost on the Federals either, one humorously writing that "every time a shell bursts the dogs in turn set up a terrible howling. They must be well supplied with dogs from the noise they make."[14]

Yet this bombardment on June 20 was different. Dana reported that "the result is to settle the question of a further attempt at present to assault the place, or to leave its reduction to the regular progress of siege operations." In all, some two hundred artillery pieces were involved from the land side, as well as the navy and guns planted on the opposite shore of the Mississippi

River. One artilleryman noted in his diary, "Precisely at 4 o'clock we opened, as so all along the lines." Some claimed that, despite it being hot and dry, "rain would fall as a consequence of this bombardment," although one Federal admitted "the clouds rendered not." There were plenty of manmade clouds, however, one Ohio battery captain writing that "the atmosphere soon became very thick with smoke . . . , and at times we could scarcely see the works we were firing at." The result was awe-inspiring, one Federal declaring that "at times the ground fairly trembled from the concussion." Dana reported that "during the attack no rebels were visible, nor was any reply made to our artillery," but another Federal lookout reported "them busy carrying off their wounded all day."[15]

Logically, such a massive bombardment brought all on both sides to think an assault was on the way. "Rumor says that we are to make another charge today, but I hope not," one Union soldier said. Many Confederates, spurred even more by odd happenings on their front, believed a charge was coming. One 38th Mississippi soldier declared that "we were very unexpectedly called into our positions in the trenches at a double quick. The alarm was caused by two impudent Yankees crawling up and looking over our parapet. We are now lying in the ditches all ready, but I think it was a false alarm." Indeed, no assault was made, the barrage not uncovering any evidence that the enemy was ready to give up. Grant thus continued on with the siege operations, although more of the same could be had at any time, with one specific point on Steele's front being discovered "from which the entire town is seen and commanded." Once a fortification rose there, Dana reported, "all the buildings in the town can be destroyed by it." Being so close, it was thought that the raised guns of the gunboat *Cincinnati* would be a perfect fit for the battery.[16]

The Confederates certainly took note of the bombardment even though there was no assault. Some reported increased activity even before daylight. "The pickets in front of the center report that the long-roll was beaten in the enemy's camp about 2 o'clock this morning," division commander M. L. Smith reported, and "also that the sound of wagon or artillery carriage wheels was heard at the same time." A Louisianan declared that, between two and four in the morning, "I made my rounds and saw a large number of signal lights in the direction of the Jackson road," and a Mississippian explained that "shortly after midnight on the morning of Saturday June 20th, there was heard an unusual bustle sound around the enemy's lines. Wagon trains were moving, drums and fifes were heard and there seemed to be a sound of tramping of many feet." Pemberton himself wrote in his diary that a "tremendous artillery fire" erupted, which was "terrific, greatly exceeding in severity anything yet witnessed since the commencement of the siege." He noted that the fire "seriously injured our works on the right." Brigade commander Hébert echoed that it was "the heaviest and most rapid cannonading we have yet undergone."[17]

The bombardment was so severe and loud that it even made quite an impact back on the rear lines. The blasts were easily heard back at Snyder's and Haynes' Bluffs. An Iowa trooper explained that "everybody listening with astonishment this morn—wondering what they mean—how anxious now to hear." An Indianan at Big Black River bridge described how he and his comrades were awakened early that morning by "the most terrible cannonading that I have yet heard." The episode not surprisingly began more rumors of Vicksburg's surrender. Even Johnston's forces miles farther away noted the new level of bombardment, one Tennessean writing that "the roar was more steady and more heavy than I ever herd there before."[18]

Yet the massive bombardment was unable to do much more than tear up the Confederate ramparts and kill or injure a few of the enemy. The casualties were soon carted off and the fortifications rebuilt by the next morning, John C. Taylor of Pemberton's staff describing how "as our parapets are destroyed we sink lower into the hill and thus each night repair the effects of their fire during the day." It seemed obvious that the Federals would not be able to blast the enemy out with artillery, so the plan returned to the tried-and-true siege operations, which were nearing their own climax.[19]

As important as the defense of Vicksburg was—and by this time perhaps the saving of the army itself even more—the two Confederate commanders involved just could not get on the same page, and a comedy of errors continued to develop. If not for the dire stakes involved, it would indeed have been humorous to watch as Johnston and Pemberton both talked past each other, neither seeming to listen. Worse, the communication delay Johnston described as "uncertain and slow" was such that messages were old and outdated by the time they were received. Each commander responded to days-old messages after they had already sent many more communications after the one that garnered the just-received response. For instance, Johnston's May 29 note did not arrive in Vicksburg until June 13, by which time Pemberton had sent four additional messages. Even more concerning was that neither would take a leadership role in doing something—anything—about the mess they were in. Most fatal, of course, was the fact that, by this point in June, Joseph E. Johnston had given up hope of doing much of anything.[20]

The Confederate relief stance was certainly cautious, Breckinridge telling one of his generals in a forward movement in early June to "move your encampment as near to the Big Black River as may not prove too hazardous [to] your command." He also ordered local natives who knew the area to join the command to scout. That cautiousness came directly from the top: "I am too weak to save Vicksburg," Johnston had plainly told Pemberton on June 16, which arrived at a shocked Pemberton's headquarters only on June 20. "Can do no more than attempt to save you and your garrison," he added. Johnston then insisted that "it will be impossible to extricate you unless you co-operate and we make mutually supporting movements. Communicate your plans and suggestions, if possible." Of course, Pemberton had been trying to do just that, urging Johnston to make some specific plans, but it seemed Johnston wanted Pemberton to do the dirty work and perhaps take the fall. A flabbergasted Pemberton called a council of war on June 21 to discuss Johnston's latest message of defeat.[21]

The shock of Johnston's pronouncement that Vicksburg was doomed and only the garrison might be saved hit Richmond as well, where Secretary of War Seddon answered that "your telegram grieves and alarms me. Vicksburg must not be lost without a desperate struggle. The interest and honor of the Confederacy forbid it." Then, he added, "I rely on you still to avert it," even if it meant "you must hazard an attack" while numerically inferior. A few days later he wrote that "the aim, in my judgment, justifies any risk and all probable consequences." For his part, Johnston simply continued his refrain of "I will do all I can, without hope of doing more than aid to extricate the garrison." Johnston was not inspiring by a long shot.[22]

Pemberton was in no position to make any plans. He was trapped within Vicksburg, where he had no idea what Johnston was doing, where he was deployed, or his strength. And Pemberton's nerves seemed to be fraying by this point in late June, with Grant's besieging forces more than enough to worry about. "On the Graveyard road the enemy's works are within 25 feet of our redan," he reported to Johnston; "also very close on Jackson and Baldwin's Ferry road." The condition of the troops perhaps concerned Pemberton even more, adding that "my men have been thirty-four days and nights in trenches without relief, and the enemy is within conversation distance. We are living on very reduced rations, and, as you know, are entirely isolated."[23]

Pemberton so informed Johnston, before the latter's "I am too weak" message arrived. An obviously shaken Pemberton described the Union firing as "the heaviest fire we have yet sustained," and the relieved general added, "but he did not assault our works." It was time for some real relief, however, Pemberton anxiously querying, "What aid am I to expect from you" and "I hope you will advance with the least possible delay." In the midst of all of it, Pemberton described hearing artillery in the direction of Snyder's Bluff, "supposed to have been an engagement with your troops."[24]

Of course, that firing was not a confrontation with Johnston, as Johnston had not moved. Rather, the Confederate general remained at his headquarters, continuing to gather, coordinate, and prepare. Despite all this, he saw fit to order minute changes in positions far to the north in Mississippi, telling Brigadier General Daniel Ruggles at Columbus that "you ought to occupy a line somewhat north of that you now hold." He also continually reorganized. He added another division of gathered brigades, assigning it to newly arrived Confederate general Samuel G. French, the division camping around the Carraway Plantation near the Livingston area. Dabbling in lower-level command, he also ordered French to promptly put one of his brigadiers, Nathan G. Evans, under arrest. Johnston also dictated newly arrived regiments joining it, such as the 39th North Carolina.[25]

It is unbelievable that Johnston made no moves given the time crunch Vicksburg was in, and especially because he knew the Federals to be extremely worried about his potential for disrupting Vicksburg's siege. Lieutenant Colonel Robert C. Wood of Wirt Adams's Cavalry reported that "the impression among the Federals is general that the attack of General Johnston will be made in the immediate vicinity of Haynes' Bluff, and dispositions have been made accordingly. Roads are being blockaded and artillery placed in position near the Bluff, in view of General Johnston's advance in that direction." While word of Union preparations might be halting to Johnston, including a list of Federal generals such as "Kimball, Smith, and a German (probably Osterhaus)," the news of almost Federal paranoia should have had an opposite effect. "Great anxiety is manifested by Federal officers to learn something authentic of General Johnston's movements and strength," Wood added.[26]

Johnston's inaction also began to gain the notice of others outside

Mississippi. P. G. T. Beauregard wrote from South Carolina about the activities in Mississippi and offered to send two generals who had fallen out of his favor. Colonel Edwin J. Harvie even wrote to Joseph Davis, the president's brother, in hopes that something might be done. He flattered Davis with talk of his "high position, great intelligence, and eminent character, to say nothing of the close relations you sustain to the chosen head of the Government." Harvie described the situation at Vicksburg as "most critical; the complication the most difficult yet presented in the history of the war." The main reason was that "the enemy have exhibited uncommon energy and activity in fortifying their rear against operations of a succoring army" and were doing so with "all the industry, ingenuity and skill of which the Yankee nation is capable." Essentially, he argued, "the Northern Government has made a point on Vicksburg, and has determined it shall fall, and with it, if in their power to accomplish it, the Mississippi Valley."[27]

The solution to all this was to raise the siege and save Pemberton's army. But Harvie argued that Johnston was too weak—"simply a physical impossibility," he said, adding that "it cannot be done, and is not in the matter of hope or calculation." Then Harvie came to the crux of the letter, apparently doing for Johnston what Johnston realized he could not do himself with the president: encourage Richmond to move Braxton Bragg's army from Tennessee to Mississippi. Johnston was of course department commander over both Pemberton and Bragg, but such a drastic reshuffling of the armies would have to have had Davis's approval and Johnston would not, and could not, seek it. So he had his staff officer make an end run through the president's brother. It was essentially, Harvie opined, "a political question between Middle Tennessee and the Mississippi Valley, which he, as the head of the Government, ought to decide. . . . It may be that the decision involves the very fate of the Republic itself."[28]

Of course, Johnston did not get Bragg's army to Mississippi, and as a result Pemberton got very little from Johnston except the note that he was too weak to save Vicksburg. Yet somehow word emerged among the troops inside the garrison that Johnston was on the way. He was "only waiting for a very important train expected hourly to Canton, and he would move." Nevertheless, a truth-knowing Pemberton responded on June 21, the day after the doleful message arrived in Vicksburg. "If it is absolutely impossible, in your opinion, to raise the siege with our combined forces," Pemberton recommended Johnston approach the enemy near Snyder's and Haynes' Bluffs, "occupying him during the entire day," while Pemberton took his garrison out of Vicksburg by the Warrenton Road to a crossing of the Big Black River at Hankinson's Ferry. Pemberton recommended Johnston send cavalry to hold that crossing and the ones to the north. He reported that this was the only way out of Vicksburg, by way of the lightly defended southern extremity where Parke's troops were supposed to have gone but was now held by only Lauman and Herron. "All the other roads are too strongly intrenched and the enemy in too heavy force for a reasonable prospect of success, unless you move in sufficient force to compel him to abandon his communications with Snyder's." This was the best Pemberton could do, but he realized he was only a subordinate, adding, "I await your orders."[29]

Those orders never came, Johnston already having made up his mind and talking of surrender. On June 22, in fact, before Pemberton's latest proposal arrived, Johnston fired off another note to Pemberton stating that Major General Richard Taylor and Lieutenant General Kirby Smith may be Vicksburg's best hope. Although he said he would "have the means of moving toward the enemy in a day or two, and will try to make a diversion in your favor," he added that "I have only two-thirds of the force you told Messenger Sanders to state to me as the least with which you think I ought to make an attack." Johnston was already shifting the blame for the coming debacle onto Pemberton and even began to speak in terms of surrender. "If I can do nothing to relieve you," he finished his missive, "rather than surrender the garrison, endeavor to cross the river at the last moment, if you and General Taylor communicate."[30]

Pemberton should have once again gotten the picture by this point that little help would be forthcoming from Johnston's so called "Army of Relief."

The fatalism Joseph E. Johnston displayed and the comedy of errors that characterized his and Pemberton's correspondence was in no way evident to the Federal high command as the third week of June came and went at Vicksburg. In fact, Grant's concern seemed to reach its tipping point then. By that time, it seemed as if Grant had done all he could. He had brought in all the reinforcements he was likely to get. He had also made his command decisions, most notably by relieving McClernand and tasking Sherman with the rearward defense. The only other major decision he had to make was when to pull the trigger on the contingency plan and send Sherman rearward. Once that was done, all he could do was wait. Ironically, the time for moving

Sherman was closer than Grant imagined. Confederate activity—and, more important, reports of Confederate activity—quickly picked up on June 21.

One rumor that Grant particularly believed in fact had nothing to do with Johnston or the rearward defense. Rather, it involved an alleged plan that Admiral Porter had been warning Grant about for some time. "Information received from Vicksburg last night confirms your theory of the probable method Pemberton will take for escaping in the last extremity," he wrote to Porter on June 21. The reports from a deserter were that Pemberton had his soldiers building boats with which to cross the river. "The rebel said they were tearing down houses to get the materials out of which to build boats," he added. Obviously, any river operations came under Porter's purview, and so Grant warned him of the possibilities evidenced by this report. Hopefully, Porter would be able to stop any crossing by large numbers of troops, but if any made it to the other side Grant also cautioned his commanders on the Louisiana shore to be ready. He still had troops under Elias Dennis, including the brigade from Sherman's corps under Joe Mower, in Louisiana and wanted "a strong picket in the river in front of Vicksburg at night." Grant recommended that Porter and Mower converse as to the best plans to make, he telling Porter, "you will find General Mower an intelligent and gallant officer, capable of carrying out any plan that may be adopted."[31]

Elias Dennis received orders to be prepared for as many as two thousand boats crossing the river at night. Of course, Porter would be key in stopping movement on the river outside of Vicksburg's guns, but the crossing might take place right in the De Soto Peninsula for that very reason—to be covered from the navy by the heavy river batteries. Grant thus wanted the peninsula covered well, and he tasked Dennis with handing that job to Mower. But Grant also warned Dennis that "it may be that should any such movement be contemplated by Pemberton, the enemy west of you will attempt assistance by attacking Young's Point simultaneously therewith." Grant wanted Dennis to be prepared for either development or both: "You will place at once in the best possible position for the defense of that place against attack from the west, and at the same time prevent any part of the Vicksburg forces from escaping by way of the Peninsula." Grant even cautioned to "get materials together to light up the river, should any considerable number of boats attempt to cross." Of course, the placement of heavy artillery on the peninsula helped that defense greatly.[32]

Even with the possibility of a westward movement, Grant's fears of that occurring paled in comparison with what was happening to the east. Knowing Johnston was due any day—or past due, for that matter—Grant kept what little cavalry he had with the army continually patrolling the roads between the Yazoo and Big Black Rivers, especially the major fords or ferries along the Big Black at Bridgeport, Messengers', Birdsong, and Bush's Ferries. It was "the roughest country I ever saw," one Iowa trooper wrote home. Yet Grant had far too few cavalry units to do the job adequately. With so much ground to cover, these troops could not possibly cover everything and opted to block with trees and debris the roadways leading from the ferries. "This is effectually done," wrote one Iowa trooper, "by choosing a defile or a steep ridge and as the timber is very thick, the trees are cut so as to fall across each other, and an army cannot pass without removing the obstruction." Another 4th Iowa Cavalry trooper described his efforts: "I took an axe & tried it awhile Cut down one little tree, raised a Blister on my hand, every one of the Boys that chopped blistered their Hands. We filled the road for over a mile. Rode back to corn & fed, got blackberries & plums. The Boys upset Bee gums for honey and made a desperate Scattering among men & horses. Stung 2 horses to death."[33]

Amid this context, Grant also received reports that Johnston was moving. "Joe Johnston's plan is at last developed," Dana excitedly reported to Washington on June 22; "he began yesterday to throw his army across the Big Black at various points above Bridgeport, and principally in the vicinity of Birdsong's Ferry." Much of this information came from "the spy of General Grant," Dana explained. And it was partially true; Johnston had crossed the Big Black with part of his force, but the reason for it was totally misinterpreted. Johnston had called Walker and Loring east of the Big Black from Yazoo City, they going into camp around Vernon on the east/south side of the river in a relocation Johnston began when he apparently decided once and for all to give up on a move down the slot itself. Federal scouts picked up on this movement, considering it a forward advance.[34]

These movements were confirmed in a small skirmish near Birdsong Ferry on June 22 in which a battalion of the 4th Iowa Cavalry under Major Alonzo B. Parkell, despite just getting brand-new Sharps carbines, was pretty roughly handled, losing several dozen killed, wounded, and missing. Sherman perhaps unfairly reported that the Iowans "must have been off their guard," so "our men got the worst, and were forced to fly." Parke sent word to Grant, describing how the troopers were driven back across Bear Creek and that "two hundred of our men are reported missing." It was not that bad, although two regiments of Confederate cavalry, Wirt Adams's and Starke's both under Lieutenant Colonel Robert C. Wood, had attacked a battalion of the Iowans at Hill's Plantation. The Confederates managed to get in behind the Iowans and capture a small 2-pound howitzer (which had been captured from the Confederates at Jackson earlier in May) posted "at the head of a narrow lane, with a high and strong fence on each side." The Iowans broke and fled when orders came for "every man to camp his own way," leaving the cannon, although the casualties were not in the hundreds but merely eight killed and sixteen wounded, with twenty or thirty captured. Reinforcing Iowans noted the chaos, one writing that they "proceeded cautiously to the scene of action. Kept finding our Boys all the way. Hid in the Brush, Corn, &ct they was afraid to venture out until they was sure who we was." One Iowa brother nevertheless had the sad duty of writing home to tell their father about his brother's death. The Confederate loss was about the same. Still, it was enough for Grant. "At once on the receipt of this intelligence," Dana reported, Grant acted and sent out a flurry of messages on June 22, all with a tinge of panic that clearly indicated his concern. It seemed the rearward defense was about to come to a climax.[35]

Grant indeed sent a flurry of messages on June 22, each carrying with it basically the same information. To Parke, now commanding the forces to the rear, he wrote: "Loring has crossed a portion of his troops below Vernon. An attack is contemplated, evidently by way of Bear Creek, and that within two days." To many of the others he wrote similar concerns, that "there is indication that Johnston will attack within forty-eight hours" or "there is some probability of an attack here by Joe Johnston within the next twenty-four or forty-eight hours."[36]

Specific orders went to specific commanders, most importantly and immediately to Parke. With word of Loring crossing the Big Black River, Grant ordered Parke to send four of his brigades out to Bear Creek "to support your cavalry and obstruct their advance as near Big Black River as possible, until all the forces to spare can be brought against them." Three of Washburn's and one of his own from Potter's division moved out toward Bear Creek, Washburn's taking a position from the Benton Road near Oak Ridge Post Office down to McCall's on the Birdsong Ferry Road. The IX Corps brigade continued the line from McCall's down to Tiffin's, covering the Bridgeport Road and connecting with pickets from Osterhaus's division at the railroad bridge. Grant's contingency plan of course was that Parke would stop the advance until all the other elements from Haynes' Bluff and Vicksburg could assemble: "The enemy once fixed upon my ground, all the forces from Haynes' Bluff can be taken to the attack and a large number from here also." The key was to stop Johnston as far out as possible, and Grant thus ordered Parke to "move out early to-morrow morning, or sooner, if you can." Parke did so, and the newly arrived soldiers soon fortified the area, especially along the roads but also on the high ground overlooking the upper reaches of Little Bear Creek. In the haste, all equipment was left behind and the troops had to bivouac; even food had to be brought forward in wagons from the bluffs.[37]

One Federal in the 61st Illinois described well the fortification process. "We went to work on the ridges with spades and mattocks," Leander Stillwell wrote,

> and constructed the strongest field fortifications that I ever saw during the war.
> We dug away the crests, throwing the dirt to the front, and made long lines of
> breastworks along our entire front, facing, of course, the northeast. Then, at
> various places, on commanding points, were erected strong redoubts for artillery,
> floored, and revetted on the inner walls with thick and strong green lumber and
> timbers. On the exterior slopes of the ridges were dug three lines of trenches, or
> rifle pits, extending in a parallel form from near the base of the ridges almost to
> the summit, with intervals between the lines. All the trees and bushes in our front
> on the slopes of the ridges were cut down, with their tops outward, thus forming
> a tangled abatis which looked as if a rabbit could hardly get through.

Covered ways also led to the rear. Yet Stillwell added that "I never did an hour's work in the trenches . . . never 'took' willingly to that kind of soldiering." He always preferred picket duty and swapping tasks with a soldier who much preferred digging.[38]

The other major orders went to Sherman, who explained how "I was summoned to General Grant's headquarters." His orders read similarly that "information just received indicates that the enemy are crossing Big Black River, and intend marching against us by way of Bear Creek." Grant explained what he had ordered Parke to do in the time between then and when Sherman would arrive. He told Sherman to start immediately to that front and that "you will go and command the entire force." Sherman was to take Tuttle's two brigades under Ralph Buckland and Joseph J. Woods, while Grant sent word to McPherson to have his brigades, all under the command of John McArthur, ready to move "on Sherman's order. Sherman goes out to meet Johnston, if he comes." McPherson readied Manning Force's, Charles Matthies's, and Alexander Chambers's brigades, one each from the three divisions, as well as artillery: "The battery should be taken out of the trenches immediately," McPherson ordered, "horses hitched up, and the battery moved over near the brigade." Troops remaining on the lines shifted to fill in the gaps made.[39]

Others received the same forty-eight hour message and were counseled to be ready too. Grant said to Ord, for example, that "Osterhaus should be re-enforced immediately with the remainder of his brigade [division], to enable him to withstand a cavalry attack. The attack will come from Black River, from above Bridgeport." Grant also informed Ord that Sherman was taking command and that Osterhaus would be under his orders and that, if pressed, he should even abandon the bridge area and move to join Sherman. Farther to the left, Francis Herron also received word to be ready to send troops if necessary: "Should the forces at present indicated be insufficient to cope with him, your division will be withdrawn and sent to re-enforce them." That was quite a statement, as Herron actually covered a good stretch of the trenches.[40]

Osterhaus certainly benefited from the chaos, he receiving on June 22 most of his other brigade under Colonel Daniel W. Lindsey. That beefed up his numbers in his somewhat isolated position, where communication was choppy and a line of supply, despite the railroad, almost nonexistent. Oster-haus did the best he could, actually repairing the railroad to the Union lines around Vicksburg and setting a reconstructed flatcar on the rails, pulled by "four mules, in lieu of locomotive." Osterhaus reported that this makeshift trolley "form[s] an essential addition to my transportation." He also finally secured a telegraphic line to the main army, one of his Illinoisans excitedly writing "so we can have the news fresh from the field of action."[41]

Despite all the activity, it seemed oddly quiet all along the Big Black at Os-terhaus's position, especially given Grant's sudden burst of fear. One Indianan described everything from playing pranks on fellow soldiers to watching the shells in Vicksburg explode and light up the low clouds that sometimes hung over the area. The main duty was standing picket, which the Union soldiers did east of the river, actually in the old Confederate works. Only very unusual occurrences shook the troops out of their blackberry-picking leisure. An acci-dental shooting in the 22nd Kentucky, for example, killed one man and badly wounded three others. One Indianan in the next regiment wondered why "a sharp report of a gun was heard over in the 22d camp and men were seen running from all directions." Constant rumors of Vicksburg's fall as well as a visit from Grant himself on June 23 kept the focus for the soldiers, however.[42]

Those currently dealing with the threat of a Confederate escape by boat received the same messages from Grant. To Admiral Porter, Grant wrote that he had put his contingency plan into effect: "I have given all the necessary orders to meet him some 25 miles out, Sherman commanding." Yet if there was an attack from the east, Grant knew that it might also involve a simultaneous advance west of the river: "Milliken's Bend, in such case, may come in for a visit also," and Grant recommended having a gunboat there. To Dennis, Grant reported the forty-eight-hour threat and told him to "exercise unusual vigilance." Dennis responded that he would take care of the situation, adding that "from what I can learn, the rebels are unquestionably building skiffs and flat-boats at Vicksburg." He told Grant, however, that "you may rest assured, general, if they intend an attack upon us, they will not catch us napping." Grant was no doubt relieved to hear that, but in reality he had moved far past worrying about the Confederates attempting to row their way out of Vicksburg. Johnston to the east was the main threat, and Grant said as much to Porter, making clear that "my hands will be very full here in case of an attack. I will direct General Dennis, therefore, to consult with you in all matters relating to defenses on the west side of the river." For their part, some Confederates did indeed mention building some four hundred boats. Pemberton himself also put carpenters to work making oars.[43]

Once all was in process, Grant focused on his two main efforts. To Parke he wrote that "Sherman goes out from here with five brigades and Osterhaus' division, subject to his orders, besides." Parke was to hold for the time being with his four brigades while Sherman made his way out with Tuttle and McArthur. "We want to whip Johnston at least 15 miles off, if possible," Grant said. In order to do so, he informed both Sherman and Parke that he would send both Lauman and Herron if needed: "I can take them from our left by leaving that in the same condition it was before the[ir] arrival," he informed Sherman.[44]

Sherman soon made his way eastward, one Illinoisan joking, "It is rumored that we are out hunting the paymaster instead of Johnston." Another was not interested in the reason and was just glad to get out of the trenches: "It seems to revive one up to get out into the open country once more and breath the fresh air that is not tainted with the stench of an old and large camp."

Sherman set up headquarters near the Trible Plantation house and began to formulate his response, meeting Parke at Templeton's on the way. Parke's four brigades, who Sherman referred to as "strange men" and "one brigade of his Yankee troops," had already moved ahead toward Oak Ridge Post Office and Little Bear Creek, where the roads and terrain were winding, rough, and narrow. Sherman wanted to meet the Confederate advance there before the Confederates reached the comparatively open and flat ground along Clear Creek's watershed farther west. Dana reported to Washington that "on this side of Oak Ridge, about the head of Clear Creek, there is a broad, open region, extensively cultivated, where a great army might deploy and fight advantageously — at least on equal terms. The effort of Sherman will be to settle the question before Joe Johnston can get to this open place." Sherman was especially concerned over Birdsong Ferry, which he deemed "the point where it was supposed Johnston designed to cross the Big Black." He explained to his wife, Ellen, that he was "out here studying a most complicated geography and preparing for Joe Johnston if he comes to the relief of Vicksburg." But that took time, and the soldiers waited, one writing in his diary that "awaiting orders to march is as tiresome as waiting at a station for a train." Others declared they were not even concerned about Johnston: "That didn't make us very uneasy. We were just waiting for a good chance to whip him."[45]

As the contingency plan developed just as Grant envisioned it, he nevertheless seemed to get even more distraught. Thinking Johnston and Pemberton had communicated, he cautioned his forces still "on the line" against an attack by the Vicksburg garrison at the same time. Turning again to the rear, he ordered Ord to cover all the crossings on the Big Black River up to Birdsong Ferry and down south of the railroad bridge as well. "The utmost vigilance should be observed in watching the crossings of the Big Black, south of the railroad bridge," he ordered. In fact, Grant even began to contemplate sending more divisions eastward than just Lauman and Herron if necessary. He mentioned to Sherman that he would send all he could "to the last man here and at Young's Point," specifically that he could also send A. J. Smith from Ord and that "two more brigades can be taken from your corps without breaking the line investing Vicksburg." He then made a telling statement about just how much he feared problems in the rear: "We want to whip him [Johnston], if the siege has to be raised to do it." The worry filtered down to some in the ranks as well, one Ohioan writing that "we are to fight him from

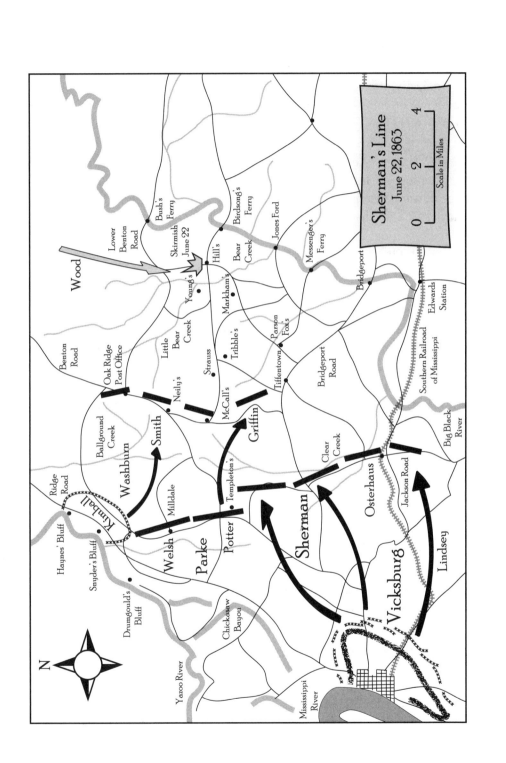

N

Wood

Lower
Benton
Road

Skirmish
June 22

Bush's
Ferry

Birdsong's
Ferry

Jones Ford

Messenger's
Ferry

Bridgeport

Benton
Road

Oak Ridge
Post Office

Young's

Hill's

Markham's

Bear
Creek

Little
Bear
Creek

Neily's

Strauss

Tribble's

Parson
Fox's

Tiffentown

Bridgeport
Road

Edwards
Station

Ballground
Creek

Smith

Washburn

Kimball

McCall's

Griffin

Clear
Creek

Southern Railroad
of Mississippi

Ridge
Road

Milldale

Templeton's

Osterhaus

Jackson Road

Big Black
River

Haynes' Bluff

Snyder's Bluff

Welsh

Parke

Potter

Sherman

Lindsey

Drumgould's
Bluff

Chickasaw
Bayou

Vicksburg

Yazoo River

Mississippi
River

Sherman's Line
June 22, 1863

Scale in Miles

0   2   4

hill to hill and bluff to bluff." Another was amazed that "they call it level here when the surface presents no greater angles than 45 degrees."[46]

Ironically, after so much planning and movement and the contingency plan going into effect like clockwork, nothing happened within those twenty-four to forty-eight hours Grant so worried about. "I hear nothing of Johnston at all; no trace of him or signs of his approach," Sherman reported to Grant. And it was the same over the next few critical hours. Parke reported to Sherman on the afternoon of June 23 that his cavalry had moved across Bear Creek and even onward, meeting only very small numbers of skirmishing Confederates and determining that most of the large Confederate elements were still in their original positions at Jackson and elsewhere. Sherman sent the news to Grant, who thankfully wrote to Ord that he "had heard nothing of Johnston up to 11 o'clock. Don't think he is this side of Big Black." The same held true the next few days, Sherman adding that "on the best evidence now procurable, he is not coming this way, or at this time." Grant confirmed as much in the next few days, one deserter informing the Federals that some forces did "come as far as Mechanicsburg" in the slot between the rivers but had since moved back across the Big Black River. Sherman confirmed that what Confederates there were had come down the slot instead of across the Big Black: "A reconnaissance of the river bank demonstrated the fact that no enemy had crossed over in any force, or had made any preparations in the way of bridges, fords, or boats."[47]

Over the next few days, all Grant could explain was that "Joe Johnston has postponed his attack until he can receive 10,000 re-enforcements, now on the way from Bragg's army. They are expected early next week." Of course, there were no reinforcements coming, but Grant was confident in his preparations; "[I] do not despair of having Vicksburg before they arrive." Sherman took it all in stride, writing that "from scouts and citizens, I became satisfied that the enemy was on the east side of the Big Black River in considerable force." Others had to backtrack as well. "The whole operation is a puzzle here," Dana admitted to Washington, later outright declaring that "the report that Joe Johnston had crossed Big Black, or was crossing, was erroneous." As more information came in, on June 25 he added that "the report from the spy of General Grant, which led to the sending out of Sherman on the 22d instant, was a mistake, though it must have had some foundation."[48]

The main culprit had been Loring and his move southward to Vernon, but his soldiers reported doing little else offensive during this time. One officer in the 31st Mississippi, Colonel Marcus D. L. Stephens, described how there was a lot of drilling and camp life, the men of the regiment even having time to found a Masonic Lodge. Another described a "General Review" with Johnston himself participating, and word even went out that one officer and three men from every company would receive short furloughs. But as for offensive actions, there was nothing that should have brought on the massive Union response and Grant's worry.[49]

Still, the threat was there, and Sherman recommended keeping a vigilant watch despite this being very good ground for a defense. The Big Black was at such a low stage that it could be crossed in many places, he reported to Grant, but the country west of it fortunately was so severely broken up that "a regiment will find difficulty in forming a front. A small force can oppose a large one." He also explained that "I have as many men as can be handled on such grounds." Sherman nevertheless wanted to stay put to see the thing through, writing Rawlins that "unless General Grant thinks my services more useful elsewhere, I had better remain, as naturally all look to me for orders." He planned in the event of an attack, however, telling Grant himself: "I take it for granted you do not want me to attempt to follow him across that river unless after a defeat."[50]

The siege and monotonous operations—now five weeks old—were beginning to grate on everyone. Even the usually levelheaded Grant was beginning to see Confederates where they did not exist, even to the point of exercising his contingency plan for nothing. But it may have been all for the better. With Vicksburg still tightly enclosed, the forces on the west side of the Mississippi River on high alert, and with Sherman and a large force fully covering the rear, Grant now had all areas fully manned and ready for whatever might happen. One of Sherman's Illinoisans wrote that "if the rebs are ever going to attack us at this place they had better come soon for we will have this point . . . well fortified as the burg in a week." Grant could perhaps now legitimately take a breath and relax—although he could not fully do so until Vicksburg was at last in his grasp.[51]

Whatever happened out on the periphery of the Union operations, the main goal was still to neutralize Vicksburg, and that primarily meant the continuation of siege operations. But those efforts were affected in some ways every day by the long nights. "It is a most glorious night," wrote Colonel Water

Gresham of the 53rd Indiana to his wife; "the moon rose clear and full about dark, shedding a mellow light over the hills and valleys, reminding me of home. I fancy I can see you at the front door to-night, as I used to, enjoying the moonlight scenes." Obviously, what went on at night revolved around what stage the moon was in, giving more or less light. "Late in the night the moon rose lighting up the surrounding scenery with almost noon day brightness," one soldier wrote during the siege. Other nights were very dark, even "intense darkness," one observer noted, especially on cloudy or stormy nights. The darkness brought fear, homesickness, or jumpiness for almost half the day, Confederate brigade commander Francis Shoup bemoaning even the lack of "light balls; have no means of lighting up."[52]

In other ways, night also brought some relief, although of short duration. One Louisianan wrote how "the days are very long now & nights very short. . . . Night falls at ½ past seven and day breaks at ½ past three—very light at 4 o'clock." But even in that short time, the threat of sharpshooters dwindled, and soldiers on the front lines, especially Confederates, could actually stand erect and walk around a little bit. One Louisianan explained how it was done, even in some of the camps in the city graveyard: "As the work & stirring about of a besieged army is to be done at night, the haste & life in that solemn place was in sad contrast with the many marks that told of the dead."[53]

Night was also the best time for generals on both sides to ride their lines. One Louisianan wrote on June 14 that he "saw Gen. M. L. Smith riding by his lines before day." Brigade commanders did the same thing: "Gen. Hébert was around the lines last night. He spoke encouragingly to the men and seems confident of our ultimate success." Federal generals did likewise, although at times riding the lines could still be dangerous to both sides even at night. "Captain Adaire, field officer of the night, was killed while making his rounds," M. L. Smith reported. One Mississippian noted he "was making his last round when he was struck."[54]

Mostly, the nights offered a chance to witness another overarching spectacle that almost everyone at Vicksburg observed and commented on: the mortar shells. Everyone seemed to have his own description of the bombardment. "We beheld them rise, go streaming across the sky like a flying meteor describe a great curve and pitch headlong into the earth, gathering momentum as they fell," one Mississippian explained. Others took pages and pages to describe every intricate part of the mystifying scene. And there was plenty for everyone. "At night the bombardment from the mortar fleet was very heavy and constant," Pemberton wrote in his diary. His staff joked that each day they were being "mortified."[55]

Just because night was a normal time of rest did not mean operations stopped when darkness fell. In fact, in certain ways they picked up. Much of the Federal digging was done at night so it could be done more safely; warnings to whisper while digging between the lines made it even more safe. "Every night we intrench a little closer to the Rebel works," one Indianan related to his mother. Many also saw things that were not there and would call out whole regiments. William Wiley explained how the 77th Illinois was frequently "called into line at all hours of the night." He described how "at such times Colonel Grier would step out of his tent and call out in that peculiar voice of his, fall in 77th." He added that "every man would jump to his feet, grab his gun and accoutrements and be in line in a moments time no matter how soundly he may have been sleeping."[56]

The Confederates were also busy digging at night, mostly in repairing what had been pummeled throughout the preceding day. "At night the engineers were busily engaged in repairing the works in front of Lee, Moore, and Hébert, which were badly shattered," Pemberton reported. He added that "the labor at night [is] becoming very severe, and is beginning to tell upon the engineers and their working parties. The daily breaching of our works by the enemy's heavy guns renders the labor of repairing them very arduous." He complained in his diary how the Federals continued to "batter our works which are nightly repaired, or new ones constructed in their stead."[57]

The work was indeed arduous. One Confederate explained that "it took all night to repair the damage done to the works during the day." And it was often done under unrelenting fire. In the 46th Mississippi, William Pitt Chambers related how, "as we worked at night, we kept one man watching for the Flash, and at the signal all 'lay down.'" Sometimes the shells would penetrate the earthworks and would still burst amid the sheltered workers.[58]

Not everything could be done at night, however, as engineers had to have light to see what needed to be repaired. Obviously, showing any light after dark was tempting death; one Illinoisan was killed when he lit a match to check the time. Thus, some work had to be done in the daytime. "General Forney directs me to say that he would like you to come out before dark or as soon as you can," one of Forney's staff officers wrote Engineer David Wintter on June 12; "the enemy is erecting new works on the Jackson road, and it is necessary that something should be done on our part. He therefore wishes to see and consult with you on the subject at once."[59]

All the work was not lost on the amazed Federals, who beheld almost new fortifications every morning. Brigade commander John B. Sanborn reported how the Confederates "kept large details at work during the nights, constructing rifle-pits, covered ways, and breastworks for batteries." Newspaperman Cadwallader remembered how "all damages would be repaired at night, and the morning sun would show a dazzling array of white cotton gunny sacks filled with dirt and sand in the breaches made the day before. These white sacks afforded excellent targets for artillery practice, and bets were daily made as to the number of shots some particular gunner would require to dislodge one. The second or third shot would generally hit the mark."[60]

Skirmishing was also common at night. Sometimes, if the light was right, sharpshooting could occur, although over time the skirmishing at night seemed to slacken as everyone realized that it was not worth it. Most skirmishing was done by pickets that both sides sent out after dark into no-man's-land to keep watch and secure the lines against any nighttime surprise attack. One Confederate officer described how "nightly our pickets were in advance of our defenses and nearly contiguous to the sentinels of the enemy." This was especially important when there was some ability to see at night, as one commented in warning against attack: "Now that the nights are light."[61]

Pickets thus went out at night, although any given soldier would have to stand picket guard only every few days. The idea was to give early warning, with orders to fire if the enemy advanced "and run in." One Mississippian dreaded that scenario each time his turn came. "I was always glad when a night was over and we were safely back in our trenches, for we would have been in almost as much danger from some of our own men, as from the enemy, in case we had to run in." Another had a different take. "I preferred this to working on the defenses," a Mississippian said, "for while this picket duty between the lines was exceedingly dangerous work, yet there was no labor about it and one could rest." That is, unless something happened to alert the enemy and call attention, as in the case of one 36th Mississippi soldier who developed "a violent cough" one night while out. "Every time our comrade would cough," another explained, "here would come a shower of bullets in reply." Most of the time, however, the pickets let each other alone: "It is very seldom that they pay much attention to us more than to send out their sharp-shooters who by their continual shooting serve to keep us from being too curious concerning the affairs of the rebels."[62]

Just posting the pickets could at times bring confrontation, as both sides wanted the same territory. At one point a Confederate officer ordered the Federal pickets off no-man's-land. They ignored him a couple of times but finally obeyed after both sides geared up for a fight. On another occasion, an Indianan described "the appearance of the officer of the rebel picket guard who came out saying boys get up out of this, the d__d Yankeys want to dig here." Humorously, on another occasion a Federal major would not give in and, "placing his hands on the shoulders of one [Confederate], he pressed him backwards." The Confederate yelled out to his men "this Yankee is posting both his own pickets and ours."[63]

Many thoughts ran through the minds of soldiers alone out on picket. "How often, when on the silent picket line, the thoughts would revert to the homes we had left in that other world outside, and an intense yearning for those peaceful scenes would come over us! And yet, amid it all, there dwelt in my heart a feeling that it was good to die for freedom," one Southerner explained. Danger also lurked in the darkness, especially as the Federals drew ever closer to the Confederate fortifications and no-man's-land continually grew smaller. "Our pickets are now nightly posted within a few feet of those of the enemy, and his sap has reached within forty yards of our works on the railroad," Pemberton nervously reported on June 22. At times confusion also set in as darkness shrouded the field. One Mississippian went to check on a neighboring regiment's pickets, which were farther back than the others. He stumbled upon them, each as surprised as the other. "The first intimation I had of their proximity (for it was a dark night) was the click of the hammers as they cocked their guns." He did not stop, but the next thing he knew "two men jumped on me and ordered me to surrender. It required considerable 'talk' to convince them that I was not a Yankee." Accidents were also common, as when "J. T. Avery shot himself through the right hand this morning while on picket."[64]

At other times the duty was just plain disgusting. One soldier between the lines described how one night his only cover was a small patch of broom sage "large enough to hide my body from sight, and behind this precarious shelter I sat all night while the enemy's bullets were spatting all around." Fortunately, he found a small mound on which to sit, making it more comfortable, but he wondered why it was "very soft and spongy." He added, "I also got occasionally a whiff of something that was not very grateful to the nostrils," and only later did he find out that he was sitting on the barely buried body of a Federal killed in the May assaults. "I was glad that I did not know of it at the time, for I would most assuredly have deserted my post."[65]

The constant required alert, especially on the Confederate lines, also produced weariness at night. A Louisianan reported that his officers were worried about night attacks, but it still afforded cover to get up out of the trenches: "If enemy were to increase occasional shots at night we would be much worried by it, for we lay low in daytime, and—scamper about at night." A Missourian described how "at the slightest alarm from any cause, we had to be ready to instantly get in line and move. As a result, we slept without taking off our shoes, with our guns within reach." Colonel Ashbel Smith of the 2nd Texas wrote that it was "prudent to keep a portion of our men (sometimes one-half, sometimes one-third) under arms during the night as well as day. All our men at all times slept on their arms, and, as they were never relieved, but remained at all times at their post, the fatigue was very great."[66]

Artillery fire was also common at night, and not just the mortar shelling. Most of this was done by the Federal artillery, pummeling both Vicksburg and the siege lines and keeping everyone up. One Mississippian even declared "it seems the Yankees are resolved we shant over sleep ourselves." Certainly most watched were the mortars:

> Oh! So pretty! First we would see a flash of light refracted over from the river, in 18 seconds would hear the report and see a speck like a star coming through the sky descending in a beautiful curve, growing larger and larger till after a serial voyage of 36 seconds it would flash forth in a round ball of flame and vanish into darkness 100 feet from the ground, after which we would begin to hear the hissing of fuse growing louder and louder and ending with an appalling noise.

Federals also wondered as "rockets were thrown up in Vicksburg last night and night before last, and they were answered from a point on the Louisiana side opposite Warrenton."[67]

Field and siege artillery also chimed in, and the Confederates also fired at night because of cover, an Illinoisan describing one shell that came over his camp:

> You could hear the rebel cannon boom in the distance, then a spark of light would make its appearance over the hill, growing rapidly larger and at last flash

out in a big blaze in the shape of a bright star, after which you would hear the report and the humming of the scattered fragments of the shell. Some of these clatter through the trees but most of them would be heard to strike the ground. One piece fell close behind me and was picked up.[68]

Still, mostly the Federal shells landed inside fortress Vicksburg, and it was not lost on the defending Confederates. "We are lulled to sleep by a lullaby of roaring cannon & bursting shells," wrote one Louisianan. Another Confederate surmised that "an occasional mortar shell from the river gives notice to the Yankees on shore that their friends are alive and kicking." In fact, the cannon fire was so common that some had trouble differentiating between thunder and cannon. There was a lot of lightning in the area in early June, and one Confederate admitted how "it is sometimes difficult to tell whether a gun has fired or a cloud has discharged its superabundant electricity."[69]

While there was sharpshooting with small arms and artillery throughout the siege, at times this skirmishing swelled almost to battle proportions— obviously more often during the night when surprise could be better achieved. Colonel Aaron Brown of the 3rd Iowa left a vivid description of one such event, writing that on this occasion "the night was dark, and a slight rain falling." The enemy suddenly appeared "and demanded a surrender," Brown explained, whereupon "our men seized their arms, sprang to their places in the trenches, and delivered a terrific fire." Much of the higher level of fighting seemed to come later in the siege and on the southern end of the lines. There, Jacob Lauman's division "repeatedly lost pickets." Grant was not overly impressed with Lauman to begin with, and often during the siege Grant had to correct his mistakes. Once Grant had the division positioned, in fact, he did not want to move it because of the confusion it might create. Lauman's approach toward the Salient Work on the Hall's Ferry Road made additional fighting necessary, however, as division commander Carter Stevenson's troops sought to keep Lauman from drawing any nearer. Unfortunately, at least according to one disbelieving artilleryman, some of the Illinoisans on that stretch of the lines "were asleep in the pits and had their cartridge boxes off!"[70]

Lauman, one Federal explained, was "almost nightly assailed by little sorties of the enemy. He loses one or two men every night, and sometimes more, generally by carelessness, and lately had one of his rifle-pits filled up by a party that made a dash upon him." Herron had problems as well, being "stopped for the last two nights by the brightness of the moonlight, which has enabled the enemy to fire at men on fatigue duty." When some of the Confederates called on them to surrender, an officer cautioned his men to simply "fix bayonets," adding, "and boys, when they come up, just take them up on your bayonets and pitch them over your heads."[71]

Confederate brigade commander Alfred Cumming was the main culprit causing this fighting, he reporting that Lauman's Union lines were far too close for comfort. "The enemy's rifle-pits in time were so extended as to almost entirely envelop the brigade front," he reported, "and were generally about 150 yards distant." Only in one sector were they closer: "At the redoubts on the Hall's Ferry road, however, they had approached much nearer, and were in possession of the foot of the slope on which one of the redoubts was constructed." This position, now within seventy yards of the Confederate line, was even more problematic; because of the lay of the land, its sap was shielded from Confederate fire by the slope of the ground. Cumming had to act.[72]

On two different nights, Lieutenant Colonel Cincinnatus S. Guyton of the 57th Georgia, aided by the 43rd Tennessee, led "sorties" on the enemy approach. Cumming reported that "on each a degree of success was attained, in the second the enemy being badly beaten." Lauman's engineer, Henry C. Freeman, described how the enemy made an attack at 11:30 P.M. on June 21 but was driven back. The same thing happened on the Hall's Ferry Road itself, the Federals there driving the Georgians back three separate times. But the next night the Confederates "fired a volley and made a sortie, rushing down the ridge in the same place and manner as on the previous night." They caught the enemy by surprise, one of the Illinoisans admitting, "feeling that everything was secure the men were allowed to lie down and some of them even went to sleep."[73]

To achieve their surprise, the Confederates crawled out and then let loose "volley after volley in quick succession"; Pemberton described it as "a gallant sortie on the Hall's Ferry road." One Federal was killed, several wounded, and six captured, including Lieutenant Colonel William Camm of the 14th Illinois, who was himself in the trench and played dead until the Georgians began to fill it up, whence he came alive and became a prisoner ultimately at the Warren County Courthouse. Others stabilized the lines, Walter Gresham writing that his 53rd Indiana boys "threw down the spades and picks, shouldered their guns, and held their ground." Lauman seemed almost more concerned about the enemy capturing "a number of our spades and picks." The Confederates filled in the trench the Federals had been digging, Federal Engineer Prime reporting that "they filled up 50 yards of our trench and began a counter-trench." Yet it was ultimately all for nothing; as Cumming reported, "it was finally deemed advisable, however, to leave the point to be occupied by them." Another Confederate was also hard-pressed to figure out what it was for: "It could not profit us anything for we could not hold it when taken." Perhaps that was because Lieutenant Colonel Frederick S. Lovell of the 33rd Wisconsin made a "bayonet charge" two nights later, Lauman writing it was "a charge and a yell." Lovell drove the Confederates away, reestablishing control of the point of the ridge and filling in a trench the Georgians had begun, although some reported they were sure "a force could have gone in [to Vicksburg] without much difficulty." Herron also "took the last rebel rifle-pits outside of their intrenchments, and captured in it a lieutenant and 9 men." Lauman's troops dug back out the trench the Confederates had filled "and found one of our men and one of the enemy buried within it, who had been killed in the fight."[74]

Most of the blame for this nonsense fell on Lauman, one Ohioan admitting, "I think Gen. Lauman's worst fault is the want of energy—a love of ease." In fact, he thought a staff officer was actually making most of the decisions. Others thought no better of the general: "Lauman is a brave man, but an ox is just as fit to command as he." Not unexpectedly, Grant himself was soon down to check on things, along with corps and division commanders.[75]

While some fighting in large proportions occurred, most contact between the two sides during the nights took on a decidedly more friendly and comical flavor, as the oft-mentioned conversations and association between the two sides were every bit as real as legend has painted it. The initial breakthrough came with the May 25 truce, and the collaboration slowly built from there. Thereafter, it was a slow, methodical, and careful feeling-out of each other that led to friendly meetings. For instance, after asking for coffee and being told to come on over and get some, a Confederate at first timidly replied: "Will you let me come back again[?]" After an affirmative answer he queried again: "But you want to shoot me yank." The Federal assured him he would not shoot and would let him return, whereupon the nervous Confederate admitted, "Well, yank I will try you[.] [Y]ou say you wont shoot now yank if you was to shoot me you would be a verry mean fellow." On another occasion, a Federal claimed that pickets crawled up so close to one another that they were on each side of a stump, where they talked for much of the night. Lots of good-natured chatter ultimately went back and forth, such as the Federals asking how they liked the bombardment, to which the Confederates answered that "they dig holes to put our ded in which saves us the trouble of making graves." Soon, both sides became used to such visitations during the nights and took additional chances. "The men have become so used to it that it would seem as if all danger were forgotten—indeed I have known the men to stand in the ditches & throw clods of dirt into the rebel fort—for the purpose of tantalizing them."[76]

Some cajoling took place initially, although at first it was heavy toward sarcasm and what the Federals would do to the Confederates. Later, one Louisianan noted that "they do not revile us as much as when they first appeared before us confident of driving us from our works at the first charge." Now, it was as tame as one Federal who hollered "haloo old reb are ye asleep?" Another called over "what o'clock is it Reb." One Southerner asked, "Are you agoing to shoot tonight[?]"[77]

The picket line was where most of the visitations took place. These forward lines were often very close, and one Federal declared that "great friendliness prevailed at night." Engineer Prime explained that

> their active defense was far from being vigorous, the object seeming to be to wait for another assault, losing in the mean time as few men as possible. This indifference to our approach became at some points almost ludicrous. We were accustomed to cover the front of our night working parties by a line of pickets or a covering party, and the enemy, while we were not nearer than 100 yards to their line, would throw out their pickets in front of it. On one occasion, in front of Ord's corps, our pickets, in being posted, became intermixed with the enemy's, and after some discussion the opposing picket officers arranged their picket lines by mutual compromise, these lines in places not being more than 10 yards apart.

While surprising, Prime admitted that the Confederates could have unleashed volleys and slowed the work and that "the advantage of this arrangement, novel in the art of war, was entirely on our side, and was not interfered with." At times, the Federals even took advantage of it, Engineer Hains describing one night when "the picket officer was directed to crowd his pickets on the enemy's, to allow the working party to push on the second parallel." That said, Prime admitted that "in Lauman's and Herron's front the enemy was

not so courteous." At other points they also captured each other. One Louisianan noted how a "Yankee sentinel in front of 26th [Louisiana was] captured.
Our sentinels were posted on one side of a log & he was on the other—so he
gave up."[78]

Over time, regiments from each side learned more of their counterparts,
who mostly did not change night after night, and a friendly relationship developed. One Mississippian noted how the skirmishers of his 38th Mississippi would meet the opposing pickets every night, and "thus the 38th and the
17th Illinois became good friends." It became so friendly that "on parting the
'boys' would shake hands and caution each other, in all seriousness, to 'keep
heads down after daylight,' when they would shoot at each other's heads with
the eagerness of sportsmen." One Wisconsin soldier told how "our pickets
are getting to be quite sociable with those of the enemy; it is quite a common
occurrence for them to meet halfway without arms to drink a cup of coffee
together, and have a long talk over matters and things in general. It very often
happens too that the rebels do not go back again, preferring to stop with our
men until they can be sent north."[79]

Trading was common in the friendliness of night, including canteens, Confederates' cedar ones for Union metal. Feelings became so friendly on Francis
Shoup's front in terms of trading goods that one Federal told a Louisianan
to "make out your requisition," and the Southerner put down what he would
like to have—"sardines, coffee a pare & bottle of whiskey." The Federal later
returned with everything but the whiskey, saying "that was some distance off
but they would get it & send it to him." At other times, the two sides would
"throw over notes & put them on wild canes & hand them to our boys." One
Louisianan marveled that "they swap knives, canteens, etc., with our men.
By agreement we do not fire upon each other unless one party commences
to work."[80]

Amazingly, on occasion family members from opposing sides also met
each other. "One night one of our boys got to joshing a rebel across the line
and found out the rebel was his father. The next night the father deserted and
came across to his son," declared an Indianan. Often, brothers would find
each other by asking if a certain regiment was across the lines and gradually
narrowing it down, meeting between the fortifications. One Confederate in
the 6th Missouri gave his brother across the lines a wad of money "to send to
the old folks in Missouri."[81]

In a most interesting anecdote, one Confederate asked if the 54th Ohio was near, and it was. He wanted to meet a certain sergeant, who soon appeared. The Confederate returned to him a letter he had picked up at Shiloh and along with it "the likeness of his sweetheart."[82]

The visiting and back and forth was often done musically. At times during the nights, various bands and singers would serenade each other. An Ohioan, John N. Bell, noted that his regiment "closed the day with singing in chorus the glorious Star Spangled Banner and other patriotic songs in the rifle pits before we were relieved, which the Rebels could hear plainly." The 3rd Louisiana had a "glee club" that would sing to friend and enemy alike. Often, the fighting would stop so that all could listen, and one nearby Mississippian explained that "the effect of such music, heard, in a living graveyard, in the shadow of night, was as weird as it was exquisitely beautiful." Often, the more humorous songs were directed at interstate rivalries within a brigade rather than the enemy, one Mississippian of Hébert's brigade noting "the Louisianans never fraternized with the Mississippians, and frequently made us the butt of their ridicule." He also noted that "'our friends the enemy' enjoyed this more than we did, and frequently applauded the singers."[83]

The back and forth between the two sides brought out the keen wit and sense of humor among many of the soldiers, the wittier and more humorous on each side rising to become unofficial spokesmen. John C. Taylor of Pemberton's staff described it as "exercising their wits at repartee." At times there would be fun and games, with some offering riddles and "conundrums" to each other, the officers being the spokesmen. The Federals got the best of the Southerners for several nights until the Confederates came up with a riddle no one could solve: "Why are greenbacks like the Jews?" The answer, after the Federals gave up, was given: "Because they have Abraham for their father and no redeemer." Some were more biting, such as when a Confederate asked "What are you doing there, Yanks?" and the reply came, "O-o-o-h, just *guarding prisoners*." The oft-repeated line with one "facetious" Federal declaring "that we had a worthy general over us now" led Confederates to ask who, and the Yankee replied: "Gen. Starvation." It was, the unthankful Confederate wrote, "a cause of much merriment on their side."[84]

The back-and-forth ran the gamut of anything and everything and was often biting in nature. When one Confederate asked how the Federals liked the "Sunny South," a Northerner responded that they liked it just fine: "Oh, bully! . . . we wear our overcoats all day." One Federal asked, "Played out[?]—Played out[?]" Another cajoled "old Rebs are ye all dead yet?" One

Confederate asked, "Well, Yank, when are you coming into town?" The re-
ply: "We propose to celebrate the 4th of July there." One Confederate asked,
"Yanks, why don't you pitch in and storm our works?" The answer came:
"We weren't brought up to pitch upon prisoners." It continued: "Where's
Hooker?"—"Alight, where's Stonewall Jackson?" A Federal asked how they
liked "Grant's Mule pen," and a Confederate retorted how they like "Jeff
Davis's 'stake & ridered' fence." Federals often asked if the Confederates
had any grease, whereupon an affirmative answer would bring: "Well grease
yourself and slide back into the Union." One Confederate asked why they
were digging ditches, and a Union soldier responded "we intend to flood it
and run our gunboats up that ditch and shell h___l out of your old town."[85]
     Union division commander Alvin Hovey described the back-and-forth:

Hello, Reb, wouldn't you like a good cup of coffee. Yes, wouldn't you like to
have Vicksburg. Yes, and we intend to have it. Can't see it. I suppose not there
is too much dirt in your eye. When do you expect to take Vicksburg? O, we are
coming into the City to celebrate the fourth of July, and take dinner with you.
Hope so, guess we will be likely to see you when you come. O yes we thought
we would notify you so you would have no excuse for we want to find you at
Home when we come. O we scarcely ever leave Home now adays. You must
have urgent business lately you stick at Home so closely you used to be such
great run-abouts. What is got the matter with you lately? We understood there
was a band of thieves round here and we want to stay and watch them. When did
you get a mail last. Last night. Guess it was a female. Have you got any more
Indianola's you want sunk? No but we've got a lot of Dummys though. . . . Well
look for us there about the 4th of July will you. Why don't you fire on us now
like you do in the daytime? Cause Gen. Grant says it aint right to fire on Prisoners. Why don't you come out? Why don't you come in? Well we will be there
soon enough for you. Has Gen. Pemberton got any more cannon he wishes to
turn over to the U.S. Government. If he has we'll 'Grant' him bread for them.

Above and beyond the back-and-forth and the muffled mortars, Hovey declared all could be heard was "the dull sound of the Pioneers Pick and Shovel
which plainly told the foe that we never slept. On the contrary we were slowly
& surely drawing nearer their works."[86]
     The high command knew such fraternization was happening and most al-
lowed it. Confederate brigade commander Francis Shoup explained that

we are on speaking terms with the enemy at the [Stockade] redan. The picket
parties at that point agree upon short truces, during which neither party is to
fire. Notes are thrown across from one party to another. Some trading going on
in coffee, &c. Have forbidden communications, but after sundown the firing
ceases and there is a good deal of talk going on between the enemy and our own
people, but principally in the brigades to my right and left. I permit it only in the
presence of the officer of the day. Brothers, relations, and friends are constantly
inquiring after each other.

One Ohioan noted that Sherman himself sometimes came to the front to listen, and had "a good laugh over it."[87]

Both Pemberton and Grant tried to stop the get-togethers, Pemberton
stipulating that "none . . . hold any conversation with the enemy across the
line." Grant ordered that "all talk conversation exchanging of Papers or other
friendly intercourse between our pickets and those of the enemy is hereby
positively prohibited, and any violation of this order by officers or men will
be summarily punished." Confederate division commander Carter Stevenson
reported that "our pickets on Lee's line were met by an officer to-night, sent
by Grant to say that he would place no more pickets in front of that line, and
would fire on ours. Our pickets were consequently withdrawn to the immediate front of the works." On another occasion, a Confederate officer came
along and barked "this won't do, boys. I give you five minutes to get back to
your posts." A Federal admitted that there followed "of course a general howl,
and a break for the rifle pits followed on both sides." Evidently, however,
Grant learned he could not stop it totally. Fred Grant told of how his father
received the Vicksburg newspaper every day and found "that there was some
communication going on between our respective lines." He tried to stop it,
particularly that between Missourians on each side. The conversation also
included "a little trade of coffee, etc., for tobacco, mingled with news from
besiegers and besieged." Grant soon found that the information could be useful, and "the illicit 'press association' was allowed to continue its work."[88]

Despite the friendliness on most sections of the line, there was still a lot
of uneasiness and concern about being tricked. Occasionally, a shot rang out
amid the festivities, when the calls of "dry that man up. Dry him up" would
ring out. Most kept their word and did not fire. In fact, when told by officers
trying to break up the friendliness to fire on the enemy, most refused, at least
initially. They would at least bellow out a warning: "Rebs hunt your holes, we
are going to fire." One Federal wrote that "the pledge is given not to fire on

each other, both sides keep the pledge sacred." Another noted "it is a point of honor with the pickets not to fire on each other unless there is some unusual demonstration."[89]

At other times, the proximity caused heated discussions and actions even though an informal truce was had. Many enjoyed throwing items over the works into the enemy's ranks, sometimes notes wrapped around bullets and sometimes more harmful objects. Some, including division commander Frank Blair, threw dirt clods at the enemy. Other items were merely intended to frighten, such as when "one day our neighbors tossed over a dead rattle-snake, and occasionally a cracker would come over with a polite inquiry as to the condition of our larder." Others more sinisterly threw grenades: "It had the appearance of a ball game, only the players never caught the balls, but fled from them." One Federal guarding the stacked guns of his comrades as they met their counterparts between the lines suddenly hurled a shovel at the Confederates. His bewildered lieutenant demanded to know what was hap-pening, and he responded, "One of thim grayback devils hit me with a clod." One Missourian explained how his lieutenant's "nose was skinned in a pretty rough manner by a lump of clay that was dried hard in the sun." There was more chance of heated arguments when the discussion turned to the war. One Federal described how the Confederates he talked to admitted a mistake but were afraid to come back into the Union because "we'd just treat them like dogs." The Federal replied that "our boys told them if they would come back they would be treated as brothers."[90]

The devotion with which each side argued their positions sometimes led to ludicrous scenes. Many discussions became heated, often with "no small amount of profanity," one Illinoisan related. But cooler heads normally pre-vailed, and, in the midst of war, each side would conclude they must separate to avoid "any fighting over the subject!"[91]

Night after night for weeks on end such curious behavior defined the Siege of Vicksburg. Yet it ended at dawn. At the end of the nights, around 4:00 A.M., Alvin Hovey explained that a volley from some two hundred guns was their "Revile" and warned the enemy to hunt their holes. A Mississippian similarly explained how "we held our ground until we could see the first scintillations of approaching dawn, and then we knew we had to get away from there." It was often a scamper among bullets to make it back to the fortifications as those who had just been talking as friends engaged one another again as enemies. Night after night such oddities went on, but the sun always rose the next morning, prompting all back to the reality of the daylight war.[92]

12

"THE DEATH HOLE"

June 23–25

By the last week of June, the Siege of Vicksburg had settled into a moribund and monotonous existence. "The same old routine of shelling and sharpshooting still continues," one Mississippian wrote. "We can do nothing during the day but eat and sleep, and but little to eat and that very common. We are nearly worn out with the ditches, but will hold out as long as provisions last." He went on: "I could endure it cheerfully if I could know how my dear ones at home are; it has now been six weeks since I heard from home; been in the trenches 27 days and no prospect of being relieved at a very early date." Another Mississippian described how "monotony does not convey all the sameness of these days." A Federal similarly declared to his diary that "the siege is dragging along its slow weary length." The soldiers in the trenches endured the same heat, tedium, and schedule day after day, with only the exchange of regiments in and out of the front lines on the Union side and the constant skirmishing while on duty breaking up the monotony. The outnumbered and confined Confederates did not even have that much time off; they continually stayed in the trenches and tired accordingly. Even Grant's line of countervallation back at Sherman's position settled into tedium, with nothing much heard from Johnston and his forces and the varying divisions taking firm positions and holding against boredom more than anything. Young Fred Grant explained that the siege went on and on "without much excitement except such as was caused by reports that Johnston was about to attack our rear."[1]

Only a few events broke the monotony, one Illinoisan describing a long day of watching with nothing stirring across the lines. Then "an old half-starved mule" wandered closer to the Union position and suddenly "off went a hundred or more muskets, and down fell the poor mule." The Illinoisan admitted how "this little incident, for a few minutes, broke the monotony." Some sharpshooting that grew to slightly larger proportions also helped, although at times both sides realized the sharpshooting and even skirmishing were making no real difference, and by the latter part of June both sides began to scale it back. One Illinoisan in Lauman's division, where much of the hottest skirmishing had taken place, described how his troops took a position on the picket line and "the rebels were at work outside this fort, countermining, while many of their men sat and lounged around the fort, in plain view. Neither them or our men said a word, but worked on in silence." That did not stop one Illinoisan from having a little fun as they continually dug, however. As he would throw a shovel full of dirt over the top, he would "jump up and wave the shovel at the rebs, then 'juke.' How the bullets would sing over while we were down behind the bank." These isolated but disproportionately loud events often brought quick queries from higher up, such as McPherson writing to Grant on June 23 how there was "heavy and rapid musketry and artillery firing on the left and center apparently of General Ord's corps. What does it purport?" Other bombardments also came as a surprise to the high command. Grant queried Herron on June 23 that "heavy firing is reported on our left. Is it in your front? What are the indications?" Herron replied: "Have just taken another rifle-pit and 13 prisoners in moving up my right line of skirmishers."[2]

The trouble came in stalemate, one Federal writing that "the rebs show no disposition to come out and fight us, and we are in no hurry to charge on their breastworks." Another declared "our men are still pecking away at Vicksburg," although all knew "the taking of Vicksburg is now only a question of time." As a result, the administrative aspects of the siege began to pick up the longer it went, if nothing more than because the commanders from Grant and Pemberton on down had more time on their hands to see to issues that had been backing up for a while now.[3]

Often, these issues led to additional troubles, but the boredom of what one Illinoisan described as "the long irksome siege" nevertheless had its effect, often resulting in punishment being meted out. "Corporal David Connor was Reduced to the ranks by order of Col [Samuel R.] Edginton for being absent without Leave," one 12th Iowa soldier reported. The boredom and increased administrative actions also led to correspondence across the lines. Grant, for instance, learned that some of the white and black Union soldiers captured at Milliken's Bend had been hanged at Richmond, Louisiana, earlier in June. The report from a captured Confederate was that "General Taylor and command were drawn up to witness the execution." Grant fired off a note to Taylor protesting the event if it occurred but nevertheless stating he was willing to take Taylor's word for it that it did not happen under his guidance, "hoping there may be some mistake in the evidence furnished me, or that the act of hanging had no official sanction, and that the parties guilty of it will be duly punished." For his part, Taylor responded that such treatment was "disgraceful alike to humanity and to the reputation of soldiers" and assured Grant he knew nothing of it, and that it was not an official act if it did take place. He added that he would "cause this matter to be thoroughly investigated."[4]

Of similar note was Grant's almost continual effort to send medical surgeons to care for and bring back Union prisoners from the Raymond and Champion Hill areas. Reports of the arrival of the Federal party went all the way up to Johnston, who desired to know what the commander on the ground told them. Others chimed in as well, including Confederate cavalry commander William H. "Red" Jackson, who reported he halted the medical party at the picket line until further instructions could be attained. In the meantime, the Federal "truce party became tired of waiting for General Johnston's reply to their communication, and withdrew beyond the Big Black, where they now are." Johnston eventually ordered a message sent to the surgeon through Osterhaus that Federal wounded would be delivered to him "at the outer chain of vedettes."[5]

Larger military concerns also continued, with Grant continually wondering about Port Hudson's defense amid rumors it had fallen. Admiral Porter was Grant's best source of news and informed him on June 24 that "there is no news of importance from Port Hudson. Garrison still holds out, and have nothing but parched corn to live on." He did inform Grant, however, that Nathaniel Banks had tried and failed in two assaults at Port Hudson, much like Grant before.[6]

Another concern of Grant's was the enemy presence to the north, in much smaller force than that at Port Hudson but aggravating nonetheless. One Confederate in particular, Captain Hiram M. Bledsoe, was causing problems along the Mississippi River around Greenville. Bledsoe had only about fifteen cavalry troops and his Missouri artillery battery, with which he fired on Union shipping. Grant asked Porter to send the Mississippi Marine Brigade to "clean Bledsoe out." He added, "They might land at Greenville and dash behind them, so as to secure the artillery, if nothing more." Porter could not spare the brigade, so Grant sent Lieutenant Colonel Samuel J. Nasmith and a small force instead.[7]

The Confederate high command also found itself swamped in minutia, perhaps because nothing else larger was occurring. Despite paperwork being reduced throughout the siege, Pemberton and his generals were not above minutia in administrative aspects, a dysentery-ridden Bowen picking a fight on June 24 over who was to blame for the debacle at the Big Black River back on May 17. He wanted Martin Green to "forward a report throwing the burden of having been the first to leave the trenches at Big Black Bridge on the shoulders of those who should bear it," namely the conscript Tennesseans of John Vaughn's brigade. He hoped this would have the effect of "wiping off this unmerited approach upon the fair fame of the brave men of this division." Better news for Bowen arrived in one of the outside dispatches on June 23: his promotion to major general.[8]

Pemberton himself tinkered with policy, forms, and troop positions, such as when Bowen moved some of Cockrell's troops (now the only reserve since Green's brigade had gone into the trenches on June 2) into the fortifications themselves. Cockrell sent half a regiment to Green's right "to fill out your line and act as a reserve" and later moved two regiments to the Jackson and Graveyard Roads each. At times, Pemberton had to move quickly, causing the ire of commanders who were not informed beforehand. He also often required commanders to correct forms and fill out vouchers correctly and had to cite, on several occasions, regulations to them as to why he could or could not do something. He and his staff also kept close watch on the status of "public funds" and army returns and rations requisitions, to make sure the same amount of precious rations were being drawn as there were troops. At times, it was also necessary to transfer supplies from department to department, such as when he ordered the superintendent of the telegraph to transfer wire to the ordnance department to make primers. The only telegraph line in Vicksburg by then ended at the fortifications, so it was not necessarily needed anyway.[9]

A similar issue Pemberton found himself involved in was city jurisdiction and the besieged civilians. He made rulings on using private entities such as the "Vicksburg Hotel" for storage and utilized the public when he had to. On one occasion, he ordered staff to "find a German to communicate with the prisoner just turned over to you and obtain his statement in writing." At another time, when a soldier killed a civilian, he ordered that affidavits be "made before a civil magistrate."[10]

Mostly, Pemberton fretted about his defense of Vicksburg and how long he could hold out. His observers had broken the Union signal codes, so he knew a lot of what was occurring on the outside. He issued orders on June 24 "to be particularly vigilant against an assault between now and to-morrow morning," and the next day he gave orders that the Confederates on the front lines not "hold any conversation with the enemy across the line, unless specifically directed."[11]

Most concerning was what began to creep into Pemberton's mind. He first used the word "terms" in the context of surrender during this time, perhaps because of Johnston's recently arrived declaration that Vicksburg was doomed. He wrote to Johnston on June 23 that, if he tried to cut his way out, he would lose the place and a lot of his army. If he stayed, he would lose the place and the entire army. "This we cannot afford," he wrote. Accordingly, Pemberton offered a plan by which Johnston would send "terms" to Grant in which Pemberton would be allowed to "pass this army out with all its arms and equipage." Pemberton argued that it would be a "result more to our advantage than either of the above actions" and suggested that Grant might accept these terms from Johnston. Pemberton added that he still hoped Johnston "by force of arms, [would be] enabled to act with me in saving this vital point," and he committed to "strain every nerve to hold out, if there is hope of our ultimate relief, for fifteen days longer." But it was clear—and was perhaps a subtle message to Johnston—that Pemberton was losing hope and was beginning to think in terms of surrendering.[12]

Grant certainly would not have accepted this offer if given, which it was not, as Johnston was still determined to refuse to accept any blame for the coming defeat. Grant would have no doubt thought back to the problems faced when Zachary Taylor had done the exact same thing to the Mexican army at Monterrey in the Mexican–American War; it only led to a larger and more brutal fight at Buena Vista as well as questions of his methods.[13]

The common soldiers were also beginning to have doubts. One Mississippian wrote how "hopes of relief from friends without had been so long deferred that our hearts sickened and sunk within." The constant upheaval of emotions with rumors of Johnston's approach led to an upsurge in morale at times but always ended with crestfallen morale when it did not pan out. One soldier declared they "hope they would be relieved by Johnson, cholera and yellow fever." Another moaned that "thirty-nine days in the trenches will kill up any set of men."[14]

Yet something was about to happen, unknown to either Pemberton or Johnston. Grant was even then working on a new way to end the campaign—and in a different manner than what Pemberton desired. It would certainly end a lot of the boredom facing both armies. Ironically, it was known to one person inside Vicksburg, at least according to what one Confederate officer described as "an old man in this place who claims to be a prophet," or what one of Pemberton's staff officers described as a "spirit medium in town." He had been making predictions that never came true, particularly about Johnston's arrival and the fighting that would result, even to the point of predicting that certain members of Pemberton's staff would be killed. The distrust of this latest pronouncement was evident, although one soldier added that "some say that in several instances his proficis have come to pass." Nevertheless, on June 24, the old man declared that something big would happen the next day, June 25, at 3:00 P.M. He gave some detail, mentioning that Johnston would attack and that "we will hear the most dreadfull cannonading that has been heard during the war." The officer was skeptical to say the least, adding, "We will see now weather or not he is a true prophet."[15]

By late June, the Union engineering efforts had reached a more professional stage. Early in the siege, an almost comedy of errors had taken place, delaying the digging war and muting its effect. In fact, while the whole reason the Federals were even there was gaining entrance into Vicksburg, many other threats developed, such as the ongoing danger to the rear, the nagging Confederate efforts west of the Mississippi River, as well as logistical concerns. At the same time, various problems on the Vicksburg lines themselves also emerged that made the effort to dig toward the Confederate fortifications less than what Grant had wanted. Ironically, that the approaches were getting uncomfortably close to the Confederates was a new issue, Engineer Hains of the XIII Corps explaining that they were "so close that every movement has to be made with the greatest caution."[16]

One lingering problem was the lack of competent engineers to direct the digging. Grant had complained about this shortage, but that had somewhat resolved itself with the arrival of new ones and the turning of West Point–trained officers, who had endured a heavy dose of Dennis Hart Mahan's engineering classes while in school, into de facto army engineers for their commands. More of a problem emerged at the top, when Grant's staff engineer Frederick Prime had to leave the army due to sickness. His replacement was Captain Cyrus B. Comstock, who had arrived June 15 and taken over the lagging effort on McClernand's, Lauman's and Herron's fronts to the south. He took Prime's place late in June and carried on the work without any disruption.[17]

The emphasis on the rear areas was also another issue; if it did not cause problems, it certainly took attention away from the besieging lines. Grant himself spent many a worried day working on the defense in the rear, even riding out at times, and of course Sherman's removal to that area took away the original XV Corps commander. Several brigades from the besieging line also went east, and Grant was willing to send more if necessary. The defense of the rear contained some engineering aspects as well, especially after the contingency plan was put into place and Sherman deployed his forces, including those pulled away from the Vicksburg lines. Sherman began to deploy his nearly 33,000 troops forward from the Big Black River railroad bridge northward to Haynes' Bluff, fortifying and manning a line facing east to secure Grant's siege forces facing mainly west. Sherman's line was a true line of countervallation.[18]

That said, there was continual development on the original siege lines, they having grown to such a state of complexity by this point that one Federal described them as "almost like a honeycomb." In fact, Ord had the XIII Corps working harder now than it ever had under McClernand, especially with Comstock and then Captain Miles D. McAlester, who took over the southern Federal lines when Comstock became army chief engineer, overseeing the work. In fact, two additional approaches began on this front in late June. Alvin Hovey began a zig-zag approach from his lines toward the Square Fort south of the Railroad Redoubt, and it was a shame that it started so late, on June 23, because Prime reported that "the ground gave cover here to within a short distance of the enemy's line." He argued that "this was one instance among many where the lack of engineer officers was shown. With a proper number of officers, the ground in all its details would have been thoroughly reconnoitered, and the best positions for approaches chosen, instead of wasting work, as in this case, when the best approaches were selected after the siege was half over." This approach was mainly constructed under the command of Engineer Hains of Ord's corps.[19]

Farther to the left, Francis Herron also began approaches toward the Confederate works on his front. A parallel took form some two hundred yards out from Stevenson's lines, from which ran the approach, begun toward the Confederate lines on June 24. It ultimately ran to within a hundred yards of the enemy fortifications. Captain Arnold Hoeppner had charge of the work here.[20]

Lauman, of course, had already begun his approach, working hundreds of men at night on the sap that was "three and a half feet deep and four feet wide." This now made five approaches on McClernand's, Lauman's, and Herron's fronts, and a grand total of twelve to date across the entire army's line. Dana reported that

> a great deal has been accomplished, especially in widening the trenches, connecting them, and making it practicable to move men and artillery through them. Ord is devoting his attention particularly to Hovey's approaches, which he thinks offer perhaps the most favorable attack in our whole line, but which McClernand has left in great backwardness. A week's labor will, however, bring them into such a condition that Hovey will probably be able to crown the rebel lines with his artillery.

Still, Dana reported on June 25 that "if there was a better supply of engineer officers, the labor would be much more effectively applied."[21]

While more approaches took form, the manner in which the engineering developed also changed in late June. For much of the siege, attention had been focused on digging the approaches toward the enemy's lines, with attending parallels run out corresponding to the Confederate fortifications. These parallels were put in place so that troops could be stationed closer to the Confederate lines in case the generals saw an opening in which an assault would succeed, such as in Grant's massive artillery bombardment on June 20 when the parallels had been filled to the brim with troops. While not always manned to such a degree on a regular basis, these parallels did allow sharpshooters to take station closer to the Confederates and made their jobs much easier and deadlier. Artillery placed in these parallels did the same thing on a much grander scale. The effect was not lost on the Confederates. A nervous Pemberton scribbled in his diary, "There was nothing today to vary or stay the steady progress of the enemy works."[22]

The arrival at the Confederate works caused even more decisions for the Federal high command, however. The fire from small arms, grenades, and

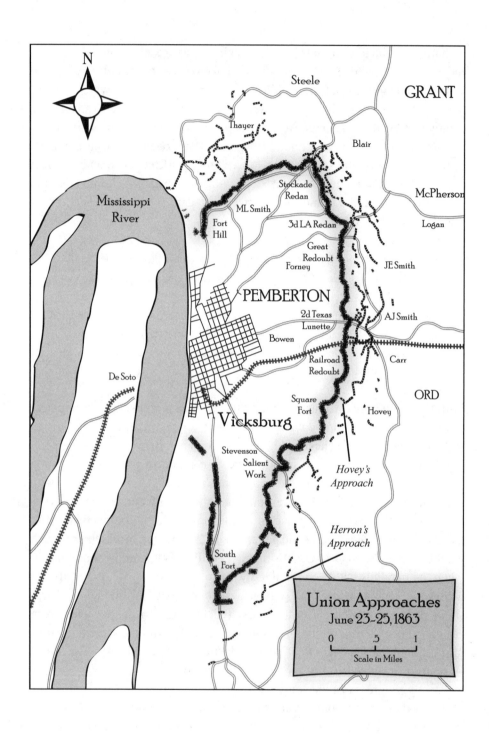

N

Mississippi
River

Steele

GRANT

Thayer

Blair

Stockade
Redan

McPherson

ML Smith

Fort
Hill

3d LA Redan

Logan

Great
Redoubt

Forney

JE Smith

PEMBERTON

2d Texas
Lunette

AJ Smith

Bowen

Railroad
Redoubt

Carr

De Soto

Square
Fort

ORD

Hovey

Stevenson
Salient
Work

Hovey's
Approach

Herron's
Approach

South
Fort

Vicksburg

Union Approaches
June 23-25, 1863

0   .5   1

Scale in Miles

sometimes even artillery was so close and hot that little more work could be done. "A great many canes have been cut," Hains explained, "however, by Minie bullets. The artillery fire caused the workmen all to leave, but they were returned at once." Hains admitted that "the saps are now about as close as they can get without first clearing the rebel works in front by means of mortar shells." At times, the Confederates even filled the ditches in front of the works, they being seen "wheeling hand-barrows along the left face." To get a better view, Hains "made a novel reconnaissance of the enemy's ditch this morning, by means of a mirror attached to a pole, being raised . . . a perfect view of the ditch was by this means obtained."[23]

The Union approaches arriving at the Confederate works also allowed for an even more unique engineering effort in late June. The whole idea to run approaches toward the enemy fortifications was for two reasons, one of which was to position large numbers of troops closer to the enemy for purposes of sharpshooting or assault. The other—a strictly engineering effort although tied to the ultimate use of troops closer for an assault—involved mining operations. Once the approaches reached a point close enough to the enemy forts (one Confederate on the right of the 3rd Louisiana Redan remarking that "they neared us until dirt fell against the Third Louisiana's dirt. The breastworks completely came together"), excavators could begin to dig underground to a point beneath the enemy's works. Obviously, this would provide more cover for those digging than a simple sap would. It would also allow for the use of large amounts of black powder that when packed into a gallery underneath the Confederate line could blow a literal hole in the Confederate fortifications, which could then be assaulted with troops from the closest parallels.[24]

This type of digging under the enemy had been a staple of siege warfare for centuries. The earliest besiegers dug under castle or city walls, carefully shoring their progress and then burning the shoring to make the mine cave in, opening a hole through the walls above as they fell into the cavity. With gunpowder's invention, siege mining changed both with the ability to knock down fortifications with cannon fire as well as blowing up mines.[25]

There were, as would be expected, numerous concerns with this type of mining warfare. The opening of the mine had to be in a covered position, both for the coming and going of the workers digging the shaft as well as for the removal of dirt from the mine itself. Similarly, the opening had to be close enough to the enemy lines that this could be done quickly, easily, and safely in terms of airflow. A mine underground for hundreds and hundreds of yards was unquestionable at this point, given the amount of dirt that had to be removed and the distances involved. But beginning mining operations from the heads of the approaches near the saps would provide a short jaunt underground to the Confederate lines.[26]

Other, scientific-related aspects also had to be considered. Plotting distances was important, because the mine needed to be at a precise point underneath the Confederate lines. Too far would do little to no damage to the enemy, and too short would endanger Union troops in the closest parallels and the head of the approach. Shoring and safety was also a concern, although the specific soil types at Vicksburg made digging easy and safe in most areas; the loess soil that retained its form and would not cave was perfect for quickly digging and needed no shoring. Then, once the powder charge was set, the tunnel also needed backfilling so that the force of the blast would go up instead of back out the shaft. And finally, there was a definite need to get the charge right. A lot depended on the size of the powder charge as to what kind of crater was formed. A lighter blast would cause a narrower and steeper hole, whereas a bigger charge would produce a wider but shallower and less steep cone. Less steep was needed if troops were intended to pour through the gaps made in the Confederate lines.[27]

The engineers began the mines, but Prime was not a fan of their efforts. While he admitted that "the compactness of the alluvial soil making lining for mining galleries unnecessary, [and] these galleries were formed with ease," he argued that "mines could not make an easier way into the enemy's line than existed already." He readily argued that "their only use was to demoralize the enemy by their explosion at the moment of an assault." While many mines were begun, Prime concluded that "more importance was attached to them by officers and men than they deserved."[28]

In all, some eight different mines were started in the various Vicksburg approaches, mostly in McPherson's and Sherman's corps areas. Only one mine was on Ord's front, at A. J. Smith's saps, indicating how the approaches in McClernand's sector had lagged behind before Ord took over. Similar mines began on McPherson's front as well, as Logan's approach reached the Confederate lines on June 22, when Hickenlooper's workers arrived at the base of the parapet of the 3rd Louisiana Redan with their new sap roller that had replaced the one burned a few days prior. A visiting Illinoisan from Lauman's division wrote home that "it is astonishing to see the work that Logan's men have done to approach the fort." A nervous Pemberton similarly jotted in his diary, "The enemy has reached the ditch in front of our works on the Jackson Road." He knew it portended trouble; indeed, the digging underground soon began. The same occurred on Sherman's front as Ewing's approach reached the Stockade Redan and then went underground.[29]

Confederate engineers were not complacent throughout all this Union engineering effort. Knowledge of these operations became apparent in mid-June, and a near-panic ensued. Some asserted that by the simple act of placing the ear to the ground "one could distinctly hear the click of pick and spade at work beneath." John C. Moore's engineer, upon learning of the mining in front of the 2nd Texas Lunette, wanted the army's engineer Samuel Lockett and others to come out "as soon as possible . . . to consult in regard to some method of stopping it as they will soon be under the fort." Confederate commanders frequently reported on the approaching Federal engineering efforts, and they were also aware that mining operations had begun. But there was just not a lot militarily that could be done about it short of advancing past their fortifications and capturing the heads of the approaches, which was not an option. Rather, the best solution was engineering efforts on their own parts.[30]

Regarded very highly around Pemberton's headquarters for the wonders he and his small band of engineers were performing, Lockett and the others soon began countermining operations near the Federal mines, most notably at Sherman's, Ransom's and Logan's approaches. Pemberton explained that "our engineers were kept constantly and busily employed in countermining against the enemy, who was at work day and night in mining on different portions of the line." In fact, a Union spy sent into Vicksburg by Admiral Porter several months previously had been detailed on an engineering squad and worked on the countermine on Sherman's front. He described it as "from the ditch of the principal fortifications, so that its explosion will leave the work unharmed, and extends toward the sap."[31]

Three results were hoped for in countermining, although none would be a permanent fix to the situation. The best hope was to locate and dig into the shafts and chambers the Federals were digging. If they could be located, obviously troops moving through the Confederate shafts could annihilate the Federals digging their shafts in what would have become a curious and miniature battle beneath the ground. This fighting might have rivaled Chattanooga's "Battle above the Clouds" for uniqueness. Although much Confederate digging took place, because of the needle-in-a-haystack chances of locating the

Union mines even by listening through the soil, no success ever came from this effort, although the Confederate work did cause the Federals to stop digging on Steele's front in order to find the culprits. Dana reported on June 26 that the digging had "been delayed for two or three days by the effort to find a mine which the enemy, starting from the counter-scarp and working from the ditch, has run under our lines." Perhaps running out of patience, Grant sent for Steele and ordered him to get on with the work, although Steele replied that it "cannot be done before tomorrow."[32]

More realistic for Confederate engineers was the secondary hope that, by digging at least near the Union shafts, blowing their own smaller charges in their own mines might loosen the nearby soil enough to collapse the Federals' tunnels and keep further work from occurring because of the loosened soil that could no longer be mined. That would entrap those digging, make the Federals start over again, and perhaps even dissuade them from even attempting a restart. Such an effort did take place later in June when Confederate engineers blew their own charge at the Stockade Redan, hoping to collapse the mine at the head of Ewing's approach. Blowing countermines also occurred at the 2nd Texas Lunette, although none did significant damage. Of course, engineers had to be careful about the size of the charge and the location of the shafts. Suddenly digging out the side of a hill near the Union lines would not be a good idea—neither would be a charge that might blow up your own fortifications. The idea was simply to loosen the nearby soil, not remove it by a large blast.[33]

The third hope for Confederate countermines—the one that really had the largest and possibly only effects during the siege—was to dig countermines close enough to the enemy's blast that the open areas and voids would assume much of the force of the Federal explosion, thereby lessening the amount of force removing the Confederate fortifications atop the ground. Unfortunately, not all the forts were built for this type of resistance. Normally, the countermines were begun in the ditches in front of the forts, allowing a head start as much as eight or ten feet deep to begin horizontal digging. At the 3rd Louisiana Redan, however, there was no ditch due to it "being on a very narrow ridge." Lockett "found it impossible to get in its front to start a counter-mine without exposing our sappers to the terrible fire from the enemy's sharpshooters and batteries, not more than 150 yards distant." Lockett thus began a vertical shaft inside the fort, from which he started horizontal galleries once he was at the right depth. One Louisianan explained that "a perpendicular shaft

was sunk near the center of the redan in order that the force of the ex
when it came would break through the walls of the shaft and thus les
effects of the explosion."[34]

The Confederate countermining ultimately accomplished little.
Hains, mining under the 2nd Texas Lunette down on the Baldwin's
Road, explained that "they are very shy about it." He listened to their
determining that "from the sounds that are heard, it is highly probable
are running a gallery from the counterscarp of the ditch, for the purpos
exploding a mine near us. I have directed a listening gallery to be run ou
the direction they appear to be, and change the direction of the sap slight
He later guessed that "they are deceived as to the direction we intend to tak
He was right, one Confederate describing how a countermine began from t
ditch in front of the parapet. The trick was getting to the countermine itse
from inside the fort, and the engineers worked that out when "a hole was cu
just large enough for a man to crawl through the breastworks to the ditch ir
front."[35]

The Confederates also responded with countermines on Sherman's front
as early as mid-June, but they did not blow them up that early. M. L. Smith
in particular had complained to Pemberton of the lack of work on his front,
and Pemberton ordered Lockett that "you had better come over to see me
on the subject at once." Lockett got the work started, and Smith reported on
June 20 that "it was the intention to explode one of the mines last night, but
there being no indications of the enemy working in immediate proximity, it
was deferred." At other times they could not get the fuses to work properly;
Smith reported two days later that "an attempt was made to spring one of
our mines last night, which failed from some peculiarity which exists in the
igniting of powder in tubes." Shoup further explained that "the train was laid
in gas-pipes; will not communicate. Find by experiment that powder, when
confined in a long tube, when ignited, will burst the tube a few feet from the
end, and will not burn further."[36]

Despite the problems, Lockett and his engineers stayed busy while the
Federals tried to dig their way into or underneath Vicksburg. The trick was
to know where to countermine and how far to go. Lockett explained that
"it was very difficult to determine distances under ground, where we could
hear the enemy's sappers picking, picking, picking, so very distinctly that it
hardly seemed possible for them to be more than a few feet distant, when in
reality they were many yards away." The other trick was to get one's own

ɔ that they would not be permanently entombed when a blast
ˋlike the larger situation itself concerning Vicksburg, those in-
l little knowledge of detail as to the timing, desires, and intents
als outside Vicksburg's walls who could pick and choose their
of action. The waiting game thus continued inside miserable

e digging and tunneling the Union forces undertook at Vicks-
es of circumvallation and countervallation, it is surprising that
nfederate fort did the Federals attempt to blow a hole through
s. Fort Hill, as it was termed then, now known as the 3rd Loui-
n the Jackson Road was the target of Hickenlooper's mine in
ificantly, this would be the first successful explosion of a mine
fortifications in American history.[38]

eering work on this front, by Logan's division of McPherson's
, under civil engineer Andrew Hickenlooper. This Cincinnati pro-
ad been in private practice before the war and was actually an ar-
n earlier in the conflict, commanding the 5th Ohio Battery at Shiloh
ing to defend the famed Hornet's Nest. He quickly found a path to
e knowledgeable duties and became McPherson's engineer. During
vious few weeks, he had directed the serpentine approach on Logan's
as it ran along the course of the Jackson Road, veering one way or the
r only to take advantage of the ground or to provide spots of relief and
er for anyone moving through the approach.[39]

Early thoughts of mining under the fort had emerged, with Logan's divi-
ion engineer Captain Stewart R. Tresilian trying to open a mine as early as
May 24 and thinking he could blow it soon, which of course turned out not
to be the case. Dana reported three days later that "McPherson's mining operations have proved much more difficult than his engineers first calculated,
and it must still be some time before the work he is digging at can be blown
up." Indeed, it was only on June 22 that Hickenlooper's workers reached the
foot of the ridge on which the 3rd Louisiana Redan sat. The approach would
have to begin to ascend the hill toward the fort, which was problematic as
it would provide less cover by the sap roller, or otherwise begin to tunnel
underground. Hickenlooper chose the latter and had his workers dig a tunnel
under the Confederate redan. It was suffocating, miserable work, although

air shafts aided the flow of oxygen and the good soil made digging a lot less troublesome than it could have been. As a result, Hickenlooper put out a call for "all the miners in the command to report to me in person." The digging then began in earnest.[40]

Once Hickenlooper cleared away a good covered position to start the mine, he went to work. Fortunately, Logan's division had many miners, such as men of the "Lead Mine" regiment, the 45th Illinois. Others came from the 124th Illinois. Thirty-five miners ultimately answered the call, and Hickenlooper divided them into three shifts working around the clock. Under the supervision of Lieutenant Thomas Russell of the 7th Missouri, the miners set to work with picks and shovels and quickly dug a three-by-four-foot shaft. Six men worked each hourlong shift, with two working the picks, two shoveling the loose dirt, and two handing the grain sacks filled with dirt back to where they would be out of the way and eventually taken out of the mine. By June 24, Hickenlooper and his men had reached the sixty-foot point they thought was under the fort, some forty-five feet of tunnel with a smaller fifteen-foot extension, as well as fifteen-foot galleries branching off each side at forty-five degree angles.[41]

The next chore, and obviously a more dangerous one, was to move the powder in. Soldiers manhandled it in its barrels to a safe point in the sap, where the kegs were broken and the powder transferred into grain sacks, making a load of about twenty-five pounds each. The trouble was that the bags had to be carried the remaining length of the sap, which was somewhat exposed. The miners did so, making about a hundred trips with the dangerous powder on their shoulders. Hickenlooper explained that the miners learned to move "during the intervals between the explosion of the enemy's shells; and so well timed were these movements that . . . all were landed in the mine without a single accident."[42]

But there were problems. Hickenlooper reported that he could "hear the rebels at work on [a] counter-mine very distinctly. Appear to be above and to the left of our gallery." In fact, during the night of June 24, while Hickenlooper was asleep, the miners "became frightened at noise made in rebel counter-mine and quit work." He had them right back on the job the next morning and finished the work, but by that time the miners reported they could "distinctly hear the conversation and orders given in the counter-mine." It was a race against time and the Confederates, and whoever lost was likely to be lost forever, buried alive in the other's explosion.[43]

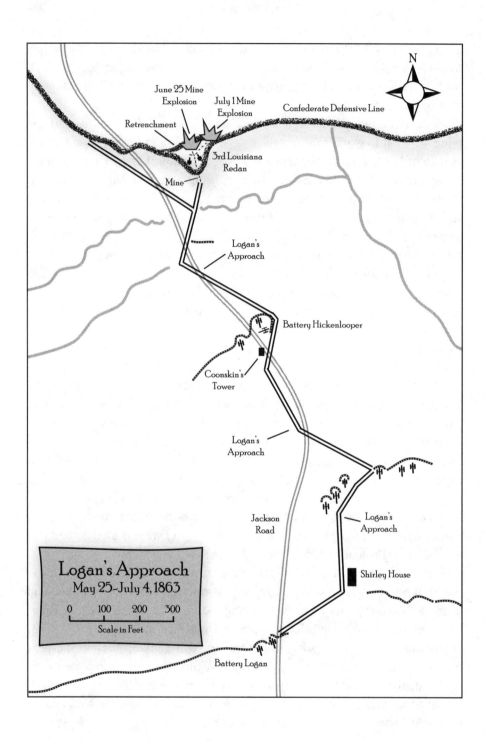

N

June 25 Mine
Explosion

July 1 Mine
Explosion

Retrenchment

Confederate Defensive Line

3rd Louisiana
Redan

Mine

Logan's
Approach

Battery Hickenlooper

Coonskin's
Tower

Logan's
Approach

Logan's
Approach

Jackson
Road

Shirley House

Logan's Approach
May 25–July 4, 1863

0   100   200   300

Scale in Feet

Battery Logan

The miners ultimately packed seven hundred pounds of powder in each gallery and eight hundred pounds in the center shaft, for a total of 2,200 pounds of powder borrowed from the navy. The amount was just a guess as to how much to use, as many factors such as soil type, air pressure, and desired shape and size of the resulting crater were all variables. Mahan had constructed a table of calculation for different soil types, but it is unknown if the civilian engineer Hickenlooper used it; it did not have any data for loess-type soil anyway. Hickenlooper connected each gallery and the center shaft with two fuses each, also obtained from the navy, "so arranged as to explode them all at the same instant." The redundancy, of course, was in case one of the fuses failed to burn. Finally, the grain bags of dirt taken out were returned and packed "in the most compact manner possible," while timbers and other shoring went in behind that, all plugging the shaft well behind where the galleries branched off so that the force would be directed upward instead of out the shaft. Behind that, the dirt was replaced in a less compact manner but nevertheless replaced. "Mine tamped with cross-timbers, sand-bags, &c., and all ready to explode at 1 p.m.," Hickenlooper reported.[44]

Once Hickenlooper reported his work done, the higher commanders took over. Grant was interested in the project and saw it as a possible way to end the campaign immediately. If Logan could break through at the gap blown in the Confederate lines and infantry could pour through, perhaps Vicksburg would be his by nightfall. That would obviously ease the situation to the rear as well, as there would then be nothing for Johnston to relieve and Grant could utilize the vast majority of his force on that front. Grant thus informed all his commanders that the mine would be "sprung" on the afternoon of June 25, somewhere between 2:00 and 4:00 P.M. "McPherson will spring . . . mines in his front this afternoon," he also informed Sherman back at the rear line. "He will try then to secure a place within the fort now in his front," he added, including erroneous information that "the mines are run about 35 feet in, and will go up with a blast of 1,000 pounds of powder."[45]

More specifics went to the other commanders on the lines. "McPherson will spring the mines in his front between 2 and 4 o'clock to-day," Grant explained to Ord, "and will try to take possession of the main fort." Ord was to "hold your troops in readiness to threaten an assault, to keep the enemy from marching on McPherson. As soon as you hear the explosion, open with artillery lively for about fifteen minutes." He wrote a similar missive to Herron, who was not affiliated with any particular corps and not serving under Ord as

Lauman was, to open with artillery and "should you discover any signs of the enemy moving troops toward . . . McPherson's, you will make such demonstrations as to lead him to believe you intend to attack him." These orders then trickled on down. Nearest the explosion, Ord to the south ordered his troops to be ready, some even moving north to support the advance. Ord advised his subordinates that he would receive another note "about half an hour before the miners are priming" and would thus give shorter notice, but when the time came he wanted "the trenches . . . manned for an assault, and the regiments and companies not therein . . . put under arms, in the best cover, for the same purpose in our front, without exposing them to fire."[46]

Additional information for Ord soon came from McPherson as well: "The mine will be exploded about 3 p. m. to-day." Ord relayed the message to his division commanders and instituted the plan by which each division, starting on the right nearest the blast, would "listen for explosions and firing of artillery on their right, at or about 3, and take up the fire at the time it reaches them, without further orders."[47]

McPherson was making much more elaborate plans. In addition to having his hand in the engineering aspects, he being a prewar professional army engineer, he also oversaw the troop dispositions that would go into action as a result of the blast. Logan's division being on this front, it obviously fell to it to make the attack once the mine blew. McPherson sent detailed orders to Logan, explaining that the mine would be touched off about 3:00 P.M. and that "if successful in destroying a portion of the enemy's works, it is important for us to take advantage of it." McPherson wanted Logan's entire division "under arms at 2 P.M.," with one brigade, Mortimer Leggett's, "in the trenches with fixed bayonets, the advance as near to the mine as they can go with safety; say, where the advanced left hand trench debouches." All the other troops would need to be in the trenches farther back, McPherson said, "to drive back the enemy in case we make an assault and our troops are repulsed." But McPherson was counting on success, adding regiments from other divisions as a reserve (one from McArthur's and two from John E. Smith's). He also stipulated that Logan should have "a working party, provided with picks and shovels, . . . in readiness to make a lodgment on the enemy's works, should we succeed in getting in."[48]

Similar orders went to McPherson's other commands. The next division to the south, between Logan and Ord's corps, was John E. Smith's, formerly Isaac F. Quinby's earlier in the siege. Smith had commanded one of Logan's brigades before moving to Quinby's division when the latter became sick. McPherson informed Smith of the 3:00 P.M. target time, ordering that he send the two regiments to act as Logan's reserve "at 2 o'clock precisely" and to hold his division under arms "in readiness to move as circumstances may require." Sharpshooters and artillery were to open up as soon as the mine exploded, "firing deliberately," he added. McPherson included a word of caution was as well: "The ground in your front being impracticable, it is not intended for you to make an assault, but a demonstration to prevent the enemy from massing on Logan's left." Similar orders went to the only present brigade of McArthur's division, Thomas E. G. Ransom's, north of Glass Bayou. The only exception was that Ransom was also to fire his artillery obliquely "on the reverse of the works in front of Logan" and that "if you can succeed in effecting a lodgment on the work on Logan's front, it will be a great point gained, and will lead to still greater advantages on the right and left."[49]

The orders trickled down the chains of command to brigades and regiments, but the only one that really mattered was the brigade that would actually do the assaulting once the mine blew. That lot fell to Brigadier General Mortimer Leggett's brigade of Illinoisans, with one regiment of Indianans mixed in. The brigade had originally been under John E. Smith before he moved to division command on June 4, Leggett taking over the same day despite being already in command of a different brigade, which fell then to Colonel Manning F. Force. The 23rd Indiana had participated in the assault on May 22, as had the 45th and 20th Illinois, none of them making any headway against the Louisianans defending their redan. The 124th Illinois had not seen any perceptible action as yet. Most of the regiments were veterans, the Indianans and 20th and 45th Illinois being at Shiloh and many battles thereafter, while the 124th Illinois was newer. Fittingly, the 45th Illinois was known as the "Lead Mine" regiment, its ranks being full of miners from the Galena, Illinois, area. This mining operation—if not assaults through craters the explosions from the mines created—was perfect for them.[50]

Leggett filled his trenches with troops on time, mostly in a leftward parallel that he had earlier constructed while the mine ran from the head of the sap itself. His orders were to "hold my command in readiness to charge and take said Fort Hill as soon as the mine should be sprung, to hold the breach made by the explosion at all hazards, and, if practicable, to charge over and drive the enemy from his works." Leggett placed the best regiment in the brigade at the forefront, the miners of the 45th Illinois, at Coonskin's Tower, as well as about a hundred men of the 23rd Indiana to their left, in the parallel with orders to "occupy the breach, and hold it, cost what it may." The remainder of the brigade supported them in the rearward approach and parallels, ready to do whatever was needed. Others on down the lines did the same, Hickenlooper describing how "as far as the eye could reach to the right and left could be seen the long winding columns of blue moving to their assigned positions behind the besiegers' works." All were in position by the 2:00 P.M. deadline. And then they waited.[51]

By this time, the Confederates could plainly see something was in the offing and got busy themselves readying for whatever might happen. "Even the rebel army seemed conscious that something startling was about to occur," one Federal wrote. They knew the Federals were tunneling, and accordingly they had sunk their own mines to try to dig into the Union chambers or at the least allow some of the pressure to vent through their own open galleries. Fully expecting a charge to be blown, although not knowing where, Lockett and his engineers had taken the extra step of constructing a supporting fortification in the rear of the 3rd Louisiana Redan, basically across the base of the V-shaped fort. Consequently, if anything but the base of the fort was blown out, the Louisianans would still have a defense at the base, carrying the main line across in unbroken fashion. If the blast blew away the entire work, base and all, then a free path into Vicksburg might emerge.[52]

The Confederates defending this redan cast nervous glances around as the afternoon wore on and everything became quiet, one Federal remembering that "hundreds of rebel infantry peered over the lines of rifle pits as if to unravel the mystery." Something was definitely up, and the soldiers of the 3rd Louisiana braced for whatever might come. Ironically, there had been little indication of much of anything different up through the night of June 24, brigade commander Louis Hébert writing that "no change was visible, except the nearer approach of saps and the addition of newly thrown-up earth at several points." That should have been a clear indication as the dirt from the tunnels had to be placed somewhere. Still, that night was calm, and "the night of the 24th passed off with little firing on my line."[53]

The next day was no more odd, Hébert reporting that "the enemy continued his labors, but no movements of troops were seen. The skirmishing was as usual." Later in the afternoon, however, glimpses of something afoot emerged, including heavy firing toward Hébert's right and the Baldwin's Ferry Road. Yet there was nothing altogether out of the ordinary, Hébert admitting that "up to about 5.30 P.M. there was no indication of a projected attack on the Jackson Road." (Obviously, there was great discrepancy between Union and Confederate timepieces.) Only a slackening of the skirmishing as well as digging seemed odd, but there was a foreboding feeling of dread sweeping the Confederates. One Louisianan admitted "a strange stillness came over everything that brought with it an uncanny feeling. Men looked inquiringly into each others faces and moved restlessly about as if vainly endeavoring to shake off this indescribable presentment of impending evil." As time moved on, it became more worrisome: "The awful truth was realized that we stood face to face with a disaster the extent of which we could hardly conjecture," one Louisiana later admitted.[54]

Obviously, Hébert was not privy to the preparations being made behind the scenes across the lines, but McPherson was even then making his way to Logan's headquarters around 2:00 P.M., ready for the show. He was especially interested, given his background, in the engineering aspects, but he was perhaps more interested in the success that might come with the effort that would erupt any minute now as the clock ticked on toward 3:00 P.M.[55]

Tension filled the Union ranks as the Federal infantry huddled in their approaches and parallels, waiting for the inevitable explosion. "The eye of every soldier in the besieging army was fixed intently upon Fort Hill or in that direction," one recalled. It could not come quick enough for some, this waiting being excruciating. Others surely wished it would never come, that the fuse would somehow fail and they would not have to assault. These lead miners had been in this very position before, on May 22, and knew the deadliness of the Confederate fire coming from the Louisianans across the way. Making the tension higher for these troops, the allotted time for the explosion soon came and went, with no sign of anything remotely resembling a blast deep beneath the earth. Hickenlooper himself "coolly yet eagerly" watched the fuse burn until it went underground, and he and a few officers then scurried hurriedly back to Coonskin's Tower. There, they watched their timepieces "and counted the seconds." Nearby infantrymen watched as the fuse burned as well: "We saw a fire running along the embankment of Fort Hill; . . . a faint smoke was visible."[56]

The officers watching the proceedings wondered too. Grant was there as far forward as Battery Hickenlooper, as was McPherson and Logan and many

lower-level officers intent on seeing the greatest show yet at Vicksburg. The
stage became even more surreal as the time approached. Hickenlooper explained that "gradually as the hour of 3 approached the booming of artillery
and incessant rattle of musketry, which had been going on day and night for
thirty days, suddenly subsided, and a deathlike and oppressive stillness pervaded the whole command. Every eye was riveted upon that huge redoubt
standing high above the adjoining works."[57]

But as they watched, the minutes on their watches continually clicked on
with no movement at all. Most had to just wait and wonder *What had happened? Had the fuse failed? Had the charge not been properly planted and
set? Had the spark been extinguished by some outside force?* "The silence
became oppressive—even painful," one of the watching Federals with Hickenlooper declared.[58]

All eyes turned to Hickenlooper, who one Federal described as "leaning
carelessly against the base of Coon Skin Tower with his eyes intently fixed
upon the hands of his watch. His face was white and there was an anxious
expression about his eyes, but I never saw him cooler or more self possessed."
Hickenlooper was actually stewing on the inside, realizing "upon its success
depended my reputation as an engineer." He had no answers; his questions
were just as numerous, although probably more scientific and engineering-
based than the others. Yet there were overarching questions on all minds that
no one seemed to want to talk about. If this attempt truly failed, how long
should it be given for a safe period so that there would be no chance of it
going off? More important, who was going to be the one that went back into
the mine and checked on things? It would be sure death for whoever did so if
the thing suddenly blew up, the fuse having worked but being only delayed.[59]

Even after a little delay, Hickenlooper was not yet ready to send someone
in. It was still much too close to the time of the lighting to do that. Perhaps
the fuse was just burning slowly, or perhaps it had stopped for some reason
and would soon take up again. No one would be going in any time soon as
Hickenlooper, clearly frustrated that it was late, nevertheless saw no reason
to hurry. Just give it time. But a nearby officer felt for him, knowing he was
thinking: "What if it should fail?"[60]

It was a good thing he gave it time, because a few minutes later, around
3:30 P.M. (many others offered a myriad of times as much as an hour later),
the earth began to rumble and then spew fire, smoke, and dirt upward. The
fuse had worked. The mine had been successful. The engineering had proven

triumphant. "Perfect success," Hickenlooper crowed, and he later proudly wrote how "it appeared as though the whole fort and connecting outworks commenced an upward movement, gradually breaking into fragments and growing less bulky in appearance, until it looked like an immense fountain of finely pulverized earth, mingled with flashes of fire and clouds of smoke, through which could occasionally be caught a glimpse of some dark objects,—men, gun-carriages, shelters, etc."[61]

Quite a show it was, as the earth belched forth all manner of debris high into the air and the ground shook as if an earthquake had hit. Logan's division surgeon Silas T. Trowbridge remembered how "I stood about 250 yards distant from the mine at the time of the explosion, and felt the tremble of the shock very perceptibly at the moment. The noise was a dull heavy thud, unlike anything I ever heard, and then a column of smoke dirt and dust ascended full 100 feet in the air." Newspaperman Sylvanus Cadwallader similarly recalled when, "for a few seconds, which seemed minutes if not hours to those engaged and to all beholders, the air was filled with dirt, dust, stockades, gabions, timbers, one or two gun carriages, and an immense surging white cloud of smoke which fairly rose to the heavens, and gradually widened out and dissipated." A nearby Illinoisan described the "explosion[,] not sharp but muffled."[62]

The explosion was much more massive inside the redan itself. Hébert simply wrote that "the enemy sprang his mine under the main redan on the left of the road, and advanced to the assault," but others inside were obviously more impacted. One Louisianan described how "suddenly the earth under our feet gave a convulsive shudder and with a muffled roar a mighty column of earth men poles spades and guns arose many feet in the air."[63]

Others watched in awe, even some well behind the Union lines, although one soldier three hundred yards away was amazed at the lack of sound: "Strange to say it made no report. I was within three hundred yards of it but could hear nothing." Farther out, one of Sherman's men described the "immense spherical dome supported by a huge pillar under its center." Another added, "We could see the poor wretches flying in every direction, in the air, mingled with timbers and guns, and almost everything you can think of." One Federal surmised that "the poor rebs thought the Day of Judgment had come, and it had, to a good many of them." Even an artilleryman way down on Lauman's front described how, having been prewarned, everyone "was on tiptoe for the explosion." He went on: "At a little after four o'clock we saw an immense cloud of black and yellow dirt thrown up to a height of at least 100 feet." Confederates also watched in amazement. A Mississippian all the way over on the left of the Stockade Redan wrote that "from where we were, we could see the dust mingled with timbers and the bodies of men." Down the line in the other direction, a Confederate officer in charge of a detail of men working on traverses became frightened and bolted back to the regiment, losing his hat in the process. When he arrived, "his eyes were almost like a pair of saucers, and he was utterly speechless." Soon recovering, he spun a yarn about how the blast had been so close it knocked his hat off with dirt and debris. The rest of the detail, without their leader, soon ambled back into camp and gave the true story that the blast had been nowhere near them. They brought the officer his hat back.[64]

As awe-inspiring as the explosion of the military engineering was, the crater that was left was also impressive at "35 feet in diameter, and carrying away a greater part of the bastion but not reaching the terre plein of the fort," one observer noted. A Federal wrote in his diary at 4:00 P.M. that "Fort Hill has just been blown higher than a kite through the air." Another wrote how "the crater appeared to me like an immense ditch more than anything else and was I should judge about 35 or 40 feet long by 25 to 30 feet wide at the top and sloping to about 8 feet at the bottom." Another described it as "triangular in shape, the base line along the rebel works about 50 feet in length, sides about 30; depth . . . about 20 feet with sloping sides." Yet the whole intent of the explosion was to provide chaos in the enemy ranks and to open a pathway into the Confederate works. Part of that was done when all those items began to fall back to earth, and more when the defending Louisianans saw the "yawning crater where the mine had been." Accordingly, Leggett sent his Illinoisans directly into the breach, he reporting that "before the dirt and smoke was cleared away the Forty fifth Illinois had filled the gap made by the explosion and were pouring deadly volleys into the enemy."[65]

The stunned Confederates had little warning of such a monumental development and accordingly had to respond on the fly. They took stock of the horrid scene as soon as they gathered their wits, and the view was shocking with the crater, smoke, upturned cannons, and dead and dying. And not all the destruction was evident. In fact, six members of the 43rd Mississippi were in their own shaft "which our engineers were digging in the redan to meet the enemy's line." In the words of brigade commander Hébert, they "were necessarily lost," buried where they worked. Miraculously few others were hurt in the blast, the Louisianans mostly having pulled back from the apex of the redan itself. In fact, Hébert reported that the shaft the Mississippians were digging did exactly as partly intended: It "served as a vent upward to the force of the blast, and thus confined the breaking up of the soil to a shorter distance in the direction of the perpendicular of the redan."[66]

Once the shock of the blast wore off, Herbert and the Louisianans took quick stock of what had happened and how bad it was. Herbert was pleasantly surprised, as he and others were sure the Federals intended assaulting "during the confusion that would exist, as he conceived, in our troops. He was, however, quite mistaken, as the explosion created no dismay or panic among our brave officers and soldiers, and every one was ready for the foe before he appeared." Even better, Hébert was afraid he would see the dust settle only to face hordes of Federals coming through his line. But the Federal advance, in his words, "was a feeble one . . . ; but few of his men could be brought to mount the breach." A watching Indianan down the line agreed, writing that there was a five-minute delay between the blast and the advance. Hébert added, "Three regimental flags alone were seen at any time, and it is my belief that the enemy never contemplated but an assault to secure the redan, and there hold."[67]

Nevertheless, Federals soon began to pour into the crater, led by Company K of the 20th Illinois (interestingly under Captain John A. Edmiston of Company E) with two heavy beams from a nearby barn and cotton gin. The company, divided into two platoons, was to tote their two huge beams with notches every two feet to poke muskets through, the beams being ten inches thick and more than twenty feet long each and referred to by those involved as "logs" or "sills." Their job was to place them atop the new parapet at the edge of the crater. They were also if possible to spike any Confederate cannons they could get to, "believing that during the confusion many of the guns of the Fort could be spiked, destroying their usefulness." The Illinoisans did so, moving through the approach trench to the crater and then they "pushed roled and skid them [the beams] up the incline to the top of the west side of the crater." One of the Illinoisans noted that "the pit being full of loose dirt and 10 to 15 feet from bottom to top was a hard thing to climb but by hard work it was done." Few if any guns were spiked, but the beams were soon in place and the beam-carriers exited so the 45th Illinois could enter. A Louisianan described the effort from the Confederate side, including the placing of the beams, and noted how the following Illinoisans would dig out enough dirt under the beams to stick a musket through. A quick-thinking Confederate ordered a nearby cannon loaded with solid shot and fired at the beams, which when hit would recoil, only to have the Illinoisans heave it right back up on top. Captain Edmiston also described how the Confederates "tried to push them back on us with bayonets."[68]

With the beams set, the lead miners flowed into the crater, but there was a reason why the Federal attempt seemed feeble: this was not the best ground to move across, complete with a crater and loose dirt on the sides. In addition, the 45th Illinois immediately lost Lieutenant Colonel Melancthon Smith and Major Leander B. Fisk amid the chaos of the advance, the former morally wounded and the latter killed instantly. Sergeant Henry H. Taylor neverthe-less charged forward with the colors and planted them on the new parapet, a feat for which he later received the Medal of Honor. Yet as the Illinoisans poured into the crater under cover of the massive artillery barrage that had by now begun and formed a line as best they could, certain observations began to dawn on them and the engineers in charge. The crater was wide and shal-low, leading to supposition that the mine was overcharged with too much powder. That turned into tangible effects for the Illinoisans, who had to ma-neuver through the dirt and debris and try to form a line under fire from the Louisianans, who were still encased within their secondary earthworks along the base of the original redan. The Confederates had been massed down the hill in rear for just such a concern, with only a few still in the main work to watch carefully. Those behind were kept ready, "resting on their arms day and night to be ready for any emergency that might arise." The mine and resulting crater was definitely such an emergency; the explosion had basically blown off the apex and most of the V-shaped fortification, although leaving the base and the new secondary line intact. The Louisianans scampered to this defense and quickly began to pour a hot fire into the Illinoisans. Lockett crowed that "a parapet had been made to meet such an event some 15 feet back of the salient." It worked perfectly.[69]

Only a few Federals even actually attempted to storm the new Confederate line. Hébert described how "but few of his men could be brought to mount the breach, and, with the exception of one officer (supposed to be a field officer, leading the forlorn hope), evinced [no] determination." Despite the bravery, he added that the officer "mounted the parapet, waved and called his men forward, but was instantly shot down." Dana reported that "some of our men climbed the parapet with a view of taking aim over it at the enemy within, but were obliged to fall back and seek protection on the outer slope of the parapet. No attempt was made to enter the work through the breach; indeed, even after the explosion, the ascent remained so steep that an assault would have encountered serious difficulties from that cause alone."[70]

Andrew Hickenlooper was right in the middle of the affair, directing the building of the parapet and leveling the floor of the crater. But all were facing overwhelming odds, and he told of an episode when one of the bravest of the Illinoisans simply had a meltdown. The man tried to turn and get out multiple times, whereupon Hickenlooper would turn him back. When he tried again and "he turned his pallid face and appealing eyes upon me in such a mute but beseeching manner that I led him to the exit and pushed him out of the crater." Hickenlooper concluded that "through some strange and sudden weakening of his nerves [he] had become panic stricken, and nothing said or done could restore his courage." Others were not fortunate enough to be able to get out, and Hickenlooper described how the "shrieks, cries and groans were truly heart rending."[71]

There was an effort to consolidate what had been gained, however, and to do so Engineer Tresilian and his pioneers moved in. "I immediately repaired to the crater," Tresilian wrote, "and began to fill up the opening through which the enemy were firing volley after volley." A company of the 45th Illinois helped in this work, with Colonel Jasper A. Maltby right there among them, but he was also wounded for his effort. Nevertheless, the casualties continued to accrue, and the Illinoisans termed the crater "the death hole."[72]

Perhaps the most notable wound and potential death was to brigade commander Mortimer Leggett himself. He was in the thick of the fighting and took a unique injury: a large splinter of wood sent flying from a cannon shot struck him in the shoulder and torso. It tore open the flesh, and at first Leggett refused to be moved, but then soldiers carried the unconscious general to the rear, where he awoke as a surgeon cleaned his wound of rocks and other debris. Although he lived, worse news came the next day as surgeons further cleaned the wound. His muscle was torn and parts of his intestines were protruding, causing a hernia he had to live with the rest of his life.[73]

With the Federal surge halted, the most intense fighting began across the parapet "between parties invisible to each other," much like that which had occurred on May 19 and 22. "After his repulse," Hébert explained, "the enemy occupied the outer slope of the works, and from there commenced, accompanied by musketry fire, a terrific shower of hand grenades upon our men." One Confederate described the grenades as "about the size and shape of goose eggs," but with a stick stuck in them to make them fly. Some of the Federals decided it would be best to have nearby artillerymen throw them, but one refused. "The idea was started of putting [me] under arrest, but no one wanted my place," one of the cannoneers wrote, "so it was not done. I told them that it could not be done too quickly to suit me, as I did not care for the job." Some grenades were thrown nevertheless, one of the throwers being "blown to pieces by the premature discharge of a shell." Tresilian recalled that "the enemy seemed disposed to come over," but a few well-placed grenades helped tamp down their enthusiasm and Tresilian explained that "our men and the enemy were then bayonet to bayonet." Some actually threw their bayonets over as well.[74]

Another problem then arose as the Confederates began hurling cannonballs down onto the huddled Illinoisans in the crater. Leggett reported that "hand-grenades were then freely used by the enemy, which made sad havoc amongst my men, for, being in the crater of the exploded mine, the sides of which were covered by the men, scarcely a grenade was thrown without doing much damage, and in most instances horribly mangling those they happened to strike." But the Federals gave as good as they got. One Federal officer described how later one 1st US Siege Gun soldier was detailed for the purpose of throwing the grenades and had thrown about twenty before he was mortally wounded. Then, a detail of three soldiers from the same regiment took up the task. Even one of Logan's staff officers got into the act, one grenade exploding right in his hand but miraculously not injuring him.[75]

With the crisis point at hand, Hébert called up reinforcements to blunt the Federal fire, Dana reporting the Confederate resistance as an "obstinate defense." There were actually places on the flanks of the 3rd Louisiana that had no troops at all, so something had to be done. With Green's brigade of Bowen's reserve division having gone into the trenches on June 2 just to Hébert's left, that left only Cockrell's Missouri brigade as the reserve. The various regiments had been doled out in several areas, the 1st Missouri fortunately taking a position of little action known as the "Peace Department." Not so with the others, as Cockrell sent Colonel Eugene Erwin and his 6th Missouri to the breach immediately after the explosion, the 3rd Louisiana moving to the left. Colonel Erwin, the grandson of Henry Clay, was sick and had just left the city and returned to his command against surgeon's orders. He was perhaps caught up in the novelty of the situation, because he "gallantly attempted to lead some of his men to follow him over the parapet." Hébert reported that "whilst at the top he was instantly killed." A Louisianan described Erwin and the Missourians moving up "with a yell that sounded above the roar of battle," and another was convinced that Erwin became disoriented, thinking there was a line of Confederates to the front. The Louisianan distinctly remembered hearing him yell, "Forward boys, don't let the Louisiana boys go further than you do." Of course, there was nothing but Federals ahead of him, and he surged right into their fire.[76]

With the arrival of Cockrell's Missourians, despite the loss of Colonel Erwin, the lines further stabilized to the point that neither side seemed to have a decided advantage. The long afternoon thus waned as the 45th Illinois soldiers consolidated their gains near the new Confederate earthworks, their line in the crater and on either side a poor match for the Confederates looming above them. But that did not stop the Illinoisans from firing as fast as they could, and one Federal reported they did so, "holding their position and fighting desperately until their guns were too hot for further use." Hickenlooper remembered how the Illinoisans formed two lines, "the front line raising their muskets over their heads and firing at random over the crest while the rear rank were engaged in reloading." With the efficiency of the regiment waning, however, and Leggett wounded, the higher authorities had a decision to make. Would they continue to hold this new progress and perhaps even break through? It was obvious by now a breakthrough had not occurred, but was it time to give up entirely? Should the regiments be withdrawn and an admission of failure be made? Logan bellowed that "they are killing my bravest men in that hole," but when someone recommended calling off the fight, he barked, "I can't; my commanding officer orders me to hold every inch of ground."[77]

No one was ready to quit just yet, especially with a good flanking opportunity to fire straight down the Confederate lines to the sides, so the only other option was to hold what had been gained and hope something might turn up. The Illinoisans thus fired as fast as they could, one describing how they "fought until our guns were so hot and foul that we could not use them." The engineers finally were able to create a larger barrier for the Illinoisans, Hickenlooper calling it "a casemate out of the heavy timbers found in the crater, and upon which the earth was thrown until it was of sufficient depth to resist the destructive effects of the exploding shells." But it was clear the 45th Illinois was about done. Accordingly, Logan withdrew the lead miners and replaced them with the 20th Illinois, which had also previously been to this area, if not out this far, on May 22. The fresh Illinoisans quickly filed into their new position and continued the fight.[78]

Soon, the afternoon sun went down, but that did not preclude the Federals from remaining and the fighting from raging. Still the horror remained, Hickenlooper writing that "the groans of the dying and shrieks of the wounded became fearful, but bravely they stood to their work." In fact, over the course of the night and the next day, Logan continually swapped out regiment after regiment. The 31st Illinois replaced the 20th Illinois later on, they losing Lieutenant Colonel John D. Reese, mortally wounded when "a hand grenade struck . . . which literally disemboweled him." Another was hurt when the Louisianans "rolled a cottonwood sapling over on our side, striking me square on the back of my neck." He admitted how, "although it was very light, I thought the whole confederacy had fallen on me, Jeff Davis along with the rest of them." The Illinoisans were in turn swapped out for the reserve 56th Illinois under Colonel Green B. Raum. These Illinoisans not only had to endure the harrowing Confederate resistance; they also quickly found their ammunition to be bad as well. Logan knew he could not leave them at the front, so he recalled them and sent in his own 23rd Indiana. The fighting continued throughout the night, the reserve 17th Iowa then going in for three hours, Major John F. Walden explaining that "I could only judge of the position we were expected to take by the glare of the bursting shells which were constantly thrown over the broken parapet by the enemy, and behind which he was safely lodged." Walden added that "instead of intimidating our men, [the grenades] served to make them fire more rapidly and fight with greater determination." These Iowans were in turn relieved by the 31st Illinois again, they holding the line until daylight when Confederate brigade commander Hébert reported that "this species of combat is still going on this morning." He added that the Federals had, "however, in the night succeeded in covering his men."[79]

Episodes of bravery and horror mixed amid the close-quarter fighting, as in the 56th Illinois when Tom Oliver crept atop the parapet and shot as fast as his comrades could load and hand him weapons. One Illinoisan estimated that he fired more than two hundred rounds, while "5 men were busy loading and handing guns to him." His bravery did not have a good ending, however: "He remained up until shot down dead." In another episode, a shell exploded right as it hit another soldier; "it tore him all to pieces and set his flesh upon fire."

On the Confederate side, brave Louisianans who were also being torn apart by the grenades realized that they could hold blankets at the corners, gingerly catch the grenades, and heave them back without the fuses detonating.[80]

Logan was not the only one to bring in fresh troops as the hours extended. Hébert also did so. Later in the night, around 10:00 P.M., Colonel James Mc-Cown arrived with his 5th Missouri, although Hébert ordered him to bivouac in the ravine behind the line. Cockrell himself arrived on Bowen's order and insisted that the troops go into the line, relieving a portion of the 3rd Louisiana, which they did. Cockrell stayed at the redan despite having regiments on Stevenson's front as well as one at the Stockade Redan. With Erwin's loss, which Bowen assumed "might dispirit his men," Bowen thought Cockrell was most needed at the 3rd Louisiana Redan.[81]

The lines solidified as the hours passed, and Grant declared that there were some civil moments. He wrote that "the soldiers of the two sides occasionally conversed pleasantly across the barrier; sometimes they exchanged the hard bread of the Union soldiers for the tobacco of the Confederates." The blast also had odd effects elsewhere as well, such as on Hugh Ewing's line up near the Stockade Redan. When the mine went off, the 4th West Virginia, ready and waiting in the trenches, gave an extraordinary cheer, which caused the Louisianans opposite them to think they were about to be assaulted. They poked their heads above the parapet, and the ready western Virginians unloaded a volley. The fire "made them disappear quick," one observer added.[82]

Word of the Federal failure made its way out to the higher command, Grant receiving word from the front: "Find it impossible to hold [this] point without great sacrifice of life. Have withdrawn men, and have opened with artillery. Think we shall yet hold it." Grant sent word to his other corps commanders, particularly to Ord, who himself was often under fire. He wrote in a couple of notes that "McPherson secured the crater made by the explosion. The cavity made was sufficiently large to shelter two regiments." He explained that the enemy fought back but that McPherson was sending in artillery, which would be operable by the next morning on June 26, and that McPherson "has been hard at work running rifle-pits, and thinks he will hold all gained." Grant wanted Ord to keep his troops ready for whatever occurred, especially at daylight the next morning, including keeping A. J. Smith's division "sleeping under arms to-night, ready for an engagement. Their services may be required, particularly about daylight to-morrow morning. There should be the greatest vigilance on the whole line." Grant also sent word to the far left to Lauman and Herron to "be in readiness all night to afford any assistance necessary," Ord adding that he wanted Lauman to keep "at least half your force not in the trenches . . . sleep[ing] on their arms, ready to move at a moment's notice." Grant added that "if we can hold the position until morning it will evidently give us possession of a long line of rifle-pits to the right, and a fair way of advancing to enfilade to the left."[83]

Yet the affair generally flamed out the next day, albeit after some twenty-six hours of fighting. Grant informed Washington of the attempt, reporting that "the fight for it [the crater] has been incessant, and thus far we have not been able to establish batteries in the breach." Dana elaborated in a missive at 10:00 A.M. on June 26, writing dejectedly that "we have made no progress in the work whatever, and have not been able either to plant a battery or open a rifle-pit, or even to ascertain what is the real practical value of the fort of which we have just got possession of one corner, and cannot tell whether the adjoining works are or are not enfiladed against fire from it." The Federals nevertheless continued to swap out regiments in the front; the original 45th Illinois went in again and held the position under lessening Confederate fire. By that time, the lines were even more stabilized, and the firing began to die down while the Federals attempted to "raise a cavalier work on the parapet of the crater formed by the recent explosion. Sand bags are to be laid up, if possible, with loop holes for sharpshooters, and short rifle-pits dug on each flank, with the design of driving the enemy from the interior of the fort." Eventually, the 124th Illinois also got into the action at what many had begun to call the "slaughter pen," one Illinoisan describing how "we had to fight hard to fire without taking any aim at all but the guns were just held up over the log and fired off in this manner." Still, by the afternoon of June 26 all could see this too was a failure. Logan withdrew the Illinoisans to prepared parallels, and the mine attempt stopped. The Confederate response also grew weaker, even brigade commander Hébert falling ill, reporting that he was "kept out at the trenches during the entire night, and afflicted to-day with a fever." Once the Federals left, however, the Louisianans and Missourians moved up to "reoccupy it this morning, the sand-bags which the enemy had placed there serving as protection to our men." Cockrell reported the line retaken but a desperate need for sandbags as he had already used "all the old tents & flies I have been able to find."[84]

The results were not that impressive on the Union side, despite the extraordinary blast and vicious fighting. "Of all the fights I have ever been in," one Illinoisan wrote, "this was the most desperate"—"and I was at Shiloh." Logan, McPherson, and Grant all realized that what was potentially a game-changer had failed. Nothing would come of it except casualties, and not many of them on the Confederate side. Pemberton listed only eighty-eight killed and wounded in the whole affair. Forney sent Hébert a message "to say that he is gratified that you appear in such good spirits." McPherson lost more: thirty-four killed and 209 wounded. One Federal bemoaned that "the affair ended in smoke and sound. Judging from the noise one would have thought the bloodiest battle of the war was in process." He later added, "I can but re-gard these demonstrations as puerile and childish, and a disgrace to our arms. We can not whip these rebels with noise and uproar as the Chinese fight their battles." No such dismissal occurred on the Confederate side, where the fight was seen as a major victory, though a costly one in terms of territory lost. Hébert reported the next day that "everything indicates that during the night the enemy did a great deal of work. . . . [H]e has given shelter in our outer ditch to his men by throwing up sand bags, &c." The result of the Federals be-ing so close was frightening. Hébert reported that the enemy "is likely to have started new mines," which would cause this scenario to be played out over and over with perhaps more devastating results. The other horror, in Hébert's words, was that "he is now in position to appear in our works at any instant."[85]

Indeed, the Federals—by both normal above-ground approaches as well as tunneling below ground and exploding the mine—had reached the very ramparts of Vicksburg and more. How Grant would take advantage would be seen in the coming days. Perhaps he should have asked the self-proclaimed prophet in Vicksburg for advice, his prophesy getting close to the idea of hearing the loudest noise of fighting yet on the afternoon of June 25 but totally missing the vision that Johnston would attack. If he was indeed a prophet from on high, it seemed even God himself could not get Joe Johnston to move.[86]

13

"We Are Drawing Nearer Every Day the End of Our Tether"

June 26–30

By the end of June, almost all could see that this great tragedy playing out down in the Mississippi Valley was coming to its end; one Pennsylvanian went so far as to describe Grant as having a "bull-dog grip" on Pemberton. Admiral Porter thought so and had written as far back as June 14, "I think the town cannot hold out longer than 22d of June." An Illinoisan wrote to his wife on June 27 that "I think the surrender will take place between this and the fourth of July." Grant himself admitted to Nathaniel Banks at Port Hudson on June 30, "I confidently expected that Vicksburg would be in our possession before this," yet he knew it could not be much longer. To Julia he wrote on June 29 that "during the present week I think the fate of Vicksburg will be decided." He elaborated that "Johnston is still hovering beyond the Black river and will attack before you receive this or never. After accumulating so large an army as he has, at such risk of losing other points in the Confederacy by doing it, he cannot back out without giving battle or losing prestige." That said, at least one Federal declared that "it would not surprise me if July or even August found us still outside the town."[1]

Even with the feeling of confidence, Grant still did not know how this would all play out. In his wildest hopes was the scenario where Johnston did nothing and Pemberton surrendered, but that seemed too much to wish for. Rather, Grant thought he would have to fight one way or another, either Johnston in the rear or assaulting the Vicksburg works again. "I expect a fight by Wednesday or Thursday," he told Julia. "There may be much loss of life but

I feel but little doubt as to the result.—Saturday or Sunday next I set for the fall of Vicksburg." That Saturday would be Independence Day.[2]

As June neared its end, thoughts of the possibility of a July 4 surrender began to take hold. Certainly, a capitulation planned for Independence Day would be ironic. Iowan James B. Mathews wrote on June 28, "I think we will have a bigg fight between this and the fourth of July on the 4th or unless the Rebbles histe the white flagg. I fear thear will be a bigg fight." Albert Chipman related how "some of our men have been talking about celebrating the 4th of July in Vixburg, but I am afraid they will slip up, but we know not what a day may bring forth." Another added, "If we plant the 'Star Spangled banner' on Vicksburg's heights by independence day it will be about as soon as I expect." Still, no one knew; one Illinoisan declared "it is only a question of time as to how long men are capable of living on nothing."[3]

Even the Confederates were becoming convinced by this point, one of Pemberton's staff officers, John C. Taylor, admitting on June 27 to his diary, "We are drawing nearer every day the end of our tether." Division commander Martin L. Smith wrote to his wife—the letter subsequently captured by Federals—that "their fate must be decided within the next ten days." A couple of deserters reported to their captors on June 27 that there were only "six days' quarter-rations left yesterday" and that "the town will surrender on the 4th of July, after the rebels fire a salute." Rations were key, but one Mississippian noted on June 26 that "some of the fattest mules were driven to the butcher pen yesterday, so we are not starved out while the mules last." He also noted "some of the soldiers are cooking and eating young cane and various kinds of weeds."[4]

By this point, the Confederates could see no way to hold out much longer and even less possibility of Johnston offering any help. Food was nearly exhausted, soldiers were tired, nerves were frayed to the point of disobeying orders, and many Confederates could hear the enemy working underground at their fortifications. One admitted on July 1, "From present prospects, our 4th of July celebration, will be a little dangerous. The fireworks will not be such as we like." Another admitted, "There is as yet no sign of Johnson but we are waiting with all patience for his appearance. It seems probable that he has abandoned Vicksburg to its fate." A staff officer related on June 27, "We have not heard Johnston *yet* but *hear* of him often." Another simply stated, "'Johnstons coming' is getting to be an old song."[5]

How it would all play out was anybody's guess, but in the interval "time hung heavily," according to one Wisconsin soldier. Some took bets on how it would all end. Brigade commander James Slack wrote to his wife that his division commander, Eugene Carr, "offered day before yesterday to bet 100$ that we would be thru by tomorrow night." He added, "I do not know what he bases his opinion on" but mentioned several mining operations then in process. Vicksburg did not surrender by the next night, of course, and Slack himself later bet that the city would capitulate by July 4—but his bet was for only ten dollars.[6]

Nevertheless, the world watched. One observer noted how all was done "with a nation watching and waiting day after day, week after week, as North and South keep wrestling there, while on the throw depends the future history of the Mississippi Valley."[7]

And perhaps the Union itself.

As June began to shrink on the calendar, the food rations inside Vicksburg began to drop even more, the griping and complaining began to rise, and the number of deserters increased. Perhaps most concerning, the ability of the soldiers in the trenches continued to fade, making it appear that a defense of Vicksburg was coming to an end even without any external pressure in the form of more mines being blown or more assaults being attempted. Just the day-by-day wear and tear and mind-numbing monotony in the context of a dangerous situation that could cost a life if not careful made morale drop significantly and, with it, the chances of Vicksburg's garrison getting away safely.

Despite rhetoric about the staunch firmness of the Confederate garrison, there was quite a bit of gloom growing, mainly on account of Johnston's nonarrival. Lieutenant William Drennan set in his own mind the early date of June 10 as the firm day by which Johnston had to arrive, but all that came that day was heavy rain. "I do not despair, by any means, yet I confess that I feel disheartened." That sinking feeling only grew as the days passed and turned into weeks with no Johnston. Making it worse, each arrival of couriers from Johnston was celebrated, the *Daily Citizen* advising of big news on June 13. "Expectation was brought up to a high pitch," Drennan confessed, but "it contained nothing at all. The consequence is that it has left the men in lower spirits than previously." Later, a Tennessean admitted that "if Johnston don't come in ten days from this time we will have to go up the spout for the want of provisions."[8]

By this stage in the siege Pemberton did little shuffling or moving of troops, mainly due to their condition. There were only a few instances of extending lines one way or another, mainly removing reserve units that had been put in the trenches for a short period. Pemberton let it be known that Cockrell's worn-out brigade should be left alone as much as possible: "It is strictly a reserve," he barked on June 28. Pemberton knew his command could not take major reshuffling, especially when talk of desertion and surrender reached him. His signal corps was adept at intercepting messages being sent between the land army and Admiral Porter's gunboats, and some of these spoke of those desertions and the coming surrender.[9]

The Federals certainly knew the dire situation in Vicksburg, the Confederate desertions coming much more frequently now than before. As early as June 21, Confederates were reporting the squalid conditions, one telling a Union picket that the "cannonading killed and wounded a great many in the rifle-pits" and that the big bombardment then convinced everyone: "They fully counted upon an assault as being intended and were prepared for it." No assault came, of course, which ironically drove down morale even more. A Confederate reported that "the troops were canvassed to see if they could be got out to attack the Yankees. They not only declined this, but those on the right . . . almost mutinied because their officers would not surrender." Apparently the Confederate officers kept the situation calm only by telling the troops there were still plenty of provisions for seven more days and that there were boats being built to take them to safety.[10]

Other deserters brought similar reports, as did captured couriers, sometimes laden with numerous letters being sent out to anxious family members. Martin L. Smith wrote dejectedly that he "expects to go North, but calculated on a speedy exchange, when he will be restored to the bosom of his family." Other lower-level Confederate letters described the hardships: "Four ounces of bacon per day, and bread made of rice and flour mixed. Corn $40 per bushel, and not to be had at that." Some still offered hope that Johnston would be their salvation, although artilleryman Colonel William T. Withers wondered why they "have been so wicked as for Providence to allow the loss of their stronghold of Vicksburg." Grant delighted in reading these letters and surmised that "their principal faith seems to be in Providence and Joe Johnston."[11]

The desertions and news of hardships became a deluge the farther June moved along. E. O. C. Ord sent Grant information taken from prisoners, including a little black boy who was trying to escape with two soldiers. They related that rations were down to "one-quarter pound of bacon and meal each for ten days past." Ord simply stated that the information "is strongly corroborated by the statements of deserters for some days past." On June 28, Herron on the extreme left flank reported that six Arkansans showed up on his lines. He said they deserted "under the impression that the town would be surrendered in a few days. They report a further reduction in rations and great dissatisfaction among men." Two days later, Herron again reported that a "deserter in to-day report provisions exceedingly scarce and a bad feeling among the troops." Others somehow got past Herron's forces, causing Grant to scold that pickets should be run to the Mississippi River bank and "as close to the enemy as possible." Soon, there was an additional tidbit of news illustrating just how bad things were inside Vicksburg: "Mules were killed this morning and the meat distributed to the troops." Herron also reported that the Arkansans declared that "next Saturday will settle the question." Interestingly, more and more deserters began to mention an Independence day surrender as they came out of Vicksburg.[12]

Constant death and threat of death loomed large in the Confederate mind as well. Drennan described how "the mortality here at this time is very great; hardly a day passes but I see dozens of men carried to their last homes. They are buried in a trench with a blanket for a shroud. Coffins can not be had for all of them. Graves are dug today for use tomorrow."[13]

In the continual spiraling of the situation into hopelessness, the never-ending death in the Confederate trenches perhaps more than anything seemed increasingly unnecessary. Many continued to fall all along the lines, some from the artillery barrages but most from the sharpshooting that remained constant and deadly. Even behind the lines it was not safe by this point, one Mississippian, James Boler of the 46th Mississippi, being hit with a Minié ball while sitting in the regiment's bombproof of all places.[14]

Officers were not immune either. In addition to Colonel Garrott killed earlier, many others lost their lives in defense of Vicksburg. Lieutenant Colonel Sidney H. Griffin commanding the 31st Louisiana and Lieutenant Colonel Thomas N. Adaire commanding the 4th Mississippi were both hit, Griffin killed and Adaire severely wounded. Colonel Leon D. Marks of the 27th Louisiana, wounded during the assaults, also fell mortally wounded later on. One member of the 38th Mississippi described how his colonel, Preston Brent, came into the trenches on June 30, wishing to "show off before his comrades." He peeped over the top and took a ball in the face, exiting his neck. Colonel Charles H. Herrick of the 21st Louisiana also perished.[15]

The loss of officers was especially felt in some regiments. Lieutenant Colonel Laurin L. McLaurin of the 27th Louisiana fell as did Major William W. Martin of the 26th Louisiana, shot above the eye by a sharpshooter while standing in the pits acting as brigade officer of the day. When Major Alexander S. Norwood fell two days later, that left the 27th Louisiana completely without any field officers; it "has but one captain for duty," brigade commander Francis Shoup explained, and he was not up to the task of commanding the regiment. "My entire command is sadly reduced in officers," he added. The 27th Louisiana was so weak, in fact, that division commander Smith asked for a regiment to be stationed to its rear to hold the trenches during the night. One was sent, but the major commanding "refuses, when called upon, to go into the trenches." Smith took the matter all the way up to Pemberton, writing that he and Shoup were merely trying to "make a position secure upon which the safety of the Lieut. General's army, to some extent, depends."[16]

Constant change due to wounds or sickness that did not result in death also weakened the Confederate command structure. Brigade commander William E. Baldwin returned on June 13 from a wound received on May 22, retaking command of his brigade in Smith's division from Colonel Robert Richardson of the 17th Louisiana. Others missed time because of sickness, such as when Francis Shoup left for a short period later in the siege, leaving the brigade under the command of Colonel Allen Thomas of the 29th Louisiana. Louis Hébert was sick for a time in late June, so Colonel William W. Witherspoon of the 36th Mississippi took command. Division commander John Bowen was also sick much of the siege, but he did not relinquish control.[17]

The most significant loss occurred on June 27, when Brigadier General Martin E. Green, commanding one of Bowen's brigades now in the trenches at the Stockade Redan, took his turn at sharpshooting. His men held the smaller redan just south of the main Stockade Redan on the Graveyard Road, which quickly became known as "Green's Redan." When the Federals began a sap on his front, he could not resist examining it; he was wounded on June 25 and missed a day or so on the lines. He was back two days later, being cautioned several times to be careful, and he supposedly responded that "the bullet was not moulded that would kill him." Around 9:30 A.M. on June 27, Green peeped over the parapet to see what was happening and paid dearly for it, a shot in the head taking his life. Green's brigade surgeon described how "a minie ball carried away a part of the occipital bone and a large part of the brain." He died quickly, and Surgeon John A. Leavy added that "we gave him as good a funeral as possible; his remains were attended by mourners & friends who sadly grieve at his loss. I had the coffin opened and secured a lock of his hair for his widow & orphaned family." Colonel Thomas P. Dockery, who took command of the brigade, asserted that "many a tear was shed at his fall." Oddly enough, across the lines that night, Merrick Wald of the 77th Illinois while on picket duty noted "we could hear the rebels digging at something and hear them playing a band of music. It seems as if they were burying some officer."[18]

Perhaps the coup de grâce for Pemberton's willingness to defend Vicksburg came in a letter written to him by one disgruntled Confederate but carrying the signature of "Many Soldiers." In the June 28 note, headlined "in trenches, near Vicksburg," the soldier told Pemberton plainly what was happening and what would happen soon:

SIR: In accordance with my own feelings, and that of my fellow soldiers with whom I have conferred, I submit to your serious consideration the following note:

We as an army have as much confidence in you as a commanding general as we perhaps ought to have. We believe you have displayed as much generalship as any other man could have done under similar circumstances. We give you great credit for the stern patriotism you have evinced in the defense of Vicksburg during a protracted and unparalleled siege.

I also feel proud of the gallant conduct of the soldiers under your command in repulsing the enemy at every assault, and bearing with patient endurance all the privations and hardships incident to a siege of forty odd days' duration.

Everybody admits that we have all covered ourselves in glory, but alas! alas! general, a crisis has arrived in the midst of our siege.

Our rations have been cut down to one biscuit and a small bit of bacon per day, not enough scarcely to keep soul and body together, much less to stand the hardships we are called upon to stand.

We are actually on sufferance, and the consequence is, as far as I can hear, there is complaining and general dissatisfaction throughout our lines.

We are, and have been, kept close in the trenches day and night, not allowed to forage any at all, and, even if permitted, there is nothing to be had among the citizens.

Men don't want to starve, and don't intend to, but they call upon you for justice, if the commissary department can give it; if it can't, you must adopt some means to relieve us very soon. The emergency of the case demands prompt and decided action on your part.

If you can't feed us, you had better surrender us, horrible as the idea is, than suffer this noble army to disgrace themselves by desertion. I tell you plainly, men are not going to lie here and perish, if they do love their country dearly. Self-preservation is the first law of nature, and hunger will compel a man to do almost anything.

You had better heed a warning voice, though it is the voice of a private soldier.

This army is now ripe for mutiny, unless it can be fed.

Just think of one small biscuit and one or two mouthfuls of bacon per day. General, please direct your inquiries in the proper channel, and see if I have not stated stubborn facts, which had better be heeded before we are disgraced.

From—Many Soldiers[19]

Some thought it could be "a bit of enemy propaganda," as the Federals did issue a leaflet, delivered by kites flown in late June over the city by the navy, directed to "our friends in Vicksburg." It told the Confederates to "cave in boys and save your lives, which are considered of no value by your officers. There is no hope for relief for you."[20]

No matter where it came from, the doleful note certainly gave Pemberton a lot to think about.

Yet another reason why it seemed the Vicksburg drama would soon be at an end was the continual pressure applied by Ulysses S. Grant. Whether it was mining, approaches, thoughts of a new assault, or just the continual sharp-shooting and artillery bombardment, Grant had many options as he contin-ued to tighten the noose around Pemberton's neck. And he was not afraid to use any of them. He even held a discussion with corps commanders Steele, McPherson, and Ord on the morning of June 30 "to take their judgment on the question of trying another general assault, or leaving the result to the exhaus-tion of the garrison." He had ordered Ord the day before: "I would like to see you at Headquarters at 10 A.M. tomorrow to meet other corps commanders." Dana reported that "the conclusion of the council was in favor of the latter policy, and as General Grant had himself previously strongly inclined to that course, it will, no doubt, be adhered to."[21]

But there was a growing despondency, perhaps because of the heat, among the Federals to continue the digging war. Captain Comstock reported to Grant that "in the present condition of the siege works, and the indisposition of the troops to work zealously in the trenches, it will require at least a fortnight to take the place by that means only." Nevertheless, Comstock hoped that the mining efforts, especially on Logan's front and a new one on Ransom's front, "may give us advantages that will expedite the catastrophe."[22]

Nerves were also fraying and bodies tiring in the Union lines, however. One high-level rift occurred as Major Ezra Taylor, Sherman's XV corps artillery chief, seemed to take on much more responsibility than he should have. He took out his frustration on his chief nemesis, Captain Peter Wood of the Chicago Light Artillery. Taylor, as the commander of the other Chicago Light Artillery Battery (there were two), had had it in for Wood and his cannoneers since Fort Donelson and claims of glory there, and he had apparently been openly unfair to them at Shiloh. Now, Taylor enjoyed commanding Wood and making the men erect "useless & unnecessary batteries in out of the way places." When Taylor and Wood tangled late in the siege and Wood loudly proclaimed in front of the troops that he commanded Wood and even Blair, Blair took the matter to Sherman, telling him he had endured "insufferable" conduct from Taylor all along but this was the final straw.[23]

Grant dealt with a myriad of other issues as the siege dragged on, including almost trivial aspects such as postal arrangements for his department. Dealings with other commanders took more of his attention, such as Hurlbut's nearly continual bemoaning of the fact that his area in West Tennessee was stripped of troops almost to the bare bone. Grant told him to "hold as much of the railroad as possible" but that if need be he could consolidate down to only a couple of points in his department, even just Memphis and Corinth. But there was nothing Grant could do at this point, he explained to Hurlbut, especially with his own two-front situation at Vicksburg. The same news went to Elias Dennis across the Mississippi River, where a small skirmish took place on June 28 at Lake Providence. Grant notified Dennis that there would be no more support forthcoming from his side of the river even though it was likely that Confederate general Kirby Smith was going to try some type of relief of Vicksburg. Grant told Dennis to concentrate his troops, "white and black," and defeat the enemy because "with Johnston in my rear, I cannot detach troops for that purpose."[24]

More of a problem was Nathaniel Banks at Port Hudson, who continually called for troops. Grant took the extraordinary step of sending a fairly high-ranking officer to Banks to explain the situation. Thomas Kilby Smith, colonel of the 54th Ohio but recently in command of a brigade in the army, went southward with Grant's arguments about Vicksburg. Smith had led one of Frank Blair's brigades in the assaults on May 19 and 22 but had been out-ranked and replaced by a newly arrived brigadier general, Joseph Lightburn. Rather than simply return to command of a regiment, Smith went on Grant's diplomatic mission. Grant basically stated that he could not send any troops at this point, although he had "much more than can be used in the investment of the rebel works," but the extras were needed in the rear to deal with Johnston. As soon as Vicksburg fell, however, he would send troops if Port Hudson still had not surrendered.[25]

Grant also kept Johnston in the back of his mind, admitting to Washington that "his movements are mysterious, and may be intended to cover a move-ment from his rear into East or West Tennessee, or upon Banks." Yet his fears eased a great deal with Sherman out to the east. Perhaps the more than thirty thousand troops Sherman had with him was the actual cause of the safe feel-ing, they keeping a close watch on all the fords across the Big Black River and often making reconnaissance marches with larger units all the way to the river and even to the other side. Still, Grant was concerned if no longer paranoid, he informing Banks that "whether he [Johnston] will attack or not, I look upon now as doubtful," but adding, "no doubt he would, however, if I should weaken my force to any extent." Yet Grant was also learning that Johnston was more show than fight. He quipped to Sherman, upon news of Johnston moving, "but this information is several days old. In the mean time John-ston may have changed his plans and the position of his troops half a dozen times."[26]

As always, despite the peripheral aspects even of such importance as Sher-man's defense of the rear, Grant kept the focus on the Vicksburg siege and the efforts to reach the Confederate works. In these last days of June the struggle for control of the mine exploded back on June 25 continued at a lesser pace, for days in fact until the 45th Illinois withdrew upon McPherson's orders on June 28. During that time, heavy fighting at times took place between the Il-linoisans of Leggett's brigade and Louisianans and Missourians in the newly refashioned 3rd Louisiana Redan. The raging fight there also affected outlying troops, one brigade of the next division to the south, John E. Smith's, being told on June 26 to "have your command in line under arms at 3.30 to-morrow morning, and remain so until 6 A.M., unless otherwise directed." There was some fear also of the Confederates attacking during the night, at which "the battle cry will be 'Logan,'" Smith explained to brigade commander John B. Sanborn. Similarly, McPherson issued orders that the battle cry for the night of June 27 would be "Grant."[27]

Yet more than just reacting to what had already happened occurred in Grant's fertile mind; he wanted continual forward movement, and it came in several ways as his troops, by this point smelling victory, moved ahead with the operations, increasingly confident of victory. Grant described his army on June 30 as "in excellent health and spirits. There is not the slightest indication of despondence either among officers or men." That said, a big blow came when on June 27 Captain Prime left the army due to sickness, Captain Comstock taking over his position as chief engineer. Captain Miles D. McAlester fortunately arrived the same day and took over Comstock's work on the southern end of the line. Dana nevertheless repeated his frequent refrain of "still a lamentable deficiency of engineer officers."[28]

One way to further the action was to keep on with the mining under the Confederate forts. Some four mines, including the one blown on June 25, had been started by this point, and by June 27 McPherson ordered yet another begun at the same 3rd Louisiana Redan. Starting a new shaft from a covered area within the former mine's crater itself, Hickenlooper pushed forward yet again, this time intent on getting far enough to take care of the entire Confederate fort, not just its apex. McPherson oversaw the project, explaining that he wanted it "on the right-hand side of the crater, leaving the present high points on the right and left of the crater standing, as well as the intermediate space." Obviously, it would take a little while, maybe days, before this new mine was ready to be sprung, but it was going ahead.[29]

The Confederates were not themselves idle in undertaking mining operations, however, touching off their own charges in front of Ewing's approach on the morning of June 26. The countermines had been ready as early as June 17, but Confederate engineers waited until an explosion could have the maximum effect. That day came in late June, when Lockett's engineers touched off two charges, one of forty-five pounds in one gallery eight feet underground and another of eighty pounds in a similar gallery nearby. While the effect was not well known inside Confederate lines, Dana reported the significant results on his side: "Enemy yesterday morning sprung a mine, which destroyed those Sherman's engineers had nearly finished, and threw the head of his sap into confusion generally. The engineers have gone back some 50 feet to run a new mine under the fort." Engineer Kossak wrote that the explosions were effective, "crushing in the roofs badly. Some gabions in the trench cavaliers were thrown down; but the charge of the mines was too small to throw up any crater which we might have taken advantage of. . . . They anyhow filled our mines and disintegrated the soil around to such an extent that further mining at that point was out of the question." Fortunately, no one was in the mines at the time and there were no deaths, although "a few men were covered by earth and gabions falling on them from the parapets, but they extricated themselves without material injury."[30]

Another way Grant kept the pressure on the defenders was by continually drawing nearer above ground as well, with some twelve different approaches already moving forward toward the Confederate lines at this point. By the end of June, there would be two more. One of the additional saps began on June 28 near the Stockade Redan. This approach, by Joseph Lightburn's brigade, which had taken the front line when the additional brigades went with Sherman to the rear, was not a full-fledged effort but rather began from one of the other approaches already in progress. Aimed at the Confederate lines between the stockade on the north face of the Stockade Redan and the 27th Louisiana Lunette to its left, this approach branched off of Buckland's existing approach and moved toward the Confederate lines there. Starting as it did that far forward, it did not have far to go to reach the enemy line. In a day or two, in fact, a mine would also be begun here. Colonel Oscar Malmborg of the 55th Illinois gave his personal attention to the effort, often getting the advice of Engineer Kossak at work on Ewing's mine. In fact, Kossak advised both Malmborg and Giles Smith, the other approach in Blair's division, to stop sapping and start mining. Confederate artillery and grenades were damaging the sap rollers, and they were as far as they could go, Malmborg in fact having to cover his approach with fascines to provide a covering roof. To aid them, Kossak got Hugh Ewing to provide sixteen men of the 4th West Virginia who had been coal miners, and they started the mines on Lightburn's and Smith's approaches. On the Confederate side, Francis Shoup described how the Federals "moled up" to their works.[31]

Another approach began on June 30, far down the line to the left on James Slack's front of Hovey's division in Ord's corps. This approach began from one of the forward parallels that Hovey's division had managed to create as they continually moved forward. Work began and moved toward an angle of the Confederate line just north of Square Fort, an area held by the 23rd

Alabama. There was a valley to cross that needed traverses to protect the workers and troops shuffling through the approach on the slope opposite the Alabamians. Cotton bales provided the needed cover, and work continued on into July.[32]

By the time July rolled around, Grant thus had thirteen different approaches moving toward the Confederate lines (the fourteenth, the Woods/Manter effort, had been stopped earlier), many of them having reached the parapets and others within mere feet of them. On six of these approaches, seven mines were begun to tunnel under the Confederate lines and blow them up, including two on Logan's approach along the Jackson Road. Just a mere look at the engineering aspects told anyone that the fighting was about to come to a climax.[33]

Digging approaches gave Grant's troops a position that was close enough to assault the Confederate lines with a good chance of success. The mining activities furthered chances of success by providing a gap through which the assault could move. Grant had assaulted twice before, but from long distances out, thereby enduring heavy casualties traversing the intermediate ground. Now Grant was close enough to simply vault over the enemy fortifications. The wheels of possibilities were already turning in Grant's head as to what to do with this development.[34]

Part of the reason Grant could concentrate on finishing up the Vicksburg siege was because his rear areas were, for the first time, comparatively safe. By the end of June, matters in the rear had settled down because of the arrival of so many new troops and because Grant had implemented his contingency plan, sending a large force out from the main army led by Sherman himself to the rear line. It was all in response to what Grant thought would be an attack within that time frame of twenty-four to forty-eight hours. Once Sherman arrived and probed ahead, however, he quickly determined there was no such threat. Still, even though matters had settled considerably, Grant remained concerned about his rear, he actually writing Hurlbut on June 27, "I have information that Johnston expects 10,000 men from there [Tennessee] in a few days. There is scarcely a shadow of doubt but I will be attacked by next Wednesday or Thursday, unless Vicksburg should fall in the mean time." Accordingly, he ordered Sherman to continue holding his positions and to be

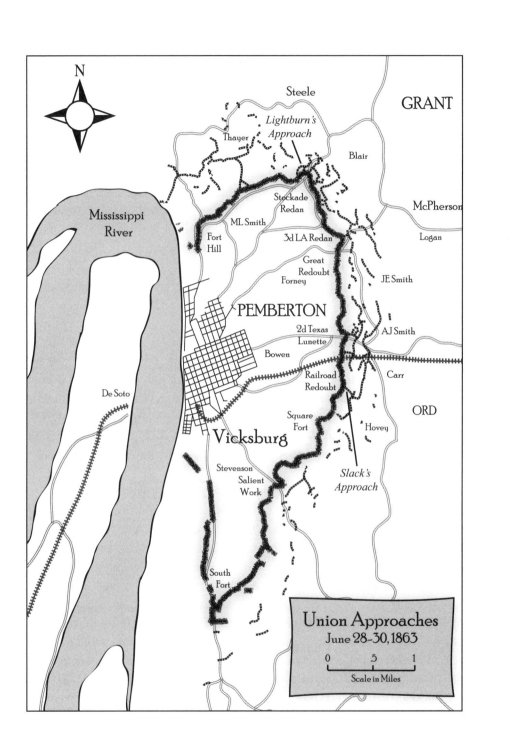

N

GRANT

Steele

Lightburn's Approach

Thayer

Blair

McPherson

Mississippi River

Stockade Redan

ML Smith

Logan

Fort Hill

3d LA Redan

Great Redoubt Forney

JE Smith

PEMBERTON

2d Texas Lunette

AJ Smith

Bowen

De Soto

Railroad Redoubt

Carr

ORD

Square Fort

Hovey

Vicksburg

Slack's Approach

Stevenson Salient Work

South Fort

Union Approaches
June 28-30, 1863

0   .5   1

Scale in Miles

ready to counter any move Johnston made. "I think it advisable to keep your troops out until Joe Johnston carries a design to move in some other direction," Grant told Sherman.[35]

Johnston of course would not move any faster than he had up to this point. He had already made up his mind that saving Vicksburg was all but impossible, and rescuing the garrison from their fate was probably impossible also. The window of opportunity to do something had long since passed. At that time—before Grant's reinforcements arrived but after Johnston's did—Johnston and Pemberton had a combined total of around sixty thousand men compared to Grant's fifty-six thousand. Just a few weeks later, no more Confederates arrived but upward of twenty-one thousand more Federals did. By that time, Johnston cited all kinds of problems such as the transportation shortage and lack of generals. And while starvation grew in Vicksburg, Johnston's organizing army was not immune, one Confederate writing that "we have no cooking utensils and sometimes have to go all day and sometimes longer without any food." That lethargy did not always translate down to the ranks, however, one of Johnston's Georgians writing in late June that "we are looking for a force[d] march every day and I don't know how soon. It may be today." Still, Johnston continued to be involved in minutia within the organization of the command instead of focusing completely on the enemy. On June 28, for example, he sent elaborate orders to division commander French about the need to disband the current officer examination boards in the division and constitute new ones.[36]

Sherman kept his force well in hand, however, and covered the entire area between the railroad bridge over the Big Black River northward to Haynes' Bluff. He even rode the lines daily. One Iowan described how "Genl Sherman rode up. talked & laughed awhile then told Col to saddle up and come with him." Another wrote to his wife that Sherman rode up to his brigade and was "saluted with applause." He then "took his straw hat and waved it to all the soldiers as he rode off"; "he is not ashamed to speak to a common private as many of our tickey assed officers are." Still, Sherman was there to work, not enjoy the praise. On June 26, in fact, he gave elaborate orders about how his line of countervallation should be set up, and then he improved things three days later on June 29. The result, in his words, "makes a connected line from the railroad bridge to Haynes's Bluff." Additional patrols and scouts covered the Big Black River farther south, but neither Sherman nor Grant thought

Johnston or Pemberton would operate in that narrow triangle of land between the Mississippi and Big Black Rivers.[37]

The key for Sherman was to cover the high ground west of the Big Black, which was in most places not a bold bluff but a gradual slope upward to the west. There was a "fertile valley on this side," Sherman wrote, before it rose onto the ridge west of the river. "It is only by familiarity with the country, its ugly ravines, its open, narrow ridges all coming to a common spur, that a comparatively small force can hold in check a large one." As a result, Sherman wanted the ridge farthest to the east held so that, even if Johnston crossed at different points, a concentration on the ridge roads could be made. Sherman predicated that, if such occurred, then "Wixon's [Plantation] will be the grand battle-field, or somewhere on Clear Creek."[38]

Once all the troops had arrived from the main army besieging Vicksburg, Sherman had a total of about thirty-three thousand troops to cover the rear. These were disposed into seven divisions under "Sooy" Smith, Nathan Kimball (both under Washburn), Thomas Welsh, Robert Potter (both under Parke), John McArthur, James Tuttle, and Peter Osterhaus. He had a conglomeration of odd sorts to be sure, but it was a force to be reckoned with. It held defensible ground through which the country roads ran from the fords on the Big Black River and the slot between that river and the Yazoo farther north. And they were watchful, one Indianan describing his patrol-word as "Ney" and the countersign as "Wagram," clear Napoleonic references.[39]

The key areas of the line were Haynes' Bluff on the Yazoo and the railroad bridge across the Big Black to the south. Osterhaus and his XIII Corps troops held the railroad bridge area behind major fortifications. One brigade had been there for the majority of the siege with another recently arrived in Grant's contingency effort. They knew the terrain well, although there was not much else to do but wait. Colonel Marcus Spiegel described some concern for Confederate movements in late June, even leaving a peaceful camping site and returning to the trenches at the end of the month. But he still admitted to his wife that "it is awfully hot here, but we stand it; we have not much to do except standing Pickets and that is much easier in the Summer than in Winter." He reveled in the produce summer brought, writing, "For the last three weeks we are having Peaches and Cream, Peach Pie, Blackberries and Cream, three times a day." He explained that "Blackberries are here by the million; you can ride for miles at a time and the Bushes look perfectly black." Even though in a veritable Garden of Eden, Osterhaus's orders were to hold his position while sending patrols along the river itself southward as far as Baldwin's Ferry and northward up to Bridgeport. He was also to connect with the next division in line to the north, but his main role if needed would be reinforcing those divisions farther north if the attack came there. Sherman could not fathom the actual attack coming at the railroad bridge or southward, so he had little concern for that position. He ordered Osterhaus rather to be ready to "act decisively on intelligence or the sounds of battle in the direction of Tiffin's or Fox's plantations."[40]

The other end of the line at Haynes' Bluff enjoyed no such fleeting concern from Sherman. He thought that the attack would come more on this end of the line than the southern flank. Holding the fortifications at Haynes' Bluff itself was the XVI Corps division under Kimball north of the Skillet Goliath, with Washburn, his parent commander, in charge of the place. Sherman believed the attack would come here and in actuality hoped it would. "That being our strongest front," he wrote, "we should invite attack in that quarter."[41]

These two focal points were immovable and had been held for the entirety of the siege. And they were secure from flank attack, the Yazoo River shielding Haynes' Bluff from anything but a frontal assault at the fortifications and the nature of the geography south of the railroad bridge precluding any logical attempt to maneuver in that area. But while the flank positions were immovable and manned continually, the line in between had not beforehand been so manned. Fortunately, Sherman's other five divisions, including his two trusted ones from the main army—some from his own corps—currently created a defensive line that was all but impregnable at this point.[42]

Sherman had inherited a quickly established line of forces from Parke when he arrived on June 22. Parke had scouted the area well, even up the Yazoo River on a gunboat. This line lay mainly west of Clear Creek, with its main forces on the Bridgeport and Benton Roads and concentrated around Milldale and Templeton's Plantation. Only the four brigades farther forward toward Oak Ridge and Bear Creek held the ground in front. Unfortunately, such a line along Clear Creek created an inward bulge in the line, with Osterhaus at the railroad bridge and Washburn at Haynes' Bluff extended out on each flank. Thus, interior lines of communication were not available.[43]

Sherman wanted the line farther east, in accordance with Grant's desire to meet Johnston as far out of Vicksburg as possible. Despite its "heavily timbered" aspects, the next creek system to the east—Bear Creek and most

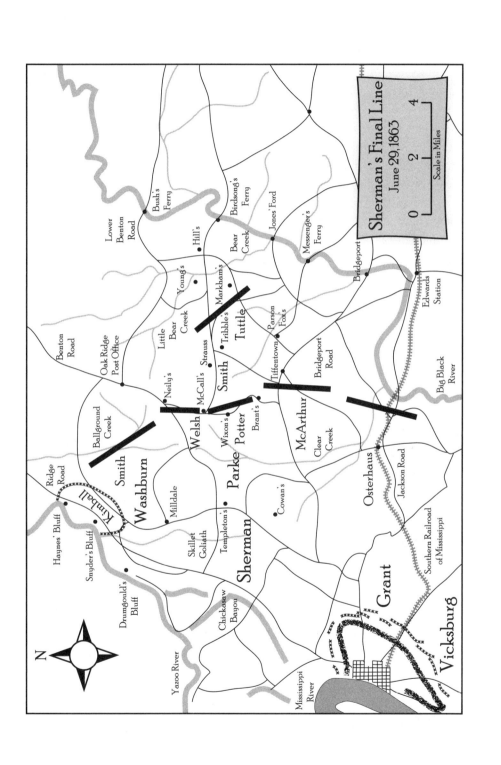

N

Sherman's Final Line
June 29, 1863

Scale in Miles
0   2   4

Yazoo River

Drumgould's Bluff

Haynes' Bluff

Snyder's Bluff

Ridge Road

Kimball

Smith

Washburn

Milldale

Skillet Goliath

Templeton's

Chickasaw Bayou

Cowan's

Sherman

Ballground Creek

Benton Road

Oak Ridge Post Office

Neily's

McCall's

Strauss

Welsh

Wixon's

Potter

Parke

Brant's

Smith

Tribble's

Tuttle

Parson Fox's

Little Bear Creek

Young's

Markham's

Hill's

Lower Benton Road

Bush's Ferry

Birdsong's Ferry

Bear Creek

Jones' Ford

Messenger's Ferry

Tiffentown

McArthur

Clear Creek

Bridgeport Road

Bridgeport

Edwards Station

Big Black River

Osterhaus

Jackson Road

Grant

Southern Railroad of Mississippi

Mississippi River

Vicksburg

importantly its westernmost tributary, Little Bear Creek—provided that opportunity for much of the proposed line. Only a few isolated areas were
cleared, mostly on the narrow ridges but also including on occasion land
down in the hollows. Accordingly, Sherman moved most of his divisions
about ten miles eastward from behind the Clear Creek shield to the Bear
Creek area where a few of Parke's brigades already were. There, Sherman
arrayed them in line along the western bluffs overlooking most of Little
Bear Creek south of Oak Ridge. North of the Oak Ridge Post Office, the
line fronted Ballground Creek, named for the plantation near the old native
Indian ballfield in the area but sometimes referred to by the soldiers as "Bald
Ground Creek." The entire line sat behind newly built fortifications the Federals or the "darkies," as one Indianan described contrabands, erected upon
arrival. A visiting Dana marveled at the energy, writing on June 27 that he
"found his [Sherman's] amazing activity and vigilance pervading his whole
force. . . . By rapid movements of his forces, also, and by deploying them on
all the ridges and open headlands, he produces the impression that his forces
are ten times as numerous as they really are." For the soldiers' part, they were
delighted with the orchards and blackberries, one concluding that "we had
made a good exchange of position."[44]

Moving south out of the Haynes' Bluff enclave, "Sooy" Smith's XVI
Corps division held a line several miles forward from Kimball's right down
to Oak Ridge Post Office on the Benton Road. This line did not front Bear
Creek, it being on the northern side of Oak Ridge rather than the south where
Bear Creek flowed toward the Big Black River. Smith's line, rather, stood on
the tall ridge overlooking Ballground Creek that flowed northward into the
Yazoo River. Smith was to keep out pickets on the main as well as the Lower
Benton roads. Sherman also ordered that it was up to Kimball and Smith, under Washburn's united command, to "effectually blockade all roads and paths
coming from the north and lying between the ridge road and Yazoo Valley
Road." Essentially, they covered the main slot between the rivers, where the
attack, if it came, would probably occur.[45]

To Smith's right, connecting with him at Neily's Plantation, came Parke's
IX Corps troops in two divisions. Most of Parke's troops had been situated
back nearer Milldale in the earliest deployment but moved forward and took
station on Smith's right when Sherman put his forward plan into effect, leaving only a small force at Milldale and Templeton's. Parke held the high Oak
Ridge northwest of Little Bear Creek from Niely's on his left through the

Wixon Plantation and down to Brant's (Bryant's) Plantation. Parke was to keep a regiment of cavalry out on the Birdsong Ferry road in his front, where the road crossed Bear Creek, with pickets even farther out at the fork in the road east of the creek.[46]

One of Parke's soldiers described the area in not-so-flattering terms:

our quarters are in a church yard. The Colonel occupies the part of the church and we have our provisions in the main body of the church. The seats have all been gone some time. They were taken out by troops that were here before us. We slept on the ground in the graveyard—among the tombs, but I saw no ghosts. It is a Baptist church. I can't imagine where they get water enough to immerse their converts unless they take them down to the Mississippi.[47]

Connecting with Parke's forces at Brant's was McArthur's division of the XVII Corps, troops fresh from the siege lines at Vicksburg. McArthur's three brigades were situated on the western hills overlooking Little Bear Creek as that watershed moved southeastward. His main force was on the Bridgeport Road at Tiffin's. This line continued southward until it met Osterhaus's troops nearer to the Big Black River. McArthur's chief function was to guard the main thoroughfare that was the Bridgeport Road and to watch that crossing of the Big Black River as well as Messenger's Ferry to the north.[48]

With a near-complete line manned by these six divisions, Sherman posted Tuttle's XV Corps division farther forward to Little Bear Creek, where it could hold closer positions to the Little Bear Creek crossings. Tuttle thus deployed around the plantations owned by the Youngs, Markums, and Tribles and held the Bear Creek crossing with more force than the others could have. His position was on "the ridge from Trible's down to Young's, . . . so as to have a full view of the fields down the valley of Bear Creek." Sherman wanted the position entrenched, particularly in the most important areas along the roadways: "[I] gave preference as a line of defense to the peculiar spurs and ridges which characterize the peninsula between Big Black and Yazoo." Tuttle covered both the Messenger's and Birdsong Roads, with a regiment advanced on both "as an outpost," Tuttle explained.[49]

This entrenched line was much better situated than the earlier one mainly because, instead of an inward bulge, there was now, if anything, an outward swell as the line went all the way to Oak Ridge Post Office and the Little Bear Creek watershed. An outward bulge provided better chances of support along the line with interior lines of communication now being possible. This slight bulge on the northern end also allowed for at least three good roads from Haynes' Bluff to be utilized for movements to other divisions farther south. This line also sealed off the slot from the Big Black River to the Yazoo River along Little Bear and Ballground Creeks, where Parke, Smith, and Kimball held the high ground on the west side of those creeks and the major roadways that crossed them. The most significant position was where all the high ground came together somewhat in the center of a star formation at Oak Ridge Post Office, where the headwaters of Little Bear, Clear, Ballground, and Skillet Goliath Creeks all emanated from. The only conceivable problem spot was the area between the railroad bridge and the mouth of Bear Creek. If Johnston crossed the Big Black River there, he could get behind the major Bear Creek line. That, of course, is why Sherman had McArthur's entire division in that area, keeping a close observation on the crossings at Bridgeport and Messenger's. In fact, Sherman told his commanders that "the commanding general, after careful personal inspection, pronounces the points from which we have most reason to apprehend danger, to be the two fords at Messenger's, and about a mile below Birdsong. Wixon's, and Neily's are the best points for concentration, and the ridges by Fox's and Markham's the best lines of operation."[50]

Sherman wanted this line entrenched, ordering that "each corps and division commander will proceed to entrench a position near his key point, sufficient for two batteries and one brigade, commanding water, and looking to the east and north." Other portions of the line were already or were to be entrenched as well. Perhaps more important, given the ground, Sherman also wanted the roads leading toward this line "obstructed, except such as are necessary for our guards and our own use." Behind this line, Sherman wanted all roads open and improved, some double-laned. "Lateral roads should also be looked to," he ordered, "to facilitate concentration and lateral movements." In all, despite some constant skirmishing with very small squads of Confederates as patrols reconnoitered the fords almost on a daily basis, Sherman felt secure: it was a line that "would . . . cost the enemy dear . . . [if] he attempted to force it." One of his soldiers echoed him, writing, "If he knows when he is well off he had better keep his distance."[51]

Of course, the best defense was quick notification, and Sherman wanted as much cavalry as possible out front. He ordered "all cavalry not absolutely needed for orderlies and patrols" to be scattered out in front of this line for early warning, a major force under Colonel Cyrus Bussey on the Benton roads to the north and the 4th Iowa Cavalry along Bear Creek farther south, watching the various fords and crossings of the Big Black River. "All cavalry pickets must keep their horses saddled and their weapons well in hand," Sherman insisted, "and a surprise will be certain ruin to the officer in charge. These pickets will be carefully instructed, and the commanders of the cavalry regiments will be responsible."[52]

With his dispositions made, Sherman gave his final instructions. He counseled speed, writing that he wanted pioneer companies and soldiers working "all the time; an hour's time now is worth a day after an enemy makes his appearance." He also waxed eloquent, writing that "the vast importance of events, now drawing to some conclusion, bids us guard against supposed combinations of the enemy rather than mere appearances. If Johnston attempts to relieve Vicksburg, which he is impelled to do by honor and the clamor of the Southern public, he will feign at many points, but attack with vehemence at some one. Let him appear at any point, he must be fought desperately." And Sherman let it be known he expected each soldier to fight well: "Re-enforcements must not be clamored for, but each commander will fight back, along the ridge he is guarding, stubbornly, reporting facts and not opinions, that the general in command may draw his own conclusions." He added, "Let all guards and sentinels be carefully instructed, all wandering about stopped, and all citizens found away from their homes be arrested and sent to the rear, Haynes' Bluff, or Vicksburg." In order to oversee it all, Sherman set up his own headquarters first near Parke's line on the Birdsong Ferry Road but then farther forward to the front near Tuttle's division of his own corps, where he received daily reports from all corps and division commanders. He rode his lines daily as well, even down to Osterhaus's position, and intended to get back to see Grant at Vicksburg but was so busy he never found the time. Some of the riding was no doubt mounted atop a brand-new "Mississippi present" from Frederick Steele, a fine horse named Duke.[53]

The troops performed the work gladly, although the hot summer weather took its toll, one Indianan writing how "the sand burns our feet when we go to the Spring." At any one time, half of each regiment was either picketing, skirmishing, or guarding along this line. One Iowan was fine with that schedule, writing, "While this duty was heavy it was a relief from the work in trenches, and was accepted as a very desirable change." Even better for the troops, some of the baggage and camp equipment left behind months before finally caught up to them. David W. Reed of the 12th Iowa reported that their "tents and camp and garrison equipage" arrived on July 2, and all went to work with a will fashioning wonderful cane beds to sleep on. The fortifications also gave a boost in morale, one Indianan writing home that "if he [Johnston] comes here we wont have to go to him and here we are behind entrenchments and him out—when if we have to hunt him it will be the reverse." The men especially enjoyed their off-duty time, some bathing in Bear Creek and one writing home that "I do nothing but eat and sleep and it tires me most to Death." An Iowan "visited a beaver dam on the creek a short distance above camp and saw some of the ingenious workmanship of those animals." Others explored their new region, one finding along Bear Creek what he described as "a rare geological specimen,—a prettified tooth, 4 by 8 inches on the face, the roots being 9 inches long, weight 8 lbs and 3 ozs."[54]

Sherman of course kept Grant apprised of his moves, to which Grant responded, "the dispositions you made are excellent. It will be impossible for Johnston to cross the Big Black River, north of the railroad without being discovered and your troops ready for him." Grant still had some "apprehensions" about the territory south of the railroad bridge but just could not fathom Johnston moving in that direction. Accordingly, Grant felt even better about his rear. Even if Johnston came, Sherman could handle him.[55]

It was a matter of whether Johnston would come—and that was not probable any time soon. Sherman reported on June 27, "Not a sound, syllable, or sign to indicate a purpose of crossing Big Black River toward us," he later describing Johnston as "vibrating between Jackson and Canton."[56]

If recent history was any indication, Johnston would not be moving westward any time soon. He seemed to be very good at organizing, training, and defending, all of which took place among his divisions as they prepared for a move westward, but the trick of turning all that preparation into an offensive seemed to be beyond his grasp. In fact, there was even by the end of June still a heavy emphasis on defending the areas already held rather than going to meet Sherman and perhaps providing relief for Vicksburg. Staff officers at Yazoo City reported on June 26 that "the works of defense at this place are progressing as rapidly as could be desired."[57]

The time had long since come when Johnston would receive no new troops of any kind. Brigades had come from all over the Confederacy, including from South Carolina and Tennessee as well as Port Hudson, but Johnston could expect no more in the future, at least not in any huge numbers. The Mississippi state government was still trying to round up militia units for service, but no more than about five hundred appeared, and Governor Pettus had actually sent many of them off chasing a cavalry raid. By the end of June, Johnston had a total of four infantry divisions with artillery and a cavalry division. The rolls on June 25 listed a total of 54,747 "aggregate present and absent," 36,315 of those being actually present and 28,154 deemed effectives. Commissary returns for rations on hand at the various depots and posts throughout Johnston's command area also showed large amounts of bacon, beef, corn, rice, sugar, and salt, with sufficient amounts of everything else from lard to flour to peas.[58]

Yet these troops lay scattered in a basic line from Jackson northward toward Yazoo City. They were not concentrated for a movement. John C. Breckinridge's division that had been transferred from Bragg's army in Tennessee was at Jackson, having arrived there on June 1. It contained three brigades of well-seasoned troops that had seen much action, including most recently at Stones River, where it made that ill-advised attack on January 2. Also near Jackson at first was William W. Loring's division that had broken away from Pemberton's army at Champion Hill on May 16. These three battle-tested brigades had marched roundabout to Crystal Springs and thence to Jackson, where they had to be rested and rearmed, the division having lost much of its armament on the trek. Loring has subsequently moved northward in June, ultimately to the Vernon area. W. H. T. Walker's division of four brigades held Yazoo City itself before being brought southward also to Vernon, these brigades being recently cobbled together into a division of four brigades from all over the map. Two of the brigades, and Walker himself, had come from Beauregard's department in South Carolina, while another had come from Bragg's army in Tennessee. The fourth was John Gregg's brigade that had been in the area a while, having moved up from Port Hudson and fighting McPherson at Raymond on May 12. The newest division was under Samuel G. French, three brigades in total forming on June 21, one each from Bragg's army in Tennessee, from Beauregard's department in South Carolina, and the last from Port Hudson. French, who arrived from his home leave and took command on June 24, maintained the middle around Livingston, where Johnston kept his headquarters near Canton. A cavalry division of two brigades under William H. Jackson had also been transferred from Bragg's army in Tennessee in late May.[59]

Johnston accordingly had been the recipient of a vast concentration of troops intended to relieve Vicksburg. And they were sent at the expense of other areas then in danger. Pemberton's army in Vicksburg certainly qualified as such in losing three of its original fourteen brigades at Champion Hill when Loring marched away. Bragg's army in Tennessee sent five infantry and two cavalry brigades to Mississippi even as it was about to face a Union advance known today as the Tullahoma Campaign. Beauregard in South Carolina sent three infantry brigades while preparing to confront Federal landings near Charleston. Obviously, Port Hudson was also facing its own problems and did so with two fewer brigades that went to Mississippi. The irony is that each of these areas sent troops to aid at Vicksburg, where they were little used, while each area eventually suffered defeat in part because they needed more manpower. One wonders whether those troops—if Johnston was not going to use them in Mississippi—would have been better off in their original areas. One Kentuckian in Breckinridge's division caught on to the lethargy and confusion, writing on June 24 that "General Johnston seems to carry out the command which says 'let not thy left hand know what thy right doeth.'"[60]

Indicating Johnston's reluctance to use the troops sent to him was his apparent opposition to saving Vicksburg itself but now, in late June, also his giving up any hope of any success. The telltale sign, in addition to outright saying so to Pemberton earlier, was that at this point Johnston began to deflect any blame from himself for what he surmised would be the eventual loss of Vicksburg and the army. For example, he sharply responded, often in cipher, to Pemberton's idea of seeking "terms" from Grant on June 27, writing that "negotiations with Grant for the relief of the garrison, should they become necessary, must be made by you. It would be a confession of weakness on my part, which I ought not to make, to propose them." Johnston did not indicate whether such an admission of weakness was a military concern over his current strength or reflected on his personal generalship.[61]

No matter, the troops were not being used, Johnny Green of the Orphan Brigade in Breckinridge's division illustrating what was actually going on. He noted, "We went into camp near a lagoon just outside of Jackson; here we had rare sport catching fish." The major effort came at night, when the boys would take out a canoe they found on the lake with a torch and patrol the banks with a blanket and catch numerous fish. It was also then that Green explained, "I tasted my first eel here." The men also swam in the Pearl River. Others went to church in Jackson's places of worship. Not so delightful, Breckinridge's

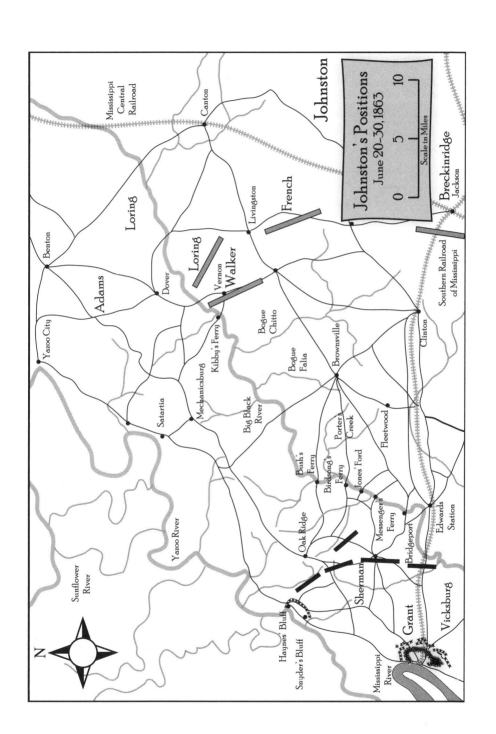

N

Sunflower
River

Yazoo City

Benton

Yazoo River

Mississippi
River

Snyder's Bluff

Haynes' Bluff

Vicksburg

Grant

Sherman

Oak Ridge

Bush's
Ferry

Birdsong's
Ferry

Messengers
Ferry

Bridgeport

Edwards
Station

Porters
Creek

Jones Ford

Fleetwood

Big Black
River

Mechanicsburg

Satartia

Kibby's Ferry

Dover

Adams

Loring

Walker

Vernon

Loring

Bogue
Falia

Bogue
Chitto

Brownsville

Clinton

Southern Railroad
of Mississippi

French

Livingston

Canton

Mississippi
Central
Railroad

Johnston

Breckinridge

Jackson

Johnston's Positions
June 20–30, 1863

0   5   10

Scale in Miles

division inhabiting Jackson also witnessed the burning of the famous Bowman House hotel next to the statehouse. Both Johnston and Grant had stayed
there in mid-May, but it went up in flames on June 9. One Kentuckian described how the building was "wrapped in flames, which roared not a little in
the stillness of the night." Staying there at the time, and just barely getting out
with injuries, was the future Confederate general Henry W. Allen.[62]

Worse, Johnston in late June also shifted the responsibility of either saving Vicksburg or saving the garrison to Kirby Smith in the trans-Mississippi.
Despite having five divisions of infantry and cavalry on the same side of
the Mississippi River as Grant, he somehow concluded in correspondence
to Pemberton that "the determined spirit you manifest, and his [Smith's] expected cooperation, encourage me to hope that something may yet be done
to save Vicksburg." Johnston wrote to Smith as much, despite complaining
to Pemberton that "Smith's troops have been mismanaged," telling the trans-
Mississippi commander that "our only hope of saving Vicksburg now depends on the operations of your troops on the other side of the river," adding
that "it is impossible with the force the Government has put at my disposal to
raise the siege of that city." Eventually, Jefferson Davis himself also became
involved, writing to Smith, "I am convinced that the safety of Vicksburg depends on your prompt and efficient co-operation." He peremptorily ordered
Smith to "move your forces to the Mississippi River, and command in person
operations for the relief of the besieged city." Whether Davis was acting on
Johnston's urging or in response to Johnston's lethargy is not known.[63]

Johnston envisioned any numbers of ways Smith could aid Vicksburg,
from "plant[ing] artillery on the Mississippi banks, driv[ing] beef into Vicksburg, or join[ing] the garrison." In a sure way not to win friends and influence people, Johnston continued that "your troops up to this time have done
nothing," but he massaged Smith's ego with talk of his "intelligence, skill,
enthusiasm, and appreciation of the mighty stake involved in the great issue
now pending." In a postscript, Johnston bluntly added that it was the opinion
around his headquarters that "if your troops could send in abundance of cattle,
and themselves (8,000) join the garrison, the place would be saved."[64]

Obviously, Johnston did not know the situation around Vicksburg and the
impossibility of moving troops or cattle across the river, especially with the
navy patrolling north and south of the city and with Federal troops, including
Mower's brigade, on the peninsula opposite Vicksburg. What he suggested
was an impossibility, and Pemberton, once he heard of it, rightly declared that

"the enemy occupies the peninsula opposite the city, and I think it would be entirely impracticable for General Taylor either to put in supplies or to cross the river, and equally so for me to cross the garrison over." Pemberton then almost begged Johnston: "Could not a combined, vigorous effort even yet raise the siege?"[65]

That said, by the end of June Johnston realized that he had to do something, even if it was to make only a show of effort to cover his reputation and to continue to deflect blame away from himself. His wife even showed concerns for his reputation as well. Johnston had pinned the lack of success thus far on Pemberton's not suggesting a course to follow, on the Davis administration for not providing him with enough troops, and now on the trans-Mississippi commanders for not doing anything about Vicksburg. He even had the gall to blame Smith for not doing anything. But now Johnston seemed ready to begin his move, although it is unclear whether he really intended to fight or wanted to show force for his own well-being. Either way, some of his divisions began to move westward on June 30. He reported how "field transportation and other supplies having been obtained, the army marched toward the Big Black."[66]

As the calendar thus rolled over into July, it seemed even more likely that a culmination was coming in the next few days.

"I have read of besieged cities and the suffering of the inhabitants," wrote Confederate surgeon Joseph Alison in his diary, "but always thought the picture was too highly painted. But now I have witnessed one and can believe all that is written on the subject." It was indeed a bleak picture, although word of the suffering inside the city among civilians and soldiers alike rarely became known on the outside. Newspapers printed letters from inside Vicksburg and any news they could get on occasion, but by and large those inside Vicksburg were left to their own plight. Yet at the same time, those civilians on the outside, but still in the area of operations, continually faced their own challenges as well. It was a rough time for the civilians, both white and black, caught up in the military operations around Vicksburg.[67]

Unquestionably, those inside the ring of fire that was Vicksburg suffered the most as the siege wore on, even from the most mundane things that compounded the misery to a much greater degree. One man described how "the heat is awful & we have no ice and have to drink warm river water which is anything but a luxury. The mosquitoes, too, are awful to behold & more so to bite and we suffer in the flesh day & night." More problematic was the continual bombardment, made even worse on particular days of heavier fire, such as on June 25 prior to the mine explosion. Pemberton noted the enemy "turned upon the city a most murderous and concentrated fire." Worse tidings came when, by late June, Elias Dennis positioned sharpshooters and artillery across the Mississippi River and they preyed on the city from the west. This new angle, not used before, created additional damage to the buildings as well as among the people. One Louisianan declared, "They shoot at anything they can see, man, woman, or child," and another described "a great many holes in the streets."[68]

Most civilians as a result stayed close to their caves, which were continually decorated as the siege went on with more and more finery brought out from their houses. One observer noted the niceties of the caves, describing carpets on the floors and pianos and organs brought inside. One soldier noted the humor in how a mother cooking in front of her cave with all her little children running around her "suddenly hearing a shell from the mortar . . . would fly with her little ones for safety like a hen with her brood when the hawk approaches." Danger lurked within as well. Lucy McRae, the daughter of the sheriff, was buried alive in a collapse caused by a cannon round exploding above. She was quickly dug out, blood rushing from her ears, mouth, and nose. Mary Loughborough also told of "a large snake curled up between the earth and the upright post" in her cave. She called a military officer who, despite it striking at him "with open jaws," managed to slice its head off with his sword. She described it as "fully as large round the body as the bowl of a good-sized glass tumbler, and over two yards long."[69]

A few refused to leave their homes and suffered the consequences. When one soldier talked to a woman about staying in her house, she coldly responded that "all the nasty Yankees in the north could not scare me away." He admitted: "I admired her grit, but did not have much respect for her discretion." Another soldier described "shattered stores warehouses, and dwellings," and Dora Miller was in her house when a shell hit and pieces of the house flew all around. "It has taken all the afternoon to get the plaster out of my hair, for my hands were rather shaky," she told her diary. "Most of the houses in the city were damaged and several burned," another explained, and one Mississippian described how "everywhere the terrible effects of the long bombardment were visible; houses torn to pieces, chimneys knocked down and trees without limbs or tops. More especially along the river front, was this wholesale destruction apparent." The Warren County Courthouse was a favorite target, and a shell actually hit it at one point, killing a couple of the 5th Mississippi State Troops who were guarding Union prisoners in the courtroom. One Louisianan described how the Mississippi militia "incontinently 'skedaddled' from such hot quarters to a more secure position." On another occasion, brigade commander Stephen D. Lee was almost killed as he sat on the porch of a residence visiting with civilians.[70]

As expected, casualties continued to mount among the civilians as the siege wore on, even including, one dentist noted, "Newman the milkman [who] had his head shot of[f] today." One Louisianan reported the roll of recent casualties: "This morning a man walking in town had his arm shot off. Maj. Reed's wife had her arm taken off by a piece of shell." He also noted that "two ladies, day before yesterday, were struck by balls from a shrapnel shell & so severely wounded as not expected to live." He also added that a shell wounded his cook and that "two kittens were killed by the same explosion." Others added their own stories to the list: "A lady in the next house was instantly killed this evening while sitting in her own door with another lady friend over whom her brains were splattered by a shell from a Parrot gun on the other side of the river." Another wrote to his daughter that a woman and three children all perished when a shell came through their roof. On another occasion, he saw a shell kill a child being carried by a slave woman, the shell taking off the woman's arm. He later described how a family of nine was buried alive when a shell hit their cave, and "there they remain to this day, no effort being made to dig them out." He continued that "nineteen women and twelve children, it is said, have been killed since the siege commenced & men & horses, mules & cattle, too many to count." One observer summed it up: "Surely this is terrible warfare which dooms the innocent lambs to inhuman slaughter." And the fear could at times be just about as bad. One little girl was told that God would protect them during the bombardment, to which she responded, "But momma, I's so 'fraid God's killed too!"[71]

The flagging sustenance and increased prices also troubled the citizens of Vicksburg. One told of "starvation prices": flour six hundred and later a thousand dollars a barrel, biscuits eight dollars per dozen, pies four dollars apiece, molasses ten dollars per gallon, rum up to one hundred dollars for a gallon. Mule meat was eventually sold at the city market. Sometimes other options were needed, and Pemberton allowed citizens to grind corn if they could get it at government mills. It became so bad, one noted, that "rats command from one to two dollars a piece," and several described rumors of subsisting "in some instances on cats & dogs." While that may not have been too common, the animals of Vicksburg did suffer with hunger and soon became fearful as well. One woman described how the dogs "on hearing the descent of a shell, they would dart aside—then, as it exploded, sit down and howl in the most pitiful manner." They were hungry, too, and Mary Loughborough noted that her servant George "carried on a continual warfare with them, as they came about the fire where our meals were cooking." She added, "It came into my mind one day, that these dogs through hunger might become as much to be dreaded as wolves. Groundless was this anxiety, for in the course of a week or two they had almost disappeared." Mules and horses were in danger as well, being scared and some wounded making the most pitiful show of pain in moaning and rearing. One surgeon described how "the stench from dead mules and horses (killed by shell) is intolerable." Those that lived were miserable as well, John C. Taylor of Pemberton's staff telling of one horse who began munching on a woman's green shawl, thinking it was something to eat.[72]

It was obviously worse as humans began to starve. "All the eating houses are closed," one chaplain wrote to his wife; "the poor in town are upon the verge of starvation. Lean and laggard famine stands at the door of the rich and knocks for admission." Fortunately, several of the better-off residents opened their resources to the poor: W. H. Stevens, Victor F. Wilson, and a German, J. Kaiser.[73]

Yet, the people of Vicksburg continued on as best they could, taking any little victory they could get. One staff officer described a "magnificent sunset—charming view from 'Sky-Parlor Hill.'" One Mississippian who went to Vicksburg on a burial detail explained how "while in the city I was amazed to meet everywhere refined, delicate ladies ministering to the sick and the wounded, and perfectly indifferent to the shells Admiral Porter was constantly raining upon the devoted city." Others tried to gain safety by any means possible. An English man flew a British flag, probably to keep safe from both sides. William Orme described him as having "no sympathy for the loyal North, but great respect for the suffering South." Confederate brigade commander John C. Vaughn similarly reported on June 30 how "a gentleman and lady attempted to pass the line under a flag, but the enemy would not allow them to enter their lines." An Ohioan explained that they were "British subjects," and the soldiers on that isolated part of the line took the chance under the truce to meet and shake hands and talk. It was Dora Miller, but Grant refused her passage, the officer delivering the message stating that "General Grant says no human being shall pass out of Vicksburg; but the lady may feel sure danger will soon be over. Vicksburg will surrender on the 4th."[74]

Grant admitted as much, writing that "by throwing shells every few minutes the people are kept continuously in their caves. They must give out soon even if their provisions do not give out. Troops are on less than half rations and many poor people without anything. I decline allowing any of them to come out." A Confederate Mississippian sympathized: "It must have been a long, tedious time to those people, shut in from the sunlight, afraid to venture abroad, for fear of being mangled to death by the ever flying missiles of the enemy." One even admitted that "if the affair went on much longer 'a building will have to be arranged for the accommodation of maniacs' because the constant tension was driving people out of their minds."[75]

A positive attitude and the simple things of life helped keep emotions in check. Dora Miller told of watching "a pair of chimney-swallows [that] have built in the parlor chimney. The concussion of the house often sends down parts of their nest, which they patiently pick up and re-ascend with." Others grew to be at ease even among the bombardment: "Grown accustomed to continual firing," one civilian wrote; "even women scarcely quailed under ordinary bombardment—mirth and even jollity occasionally lessened the tension of the times." One even admitted, "Still, we had nothing to complain of in comparison with the soldiers." Humor also helped, if it could be found. Lida Lord told of her father dodging the sparks of a fuse on a mortar shell for far too many seconds, wondering when it would explode, only to realize it was actually a lightning bug or fire fly. On another occasion, one woman drew giggles when she protected herself with a blanket: "All laughed heartily at my wise supposition that the blanket could be any protection from the heavy fragments of shells."[76]

Still, life was horrible, and there was no way to cover it up. "The screams of the women of Vicksburg were the saddest I have ever heard," declared Mary Loughborough. Added to the doldrums were the low tones of the church bells and courthouse as they tolled the deadly minutes and hours away. "And so the weary days went on—the long, weary days," Loughborough added.[77]

It was certainly cause for concern that Johnston was Vicksburg chief's source of hope, because he proved woefully late. And he provided no better protection for the civilians in the rear areas of the Union operations either:

they faced increased turmoil as a result of larger and larger Union numbers back on the rear line as well as their continual movement eastward. By July, Federals had taken full possession of almost all the territory between Vicksburg and the Big Black River and up the Yazoo River past Haynes' Bluff.[78]

Those civilians outside of Vicksburg were told good news perhaps to bolster their morale: "The last couriers from Vicksburg report very favorably," one wrote; "the word is, we have plenty of ammunition and provisions, and the officers and soldiers are in the best of spirits." Not all were buoyed, however, one writing that "back in the country here we stand affected according to our different temperaments—but there is a general feeling of uneasiness, from the fear that Johnston has not sufficient force to meet Grant in the field, or to attack him in his trenches. I share in this apprehension."[79]

The waiting brought contact, and when it did, any number of responses and results could happen. Many Confederate Mississippians refused to give up. One lady who owned the house where one general made his headquarters "wears a small dagger at her side, and carries a pistol in her trunk.—She talks fierce," the general admitted. Sherman noted to his wife: "I doubt if history affords a parallel to the deep and bitter enmity of the women of the South." The Federals could give right back, one describing the attention given a mentally challenged civilian: "Stopped and fed at noon where the Idiot-Boy lives. He is a curiosity."[80]

In his new position, Sherman had a lot of interaction with the civilians in the rear areas. Near his line along Bear Creek was the John Klein farm, whose wife was the daughter of Sherman's brother-in law's sister. It was a tortured connection to be sure, but a connection nevertheless. "I used frequently to drop in and take a meal with them," he remembered, "and Mrs. [Elizabeth] Klein was generally known as the general's cousin, which doubtless saved her and her family from molestation, too common on the part of our men."[81]

The Messenger family who lived near the ferry on the Big Black River did not fare quite so well. Sherman described them as "the family consisting of many women, whose husbands and brothers were evidently serving an easy purpose of keeping up communications, so I moved them all by force, leaving a fine house filled with elegant furniture and costly paintings to the chances of war." Colonel William W. Belknap and the 15th Iowa was sent to move them, and brigade commander Colonel Alexander Chambers and division commander John McArthur both accompanied the regiment. Belknap reported: "Mrs. Messenger and family, together with four other families of white persons on the place, numbering in all 14 persons, and the colored people, were removed and brought within our lines." They left three blacks who were unable to travel and also brought "four wagon loads of property." Belknap interestingly reported finding a Vicksburg *Sun* newspaper from May 4, 1861, stating that "Col. George Messenger" had given money and would give his entire million-dollar estate "to uniform and equip our volunteer companies . . . to maintain Southern rights, honor, and independence. This is what we call showing a man's 'faith by his works.'"[82]

Once the family was gone, plunderers set in. An Iowan reported "parties from other commands, under command of commissioned officers, did, during the day, enter the Messenger house and take articles of furniture and clothing." One of those was from the 114th Illinois, who wrote home that his regiment was camped at the Messenger Plantation and that "we have taken the Furniture out of mans house that ownes the Negroes[.] John Wood and I sleeps on a Spring Bed." This type of plunder was common. Two Federals who were brought to A. J. Smith for stealing chickens heard him bellow, "O, damn 'em, let 'em go. There ain't any tree here high enough to hang 'em on." His headquarters were incidentally situated in a lovely stand of "stately poplars." Another soldier told about orders to take only the top rail of a fence for firewood, and the "order was obeyed to the letter." Of course, the entire fence was soon gone, as each rail became the top as the one above it disappeared.[83]

The Hill family near Birdsong Ferry, being suspected of clandestine activity, received similar treatment. "The family of Hill, with other war widows, at a place on the Birdsong road, is removed to a harmless place within our lines," one Federal explained. Sherman cautioned Grant about being too lenient on these Confederate-leaning civilians. "These may appeal to the tender heart of our commanding general, but he will not reverse my decision when he knows a family accessible to the enemy—keen scouts—can collect and impart more information than the most expert spies." Part of the issue was the talkative Federals themselves: "Our volunteer pickets and patrols reveal names and facts in their innocence which, if repeated by these women, give the key to our points." Others were more at a loss on how to treat civilians; Osterhaus down at the railroad bridge by his own admission did not always know what to do.[84]

Similar was the case of the Wilkinsons, who were "refugeeing" at another local house. Sherman had had one of the Wilkinson sons as a student in Louisiana before the war and inquired at one house as to their whereabouts.

Two young girls confirmed who they were, relating that their mother was at Parson Fox's for the day. Sherman went there and rode into the yard, inquiring if it was indeed Parson Fox's, a "fine-looking, venerable old man" rising and stating that he was the parson. Sherman then asked for Mrs. Wilkinson, who popped up and took on the conversation. He asked if she was the one who had a son at the military school in Alexandria "when General Sherman was superintendent," and she confirmed as much. Sherman related who he was and asked about his welfare, she stating that he was an artillery officer inside Vicksburg. When he asked about her husband, she burst into tears and yelled, "You killed him at Bull Run, where he was fighting for his country!" Sherman politely "disclaimed killing anybody at Bull Run," but all the other dozen or so ladies joined Mrs. Wilkinson in "loud lamentations, which made it most uncomfortable for me, and I rode away."[85]

That was not the end of the dealings with Mrs. Wilkinson. On July 3, as the Vicksburg effort was coming to a climax, Sherman sat atop his horse along one of the major roadways his troops were defending and saw "a poor, miserable horse, carrying a lady, and led by a little negro boy, coming across a cotton-field toward me." It was Mrs. Wilkinson, whom Sherman helped to dismount. He inquired "what had brought her to me in that style," and she admitted she knew Vicksburg was about to fall and she was going to see her son. "I tried to console and dissuade her, but she was resolved," Sherman remembered. He gave her a letter of introduction to Grant and later found out that it had helped her in her cause.[86]

Some contact was more comical. One group of Federals out hunting for blackberries interestingly ran up on a birthday party, "brightened by the presence of no less than eleven young ladies." They asked where the men were and got the customary answer—"out hunting yanks." One Illinoisan noted "they were very nice rebel girls, though I think the color of the eyes of one of them was what I might call *true blue*." The Federals remained for lunch, and despite being assured the girls were all loyal, they kept "one eye on the girls and the other on the window." He concluded that they were Unionists, joking that "no doubt they will be whenever their 'boys' come home."[87]

Most civilians caught up in the horror thus tried to get along as best they could, a few remaining on their farms instead of heading to safety. These included Joseph E. Davis, the president's brother, whom Samuel French reported having breakfast with. Others tried to make a living off the Federals, including some selling vegetables by permit. Others tried to get aid from the

Confederate authorities, who were all but powerless in no-man's-land. One woman wrote to Governor John J. Pettus asking that he get her husband, a civilian, released from Federal custody. She declared he was "heavily chained and fed upon bread and water," and she was thus "without a home, the Federals having placed me in this situation, and carried my husband off prisoner." She wanted him released so he could obtain a home but assured the governor that once he provided a home he would "then join the army, which I am sure he will do, though not a conscript." Nevertheless, she added that "the Ladies daily prayers here, is for the safety of Vicksburg."[88]

14

"I Only Wonder It Has Held Out So Long"

July 1–2

While building to a climax for the armies operating around Vicksburg, the first few days of July were anything but calm elsewhere in America. Brigadier General John Hunt Morgan's raid was ongoing, an Indianan at Vicksburg writing to his wife: "I hope the Rebel raiders have not scared you out of your wits." At the same time, the large and important Tullahoma Campaign was ongoing in Middle Tennessee. Most famous in those three days was the fighting around Gettysburg in far-off Pennsylvania. The soldiers of both North and South around Vicksburg were just as interested in what was happening there as those soldiers in Pennsylvania were about the events around Vicksburg. News came slowly, however, and it was several days before anything more than rumors surfaced. "News is old by the time it reaches us," Union brigade commander William Orme wrote; he described reading papers up to June 19 on June 24.[1]

The Union debacle at Chancellorsville earlier in May and the Confederate invasion of Pennsylvania garnered most of the soldiers' attention. "I have just heard that Lee is in Pennsylvania and that Hooker is falling back on Washington," Colonel Walter Gresham of the 53rd Indiana wrote home. "I hope it is true, for I want something done that will make the North realize what is going on." Another wrote that "things look somewhat 'scarey' in the east in Pennsylvania but I do think if the Rebels attempts an invasion on the north it will be the best thing they could do for the 'Union' for I think it will arouse & bring to light the slumbering 'patriotism' & 'war spirit' of the north & I think probably they may find it an easier matter to advance than to retreat success-fully." Another simply added, "I would like very much to hear how the Rebel raid into Pennsylvania terminated."[2]

There was of course a special connection between the two operations. Part of the reason for Gettysburg was Vicksburg. The idea of sending troops to Mississippi to take pressure off Pemberton spurred a plan by Robert E. Lee to invade the North to accomplish the same goal. Rumor said that Jefferson Davis even thought of going to Mississippi to take command himself, although his health was very bad in May.[3]

Watching events in the East gave ample opportunity for these westerners to show the bias they had developed against easterners. There had always been some cajoling between the two; the 32nd Ohio in McPherson's corps were even talked about as "Harper's Ferry cowards" because of their surrender there in 1862. One Illinoisan noted, "We hear now that Hooker is repulsed and forced to recross the river." He added: "Why is it that Grants army is victorious while the army of Virginia is defeated in every movement?" Another noted the defeats in May, writing, "It was only what we have learned to expect from the Army of the Potomac." An Ohioan pointedly admitted that "I am happy to say that we do not belong to the Army of the Potomac now for while they are being defeated time and again we are gaining victories after victory." An Iowan even planned ahead: "When we get Vicksburg we can go right on east and take them places that the Eastern Army have been fooling around so long."[4]

There was some good feeling between the easterners and westerners, however, even if somewhat backhanded. One westerner was bold enough to praise easterners for at least still fighting: "Any but the finest kind of an army would be perfectly demoralized after so many disasters." Another explained that new eastern troops "think a heap of Grant and say if he was sent over to the Potomac he would do something." He lamented that they kept getting beat in the East and thus "I guess I will get to serve my time out."[5]

Even though easterners had their own fighting to take part in, they nevertheless watched carefully the events around Vicksburg as well. Major General Lafayette McLaws, one of Lieutenant General James Longstreet's division commanders, wrote on June 5 that "the news from Vicksburg is so meager and unsatisfactory that it carries much uneasiness. Its fall would be so discouraging and its successful defense so inspiring that everything concerning it, is looked for with the greatest anxiety." Another Confederate noted, "No news from Vicksburg though a spirit of confidence seems to prevail. If it falls, in my humble opinion, it will be the death blow to our independence."[6]

Yet even as those great events transpired in Pennsylvania in the first three days of July, the combatants around Vicksburg turned their attention to the looming Fourth of July. As early as June 24, one Louisianan wrote how "we are beginning to fear that our 4th of July may be spent here." Union brigade commander Adolph Engelmann had remarked back in late June that "it is impossible to tell how long Vicksburg may hold out, but I confidently hope that it will be ours by the 4th of July." That looked less and less likely as the troops in the rear near Haynes' Bluff received little news of what was happening at Vicksburg and the troops of his brigade prepared to celebrate Independence Day: "We are so short of news here," Engelmann wrote on July 3, "that all I know to tell you is that we are going to raise our large flag tomorrow. It is the flag that General Brayman got for the Post of Bolivar and it is 10 feet wide and 20 feet long."[7]

Inside Vicksburg itself, optimism was fading as July 4 loomed. Johnston was the last hope, and most had given up on him by this time. One Confederate admitted there was "no Johnston yet, and if not soon *we* will have no use for him." Staff officer William Drennan similarly confessed by July 3 that "in my own mind I have given up Johnston." In fact, he had settled on captivity: "I will make the best of the confinement."[8]

Obviously, the main focus of the whole operation was Vicksburg itself. And the siege operations continued on without a pause, Grant moving closer and closer with more men and firepower, including the naval support in the river. "Brigadier General Hovey informs me that the firing from the mortar boats this morning has been exceedingly well directed," Grant wrote to Admiral Porter on July 2; "one shell fell into the large fort, and several along the lines of the rifle pits. Please have them continue firing in the same direction and elevation."[9]

A lot more than just naval and even land artillery bombardment was needed, however, and Grant continued with his engineering operations in order to gain every advantage he could. Chief among these were the thirteen active major approaches, mainly the ones that had mines, although Engineer Frederick Prime reported there was also work done on other areas that did not develop into major approaches. More important, tunnelers were digging mines on Thayer's, Ransom's, Lightburn's, Ewing's, Giles Smith's, Logan's, and A. J. Smith's approaches. The Confederates had countered with their own mines at various places, including one on the Hall's Ferry Road, two in front of Square Fort, two on the Baldwin's Ferry Road, one on the Jackson Road, two on Green's front, and three on Shoup's front, where "a Yankee Dutchman who was drunk put his head & shoulders over & told the men they had better leave, that there was no use of their tunneling." All mines were six to nine feet underground and charged with a hundred to a hundred and twenty-five pounds of powder.[10]

Yet only a few were blown in late June on Ewing's and Smith's lines and on July 2 on Ord's front. Charles Dana reported the latter "exploded . . . before a sap of ours, doing us no damage, but giving us the advantage of carrying the trench into the crater." Confederate engineer Samuel Lockett explained that "the explosion was premature, and the enemy's sap was hardly near enough to be much injured." Worse damage came on Ewing's approach, where Prime reported that "the explosion of the enemy's mines, crushing our first gallery, had shattered the earth for 30 feet around, [and] a detour was made to avoid this shaken earth." But it was far too little and far too late, Prime character-izing the countermines as "feeble ones, their charges always light, and rarely doing other damage than making the ground where they had been exploded impracticable for our own, as we did not use gallery frames or sheeting." A Confederate staff officer agreed, writing how one attempt "failed by 6 feet, we will try again." Still, just the mere thought of countermines halted other work, Prime reporting on Thayer's approach that "when near the salient ap-proached, the officer in charge of the approach thought he heard the ene-my's miners at work. Accordingly, work in the sap was stopped, and a mine begun."[11]

The most work took place on Ewing's approach toward the Stockade Re-dan, where Engineer William Kossak used some trickery to "mislead the en-emy." The Confederate division commanders had a hard time determining where to send reinforcements as a result, Forney telling Pemberton that he had asked Smith's neighboring division for help but that "the call will not be made for troops unless our positions are carried or we are hard pressed." Keeping details of infantry working on the rearward trenches and approaches and pioneers on the work up front, Kossak started a lengthy mine "on a cir-cuitous route, to keep . . . out of their radius of rupture." After digging well over a hundred feet to the northwest, he made a ninety-degree turn into the

northeastern face of the redan. With such a long distance for wheelbarrow-
ing the dirt, the miners had to establish a new dump for the dislodged earth,
conveniently behind a large log that hid it from view. They also had to dig
new air holes because "[of] the candles being extinguished by the extreme
heat and foulness of the air." The new air holes and dump "brought plenty of
circulation of air into the mine."[12]

Once the run in toward the fort began, it took seventy feet of digging to
reach a point under the Confederate bastion. The mine shaft itself was only
four and a half feet high while a mere three feet wide at the bottom and an
even tighter two and a half feet wide at the top. Every four feet were braces
with sheeting on the top of the shaft. The miners moved on in the ensuing
days, working in six-hour shifts, all the while "suffering from the extreme
heat and want of air" the farther the mine went. As the shaft drew closer to the
Confederate lines, Kossak prepared everything else he would need to blow it
up, including backfill and 2,200 pounds of powder.[13]

While Kossak's mine never went off, the only other Union mine to be
sprung at Vicksburg was the second one started on Logan's approach at the
3rd Louisiana Redan. Confederate division commander Forney noted that,
after the fight in the crater, "work was resumed by the enemy and by us, they
mining and we countermining." Captain L. B. Taylor of Hébert's staff also
burned another sap roller on the Jackson Road on the night of July 1, doing it
"by means of fire balls." Hickenlooper had sent his mining crew over to Ransom's position after the work was done on the Jackson Road, but he recalled
them to start another mine to the northwest on June 28: "We have concluded
to spring another mine under parapet to left [north] of crater, for the purpose
of uncovering their work." Lockett divined their intention and had the Louisianans throw grenades at the opening of the mine where sappers went in and
out and the dirt was dumped, but the wily Federals countered with "a timber
shelter, to protect their sappers from our hand grenades." Lockett ordered "a
barrel containing 125 pounds of powder" lit with a fifteen-second fuse and
rolled it over the parapet. A proud Lockett noted that the fuse "was touched
off by myself with a live coal." He added how "the effect of the explosion was
very severe, and fragments of sap-rollers, gabions, and pieces of timber were
thrown into the air." But it did not stop the work. Within a couple of days this
new mine was ready as well, and McPherson notified Grant on July 1: "The
mine on Logan's front is ready, and the enemy appear to be digging in toward
it. Shall I explode it?" McPherson also wanted guidance on what to do after

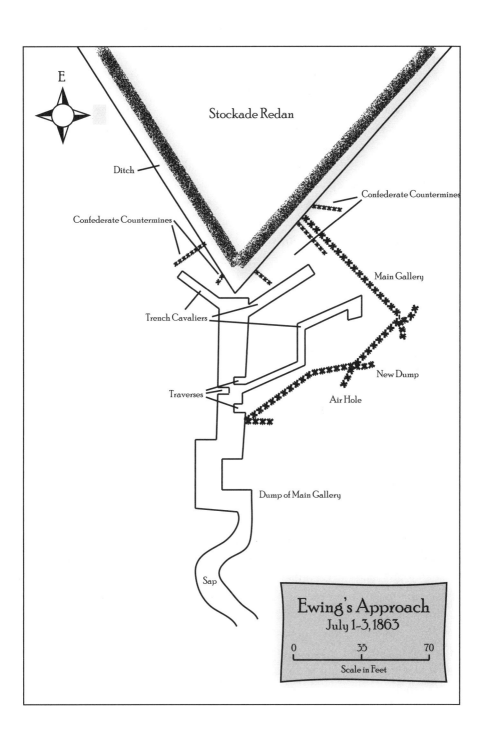

E

Stockade Redan

Ditch

Confederate Countermines

Confederate Countermines

Main Gallery

Trench Cavaliers

New Dump

Traverses

Air Hole

Dump of Main Gallery

Sap

Ewing's Approach
July 1–3, 1863

0   35   70

Scale in Feet

the mine was sprung "and what disposition do you desire me to make of my troops; anything more than having the rifle pits filled with sharpshooters?"[14]

Engineer Prime explained that the mine was supposed to be charged and exploded when a general assault occurred, but those digging heard mysterious sounds coming under the ground from the Confederate side. "The enemy's miners being heard at work near it," a sick Prime nevertheless reported, "and it being feared that they might crush our galleries, which were not lined, the mine was loaded and fired." Hickenlooper was by this time also sick from the constant work and confined to his bed, where some feared he might not recover. Grant even came to see him, asking if he knew who he was. Hickenlooper replied, "Certainly I do, you are General Grant." Tresilian took over and finished the mine. In total, workers placed some eighteen hundred pounds of black powder inside.[15]

Grant faced another decision, but this one was fairly easy. Not wanting to press the issue just yet—certainly not until everything was ready on all other fronts—Grant did not want an assault in coordination with the mine explosion. Some of his commanders, particularly Herron on the far left, told him as much as a week earlier that "I believe I can go into the enemy's works from this position to-morrow night." But Grant was only willing to scare the enemy: "Explode the mine as soon as ready," he responded, adding, "notify Ord the hour, so that he may be ready to make a demonstration should the enemy attempt to move toward you." Then putting a halt to any idea of an assault, Grant ordered, "You need not do more than have rifle-pits filled with sharpshooters. [But] take all advantage you can, after the explosion, of the breech made, either to advance guns or your sharpshooters." With the go-ahead, McPherson alerted Grant that the mine would be sprung at 3:00 P.M. He also sent orders down the chain of command to Logan, cautioning that "it is not intended to make any assault, but simply to have the rifle pits lined with sharpshooters, and the command under arms, ready to take advantage of any chance in our favor or repel any sortie of the enemy."[16]

With that, McPherson gave the order, and the mine blew. Prime reported that the eighteen hundred pounds of powder had their effect, despite some of it being bad, and a crater thirty feet wide emerged where a portion of the 3rd Louisiana Redan had previously been. Unlike the June 25 mine, this crater produced many different explanations in terms of measurements, and few resembled one another. As a result, it is unknown whether Tresilian undercharged or overcharged the mine or if the correct amount of powder was used.[17]

Union engineer Prime reported that "the right flank fort was cleared off by it, so that Ransom's shells had free way into the work. Many rebels were killed, but McPherson has not yet got possession of the fort." Some claimed to have seen as many as twenty Southerners in the air at one time, and Prime also noted that the blast "crushed the enemy's galleries" and that some twenty-five Confederates were casualties, including "six rebels [who] were thrown into our lines by the explosion; all dead but one, a negro." A 124th Illinois soldier put it more bluntly, writing that "it threw 3 dead men and one live nigger over on our side from the Rebels." An Indianan countered that it threw four slaves and three white men into Union lines, one of the whites being safe. He tried to "crawl back inside the works again, when one of our sharpshooters put an end to his existence with a minie." Another Illinoisan noted that a dog was also thrown into their lines, but it was killed. Lockett countered that only one private and seven blacks who were "sinking a shaft" were killed.[18]

All agreed that the one survivor was a slave named Abe. An Illinoisan wrote that "the black man was scared so bad he was almost white." Logan's medical director described him as "badly bruised, and for some days I thought his chances to live very doubtful." He recovered, the surgeon attributing it to his falling on "soft ground, and evidently on the back part of his head and shoulders as there were the most serious injuries." Abe was up and walking in a week, and Logan summoned him. Abe explained where he had been when the explosion occurred, "mighty close under the breastworks, sleeping in the shade." When Logan asked why he did not "hold on to something," Abe replied, "I dun gone hel on a bush Sa, but it blowd up too." When asked how high he went, Abe responded, "Dun know Sa, spek bout 3 or 4 mile." To an Ohioan Abe answered the same question: "Dun'no, Massa, when I'se coming down others were goin' up." Another Federal wrote home that he said he "'met a white man going up as he come down' & told him he 'needn't go up dar 'cause he couldn't get to stay dar.'" Surgeon Trowbridge described Abe as "the dumbest mortal I ever saw," but some smart Federals took advantage and charged five cents a head for a look at him. Historian Terry Winschel has humorously described Abe as "America's first man in space."[19]

Confederate reactions were more awestruck. Willie Tunnard of the 3rd Louisiana explained how "at first there was a general rush to escape the huge mass of descending earth." Lockett surmised that "the charge must have been enormous, as the crater was at least 20 feet deep, 30 feet across in one direction and 50 in another." He added that "the original faces of the redan were almost completely destroyed, and the explosive effect extended to a parapet I had made across the gorge of the work, making in it almost a practicable breach for an assault." He later admitted that the breach was as large as twenty feet long. Brigade commander Francis Cockrell himself had been blown into the air and was stunned but not badly hurt, but he had the presence of mind to bring forward his Missourians. He had just switched out the 6th Missouri with the 2nd Missouri for duty when the blast occurred, and Cockrell yelled, "Forward, my brave old Second Missouri, and prepare to die!" Some did, including Lieutenant Colonel Pembroke S. Senteny of the regiment, who peered over the parapet and took a bullet in the head. There was much confusion as a result, and had Grant readied an assault this time it might have broken through. He did not, and Lockett explained, "I went to work immediately to repair damages as well as possible." But just because no assault came did not mean the fire against the parapet and breach was not heavy, and Lockett explained that the Confederates first tried to fill the gap "by heaving dirt into the breach with shovels from the two sides, but the earth was swept away by the storm of missiles faster than it could be placed in position." Lockett then tried sandbags, "but they, too, were torn to shreds and scattered." Finally, Lockett managed to fill "tent flies and wagon covers" with earth and rolled them into position; "finally," he wrote, "at last we had something between us and the deadly hail of shot and shell and minie-balls."[20]

Night helped more than anything. By dawn the next morning, "the breach was filled and the redan still tenable," Pemberton and Bowen both visiting to check. The 6th Missouri of Cockrell's brigade manned the line at that time, and John Forney could only surmise: "Perhaps he only wished to destroy life and weaken the position. In this he has succeeded but too well. The redan itself is entirely gone, and the interior line considerably weakened." Indeed it was, he later reporting that this blast was "much heavier than the first. The result was the entire demolition of the redan, leaving only an immense chasm where it stood. The greater portion of the earth was thrown toward the enemy, the line of least resistance being in that direction. Our interior line was much injured. Nine men who were countermining were necessarily lost, and a large number of those manning the works were killed and wounded."[21]

Casualties were numerous. "Badly bruised in the explosion," Cockrell reported that two lieutenants died, one buried in the explosion, and several privates also perished, "some of whom were blown high up into the air and buried in the wreck." Others were also thrown upward but survived: "A large number of the Sixth Missouri Infantry were blown up and thrown over the brow of the hill." The rest were stunned, Cockrell writing of the blast "knocking off their hats and their guns out of their hands, bruising and wounding quite a number." Yet most found whatever musket was nearest and, with a cheer first raised by the Louisianans and then taken up by the Missourians as well, rushed back to what was left of the parapet. Perhaps worse, the Confederate engineer in that sector, a lieutenant named Blessing, was wounded about that time, and Hébert wrote, "I earnestly ask that some other officer be immediately sent to replace him." Others were also rotated in and out of the position as the hours moved on, and the 1st Missouri also took station nearby, in six-hour shifts on duty and twelve hours off.[22]

The Confederate defenders of the 3rd Louisiana Redan, mainly the Louisianans themselves and the accompanying Missourians, braced for an assault, but it never came. Hébert reported that although they were shocked at the blast, which he noted removed "the entire left face, part of the right, and the entire terre-plein of the redan . . . , leaving an immense deep chasm," the men nevertheless faced no assault "to the disappointment of our brave soldiers." There was confusion as to why not, although word from other sectors of the field indicated something may still be up even after the mine blew. Colonel Thomas P. Dockery, who was near the Stockade Redan on the Graveyard Road, having taken command of the brigade when General Green was killed a couple of days earlier, notified division commander John Forney that enemy troops were heading to the left, although "I cannot see enough of the force to judge of its strength." Forney braced for an attack, even making plans to call on neighboring Martin L. Smith's division for reinforcements. He asked Smith "to hold a portion of his troops in readiness to move to our assistance." One battered Louisianan noted in his diary: "What a record for the opening of a new month!"[23]

Back at the breach, the main problem developing for the Federals was that their line near the new crater was significantly below the Confederate forces, and gravity aided the Louisianans as they pummeled the Federals with grenades that Leggett's men could not return, the distance being too great. There was nothing else that could aid these Federals in such a tight spot until Engineer Tresilian developed an ingenious way to deliver almost vertical fire behind the Confederate lines, matching the grenades coming out of their midst. Tresilian, a civilian engineer before the war, had his pioneers cut large bolts from trees and "by shrinking iron bands on cylinders of tough wood, and boring them out for 6 or 12 pound shells," created instant small mortars. In all, he created three of them, one 6-pounder and two 12-pounders, with which he ultimately fired 468 shells and was later assured by Hébert's engineer that he had caused twenty-one killed and seventy-two wounded. Prime reported that "these mortars stood firing well, and gave sufficiently good results at 100 or 150 yards distance." Dana marveled that "in the absence of ordinary mortars, he has constructed several of wood, throwing 12-pounder shells effectively." And they did horrible work, Forney writing of what he supposed "to be a Cohorn mortar, which throws its missiles among the men with great accuracy, killing and wounding many, and tending much to dishearten the men." Bowen asked for emergency movement of howitzers to battle these guns.[24]

The idea caught on elsewhere as well. Without any Cohorn mortars of his own, Engineer Hains on Ord's front told his workers "to make some of these also," he writing that he found gum trees to work best. The wood guns were not perfect, however, Hains finding they worked well for only about a hundred rounds. Others had accidents. One pioneer reported on July 2 that "on account of a defective shell, one of the wooden mortars was blown to pieces today." He added that another was disabled as well. Still, they were better than nothing and actually served well. Hains also experimented with "spring boards," something like miniature catapults.[25]

In the larger context, Grant did not want to move until ready, although he did query McPherson: "Can't you take possession of the ground gained by the explosion today, after dark; and hold it without much sacrifice of life?" Yet Grant was nearing a major decision. Many of his approaches, including those so far behind on McClernand's former front, were now close up to the Confederate works. Even Smith's and Carr's approaches along the railroad were within mere yards or even in the Confederate ditches. More digging would likely accomplish little, Prime reporting that "little farther progress could be made by digging alone." It was time to seriously think about blowing the whole Confederate line out with mines or assaulting from the approaches so near the Confederate fortifications.[26]

Despite later writing of "the experience of the 25th admonishing us," Grant mostly did not assault in coordination with the mine on July 1 simply because he had bigger ideas. He was thinking of another assault—but not yet. Dana reported as early as June 17 that "General Grant will make another general assault as soon as McClernand's, Lauman's and Herron's lines are brought up close enough." He wanted the approaches moved far enough forward on all fronts and only then prepared for an assault. Orders thus went forward in the early days of July to prepare, Dana reporting that "orders have been given to abandon all attempts to push forward saps with a view of entering the enemy's works by that means, and to devote the labor of working parties to widening the covered ways and carrying them as near the rebel lines as practicable, in order to afford cover for storming columns." Division commander Frank Blair, for instance, received orders on July 1: "General Steel directs me to say that Major General Grant orders that all the approaches in your front be widened to 8 feet, so that a column of four (by the flank) can march therein." Chief engineer Cyrus Comstock elaborated on the orders the next day, telling commanders that Grant wanted the approaches "placed at once in such condition as to allow the most rapid movement of troops by fours along them, and the equally rapid debouche of troops." In order to make them so, Comstock ordered "the heads of trenches, for 60 feet, should be cut with gentle steps, so that troops can leave the trenches rapidly and in order. . . . Preparations should also be made for crossing ditches, planks should be obtained and held in readiness, and sand bags, solidly stuffed with cotton, tried, to see if they will not make, when thrown in ditches, a sufficiently solid roadway for infantry." He also wanted "the ground in rear of the enemy's works . . . carefully examined from different points . . . for the use of generals commanding divisions and the corps." Specific orders went to Captain Miles McAlester, who had taken over Comstock's job of seeing to the work on Ord's, Lauman's, and Herron's front, and a surgeon declared that Grant "pressed all his wagons in the service of hauling ammunition from the Yazoo landing." Others mentioned fashioning "scaling ladders and frames."[27]

It all sounded a lot like preparations for an assault, which it was. While the May assaults had been bloody, there was always the possibility of new ones. Sherman, in fact, had earlier notified his senator-brother John Sherman that "if we did not apprehend an attempt on our rear, we could wait patiently the slow process of besiegers; but as this danger is great [Johnston], we may try and assault again." Prime also gave his rational: "The enemy's works were weak, and at ten different points we could put the heads of regiments under cover within from 5 to 100 yards of his line. The assault would be but little easier if we waited ten days more." Comstock thus added in his orders that all these preparations should be done quickly: "[S]uch details must be used as will secure the completion of the work in three days, say by July 5." That was because Grant had made up his mind: he scheduled an army-wide assault for July 6.[28]

While matters were coming to a conclusion on the siege lines around Vicksburg, the same was occurring out east on the Sherman/Johnston front. "Sherman is wide awake for him and will give him a sound whipping when he undertakes the job," concluded one Federal out with Sherman on Bear Creek. Although rumors put Johnston heading for an attack on Memphis, Sherman had his lines well laid out in very defensible territory and was confident of his ability to hold. That confidence would soon be tested, as Johnston had finally begun a movement westward in the last days of June, one Mississippian accurately terming it a "gradual approach." By the first days of July, Johnston's divisions were nevertheless on the move, leaving their tents and camp equipage behind. A relieved Johnny Green of the Orphan Brigade in Breckinridge's division simply noted in his journal: "On July 1st 1863 we marched towards Vicksburg," although one of his fellow Kentuckians noted it was "the hottest march we have ever made."[29]

Johnston had major trouble getting his troops moving. One Kentuckian in Breckinridge's division talked "about the most trying march we ever made." Despite high confidence in Johnston himself, the Kentuckians found "the sand was shoe mouth deep & so hot it actually blistered our feet." Many straggled, he adding how "we nearly perished for water." Another noted that "perhaps troops never suffered more during the war, on account of extreme heat and dust and scarcity of water; men fell on the march, utterly exhausted and famished for want of water."[30]

The Confederate movement was thus a muted one. French moved toward Brownsville, first stopping on Bogue Filia Creek the night of July 1 and then the next day moving on to Brownsville and camps on Porter Creek. Breckinridge moved to Clinton the first day and on to the Bolton area on July 2. Loring and Walker set out from Vernon on the Big Black River on July 1, camping that night on Bogue Filia and Bogue Chitto Creeks before heading the next day to camps on Porter Creek north of French's division. The long

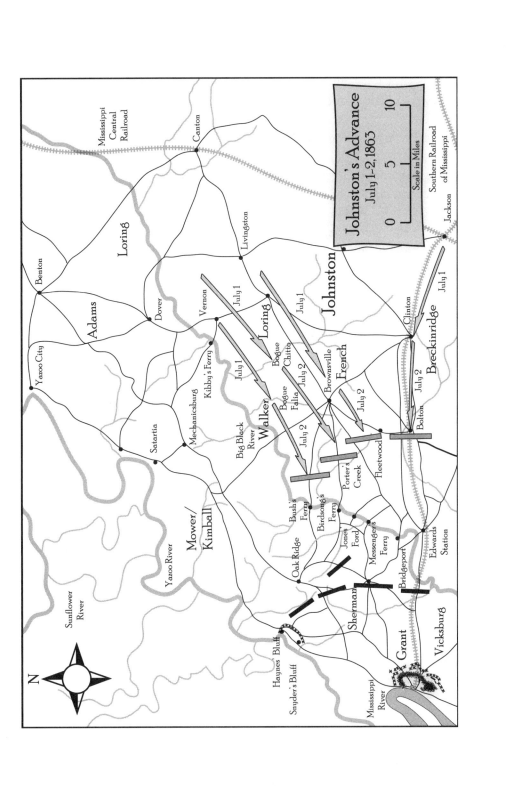

N

Johnston's Advance
July 1-2, 1863

Scale in Miles
0   5   10

Mississippi
Central
Railroad

Southern Railroad
of Mississippi

Canton

Loring

Benton

Adams

Yazoo City

Livingston

Dover

Vernon

July 1

Loring

July 1

Johnston

Mechanicsburg

Kibby's Ferry

July 1

Bogue
Chitto

Brownsville

French

July 2

Clinton

Breckinridge

July 1

Jackson

Satartia

Big Black
River

Walker

Bogue
Falia

July 2

July 2

Porter's
Creek

Fleetwood

July 2

Bolton

July 2

Mower/
Kimball

Yazoo River

Bush's
Ferry

Birdsong's
Ferry

Jones
Ford

Messenger's
Ferry

Edwards
Station

Sunflower
River

Oak Ridge

Bridgeport

Sherman

Grant

Vicksburg

Haynes' Bluff

Snyder's Bluff

Mississippi
River

stretches between creeks was tough, one of Loring's Mississippians describing how they left camp with three days' rations and "had plenty of rations but no water." Whether Johnston every really intended to attack Sherman's positions or even cross the Big Black River is unknown, but the movement itself was tardy, small, and not at all overpowering or even continuous.[31]

In fact, what fighting occurred erupted among the Confederates themselves, even between division commanders within Johnston's army. W. H. T. Walker somehow managed to get in front of William Loring's troops, and the combative Loring complained to Johnston. Walker shot back, "I am sorry that by a mismanagement of mine the general was subjected to any inconvenience," and then with the sarcasm over he lambasted Loring. Walker blamed the delay on artillery batteries watering their horses and also found fault with Loring himself declaring there were no quartermasters in Walker's command. Walker barked that "he was just as liable to be mistaken as the division quartermaster, and I trust the next time he comes into my division to hunt up quartermasters, he will be sure of his report before he accuses officers of not being in their places." With friends such as these, who needed Sherman's opposition?[32]

The war of words continued between Johnston and Richmond as well, a new argument flaming up around this time over Johnston's belief that his transfer to Mississippi removed his ability to command in Tennessee, in particular to transfer troops from Bragg's army to Vicksburg. Davis took him to task over it, calling it a "strange error" of judgment, but Davis then took the opportunity presented and worked on removing Johnston from full department command. For his part, Johnston argued that "an officer having a task like mine, far above his ability, cannot in addition command other remote departments. No general can command separate armies." Johnston biographer Craig Symonds simply labeled the affair a "silly quarrel."[33]

By July 3, Johnston's force had reached the Brownsville area, most camping between that hamlet and the Big Black River. Then all stopped, as the next several days were spent in sending out scouts and reconnaissances, mainly toward the Big Black River crossings that Sherman had covered so well. Forward scouts reported the enemy fortifications very strong: "as far as he could see line of intrenchments extending in the direction of Bovina. Fortifications on the hills and timber cleared away in the direction of Big Black." In fact, Johnston found the roads so blocked that he admitted "the reconnaissances, which occupied the 2d and 3d, convinced me that attack north of the railroad

was impracticable. I determined, therefore, to make the examinations necessary for the attempt south of the railroad; thinking, from what was already
known, that the chance for success was much better there, although the consequences of defeat might be more disastrous."[34]

Finding roads to move on also presented a problem, which was also an
omission of Johnston and his faulty staff work. The question was: Why had
all this preparation work not been done before now, causing two full days of
delay? French related that on July 3 he rode over to Johnston's headquarters
on Carney Creek and met him. Also present were Loring, Walker, and cavalry
commander Jackson. French related the frustration of chaos, writing in his
diary that "if there be any one thing in this part of the country more difficult
than all others, it is to find a person who knows the roads ten miles from his
home." He went on: "*Nine* hours were spent in vainly attempting to get accurate information from the citizens respecting the roads and streams. But
little could be learned of the country on either side of the Big Black that was
satisfactory, because it was so contradictory."[35]

An obvious explanation for the needless delay was that Johnston was not
really intent on doing much more than showing a force to the Federals and
anyone else who might try to blame him for the ultimate fall of Vicksburg,
which by this time was, to his mind, a done deal. Wasting more time, Johnston
simply sent a courier, who was ultimately captured by the Federals, to Pemberton on July 3 carrying a message stating that he would create a diversion
so Pemberton could "cut his way out, and that I hoped to attack the enemy
about the 7th." It could have been done if Johnston wanted to, one of his
Confederates writing that they were so near the enemy that "we can pick up
a cheap fight just any time a fighting fit comes on."[36]

An analysis of Johnston's effort indicates he was more interested in showing force than actually using it. Pemberton had informed Johnston on June 15
that he was "living on greatly reduced rations, but I think sufficient for twenty
days yet." If that day was counted, twenty days from then was July 4. Pemberton had followed that up with another message on June 22 or 23 (Johnston
said June 22, but the version in the *Official Records* says June 23, although it
did not appear in Pemberton's letter book at all). In that note, he stated that he
would "strain every nerve to hold out, if there is hope of our ultimate relief,
for fifteen days longer." If the day it was written according to Johnston's account is included, that would put fifteen days at July 6. It is significant that, either way, Johnston waited until the last minute to help, probably knowing he

would not make any difference. And there is the chance that he set the July 7 day of attack with a firm belief that Pemberton could only hold out those twenty days from June 15 (July 4) or even fifteen days from June 22 (July 6), both of which put Johnston's relief effort *after* Pemberton's longest self-stated chance of holding out.[37]

Johnston's lethargy was exactly what Sherman and Grant wanted, of course, but even that was misconstrued. One Federal noted the captured messages stated that Pemberton told Johnston he could hold out until July 4. He wrote on July 1: "According to that they have but 3 days to go." Especially perplexing were the misinterpreted probings south of the railroad, Osterhaus and others detecting these efforts and sending messages of panic up the chains of command. Small skirmishes were frequent, with the Confederates often laying an "ambush" for the scouting Federals. Word of a Confederate force of twelve thousand men moving southward toward Hankinson's Ferry eventually emerged, mostly emanating from civilians in the area, although there was a small but "obstinate conflict," according to Major James Wilson, with the 15th Illinois Cavalry. Grant alerted Sherman of reports, "on information received from citizens east of the river, that 12,000 of Johnston's troops have passed south of Baldwin's ferry." Grant added, "I place no great reliance in the information, but it may prove true. Do you learn anything from Johnston?"[38]

While such news was seemingly impossible or at best illogical, Grant nevertheless erred on the side of caution and sent troops to make sure of his rear south of the railroad. Herron dismissed the force as "probably a scout of their cavalry," but Ord asked, "shall I send out a brigade with artillery to the south, to meet the reported march?" Grant thought it was a good idea, telling Ord "if it is really true that the enemy have 12,000 troops at Hankinson's ferry, they should be met." Ord sent Michael Lawler's brigade, and Grant cautioned Herron to prepare one of his to go in support if necessary. Updating Sherman, Grant explained that Ord was sending the brigade and surmised that "they may try a direction to the south of the city, with a view of drawing as much force in that direction as possible. I will let you know all that takes place as early as possible."[39]

The heavily rotund Michael Lawler led his brigade southeastward to the Big Black River, but he saw or heard very little. It was mostly just a hard march for his troops. Not all liked him as a result of how the affair was handled, one Iowan describing him as "a General on horseback, who had never marched a mile in his life on foot." Worse was when Lawler found nothing at the river and returned on just as hard a march. "As the General was still on horseback, and anxious to get back to his quarters, it was again a forced march," one of his disgruntled soldiers complained.[40]

Sherman appreciated the help but left nothing to chance. He informed Osterhaus of the rumored developments south of the railroad, stating, "It becomes us to leave nothing to conjecture." Still, he concluded, "I don't think he [Johnston] will put his army in such a pocket." But Johnston was somewhere, and the fact that Sherman could not locate him was a problem. "I have been along my front," Sherman added, "and the silence and absence of an enemy is more ominous to me than the sharpshooting at Vicksburg. We must discover the whereabouts of our enemy positively." He particularly wanted his best scout, named Tuttle, sent out to the south: "If an army is passing or has passed, he can easily distinguish the fact by signs, or he may in his own way personate a straggler, and find out all from some farmer or negro." At the same time, Sherman kept his divisions busy continually fortifying and blocking roads, one Ohioan describing how it was done: "The process is very simple—fell all the trees in the neighborhood." Parke's easterners did much of the work, one Pennsylvanian admitting that the labor "nearly killed us, the climate of Mississippi being so much warmer than we had been accustomed to." A New Hampshire soldier similarly declared that his regiment was not so used to work and that "acres and acres were laid low; trees were felled in all directions; and the wonder is that half of the men were not killed. Some did cut their feet, and others were injured by falling trees."[41]

Eventually, the rumors to the south faded away, prompting one frustrated Federal cavalryman to write "we are getting tired of waiting and watching for him." That the weather was increasingly hot and dry made the waiting even worse, one Massachusetts soldier in Parke's corps telling of the lack of water and the bitterness when it was found that the landowner where they were camped had hidden a spring with a cover and three inches of dirt. A slave told the soldiers and they uncovered it, the New Englander writing, "If I had my way he would be shot or hung on the nearest tree." Even so, Confederates in small numbers eventually began to appear on Sherman's front as Johnston's forces trudged westward and then stopped to scout, producing some slight skirmishing around the river crossings at Bridgeport and Messenger's. McArthur reported Confederates on his front at Hooker's Ferry on July 2. "General McArthur reports the enemy preparing a battery on the bluff opposite

Hooker's, looking to that passage also," Sherman informed Osterhaus. This was more of what Sherman expected, and he was ready. To the Osterhaus note he added, "We cannot prevent the passage of Big Black River, but must attack his column or columns [as] they make their appearance."[42]

As the land armies vacillated, the navy continued its important work on the rivers. In fact, one of the most underemphasized cogs in the Vicksburg Campaign was the United States Navy. The mere fact that the Federals had one—a large and powerful one at that—and the Confederates had nothing in comparison is evidence enough that the navy was a factor. While the navy's roles in passing the Vicksburg batteries earlier in April and ferrying the army across the river to Bruinsburg were perhaps the height of its importance, the navy's role in the siege was also of mammoth consequence. Despite most of the fighting being done by the army on land, prompting Admiral Porter himself to lament that "the Navy has necessarily performed a less conspicuous part in the . . . [siege] than the Army," the water service's role was nevertheless integral. And for what it did, Porter added, "it has been employed in a manner highly credible to all concerned."[43]

The navy under Admiral Porter, with his flag flying from the *Black Hawk*, assumed numerous duties during the siege of Vicksburg. Not the least among these was the continual ferrying of supplies safely to the army at Vicksburg. Grant always knew the key to taking Vicksburg was acquiring an open supply line via the Yazoo River at Snyder's and Haynes' Bluffs and Chickasaw Bayou. Porter agreed, and soon supplies began to flow, in fact even before the failed May 22 assaults. The vessels also brought tens of thousands of troops to Vicksburg. Porter was instrumental not only in moving the great loads of cargo to the landing areas but also in guarding the movement of the transports and supplies along a thin line of easily corrupted river miles from Memphis down to Vicksburg: "I stationed the smaller class of gunboats to keep the banks of the Mississippi clear of guerillas, who were assembling in force and with a large number of cannon to block up the river and cut off the transports bringing down supplies, reinforcements, and ammunition for the army," Porter explained.[44]

The fighting of course garnered more coverage, and the navy did not fail to do its duty there as well. Essentially, Porter had two flotillas in the Mississippi Squadron, consisting of those vessels above and below Vicksburg.

Running the batteries was not a welcomed idea, so those gunboats and transports that had done so on April 16 and 22 and others that had found themselves south of Vicksburg beforehand made up one part of Porter's force. The senior commander down there was at first Commander Selim E. Woodworth onboard the *General Price* and then Lieutenant Commander James A. Greer, commanding the gunboat *Benton*. Woodworth and Greer had the bulk of the major gunboats with them, they having passed the batteries in April to battle Grand Gulf's big guns and ferry the army across the river. Included among them was Greer's own *Benton* as well as the gunboats *Carondelet*, *Lafayette*, *Louisville*, *Mound City*, *Pittsburg*, and *Tuscumbia*, as well as smaller vessels such as the *General Price* and *Switzerland*, some of them captured from the Confederates earlier in the war, mostly at Memphis. Being away from Porter, both officers sent detailed daily reports to the admiral who remained north of Vicksburg.[45]

North of the city was a much smaller flotilla, and it had numerous duties both on the Mississippi River confronting Vicksburg's northern defenses as well as patrolling and operating on the Yazoo River. Since most of the heavy ironclads had gone south, only a few gunboats remained north of the city, including Porter's flagship *Black Hawk* as well as the *Baron de Kalb* and *Cincinnati* before it sank on May 27. Several smaller armed vessels without the ironclad plating also patrolled this portion of the Mississippi and Yazoo Rivers. Also operating in the northern zone were the seven vessels of the Mississippi Marine Brigade under Brigadier General Alfred W. Ellet.[46]

Added to the normal riverine vessels were the many mortar boats, and they primarily carried out their major duty north and west of Vicksburg, bombarding the city and the Confederates mercilessly despite the rumor that each shot cost thirty dollars. "The mortar boats have been at work for forty-two days without intermission," Porter reported, "throwing shells into all parts of the city, even reaching the works in rear of Vicksburg and in front of our troops, a distance of 3 miles." The mortar boats under Gunner Eugene Mack poured an almost constant barrage of projectiles into the city. One paroled Federal who had been inside Vicksburg told him, "I came near planting a shell in the headquarters of General Pemberton, and that a little more powder would reach them." Mack confessed, "That was good news to me." Porter was satisfied, reporting to Washington that "the mortars keep constantly playing on the city and works, and the gunboats throw in their shell whenever they see any work going on at the batteries, or new batteries being put up." Late in the siege, Alfred Ellet described how "your mortars are doing good work this morning. Every shell is thrown into the city, or bursts immediately over it. But few people can be seen moving about."[47]

While most of that firing fell to the mortar boats, the gunboats patrolled and fired on targets of opportunity, although Porter cautioned his commanders not to waste ammunition. "I am told there is a party of rebels at work burning rifle pits down toward the water and in the direction of one of the lower batteries," Porter wrote. "I want these workers annoyed as much as possible without wasting shell. The *Mound City* and *Benton* will reconnoiter constantly, one at a time, and when any workers are seen, drive them out. Fire but seldom and then with effect." In addition, crews placed three huge guns on scows, a 9-inch, a 10-inch, and a 100-pound rifle. These could be maneuvered to where they were needed and did heavy damage to the Confederate water batteries.[48]

At times, special targets appeared that Porter wanted taken out. One such worrisome cannon was the Confederate artillery piece nicknamed "Whistling Dick" in one of the southernmost river batteries. Porter wanted shots sent toward it often, he telling Greer that "our long ranges are better than his." Nearby was also an area Porter determined contained the cattle herd for the garrison and city. "The enemy have sent all their cattle up there," he told Greer; "they are below the hill, on this side of it, in the hollow. We have killed a good many of their beeves with mortar shells, which are running short, so we must keep up the fire with the gunboats." Porter added, "The object is to burst the shells about 50 feet above the ground."[49]

Porter scolded Greer at times, writing on June 4 that "I took your bearings last night" and determined that the "shells all fell short." He continued, "If you want to do any good, you will have to move up closer than that." For his part, Greer reported that he had seen the Confederates moving their cattle, horses, and mules and that he was surprised by Porter's note: "Had I been asked previous to receiving your letter, I would have been willing to swear that our shells fell into the town."[50]

On numerous occasions, the navy's bombardment was at the behest of army commanders on land, and their heavy ordnance severely damaged the Confederate works. This was especially so with the commands nearest the river, Herron's division to the south and Steele's division of Sherman's (later Steele's own) corps to the north. Sherman, Steele, and Herron frequently corresponded with naval commanders about where to fire and where not to, and at times the army and navy coordinated by sending officers to each other for collaboration. A "system of night pickets" was also developed between those on the river and shore, and signs and countersigns were established.[51]

The biggest coordinated bombardment came on June 20. Grant requested Porter's flotilla to join in, and Porter did with gusto, opening with his mortars as well as the gunboats and even artillery placed on the De Soto Peninsula. "There was no response whatever," Porter recalled. There was also a delay, given that a heavy fog had rolled in during the night that did not lift until later in the morning. Lieutenant Byron Wilson, commanding the *Mound City*, reported, "We were obliged to lie there some time, owing to the intense fog which hung over the hills, and it was not till 7:35 that we were enabled to throw a shell with any certainty."[52]

There were times when the naval firing came a little too close and the army had to gingerly ask for redirection. Grant wrote to Porter on May 27, for example, that "General Lauman, on our left, informs me that your firing to-day did good execution, but several shots were too far to the left, your right going into his camp." Before his removal, McClernand similarly wrote to Grant: "I am happy to congratulate Admiral Porter through you on the improved and successful effect of the fire of this evening. Many of the shells have exploded over the enemy's works. Any higher elevation would probably bring them upon my lines; perhaps their effect would be increased by lowering their range." Herron similarly wrote, "The boats could move a little farther up while shelling. The enemy have a mortar in that work that is annoying us terribly."[53]

A novel way the navy supported the bombardment on land was by actually bringing guns ashore and working them with navy crews. The most notable was the one on Sherman's front, which the general had not at all been excited about but allowed due to interservice goodwill. Lieutenant Commander Thomas O. Selfridge, Jr., who had been in command of the ill-fated *Cairo* when it sank in the Yazoo River in December, set up two 8-inch guns on the northern reaches of the Union lines, although it was arduous and Selfridge claimed he had little help from the army. "As usual," he bemoaned, "the army promises everything, but I have had to do all the work." He was able to get one gun in action by June 5, although the other was delayed by a missing bolt, "which is indispensable," a frustrated Selfridge reported. Still, he was excited about his chances of getting into action: "There is a long 42-pounder in front of me that I shall endeavor to knock down," he explained to Porter, "afterwards I shall direct my fire upon the town." Later, he added that "our firing thus far has been excellent, though we have nothing especial to fire at." Still, he managed to get off about 150 shots a day and some even during the night, every fifteen minutes. Selfridge later described how his men worked hard: "The labor imposed upon them was very arduous, working their guns under a hot sun, and frequently employed half the night repairing the damage inflicted during the day."[54]

Two other naval batteries also went up, although army cannoneers crewed some of them. One was on McPherson's lines in Logan's division on the Jackson Road and the other on Herron's front. Logan's guns were 9-inch Dahlgrens, and the guns sent to Herron were two 32-pounders, complete with both ten- and fifteen-second fuses. Acting Master J. F. Reed of the *Benton* accompanied the guns to command the pieces, even though they had army crews. Herron named the battery after the gunboat: Battery Benton. Eventually, Porter had as many as thirteen naval guns on shore on the Vicksburg side of the river, including some of the guns from the sunken *Cincinnati* put into batteries atop the ridges as well as in fortifications built on the shore next to the sunken vessel, which provided a new angle of bombardment for Vicksburg as well as cover for those working on the boat itself. The navy also facilitated the movement of other large siege cannons for the army, Grant informing McClernand of one such deposit on land and bidding him to hurry and get them as "they are in danger of being lost from the caving in of the bank."[55]

Additionally, Porter placed a 20-pound Parrott "on the point opposite Vicksburg" for the purpose of taking out a steam-powered factory in the city. Captain Thomas C. Groshon commanded the piece, and Alfred Ellet reported that, despite return fire from at least five Confederate cannons, "the gun accomplished all for which it was intended. The work at the foundry was stopped, the boiler having been exploded by a shot, and considerable damage was done to that and other buildings." Ellet surmised that "we had reached some tender spot, of which the enemy are particularly watchful."[56]

Porter himself sometimes came on land, including the early episode when he became overheated and had to return to the *Black Hawk*. Later in the siege, in mid-June, he also tried to go to Grant's headquarters, but a watchful picket turned him away. "I regret the stupidity, of the picket in preventing you getting out to camp yesterday," Grant apologized, but added, "the propensity of officers as well as men to loaf off to the Steamboat landing makes it necessary to give strict orders against persons passing without permits. . . . I hope Admiral you will not be deterred by your experience of yesterday from making us another call." For his part, Porter took it in stride, telling Grant, "I hope Joe Johnston may have as hard a time as I had," although he readily admitted that the picket "saved my neck, my horse had been dancing about and standing on his hind legs for some time, and it was very uncertain how long it would be before he landed me in Chickasaw Bayou." An officer with Porter joked that "he thinks I was glad of an excuse to turn back, he admits that he was; as his horse was rather more frisky than suited the habits of a sailor." In another episode, Porter's men somehow obtained a pool table, apparently from the neighborhood, one writing, "I suppose that after Vicksburg is ours General Grant and the Admiral will have a game of billiards on board the *Black Hawk*."[57]

When the theory of the Confederates escaping on hundreds of skiffs emerged, Porter was energetic in trying to stop it, even ordering bonfires ready to be lit on the banks when it happened. "I wish you to keep the strictest lookout at night and see that no skiff or boat comes out from Vicksburg or attempts to cross the river," Porter ordered. Later, when the plan really became a major fear, he tasked the gunboats to keep a vigilant watch and, if Confederates appeared, to "go right in amongst them and give them grape and canister right and left, fore and aft. . . . I need not tell you the importance of using great vigilance." In another note, Porter again warned to "push up amidst them" but cautioned "looking out that they are not boarded." He also admonished not to take time to pick any Confederates out of the water. Porter similarly warned, at Grant's behest, of a possible attack on the Louisiana side "when Johnston attacks our outposts."[58]

In order to aid the destruction of Confederate morale, Porter and his officers also devised leaflets to be sent into Vicksburg, and Commander Woodworth created an easy way of doing it. "I am having a number of kites made, and shall have them landed into Vicksburg to-night or to-morrow morning." Woodworth thought this idea "will be more sure of reaching the parties for whom they are intended than the shell."[59]

The intense work required of the naval crews was difficult, but there were additional problems that periodically developed that caused Porter to have to adapt as the siege wore on. Some were of the bizarre and novel type, such as floodwaters washing out the shore where Union dead had been buried at Grand Gulf. "The bank caved in," one officer wrote, "and the coffins have tumbled out. It is a sad sight, and humanity and respect for our fallen comrades demand this duty." On another occasion, a leak in the *Louisville*'s "bread room" caused the loss of six hundred pounds of bread as well as some beef and flour.[60]

Other problems were more serious, such as at times a dire lack of ammunition, everything from shell to rockets used to communicate. Gunner Mack commanding the mortars reported on June 9 that he fired "175 mortars from daylight until 11:30 a. m. I would have continued the firing this afternoon, but our ammunition commenced to look small, together with being taken quite unwell myself. The men also complained of being overworked a little too much, and I thought a good rest would be an improvement." The Confederates noticed, asking, "what was the matter?" All sorts of rumors explained away the peace, but the civilians and soldiers inside Vicksburg nevertheless took advantage of the slowdown in mortar firing, and one Confederate chaplain noted that "the whole town seemed to breathe freer. Now one could see ladies walking the streets at their leisure—not with the hurried, uneasy step that marked their gate during the bombardment." Then he noted, "But, alas! This quiet did not last long." On another occasion, Mack reported that "the heavy rain this morning has made the men very wet and uncomfortable," but the main issue was that "there is a general murmur among the men about the meat ration not being enough, and they say they only average meat once a day. . . . These men are continually grumbling about hard work and little meat."[61]

The ordnance used also proved problematic. In reporting how his mortar crews fired 193 shells on June 11 at five-minute intervals, Mack added that "the fuses which we are now using are some of the kind used against Island No. 10, and I have found out that many of them are so poorly manufactured that the composition is soft and mealy, which accounts for the many close explosions of shell to the mortar boats and halfway to the city."[62]

Other issues also took vessels out of service periodically. Recoaling and cleaning boilers was a necessary but time-consuming process. Greer requested permission to take the *Benton* out of service to clean the boilers on June 16, arguing that "it is forty days since they were cleaned." Fuel was another issue, one officer reporting "not a pound of coal to move his vessel." Another officer reported that the *Mound City* on June 20 had "barely sufficient [coal] to take her back to her position but she will cut wood enough to prepare herself for any brief emergency." Although the gunboats used much less coal while sitting stationary in the river on guard duty, part of the fuel problem was fixed by locating and retrieving coal from the sunken vessels in the river, especially the barges that were floated southward and had been sunk by Confederate fire.[63]

Then there were problems with the crews themselves. "I am sorry to say," Porter reported to Washington, "the health of the squadron is not good. We have many sick officers and men, and the duty has been incessant and most laborious, working in a very hot sun." One sailor described how "it is very hot down here so I slept on the hurricane deck for the past three nights." Porter went on to say, "Still, the men and officers never murmur, and stand their posts until they can stand no longer." That was not the full story, however, as desertions did occur. Lieutenant Commander Elias K. Owen commanding the *Louisville* described losing two crew members: "Whilst at Rodney 2 of my men deserted. They were perfectly worthless." Another commander reported "the desertion of two white boys." Of course, it cut the other way too, and many deserting Confederates tried to flee to safety along the river and fell right into Union hands. One officer sent Porter several "very equivocal individuals who gave themselves up to Captain Wilson, of the *Mound City*." In one episode, the navy picked up a professed Confederate deserter who later "confessed he is a deserter from the Fifty-third Indiana Volunteers."[64]

Other myriad problems also cropped up as the weeks passed, such as the falling water levels in the river. Porter had to warn the southern flotilla: "I do not think it safe any longer for the gunboats to go up above the towheads or on the opposite side unless specifically ordered to do so. The water is falling very fast, and you will hereafter keep on the canal side." Other problems emerged in communication with the land forces, especially Joseph Mower on the peninsula opposite Vicksburg. Commander Woodworth informed Porter that "Colonel Ellet and myself have made several attempts to find General Mower, to obtain each night the countersign for our pickets and picket boat, but we have been unable to do so."[65]

Even as Grant and Dana were keeping the War Department apprised of the situation, Porter was doing the same with Secretary of the Navy Gideon Welles. "The army is still advancing close to the works," he reported on June 9. "General Sherman is so close that he can not get nearer without going in." Porter added that victory was sure except for the chance of relief from the rear: "If the city is not relieved by a much superior force from the outside, Vicksburg must fall without anything more being done to it. I only wonder it has held out so long. If the city is relieved, and our army have to retire, we will lose everything we have. . . . If we do not get Vicksburg now, we never will." Another report on June 26 sounded Porter's impatience: "I was in hopes ere this to have announced the fall of Vicksburg, but the rebels hold out persistently, and will no doubt do so while there is a thing left to eat." Porter related that the enemy's only hope was in Johnston—and that was a false hope.[66]

In short, the navy acquitted itself wonderfully. Porter reported as of July 4 that "the mortars have fired 7,000 mortar shells, and the gunboats 4,500; 4,500 have been fired from the naval guns on shore, and we have supplied over 6,000 to the different army corps." The reduction of Vicksburg was certainly not an all-army show, and a grateful Grant later articulated

> an expression of thankfulness for my good fortune in being placed in co-operation with an officer of the Navy who accords to every move that seems for the interest and success of our arms his hearty and energetic support. Admiral Porter and the very efficient officers under him have ever shown the greatest readiness in their co-operation, no matter what was to be done or what risk to be taken, either by their men or their vessels. Without this prompt and cordial support, my movements would have been much embarrassed, if not wholly defeated.

Put simply, Grant later stated "the navy under Porter was all it could be."[67]

Porter agreed, telling a gathering of navy veterans meeting on the twenty-fifth anniversary of the passing of the Vicksburg batteries (April 16, 1888) that "Vicksburg was a hard place to take, but there were Western sailors there with hearts of oak, in Western iron walls." He concluded that "the opening of the passage by those forts, and of the river down to New Orleans, was one of the grandest achievements of the war, not only for the dangers that were run, but for the fortitude and endurance exhibited throughout the whole contest by Western officers and men, who never had any superiors on the face of the earth."[68]

As much as Ulysses S. Grant was the mastermind behind Union success, he nevertheless did not do it alone. On land, he had a large cadre of general officers to command corps, divisions, and brigades, and even though all were not first rate, there were enough to leaven the entire army and make it successful.

Yet what is truly remarkable is not the ability of the general officers—which perhaps dwindled slightly with the infusion of so many reinforcements (there was a reason, perhaps, that certain XVI Corps units had been initially left behind)—but the adaptability of the army and its commander to navigate a huge number of changes amid the army's high command. During the siege, two of Grant's three corps commanders, two of ten division commanders, and numerous brigade commanders changed, and that was just in the army that he approached Vicksburg with. Those arriving units of the IX and XVI Corps as well as Herron's division brought brand-new officers that had to be amalgamated into the army system Grant used. He most effectively did this by placing new units in the rear, although a few of these new troops wound up almost seamlessly on the front lines at Vicksburg as well.

Those generals did the best they could amid trying circumstances, some-times of their own making. Of course, the McClernand affair netted a change in the XIII Corps, but not before McClernand put his stamp on the activi-ties of the corps. He had originally made his headquarters on May 25 at "a cleaner, higher place" and then later moved to "a more agreeable and pleasant location." There were always interesting events around McClernand's head-quarters, including an escaped prisoner who was caught, McClernand having him tied up until morning. McClernand's temperament also kept things on edge; Lieutenant Colonel Don Pardee of the 42nd Ohio noted, "He is a petu-lant, cross old cuss, and when he talks to me as I have heard him talk to some others of his staff, there will be a row." More interestingly, McClernand's wife arrived on June 1 for an overnight visit, causing some stir. "She is a very handsome woman—about 20—not more," wrote one astonished staff officer. "The Gen'l is near 48."[69]

Times were lively around Logan's headquarters in the XVII Corps as well. One Federal noted he went to headquarters "to examine his approaches and hear the General *cuss things generally*." Logan often drank, especially in nearly nightly trips to Grant's headquarters to drink with the army's medical director. One night reportedly saw Logan playing the fiddle and several black servants dancing joyously. Logan's headquarters sat on the south side of the Jackson Road near Battery Logan, which included the two navy Dahlgrens. It was here that he was apparently hit in the back of the thigh by a glancing bullet while leaning back in a chair in his tent. He had a surgeon dig the bullet out but swore him to secrecy. It kept him from getting in the saddle for only a few days.[70]

Other generals were not so vocal and amusing—perhaps only the politicians were—but all had their own way of doing things, and some relished the thrill of being at the front. Many were often in the works. One Federal reported how he scampered through small trenches and covered ways to a forward battery only to surprisingly find brigade commander Giles A. Smith there. Grant and Sherman were often together, at times at the front as well. One Illinoisan noted that "almost every day Gen. Grant came to our front, very often accompanied by Gen. Sherman."[71]

Others moved about in the boredom, one Federal describing how "division and corps commanders are riding leisurely around the lines. We gaze upon them as they pass with a suspicious look think they will require some unpleasant work of us some future day." Another described how "old Gen. Smith was out looking at things tonight." Others stayed to themselves in camp, reading and relaxing, while many visited one another. Giles Smith, still hurting from his hip wound from the May 19 assault, ate lunch with William Orme on occasion.[72]

Much of the change in high command leadership came on the divisional and particularly brigade level. In McClernand's XIII Corps, in addition to McClernand and Ord switching places, there was actually less change than in the other corps. There was some sickness among the commanders, including division commander Eugene Carr, who had a myriad of problems, not the least of which were reoccurrences of malaria. He also had a urinary/prostate issue that forced him to take medicine that caused diarrhea. He was hardly able to perform his duties by late in the siege. Similarly, Brigadier General William P. Benton went home from his brigade on May 31 due to "chronic dysentery of long standing"; Colonel Henry D. Washburne of the 18th Indiana first took command of the brigade and then gave way to Colonel David Shunk of the 8th Indiana (Benton arrived back before the siege ended). A slightly wounded Lieutenant Colonel Job Parker left the 48th Ohio, but its original colonel, Peter Sullivan, who was wounded dreadfully at Shiloh, soon appeared to command the regiment.[73]

More change took place in Sherman's XV Corps. Sherman himself left to take command of the rear on June 22, leaving the corps to ranking division commander Frederick Steele, who was himself somewhat ill. Steele's ascension opened the division command to the ranking brigadier, John Thayer, whose brigade then went to a new commander as well. Also in that division, Colonel Francis Manter was outranked when Colonel Bernard G. Farrar arrived back with the army, Manter taking a position on Steele's staff. Battery commanders were also susceptible to changes when injuries occurred, such as when the "Flying Dutchman," Captain Clemens Landgraeber, was wounded.[74]

Frank Blair's division also saw changes, Blair himself leaving for a few days to command the first major foray to the rear in late May. A major change occurred when Brigadier General Joseph A. J. Lightburn took command of Colonel Thomas Kilby Smith's brigade on May 24, causing him to be relieved. Smith had shown some concern earlier, writing to his mother that "there are brigadier-generals here, with bright, new stars upon their shoulders, but without command, who are doubtless eagerly seeking my place. Perhaps I shall be compelled to give way." Once it happened, he queried Sherman, "it is of vital interest to me to know if the order relieving me can be construed as a reflection on my conduct of the command or my personal bearing in the late engagement." (His mother also wrote a flurry of letters, including to the secretaries of war and treasury and to Lincoln himself.) Sherman replied that it was nothing of the kind but was mandatory because Lightburn was a brigadier general and had been assigned to him for Blair's division, and there was no other place to put him. Smith was not assuaged and threatened to resign, but Grant allowed him an out so that he would not have to embarrassingly return to his regiment after commanding a brigade. Grant made him a staff officer and sent him on several errands, including to Port Hudson to deal with Nathaniel Banks. For his part, Lightburn, a corporal in the Mexican–American War, "appears to be a very nice man great big stout healthy man." That said, one of Smith's soldiers described him as a "total stranger" and called it an "unwelcome assignment." Field officers also changed, including Colonel Benjamin Spooner's command of the 83rd Indiana.[75]

James Tuttle's division saw two brigades change hands. Colonel Joseph J. Woods of the 12th Iowa took command of the brigade in Sherman's corps when Charles Matthies left to command a brigade in the XVII Corps. Similarly, Ralph Buckland left his brigade because of a high fever in late June, with the ranking colonel, William L. McMillen of the 95th Ohio, taking over. Lower-level commanders also changed, such as Colonel Andrew J. Weber of the 11th Missouri being mortally wounded on June 29 across the river, he "being struck on the head with a piece of shell from the enemy's guns."[76]

McPherson's XVII Corps also saw a good deal of change, including a division commander. Isaac Quinby had earlier in the campaign gone home sick, replaced by Marcellus M. Crocker. Crocker then became sick himself and returned the division to Quinby, who was actually not fully recovered. He lasted only through June 3, when he left the army, never to return due to "almost utter inability for physical exertion" and for "chronic diarrhea." McPherson sent Brigadier General John E. Smith from one of Logan's brigades to take over the division, he writing to his wife that "my command consists of 12 Regiments and 4 Batteries and will keep me busy." In that division, brigade commander Colonel Samuel Holmes went home for medical reasons and Colonel Green B. Raum took over. Similarly, a shuffle took place to replace George Boomer, who had been killed on May 22, the brigade first going to Colonel Holden Putnam. Soon, a brigadier general, the aforementioned Charles Matthies, arrived from Sherman's corps to command.[77]

Of course, Smith leaving Logan's division for his own command necessitated a change in that division, with Brigadier General Mortimer D. Leggett, who actually commanded a different brigade in the division, taking Smith's old one and fighting with it at the crater on June 25. One of his new soldiers remarked that "he is a nice man." To replace Leggett, Logan gave the brigade command to Colonel Manning F. Force of the 20th Ohio. Force received a nice note from Leggett upon assuming command: "Enclosed find order, assigning you to command of the 2d brigade. You may be assured I leave the Brigade with feelings of sadness—but to no other hand would I be so willing to yield its command as to yours. You have my best wishes for your complete success & I hope the day is not far distant when your *rank* shall correspond with your new command." Lower-level field officers also changed, such as when Colonel Francis Hassendeubel of the 17th Missouri was in the forward trenches talking with General Leggett and others when a grenade exploded and tore into his chest. He was carried to the rear and to "words of solace while being carried out . . . answered quietly 'I am done for.'" Conversely, the colonel of the 124th Illinois, Thomas J. Sloan, had been under arrest since May 13. Lieutenant Colonel John H. Howe was then in command, but Sloan was released on June 18.[78]

In McArthur's division, Colonel Alexander Chambers, who had been on leave, returned and took command of William Hall's brigade. The brigade was by then back from the expedition eastward and took a position in reserve aiding Ransom's men. In Ransom's brigade, attrition was so high that a lieutenant commanded the 11th Illinois after the assaults.[79]

Many other changes also came to the field officers at the regimental level, and perhaps that was where it was felt the most. One Indianan wrote home that his major's bravery "makes us tremble. I have seen him walk along in front of our advanced skirmishers just as quiet and cool as if nothing were going on, while the rebels were pouring a perfect shower of bullets all around him." While no general officers were killed in the siege itself, George Boomer perished in the May 22 assault before siege operations formally began. At that time, many field officers were also killed and wounded, producing change much closer to the men in the ranks. Others fought continual pain, one Illinoisan describing how an officer in the 15th Illinois made his rounds with his "corkleg squeaking like a shutter in windy weather."[80]

By July 1, John Pemberton knew the game was about up, one courier describing how he "expects in a very short time to have to fight enemy with bayonets." The "Many Soldiers" letter had left him shaken, and he could tell matters were coming to a head. Others gave the same indications, one of his engineers who had been up to the works on the Graveyard Road declaring to him that they "were no longer tenable," to which Pemberton responded that the same was true almost everywhere. Another declared that with the Federals so close—within hearing distance—that only "with difficulty I could keep the men at work, only doing so by making frequent changes of men." Pemberton explained: "I felt satisfied that the time had arrived when it was necessary either to evacuate the city and cut my way out or to capitulate upon the best attainable terms." Conditions were about to bottom out in Vicksburg, and Johnston of course showed no signs of help. Surrender or escape seemed to be the only choices, and "my own inclination," Pemberton wrote, "led me to favor the former." The indecisive general wanted backing, however, and thus wrote each of his division commanders for their opinions. To Bowen, Stevenson, Forney, and Smith went the query directing them to "inform me with as little delay as possible as to the condition of your troops, and their ability to make the marches and undergo the fatigues necessary to accomplish a successful evacuation." He cautioned them, in case the garrison needed to hold out longer, to "use the utmost discretion while informing yourself through your subordinates upon all points tending to a clear elucidation of the subjects of my inquiry."[81]

The responses were quick and decisive, each one being dated the next day, July 2. Carter Stevenson noted that his men had high morale, "but from long confinement (more than forty-five days) in the trenches on short rations [they] are necessarily much enfeebled, and a considerable number would be unable to make the marches and undergo the fatigues which would probably be necessary to make a successful evacuation of this city." He said most men would not be able to make the Big Black in one day if pressed, although "most of them, rather than be captured, would exert themselves to the utmost to accomplish it." He passed on his brigade commanders' thoughts as well, which were unanimous in their opinion that the troops would want to cut their way out but that it would be suicidal: "If an honorable capitulation could be effected it would be the best and wisest course, considering the condition of the men." Only Stephen D. Lee made any dissent, writing on July 3, "I do not think it is time to surrender this garrison and post yet. . . . I still have hopes of Johnston relieving the garrison."[82]

John Forney echoed Stevenson. "As heartrending as the reply may be," he said, "I have to state that I concur in the unanimous opinion of the brigade and regimental commanders, that the physical conditions and health of our men are not sufficiently good to enable them to accomplish successfully the evacuation." That said, he noted the morale of the men was still "unshaken" and that they would cheerfully continue the defense in the siege. Of particular concern in regard to a breakout attempt, as expressed by Forney's brigade commander Hébert, was that "most of my brigade are Mississippians, who I am confident will leave the ranks, and, throwing away their arms, make their way home the moment we leave our works."[83]

Martin L. Smith went farther than the others. He agreed that "a secret evacuation I consider almost impossible, on account of the temper of many in my command. . . . In other words, while under the impression that the troops will to-day resist an assault as obstinately, or perhaps more so, as when they first manned the trenches, I do not think they would do as well out of them and in the field." Then he noted that, with no evidence of relief from Johnston, "I see no chance of timely relief from him" and that "I deem it best to propose terms of capitulation before forced to do so from want of provisions." That said, one of his brigade commanders, William E. Baldwin, went on record: "I object to a surrender of the troops, and am in favor of holding the position, or attempting to do so, as long as possible."[84]

Bowen went the farthest, writing plainly that, while his men were in as good condition as any inside Vicksburg, "I do not consider them capable (physically) of enduring the hardships incident to such an undertaking.

Forty-five days of incessant duty day and night, with short rations, the wear of both mind and body incident to our situation, has had a marked effect upon them, and I am satisfied they cannot give battle and march over 10 or 12 miles in the same day." He then added, like Smith, Johnston "has never held out the slightest hope to us that the siege could be raised" and therefore "I see no alternative but to endeavor to rescue the command by making terms with the enemy." He thus recommended an "immediate proposition be made to capitulate. If accepted, we get everything we have any right to hope for; if rejected, we can still hold out stubbornly for some days, and our enemy may make the proposal to us." He argued, "If the offer is made at once, we have a better chance of making terms than when we have only one day's resistance in store in case of refusal."[85]

It seemed abundantly clear that morale was still remarkably good in the army, and the soldiers would gladly man the trenches and defend the city longer despite the obvious feeling of festivity they could hear across the lines in the Union camps. Some reported hearing bands playing. "With sufficient provisions we could hold the city long against the cowardly enemy—for their attempts to charge us have not been as bold as Hector's attack upon the Grecian walls with his brave Trojans," one confirmed. Yet lack of strength was a major concern, especially if the army had to maneuver. One Mississippian described the effects of "weeks of crouching behind our works." And the Federals used that to every advantage. One Confederate described how the "Yankees place two loaves of bread on a pole in front of our lines to tempt or tantalize hungry eyes."[86]

To make absolutely sure, Pemberton then called in his division commanders for a council of war on the night of July 2, staff officer John C. Taylor writing that it was "at the suggestion of several of his major generals." Establishing that all were unanimous that cutting their way out was impossible, he laid before them Johnston's dispatches and queried them about the potential for relief. Bowen and Smith again asserted that "I have no hopes of his doing so" and "I see no probability of his being able to raise the siege." Just to make sure once more, Pemberton reread Johnston's dispatches, which actually upon further reflection made Pemberton think "there is a more cheerful tone in his last dispatch." None of the division commanders changed their minds, however. Pemberton summed up that no one thought Johnston was a factor any longer, "whatever he may have intended."[87]

Then Pemberton went to the next subject, that is, "how long we can remain in status quo, remain as we are until we are minus food, and surrender, or make proposition." Various staff officers and heads of departments reported a dismal situation—little food and fortifications in disarray. Bowen piped up and repeated his desire "to propose to General Grant now, and then we can have some alternative after, if he refuses." The other three division commanders readily agreed. Pemberton then asked what terms to propose, and the group decided on asking that the army be able to march out with arms, personal effects, baggage, and eight days' rations. Pemberton then queried whether he himself should open the dialogue or if a commission of three officers should meet a group appointed by Grant. The generals decided on the commission, with one division commander, Bowen, among them. Bowen had known Grant in St. Louis well before the war.[88]

Pemberton also queried Colonel Edward Higgins, who commanded the river batteries, and he responded that "having no hope of General Johnston's relieving the garrison, and believing that we are unable to cut our way out," he counseled surrender. Samuel Lockett was also present, he later noting that, in terms of the engineering, "the Federal forces were within less than a minute of our defenses, so that a single dash could have precipitated them upon us in overwhelming numbers." Pemberton took it all in and elaborated that "so far as I know, not a solitary brigade or regimental commander favored the scheme of cutting out." The division commanders were all for capitulation. And Pemberton agreed—"reluctantly, I think," Stevenson added. Pemberton said that it should be done "while we still had ammunition enough left to give us the right to demand terms," but reality was not far behind when he dolefully admitted, "a surrender with or without terms was the only alternative left me."[89]

15

"VICKSBURG HAS SURRENDERED"
July 3–4

Independence Day was a special event in the United States every year, but the added patriotism of the Civil War years made it even more celebratory. For those in the North, it was a reminder of the birth of the nation and why this current war was worth fighting. In fact, there was a desire on the part of some of the naval forces to hold ceremonies on the vessels on that day, reading the Declaration of Independence. The only problem was that a copy could not be found. One of the steamboat overseers queried Grant's headquarters to see if there was one available and if they could send it along. Amid all the other issues going on at the time, John Rawlins responded, "I will if I can find one." At the least, Grant gave orders that his troops should fire a "national salute" early on the morning of July 4. For those in the South, the day was also their common heritage of independence, but it added a thought of what the Confederacy could likewise do in this "Second War of Independence."[1]

This eighty-seventh anniversary of the 1776 Declaration of Independence ("four score and seven years ago") was perhaps the most important of them all, as big events were taking place in July 1863. In Pennsylvania, Major General George G. Meade and the Army of the Potomac had just blunted the climactic Confederate attack at Gettysburg, and Robert E. Lee's Army of Northern Virginia was huddled in defensive array awaiting a counterattack and then withdrawing in defeat. In Washington, President Abraham Lincoln issued on this day a proclamation: "The President announces to the country that news from the Army of the Potomac . . . is such as to cover that army with the highest honor. . . . [H]e especially desires that on this day, He, whose will, not ours, should ever be done, be everywhere remembered and ever

reverenced with profoundest gratitude." Lincoln had waited at the War Department deep into the morning on this July 4, when the first inkling of good
news arrived. Later, he went out to the Soldier's Home.[2]

In Middle Tennessee, the Army of Tennessee under Braxton Bragg saw
itself being out-generaled as William S. Rosecrans's Army of the Cumberland
drove Bragg back toward Chattanooga in the Tullahoma Campaign, some
skirmishing still taking place even this day. Additionally, there was some
fighting attendant to John Hunt Morgan's famed raid into Union territory.[3]

There was no lack of action in the Mississippi Valley either. Confederates
under Major General Sterling Price attacked Benjamin Prentiss's garrison at
Helena, Arkansas, on the Mississippi River on July 4. It was a late and limited
attempt to aid the Vicksburg garrison, and the Confederate defeat added nothing to the chances of survival at Vicksburg. "We did the best work here on the
morning of the 4th that has been done since the war began," a boastful Federal
wrote home from Helena. Porter had warned Grant earlier of a potential attempt to cut off his supplies, and a weary Grant now had yet another concern
to fill his mind: "Your letter of yesterday places the possible intentions of
the rebels in a light I had never thought of before," he admitted to the admiral. Closer to Vicksburg but still across the river, Kirby Smith was writing
Joseph E. Johnston that very day that "the relief of Vicksburg from this side
. . . is, with the means now at my command, absolutely impracticable," also
stating that he had told Pemberton that he should "expect no aid from this
side."[4]

Likewise, the attending operations at Vicksburg went on as usual on this
Independence Day. In the Haynes' Bluff defenses, one Wisconsin soldier was
ordered to dig a trench with a buddy, but he admitted how "as it was a holiday
we did not over-exert ourselves and when night came the trench was far from
being done, so the next day two other men had to finish it." There was skirmishing on the rear line as well, when four companies of the 16th Iowa and
a detachment of the 11th Illinois Cavalry crossed the Big Black River "for
the purpose of clearing the road to Cowan's house," some two miles beyond.
A half-mile across they met the enemy, "whom they drove before them in a
slight skirmish." The Federals took position at the Cowan House and posted
pickets on the roads, only to have a larger Confederate force show up with
artillery. The Iowans fell back to the river and crossed it, covered by the 10th
Ohio Battery. That said, those on the rear lines found it odd that the continual
rumble of bombardment that emanated from Vicksburg even this far out was

absent this day; a Kentuckian in Breckinridge's division ominously noted in his journal "all quiet to-day," while one civilian in the area where Breckinridge's troops camped around Bolton noted in her diary, "General Breckinridge's division was encamped here; the soldiers being very troublesome by injuring orchards and gardens."[5]

Operations also continued at Vicksburg, although all could tell something was happening, especially with the frequent flags of truce. One Indianan declared it was yet another burial effort because of the heavy fighting around the Jackson Road in the last few days. Many others thought it might have something to do with a potential surrender of the place, but it being so near or even on July 4 it seemed just too perfect for the Federals and too harsh for the Confederates to be real. "Won't it be a joyous fourth [if so]," one wrote, "but you know we can't believe anything." Despite these odd happenings and even a no-fire truce, work went on as if nothing was certain. As an example, Colonel Oscar Malmborg continually dug toward the Confederate lines in the mine at Lightburn's approach but could tell something was amiss. He could hear odd sounds and sent Engineer William Kossak word that "he believed he was countermined by the enemy, and asking my advice." Kossak went immediately and "ascertained that the enemy was working in gallery on his right flank, 8 feet distant, on the same horizontal plane." Kossak recommended "to head the enemy's countermines by turning and crushing him." Kossak sent Malmborg two hundred pounds of powder and a fuse to do so," but before it could be touched off other events intervened.[6]

Sadly, death also continued. In the 8th Wisconsin, Henry Wingate was in the trenches merely examining a rifle when it somehow went off and killed him. A comrade related to the hometown newspaper that "I saw him after he was killed. He was interred in a metallic case. I think his brother John intends to send his remains north." In the 32nd Ohio, two men died that day of disease.[7]

All this continued work aimed at the ultimate reduction of Vicksburg. Whether it would be done by Confederate capitulation sooner or Union assault later, it would be done. And the second option would not be all that much later in coming, as Grant had by this time begun preparations for the new assault to take place on July 6. By this time, the Union lines were so close to the Confederate fortifications that a short sprint would put them over the parapets within seconds, not the long minutes under fire that the Federals had endured in the May assaults. One Mississippian declared that "the two lines were so close that the dirt from the two ditches blended together." Grant also had numerous mines ready to blow, which would aid the assaults with all coordinated into one massive blast, one Federal remarking that "it will be a good way to celebrate the 4th of July for Johnny Reb." Grant had been thinking more and more about finishing this up soon one way or another, and he left no stone unturned, even writing Herron that "a reconnaissance under the bluffs [on the far left] might disclose a weak place, where troops can be got into the City without loss. I wish you would have such reconnaissance made."[8]

Yet, signs of something huge going on at the same time were unmistakable. "There is something up at Vicksburg this morning," one Federal wrote to his wife in a postscript to a letter he was finishing, "and when I find out what [it] is I will write it." An out-of-the-loop Confederate surgeon scribbled in his diary, "Strange to say all is quiet this morning, but how long it will last no one knows." He labeled it "the only quiet we have had in 47 days." In fact, he added: "I still look for relief, but fear Johnston will put it off until the last moment."[9]

It was about time for a summation of this Vicksburg effort, one way or the other. Obviously Grant hoped for the least bloody course of action, which would be a Confederate voluntary surrender rather than an assault. Fortunately for all involved, John C. Pemberton was thinking the same thing.

There was, in fact, a lot on Pemberton's mind. Obviously, he had the entire weight of the Vicksburg garrison—both now and in history—on his shoulders. Lives were certainly at stake. He also had more personal concerns as well that wore on his conscience, even though they paled in comparison to his duty to his soldiers and the Confederacy. That dedication never wavered, but it was still a concern that no human could help but let cross their mind. Accordingly, as Pemberton began the process of capitulation well before that July 4, he wrote a note and read it to his assembled officers on the night of July 2—which all approved. He laid the issue before them and then, according to an ill Louis Hébert, "withdrew to an adjoining room." The officers backed surrender, so it was a distraught commander who opened negotiations with Grant early the next day, July 3.[10]

Pemberton certainly showed his humanity in the meeting with his officers, but also his dedication to his soldiers: "Well, gentlemen, I have heard your

votes and I agree with your almost unanimous decision, though my own preference would be to put myself at the head of my troops and make a desperate
effort to cut our way through the enemy." Whether he was genuine or just
talking boldly is not known, but he certainly had his reputation in mind when
he admitted "that is my only hope of saving myself from shame and disgrace.
Far better would it be for me to die at the head of my army, even in a vain
effort to force the enemy's lines, than to surrender it and live and meet the
obloquy which I know will be heaped upon me." Of course there were more
lives at stake than Pemberton's or his sole reputation, and he added, "but my
duty is to sacrifice myself to save the army which has so nobly done its duty
to defend Vicksburg. I therefore concur with you and shall offer to surrender
this army."[11]

Accordingly, a flag of truce went to Grant around 8:00 A.M. on July 3.
Orders went out among the Confederate troops beforehand that "in case a
flag of truce is sent into our lines by the enemy, or sent to them from our
lines, you will immediately give orders to the regimental commanders not to
allow the men to leave the trenches or to hold any conversation with the enemy, and to require the enemy to keep his ordinary distance from our lines."
Thinking the soldiers might mutiny if they suspected surrender negotiations,
one chaplain even described a circulating rumor that it was merely to remove
some women and children from the lines. Yet, as one Missourian explained,
"we all knew the fatal hour had arrived." Pemberton and the division commanders of course knew the flag of truce was for the purpose of surrender,
and one of Pemberton's generals, John S. Bowen, accompanied by Colonel
Louis M. Montgomery of Pemberton's staff, carried the note across the lines
at the Baldwin's Ferry Road. It was a wise move by Pemberton. He thought
that Bowen might perhaps have a better chance of getting good terms from
Grant because of a prewar friendship when both lived near St. Louis. "I had
been a neighbor of Bowen's in Missouri, and knew him well and favorably
before the war," Grant later noted. But that did not help in this case, and in
fact Bowen almost died in the attempt. The Federals fired on the two officers
because Montgomery forgot to unfurl the flag of truce. One watching Confederate noted, "The officer turned deliberately to the courier and caused him to
unfurl the flag." Bowen then "leaped across the ditch and rode rapidly down
the hill to the Federal lines."[12]

The resulting truce itself was an amazing sight. One artillery commander
was firing away, but

my attention was at last attracted to great numbers of men standing up in plain
view of each other, in both the rebel works and ours up on Hovey's front and
farther to the right of it. . . . Soon the works on both sides were lined with men,
standing up and sitting down. Our advanced works are within 100 feet of the rebels and here there was a large crowd of our boys collected and they soon opened
a conversation with about an equal number of rebels on their works. The sight all
along the line was a most curious one, and well worth seeing.

An Illinoisan related that the sight of Confederates mounting their fortifications "put me in mind of turtles coming out to sun themselves after a rainy
day and gather on logs on the Rivers edge." Another used a similar analogy,
describing how "the rebels had come out like snakes on a sunny day and
were all along their works." Lots of interaction took place despite prohibitive
orders and a random shot here or there that led to the call of "down heads"
for a time, one Illinoisan describing how "in an instant our troops had mixed
with the rebel troops and one wondered what was taking place. There was a
shaking of hands, each with the other, as though they never had been enemies
and that they had always been old acquaintances and good friends." The fond-
ness only went so far, however. One Federal described how "a colonel came
down from the Vicksburg side and in no very mild terms ordered his men to
go back to their works." Elsewhere, battery commander Lieutenant Anthony
Burton of the 5th Ohio Battery took the opportunity to spy on the lay of the
land between the forces, which caught the Confederates' attention. "The rebs
didn't seem to like my spying with the glass and said that 'the less we saw of
those works the better it would be for us.'" Another "sarcastically remarked
that I was looking for another hospital to shell."[13]

In an amazing occurrence, two grizzled sharpshooters also climbed out
of their holes on the front lines, spying each other and figuring out quickly
that they had been shooting at one other for days but with no success. "You
spattered some dirt in my eye now 'n' then," the Confederate confessed, and
the Federal replied, "So'd you mine." An unfortunate shot from somewhere
else quickly made everyone nervous and return to their holes, although they
soon came out again.[14]

The truce produced an odd silence. "Not a gun could be heard. . . . Yankees could be seen on the parapets basking in the Sunshine & the thought of
taking the place they most desired." One Federal surgeon described the quiet,
writing that "the cessation of firing produced a very peculiar and anxious

stillness—a sanctified Sunday had fallen upon us in mid-week—and every mouth and ear was asking and listening for the next announcement." A Mississippian agreed, remarking on "the strange sensation produced by the sudden transition from the thunder of battle to a silence almost like that of the tomb." A Texan declared that "several of our men wept because they could not sleep as it was so quiet."[15]

In the note Bowen carried, Pemberton proposed an "armistice . . . with a view to arranging terms for the capitulation of Vicksburg." He also proposed that three commissioners on each side meet to work out the details and noted in bold talk that "I make this proposition to save the further effusion of blood, which must otherwise be shed to a frightful extent, feeling myself fully able to maintain my position for yet an indefinite period." When the note finally reached Grant, he more than likely rolled his eyes at the bravado, wondering if Pemberton was so able to hold out why he wanted to surrender. Still, it was, one Federal wrote, the "long-looked for white flag."[16]

Bowen met the initial Federals on the skirmish line, and they immediately blindfolded the two Confederates and took them to the nearest brigade headquarters, Stephen Burbridge's. As they were crossing the Union siege line, Bowen tripped and fell, causing a nervous reaction from the Federals who were responsible for him. He waved it off, remarking that "I never expected to cross Yankee breastworks without something happening, and I feel truly thankful that it was no worse." They soon reached headquarters, but Burbridge was sick and in bed, so he sent for William Landram, who had his headquarters a mere sixty or seventy yards away. Landram soon appeared and learned of the mission, immediately calling his division commander, A. J. Smith, who came as well. Fred Grant later claimed to have had a front-row seat to these events, even going to meet Bowen with A. J. Smith and Colonel Clark Lagow. He recalled that, even as they met, the guns still roared, particularly the navy's, and someone ordered them to stop. One of the Confederates, Colonel Montgomery, "begged them not to interfere, assuring us that our fire did little to no harm." In fact, Montgomery would only admit, when asked if the barrage was not doing major damage, that "during the previous week we had actually killed a cow." Fred remembered how "later on, when we entered the city, we suspected that Colonel Montgomery had been guilty of a little boasting."[17]

Montgomery must have been full or remorse or indignation, because numerous sources mentioned his combativeness that day. One nearby Ohioan at the headquarters recalled that he thought Bowen was an ideal-looking man, in fact "more like a preacher than a soldier," which may have come from a rebuke Bowen gave Montgomery when he blurted out once in the Union lines that they "must have the whole damned country around them dug up."[18]

Bowen and Montgomery remained at Burbridge's headquarters while Smith quickly took the note to Grant and returned with his answer. In the meantime, "the time was pleasantly occupied during his absence in discussing the battles of Port Gibson, Baker's Creek (Champion's Hill) and other engagements, General Bowen especially talking freely and unreservedly about everything that had no reference to the siege." Eventually, Smith returned with an envelope and note, which Bowen read silently: "The useless effusion of blood you propose stopping by this course can be ended at any time you may choose, by an unconditional surrender of the city and garrison. Men who have shown so much endurance and courage as those now in Vicksburg will always challenge the respect of an adversary, and I can assure you will be treated with all the respect due to prisoners of war." Grant also added: "I do not favor the proposition of appointing commissioners to arrange terms of capitulation, because I have no terms other than those indicated above." One Federal remembered that it was "about the same reply he did at Donelson."[19]

Bowen was disappointed that all he had gotten in return for his work was Grant's familiar refrain, as one Federal said "true to his reputation"— "unconditional surrender." Of course, Pemberton and the Confederates wanted better terms than that, hopefully parole with their arms and equipment. Knowing his commander would never accept unconditional surrender, Bowen pressed forward in the effort to stall and get better terms. He actually "expressed a strong desire to converse with General Grant," but despite their prewar friendship Grant would not see him. As protocol dictated, he would meet no one lower in rank and command than himself.[20]

Bowen thus saw an opening and took it. He informed the Federals that Pemberton would like to meet with Grant himself, giving the idea that it was Pemberton's suggestion. Ord, who was there by now, reported, "Bowen told General [A. J.] Smith that he knew General Pemberton would be glad to meet General Grant." Word went back to army headquarters and Grant agreed; he would meet with a fellow army commander. Bowen proposed the meeting occur at "the point where the Jackson and Vicksburg road crosses the rebel trenches as the place where the white flag would be raised at 3 p. m." General Ord reported "this point is in front of General McPherson's." But there was some concern over timing. Watches were notoriously different at the time, necessitating Grant to set all according to his on May 22 for the grand assault. Now, Ord reported that "the rebel time is forty-eight minutes faster than mine. I will send you my time."[21]

Bowen and Montgomery prepared to return and were once more blind-folded and led back to the entrance of the Union fortifications. "The walking through the intrenchments was tiresome and worried Bowen considerably," Landram noted, and he removed the bandages once out into no-man's-land. "After lighting our cigars and a pleasant shake of the hand we separated," Landram explained, "with a friendly good-by." But as Bowen slowly rode back to his own lines, he had to quickly come up with a way to convince Pemberton to meet with Grant, which Pemberton had never proposed. Once he reported to Pemberton, Bowen just plain-out lied and told him that Grant wanted to meet with him, which Pemberton accepted. Pemberton later ex-plained: "I was not aware that the suggestion had originated with General Bowen, but acceded to the proposed meeting at the joint request of my four division commanders." Thus, both commanders went into the meeting think-ing the other had called it.[22]

The high-level courier and flag of truce quickly made all who saw or heard of it know something was happening, although the details were known only by a few, not even Landram. Yet, the timing was an almost sure giveaway. "A flag of truce gone out we Know not its object and various are the conjectures in regard to it," one Louisianan wrote in his diary. He added, "The prevail-ing opinion is that it is for a Surrender of the place." Others picked up on the reason as well, although Confederate officers who knew no more than the private soldiers tried to keep a bold face for their own troops. "Numberless conjectures were indulged in as to what was on foot," Mississippian William Pitt Chambers wrote. "I felt assured that negotiations for a surrender were in progress; but when I expressed such a conviction, I was hooted at by the regi-mental and company officers." He continued: "Some of them even went so far as to state in detail the object of the truce and the result of the negotiations. It would be amusing, if not so repugnant to candor, to witness the subterfuges resorted to keep the men in ignorance of things of an unpleasant nature."[23]

Northern soldiers who viewed the event or heard of it as it spread like wildfire also knew what it probably meant. "It was a glorious sight to officers and soldiers on the line where these white flags were visible," Grant wrote. And the news soon spread to all parts of the command. The troops felt that their "long and weary marches, hard fighting, ceaseless watching by night and day, in a hot climate, exposure to all sorts of weather, to diseases and, worst of all, to the gibes of many Northern papers that came to them saying all their suffering was in vain, that Vicksburg would never be taken, were at last at an end and the Union sure to be saved." Some shouting invariably occurred, at which time "all rushed from the camps to see what could be seen."[24]

That watchful feeling slowly spread as the day wore on and negotiations began to take place in earnest, although out of sight from most of both armies. "About nine o'clock flag of truce sent out by us," a Louisianan described the events of the day, but then firing started back up as Pemberton alerted his commanders that "the Flag has returned and the truce is at an end." Then the mood changed as the hours rolled on: "Towards the middle of the day & early evening it began to be whispered that Pemberton was making terms of surrender & by night on account of an order being received that during the night there should be no firing it was confirmed in the minds of all." Yet the delay on July 3 brought another possibility to mind: an actual surrender on July 4. One Louisianan talked with a Yankee "twenty feet off" and lamented that they would surrender "on the 4th of July on a day that would particularly gratify the Yankees."[25]

Even though negotiations were taking place, work still went on as if fighting could restart at any moment, which it actually did after Bowen and Montgomery returned to their lines. Even during the truce there was occasional inexplicable firing, one shot killing a cannoneer in the 6th Wisconsin Battery. Conversely, Confederate brigade commander Francis Shoup wrote of the good that came of the truce: "We can now see more clearly what the enemy is about." He also related that the Federals were still mining, writing that the enemy "is hard at work to-day." He added, "We follow his example. The question is, which shall explode first?" Of course, heavier fighting could restart at any time; Union orders went out "to be extremely guarded against a sortie, or attempt of the enemy to cut his way out," one Union commander wrote. "My troops were under arms," he added, "but nothing unusual occurred."[26]

Matters thus quieted as all waited on the midafternoon meeting. One watching Mississippian noted "how glad I would have been to have heard once more the booming of the cannon. A sound once so annoying, yet now so welcome, for it would have told the glad news that our devoted city had not yet been surrendered." Events soon picked up once more as the meeting time neared. Grant and his entourage arrived on time and waited in front of the lines of McPherson's corps, one officer noting that Grant looked "evidently annoyed" when Pemberton did not show up on time. Fred accompanied Grant and his staff to meet Pemberton and remembered that "soon a white flag appeared over the enemy works, and a party of Confederates was seen approaching." He also noted, "The works on both sides were lined with soldiers." Pemberton thus arrived in front of John Forney's lines at the Great Redoubt, resplendent in a brand-new uniform. With him were Bowen and Colonel Montgomery. Both parties moved forward, and Bowen introduced the two generals under what Grant described as "a stunted oak-tree, which was made historical by the event. It was but a short time before the last vestige of its body, root and limb had disappeared," Grant later joked, "the fragments taken as trophies. Since then the same tree has furnished as many cords of wood, in the shape of trophies, as 'The True Cross.'" A watching Confederate simply responded, "This looks suspicious."[27]

For his part, Confederate brigade commander Francis Shoup thought Pemberton "blundered horribly" by going to meet Grant and negotiating. He thought the momentum was all on Pemberton's side and that he was giving in. The way it stood, Pemberton had offered to capitulate, and if Grant denied it he would never lose more troops in an assault "while he had an offer of surrender in his pocket." When that became public, Grant would be raked over the coals. Pemberton went anyway.[28]

Bowen tried to break the ice in an extremely tense situation, but in reality there was no need for introductions, as Grant knew Pemberton well. He wrote that he and Pemberton had served in the same division in Mexico and "I knew him very well therefore, and greeted him as an old acquaintance." Pemberton explained that "after a few remarks and inquiries on either side, a pause ensued, which was prolonged on my part in expectation that General Grant would introduce the subject." After all, in Pemberton's mind, Grant had called this meeting. Grant not taking the lead, Pemberton mentioned that he "understood that he had expressed a wish to have a personal interview with me." Grant said he had not, whereupon Pemberton turned to Bowen and snapped, "Then there is a misunderstanding; I certainly understood differently."[29]

Taking the lead in the embarrassing situation, Pemberton asked if Grant's unconditional surrender was still his terms, which Grant affirmed, and Pemberton barked, "Then, sir, it is unnecessary that you and I should hold any further conversation." Then Pemberton did just that by blurting out, "We will go to fighting again at once," adding, "I can assure you, sir, you will bury many more of your men before you will enter Vicksburg." From Grant's perspective, he reported that when Pemberton asked for terms and he replied the same as in his letter—unconditional surrender—Pemberton replied "rather snappishly, 'the conference might as well end,'" to which Grant agreed "very well." Charles Dana, who accompanied Grant, affirmed as much, writing that "we could, however, see that Pemberton was much excited, and was impatient in his answers to Grant." His answers were also defiant. An observant Union officer noted how "on this rock they split."[30]

With things spiraling out of control, Bowen intervened again and proposed that lower-level officers meet. Indeed, one watching Missourian noted that it was mostly Bowen and McPherson who did the talking. Both army commanders agreed, although both also let it be known that they were in no way bound by the results of the commission. As the lower officers hashed out a deal, Grant and Pemberton continued to visit, Pemberton presumably having calmed down by this time. Grant remembered that he and Pemberton "moving a short distance away towards the enemy's lines were in conversation." Pemberton explained that they were "conversing only upon topics that had no relation to the important subject that brought us together."[31]

One Mississippian watching intensely from the fortifications described how the two met "not over thirty yards from our works." He explained,

> I knew General Pemberton and recognized General Grant by descriptions I had seen of him. He was dressed in a plain uniform that had seen service, while General Pemberton's was new and elegant. General Grant wore a full beard cropped short, and I could see that it was sprinkled with gray. General Pemberton's was long and flowing, and he pulled it nervously during the entire interview. General Grant had a cigar in his mouth, but he was not smoking it, and appeared calm and stolid.

Another Federal also described Pemberton as animated while Grant smoked calmly, "pulling up tufts of grass." Yet another remarked on how

> they stood just in front of our battery for some time, and the rebel soldiers—whom we had not seen for weeks came upon the breastworks to look over. We did the same thing. It was a beautiful sight—down the line of fortifications as far as we could see were the soldiers in blue on one side and the rebels in gray on

the opposite side all standing in bold relief, where but a few moments before not one on either side dared to show his head.[32]

Meanwhile, the conference met and returned, whereupon their joint recommendation was heard. The officers reported very generous terms for the Confederates, Grant writing that "of course I rejected the terms at once." Grant and Pemberton then parted, Grant telling Pemberton he would hear from him by 10:00 P.M. that night with his final offer. Obviously, by drawing out the negotiations, a surrender would not take place that day. The almost unthinkable—joyous for the Federals and humiliating for the Confederates—was becoming more and more likely: a July 4 surrender.[33]

Firing had restarted after Bowen returned to the Confederate lines on his initial visit and had actually occurred in isolated instances even during it. One Confederate told of how they were all sitting atop their trenches when a shot rang out, at which time "we involuntarily rolled into the ditches like turtles off a log." Yet as 3:00 P.M. neared and Grant and then Pemberton emerged from the works, it stopped altogether. And once the generals returned to their lines this time, it did not restart as before. An all-out armistice was in effect, making one Ohioan muse: "I don't know the result of the conference but as there has been no firing since, it looks like the end of the siege." He also remarked on the quiet, writing that "after 47 days of constant cannonading and rifle firing day and night, it seems very strange to have complete quiet." He added, "It is so still and quiet, I fear we will not sleep much."[34]

Yet there was still a lot that had to be done on both sides before any surrender could be finalized, namely both commanders meeting with their officers to get recommendations on how to proceed. Grant met with his generals over the course of the rest of the afternoon and evening, although he explained that it was no formal council of war: "This was the nearest approach to a 'council of war' I ever held," he noted, he only telling them of the correspondence but that he "would hold the power of deciding entirely in my own hands." He later explained that "curiosity led officers of rank—most all the general officers—to visit my headquarters with the hope of getting some news. I talked with them very freely about the meeting between General Pemberton and myself, our correspondence, etc., but in no sense was it a council of war." Still, an amazed Fred recalled that the group of officers was "the largest assemblage of general officers which I had ever seen."[35]

Although he later changed the story in his memoirs, Grant was adamant about sending the Confederates to prison camps, perhaps in keeping with the "unconditional surrender" mantra he had gained. Only Frederick Steele agreed, the vast majority of the other officers, including Admiral Porter, counseling parole and release. Oddly enough, Grant's protégé McPherson led the swell of voices to parole the Confederates. With such a weight against him, Grant agreed "reluctantly," writing Porter that "my own feelings are against this, but all my officers think the advantage gained . . . more than counterbalance the effect of sending them north." And there were good reasons, which Grant enumerated in his report. It would cost huge amounts of money to move the prisoners, feed them, and parole them. Then there was the hope that leaving them so near their homes would induce many Confederates to simply vanish and never return to the war. Finally, not having to see to so many prisoners and their transportation would free up the army and the navy for future operations. It did make sense, and Grant acquiesced.[36]

Grant sent his final offer to Pemberton that night, carried by John Logan and staff officer James H. Wilson: "On your accepting the terms proposed, I will march in one division as a guard, and take possession at 8 a. m. tomorrow. As soon as rolls can be made out, and paroles signed by officers and men, you will be allowed to march out of our lines." Officers could keep sidearms and horses and the men their clothing. Also, he allowed "any amount of rations you may deem necessary . . . from the stores you now have, and also the necessary cooking utensils for preparing them," along with a few wagons. The key, however, was that "the paroles . . . must be signed . . . while officers are present authorized to sign the roll of prisoners." That could take days.[37]

During the delay, Grant also took part in some clandestine psychological work, telling his commanders to "permit some discreet men on picket to communicate to the enemy's pickets the fact that General Grant has offered, in case Pemberton surrenders, to parole all the officers and men, and to permit them to go home from here." He especially told Herron to do so and to watch diligently during the night "lest he may attempt to get out by your front." In the remote chance of a breakout attempt, Grant thought it would come to the south. Nevertheless, with the negotiations delayed, Grant decided it was best to cancel the 5:00 A.M. July 4 "national salute," although some batteries still fired it hoping "may we fire nothing but blank cartridges next year." One Chicago Mercantile Battery artilleryman was amazed that the Confederates who had come out of their works because of the truce were still there during the salute: "At 5 we opened—expecting to see the Rebs drop down into their holes but as the smoke cleared away there they set as cool as ice."[38]

Pemberton had to decide what to do, although the officers who brought back Grant's reply had bought him some time, telling the Federals that "it would be impossible to answer it by night." With the final offer in hand and some time to spare, Pemberton met again with his generals, calling an official council of war of division and brigade commanders on the night of July 3 to go over the proposed terms Grant sent back at 10:00 P.M. The indecisive Pemberton had never been shy about calling councils of war, a clear indication that he was groping for help and not confident in his own ability. The officers haggled over the right wording of a response, Francis Shoup, who was admittedly "young and perhaps a little bumptious," even writing out his own proposed terms. He had signatures on his document when Grant's final proposal came in, which ended discussion, Pemberton taking Shoup's paper and writing a draft of his own response over the signatures. Most approved, although Stephen D. Lee and William E. Baldwin would not go on record supporting surrender but gave no reason why. Haggling over wordage of the response, Pemberton finally dismissed everyone and wrote his own note, which went to Grant early on July 4, "a little before peep of day," Charles Dana wrote. Once again, high-level commanders made the delivery, including at times division commander Martin L. Smith and Engineer Samuel Lockett. One Federal described to his family how, after the initial flag of truce, "they have been running back and forth with flags of truce ever since." Grant's engineer James H. Wilson carried one of them, to be met by counterpart Samuel Lockett, who had been with him at West Point. Meanwhile, all found ways to entertain themselves, one captain in the 33rd Wisconsin reading the Declaration of Independence word for word from atop the Union fortifications and inviting the Confederates to join in three cheers when he was done. The Confederates across the way declined.[39]

Pemberton wrote that "in the main, your terms are accepted." Then there was a "but." Pemberton wanted to amend Grant's final offer, writing that "at 10 A.M. to-morrow I propose to evacuate the works in and around Vicksburg, and to surrender the city and garrison under my command, by marching out with my colors and arms, stacking them in front of my present lines, after which you will take possession." He added, "Officers to retain their side arms and personal property, and the rights and property of citizens to be respected." The note arrived deep in the morning, and an aggravated Grant had to send

out orders to keep his troops at bay at dawn; staff officer Wilson sent a message to McPherson, warning "don't open fire till further orders—Genl. Pemberton accepts the terms but makes a wry face, and one or two unimportant
amendments."[40]

By this time, Grant decided it was time to put an end to this back-and-
forth. He wrote early the next morning, July 4, that "the amendment proposed
by you cannot be acceded to in full." Thinking Pemberton had proposed that
the Confederates stack arms and march away, he reiterated most importantly
that "it will be necessary to furnish every officer and man with a parole signed
by himself, which, with the completion of the rolls of prisoners, will necessarily take some time." He added, "If you mean by your proposition for each
brigade to march to the front of the lines now occupied by it, and stack arms
at 10 a. m., and then return to the inside, and there remain as prisoners until
properly paroled, I will make no objection to it." He also made clear that he
could not be bound by any agreement concerning the citizens of Vicksburg.
"Should no notification be received of your acceptance of my terms by 9 A.M.,"
he finished, "I shall regard them as having been rejected, and shall act accordingly. Should these terms be accepted, white flags should be displayed
along your lines to prevent such of my troops as may not have been notified
from firing upon your men." To lessen that chance, Grant sent out a circular:
"Should white flags be displayed upon the enemy's works at 10 o'clock this
morning, it will be to signify the acceptance of the terms of capitulation."[41]

Grant's note was pretty plain, and Pemberton sent back a simple message
early that morning: "I have the honor to acknowledge the receipt of your communication of this day, and in reply to say that the terms proposed by you are
accepted." Grant and Fred were in their tent when Pemberton's last message
arrived. "I remained in the tent, sitting on my little cot, and feeling restless,
but scarce knowing why," Fred recalled. "Father sat at his table writing." A
messenger arrived with a note, which Grant opened. He "gave a sigh of relief,
and said calmly: 'Vicksburg has surrendered.'" Fred explained, "I was thus
the first to hear the news officially announced . . . and, filled with enthusiasm,
I ran out to spread the glad tidings. Officers rapidly assembled, and there was
a general rejoicing."[42]

So it would happen on July 4 after all, although it was a day like all the
rest. One soldier described how "the day was clear and extremely warm,

the dust deep and stinking with the accumulated filth." It obviously became even uglier for the Confederates when it began to appear for sure that this of all days would be the day they would surrender. One Louisianan wrote early on July 4 that "the object of the flag of truce not yet (9 o'clock A.M.) transpired—We got no bread rations at all to-day[.] Our prospects every day become more gloomy." Another wrote, "The glorious fourth! God grant that we be not surrendered on this day." It was especially galling in another way for Joseph Westbrook of the 4th Mississippi and his comrades, who had also been captured at Fort Donelson: "This was my second capture by Grant."[43]

Obviously, Pemberton's Northern birth was of prime importance in how many on both sides viewed the surrender coming on Independence Day. Although Charles Dana reflected that "it must have been a bitter moment for the Confederate chieftain," most were not so caring. It did not help when Pemberton's words later leaked out, Engineer Lockett remembering Pemberton saying, "I am a Northern man; I know my people; I know their peculiar weaknesses and their national vanity; I know we can get better terms from them on the 4th of July than any other day of the year. We must sacrifice our pride to these considerations." Yet it is clear that the negotiations started on July 3, and Pemberton did not purposefully delay them to get to July 4. Obviously, the delay came in struggling over terms, which Samuel Lockett later explained was a result of the Confederates being able to read signals from Grant to Porter. They had broken the code and, according to Lockett, knew Grant wanted to send the Confederates northward to prison camps while Porter argued that he did not have the transportation to do so and paroling them would free everyone up for more operations. "This helped to make General Pemberton more bold and persistent in his demands," Lockett wrote.[44]

Still, the deed was done, and it was now time to tell the troops and have them carry out their part of the morning events. "At 10 o'clock A.M. today," orders from Confederate division commander John Forney read on Independence Day, "each Brigade will be marched out in front of its respective position, stacking arms. It will then return and bivouac in rear of the trenches until the necessary rolls can be completed. . . . So soon as this order is received, you will cause white flags to be displayed." He added, "You will please state to your troops that these terms are concurred in by the general officers and you will caution your men not to avoid being paroled as it is to their advantage." Forney more specifically told Louis Hébert the news. "I am directed by the lieutenant general commanding to inform you that the terms of the capitulation of Vicksburg and garrison have been completed." He enumerated the actual terms and told Hébert to have his brigade ready to march out of the works at 10:00 A.M. to stack arms and return inside until the parole rolls could be finished: "So soon as this order is received you will cause white flags to be displayed along your line."[45]

The news was not well received in the Confederate army that had defended Vicksburg for more than forty days now. One Arkansas captain handed the note he received to a subordinate to read to the troops "and watched the effect it would have on them." He reported that "some seemed pleased, while others said words which would not have sounded well in Sunday school and still others shed tears." The wounded Colonel Winchester Hall of the 26th Louisiana, in bed in Vicksburg, admitted that "I wept like a sick girl." Many broke their muskets against trees rather than surrender them, and Missourian Ephraim Anderson declared one of his regiment committed suicide by drinking "a bottle of laudanum." While most knew they were worn out—one describing the men as "so weak from starvation that they staggered like drunken men as they walked"—most just could not conceive of why it had to be July 4. "At 10 o'clock was astounded to hear the city was surrendered to Grant and we had to stack arms outside the works," wrote one Louisianan. "He [Pemberton] should be stricken from the rolls of our army." Alvin Hovey reported one Confederate placing the white flag on his works and yelling, "Holler you d____d Yankees. Holler until your throats burst every one of you." Hovey admitted that "the Rebs advice was followed, for we could not help but 'Holler' as the white flags appeared along the whole line."[46]

The Federals had been given the same news: white flags would be displayed if the surrender would occur. An Illinoisan in Steele's corps described how a little before ten they first began to see signs of surrender: "At length our eyes caught glimpses of white flags fluttering in the rear of their works. About this moment Col. Farrar our brigade commander rode past saying as he rode by '10 o'clock boys will tell the story, whether they comply with our terms.[']" He added, "In a few moments we saw a white flag floating over their works opposite our extreme right." It was unmistakable. "That sign was eagerly watched for," one Missourian recalled, "and about ten o'clock the flags began to appear." Iowan John Hughes displayed his excitement in his diary as he updated the day's entry at intervals throughout the hours: "10 A.M. White flags are displayed!" A member of the 3rd Iowa similarly described how "about ten o'clock, from the position of our regiment, with a field glass, the enemy might be seen to take down his flag . . . , and hoist a white flag in its stead. Then two men started, each with a bundle of white flags, and proceeded either way, hoisting them along the works." A few noticed them at first, and then the entire Federal army lunged to their works to see, letting out a huge roar of cheers. It was "a hurrah along our entire front; not only that, but the drums and fifes that had for so many weeks been silent all of a sudden opened up and such a jubilee made everybody glad they were still living on this particular Fourth of July, 1863!"[47]

There was some uncertainty on how to proceed after that. In front of the 3rd Louisiana Redan, a Missouri colonel—probably Francis Cockrell—asked "if he should have his men march outside and stack their arms and he was told that was the understanding." Forney was there, with arms folded and, as described by one Federal, "was walking a little distance aside and seemed to be meditating over the situation." Bowen and Montgomery were also there, Montgomery taking offense to the 45th Illinois band, which struck up "The Star-Spangled Banner" right at 10:00 A.M. "That's damned humiliating, general," he barked to Bowen, but Bowen retorted: "Oh, I don't know! . . . we can't always win; we will live in hopes and try again." On Stevenson's front, Colonel Alexander Reynolds's Tennesseans went to the brigade headquarters to stack their arms. The artillery limbered up and parked their vehicles where they could.[48]

It was a solemn sight as the ceremonies took place all up and down the lines. One Federal described how

it was a sight that will not quickly be forgotten by those who witnessed it. Promptly at the hour named each regiment the men dressed each in his best uniform left the works they had so well defended so long. They marched as regularly as if on dress parade or review & at the command each was halted in front of the position they had occupied in the line. The lines were well 'dressed.' The word 'stack arms' was given 'two pairs to the rear march,' 'left face' 'forward march' & the rebel garrison of . . . Vicksburg was disarmed & prisoners of war.

Another described how the Confederates "looked like a flock of dirty sheep."[49]

As the men stacked their arms and hung their accouterments on the bayonets and draped their flags over the tops, hatred, humiliation, and resentment rose to the surface. Brigade commander Shoup reported "the men are full of indignation. . . . The tone has always been 'This is pretty hard, but we can stand it.'" Another wrote that "my command marched over the trenches and stacked their arms with the greatest reluctance, conscious of their ability to hold the position assigned them for an indefinite period of time." A Mississippian went into detail about his feelings:

> We performed the humiliating task of marching in front of our works and stacking arms in full view of the enemy, and under the direction of a Federal officer. Some of us wept as we did this for we realized that this was the end of all our sacrifices. For this ignoble ending we had fought, had watched, had hungered and shed our blood, and many a brave comrade had gone to an untimely grave. . . . To intensify the humiliation of the men, was the suspicion—to many it was a conviction, if they expressed themselves correctly—that our Commanding general had been false to the flag under which he fought.[50]

Others simply reported the events matter-of-factly, one even arguing that Pemberton "virtually surrendered" when he opened communications with Grant the day before. Colonel Thomas N. Waul reported that "at 10 o'clock of the day of the capitulation the command marched out of the intrenchments with their colors flying and band playing. Having saluted their colors, they stacked arms and returned—prisoners under parole—into camp." John Forney similarly agreed: "In accordance with the terms of the capitulation, my troops were marched by regiments over the intrenchments, their arms stacked and left in possession of the enemy, while they returned to bivouac in rear of the trenches." One Louisianan could only think of the danger that had passed: "We stacked our arms and left the place, meeting no minie balls or shells for the first time in 46 days, during which time you could not get out without them whistling around you like they were going to hit you, and shells, and no end to them, flying around." Samuel Lockett bemoaned the fact that in his countermines "the fuses were set and everything was primed and ready." He mused that "the efficiency of our preparations were not tested."[51]

One Indianan was moved at the sight, relating that "we watched them march outside their works, form in line, their band played honors to their colors, then they stacked their arms. It was one of the most solemn and affecting scenes I have ever beheld." It must have been a particularly interesting site on the Jackson Road, where the Missourians of Cockrell's brigade stacked their arms on the north side of the road with Ulysses S. Grant himself there to watch. One Missourian noted that "General Grant sat upon his horse within ten steps of the point at which the company laid aside its guns and accoutrements, and saw the tattered and worn, but proud old battle-flag of the regiment droop quietly upon its standard, and rest its scarlet folds peacefully upon the stack of arms, no longer grasped firmly to sustain and uphold it." Also there was Andrew Hickenlooper, who had begged to be taken from what just days ago seemed to be his deathbed. He was put in an ambulance and taken to the Shirley House and from there by stretcher to the fort bearing his name, where he watched the solemn proceedings.[52]

One particularly sad episode occurred as the 38th Mississippi stacked their arms. A detail went back to gather the wounded soldiers' arms still lying about the trenches, and they were piled in a stack. One was loaded and went off, killing a Mississippian "in the act of surrendering." A musket with buckshot went off and hit the man in the back, he turning to ask who did it but then falling. One of his comrades noted that "there was something peculiarly pathetic in such a death, and it touched deeply the grim soldiers who witnessed it." A member of the burial detail added, "He was removed to our side and buried." Others were more obstinate, Colonel Claudius W. Sears noting in his diary "most of our light artillery disappeared on night of 3' — supposed to have fallen into the river." A Union artilleryman across the river on De Soto Point testified that "wagon loads of ammunition [were] thrown into the river and the big shot rolled down the hill into the river."[53]

Stacking their arms was only part of the humiliating process for the defenders of Vicksburg, and next came something even worse: the Federals marched in and took possession of the city. A Louisianan described how "at ½ past 10, enemy saw their flag as it is put over our works — bitter humiliation to us who have suffered for 47 days in defending them." Even that brought some argument, however, as the 8th Missouri and 47th Illinois tussled over who had the right to plant their flag first on the Confederate works near the Stockade Redan. Nevertheless, soon the various flags of the Union regiments stood tall atop the parapets of the Confederate earthworks. One Indianan could only reflect: "Long may it wave." Then the Federals began their entrance. A Mississippian described how "about 12 noon the Federal Army commenced marching in. Dressed in bright new uniforms, and with numerous bands playing the national airs, they made a great display of martial pomp." Indeed, even while cautioning his men to keep a good lookout before the armistice, McPherson notified his command, "as it is very probable we will take possession of the place this afternoon, have the men who are in camp clean up and put their arms, clothes, &c., in good trim, so as to present a good soldierly appearance when we march in." One of his soldiers reported that "all the finery we had, whether paper collars or white gloves, was in speedy requisition." McPherson also ordered that the bands be ready "so that they can take their proper position when the orders arrive. Field music will, of course, accompany the regiments."[54]

In a classic case of using Sherman when force was necessary and McPherson when finesse was better, Grant tasked McPherson's XVII Corps and Herron's division, with McPherson in overall command, with occupying the city. They quickly moved in with the bands playing "Hail, Columbia" and the "The Star-Spangled Banner." The first troops in were Logan's, he being the ranking division commander in the army. The road was dusty, one Illinoisan in the division noting that "we must keep our mouths shut." But it was worth it. "By order of Major-General Logan, my brigade, led by the Forty-fifth Illinois, was honored with the privilege of being the first to enter the garrison, and the flag of the Forty-fifth the first to float over the conquered city," reported a proud Mortimer D. Leggett, who had to be helped onto his horse because of his wound on June 25 but was not about to miss this day. McPherson himself had designated that regiment be first, writing Grant that it "has borne the brunt of the battle oftener than any other in my command, and always behaved nobly." Lieutenant John P. Jones of that regiment wrote to his wife: "Quite an honor wasn't it? . . . Didn't I strut? I guess I did." Others claimed it was the 4th Minnesota's flag that went up first.[55]

As Logan's division moved in, the rest of the army stood down, even to the point of hauling the batteries out of line: "In the course of the day [they] were withdrawn to the camp of the battery." In entering the stronghold, of course, the Federals took notice in detail of what they had only seen at a distance. Artillerymen noticed Confederate guns they had no idea were there and had never been fired; "'they didn't want us to know it was there' they said," one Ohioan wrote, adding that "probably in case of an assault we would have discovered it to our cost." Of particular interest were the Confederate fortifications these Federals had been deprived a close look at. One member of Herron's division noted that "several of these works were well built, and from their strength could not have been carried by assault without heavy loss." Another noted: "I think it would have been very doubtful whether or not we could have carried it by assault. If it had been attempted we might have lost 10 or 15,000 men and still failed." Others had different opinions. One

Illinoisan was in wonder when he observed what he described as thin Confederate fortifications: "We could have charged them any time." The Federals also noticed the defenders of those works, one explaining that Confederate officers "had mostly on that day the look of men who have been crying all night," and Dana described "one major, who commanded a regiment from Missouri, burst into tears as he followed his disarmed men back into their lines after they had surrendered their colors and the guns in front of them." Of particular interest were the many skiffs the Confederates had been rumored to be building for escape on the river: "On entering the city we found a large number of very rudely constructed boats," Grant wrote.[56]

Numerous remarkable episodes occurred as the Federals took possession of the city and the Confederates congregated along the roads to watch the parade. One Federal asked to be taken to the camp of the battery his regiment had captured at Champion Hill. Others found "acquaintances" they had met between the lines during the siege. As one regiment of Missourians marched into town, one of the member's brothers in a Confederate unit "was there to meet the boy in our regiment." It was a touching scene as "our boy fell out of ranks, and they walked together, arms around each other's waists." He added that "it was a sight most impressive and one to remain vivid a life time—the one in blue with uniform fresh, buttons shining, gun and bayonet bright; the other in gray, ragged uniform, barefoot and grimy. It was enough to make one feel sad that such things had to be." Others reported meeting up with long-lost kinfolk as well, and many made new acquaintances, all with surprise seeing as how "they tried to kill one another a few hours ago." Colonel Walter Gresham on the 53rd Indiana met several "old college mates," one of whom was a battery commander exactly where Gresham held the line and exclaimed, "Have we been fighting each other? I wouldn't have killed you, and known it, for the world!"[57]

The civilians were also involved, one Federal remarking that "the rebel women scowled, made faces and spit at us." The response from a "fat old colored woman" was more welcome, she jumping for joy and shouting "heah day come. Heah day is. Jes' you look at 'em, none your little yaller faced sickly fellers, but full grown men, wid blood in 'em."[58]

James McPherson was a good choice to oversee the surrender and occupation, he being extremely polite and proper. In fact, one Confederate general illustrated this fact. Brigade commander Louis Hébert was sick and ill and was about to collapse. Showing tenderness to a fellow officer, McPherson himself took Hébert under his care. Hébert later recalled "McPherson, who, I must acknowledge, treated me with much courtesy and kindness. I was worn out and ill; he accompanied me to the place where the paroling of the Confederate troops took place, and saw that I was not made to wait long at the spot." He added: "I have in my heart a grateful feeling for him." Others also had high-level interaction even if it did not turn out so well, such as when Colonel David Grier of the 77th Illinois asked Pemberton himself about their flag lost on May 22. Pemberton simply responded that "there was not enough of it left to tell it had ever been a flag, even the flag staff was all shattered, and it was thrown away to one side as not worth keeping."[59]

The most iconic event occurred when two Federal officers and a few escorts moved to the courthouse and, despite one of the pillars that braced the cupola being shot away, replaced the Confederate flag with the Stars and Stripes. William E. Strong and George Coolbaugh went in with Logan's division and McPherson sent them on to the courthouse. They carried with them the flag of the 45th Illinois but found getting to the courthouse harder than they imagined. "The streets were thronged with citizens and soldiers who scowled upon us," Strong wrote, "and vile epithets came to our ears from every side." One woman went so far as to yell, "Yanks! Yanks! You think you're smart, don't you! Vicksburg is only a fair exchange for Washington." The Federals moved on but found the courthouse "fairly surrounded and shut in by citizens and soldiers." The group had to push through but nothing happened, and the two officers and two escorts soon went up the stairs to the cupola of the courthouse. There, a vista of beauty emerged: "The scene that burst upon us as we gained the great bell in the cupola, the highest point attainable, was indescribably beautiful," Strong explained. "For a moment we forgot our mission and were fairly wrapped up in the grand panorama which lay spread out before us." They soon remembered their duty, however, and attached the flag (one said replacing a white flag) "to one of the pillars which supported the roof and weather vane of the cupola." Strong described how "when it was firmly tied I gathered it up in both hands and stepping to the railing tossed it out vigorously with the wind which was blowing quite fresh from the North East." He added that "it floated out grandly!"[60]

The Federals thus occupied the city with Logan's division, Logan being named commander of the post; a regiment went on duty as city guards to maintain order while portions of the 2nd Illinois Cavalry patrolled the streets. Most of the troops ringed the city around the old Confederate works,

McPherson's men spreading out to cover the areas Steele's and Ord's troops had vacated first by going to camp and then by being ordered eastward to join Sherman. This was to "prevent the escape of prisoners and the ingress and egress of citizens." McPherson later told division commander John E. Smith to "exercise increased vigilance on your front tonight preventing the possibility of escape to a single prisoner."[61]

Grant himself went in at 11:10 A.M., after watching the pageantry of the stacking of arms for a few moments on the Jackson Road. He soon met Pemberton and his staff while they sat on the porch of one of Pemberton's division commander's headquarters at the "Rock House." One Federal described the Confederate commander as "a very tall and heavy man, fine looking," although the weight of the world must have appeared in his face. Grant "was received by Pemberton with more marked impertinence than at their former interview," Charles Dana explained. "Grant bore it like a philosopher, and in reply treated Pemberton with even gentler courtesy and dignity than before." Fred described Grant's reception from Pemberton as "most frigid." Grant asked for water and was told "to go hunt for it in the kitchen." The boy thought that "this surly reception to the man who would not allow his men to celebrate their victory, was deeply resented by the members of General Grant's staff, but father was satisfied with his success in capturing Vicksburg and manifested no resentment." Eventually, Grant went on down to the river to meet Porter and later established headquarters inside Vicksburg at the Lum House. All others were wide-eyed, Dana looking at everything he could: "I found the buildings of Vicksburg much less damaged than I had expected." At the river, Federal boats pushed into the bank: "In a short time these line the levee up and down the river for nearly a mile in distance. They are loaded with provisions of every kind."[62]

Grant showed little emotion as he went about his business. Porter described his arrival onboard the flagship, carefully noting that he declined a drink of champagne everyone else was having. "There was a quiet satisfaction in his face that could not be concealed," Porter added, "but he behaved on that occasion as if nothing of importance had occurred."[63]

Accounts differed as to the reaction of the Federals once inside Vicksburg, including how shot up the city was. Some described the horrendous appearance, but at least one declared "it is a very good city damaged but little by shells." There were also numerous accounts of Federal plunder. One Confederate staff officer described how "then brigades of enemy marched in under the flags & to foreign music. Their arms stacked, they commenced plundering every house. They came in my room, stole my pistol in presence of officers & men—stole Lieut. Dubois' hat. Such a people! Such a people!" As he walked down to the river to see the gunboats, he mused "oh, my heart sickens at the sight!" Another related that he had his horse stolen "from the negro while bringing him to me." He added that "before long the sacking of the town began[.] On Washington Street numerous stores were broken open by Yankees with large stones & the contents taken, Yankee officers looking on." There was corroboration from the Federals, Ord writing: "Am of opinion many men broke by the guards and went into town." He later confirmed as much, reporting to Grant that "there are no guards along the rebels works to keep either party from crossing, . . . the town is full of our men plundering & the rebels are straggling out."[64]

The plundering took some odd twists. One Federal of the 47th Ohio took one of the white flags the Confederates had placed on the works and took it home with him as a souvenir. More ghastly, one Confederate declared that Federals broke into the family vaults in the city cemetery and removed valuable rings, which could be plainly seen through looking glasses in the crypts that were broken open to acquire the jewels.[65]

The plundering was by all accounts limited and obviously not army-sanctioned. More widespread was the respect shown for the Confederates in the form of not cheering, except at the initial sight of the white flags, at the major victory just won. This was on firm orders from Grant, who even while going inside the city, at the head of Logan's division, heard some firing he thought were salutes and quickly had them stopped. Federals across the river nevertheless reported that they "cheered and sang until hoarse." It was less widespread east of the river. One Iowan declared that "although cheer was in the heart of every Union officer and soldier it was repressed as being undignified to exult over a fallen and humble foe who had so worthily defended his trust." The newly surrendered Confederates appreciated the act, or lack thereof. One reported that as they stacked arms the Federals "witnessed the scene without cheering." Another added that they fired salutes, but "among all the Federals that came in the city, not one rejoiced or exulted over their success, but acknowledged that we deserved much praise for our gallant defense of the place." A few accounts mentioned some muted celebration, Samuel Lockett later writing that "my recollection is that on our right a hearty cheer was given by one Federal division 'for the gallant defenders of Vicksburg!'" Another mentioned "the Yankees cheering a little but generally well [behaved]." One Illinoisan declared that there was some cheering, but "they hallooed about as much as our men." Grant added that "the men had behaved so well that I did not want to humiliate them. I believed that consideration for their feelings would make them less dangerous foes during the continuance of hostilities, and better citizens after the war was over."[66]

That good feeling continued after the formal surrender and stacking of arms. With nothing to do until paroled, which would take time, the Confederates were allowed to do as they pleased, only staying inside the fortification lines. Grant recalled that "no restraint was put on them except by their own commanders." A grateful Confederate explained how "our captors allowed us the full privilege of the place inside our lines—to come and go where our fancy carries us, within that limit." Many lined the road and watched the triumphal entry of Logan's division. One Confederate walked down to the river and noted "it is a beautiful sight to look along the river at night now, (but humiliating and depressing to me) when their boats are all lighted up." They also had to listen to the Union bands that played in town.[67]

As would be expected, all the soldiers soon came into close contact, but perhaps not so expected were the niceties exchanged. Samuel Lockett explained that "a few minutes after the Federal soldiers marched in, the soldiers of the two armies were fraternizing and swapping yarns over the incidents of the long siege." One Federal met Lockett, who rode a small white pony and recognized him: "See here, Mister,—you man on the little white horse! Danged if you ain't the hardest feller to hit I ever saw; I've shot at you more'n a hundred times!" The men of the 38th Mississippi were glad to once again find their friends of the 17th Illinois, with whom they had spent so many nights conversing. One Mississippian noted that the Illinoisans "aided us greatly by many acts of kindness." He explained how "they would go out to their sutler's tent with the greenbacks we had borrowed from their dead comrades and purchase food for us."[68]

The most amazing part of the fraternization was the food given to the famished Confederates. One Mississippian described how one "genuine son of the Emerald Isle" asked "how are you Johnings?" He asked if they were hungry and "emptied his haversack, which contained crackers, bacon coffee, etc." Others did the same "until we had enough to make a good meal—the first good one we had enjoyed for a long time." Grant wrote that "I myself saw our men taking bread from their haversacks and giving it to the enemy they had so recently been engaged in starving out. It was accepted with avidity and with thanks." A Confederate noted the only limitation: "Yankees treat us very well but will not sell us anything. Confederate money selling from 3 to 10 for one greenback U.S. money. Had chicken, oysters & sardines tonight—quite a rarity."[69]

One Mississippian described how he requested to go to the Union sutler but was turned down by a nice officer who said regulations required him to forward an application for a permit. The Mississippian responded that "I would be dead some days before its return," which made the Federal laugh. The officer then said he could only offer him some of the "trash" in his haversack, and the Mississippian made a good meal on the pitiful trash that was left over in the Federal's knapsack.[70]

It was odd to say the least, that these two foes who only hours before had been trying to kill each other were now mingling with the utmost cordiality. Grant went so far as to note that the two armies "fraternized as if they had been fighting for the same cause." And it extended beyond the soldiers. Grant allowed families of soldiers to depart the city if they had their own transportation. Another instance of Grant's favor toward civilians developed when the wife of Colonel Thomas P. Dockery, who had taken command of Martin Green's brigade when the latter was killed late in the siege, found Grant himself on July 5 and asked about the fate of her husband. Grant of course did not know personally but sent a note to Pemberton, who replied that Dockery was safe and sound.[71]

W hile Grant was most concerned about the events around Vicksburg itself, he had additional troops in other areas who needed to be kept informed. He had men all up and down the Mississippi River and garrisons in Louisiana at various places, as well as the navy in the rivers. He had to keep all informed because many of these—particularly within range of Vicksburg itself—had been firing into the city. Particularly, the navy as well as batteries on the opposite shore of the river needed to be kept in full awareness of what was going on and when and when not to fire.

Grant kept in close touch with Admiral Porter on the river, telling him as soon as he received the note from Pemberton that "the enemy have asked armistice to arrange terms of capitulation. Will you please cease firing until notified, or hear our batteries open?" As the negotiations proceeded, he also asked Porter to keep a boat ready to send the news southward to Nathaniel Banks at Port Hudson as well as north to Memphis, which was ordered: "Hold the boat until Mr. Dana arrives." Of course, Grant and Porter also discussed the problem of the prisoners of war and what to do with them, Porter giving advice to parole them rather than tying up almost all river vessels transporting them north. As the peace negotiations lingered on, Porter could not help but ask "what prospect is there of a Surrender to day[?]" Other naval officers were also anxious to hear what was going on, Rawlins telling one "don't go off half cocked." Once Pemberton accepted the surrender terms, Grant advised that "the enemy has accepted in the main my terms of capitulation, and will surrender the city, works, and garrison at 10 A.M." Porter responded, "I congratulate you in getting Vicksburg on any honorable terms."[72]

Grant similarly notified Nathaniel Banks at Port Hudson. "The garrison of Vicksburg surrendered this morning," he wrote, explaining that "although I had the garrison of Vicksburg completely in my power, I gave them the privilege of being paroled at this place. . . . I regard the terms really more favorably than an unconditional surrender."[73]

By far, the vast majority of Grant's apprehension lay with Sherman to the east. The concern was not so much about Sherman's safety, although he now faced the largest concentration of still-operable Confederates commanded by the respected Joseph E. Johnston. Still, Sherman could take care of himself and had ample troops to defend the rear. What Grant was more concerned about was taking the fight to Johnston as soon as Vicksburg surrendered. With one prong of the Confederate potential threat neutralized, he wanted to beef up the other and unleash it all on Johnston. Grant thus informed Sherman the minute he received Pemberton's note, writing that "I judge Johnston is not coming to Vicksburg . . . from the fact that I have just received a proposition from Pemberton to appoint three commissioners to arrange terms of capitulation, to save effusion of blood, &c." Grant told Sherman he wanted him to go after Johnston as soon as the surrender was official: "I want Johnston broken up as effectually as possible." In another note he gave more detail: "I want you to drive Johnston from the Mississippi Central Railroad; destroy bridges as far as Grenada with your cavalry, and do the enemy all the harm possible."[74]

Grant accordingly kept Sherman well informed throughout July 3 and into the next day. Later, Grant telegraphed, "There is but little doubt but the enemy will surrender to-night or in the morning; make your calculations to attack

Johnston." Sherman noted that on the "first hint of the capitulation of Vicksburg, . . . I immediately concentrated on the three best points for passing Big
Black River," meaning the railroad bridge, Messenger's Ford, and Birdsong
Ferry. He had bridges built at Messenger's and Birdsong, while one already
existed at the railroad bridge.[75]

Sherman's force, as large as it was, would not be all his assets, however.
Grant promised support from the army at Vicksburg once it surrendered.
Grant even sent Sherman the pontoon train, but troops were the most important resources, and Grant let Sherman pick which ones he wanted. Sherman
wanted all he could get and asked for both his own XV Corps now under
Frederick Steele and Ord's XIII Corps and verified that he could take Parke's
IX Corps as well. "I will concentrate at Bolton and strike from there," he
notified Grant. He also needed maps, noting that "I sent my old ones off, supposing we were done with them."[76]

Sherman spent a nervous few hours waiting on word from Grant, even
keeping "a swift officer at the telegraph office 3 miles back, to bring me the
earliest intelligence." Knowing that Vicksburg was about to fall would make
him prickly enough, but also knowing that Vicksburg's fall meant the beginning of another campaign made it all the more consuming for Sherman. "If
you are in Vicksburg, glory, hallelujah!," he telegraphed late on July 3, not
knowing the proceedings were dragging out. Still, he termed the event, even
if the surrender took place on July 3, "the best Fourth of July since 1776."
Then he nervously lectured his friend Grant: "Of course, we must not rest
idle, only don't let us brag too soon," ending with "[I] await with anxiety
your further answer."[77]

An obviously nervous Sherman wrote again that night, expounding more
fully on what he thought should be done. "The news is so good I can hardly
believe it," he gushed; "if Vicksburg is ours, it is the most valuable conquest
of the war, and the more valuable for the stout resistance it has made; if
complete, we should follow up rapidly, but should leave nothing to chance.
Of course we should instantly assume the offensive as against Johnston."
Sherman even mentioned a campaign as far as Meridian, on the other side of
the state, and bristled at sending troops to Banks at Port Hudson. Even if that
place was not surrendered yet, it was "now well invested, and an increased
force there could do less good than the destruction of the only army that can
afford them relief, viz, Johnston's."[78]

At other times, Sherman heard artillery at Vicksburg, confusing him as to what was actually going on. He asked Grant; and he had Parke, who was actually at the telegraph office, send still another note. Grant replied that the "flag of truce only covered bearer of dispatches; firing was continued by balance of the line." Later, Grant tried to keep his anxious subordinate in the loop at all times, writing early on July 4, "Pemberton's reply is momentarily expected. If he does not surrender now, he will be compelled to by his men within two days, no doubt." For their part, Sherman's soldiers knew little of what was going on and contented themselves with the vast array of blackberries, apples, and peaches that were just becoming ripe.[79]

Great news soon came on July 4. Rumors first floated around, but the troops had learned not to believe them. Then came an official pronouncement from Sherman himself. He basked in the victory even though he was not there, writing that "personal curiosity would tempt me to go and see the frowning batteries and sunken rifle pits that have defied us so long and sent to their silent graves so many of [our] early comrades in the enterprise." But he vowed to stay "in my solitary camp out in the wood, far from the point for which we have jointly striven so long and so well." He well knew that "I must again [go] into the bowels of the land to make the conquest of Vicksburg fulfill all the conditions it should in the progress of this war." Not being at the telegraph office himself, he told Parke to "tender his warmest congratulations." Parke added, "Please accept my own."[80]

Yet there was no time to gloat. The Confederates had surrendered, and the troops Sherman requested would be moving eastward soon: "We will have to move light and rapid to interpose between Johnston's scattered forces," Sherman advised Parke. Still, the slight delay provided some time for those already in the rear to celebrate. "This is a glorious day for our noble boys here," Colonel Marcus Spiegel of the 120th Ohio wrote to his wife from the Big Black River on July 4; "all of us feel wild with enthusiasm." He added, "We raised a Liberty Pole in my Regiment, made Speeches and hurrah and so forth." Levi Bennett of the same brigade wrote that Lieutenant Colonel Oran Perry "called the boys up to his tent and read an order from Vicksburg," including how many generals, colonels, and others had surrendered. He added, "We are a happy set of boys in general." A 93rd Illinois soldier described how the "men were wild with joy and excitement. They would embrace and hug each other, throw up their hats, yell and embrace again." Their brigade commander, Charles Matthies, "felt so good that he bought a barrel of whiskey for each regiment to celebrate the 'Fourth' with, and I tell you they did celebrate."[81]

Such happiness lasted only a short time, and even less for Steele's and Ord's troops, who shuffled almost immediately eastward to join Sherman. Alvin Hovey admitted that after all they had done "we fancied we could rest awhile. But Gen Grant thought not." An Ohioan added: "I could enjoy the victory much better but the report is around camp that Steele's division is ordered to draw ten days rations and leave soon for Black River—perhaps after Johnston. I wish they would let us rest in Vicksburg awhile. We need rest and besides are curious to see how Vicksburg and the fortifications around it look." "No rest for the wicked," another concluded. One even wrote "we were not to be permitted to see the land of promise at last," although Colonel David Grier of the 77th Illinois allowed his boys to go into town on the afternoon of July 4 provided they promise to be back that evening to march eastward after Johnston. He thought "that it was too bad for the boys not to get to see the place after battling so long for its possession, he told the boys that if they would all be back before that time he would take responsibility to let them go and see the town." Others took matters in their own hands, one Federal admitting in his diary, "In the afternoon I run the guards and visited the fallen city." A sick Hovey even "tried hard to get his division in camp but it was no use," although most did not march until the next day. The Federal troops were not surprisingly in a foul mood because of the new efforts: "The men were inclined to think that the results accomplished by this army in two months . . . entitled them to a full holiday on the 4th of July, with the privilege of marching into Vicksburg and beholding with their own eyes the fruits of the victory." One soldier complained, "but Grant and Sherman were never content to rest on victories won, while an enemy was in sight." Thus, these troops marched on the holiday. Colonel Spiegel, who had planned on a leave when Vicksburg was taken, similarly had to inform his wife of the delay: "I will have to postpone my going home until we get to some place where we stop awhile." Another simply added, "We are going back to Black River to capture Joe Johnston & send him and his army up with the rest."[82]

Sherman thus set out eastward after Johnston, one Federal left behind in the convalescent camp at the railroad bridge writing that "they left the tents and everything stand as they were." Sherman accordingly began an entirely new campaign, ultimately with his own and Ord's corps, with Parke's

("Sooy" Smith's division attached) as a reserve. Most of the army's cavalry went as well. The troops had five days' rations and a train of two hundred wagons to support them. Steele's troops moved toward the Big Black River for a crossing at Messenger's Ferry, while Parke moved eastward toward Birdsong's Ferry. Despite a slight illness manifested mostly in a cough, Ord and his men left late on July 4 and early the next morning. They moved to the railroad bridge and thence on out through Edwards Station and the Champion Hill battlefield, which Hovey declared they found "still reeking with stench from the dead carcasses of horses and mules." Osterhaus made a quick trip to Vicksburg on July 4 to find out the particulars (others such as Cadwallader Washburn from Haynes' Bluff did as well) and then joined the movement while McArthur's division of McPherson's corps, which soon included Ransom's brigade marching out from Vicksburg, took over at the railroad bridge. McArthur formed the area into a depot for Sherman's movement eastward. In all the shuffling, it occurred to Sherman that, with the change of command from McClernand to Ord, Osterhaus had never even met Ord. Sherman notified Osterhaus: "I will see General Ord before we actually cross Big Black River, and will mention you, as I believe you are comparative strangers." Eventually, all was worked out and Sherman's force vaulted across the Big Black River in pursuit of Johnston despite Sherman reporting "day excessively hot & troops suffered exceedingly from heat & dust." Ironically, the major impediment was the Big Black River, which rose four feet that day and partially damaged one of the bridges. Obviously, the rise came from rains farther up the watershed in central Mississippi. Another issue that irritated Sherman was Parke's slowness. He reported that for "some inexplicable cause the 9th corps is not yet up & I have no assurance that it is on this side of Black River."[83]

The news of Vicksburg's fall took a little longer to reach Johnston, although the sudden cessation of any noise coming from the west was a huge indication. Pemberton and Johnston had no such instantaneous communication like that utilized by Grant and Sherman, and Sherman of course wanted no advantage given Johnston. One Illinoisan, in fact, related that cannons could still be heard along the Big Black River even after news of Vicksburg's surrender came to the Federals: "I guess that old Joe Johnson is giving some of the boys a chance for to celebrate the forth, but I don't care about doing any thing of the kind." News nevertheless reached Johnston several hours later. The southernmost division of his force—Breckinridge's—had reached

Bolton with Wirt Adams's cavalry farther forward almost to Edwards itself. The others were fanned out to the north nearer to the Big Black River.[84]

What Johnston had in mind is conjecture, although division commander Samuel French reported that "the order of Gen. Johnston to cross the Big Black and attack Grant's new line *was issued*." It is doubtful that Johnston actually intended for the orders to be carried out. It is also possible that Johnston already knew of the surrender when he issued those orders but did so to illustrate to history that he was actually doing something.[85]

Early on July 5 the troops were "awakened with great silence." They thought they were heading for an attack on the Vicksburg besiegers but instead found orders to "about face": Vicksburg had surrendered, and as one Kentuckian noted, "we now had a foot race before us to beat a column of Grant's forces back to Jackson." A Mississippian similarly wrote, "After marching around a few days from place to place seeking a crossing, the astounding news came that Vicksburg had capitulated. Then a foot race was at once inaugurated between Johnston and Sherman to see who would reach Jackson first." A Federal took a different slant, writing that "he started as quick as his boots would let him go." Johnston sent out orders to Breckinridge that "you will immediately retrace your steps, and march your division toward Jackson. You will send the supply train and the pontoon train in advance. Lose no time in executing this order. Vicksburg has fallen, and the enemy is threatening an immediate advance." Breckinridge passed on the need to rush, writing to his brigade commanders: "Vicksburg has fallen, and the movement requires both celerity and vigilance." The other divisions received similar orders.[86]

Federal cavalry quickly noted Johnston's movement, one writing in his diary, "He is on a big skidaddle I guess." Unfortunately for both sides, these moves came amid the most horrible weather of the summer yet, with little water to be had. "I fear the dust, heat, and drought quite as much as the enemy," Sherman admitted. Breckinridge had to send out a circular in his division because of "the straggling which prevails in this command." Worse, these straggling soldiers were taking their angst out on the local people, Breckinridge himself spying "hundreds of men wandering through the country, many of them miles from their camps." Complaints from the locals poured in, and Breckinridge admitted that "the preens of the army will be regarded as a curse instead of a protection." He ordered his commanders to beef up the guards, have more frequent roll calls, "and [use] other suitable means . . . to put a stop to the irregularities above mentioned."[87]

Johnston also notified Richmond of the defeat: "Vicksburg capitulated on the 4th instant. . . . In consequence, I am falling back from the Big Black River to Jackson." To cover himself, he assured Richmond that "there has been no voluntary inaction." Johnston had done as little as possible but enough to make a show of effort, planning all the while never to get close enough to risk his force in a fight or, by extension, help Vicksburg's garrison in any meaningful way. One Union cavalryman wrote to his wife as early as May 28 that "there is a report that the Secesh is coming in with heavy reinforcements, but I think this is all bosh." How right he was.[88]

Ironically, Grant later confessed that, had he known Johnston was making a move forward, he would have "told Pemberton to wait in Vicksburg until I wanted him, awaited Johnston's advance, and given him battle." He added: "I would have destroyed two armies perhaps."[89]

In this case, one was good enough.

16

"GEN. GRANT HAS 'CAUGHT THE RABBIT'"

After July 4

"Vicksburg Is Ours!!," Union brigade commander Adolph Engelmann wrote to his wife on July 4, just as soon as the news broke. What had seemed the impossible and just too good to be true had actually come about. One Federal explained how "we all felt and expressed a good deal of surprise that the rebels did not manage to come down on some other day than this, either the day before or the day after at least; but necessity knows no law." The only cause for sadness in the Union army was that it would take days for the news to reach the Northern states, and they would not know such glorious happenings on Independence Day itself. Ohioan Charles A. Willison declared, "I wish the people up north would hear the news to-day. Wouldn't there be some rejoicing!" Another noted that, having seen announcements of coming July 4 celebrations in Iowa papers, "I would have given anything almost if I could by some means, have been conveyed from here, there and given the joyful news. What a celebration there would have [been] had you only known the situation here."[1]

It did take several days for the news to spread. It first went by word of mouth around the local area, Matilda Champion writing, "It is needless for me to speak of the gloom that encompassed us on hearing of the fall of Vicksburg." One civilian lady in Brownsville expressed astonishment in her diary:

> while sitting on the front gallery after breakfast several officers came riding
> up, warm and evidently fatigued. Their first remark, "Do you know Vicksburg

has fallen," was like a death blow. I do not know that I ever before experienced such sensations. It was so hard to believe yet I knew it must be so. They were of Johnston's army which was in full retreat. We gave them something to eat and they went on, to be succeeded by others continually the live-long day, all telling the same sad tale, "Vicksburg has fallen," some believing and a very few still expressing doubt. It was with sad hearts that we saw this day draw to a close.[2]

Newspapers picked up the story and spread the news around the nation faster than word of mouth ever could. Vicksburg had been on the front page of *Harper's Weekly* for four straight weeks in June, so the public was attuned to the operations. And they could not get enough as papers large and small began to carry stories of the surrender and final days of the siege, as well as the possibility of future action. The news also filtered out into the entire country after it reached the urban areas by paper or telegraph. Near St. Louis, Julia Grant was sitting chatting with friends in an upstairs room when they were startled by "a perfect salvo of artillery." She hurriedly called out the window to her Confederacy-favoring father sitting on the porch if he thought Vicksburg had surrendered. He replied, "Yes, I should not wonder if both Vicksburg and Richmond had fallen from the infernal noise they are making." Word even filtered across the Atlantic. One Confederate in Europe wrote, "The news that we have received by the way of New York is of such later date and is of such a character as that to cause many Confederates on this side of the water to despair of our success."[3]

News went out more slowly in soldier's letters, which numbered in the tens of thousands. It seemed that almost everyone wanted to write their loved ones and acquaintances and tell their part of the story. "Vicksburg is ours and every thing in it," one excitedly wrote. "Thank God Vixburg has fallen into our hands at last," another told his wife. "I wish I could describe to you how our troops feel and act. All feel that we have done a *big thing* and want to rejoice over it," another bragged. On and on their letters went, one even opining, "Is the Lord on our side?" Another religious Federal wrote about "a quiet Sabbath once more, no cannonading no bursting boms attract our attention but as is as still as death. One is reminded of a Sabbath at home, though no church bell is heard."[4]

Generals also wrote their loved ones unofficial letters. John Logan wrote to his wife simply that "the long struggle is over." Sherman even told his devout wife, Ellen, to celebrate and "get tight." Yet one of his soldiers added

508   CHAPTER SIXTEEN

that "the 4th of July was a Glorious one to us although we could not celebrate it any other way than by marching towards Jackson to fight for our Country."[5]

Of course, Washington waited for official word from Grant or Porter, and it took a few days to reach the East. Memphis got the word by July 6, with confirmation the next day. Unfortunately, the telegraph was dead, so the bearer continued up the Mississippi River to Cairo, where it went out on July 7. Grant had written Halleck as soon as the surrender took place, at 10:30 A.M. in fact. "The enemy surrendered this morning," he wrote. "The only terms allowed is their parole as prisoners of war. This I regard as of great advantage to us at this juncture. It saves probably several days in the captured town; leaves troops and transports ready for immediate service." He also added that Sherman was off to Jackson and that he would send troops to Banks and Burnside. Grant's action sparked some question as to legality of paroles, but Halleck was soon satisfied and was as happy as anyone. When Lincoln received word, on July 7 from Secretary of the Navy Gideon Welles, the president "caught my hand, and, throwing his arm around me exclaimed . . . 'I cannot, in words, tell you my joy over this result. It is great, Mr. Welles, it is great!'"[6]

Word also drifted down to Port Hudson, Grant sending the news to Banks just as quickly in the hopes that the Confederates there would likewise give in. That news arrived on July 7, and Banks sent it to the troops, who responded with cheers. A salute of a hundred guns also rang out, and the bewildered Confederates wanted to know what all the fuss was about. Port Hudson's commander, Major General Franklin Gardner, sent a flag of truce to Banks, who sent back a copy of the dispatch. Gardner then surrendered on July 9. Thus another round of celebration occurred, Sherman writing to his senator-brother that "the fall of Vicksburg and consequent capitulation of Port Hudson, the opening of the navigation of the Mississippi, and now the driving out of this great valley the only strong army that threatened us, complete as pretty a page in the history of war and our country as ever you could ask my name to be identified with." A lower-level Federal said it more bluntly: "We have cleared out the Rebs from this country so thoroughly I think they will not attempt to come back soon again, for fear of another Vicksburg trap being set for them." Another added, "I hope that this victory may settle the Copperheads."[7]

The mood was much different in Richmond and across the South. Jefferson Davis also received word on July 7, the secretary of war "announcing the disastrous termination of the siege of Vicksburg, received same day."

Mississippian Thomas J. Wharton had traveled to Richmond and arrived right as word of Vicksburg's fall came in. Trying to put it all together, and perhaps to start laying blame, Davis, on his sickbed, asked Wharton how the people of Mississippi viewed Pemberton. Wharton "candidly" reported that many "doubted his loyalty to the cause." A frustrated Davis also demanded answers from Johnston: "Painfully anxious as to the result, I have remained without information from you as to any plans proposed or attempted to raise the siege. Equally uninformed as to your plans in relation to Port Hudson, I have to request such information in relation thereto as the Government has a right to expect from one of its commanding generals in the field." Johnston simply informed Davis a couple of days later that Port Hudson also fell on July 9. A distraught Mississippi governor John J. Pettus also corresponded with Richmond about the debacle and the ensuing one at Jackson.[8]

Few noticed amid all the national hoopla and despair a small declaration in the Vicksburg *Daily Citizen*. Editor Swords had his July 2 issue still laid out at the typesetters' station, and it contained a boastful admonition: "The Great Ulysses—the Yankee Generalissimo—surnamed Grant—has expressed his intention of dining in Vicksburg on Sunday next, and celebrating the 4th of July by a grand dinner. . . . Ulysses must get into the city before he dines in it. The way to cook a rabbit is 'first to catch the rabbit.'" An Indianan familiar with newspaper printing wandered into the office and read the declaration. He could not resist answering the boast, and he put out a July 4 edition with only slight changes, mainly corrected spelling and a small note boxed in at the bottom:

> Two days bring about great changes. The banner of the Union floats over Vicksburg. Gen. Grant has 'caught the rabbit;' he has dined in Vicksburg, and he did not bring dinner with him. The 'Citizen' lives to see it. For the last time urge Southern warriors to such diet never-more. This is the last wall-paper edition, and is, excepting this note, from the type as we found them. It will be valuable hereafter as a curiosity.[9]

So the rabbit was finally caught. And not surprisingly, after the shock wore off and reality set in, many Confederates were just glad to finally be out from the ordeal—win or lose. One admitted it was "pleasant to be able to move around without being obliged to dodge to keep our cranium safe." Some even had mixed feelings after it was all said and done. A Confederate, talking to a Federal, spied a Union flag float out in the breeze and admitted, "O the Old Stars & Stripes look so 'poorty.'" Still the Confederates had fought well and were proud of their defense, especially under such harsh circumstances. "But I can say we gave them Hail Columbia for forty-eight days and nights," one reminded anyone who would listen. Even Confederates in the east applauded the effort: "Our soldiers in the Army of [Northern] Va. look with pride on the men who have so gallantly defended the Key to our Mother State."[10]

The full measure of the victory and defeat became apparent as the numbers finally started coming in. Pemberton ultimately surrendered 29,491 troops, most of them signing paroles but a few refusing to do so and being sent north to prison. Yet the numbers were a bit misleading, as many of those Confederates were not available for the front lines, either being detailed in town or sick in the hospitals. Stephen D. Lee believed no more than 15,500 men were actually on the lines, with 19,500 total for duty. The rest came from sick and others: "The city having been a base of supplies, where the largest Confederate army was kept for a long time before the investment, was full of sick and wounded men, quarter-master, commissary employees and extra duty men, and hangers on of every kind, who were suddenly shut in by Gen. Grant's rapid movement." The haul also included Captain David Todd, Mary Todd Lincoln's half-brother.[11]

In addition, there was an immense amount of military equipment, although not in the best of shape. One Federal described capturing "a great many almost starved mules and rickety wagons." A wealth of artillery fell with the Vicksburg garrison, a total of 102 field guns reported by Confederate authorities, although Grant explained later that "there is much more artillery than we thought; the field pieces are given at 128, and about 100 siege guns." A final tally of 172 total pieces ultimately came about, including both field and siege weaponry. Of course, all the ammunition for those guns was also captured. Grant also listed about fifty thousand "small-arms of good quality."[12]

The number of captured of course did not take into account those lost earlier in the siege (or the entire campaign, for that matter). Differing numbers appear in various places, but the Confederates reported, with three brigade returns missing, a total of 2,872 casualties during the siege itself, 805 of those killed and 1,938 wounded, with a mere 129 missing, which most certainly does not account for all the desertions. With little means of getting news out during the siege, word of those killed and wounded at Vicksburg finally filtered out with the Vicksburg prisoners for the first time. On the other side, out of a total of 71,141 troops Grant reported at Vicksburg on June 30, along with 248 guns, Federal returns reported a mere 530 casualties in the siege, which is certainly low as well, one volume putting the total at 4,910. Ironically, Grant's numbers grew slightly as the surrender took place; Union prisoners held inside Vicksburg were released when the Confederates surrendered the city.[13]

With such a haul, there were obvious congratulations for almost everyone involved on the Union side. Both Sherman and McPherson issued congratulations to their corps, no doubt careful to follow all regulations after the McClernand episode. Ironically, both were very congratulatory, much like McClernand's. Sherman crowed a little in all they had accomplished, expressing to Ellen that "had the eastern armies done half as much [the] war would be substantially entered up."[14]

The almost giddy Union high command sent messages crisscrossing all over the army and navy, offering congratulations. An energetic Sherman preparing to move from his Bear Creek line toward Jackson could hardly contain himself. He wrote to Porter, "No event in life could have given me more personal pride or pleasure than to have met you to-day on the wharf at Vicksburg—a Fourth of July so eloquent in events as to need no words or stimulants to elevate its importance." But he added: "I can appreciate the intense satisfaction you must feel at lying before the very monster that has defied us with such deep and malignant hate and seeing your once disunited fleet again a unit; and better still, the chain that made an enclosed sea of a link in the great river broken forever." Francis Herron also congratulated Porter and thanked him for his aid to his division while "reducing the Sebastopol of Rebeldom." Navy secretary Welles himself praised Porter and the navy and basked at the "speedy, uninterrupted navigation of the rivers which water and furnish the ocean outlet to the great central valley of the Union."[15]

Most of the congratulation went to Grant. His soldiers did not refrain from his praise, one writing, "Gen Grant is the man for me." Another declared that "General Grant and July 4th 1863 will from this time be household words." Sherman offered his own praise, writing, "I can hardly contain myself." Being close friends, he added that there was no use in providing "wanton flattery" and even warning Grant against others who might do so. The plaudits came from unfamiliar sources as well. Halleck wrote that "we cannot fail to admire the courage and endurance of the troops and the skill and daring of their commander. No more brilliant exploit can be found in military history." He also sought to tamp down rumors: "It has been alleged, and the allegation has been widely circulated by the press, that General Grant, in the conduct of his campaign, positively disobeyed the instructions of his superiors. It is hardly necessary to remark that General Grant never disobeyed an order or instruction." Halleck's most effusive praise went to the general himself. He wrote that "in boldness of plan, rapidity of execution, and brilliancy of results, these operations will compare most favorably with those of Napoleon about Ulm. You and your army have well deserved the gratitude of your country, and it will be the boast of your children that their fathers were of the heroic army which reopened the Mississippi River." In response for their victories, Grant was made a major general in the regular army and Porter gained the full rank of rear admiral.[16]

The common soldier crowed as well in letters home and even in verse. One foot soldier from Illinois gave his opinion that this campaign was "one of the grandest events of the war, and will make one of the brightest pages in history when recorded for its bold and daring beginning, its skillful management, and the brave fighting of the soldiers clear through the siege. It is unequaled." Another declared, "This campaign which has ended with the capture of Vicksburg I think is the most brilliant in the history of the world." One specifically spoke of the siege, writing that it was "the crowning achievement of this most brilliant campaign." An Illinoisan added, "Never did the sun shine on a more resilient and glorious army. Napoleon never had a superior one." Thomas Watson put it into a larger context: "The war [has] not ended yet, but it looks more like ending."[17]

The victorious Federals also had some praise for the defeated. "They are pluck to the bone," one Federal admitted. Another wrote that "the rebs stood up and fought like tigers as long as they had any thing to eat." They were also cognizant of the need for respect. "Not one time did I hear a soldier say, 'We have taken Vicksburg!,'" explained a Mississippian, but rather "you have made a wonderfully brave defense." Another admitted, "There was no yelling, nor exulting—that is outwardly—over our discomfiture; not even when the stars and stripes were seen floating from the Court House. There were no mortifying jokes, no juts, or comparisons at our expense." There was also no personal gain among the Federals. Grant ordered Herron to gather the arms and equipment as well as flags of the enemy but stipulated that "none of the colors are to be taken by any individual; they are all to be sent to Washington."[18]

While plenty of congratulations went back and forth in the Union army, there was little to congratulate in the Southern forces, except perhaps the bravery and stamina of the army that defended Vicksburg all those weeks. Rather, there was a good deal of castigation and blame tossed around. And unsurprisingly, most of it rested on John C. Pemberton.[19]

Although a few later took up for Pemberton, brigade commander Francis Shoup writing that "he had a hard place to fill," most found Pemberton to be the obvious and convenient person to blame for the disaster. One fumed at the "surrender on the 4th of July to Grant by Pemberton without the knowledge or consent of the men who had fought so gallantly and endured such hardships for 48 days. Sold by a traitor." Other complaints had no credibility whatsoever, such as the rumor that Pemberton had sold Vicksburg to Grant for "2 million in gold." One Federal noted: "I tried to convince them to the contrary but they firmly believe it." A civilian later gossiped that Pemberton had been seen "crawling out of a cave," and a surrendered soldier declared that "a child would have known better than to shut men up in this cursed trap to starve to death like useless vermin."[20]

Certainly, the notion that Pemberton was a Yankee in disguise permeated the Confederate troops, especially with the surrender on July 4 of all days. His later comments on the subject did not help, and many just could not get past the way it all turned out. "I had certainly believed Pemberton to be a traitor for he certainly could have had it later or on a day sooner," one Louisianan confessed. Mississippian William Pitt Chambers agreed: "Oh, how burned the haggard cheek with shame and indignation to realize that on that day of all others Vicksburg should be surrendered! Why could not the deed have been consummated yesterday or tomorrow?"[21]

Pemberton made a solid defense in his report and later in an unfinished letter after the war seeking to exonerate himself. But nothing would ever change the tide of public opinion. Pemberton later reported to Richmond, and Davis devised a plan to put him in command of a corps under Bragg, but Bragg demurred, wanting to talk to his officers. He later replied that "it would not be advisable." Davis still thought highly of Pemberton, especially when he resigned his commission as a lieutenant general and rejoined the army as a lieutenant colonel. There, he fought in Virginia, and Postmaster General

John Reagan observed him bravely exposing himself to fire, so much so that "our speculation was that the criticisms of his surrender at Vicksburg had so wrought on his mind that he was seeking death on the battlefield."[22]

Historians ever since have not been any more kind, one writing with evident scorn: "In an unfamiliar situation, Pemberton had wilted in the heat of his great responsibility and found refuge in the familiar—fortifications—and turned defeat into catastrophe by losing the army as well as the city." Perhaps the biggest insult came from perhaps the most famous source: later in the Overland Campaign in Virginia, while fighting against Robert E. Lee, Grant remarked once that Pemberton was his "best friend."[23]

More than just Pemberton came in for blame, however, and rightly so. The Davis administration also endured some heated comments. Sid Champion, who had lost almost as much as anybody in the campaign, wrote: "I feel that the President has shamefully neglected us in every particular." Some hit both, such as a Tennessean seething at lying behind the works while their arms were stacked in front. With Union sentries on guard atop the fortifications, he wrote plainly: "This lesson ought to teach President Davis that it won't do to place a Yankee general over a Southern army. We all believe we were sold and will never believe anything else." Pemberton's staff officer John C. Taylor not surprisingly shifted focus from Pemberton, writing that the blame should fall "with the administration or Genl Johnston."[24]

Indeed, Johnston also received some blame—exactly what he had feared. "I thought that Johnston would do something but he done nothing," James Skelton wrote to his sister. Davis openly questioned him, to which Johnston argued that Pemberton's lack of "co-operation" as well as the difficulty in communication, along with paltry numbers, a lack of transportation, and sundry other issues, "rendered co-operation next to impossible." He also reminded Davis that Pemberton had disobeyed his order to evacuate Vicksburg before the siege, something against Davis's wishes, of course, adding bitingly and sarcastically: "It is a new military principle that, when an officer disobeys a positive order of his superior, that superior become responsible for any measure his subordinate may choose to substitute for that ordered." Given Johnston's clout at the time, most of the blame has come from historians ever since. It seems his late movement had done enough to mostly take the blame off of himself at the time, although Pemberton never agreed and waged a war of words with Johnston for the rest of his life. Historians have taken up the task, one arguing that "Johnston had effectively refused to do his job and to accept the command given him." In his expert analysis, Terry Winschel found major fault with Johnston, arguing that he took four "precious" days to respond to Pemberton's June 23 message reporting fifteen days as the ultimate limit of holding out. And then it was four more days before he moved. Winschel has written that Johnston seemed "prompted only by the realization that if he permitted Vicksburg to fall without making an attempt to save the city and its garrison, his reputation would be destroyed and his military career finished." Thus, he waited until the last of the fifteen days to make a major move, putting on record a message to Pemberton (which he never received) that he would attack on July 7—the extreme limit of Pemberton's fifteen days. And after the July 1 move, he stopped again for a couple more days on July 3–4. Winschel argues that Johnston "so delayed as long as he thought prudent to save his reputation without risking the possibility of battle."[25]

Some historians have taken up for Johnston, one writing that "it was useless to sacrifice two armies for an illusory hope of saving one." Yet if the blow landed by losing the one would be crippling, the attempt at this stage of the game in June 1863, much like at Shiloh in April 1862, almost *had* to be made. Albert Sidney Johnston had realized that an attack at Shiloh—even as a gamble and a long shot—had to be made because no other better chance loomed in the future. He thus rode into battle with the mantra "conquer or perish." In much the same circumstances in the summer of 1863, Joseph E. Johnston's mantra seemed rather to be "look out for number one." Perhaps Davis said it best in arguing that the lack of provisions was a cause for the surrender: "Yes, from want of provisions inside, and a general outside who wouldn't fight."[26]

Blame and defeat were not limited just to the Confederates, however. John A. McClernand also found himself castigated and defeated, even though he was on the winning side. Surprisingly, Grant did not let the issue lie but continued to berate McClernand even after the victory, perhaps in justification to himself of his subordinate's removal. When McClernand turned in his report of the actions of his corps, Grant cautioned that "this report contains so many inaccuracies that to correct it, to make it a fair report to be handed down as historical, would require the rewriting of most of it. It is pretentious and egotistical." Others even took aim at those associated with McClernand, such as his staff officer Lieutenant Colonel Henry C. Warmouth, who had been wounded on May 22 and left the army. Some argued he had overdone his wound and just wanted a leave.[27]

McClernand was hardly quiet, perhaps causing some of Grant's continued animus. After returning to Springfield, he asked a week later for Halleck to restore him to command "at least until Vicksburg shall have fallen."
He reminded Halleck that, just two days prior to "my banishment," Grant
had increased his corps by giving him command of Lauman's division as
well. McClernand argued that this fact "cannot consistently object upon the
score of distrust of my fidelity or ability." Halleck refused. Getting nowhere,
McClernand went to Grant directly, writing that the "ostensible motive" for
removal was the press release, but "the motive for so unwarranted an act
was hostility—*personal* hostility." In a questionnaire letter that summer, Mc-
Clernand listed the reason as "jealousy and general bad feeling against his
continued success assigned as the cause of this arbitrary act." He later added
that the hostility grew "out of the early connection of my name with the Mississippi River expedition."[28]

Making the situation more difficult, McClernand had supporters—and
high-level ones at that. McClernand showing up in Springfield posed a problem for Governor Richard Yates. "Major-General McClernand arrived here
on the 26th instant," he wrote to Lincoln. "He has been received by the people
here with the greatest demonstrations of respect, all regretting that he is not
now in the field." Searching for a solution, Yates advised: "I desire to suggest
that if General McClernand, with some Western troops, was put in command
of Pennsylvania, it would inspire great hope and confidence in the Northwest,
and perhaps throughout the country." Lincoln responded that he had no command to give him, even writing to McClernand himself: "I doubt whether
your present position is more painful to you than to myself." Yet he remained
firm, adding that to "force you back upon General Grant" would cause him
to resign, and there were many others just like McClernand who had people
lobbying on their behalf for new commands: "Fremont, McClellan, Butler,
Sigel, Curtis, Hunter Hooker, and perhaps others."[29]

McClernand eventually asked for an investigation and repeated the inquiry
when he heard nothing from Stanton. Lincoln refused to grant any investigation, although based on the questionable issue that it would "necessarily
withdraw from the field many officers whose presence with their commands
is absolutely indispensable to the service." An astute McClernand knew that
Lincoln's response meant that the president had moved on from his fellow Illinoisan. Grant was his man now. McClernand kept writing nevertheless, later
in September offering a "protest against portions of Major-General Grant's

[Vicksburg] report." By that time it was over for him, however. McClernand was shattered and had to leave "my public actions and my character, which is worth more to me than my life, for the impartial judgment of my military superiors and of the country and history."[30]

The removal did not officially end McClernand's military career, although Ord's position as XIII Corps commander became official when the presidential appointment took place on July 10. McClernand returned for a brief command of the XIII Corps during the Red River Campaign, but for all practical purposes his influential military career was over.[31]

Recriminations and blame aside, what was the real story of why Vicksburg fell? Many argued that the city was starved out, which seemed to be Grant's intent early on. Others agreed. "After 48 days of fighting we yielded for lack of provisions," one Confederate wrote home. A Federal believed the lack of food story, commenting: "I don't remember of seeing a single dog in the city."[32]

Yet the lack of food was not as great as sometimes argued. There was a lack of available food for the army, and many Confederate diaries and accounts displayed the paltry, and continuously dwindling, portions over the course of the siege. But that did not mean there was not more available in reserve. Pemberton purposefully kept back a certain amount in case his forces suddenly were called on to make an escape attempt. They would need provisions to take with them, and so he held back ample supplies in reserve. The surrender thus came at the depletion of the usable stock, not the full store of food. Pemberton, in fact, reported that at the time of the surrender there were "about 40,000 pounds of pork and bacon, which had been reserved for the subsistence of my troops in the event of attempting to cut my way out of the city; also 51,241 pounds of rice, 5,000 bushels of peas, 92,234 pounds of sugar, 3,240 pounds of soap, 527 pounds of tallow candles, 27 pounds of Star candles, and 428,000 pounds of salt." While that sounds like a lot of food, it was only about five days' worth of pork if issued at the reduced four ounces per day to the entire thirty thousand–man garrison. Grant agreed, reporting separately that he found inside Vicksburg "about four days' rations of flour and bacon, and 250 pounds of sugar." Of course, the irony is that this food, while held in reserve, was never used.[33]

The argument that the Confederates ran out of ammunition was also made, probably based on the calls for conservatism in using it throughout the siege. The Federals thought so, one taking exception to what he thought was a heavy fire of cannon, writing that "if they keep it up at this rate, I think they will soon have them all used up." More persuasively, Engineer Frederick Prime attested, "We attributed during the siege the silence of their artillery to the lack of ammunition." Yet the Federals found ample ordnance supplies as well when they took control of the city, and it could have made a difference if used. Prime predicted that "if at almost any point they had put ten or fifteen guns in position, instead of one or two to invite concentration of our fire, they might have seriously delayed our approaches." He added that "a small portion of this judiciously used, would have rendered our approach much slower." Thus only musketry resulted, "and even this was used sparingly in comparison with our own." The more pressing concern, of course, was the lack of percussion caps, but couriers bringing in more throughout the siege remedied that concern at least to some degree.[34]

The main reason Pemberton surrendered when he did was because of the state of affairs from the tactical standpoint, and that was twofold. Pemberton wrote that "not because my men were starved out, not because I could not hold out yet a little longer, but because they were overpowered by numbers, worn down with fatigue, and each day saw our defense crumbling beneath their feet. The question of subsistence, therefore, had nothing whatever to do with the surrender of Vicksburg." Certainly, Pemberton's comments came as he was under a cloud for not stockpiling more supplies in Vicksburg; he used his report as a lengthy justification of just how much war material he had actually hoarded inside Vicksburg and how well he had supplied the city for months beforehand. He concluded several times that the lack of certain provisions was not his fault; he used language such as "caused by circumstances wholly beyond my control," "I am not responsible for that deficiency," and "I only desire that I may not be held responsible for what the Government could not furnish."[35]

Plenty of Confederates agreed with the assertion that the troops were just too worn out to resist much longer and certainly to cut themselves out. "We endured as much as mortals ever endured in an army—every day from daylight until late in the night," one Tennessean asserted. Division commander John Forney agreed, writing, "The siege of Vicksburg was a contest which tried more the endurance and resolution of the men and their company and regimental commanders than the skill of their generals." One of his brigade commanders, John C. Moore, added how "by this time their minds and bodies seemed exhausted, and many remained at their post in the trenches who were fit subjects for the hospitals. Only those who have tried it can tell the effects produced on men by keeping them forty-seven days and nights in a narrow ditch, exposed to the scorching heat during the day and the often chilly air and dews of night." Yet the idea that the Confederates could stand several days or weeks more in the trenches was common. Francis Cockrell argued that the troops, even though tired, were "in no wise whipped, conquered, or subjugated."[36]

If sheer exhaustion was part of the twofold problem but not sufficient in itself to cause surrender, the other major factor was the ability of the Federals to launch a quick assault, either with or without mine blasts. The Federal engineering effort had been amazing and had put Grant's soldiers in perfect position to assault on July 6 — an attack that no doubt would have made quick, if bloody, work of the Confederate defenses. It conceivably could have come even sooner, as Prime argued that "we might have been ready for an assault two or three weeks earlier, if there had been a sufficient supply of engineer officers to watch that no time was lost or useless work done; to see that every shovelful of earth thrown brought us nearer to the end, and personally to push and constantly supervise the special works to which they were assigned."[37]

The result was that the exhausted Confederates could not break out and, most likely, would have faced the looming assault that they could not have repulsed in a matter of days. One soldier rightly stated that "the city was surrendered as much from fear of an assault on the fourth of July as from Starvation." Similarly, historian Justin Solonick has made a convincing argument that the Confederates in Vicksburg "were not starved out, they were dug out." Obviously, the lack of relief from Johnston, an entirely different issue, also played a part.[38]

The impact of these long days of brutal warfare on the structures and people of Vicksburg, and beyond, became more clear after the fighting ended. The Federals were now able to enter the city and see what all their bombardment had actually done. The destruction was immense. "There is hardly a house in the city but what has a cannon ball through it," one amazed Federal wrote to his family. Another described how Vicksburg appeared "as though a tornado had passed through." A scoop-gathering newspaper correspondent went into more detail: "The citizens insist that the damage is trifling, . . . but nearly every house in the city has been perforated by conical and round shot and shells. The pillars of piazzas are knocked down, doors and windows smashed, floors torn up, and damage done in every shape and form." He went on to say that "the city, which has been really a handsome place, is now pre-eminently war-worn—some degree and kind of devastation marks every thing you see." One soldier concluded, "This has been a living Hell on earth."[39]

Another newshound corroborated the stories. "It is said that there are some houses in the city that have escaped unscathed; but in my rambles through the streets I could not find them." Even Pemberton's headquarters had been hit, which was a special sight to see, including "a hole in the first room you enter on the left side of the hall which a mule could crawl through without diffi- culty." He went on to describe how "the northern portion of the city suffered most, and I cannot convey any idea of the damage sustained better than by saying it has been smashed." The results of the mortars were evident, but the people apparently feared them much less as they were lobbed toward them than the horizontal firing of the Parrott rifles from across the river: "Those fired from the mortars had become favorites with the people. Shots from Par- rott guns were not so popular." An Indiana soldier concluded, "It is a sight worth seeing to just go through town to see how things are torn up."[40]

Another correspondent similarly wrote of viewing the damage, one civil- ian showing where three shells had gone through his house yet no one was injured. They had a cave, but the man admitted "the greatest trouble was with my children. They did not appreciate the danger, and it was hard to keep them out of it." The correspondent asked one of the children, then five years old and swinging on a gate: "Are you a rebel?" The boy shot back, "Yeth thir." He asked next "are you going to be a soldier when you grow up." The boy responded again "yeth thir." He added that "many of the adult prisoners, however, are not so positive as this youngster. You may find plenty of them here who frankly confess they made a woeful mistake when they took up arms against the government of their country." Others particularly noted the sadness. Lucy McRae described how arms were stacked in the streets and a Tennessee regiment deposited its band instruments in their yard. A drummer boy gave his drum to her brother and another gave her his horse, but both were soon confiscated.[41]

Other problems surfaced besides the physical damage, which the citizens ignored and so began to move back into their houses. Many citizens took the oath of allegiance, particularly, one Confederate remembered, the German Jews. There was one exception who lost his store and goods for not doing so, he being labeled an "honorable exception," although it cost him around forty thousand dollars. Prices shot even higher, and some in Vicksburg were accused of extortion. Even catching fish was problematic, one lady remembering that "the fish in the river grew fat feasting on the bodies of the unfortunates that were killed or drowned, and it was many years before I could summon up courage to taste one." And then there were the ladies of Vicksburg, many of whom would not submit to Federal authority. One Federal wrote, "there is many a pretty young ladie in this place but they hait the Yankees worse than the devil." Even Grant himself was supposed to have told one that, "as for the women of the South . . . they cannot be conquered."[42]

The civilians outside the city also sought calm in the changing times. Sherman reported to Grant that "the farmers and families out here acknowledge the magnitude of this loss, and now beg to know their fate. All crops are destroyed and cattle eaten up. You will give their case your attention as soon as more important business is disposed of. At least I promise them this." Some feared for the final result. One soldier noted that "the Citizens of Miss. come out plainly and say that it isn't worth while to fight any longer." One of the civilians admitted that "the Yankees have ruined this country completely and I am afraid this Confederacy is gone also."[43]

Not all were ready to give in. A civilian man returned home, found a Federal on his couch, and barked, "By what authority, sir, do you take possession of another man's house?" The Federal replied, "That's none of your damned business," adding: "Who are you?" He replied, "I'm the owner of this house," whereupon the Federal asked if he was loyal. "That is none of your damned business," he spouted. It was later found out that the Federal was Grant's medical director, Surgeon Madison Mills; after the man went directly to Grant, Mills had to move to another house. Similarly, out in the rear areas, a young lady dying of consumption railed against the 4th Iowa Cavalry troops as she lay dying, "a death like pallor . . . keeping vigil o'er her wan and childish face." She managed to mouth, "I could live two weeks longer if I could know of General Johnston mopping you off as the sun mops off the morning dew." Those were her last words, and an Iowan reported, "I am proud to say she did not hear one word of reproof from our soldiers." The victorious Federals found many such civilians verbose and "spunky as rats." Others were simply trying to survive amid the personal changes in life, one writing that "Vicksburg fell on the day the baby was born."[44]

A major change also came over the newly freed slaves in the area, who were not shy about voicing their satisfaction with what had just happened. Obviously, the nearness of Federal troops helped them take such bold stances, one former slave bellowing "de long-looked-fer done come at lass." Many Mississippians found their freed slaves to be "arrogant," now with their new-found protection. That was only for the town slaves, however, at least according to one Mississippian who declared that the plantation slaves wanted nothing more than to go back home.[45]

The change in the blacks was evident, some conflict taking place as they found new freedom and acted on it. One Mississippian told of a group of freed black women who came to a house and began rummaging around. When told to leave they began cursing, saying "they were free and has as much right there as he had." The white man shot one of them in the leg after they "used the most violent language against the lady of the house," whereupon "pretty soon down came a crowd of black men, cursing and swearing and threatening." The man tried to shoot again, but the gun misfired. The blacks rushed him and "cowhided him severely," one of them holding a pistol to his head and forcing him to call him master. The man refused, telling the contraband to shoot him instead. Nothing happened, but the lady added: "I am surprised that he escaped alive but he did."[46]

The Federals quickly put the former slaves to work. "The Yankees are busy with negroes filling up the rifle pits in the streets and cleaning up the city," one disgusted Louisianan declared. Yet their gait was not always satisfactory, one Ohioan of a pioneer company that worked them writing of viewing a "negro dance." He noted, "If they would take as much interest in their work as they do in their dancing they would get more done."[47]

The most logical place to employ the male slaves was in the army, and Vicksburg quickly filled with black soldiers in blue. One Louisianan could not stand the sight when he "saw negroes standing up in two ranks & Yankees taking down their names. They pressed all the negroes of our army into their service today." Most thought the Federals were forcing the slaves to enter the service, but it could also have been for "working parties." Nevertheless, this newfound clout also added to the confidence the former slaves felt. Another Louisianan watched as "a Yankee negro sergeant . . . drew his pistol on one of the Yankee soldiers' white men." Still trying to make sense of the huge social changes occurring, mainly regarding racial issues, he could only think about how, "if this is permitted, what will soon befall this nation?"[48]

Just because Vicksburg surrendered did not mean all military movement ended. There was, after all, an active campaign against Joseph E. Johnston even then starting, and over the next couple of weeks it would result in campaigning all the way back to Jackson and then a semi-siege of that city, with Johnston ultimately withdrawing in mid-month. Sherman "pitched on to him before he knew it and chased him clear out of the country. Bully for Sherman," one Federal exclaimed. The campaign produced some fighting but little result beyond a major falling-out between Ord and Lauman, with charges preferred against the latter. Still, the maneuvering took the armies across much of the land already fought over, especially between Big Black River and Jackson. Many Federals marched back across the Champion Hill battlefield and were abhorred at the site of washed-open graves. Also interesting to the Federals, Hugh Ewing discovered some of Jefferson Davis's papers on his and his brother's alternate plantations that sat along the routes of march and where they camped.[49]

Grant also sent out other parts of his army for other military errands, although by the time reinforcements were ready to leave for Port Hudson that bastion had surrendered as well. Instead, Grant sent Herron's division up to Yazoo City to clear that valley of enemies. Troops also moved to Natchez and occupied that city, while Nathan Kimball's division moved north to Helena to stabilize that area. Eventually, after the Jackson operations ended, John Parke's IX Corps troops returned to Kentucky. One Massachusetts officer, William F. Draper, admitted that serving in the IX Corps was "a big class in Geography, and I think if we keep on we shall see pretty much all the United States before the war is over."[50]

Most occupation attention focused on Vicksburg itself, especially after Sherman returned from the Jackson effort. And a myriad of tasks awaited Federal attention. Commerce was now heavy on the river, one Federal noting eighty-seven steamers at Vicksburg at one time. Others were interested in returning the bodies of those who had died in the assaults and siege to loved ones up North, although one explained: "I have been advised by my superiors not to attempt to send his body home until cool weather. For now he would be nothing but a perfect mess of corruption." Some of the more disgusting effects of the siege were not even hidden in graves, such as one Ohioan who saw a corpse floating in the river the day after the surrender. More digging went on as well: "At the same time those parts of the fortifications which we were now to defend were selected, and the men began to obliterate the siege approaches at which they had worked so hard and so long."[51]

Sickness was also a problem for both sides, those Confederates who were already there remaining in their hospitals and Union sick and wounded being moved in some cases into town for better facilities. There was a particular rash of requests for medical leaves among the Union high command now that the fighting was over, all with surgeon's statements to attest to their need. Michael Lawler suffered from "Hepatitis with Diarrhea," Eugene Carr was "hardly able to walk," and James Tuttle had "acute dysentery which has become chronic." John McArthur requested leave to visit family and attend to personal affairs. Sherman remarked to his brother that "every general officer but two has gone on furlough, and everybody wants to go." Many of lower rank left too, although some merely let their families know of their health. Peter Osterhaus, it turned out, had been reported as having been killed back home.[52]

James B. McPherson oversaw the entire effort, he being the ranking corps commander still in Vicksburg with Sherman, Steele, and Ord off at Jackson. His division commander Logan acted as official commander of the Post of Vicksburg. Perhaps another reason McPherson was retained and Sherman sent to Jackson was because of their different personalities, Grant needing Sherman to be forceful in the military effort while he needed McPherson to be gracious in his social work. It worked, as all found that McPherson was a gentleman. One Confederate noted he was "without doubt, the only real gentleman among the Federal Generals to whom we were introduced. He was very polite, never using the epithet 'rebel' in the presence of our officers or soldiers, and avoided, as much as possible, any expression of exultation at the fall of Vicksburg when in our company." A civilian similarly noted how "the officers were uniformly kind and considerate. General McPherson especially exerting himself to make the lot of paroled prisoners and unfortunate people more endurable."[53]

Contrary to the one Confederate's assertion that McPherson was the only gentleman among Union officers, other Confederates attested to many other Federal general officers treating them well. General William Orme made his headquarters in the lower floor of the house where Colonel Winchester Hall was recovering from his wound. Orme found out who was upstairs and sent food regularly, which, Hall admitted, "I was too polite and too hungry to refuse." Orme wanted to fly the American flag, but as the sergeant who raised and lowered it had to go through Hall's room, Orme asked Hall's permission, which he granted.[54]

McPherson particularly oversaw the process of dealing with the Confederates still inside Vicksburg while the parole process was being completed. One newspaper reported that "the rebel soldiers, instead of lying close in their trenches, are roaming about the city unarmed, in unrestrained but amicable intercourse with those of our own army who have been permitted to enter the town." One Federal was amused at the suddenly free Confederates moving about: "They put me in mind of a gang of Hounds that was kept tied for several days and turned loose."[55]

It certainly helped that Grant was providing rations for the prisoners, one Confederate gladly attesting that "once more our nostrils were greeted with the delightful odor of coffee, fried bacon, etc." He admitted that "prisoners of war were never treated more royally than we were." One famished Confederate described how "we would eat until we were literally stuffed, then lie down and sleep until we had digested the food, and then start eating again, this being kept up both day and night. After about three days of this performance, we began to feel as though we had eaten a square meal." Another explained how he strengthened quickly with good food: "I improved as does a pig that is placed in a pen and fed on rich slop." With such good treatment, Grant was of course trying to get them not to return to Confederate service and perhaps was already thinking of Reconstruction as well.[56]

There was a lot of interaction between the two sides. One Tennessean who had lost his dog in the early stages of the siege talked with a Federal from the 9th Iowa, who eventually realized they had occupied the Tennesseans' camp. The Southerner asked about the dog, and the Iowan declared, "I am quite sure from your description that I got that dog." The Tennessean asked what he did with him, and the Iowan said he sent him home to Iowa, whereupon the Confederate added, "As I could not have him, I am glad you have him," and satisfied himself that "little 'Bob Hatton' had a long ride on a steam boat up the Mississippi, and found a good home in Iowa." Others enjoyed humorous episodes with the sometimes geography-challenged Southerners. One Illinoisan tried to explain how far north he was from but got the serious response from one Mississippian, "I have been as far [north] as Holly Springs."[57]

Despite such good interaction, there could at times also be trouble. Several Mississippians learned they still had some powder and that they could make roman candles "except the coloring" by poking holes in all the joints of cane and alternating wet and dry powder in them. Grant supposed they were somehow signaling Confederates on the Louisiana shore and had it stopped, saying he would send them to prison camps if it continued. "We took him at his word, and shot no more sky rockets," one declared. Some of the trouble could be more sinister. Fights broke out on the streets on occasion, and, at least according to one Confederate, a couple of Federals were killed. Desperate men also stole from one another. Colonel Claudius W. Sears of the 46th Mississippi had a mule stolen from him.[58]

All on both sides were simply marking time, however, waiting on the parole process to unfold. It took time as it went on over the course of several days after the surrender, "one man at a time," wrote a disgruntled Alabamian. Grant wanted McPherson to hurry up so he could get the Confederates off his hands, and he allowed that "every printing press that can be had . . . will [be] put into requisition for the printing of the necessary blanks." Grant asked that McPherson "hurry the same forward with all possible dispatch."[59]

Generals and staff were paroled quickly, as early as the afternoon of July 4. "There I saw Genl. Pemberton for the first time," one soldier confessed; "he had a care worn, anxious & nervous look." Eventually, the time for signing the paroles came to the individual regiments as well, and their officers prepared the men for the process. Colonel Waul gave his Texans a speech, telling them "if we went through the Northern lines, we would have furloughs. He warned us not to swear anything against the South. He said that we had been good soldiers. Still the tension is great. No one knows what will happen to us." The day finally came for each: "Our parole was taken up in one regiment after the other. Each man was to swear an oath that he would not take up arms against the North, and do no service for the South until he was exchanged. Each one signed his name and received his parole certificate." A Louisianan described how "our company was paroled at 5 o'clock this evening. Each man was given a parole, & then the company stood up in line & with right hand raised, swore to the terms & articles stated in the parole."[60]

Once all his soldiers were officially paroled, Pemberton was allowed to march his troops out of the lines on July 11. "On Saturday morning, at half-past eleven o'clock, the Confederate soldiers took up their line of march," one soldier explained.

It was a mournful and harrowing sight. The soldiers felt their disgrace, and there
was not one gallant heart in the mass of men, that did not feel half bursting
with sorrow and humiliation at being compelled to march through the enemy's
guards who were stationed on both sides of the road to some distance beyond the
entrenchments. But nothing could avert the degradations so with downcast looks,
and countenances on which a knowledge of the bitterness of their defeat could be
seen plainly stamped, they filed past the enemy, who gathered in large numbers
to witness their departure.[61]

The last hurdle was stopping at the fortifications for the rolls to be called
and the men to be checked off. "We had to go out like Sheep one at a time,"
one explained. But it was an orderly event, and "not a cheer went up, not a
remark was made that would give pain," a proud Grant recalled. Orders had
been issued as such, "to be orderly and quiet as these prisoners pass, to make
no offensive remarks, and not to harbor any who fall out of ranks after they
have passed." Grant would not do everything in his power for the Confederates, however. Pemberton wanted Grant to give him arms for a battalion to
keep the marching Confederates in line on the way to a parole camp. Grant
refused, wanting them to go home: "It was precisely what I expected and
hoped that they would do."[62]

The only minor problems attendant to the march outside the lines arose
over the Confederates taking their slaves with them. There had been many
high-level communications about the slaves, and Grant limited the number
that could leave with their masters and made it obligatory that it be by their
own choice. "Soldiers and officers are very uneasy about their slaves, fearing they cannot carry them out," one Louisianan described, and many who
wanted their slaves were not allowed to take them. Some found other ways
to escape; one slave gave his master his watch and money and made plans to
meet the next day if the Federals would not allow them to go out together.[63]

"Our baggage was inspected before we passed the lines," a Confederate
explained, and several slaves were removed from the column even at this last
minute, even though they expressed their desire to go out with the Confederate army. One described a slave who "had asked for a parole every day since
the surrender—had been put off on [one] pretext or another." He nevertheless went out with the troops huddled around him so he would not be seen,
but before they got by the Union soldiers "one of them saw the negro, and
elbowing his way among us, seized the negro by the collar, and led him out

of the ranks." Another "brought his negro through the lines by having him lie down on the bottom of the wagon bed and piling boxes of crackers around him." One soldier also brought out the 46th Mississippi flag, by then "a mass of shreds and rags"; a captain "took the tattered thing from its staff, wrapped it around his body under his shirt, and thus brought it away."[64]

Whether accompanied by slaves or not, the Confederate army thus exited the city, and "never was an army more grateful than ours upon leaving Vicksburg," one Confederate confessed. Yet not all left, particularly those too sick to travel and who remained in the hospitals. Some of the convalescents did not leave Federal custody until Christmas, they finding the life good in captivity. One described how they "issued me a suit of hospital clothes, one shirt and one pair of drawers. I then could change my clothes. We could get greenback in exchange for Confederate money. One dollar in greenback for ten dollars in Confederate money." They could also buy from sutlers with purchase orders. Division commander M. L. Smith remained behind to oversee them and set up shop at what he described as "Head Quarters Paroled Prisoners."[65]

Once the Confederate soldiers were past the Federal lines and all forms had been completed and the rolls checked, the army was once again in Pemberton's hands. Not surprisingly, all order soon disappeared and many went their own way—exactly what Grant had hoped. Pemberton tried to keep order and march them to Enterprise, Mississippi, or Demopolis, Alabama, where parole camps were to be set up, but hopes of an orderly and organized march quickly disappeared. Pemberton notified Johnston that "many of the men are leaving without authority for their homes."[66]

The continuing operations around Jackson hindered the march initially. The paroled prisoners moved along the railroad as far as the Big Black River Bridge, where a Federal in the convalescent camp there reported that "the paroled prisoners are coming down the rail road track by thousands yesterday and to-day. They parole them and send them outside of our lines. Gen. Pemberton and staff passed here yesterday evening." Moving on, the columns or groups bypassed the capital mainly to the south but "heard cannons in the direction of Jackson." Despite not liking the Federals' plundering, they occasionally did the same, as desperate men will sometimes do.[67]

Some marched to Enterprise, but many headed for their homes, "the place so long looked for." Once past the guards, for example, the Louisianans "disregarding the commands and expostulations of their officers, set their faces homeward and filed to the right." Confederate officers continually appealed to the Federals for help in keeping the men heading eastward, but they "were laughed at in reply." One Louisianan explained how "most of regiment have left for Louisiana without going to camp to be furloughed." Another added that those who went across the Mississippi found nothing but "poor people and red bugs." Some Louisiana units even set up their own parole camps in that state. Texans also crossed the river and headed west, noting that the land in Louisiana was "vacant and empty. There was nothing more than ruins." At one farm there were no whites, only a few blacks, yet "they took us in friendly and cared for us as well as possible. But they would take only Northern money."[68]

Tennesseans headed north, most swimming the Big Black River; one group pushed along a comrade, who could not swim, on a raft. Some were arrested in Kosciusko, Mississippi, by "home guards" who thought they were deserters. One of them described how they took exception, especially to being captured by "such a class of soldiers," adding that it was worse since they "were veterans who had just passed through the siege of Vicksburg." One Federal in Corinth reported that a Confederate "paroled prisoner passed through our lines from Vicksburg, going home."[69]

Much of the army was made up of Mississippians, who filtered out in all directions. Many marched eastward, but "no order was attempted," and some stayed for a time with a Mr. Catchings, "whose unfeigned and unstinted hospitality was touching to us." Perhaps it was because his "two noble boys had gone forth at the call of duty, and both had fallen in Sunday's fight at Shiloh." At another place where the kind folks had aided another Confederate, he left behind a nice note when he departed: "Kind Lady, I would like to make all the time I can, so I will be off. Many thanks and may God reward you is the prayer of Jos. F. Owens. P. S. Good-Bye and Good Luck to All."[70]

One group of Mississippians experienced many adventures on their way home to Decatur. At one point a comrade went foraging and came back with fifteen roasting ears of corn he somehow found. He would not share, declaring that "there was no more than he needed for himself." The man proceeded to eat all fifteen ears at once, his amazed comrades admitting that "we expected to find him dead the next morning but he arose shook himself and declared he never felt better in his life." Everywhere they stopped they were met with some suspicion, although most people were more than generous.

For those who were not so giving, there were sharp words at times. There was, for example, "a spirited quarrel with the man on whose premises we had slept, about the use of some of his out houses."[71]

Later, once past Jackson, the Mississippians boarded a train, but the conductor ordered them off unless they had tickets. They showed their paroles, which was not good enough for the conductor, who declared he would not move the train until they exited. "O' that's all right," one scoffed, "we are used to camping a good while in one place, and we can stay here as long as you can." One of the group declared that "this was followed by an interval which was filled with a considerable amount of mutual 'cussing' of an extremely vigorous type." Finally, the conductor cursed and pulled out after an hour, the soldiers giving three loud cheers. Later, the conductor pulled the train onto a siding for the night, declaring it would not move until they were gone. He came back the next morning, and "it would have curdled the blood in the veins of one not accustomed to it, to have heard the stream of tangled up words that flowed from the mouth of the irate conductor, when he discovered that we were still there—that we had not vacated his precious car." The conductor gave in again, although one declared that the conductor would have won if he had waited just an hour more because the group had decided to move on by foot. Nevertheless, the soldiers reached Newton, where they detrained, thanking the conductor for the ride. "In reply," one noted, "he 'cussed' us again."[72]

Nearer to Decatur, the group had a huge breakfast provided by the owner of a large mansion, although the ladies of the house would have nothing to do with the vermin-ridden soldiers and brashly marched upstairs. "This, however, did not long impair our appetites and with ineffable satisfaction we made one more square meal." The leader sternly warned one of the group "who had an inveterate habit of pocketing spoons, knives, combs, and any other article that he could." The leader of the group caught him trying to hide a silver spoon, and the "light fingered friend" put it back.[73]

Sadly, not all made it to their destinations. One Confederate declared that "some of our boys killed themselves eating roasting ears before reaching home." One particularly sad case was that of Alabamian Alexander F. McGahey. He was sick and needed to stay in Vicksburg, which his comrades tried to convince him to do. He refused: "He was so anxious to get home that he would not consent to remain." After four miles he completely broke down and his comrades had to leave him at a civilians' residence, where he died.

Elizabeth Parkman informed his widow that he was buried on their place and sent her the thirty dollars he had on him, as well as his pocketbook and letters and a lock of his hair.[74]

Similarly, division commander John S. Bowen made it only as far as Raymond. He had become sick during the siege and while being transported in an ambulance became much worse at Raymond, where he stopped for care. He died there of chronic dysentery. Saddest of all was the fact that three Missouri wives had earlier come to Vicksburg to see their husbands but had been evacuated before the siege. Now the wives of Colonel Erwin, Lieutenant Colonel Senteny, and Bowen were all widows—the tragic results of Vicksburg. Grant himself gave special attention to Erwin's wife and two daughters and provided them with passes to any point they selected. He also assigned them a guard and fifty dollars.[75]

Most made it home or to Enterprise, some moving on to Demopolis, Alabama, where Pemberton himself went, his wife and children being there. On the way, however, Pemberton had one more major duty to attend to. His parole required him to report to his superior officer, which was Johnston, now at Morton after having evacuated Jackson and fallen back eastward. When Pemberton walked in, Johnston extended his hand and retorted, "I am glad to see you." Pemberton simply saluted, saying that his terms of parole required that he report. "I have done so," he snapped, then turned and left.[76]

EPILOGUE

"The Fate of the Confederacy Was Sealed When Vicksburg Fell"

The effects of the victory and defeat at Vicksburg were clear to those involved if not to a general public that was increasingly drawn to the simultaneous events at Gettysburg. Those involved at Vicksburg, however, certainly had their own thoughts about the effects of their work. Sherman wrote that "the news is so good I can hardly realize it, though I have wished for it now fully six months. Jeff Davis made it a test question, and I know its influence on the great West will be more than the capture of Richmond." Admiral Porter added his perspective: "The effect of this blow will be felt far up the tributaries of the Mississippi. The timid and doubtful will take heart, and the wicked I hope will cease to trouble us for fear of the punishment which will sooner or later overtake them." Even Grant himself noted that "the fate of the Confederacy was sealed when Vicksburg fell," adding, "it looks now as though Providence had directed the course of the campaign while the Army of the Tennessee executed the decree."[1]

The actual components of those broad arguments were extensive. The fall of Vicksburg severely damaged Confederate morale and military power in the Mississippi Valley, especially with a full army and all its weaponry and equipment lost. "It looks like they take every place that they want and we have retreated until we have got no place to retreat to," one Confederate admitted. The geographical splitting of the Confederacy was also huge, mostly because supplies were no longer brought across from the Red River. Huge amounts of goods had been moved across from there even as the Confederate stretches of the river continually dwindled. But as long as the Red River's mouth sat between Vicksburg and Port Hudson, that avenue of supply was open and heavily utilized, as was the only major rail line touching the river between Memphis and New Orleans—at Vicksburg, of course. Historian Terry Winschel has described the three forms of "white gold" that came across the river in abundance: cotton, salt, and sugar. But all of that ended with the closure of the river and the cleaving in two of the Confederacy. "They had the place fixed well for us but thank God we have it at last and have the Mississippi River open," Ohioan Eli Todd wrote to his brother. Another predicted major results: "We have now cut their Confederacy in too and it wont be long till several of their states are back into the Union."[2]

Fittingly, Grant's reputation soared, many in addition to Halleck's comparison to the Ulm campaign also associating him with Napoleon. "Thus ends one of the most brilliant campaigns the world has known since the days of Austerlitz," one Federal wrote. Salutes all over the nation took place with Grant on the mind and lips of revelers, although in Corinth one man was injured in an accident while celebrating the news of Vicksburg's fall. "Gen. Grant is the man of this war," one Federal declared, but the general explained humbly that "the movements of an enemy necessarily determine counter-movements." And he was ready to head out on new campaigns, telling Julia that she and the children could visit after Vicksburg "when I am still. I do not expect to be still much however whilst the war lasts."[3]

Even the level-headed Grant took pleasure in one particular accolade he received, from none other than the president himself. Now, the similarly humble Lincoln wrote to Grant one of the classic presidential letters of all time:

To Major-General Grant:

My dear general: I do not remember that you and I ever met personally. I write this now as a grateful acknowledgment for the almost inestimable service you have done the country. I wish to say a word further. When you first reached the vicinity of Vicksburg, I thought you should do what you finally did—march the troops across the neck, run the batteries with the transports, and thus go below; and I never had any faith, except a general hope that you knew better than I, that the Yazoo Pass expedition and the like could succeed. When you got below and took Port Gibson, Grand Gulf, and vicinity, I thought you should go down the

river and join General Banks; and when you turned northward east of the Big
Black, I feared it was a mistake. I now wish to make the personal acknowledgment that you were right and I was wrong.

  Yours very truly,

  A. Lincoln[4]

Historians have over the decades placed more importance on Vicksburg as
well; even some Gettysburg-oriented scholars have admitted that Vicksburg
had more importance. Historians such as Edwin C. Bearss, Michael B. Ballard, and Terrence J. Winschel have written extensively on the importance of
Vicksburg, and even an Army of the Potomac scholar (as well as of Grant),
Bruce Catton, admitted "the real pull of fate was at Vicksburg. Lee took the
eye but the pivot of the war was down here by the great river."[5]

Just as much gloom filtered through the South as joy in the North. Officials in Richmond had been watching the progress of the siege and relief
for weeks, like everyone else placing their trust in Johnston. Rumors had
abounded of the city's fall and Grant's death, but all proved untrue. The general idea that things were not getting better came with Johnston's continuous
dispatches that he could do nothing, prompting War Department clerk John
B. Jones to admit on June 12 that "nothing but a miracle can save Vicksburg!"
The eventual loss came as a shock nonetheless. When the news broke in Richmond, Jones scribbled in his diary, "But, alas! We have sad tidings from the
West" and later "the fall of the place has cast a gloom over everything." And
when the true nature of the defeat at Gettysburg was realized as well, it was
all the more devastating, Jones writing that "the fall of Vicksburg, alone, does
not make this the darkest day of the war, as it is undoubtedly. The news from
Lee's army is appalling." There was a lot of truth to the oft-repeated quote of
Josiah Gorgas: "Yesterday we rode on the pinnacle of success—to-day absolute ruin seems to be our portion. The Confederacy totters to its destruction."[6]

But time moved on, and neither Vicksburg nor Gettysburg ended a war that
would last nearly two more years. The participants and people moved on as
well. The Union armies went into occupation mode for a time, but most eventually moved on to participate in other campaigns in Georgia and elsewhere.
The Confederates were exchanged, the general officers including colonels
commanding brigades declared so on July 13. It took longer for the common
soldiers to be exchanged, and after a furlough of forty days by presidential
proclamation, many of the masses of lower-level Confederates met again in

September at Enterprise, where they were also officially declared exchanged. Many went on to participate in the Chattanooga battles in November 1863 and certainly in the Atlanta Campaign in 1864.[7]

As for Vicksburg itself, it became a backwater position in the war, the press and the nation's attention following the armies to newer fields of battle. Even the physical scars of the siege soon began to disappear as houses and buildings were repaired. Despite the declaration of one Illinoisan that the fortifications were "a prodigious piece or work and will remain for generations as a curiosity and an evidence of the labor necessary to fortify and reduce the place," even the fortifications were destroyed to a large degree, certainly those that could be used by a Confederate army to lay siege to the now Union-occupied Vicksburg. Even many of the old Confederate defensive works, battered as they were, were replaced with newer and more dominating fortifications so that the Federals could more easily hold the city. Sometimes relics and more were discovered in this process, such as at the area around the 3rd Louisiana Redan. As it was being cleared after the war and made into a field, several bones emerged—those who had been buried alive when the mines blew.[8]

Some evidence of what had happened at Vicksburg nevertheless survived. Many shells could be seen lying around the city, some being used as ornaments on gateposts. "My suggestion is that," one Louisianan declared, "if we are successful, a monument be raised, composed entirely of these missiles; I am sure a lofty one could be erected." Obviously, he and the Confederates were not successful, but those who were victorious raised their own type of memorial. To mark the anniversary of the surrender, a marble shaft found in a Vicksburg stonecutter's shop and originally intended as a memorial for Mexican-American War veterans was altered and put up on July 4, 1864. There was an elaborate dedication with a formal address from Major Abner E. Barns of the United States Colored Troops (but formerly of the 72nd Illinois). The organizers placed the shaft to mark the Grant/Pemberton meeting site and event, although unfortunately the date was wrong. The monument cited July 4, 1863, when the actual interview had taken place the day before. Nevertheless, the monument—on the site where the long-gone tree once stood—was "enclosed by masonry and surmounted by an iron fence." Unfortunately, locals started chipping away at the monument, and it was later replaced with a cannon shaft. Others had more idealistic hopes for the next year, more than a simple monument dedication. "Maybe the next fourth, Richmond will fall, but I hope sooner," Indianan James Vanderbilt wrote to his mother on July 4, 1863.[9]

Over the years, the scene of such historic events became memorial and tourist enclaves. "After the war," one Ohioan predicted to his parents, "Vicksburg will be quite a point of interest, as no idea can be formed of the amount of digging we have done already and are still doing, and also the amount they have dug and are still doing." Even William T. Sherman drummed up visitors for such an important site. In trying to talk his senator-brother into coming down for a visit, Sherman told John that "Vicksburg is worth seeing, and a glance will tell you more than reams of paper why it took us six months to take the place." The federal government also set aside a different kind of memorial in 1866: the Vicksburg National Cemetery for reburial of Union dead from the campaign. Many tourists eventually flocked there, as well as to see what was left of the lines of fortifications. Even former president Ulysses S. Grant returned to Vicksburg in 1880, although he did not travel out to the fortification lines but merely to the cemetery. Others came as pure tourists, whether younger Americans or veterans who flocked to the battlefields or remembered their actions in volume after volume and even in song and verse. But nothing could compete with the actual ground where it occurred, "every foot of it a volume of history."[10]

Eventually, more memorials appeared and, finally, Vicksburg National Military Park, established by Congress in 1899 as part of the wave of military parks that decade. A commission of veterans including former Union captain William T. Rigby and Confederate general Stephen D. Lee oversaw the project, and soon the commission and individual states began to mark the park with iron and bronze tablets, obsolete Civil War–era cannons, and beautiful stone memorials. The lines of both sides were clearly marked despite much of the original fortifications having been removed over the decades, although the Civilian Conservation Corps later dug a lot of earthworks in the 1930s to display what some may have looked like. The park marked the places of conflict for the assaults and siege but also commemorated the entire Vicksburg Campaign; parts of those outlying battlefields have been added to the park over the years.[11]

The battlefield itself became a haven for reconciliation over the decades, with the speeches at the memorial dedications offering goodwill from both sides, including a Peace Jubilee in 1917. Another example came on May 21 and 22, 1937, when many met as "Descendants of the Participants of the

Campaign, Siege and Defense of Vicksburg," including John C. Pemberton III and Ulysses S. Grant III. As the decades passed and the old veterans of Vicksburg began to fade away, many still returned to the Mississippi River bastion in their minds if not in body. "As I look back upon the field of action of 39 years ago it seems like a dream," one visitor recalled with obvious emotion. Another could only wonder about his old comrades: "I live a good deal of my time in the past." One unique account of a Confederate shot in the eye through a small hole in a boilerplate he was using for cover even emerged. Years later he coughed it up, the episode making the news. A Union veteran in Indiana read the account and surmised he had shot the famous bullet and wrote the Confederate, the two trading photos and letters for years. "The two veterans have enjoyed a considerable correspondence over the incident," a newspaper reported.[12]

Others could only reminisce with emotions running wild, especially so when they visited the battlefield they made famous so many years ago. "Long years have passed and each returning spring brings grass and flowers to hide the scars," one veteran wrote. "The sulfurous battle smoke has gone. The roll of the heavy machinery of death is still. The great river that flows on its way to the sea sings the requiem of the gallant dead that sleep on either side of the line of blood that marked the defenses of Vicksburg."[13]

One illustrative Illinoisan who returned in 1906 had an especially moving experience when he went to the National Cemetery. There he found the grave of "James W. Ditto, an intimate comrade of mine." As he stood at the grave of his dear friend of so many years before, he could only think of him "as he looked just before he fell forty-three years ago, a fine, manly, young fellow, scarcely eighteen years old, the idol of the company." Patriotism, emotion, and thoughts of mortality all overcame him at that point as he connected once again with the cherished spot on the banks of the mighty Mississippi so fought over those many years ago. He added simply: "My eyes filled with tears."[14]

Appendix A

UNION ORDER OF BATTLE AT VICKSBURG, MAY 23–JULY 4, 1863

Union Forces

ARMY OF THE TENNESSEE
　Major General Ulysses S. Grant

Escort
　4th Illinois Cavalry, Company A

Engineers
　1st Battalion Bissell's Engineer Regiment of the West

HERRON'S DIVISION
　Major General Francis J. Herron

First Brigade
　Brigadier General William Vandever
　　37th Illinois
　　26th Indiana
　　20th Iowa
　　34th Iowa
　　38th Iowa
　　1st Missouri Light Artillery, Battery E
　　1st Missouri Light Artillery, Battery F

Second Brigade
　Brigadier General William W. Orme
　　94th Illinois
　　19th Iowa

20th Wisconsin
1st Missouri Light Artillery, Battery B

IX ARMY CORPS
Major General John G. Parke

FIRST DIVISION
Brigadier General Thomas Welsh

First Brigade
Colonel Henry Bowman
36th Massachusetts
17th Michigan
27th Michigan
45th Pennsylvania

Third Brigade
Colonel Daniel Leasure
2nd Michigan
8th Michigan
20th Michigan
79th New York
100th Pennsylvania

Artillery
1st Pennsylvania Light Artillery, Company D

SECOND DIVISION
Brigadier General Robert B. Potter

First Brigade
Colonel Simon G. Griffin
6th New Hampshire
9th New Hampshire
7th Rhode Island

Second Brigade
Brigadier General Edward Ferrero
35th Massachusetts
11th New Hampshire
51st New York
51st Pennsylvania

Third Brigade
   Colonel Benjamin C. Christ
      29th Massachusetts
      46th New York
      50th Pennsylvania

Artillery
   2nd New York Light Artillery, Battery L

Artillery Reserve
   2nd United States Artillery, Battery E

XIII ARMY CORPS
   Major General John A. McClernand
   Major General Edward O. C. Ord

Escort
   3rd Illinois Cavalry, Company L

Pioneers
   Patterson's Kentucky Company of Engineers and Mechanics

NINTH DIVISION
   Brigadier General Peter J. Osterhaus

First Brigade
   Colonel James Keigwin
      118th Illinois
      49th Indiana
      69th Indiana
      7th Kentucky
      120th Ohio

Second Brigade
   Colonel Daniel W. Lindsey
      54th Indiana
      22nd Kentucky
      16th Ohio
      42nd Ohio
      114th Ohio

Cavalry
    2nd Illinois (five companies)
    3rd Illinois (three companies)
    6th Missouri (seven companies)

Artillery
  Captain Jacob T. Foster
    7th Battery Michigan Light Artillery
    1st Battery Wisconsin Light Artillery

TENTH DIVISION
  Brigadier General Andrew J. Smith

Escort
    4th Indiana Cavalry, Company C

First Brigade
  Brigadier General Stephen G. Burbridge
    16th Indiana
    60th Indiana
    67th Indiana
    83rd Ohio
    96th Ohio
    23rd Wisconsin

Second Brigade
  Colonel William J. Landram
    77th Illinois
    97th Illinois
    130th Illinois
    19th Kentucky
    48th Ohio

Artillery
    Chicago Mercantile Battery
    17th Battery Ohio Light Artillery

TWELFTH DIVISION
  Brigadier General Alvin P. Hovey

Escort
    1st Indiana Cavalry, Company C

First Brigade
    Brigadier General George F. McGinnis
    Brigadier General William T. Spicely
        11th Indiana
        24th Indiana
        34th Indiana
        46th Indiana
        29th Wisconsin

Second Brigade
    Colonel James R. Slack
        87th Illinois
        47th Indiana
        24th Iowa
        28th Iowa

Artillery
        1st Missouri Light Artillery, Battery A
        2nd Battery Ohio Light Artillery
        16th Battery Ohio Light Artillery

FOURTEENTH DIVISION
    Brigadier General Eugene A. Carr

Escort
        3rd Illinois Cavalry, Company G

First Brigade
    Brigadier General William P. Benton
    Colonel Henry D. Washburne
    Colonel David Shunk
    Brigadier General William P. Benton
        33rd Illinois
        99th Illinois
        8th Indiana
        18th Indiana

Second Brigade
    Brigadier General Michael K. Lawler
        21st Iowa
        22nd Iowa
        11th Wisconsin

Artillery
> 2nd Illinois Light Artillery, Battery A
> 1st Battery Indiana Light Artillery

XV ARMY CORPS
> Major General William T. Sherman
> Major General Frederick Steele

FIRST DIVISION
> Major General Frederick Steele
> Brigadier General John M. Thayer

First Brigade
> Colonel Francis H. Manter
> Colonel Bernard G. Farrar
>> 13th Illinois
>> 27th Missouri
>> 29th Missouri
>> 30th Missouri
>> 31st Missouri
>> 32nd Missouri

Second Brigade
> Colonel Charles R. Woods
>> 25th Iowa
>> 31st Iowa
>> 3rd Missouri
>> 12th Missouri
>> 17th Missouri
>> 76th Ohio

Third Brigade
> Brigadier General John M. Thayer
>> 4th Iowa
>> 9th Iowa
>> 26th Iowa
>> 30th Iowa

Artillery
> 1st Battery Iowa Light Artillery
> 2nd Missouri Light Artillery, Battery F
> 4th Battery Ohio Light Artillery

Cavalry
Kane Canty (Illinois) Independent Company
3rd Illinois, Company D

SECOND DIVISION
Major General Frank P. Blair, Jr.

First Brigade
Colonel Giles A. Smith
113th Illinois
116th Illinois
6th Missouri
8th Missouri
13th United States 1st Battalion

Second Brigade
Colonel Thomas Kilby Smith
Brigadier General Joseph A. J. Lightburn
55th Illinois
127th Illinois
83rd Indiana
54th Ohio
57th Ohio

Third Brigade
Brigadier General Hugh Ewing
30th Ohio
37th Ohio
47th Ohio
4th West Virginia

Artillery
1st Illinois Light Artillery, Battery A
1st Illinois Light Artillery, Battery B
1st Illinois Light Artillery, Battery H
8th Battery Ohio Light Artillery

Cavalry
Thielemann's (Illinois) Battalion, Companies A and B
10th Missouri, Company C

THIRD DIVISION
    Brigadier General James M. Tuttle

First Brigade
    Brigadier General Ralph P. Buckland
    Colonel William L. McMillen
        114th Illinois
        93rd Indiana
        72nd Ohio
        95th Ohio

Second Brigade
    Brigadier General Joseph A. Mower
        47th Illinois
        5th Minnesota
        11th Missouri
        8th Wisconsin

Third Brigade
    Brigadier General Charles L. Matthies
    Colonel Joseph J. Woods
        8th Iowa
        12th Iowa
        35th Iowa

Artillery
    Captain Nelson T. Spoor
        1st Illinois Light Artillery, Battery E
        2nd Battery Iowa Light Artillery

Unattached Cavalry
        4th Iowa

XVI ARMY CORPS
    Major General Stephen A. Hurlbut (in Memphis)
    Major General Cadwallader C. Washburn (commanding Smith and Kimball)

FIRST DIVISION
    Brigadier General William "Sooy" Smith

First Brigade
    Colonel John M. Loomis
        26th Illinois
        90th Illinois

    12th Indiana
    100th Indiana

Second Brigade
    Colonel Stephen G. Hicks
        40th Illinois
        103rd Illinois
        15th Michigan
        46th Ohio

Third Brigade
    Colonel Joseph R. Cockerill
        97th Indiana
        99th Indiana
        53rd Ohio
        70th Ohio

Fourth Brigade
    Colonel William W. Sanford
        48th Illinois
        6th Iowa

Artillery
    Captain William Cogswell
        1st Illinois Light Artillery, Battery F
        1st Illinois Light Artillery, Battery I
        Cogswell's Illinois Battery
        6th Indiana Battery

FOURTH DIVISION
    Brigadier General Jacob G. Lauman

First Brigade
    Colonel Isaac C. Pugh
        41st Illinois
        53rd Illinois
        3rd Iowa
        33rd Wisconsin

Second Brigade
    Colonel Cyrus Hall
        14th Illinois
        15th Illinois
        46th Illinois

76th Illinois
53rd Indiana

Third Brigade
Colonel George E. Bryant
Colonel Amory K. Johnson
28th Illinois
32nd Illinois
12th Wisconsin

Cavalry
15th Illinois, Companies F and I

Artillery
Captain George C. Gumbart
2nd Illinois Light Artillery, Battery E
2nd Illinois Light Artillery, Battery K
5th Battery Ohio Light Artillery
7th Battery Ohio Light Artillery
15th Battery Ohio Light Artillery

PROVISIONAL DIVISION
Brigadier General Nathan Kimball

Engelmann's Brigade
Colonel Adolph Engelmann
43rd Illinois
61st Illinois
106th Illinois
12th Michigan

Richmond's Brigade
Colonel Jonathan Richmond
18th Illinois
54th Illinois
126th Illinois
22nd Ohio

Montgomery's Brigade
Colonel Milton Montgomery
40th Iowa
3rd Minnesota
25th Wisconsin
27th Wisconsin

XVII ARMY CORPS
Major General James B. McPherson

Escort
Captain John S. Foster
4th Company Ohio Cavalry

THIRD DIVISION
Major General John A. Logan

Escort
2nd Illinois Cavalry, Company A

First Brigade
Brigadier General John E. Smith
Brigadier General Mortimer D. Leggett
20th Illinois
31st Illinois
45th Illinois
124th Illinois
23rd Indiana

Second Brigade
Brigadier General Mortimer D. Leggett
Colonel Manning F. Force
30th Illinois
20th Ohio
68th Ohio
78th Ohio

Third Brigade
Brigadier General John D. Stevenson
8th Illinois
17th Illinois
81st Illinois
7th Missouri
32nd Ohio

Artillery
Major Charles J. Stolbrand
1st Illinois Light Artillery, Battery D,
2nd Illinois Light Artillery, Battery G
2nd Illinois Light Artillery, Battery L
8th Battery Michigan Light Artillery
3rd Battery Ohio Light Artillery

SIXTH DIVISION
  Brigadier General John McArthur

Escort
      11th Illinois Cavalry, Company G

Second Brigade
  Brigadier General Thomas E. G. Ransom
      11th Illinois
      72nd Illinois
      95th Illinois
      14th Wisconsin
      17th Wisconsin

Third Brigade
  Colonel William Hall
  Colonel Alexander Chambers
      11th Iowa
      13th Iowa
      15th Iowa
      16th Iowa
      63rd Illinois
      87th Illinois

Artillery
Major Thomas D. Maurice
      2nd Illinois Light Artillery, Battery F
      1st Battery Minnesota Light Artillery
      1st Missouri Light Artillery, Battery C
      10th Battery Ohio Light Artillery

SEVENTH DIVISION
  Brigadier General Isaac F. Quinby
  Brigadier General John E. Smith

Escort
      4th Missouri Cavalry, Company F. Lieutenant Alexander Mueller

First Brigade
  Colonel John B. Sanborn
      48th Indiana
      39th Indiana
      4th Minnesota
      18th Wisconsin

Second Brigade
  Colonel Samuel A. Holmes
  Colonel Green B. Raum
    56th Illinois
    17th Iowa
    10th Missouri
    24th Missouri
    80th Ohio

Third Brigade
  Colonel Holden Putman
  Brigadier General Charles Matthies
    93rd Illinois
    5th Iowa
    10th Iowa
    26th Missouri

Artillery
  Captain Frank C. Sands
  Captain Henry Dillon
    1st Missouri Light Artillery, Battery M
    11th Battery Ohio Light Artillery
    6th Battery Wisconsin Light Artillery
    12th Battery Wisconsin Light Artillery

Unattached Cavalry
  Colonel Cyrus Bussey
    5th Illinois Cavalry
    3rd Iowa Cavalry
    2nd Wisconsin Cavalry

CONFEDERATE ORDER OF BATTLE AT VICKSBURG, MAY 23–JULY 4, 1863

Confederate Forces

ARMY OF VICKSBURG
Lieutenant General John C. Pemberton

STEVENSON'S DIVISION
Major General Carter L. Stevenson

First Brigade
Brigadier General Seth M. Barton
40th Georgia
41st Georgia
42nd Georgia
43rd Georgia
52nd Georgia
Hudson's (Mississippi) Battery
Pointe Coupee (Louisiana) Artillery, Company A (section)
Pointe Coupee (Louisiana) Artillery, Company C

Second Brigade
Brigadier General Alfred Cumming
34th Georgia
36th Georgia
39th Georgia
56th Georgia
57th Georgia
Cherokee (Georgia) Artillery

Third Brigade
　Brigadier General Stephen D. Lee
　　20th Alabama
　　23rd Alabama
　　30th Alabama
　　31st Alabama
　　46th Alabama
　　Waddell's (Alabama) Battery

Fourth Brigade
　Colonel Alexander W. Reynolds
　　3rd Tennessee (Provisional Army)
　　39th Tennessee
　　43rd Tennessee
　　59th Tennessee
　　3rd Maryland Battery

Attached
　　Waul's Texas Legion
　　1st Tennessee Cavalry (Carter's)
　　Botetourt (Virginia) Artillery
　　Signal Corps

FORNEY'S DIVISION
　Major General John H. Forney

Hébert's Brigade
　Brigadier General Louis Hébert
　　3rd Louisiana
　　21st Louisiana
　　36th Mississippi
　　37th Mississippi
　　38th Mississippi
　　43rd Mississippi
　　7th Mississippi Battalion
　　2nd Alabama Artillery Battalion, Company C
　　Appeal (Arkansas) Battery

Moore's Brigade
　Brigadier General John C. Moore
　　37th Alabama
　　40th Alabama
　　42nd Alabama

35th Mississippi
40th Mississippi
2nd Texas
Sengstak's (Alabama) Battery
Pointe Coupe (Louisiana) Artillery, Company B

SMITH'S DIVISION
Major General Martin L. Smith

Baldwin's Brigade
Brigadier General William E. Baldwin
17th Louisiana
31st Louisiana
4th Mississippi
46th Mississippi
Tobin's (Tennessee) Battery

Vaughn's Brigade
Brigadier General John C. Vaughn
60th Tennessee
61st Tennessee
62nd Tennessee

Shoup's Brigade
Brigadier General Francis A. Shoup
26th Louisiana
27th Louisiana
28th [29th] Louisiana
McNally's Battery

Mississippi State Troops
Brigadier General Jeptha V. Harris
5th Regiment Minute Men
3rd Battalion Minute Men

Attached
14th Mississippi Light Artillery Battery
Mississippi Partisan Rangers
Signal Corps

BOWEN'S DIVISION
Major General John S. Bowen

First Brigade
Colonel Francis M. Cockrell
1st Missouri
2nd Missouri
3rd Missouri
5th Missouri
6th Missouri
Guibor's (Missouri) Battery
Landis's (Missouri) Battery
Wade's (Missouri) Battery

Second Brigade
Brigadier General Martin E. Green (k)
Colonel Thomas P. Dockery
19th Arkansas
20th Arkansas
1st Arkansas Cavalry Battalion
12th Arkansan Battalion (Sharpshooters)
1st Missouri Cavalry
3rd Missouri Cavalry
3rd Missouri Battery
Lowe's (Missouri) Battery

RIVER BATTERIES
Colonel Ed Higgins
1st Louisiana Artillery
8th Louisiana Heavy Artillery Battalion
22nd Louisiana
1st Tennessee Heavy Artillery
Caruthers's (Tennessee) Battery
Johnston's (Tennessee) Battery
Lynch's (Tennessee) Battery
Vaiden (Mississippi) Battery

MISCELLANEOUS
54th Alabama (detachment)
City Guards
Signal Corps

ARMY OF RELIEF
General Joseph E. Johnston

BRECKINRIDGE'S DIVISION
Major General John C. Breckinridge

Gibson's Brigade
Colonel Randall L. Gibson
32nd Alabama
13/20th Louisiana
16/25th Louisiana
19th Louisiana
14th Louisiana Battalion Sharpshooters

Helm's Brigade
Brigadier General Benjamin H. Helm
41st Alabama
2nd Kentucky
4th Kentucky
6th Kentucky
9th Kentucky

Stovall's Brigade
Brigadier General Marcellus A. Stovall
1/3rd Florida
4th Florida
47th Georgia
60th North Carolina

Artillery
Major Rive E. Graves
Johnston's (Tennessee) Battery
Cobb's (Kentucky) Battery
Washington (Louisiana) Artillery, 5th Company

FRENCH'S DIVISION
Major General Samuel G. French

McNair's Brigade
Brigadier General Evander McNair
1st Arkansas Mounted Rifles
2nd Arkansas Mounted Rifles
4th Arkansas

25/31st Arkansas
39th North Carolina

Maxey's Brigade
Brigadier General Samuel B. Maxey
4th Louisiana
30th Louisiana
42nd Tennessee
46/55th Tennessee
48th Tennessee
49th Tennessee
53rd Tennessee
1st Texas Battalion, Sharpshooters

Evans's Brigade
Brigadier General Nathan G. Evans
17th South Carolina
18th South Carolina
22nd South Carolina
23rd South Carolina
26th South Carolina
Holcombe Legion

Artillery
Fenner's (Louisiana) Battery
Palmetto (South Carolina) Artillery, Company B
Palmetto (South Carolina) Artillery, Company C

LORING'S DIVISION
Major General William W. Loring

First Brigade
Brigadier General John Adams
1st Confederate Battalion
6th Mississippi
15th Mississippi
20th Mississippi
23rd Mississippi
26th Mississippi
Culberson's (Mississippi) Battery
Cowan's (Mississippi) Battery

Second Brigade
    Brigadier General Winfield S. Featherston
        3rd Mississippi
        22nd Mississippi
        31st Mississippi
        33rd Mississippi
        1st Mississippi Sharpshooter Battalion
        Wofford's Mississippi Battery
        Charpentier's (Alabama) Battery

Third Brigade
    Brigadier General Abraham Buford
        27th Alabama
        35th Alabama
        54th Alabama
        55th Alabama
        9th Arkansas
        3rd Kentucky
        7th Kentucky
        8th Kentucky
        12th Louisiana
        3rd Missouri Battalion
        Pointe Coupee Louisiana Artillery, Company C
        Lookout (Tennessee) Artillery

WALKER'S DIVISION
    Major General William H. T. Walker

Ector's Brigade
    Brigadier General Matthew D. Ector
        9th Texas
        10th Texas (dismounted cavalry)
        14th Texas (dismounted cavalry)
        32nd Texas (dismounted cavalry)
        Alabama Battalion Sharpshooters
        Mississippi Battalion Sharpshooters
        McNally's (Arkansas) Battery

Gregg's Brigade
    Brigadier General John Gregg
        3rd Tennessee
        10th Tennessee
        30th Tennessee

41st Tennessee
50th Tennessee
1st Tennessee Battalion
7th Texas
14th Mississippi
Bledsoe's (Missouri) Battery

Gist's Brigade
Brigadier General States Rights Gist
46th Georgia
8th Georgia Battalion
16th South Carolina
24th South Carolina
Ferguson's (South Carolina) Battery

Wilson's Brigade
Colonel Claudius C. Wilson
25th Georgia
29th Georgia
30th Georgia
1st Georgia Battalion Sharpshooters
4th Louisiana Battalion
Martin's (Georgia) Battery

Escort
Nelson's Independent Georgia Cavalry Company

JACKSON'S CAVALRY DIVISION
Major General William H. Jackson

First Brigade
Brigadier General George B. Cosby
1st Mississippi Cavalry
4th Mississippi Cavalry
28th Mississippi Cavalry
Wirt Adams's Mississippi Cavalry
Ballentine's Mississippi Cavalry
17th Mississippi Battalion
Clark's (Missouri) Artillery

Second Brigade
    Brigadier General John G. Whitfield
        3rd Texas Cavalry
        6th Texas Cavalry
        9th Texas Cavalry
        1st Texas Legion
        Bridges's Arkansas Battalion

Escort and Guards
        Company A, 7th Tennessee Cavalry
        Independent Company Louisiana Cavalry
        Provost Guard

Reserve Artillery
        Columbus (Georgia) Battery
        Durrive's (Louisiana) Battery

GLOSSARY

Most definitions in this glossary are taken from Dennis H. Mahan, *A Treatise on Field Fortification, Containing Instructions on the Methods of Laying Out, Constructing, Defending, and Attacking Intrenchments, with the General Outlines Also of the Arrangement, the Attack and Defence of Permanent Fortifications* (New York: John Wiley, 1861), with additional information from Justin S. Solonick, *Engineering Victory: The Union Siege of Vicksburg* (Carbondale: Southern Illinois University Press, 2015), 231–233.

approach—A trench dug toward an enemy fortification, often in a zig-zag pattern for protection.

circumvallation, line of—An unbroken line of intrenchments entrapping the enemy, composed of the most simple elementary parts, as tenailles, redans, and the like, with a slight profile.

countermine—Used by defending forces against enemy mines for the purpose of softening blasts or disturbing the soil so that mining operations may fail.

countervallation, line of—A line of detached works in rear of the besieging force's camps and line of circumvallation. It is intended to defend against any relief force raising the siege.

covered way—Trenches, parallels, or other dug-out features that offer troops safety in moving behind their front lines.

embrasure—An opening made in the parapet for a cannon to fire through.

fascine—A bundle of twigs closely bound up. There are two sizes of fascines; one size is nine inches in diameter and about ten feet long; the other, which is generally termed a "soucisson," is twelve inches in diameter and twenty feet long.

gabion—A round basket of a cylindrical form, open at each end; its height is usually two feet, nine inches and diameter two feet.

headlog—A trunk of a tree or beam placed on top of rifle pits and fortifications to protect skirmishers and sharpshooters from enemy fire. Often notched so that small arms can be stuck through to fire.

lunette—A crescent-shaped fortification consisting of two faces and two flanks.

mine—Underground tunnels used to burrow underneath enemy fortifications for the purpose of filling chambers with powder and blowing up enemy fortifications.

mortar—A small cannon that fires a projectile on a high, arching path.

parallel—A long line of trench concentric with, or parallel to, the works of the point of attack, which it envelopes.

redan—A work consisting of two faces; the gorge, or entrance in the rear, being open.

redoubt—Any enclosed work of a polygonal form, without re-entering angles.

rifle pit—Trenches dug between major forts and used to cover the expanses between major and even minor fortifications.

sap—Approaches carried forward toward the enemy fortifications from the nearest parallel.

sappers—Engineering troops who carry forward a sap behind a sap roller.

sap roller—A large gabion stuffed with fascines or wool; it is rolled forward for protection as sappers gradually advance.

traverse—An earthwork inside of and at perpendicular angles to the outside walls of the fortifications, which offers cover from flanking fire inside the work.

NOTES

ABBREVIATIONS

AC	Anders Collection (located at the USAHEC)
AC	Augustana College
ADAH	Alabama Department of Archives and History
AHC	Atlanta History Center
ALPL	Abraham Lincoln Presidential Library
AU	Auburn University
BU	Baylor University
CHM	Chicago History Museum
CHS	Cincinnati Historical Society
CU	Chapman University
CWD	Civil War Documents Collection (USAHEC)
CWTI	Civil War Times Illustrated Collection (USAHEC)
DU	Duke University
EU	Emory University
FHS	Filson Historical Society
GDAH	Georgia Department of Archives and History
HCWRT	Harrisburg Civil War Roundtable Collection (USAHEC)
HL	Huntington Library
IHS	Indiana Historical Society
ISL	Indiana State Library
ISU	Iowa State University
IU	Indiana University
KCPL	Kansas City Public Library
LC	Library of Congress
LMU	Loyola Marymount University
LSU	Louisiana State University
MDAH	Mississippi Department of Archives and History
MHS	Missouri Historical Society
NC	Navarro College

NL	Newberry Library
OCM	Old Courthouse Museum
OHS	Ohio Historical Society
OR	War of the Rebellion: A Compilation of the Official Records of the Union and Confederate Armies. Washington, DC: US Government Printing Office, 1880–1901.
ORN	The Official Records of the Union and Confederate Navies in the War of the Rebellion. 30 vols. Washington, DC: US Government Printing Office, 1894–1922.
SHSI	State Historical Society of Iowa
SHSMC	State Historical Society of Missouri–Columbia
SHSMS	State Historical Society of Missouri–St. Louis
SIU	Southern Illinois University
SNMP	Shiloh National Military Park
SU	Stanford University
TSLA	Tennessee State Library and Archives
TU	Tulane University
UA	University of Alabama
UCSB	University of California Santa Barbara
UGA	University of Georgia
UIA	University of Iowa
UMB	University of Michigan–Bentley Library
UMC	University of Michigan–Clements Library
UMEM	University of Memphis
UNC	University of North Carolina
UNT	University of North Texas
USAHEC	United States Army Heritage and Education Center
USGPL	Ulysses S. Grant Presidential Library
UT	University of Tennessee
UTA	University of Texas
UVA	University of Virginia
VICK	Vicksburg National Military Park
WRHS	Western Reserve Historical Society

Preface

1. For the assaults, see Timothy B. Smith, *The Union Assaults at Vicksburg: Grant Attacks Pemberton, May 17–22, 1863* (Lawrence: University Press of Kansas, 2020).

2. For Pemberton, see Michael B. Ballard, *Pemberton: The General Who Lost Vicksburg* (Jackson: University Press of Mississippi, 1991).

3. For Johnston, see Craig L. Symonds, *Joseph E. Johnston: A Civil War Biography* (New York: Norton, 1992).

4. For Davis, see William C. Davis, *Jefferson Davis: The Man and His Hour, A Biography* (New York: HarperCollins, 1991).

5. Smith, *The Union Assaults at Vicksburg*, 352–356.

6. For Lincoln, see David Herbert Donald, *Lincoln* (New York: Simon and Shuster, 1995).

7. W. A. Rorer to Susan, June 13, 1863, W. A. Rorer Letters, DU; George Hildt to parents, June 19, 1863, George H. Hildt Papers, OHS; George Messer to Lottie, May 31, 1863, George Messer Papers, WKU; Don Pardee to unknown, May 31, 1863, Don A. Pardee Papers, TU; Chase Dickinson to friends, June 3, 1863, Chase Hall Dickinson Papers, NL; Thomas B. White to mother, June 8, 1863, Thomas B. White Letters, OCM.

8. Chase Dickinson to friends, June 3, 1863, Chase Hall Dickinson Papers, NL; John A. McLaughlin to sister, June 15, 1863, McLaughlin-Jordan Family Papers, HIS.

9. "Concerning the Siege at Vicksburg," *Confederate Veteran* 2, no. 10 (October 1894): 295.

10. For a good overview of the campaign, see Terrence J. Winschel, "The Vicksburg Campaign," in *The Cambridge History of the American Civil War*, 3 vols., Aaron Sheehan-Dean, ed. (Cambridge: Cambridge University Press, 2019), 1:246–268. For the siege itself, see A. A. Hoehling, *Vicksburg: 47 Days of Siege* (Upper Saddle River, NJ: Prentice Hall, 1969); Michael B. Ballard, *Grant at Vicksburg: The General and the Siege* (Carbondale: Southern Illinois University Press, 2013); Justin S. Solonick, *Engineering Victory: The Union Siege of Vicksburg* (Carbondale: Southern Illinois University Press, 2015); Steven E. Woodworth and Charles D. Grear, eds., *Vicksburg Besieged* (Carbondale: Southern Illinois University Press, 2020). For historians who downplay Vicksburg's significance, see Donald Stoker, *The Grand Design: Strategy and the U.S. Civil War* (New York: Oxford University Press, 2010), 275; Albert Castel, "Vicksburg: Myths and Realities," *North and South Magazine* 6, no. 7 (November 2003): 62–69; Archer Jones, *Civil War Command & Strategy: The Process of Victory and Defeat* (New York: Free Press, 1992), 162–163.

11. Terrence J. Winschel, "Applicability in the Modern Age: Ulysses S. Grant's Vicksburg Campaign," *Journal of Mississippi History* 80, nos. 1 and 2 (Spring/Summer 2018): 35–47.

PROLOGUE: "NO GREATER TOPOGRAPHICAL PUZZLE"

1. Ballard, *Pemberton*, 57; Ronald C. White, *American Ulysses: A Life of Ulysses S. Grant* (New York: Random House, 2016), 282; Ron Chernow, *Grant* (New York: Penguin Press, 2017), 51–52; Solonick, *Engineering Victory*, 25–26. For Vera Cruz, see Timothy D. Johnson, *A Gallant Little Army: The Mexico City Campaign* (Lawrence: University Press of Kansas, 2007), 30–51.

2. Solonick, *Engineering Victory*, 30–31.

3. D. H. Mahan, *A Complete Treatise on Field Fortifications, with the General Outlines of the Principles Regulating the Arrangement, the Attack, and the Defense of*

Permanent Works (New York: Wiley and Long, 1836); Solonick, *Engineering Victory*, 3, 12–13, 15, 21.

4. Solonick, *Engineering Victory*, 17, 218.

5. *OR*, 24(2):176; William R. Eddington Memoir, undated, ALPL, 10; Solonick, *Engineering Victory*, 18, 55, 80, 96–97, 118. There were also differing types of saps, such as "flying saps," "full saps," and "double saps."

6. Solonick, *Engineering Victory*, 19, 173–174.

7. *OR*, 24(2):176, 208; Joseph Child Diary, June 9 and 27, 1863, UIA.

8. *OR*, 24(2):176, 208; George Carrington Diary, June 4, 1863, CHM; Joseph Child Diary, June 9 and 27, 1863, UIA; Thomas Christie to sister, June 7, 1863, James C. Christie and Family Papers, MNHS; Andrew Hickenlooper Reminiscences, undated, Hickenlooper Collection, CHS, 139; Josiah W. Underhill Diary, June 7, 1863, IHS; Aurelius L. Voorhis Diary, June 7, 1863, IHS; F. H. Mason, *The Forty-second Ohio Infantry: A History of the Organization and Services of That Regiment in the War of the Rebellion; With Biographical Sketches of Its Field Officers and a Full Roster of the Regiment* (Cleveland: Cobb, Andrews and Co., Publishers, 1876), 228.

9. *OR*, 24(2):176; Thomas Christie to sister, June 7, 1863, James C. Christie and Family Papers, MNHS; Andrew Hickenlooper Reminiscences, undated, Hickenlooper Collection, CHS, 139–140.

10. *OR*, 24(2):176; Wilbur F. Crummer, *With Grant at Fort Donelson, Shiloh and Vicksburg, and An Appreciation of General U.S. Grant* (Oak Park, IL: E. C. Crummer and Co., 1915), 118; Andrew Hickenlooper Reminiscences, undated, Hickenlooper Collection, CHS, 140.

11. *OR*, 24(2):176; Andrew Hickenlooper, "The Vicksburg Mine," in *Battles and Leaders of the Civil War*, 4 vols. (New York: Century Company, 1884–1887), 3:540; Mason, *The Forty-Second Ohio Infantry*, 227–228.

12. Andrew Hickenlooper Reminiscences, undated, Hickenlooper Collection, CHS, 146; *War of the Rebellion: A Compilation of the Official Records of the Union and Confederate Armies* (Washington, DC: US Government Printing Office, 1880–1901), Series 1, Volume 24 (Part 2):169. Hereafter cited as *OR*, with all references to series 1 unless otherwise noted, followed by volume and part number.

13. *OR*, 24(2):169.

14. For a discussion of the Confederate works and their creation, see S. H. Lockett, "The Defense of Vicksburg," in *Battles and Leaders of the Civil War*, 4 vols. New York: Century Company, 1884–1887), 3:482–492.

15. *OR*, 15:11; Lockett, "The Defense of Vicksburg," 482; Edwin C. Bearss, *The Vicksburg Campaign*, 3 vols. (Dayton, OH: Morningside, 1985), 3:739; Samuel H. Lockett to wife, November 25, 1862, Samuel H. Lockett Papers, UNC.

16. Lockett, "The Defense of Vicksburg," 484.

17. Lockett, "The Defense of Vicksburg," 3:488; *OR*, 24(2):330; William Lovelace Foster to wife, June 20, 1863, William L. Foster Letter, UA, copy in Journals/Letters/Diaries File, VICK; Theodore D. Fisher Diary, May 17 and 18, 1863, Civil War Collection, MHS, copy in 1st Missouri File, VICK.

18. Jerry Evan Crouch, *Silencing the Vicksburg Guns: The Story of the 7th Missouri Infantry Regiment As Experienced by John Davis Evans Union Private and Mormon Pioneer* (Victoria, BC: Trafford Publishing, 2005), 99; George Crooke, *The Twenty-first Regiment of Iowa Volunteer Infantry: A Narrative of Its Experience in Active Service, Including a Military Record of Each Officer, Non-Commissioned Officer, and Private Soldier of the Organization* (Milwaukee: King, Fowle & Co., 1891), 104.

19. For the assaults, see Smith, *The Union Assaults at Vicksburg*, and J. Parker Hills, "Haste and Underestimation: May 19," in *The Vicksburg Assaults: May 19–22, 1863*, Steven E. Woodworth and Charles D. Grear, eds. (Carbondale: Southern Illinois University Press, 2019), 7–26, and J. Parker Hills, "Failure and Scapegoat: May 22," in *The Vicksburg Assaults: May 19–22, 1863*, Steven E. Woodworth and Charles D. Grear, eds. (Carbondale: Southern Illinois University Press, 2019), 27–56.

20. Map of the Siege of Vicksburg, War of the Rebellion Collection, BU. For detail placements of the smaller forts, see George B. Davis, Leslie J. Perry, and Joseph W. Kirkley, *Atlas to Accompany the Official Records of the Union and Confederate Armies* (Washington, DC: US Government Printing Office, 1891–1895), plates 36 and 37.

21. *OR*, 24(2):179; Simeon R. Martin Reminiscences, undated, OCM, 69, copy in 46th Mississippi File, VICK.

22. Warren E. Grabau, *Ninety-Eight Days: A Geographer's View of the Vicksburg Campaign* (Knoxville: University of Tennessee Press, 2000), 408–409.

23. Smith, *The Union Assaults at Vicksburg*, 136–137.

24. *OR* 24(1):56–57; *OR*, 24(2):177–178; Solonick, *Engineering Victory*, 45; John Y. Simon and John F. Marszalek, eds., *The Papers of Ulysses S. Grant*. 32 vols. to date (Carbondale: Southern Illinois University Press, 1967–present), 8:331, 383, hereafter cited as *PUSG*; John F. Marszalek, David F. Nolen, and Louie P. Gallo, *The Personal Memoirs of Ulysses S. Grant: The Complete Annotated Edition* (Cambridge: Harvard University Press, 2017), 371; H. W. Halleck to Cyrus Comstock, June 8, 1863, Cyrus B. Comstock Papers, LOC.

25. Solonick, *Engineering Victory*, 2.

CHAPTER 1. "THE GREAT PROBLEM"

1. Robert Harris to Mattie, March 26, 1863, Robert H. Harris Letters, GHS; Simon, *PUSG*, 7:463, 480.

2. David Dixon Porter, *Incidents and Anecdotes of the Civil War* (New York: D. Appleton and Company, 1885), 96.

3. M. D. Gage, *From Vicksburg to Raleigh; Or, A Complete History of the Twelfth Regiment Indian Volunteer Infantry, and the Campaigns of Grant and Sherman, with an Outline of the Great Rebellion* (Chicago: Clarke & Co., 1865), 78; Michael B. Ballard, *Vicksburg: The Campaign That Opened the Mississippi* (Chapel Hill: University of North Carolina Press, 2004), 3–5; Unknown to John L. Hancock, June 27, 1863, John L. Hancock Papers, CHM; Robert Harris to Mattie, March 26, 1863, Robert H. Harris Letters, GHS.

4. R. W. Memminger, "The Surrender of Vicksburg—A Defense of General Pemberton," *Southern Historical Society Papers* 12, no. 7–9 (July–September 1884): 358. For more on the Southern Railroad, see Southern Railroad Records, AU; Southern Railroad Currency, 1861, Baker Library, HU; Robert C. Black III, *The Railroads of the Confederacy* (Chapel Hill: University of North Carolina Press, 1952).

5. Smith, *Gallant in the Extreme*, 19–21.

6. Smith, 21–25.

7. For Grant's struggles just getting to Vicksburg, see Timothy B. Smith, *"The Decision Was Always My Own": Ulysses S. Grant and the Vicksburg Campaign* (Carbondale: Southern Illinois University Press, 2018).

8. Alonzo L. Brown, *History of the Fourth Regiment of Minnesota Infantry Volunteers During the Great Rebellion, 1861–1865* (St. Paul: Pioneer Press Company, 1892), 247. For operations on the river, see Gary D. Joiner, *Mr. Lincoln's Brown Water Navy: The Mississippi Squadron* (New York: Rowman and Littlefield, 2007), and Barbara Brooks Tomblin, *The Civil War on the Mississippi: Union Sailors, Gunboat Captains, and the Campaign to Control the River* (Lexington: University Press of Kentucky, 2016).

9. *OR*, 15:810–811; Thomas L. Connelly, *Army of the Heartland: The Army of Tennessee, 1861–1862* (Baton Rouge: Louisiana State University Press, 1967), 25–27. For the Tennessee Valley campaigns, see Timothy B. Smith, *Grant Invades Tennessee: The 1862 Battles for Forts Henry and Donelson* (Lawrence: University Press of Kansas, 2016), Timothy B. Smith, *Shiloh: Conquer or Perish* (Lawrence: University Press of Kansas, 2014), and Timothy B. Smith, *Corinth 1862: Siege, Battle, Occupation* (Lawrence: University Press of Kansas, 2012).

10. Raimondo Luraghi, *A History of the Confederate Navy* (Annapolis: Naval Institute Press, 1996). For Memphis, see Edward B. McCaul, Jr., *To Retain Command of the Mississippi: The Civil War Naval Campaign for Memphis* (Knoxville: University of Tennessee Press, 2014).

11. *OR*, 10, 2:430; *OR*, 15:811; John Kinsel to friend, June 28, 1863, John Ruckman Letters, Journals/Letters/Diaries Series, VICK. For the Delta, see James C. Cobb, *The Most Southern Place on Earth: The Mississippi Delta and the Roots of Regional Identity* (New York: Oxford University Press, 1994).

12. *The Official Records of the Union and Confederate Navies in the War of the Rebellion*, 30 vols. (Washington, DC: US Government Printing Office, 1894–1922) Volume 18:152, hereafter cited as *ORN*; *OR*, 6:504; Chester G. Hearn, *The Capture of New Orleans 1862* (Baton Rouge: Louisiana State University Press, 1995), 209–236.

13. *ORN*, 18:159; Jonse to sister, July 7, 1862, 17th Louisiana File, VICK.

14. *ORN*, 1, 18:492, 610; *OR*, 15:13. For this first action around Vicksburg, see Edwin C. Bearss, *Rebel Victory at Vicksburg* (Vicksburg: Vicksburg Centennial Commission, 1963); Jonse to sister, July 8, 1862, 17th Louisiana File, VICK; Aaron S. Oberly to unknown, May 21, 1862, Aaron S. Oberly Papers, AU.

15. Ezra Greene to mother, July 13, 1863, Ezra Greene Papers, FHS; Jonse to sister, July 7, 1862, 17th Louisiana File, VICK. For Porter, see Chester G. Hearn, *Admiral David Dixon Porter: The Civil War Years* (Annapolis: Naval Institute Press, 1996).

16. *OR*, 6:513, 515–516; Hearn, *The Capture of New Orleans 1862*, 237–248.

17. *OR*, 6:624, 651.

18. *OR*, 15:810–811; Lockett, "The Defense of Vicksburg," 482.

19. *OR*, 6:515, 567, 570, 884; *OR*, 10, 2:481; *OR*, 15:6–7, 811; Lockett, "The Defense of Vicksburg," 482.

20. *OR*, 15:6; *OR*, 15:849–853; Lockett, "The Defense of Vicksburg," 483–484; Samuel H. Lockett to wife, August 4, 1862, Samuel H. Lockett Papers, UNC.

21. *OR*, 15:848, 852; Lockett, "The Defense of Vicksburg," 484; Samuel H. Lockett to wife, September 22, 1862, Samuel H. Lockett Papers, UNC.

22. Timothy B. Smith, *The Real Horse Soldiers: Benjamin Grierson's Epic 1863 Civil War Raid Through Mississippi* (New York: Savas Beatie, 2018), 231–232.

23. Lockett, "The Defense of Vicksburg," 484; John Kinsel to friend, June 28, 1863, John Kinsel Letters, Journals/Letters/Diaries, VICK; Allen C. Richard, Jr., and Mary Margaret Higginbotham Richard, *The Defense of Vicksburg: A Louisiana Chronicle* (College Station: Texas A&M University Press, 2004), 83.

24. *OR*, 17(2):294, 296; Marszalek et al., eds., *The Personal Memoirs of Ulysses S. Grant*, 289.

25. *OR*, 17(2):315; *OR*, 17(1):467; Bearss, *The Vicksburg Campaign*, 1:21–112.

26. Henry W. Halleck, *Elements of Military Art and Science: Or, Course of Instruction in Strategy, Fortification, Tactics of Battles, &c.; Embracing the Duties of Staff, Infantry, Cavalry, Artillery, and Engineers. Adapted to the Use of Volunteers and Militia* (New York: D. Appleton and Company, 1846).

27. *OR*, 17(2):347, 392; Marszalek et al., eds., *The Personal Memoirs of Ulysses S. Grant*, 294. For McClernand, see Richard L. Kiper, *Major General John Alexander McClernand: Politician in Uniform* (Kent, OH: Kent State University Press, 1999).

28. *OR*, 17(2):434; *OR*, 17(1):468; William T. Sherman, *Memoirs of General William T. Sherman: Written by Himself*, 2 vols. (New York: D. Appleton and Co., 1875), 1:284–285. For the *Cairo*, see Edwin C. Bearss, *Hardluck Ironclad: The Sinking and Salvage of the Cairo*, rev. ed. (Baton Rouge: Louisiana State University Press, 1980).

29. Mildred Throne, ed., *The Civil War Diary of Cyrus F. Boyd Fifteenth Iowa Infantry, 1861–1863* (Baton Rouge: Louisiana State University Press, 1998), 95–96; Marszalek et al., eds., *The Personal Memoirs of Ulysses S. Grant*, 301–302; Bearss, *The Vicksburg Campaign*, 1:231–348; William M. Standard Diary, December 20, 1862, AHC.

30. *OR*, 17(1):613; Sherman, *Memoirs of General William T. Sherman*, 1:295; Bearss, *The Vicksburg Campaign*, 1:113–230; Robert J. Henderson Report, January 4, 1863, George H. Daniel Correspondence, AHC.

31. D. W. Wood, *History of the 20th O. V. V. I. Regiment, and Proceedings of the First Reunion at Mt. Vernon, Ohio, April 6, 1876* (Columbus: Paul and Thrall, Book and Job Printers, 1876), 19.

32. *OR*, 17(2):528–529, 553, 555; *OR*, 24(3):5.

33. *OR*, 17(2):555; Marszalek et al., eds., *The Personal Memoirs of Ulysses S. Grant*, 299.

34. Marszalek et al., eds., *The Personal Memoirs of Ulysses S. Grant*, 307–309.

35. Simon, *PUSG*, 7:268, 270, 276, 357–358, 411, 489.

36. *OR*, 24(3):9, 12; *OR*, 24(1):10; Simon, *PUSG*, 7:311, 366, 383–384; Marszalek et al., eds., *The Personal Memoirs of Ulysses S. Grant*, 309; Robert Harris to Mattie, March 26, 1863, Robert H. Harris Letters, GHS.

37. *OR*, 24(3):9, 12, 38, 65, 126; *OR*, 24(1):10, 44; Simon, *PUSG*, 7:311, 366, 383–384; Marszalek et al., eds., *The Personal Memoirs of Ulysses S. Grant*, 309.

38. *OR*, 24(3):18, 32.

39. *OR*, 24(3):131; Marszalek et al., eds., *The Personal Memoirs of Ulysses S. Grant*, 311.

40. *OR*, 24(3):6; *OR*, 24(1):14, 45; Simon, *PUSG*, 7:409, 463. For Yazoo Pass, see Timothy B. Smith, "Victory at Any Cost: The Yazoo Pass Expedition," *Journal of Mississippi History* 67, no. 2 (Summer 2007): 147–166.

41. *OR*, 24(3):112, 119; *OR*, 24(1):21; Marszalek et al., eds., *The Personal Memoirs of Ulysses S. Grant*, 313–314.

42. *OR*, 24(3):168; *OR*, 24(1):24; Simon, *PUSG*, 7:489; Simon, *PUSG*, 8:110.

43. Bruce Catton, *Grant Moves South* (Boston: Little, Brown, and Company, 1960), 407.

44. Marszalek et al., eds., *The Personal Memoirs of Ulysses S. Grant*, 319; David S. Scott to Kate, April 10, 1863, David S. Scott Papers, IHS.

45. Marszalek et al., eds., *The Personal Memoirs of Ulysses S. Grant*, 374.

46. *OR*, 24(3):152; Sobieski Jolly Memoir, undated, Sobieski Jolly Papers, CHS, 34–35; James F. Elliott Diary, April 22, 1863, IHS; A. Achen to Ohio Union, April 25, 1863, A. Achen Letter, CHM; James McLaughlin to father, May 11, 1863, James McLaughlin Papers, ISL. For Grierson's Raid, see Smith, *The Real Horse Soldiers*.

47. *OR*, 24(3):279.

48. John Russell Young, *Around the World With General Grant: A Narrative of the Visit of General U.S. Grant, Ex-President of the United States, to Various Countries in Europe, Asia, and Africa, in 1877, 1878, 1879. To which are Added Certain Conversations with General Grant on Questions Connected with American Politics and History* (New York: American News Company, 1879), 2:621.

49. *OR*, 24(1):50.

50. *OR*, 24(1):50; Marszalek et al., eds., *The Personal Memoirs of Ulysses S. Grant*, 349; Elizabeth J. Whaley, *Forgotten Hero: General James B. McPherson* (New York: Exposition Press, 1955), 133; James Slack to Ann, May 25, 1863, James R. Slack Papers, ISL.

51. Simon, *PUSG*, 8:228; Unknown to father, May 27, 1863, Leeson Family Papers, ISL. For detail on Champion Hill, see Timothy B. Smith, *Champion Hill: Decisive Battle for Vicksburg* (New York: Savas Beatie, 2004). For Big Black River Bridge, see Timothy B. Smith, "'A Victory Could Hardly Have Been More Complete': The Battle of Big Black River Bridge," in *The Vicksburg Campaign: March 29–May 18, 1863*, Steven E. Woodworth and Charles D. Grear, eds. (Carbondale: Southern Illinois University Press, 2013), 173–193.

52. *OR*, 24(3):201; L. S. Willard to brother, April 19, 1863, L. S. Willard Letters, NL.

CHAPTER 2. "WE HAVE DONE VERY LITTLE, BUT MADE A GREAT NOISE IN DOING IT"

1. John F. Marszalek, *Sherman: A Soldier's Passion for Order* (New York: The Free Press, 1993), 160–168.

2. *OR*, 24(3):179–180, 201; Sherman, *Memoirs*, 1:315; Marszalek et al., eds., *The Personal Memoirs of Ulysses S. Grant*, 374; Brooks D. Simpson, *Ulysses S. Grant: Triumph Over Adversity, 1822–1865* (Boston: Houghton Mifflin Company, 2000), 174.

3. *OR*, 24(1):70–71; Simon, *PUSG*, 7:480; Bruce Catton, *U. S. Grant and the American Military Tradition* (Boston: Little, Brown and Co., 1954), 98; Young, *Around the World With General Grant*, 2:616. For Sherman's missteps in the North Carolina surrender, see Mark L. Bradley, *This Astounding Close: The Road to Bennett Place* (Chapel Hill: University of North Carolina Press, 2000).

4. Henry J. Seaman Diary, June 1, 1863, CWTI, USAHEC, copy in 13th Illinois File, VICK; Marszalek et al., eds., *The Personal Memoirs of Ulysses S. Grant*, 365.

5. Charles Bracelen Flood, *Grant and Sherman: The Friendship That Won the Civil War* (New York: Farrar, Straus and Giroux, 2005), 127–129.

6. Marszalek et al., eds., *The Personal Memoirs of Ulysses S. Grant*, 365; Isaac Williams to brother, June 18, 1863, Isaac T. William Papers, Brookes Collection, USAHEC.

7. *OR*, 24(3):322; Sherman, *Memoirs*, 1:323–324; J. H. Wilson, "A Staff Officer's Journal of the Vicksburg Campaign, April 30 to July 4, 1863," *Journal of the Military Service Institution of the United States* 43, no. 155 (September–October 1908): 261; Sylvanus Cadwallader, *Three Years with Grant*, Benjamin P. Thomas, ed. (Lincoln: University of Nebraska Press, 1996), 83; Stephen D. Lee, "The Siege of Vicksburg," *Publications of the Mississippi Historical Society*, 3 (1900): 57.

8. *OR*, 24(2):17; Mason, *The Forty-second Ohio Infantry*, 218.

9. *OR*, 24(3):329; *OR*, 24(1):55, 154; *OR*, 24(2):170, 267; Marszalek et al., eds., *The Personal Memoirs of Ulysses S. Grant*, 366; J. F. C. Fuller, *The Generalship of Ulysses S. Grant* (Bloomington: Indiana University Press, 1958), 154; Simon, ed., *PUSG*, 8:237; Special Field Orders, May 19, 1863, John A. Rawlins Papers, CHM; George M. Rogers Diary, May 19, 1863, ISL; Calvin Ainsworth Diary, May 19, 1863, UMB.

10. *OR*, 24(1):153–154; Bearss, *The Vicksburg Campaign*, 3:774; *OR*, 24(2):17–18, 230–231; James Keigwin to W. T. Rigby, March 5, 1902, 49th Indiana File, VICK; Jean Powers Soman and Frank L. Byrne, eds., *A Jewish Colonel in the Civil War: Marcus M. Spiegel of the Ohio Volunteers* (Kent, OH: Kent State University Press, 1985), 281; Mahlon Rouch Diary, May 19, 1863, 120th Ohio File, VICK; James B. Taylor Diary, May 19, 1863, 120th Ohio File, VICK; James Leeper to wife, May 23, 1863, James Leeper Papers, IHS; Paul H. Hass, ed., "The Vicksburg Diary of Henry Clay Warmoth: Part II (April 28 1863–May 26, 1863)," *Journal of Mississippi History* 32, no. 1 (February 1970): 72; Edward J. Lewis Diary, May 18, 1863, 33rd Illinois File, VICK.

11. *OR*, 24(2):297, 299–300; Seth J. Wells, *The Siege of Vicksburg from the Diary of Seth J. Wells, Including Weeks of Preparation and of Occupation After the Surrender* (Detroit: William H. Rowe, Publisher, 1915), 65–66; Bearss, *The Vicksburg Campaign*,

3:777–778; *OR*, 24(2):292; Gould D. Molineaux Diary, May 19, 1863, AC; Edmund Newsome Diary, May 19, 1863, MDAH, copy in OCM; S. H. M. Byers, *With Fire and Sword* (New York: Neale Publishing Company, 1911), 88–89; H. M. Trimble Diary, May 19, 1863, 93rd Illinois File, VICK; Elbert Willett Diary, May 19, 1863, ADAH, copy in OCM; Jeff T. Giambrone, *Beneath Torn and Tattered Flags: A History of the 38th Mississippi Infantry, C.S.A.* (Bolton, MS: Smokey Row Press, 1998), 71–72; Lydia Minturn Post, ed., *Soldiers' Letters. From Camp, Battle-field and Prison* (New York: Bunce and Huntington, Publishers, 1865), 205; John Crane to Colonel Kirby, November 13, 1906, 72nd Illinois File, VICK; "War Diary of Brevet Brigadier General Joseph Stockton," Coco Collection, HCWRT, USAHEC, 15.

12. *OR*, 24(1):755. For a concise overview of the May 19 assault, see J. Parker Hills, "Haste and Underestimation: May 19," in *The Vicksburg Assaults: May 19–22, 1863*, Steven E. Woodworth and Charles D. Grear, eds. (Carbondale: Southern Illinois University Press, 2019), 7–26.

13. Simon, *PUSG*, 8:164; William E. Parrish, *Frank Blair: Lincoln's Conservative* (Colombia: University of Missouri Press, 1998), 162, 164; Marszalek et al., eds., *The Personal Memoirs of Ulysses S. Grant*, 396.

14. George Powell Clarke, *Reminiscence and Anecdotes of the War for Southern Independence* (N.p.: n.p., n.d.), 100; William Lovelace Foster to wife, June 20, 1863, William L. Foster Letter, UA; *OR*, 24(1):163, 756; *OR*, 24(2):257, 261.

15. Edwin C. Bearss and J. Parker Hills, *Receding Tide: Vicksburg and Gettysburg, The Campaigns That Changed the Civil War* (Washington, DC: National Geographic, 2010), 236; Henry R. Brinkerhoff, *History of the Thirtieth Regiment Ohio Volunteer Infantry, From Its Organization, To the Fall of Vicksburg, Miss.* (Columbus: James W. Osgood, Printer, 1863), 69; Thomas J. Taylor to W. T. Rigby, March 19, 1903, 47th Ohio File, VICK; *OR*, 24(2):281; Thomas H. Barton, *Autobiography of Dr. Thomas H. Barton, The Self-made Physician of Syracuse, Ohio: Including a History of the Fourth Regt. West Va. Vol. Inf'y, with an Account of Col. Lightburn's Retreat Down the Kanawha Valley, Gen. Grant's Vicksburg and Chattanooga Campaigns, Together with the Several Battles in Which The Fourth Regiment Was Engaged, and Its Losses by Disease, Desertion and in Battle* (Charleston: West Virginia Printing Co., 1890), 152; Ephraim McD. Anderson, *Memoirs: Historical and Personal Including the Campaigns of the First Missouri Confederate Brigade* (St. Louis: Times Publishing Co., 1868), 329; Joseph A. Saunier, *A History of the Forty-seventh Regiment Ohio Veteran Volunteer Infantry, Second Brigade, Second Division, Fifteenth Army Corps, Army of the Tennessee* (Hillsboro, OH: Lyle Printing Company, 1903), 144.

16. *OR*, 24(2):264, 406; Charles E. Affeld Diary, May 19, 1863, Journals/Letters/Diaries, VICK; J. J. Kellogg, *The Vicksburg Campaign and Reminiscences, "Milliken's Bend" to July 4, 1863* (Washington, IA: Evening Journal, 1913), 28–29; Jim Russell to mother, May 27, 1863, Frederick W. Russell Letters, CHM.

17. *OR*, 24(2):267; Will Jolly to parents, June 1, 1863, Journals/Letters/Diaries, VICK.

18. *OR*, 24(2):397–398, 402, 406, 414–415; Richard and Higginbotham, *The Defense*

of Vicksburg, 154, 161; S. D. Lee to W. T. Rigby, January 26, 1903, 27th Louisiana File, VICK; William Lovelace Foster to wife, June 20, 1863, William L. Foster Letter, UA; Theodore D. Fisher Diary, May 23, 1863, Civil War Collection, MHS, copy in Journals/Letters/Diaries, VICK and OCM; Samuel Fowler Diary, May 19, 1863, SU; Louis Guion Diary, May 19, 1863, LSU; Clarke, *Reminiscence and Anecdotes*, 100.

19. Saunier, *A History of the Forty-seventh Regiment Ohio Veteran Volunteer Infantry*, 145; John M. Roberts Reminiscences, undated, IHS, 37; *OR*, 24(2):268–270, 274; J. Grecian, *History of the Eighty-third Regiment, Indiana Volunteer Infantry. For Three Years With Sherman* (Cincinnati: John F. Uhlhorn, printer, 1865), 30–31; J. R. Grassmeire to friend, May 27, 1863, Andrew McCornack Papers, Sword Collection, USAHEC; Benjamin Spooner to madam, June 7, 1863, Benjamin Spooner Letters, ISL. For casualties by name in the 83rd Indiana, see Benjamin Spooner to sir, May 24, 1863, Benjamin Spooner Letters, ISL.

20. *OR*, 24(2):267; Walter George Smith, *Life and Letters of Thomas Kilby Smith, Brevet Major-General United States Volunteers, 1820–1877* (New York: G. P. Putnam's Sons, 1898), 295; *OR*, 24(2):268, 376; Robert Oliver to W. T. Rigby, April 6, 1902, 55th Illinois File, VICK; David W. Reed, *Campaigns and Battles of the Twelfth Regiment Iowa Veteran Volunteer Infantry From Its Organization, September, 1861, to Muster Out, January 20, 1866* (N.p.: n.p., 1903), 122; *The Story of the Fifty-fifth Regiment Illinois Volunteer Infantry in the Civil War, 1861–1865* (Clinton, MA: W. J. Coulter, 1887), 237–239.

21. *OR*, 24(2):282, 376; Thomas J. Taylor to W. T. Rigby, March 19, 1903, 47th Ohio File, VICK; Unknown to Judy, May 24, 1863, John H. Wickizer Papers, ALPL; Andrew McCormack to family, May 24, 1863, Andrew McCormack Papers, NC.

22. *OR*, 24(2):269; *The Story of the Fifty-fifth Regiment Illinois Volunteer Infantry in the Civil War*, 236.

23. "Opening of the Mississippi," November 2, 1905, *National Tribune*.

24. Bearss, *The Vicksburg Campaign*, 3:775–776, 778; Richard and Richard, *The Defense of Vicksburg*, 161; Sherman, *Memoirs*, 1:325; Terrence J. Winschel, *Triumph and Defeat: The Vicksburg Campaign* (Mason City, IA: Savas Publishing Company, 1999), 127; Hugh Ewing Diary, May 19, 1863, OHS.

25. Clarke, *Reminiscence and Anecdotes*, 101; Lee, "The Siege of Vicksburg," 59.

26. *OR*, 24(3):334. For a concise overview of the May 22 assaults, see J. Parker Hills, "Failure and Scapegoat: May 22," in *The Vicksburg Assaults: May 19–22, 1863*, Steven E. Woodworth and Charles D. Grear, eds. (Carbondale: Southern Illinois University Press, 2019), 27–56. For a discussion of tactics, including attacking by the flank, see Earl J. Hess, *Civil War Infantry Tactics: Training, Combat, and Small-Unit Effectiveness* (Baton Rouge: Louisiana State University Press, 2015).

27. William Jolly to parents, June 1, 1863, William H. Jolly Letters, Journals/Letters/Diaries Series, VICK; "George Theodore Hyatt," 1897, 127th Illinois File, VICK.

28. William Jolly to parents, June 1, 1863, William H. Jolly Letters, Journals/Letters/Diaries Series, VICK; "George Theodore Hyatt," 1897, 127th Illinois File, VICK; Hugh Ewing Diary, May 22, 1863, OHS.

29. Charles A. Willison, *Reminiscences of a Boy's Service with the 76th Ohio, In the*

Fifteenth Army Corps, Under General Sherman, During the Civil War, By That "Boy" at Three Score (Menasha, WI: George Banta Publishing Company, 1908), 56; Stuart Bennett and Barbara Tillery, eds., *The Struggle for the Life of the Republic: A Civil War Narrative by Brevet Major Charles Dana Miller, 76th Ohio Volunteer Infantry* (Kent, OH: Kent State University Press, 2004), 96, copy of diary in Journals/Letters/Diaries File, VICK; Henry Seaman Diary, May 21, 1863, 13th Illinois File, VICK; James F. Mallinckrodt Diary, May 22, 1863, OCM; James Thomas to Jones, May 26, 1863, Robert T. Jones Letters, UTK.

30. Smith, *The Union Assaults at Vicksburg*, 180–205. For political generals, see David Work, *Lincoln's Political Generals* (Urbana: University of Illinois Press, 2009).

31. *OR*, 24(1):710; Ira Blanchard, *I Marched with Sherman: Civil War Memoirs of the 20th Illinois Volunteer Infantry*, Nancy Ann Mattingly, ed. (New York: toExcel, 1992), 96; Gilbert Young to mother, May 28, 1863, Gilbert N. Young Letters, Journals/Letters/Diaries Series, VICK.

32. *OR*, 24(2):361, 376; *Supplement to the Official Records of the Union and Confederate Armies*, 100 vols. (Wilmington, NC: Broadfoot, 1994), 4:417; F. M. Smith to W. T. Rigby, January 9, 1905, 81st Illinois File, VICK.

33. *OR*, 24(1):55, 174–175; *OR*, 24(2):34, 37, 39, 236; R. B. Scott, *The History of the 67th Regiment Indian Infantry Volunteers, War of the Rebellion* (Bedford, IN: Herald Book and Job Print, 1892), 37; J. G. Jones to parents, May 29, 1863, John G. Jones Correspondence, LC.

34. *OR*, 24(2):20, 232; Mason, *The Forty-second Ohio Infantry*, 221–222; E. L. Hawk to W. T. Rigby, April 21, 1914, 114th Ohio File, VICK.

35. "Military History of Eugene A. Carr," Eugene A. Carr Papers, RG 94, E 159, NARA; John H. Burnham, *The Thirty-third Regiment Illinois Infantry in the Civil War, 1861–1865; Prepared by Capt. J.H. Burnham at the Request of the Directors of the Illinois Historical Society for the 1912 Annual Meeting of That Society* (N.p.: n.p., 1912), n.p.; *OR*, 24(2):39, 367, 382, 388; J. G. Jones to parents, May 29, 1863, John G. Jones Correspondence, LC.

36. J. M. Pearson to S. D. Lee, May 17, 1902, 30th Alabama File, VICK; *OR*, 24(2):141, 238; *OR*, 24(1):154–155; *Supplement to the Official Records of the Union and Confederate Armies*, 4:405; Jesse Sawyer to W. T. Rigby, February 14, 1903, 77th Illinois File, VICK; John W. Carroll to comrades, October 28, 1902, 77th Illinois File, VICK; Joseph F. Parker to J. H. Robinson, June 24, 1902, 130th Illinois File, VICK.

37. *OR*, 24(1):55–56; Wimer Bedford Memoir, undated, Wimer Bedford Papers, LC, 46; Carlos Colby to sister, June 19, 1863, Carlos W. Colby Papers, NL.

38. *OR*, 24(1):55–56, 163, 172–173; Simon, ed., *PUSG*, 8:253; Kiper, *Major General John A. McClernand*, 261; John A. McClernand to U. S. Grant, May 22, 1863 and U. S. Grant to John A. McClernand, May 22, 1863, John A. McClernand Papers, ALPL; Sherman, *Memoirs*, 1:327; Kiper, *Major General John A. McClernand*, 261.

39. Smith, *The Union Assaults at Vicksburg*, 273.

40. *OR*, 24(2):252; *OR*, 24(1):757; James Thomas to Jones, May 26, 1863, Robert T. Jones Letters, UTK; Charles A. Willison to mother, June 26, 1863, 76th Ohio Volunteer

Infantry Papers, OHS; R. W. Burt to Mr. Editor, May 30, 1863, 76th Ohio Volunteer Infantry Papers, OHS; Joseph Child Diary, May 23, 1863, UIA.

41. Carey Campbell Wright, "The Civil War Letters of Carey Campbell Wright," undated, Wright Family Papers, AU, 135; *OR*, 24(1):757, 760, 768; *OR*, 24(2):273; Dennis W. Belcher, *The 11th Missouri Volunteer Infantry in the Civil War: A History and Roster* (Jefferson, NC: McFarland & Company, Inc., 2011), 124; G. C. Adams to sister, May 25, 1863, John P. Reese to wife, May 25, 1863, Journals/Letters/Diaries, VICK; J. W. Greenman Diary, May 23, 1863, MDAH.

42. *OR*, 24(2):264; Kellogg, *The Vicksburg Campaign and Reminiscences*, 41; John Frist to W. T. Rigby, October 15, 1902, 113th Illinois File, VICK; Jim Russell to mother, May 27, 1863, Frederick W. Russell Letters, CHM.

43. L. P. Brockett, *The Camp, The Battle Field, and the Hospital; Or, Lights and Shadows of the Great Rebellion* (Philadelphia: National Publishing Company, 1866), 512; *OR*, 24(1):710.

44. William Lovelace Foster to wife, June 20, 1863, William L. Foster Letter, UA; Edward P. Stanfield to father, May 26, 1863, Edward P. Stanfield Papers, IHS; *OR*, 24(2):67–68, 316, 389; J. Q. A. Campbell Diary, May 22, 1863, 5th Iowa File, VICK; Mary Amelia (Boomer) Stone, *Memoir of George Boardman Boomer* (Boston: Press of Geo. C. Rand & Avery, 1864), 257.

45. Peter C. Hains, "An Incident of the Battle of Vicksburg," in *Military Order of the Loyal Legion of the United States, Commandery of the District of Columbia, War Papers* 1 (N.p.: n.p., 1887), 69–72; *OR*, 24(2):141, 358; William Lowery Diary, May 22, 1863, ADAH; C. M. Shelley to S. D. Lee, September 2, 1902, 30th Alabama File, VICK; A. E. Cook Statement, undated, 21st Iowa File, VICK; A. C. Lenert Diary, May 22, 1863, UNT.

46. Cadwallader, *Three Years with Grant*, 91–92; William L. B. Jenney, "Personal Recollections of Vicksburg," in *Military Essays and Recollections: Papers Read Before the Commandery of the State of Illinois, Military Order of the Loyal Legion of the United States, Volume 3* (Chicago: Dial Press, 1899), 261; Flood, *Grant and Sherman*, 168; *OR*, 24(1):757; Adam Badeau, *Military History of Ulysses S. Grant, From April, 1861, to April, 1865*, 2 vols. (New York: D. Appleton & Co., 1881), 1:671, 674.

47. William M. Reid Diary, May 23, 1863, ALPL, copy in Journals/Letters/Diaries Series, VICK; William Lovelace Foster to wife, June 20, 1863, William L. Foster Letter, UA; Bearss, *The Vicksburg Campaign*, 3:816, 858; Samuel D. Pryce, *Vanishing Footprints: The Twenty-Second Iowa Volunteer Infantry in the Civil War*, Jeffry C. Burden, ed. (Iowa City: Camp Pope Bookshop, 2008), 126–127; David Grier to Anna, May 30, 1863, David P. Grier Papers, MHS; Flavius J. Thackary Diary, May 22, 1863, OHS.

48. Richard and Richard, *The Defense of Vicksburg*, 165; Louis Guion Diary, May 23, 1863, LSU.

49. William L. Roberts Diary, May 23, 1863, ADAH; Richard and Richard, *The Defense of Vicksburg*, 165; Louis Guion Diary, May 23, 1863, LSU; John H. Wickizer to "My Dear Judge," May 24, 1863, John H. Wickizer Letters, ALPL.

50. William J. Kennedy to wife, May 27 and June 3, 1863, William J. Kennedy Papers, ALPL; Albert C. Boals Diary, May 25, 1863, ALPL.

51. Jenkin Lloyd Jones, "An Artilleryman's Diary," *Wisconsin History Commission: Original Papers, No. 8* (February 1914): 62–63, copy in WHS and letters of same in Jenkin Lloyd Jones Papers, University of Chicago; Lewis Love to Thomas Fogg, May 26, 1863, Clarkson Fogg File, Journals/Letters/Diaries Series, VICK; Henry Kircher to mother, June 17, 1863, Engelmann-Kircher Family Papers, ALPL; John G. Sever to Mrs. Piper, undated, 99th Illinois File, VICK; James S. McHenry Diary, May 23, 1863, ALPL.

52. Olynthus B.Clark, ed., *Downing's Civil War Diary* (Des Moines: Historical Department of Iowa, 1916), 116.

53. Jesse Sawyer to W. T. Rigby, February 14, 1903, 77th Illinois File, VICK.

54. Stanley D. Buckles, *Not Afraid to Go Any Whare: A History of the 114th Regiment Illinois Volunteer Infantry* (Bend, OR: Maverick Publications, 2019), 50; William Russell to Spencer, June 15, 1863, Russell Family Papers, ALPL; *OR*, 24(3):349; Samuel Eells to unknown, June 2, 1863, Samuel H. Eells Papers, LC; "History of the 99th Illinois Vols.," 1901, George S. Marks Papers, CWD, USAHEC, 7.

55. John M. Sullivan to wife, June 21, 1863, John M. Sullivan Papers, OHS; John F. Marszalek, *Commander of All Lincoln's Armies: A Life of General Henry W. Halleck* (Cambridge: Harvard University Press, 2004), 177; Joseph Bowker Diary, May 23, 1863, 42nd Ohio File, VICK.

CHAPTER 3. "I THINK WE WILL SIEGE THEM OUT"

1. Richard and Richard, *The Defense of Vicksburg*, 164; Louis Guion Diary, May 23, 1863, LSU; Rowland Chambers Diary, May 22, 1863, LSU; Jesse M. Lee Diary, May 23, 1863, 59th Indiana File, VICK.

2. Edward J. Lewis Diary, May 23, 1863, 33rd Illinois File, VICK; Gordon A. Cotton, ed., *From the Pen of a She-Rebel: The Civil War Diary of Emilie Riley McKinley* (Columbia: University of South Carolina Press, 2001), 14 (copy in manuscript form as Emilie R. McKinley Diary, MHS).

3. Samuel S. Irwin Diary, May 24, 1863, ALPL; William M. Reid Diary, June 9, 1863, ALPL, copy in Journals/Letters/Diaries Series, VICK; Theodore F. Davis to W. T. Rigby, March 31, 1902, 83rd Indiana File, VICK; Alvin Hovey Memoir, undated, IU, 59; Unknown to family, June 10, 1863, Civil War—Campaigns and Battles—Vicksburg, ISL.

4. Lockett, "The Defense of Vicksburg," 3:488.

5. *OR*, 24(3):910.

6. Theodore D. Fisher Diary, June 3, 1863, Journals/Letters/Diaries Series, VICK, copy in Missouri File, VICK; W. R. McRory Diary, May 26, 1863, Journals/Letters/Diaries Series, VICK.

7. W. R. McRory Diary, May 23, 1863, Journals/Letters/Diaries Series, VICK.

8. *OR*, 24(3):909.

9. *OR*, 24(3):913; *OR*, 24(1):276; Leonard B. Plummer, ed., "Excerpts from the Hander Diary," *Journal of Mississippi History* 26, n0.2 (May 1964): 145, original diary in Christian Wilhelm Hander Diary, UTA.

10. Jeptha V. Harris, "The State Troops," undated, J. F. H. Claiborne Papers, UNC.

11. *OR*, 24(3):914; L. B. Claiborne Memoirs, undated, CWTI, USAHEC, 14; S. N. Pickens to W. T. Rigby, April 16, 1902, 27th Louisiana File, VICK.

12. *OR*, 24(1):57.

13. *OR*, 24(3):909; John Forney notes, May 23–28, 1863 Dabney Maury Order Book, CHM, 283–294; William Baldwin to major, June 20, 1863, John C. Pemberton Papers, RG 109, E 131, NARA; J. C. Taylor to Edward Higgins, and R. W. Memminger to John H. Forney, May 23, 1863, Letters and Telegrams Sent, Department of Mississippi and East Louisiana, 1863, RG 109, Chapter II, Vol. 60, NARA.

14. *OR*, 24(3):910; John Forney to R. W. Memminger, May 24, 1863, Dabney Maury Order Book, CHM, 285.

15. *OR*, 24(3):911.

16. *OR*, 24(3):911; *OR*, 24(2):331.

17. *OR*, 24(3):915; *OR*, 52(2):483; *OR*, 24(2):362; John Forney to R. W. Memminger, May 29, 1863, Dabney Maury Order Book, CHM, 294.

18. *OR*, 24(3):910, 912–915, 917; *OR*, 52(2):484; A. L. Slack Diary, May 18, 1863, Letters, Journals/Letters/Diaries Series, VICK, 16–17; John Forney to Carter Stevenson, May 25, 1863, Dabney Maury Order Book, CHM, 286.

19. *OR*, 24(3):910, 912–915, 917; *OR*, 52(2):484; A. L. Slack Diary, May 18, 1863, Letters, Journals/Letters/Diaries Series, VICK, 16–17.

20. *OR*, 24(3):914; Henry P. Whipple Diary, May 26, 1863, WHS. For broken messages, see the John C. Pemberton Papers, RG 109, E 131, NARA.

21. *OR*, 24(3):913, 915, 919.

22. James L. Power Diary, June 12, 1863, MDAH; Charlie Moore to parents, June 26, 1863, Charlie Moore Letter, Journals/Letters/Diaries Series, VICK, 51.

23. *OR*, 24(3):346; *OR* 24(1):56; Marszalek et al., eds., *The Personal Memoirs of Ulysses S. Grant*, 368; George Hildt to parents, June 19, 1863, George H. Hildt Papers, OHS; Henry Kircher Diary, May 27, 1863, Engelmann-Kircher Family Papers, ALPL; Edmund Newsome Diary, May 30, 1863, MDAH; J. H. Pepper Diary, June 13, 1863, MDAH, copy in Journals/Letters/Diaries Series, VICK.

24. *OR*, 24(3):346; *OR* 24(1):56; Marszalek et al., eds., *The Personal Memoirs of Ulysses S. Grant*, 368; George Hildt to parents, June 19, 1863, George H. Hildt Papers, OHS; Henry Kircher Diary, May 27, 1863, Engelmann-Kircher Family Papers, ALPL; Edmund Newsome Diary, May 30, 1863, MDAH; J. H. Pepper Diary, June 13, 1863, MDAH, copy in Journals/Letters/Diaries Series, VICK.

25. Simon, ed., *PUSG*, 8:261; *OR*, 24(1):87; Charles A. Dana, *Recollections of the Civil War* (New York: D. Appleton and Co., 1898), 61, 82; Sherman, *Memoirs of General William T. Sherman*, 1:328; M. Ellis to uncle, June 2, 1863, Hubbard T. Thomas Papers, IHS; *OR*, 52(1):379. For Dana, see Carl J. Guarneri, *Lincoln's Informer: Charles A. Dana and the Inside Story of the Union War* (Lawrence: University Press of Kansas, 2019).

26. Levi Williams to uncle, May 29, 1863, Richard Emerson Blair Letters, IHS; Calvin Ainsworth Diary, May 23, 1863, Journals/Letters/Diaries Series, VICK; Thomas Latimer to parents, June 27, 1863, Thomas P. Latimer Letters, Latimer Collection, USAHEC.

27. *OR*, 24(3):339; Josiah W. Underhill Diary, May 25, 1863, IHS.

28. *OR*, 24(3):339–340, 343.

29. William M. Stone Manuscript, undated, MDAH; Carl Forbes to Mary, June 6, 1863, Carlos Forbes and Mary Jane Pond Collection, OHS; T. Northrop to Ira, May 26, 1863, 23rd Wisconsin File, VICK.

30. *OR*, 24(3):341–342; *OR*, 24(1):758; "History of the Corps," February 16, 1893, *National Tribune*; William Murray Diary, May 25, 1863, Journals/Letters/Diaries Series, VICK; John N. Bell Diary, May 23, 1863, OHS; Chase Dickinson to father, May 25, 1863, Chase Hall Dickinson Papers, NL; John Bering to brother, May 28, 1863, 48th Ohio File, VICK.

31. *OR*, 24(3):340; Don Pardee to unknown, May 25, 1863, Don A. Pardee Papers, TU.

32. *OR*, 24(3):343, 348; John T. Buegel Diary, undated, SHSMC, 30.

33. *OR*, 24(1):277; Fuller, *The Generalship of Ulysses S. Grant*, 156; John C. Taylor Diary, May 28, 1863, UVA; James Sinclair Diary, May 26, 1863, CHM.

34. Solonick, *Engineering Victory*, 57, 120; Robert L. Bachman Memoir, undated, OCM, 20; Calvin Ainsworth Diary, June 3, 1863, Journals/Letters/Diaries Series, VICK; *OR*, 24(3):339; 186; Kenneth J. Heinman, *Civil War Dynasty: The Ewing Family of Ohio* (New York: New York University Press, 2012), 186; Henry J. Seaman Diary, May 24, 1863, CWTI, USAHEC, copy in 13th Illinois File, VICK.

35. William Sherman to wife, May 25 and June 2, 1863, William T. Sherman Papers, LOC, published in M. A. DeWolfe Howe, ed., *Home Letters of General Sherman* (New York: Charles Scribner's Sons, 1909); Marszalek, *Sherman*, 227.

36. *OR*, 24(3):343–344; *OR*, 24(2):188.

37. *OR*, 24(2):172; Saunier, *A History of the Forty-seventh Regiment*, 156; Christian Lockbihler to Cyrus Comstock, July 18, 1863, Cyrus B. Comstock Papers, LOC.

38. *OR*, 24(2):172, Frederick Prime order, June 18, 1863, General Orders No. 48, June 19, 1863, and Christian Lockbihler to Cyrus Comstock, July 18, 1863, Cyrus B. Comstock Papers, LOC.

39. *OR*, 24(2):188.

40. *OR*, 24(2):168; William E. Strong, "The Campaign Against Vicksburg," in *Military Essays and Recollections: Papers Read Before the Commandery of the State of Illinois, Military Order of the Loyal Legion of the United States, Volume 2* (Chicago: A. C. McClurg and Company, 1894), 337; George Carrington Diary, May 24, 1863, CHM.

41. *OR*, 24(2):172.

42. *OR*, 24(2):199; Barton, *Autobiography*, 156.

43. *OR*, 24(2):173, 199; George Carrington Diary, June 3, 1863, CHM.

44. Hickenlooper, "The Vicksburg Mine," 540.

45. *OR*, 24(1):276; *OR*, 24(2):331; Francis R. Baker Diary, May 23, 1863, ALPL; Anthony B. Burton Diary, May 24, 1863, ALPL, copy in Journals/Diaries/Letters, VICK; Personal Memoirs of I. V. Smith, 1902, SHSMC, 31.

46. *OR*, 24(2):181; William Sherman to wife, June 11, 1863, William T. Sherman Papers, LOC.

47. Pryce, *Vanishing Footprints*, 132; Edward Stanfield to father, June 22, 1863, Edward P. Stanfield Papers, IHS.

48. *OR*, 24(2):176–177.

49. *OR*, 24(2):171, 177; Grabau, *Ninety-Eight Days*, 410–411; Solonick, *Engineering Victory*, 94.

50. *OR*, 24(2):171, 177; C. Barney, *Recollections of Field Service with the Twentieth Iowa Infantry Volunteers; Or, What I Saw in the Army* (Davenport, IA: Gazette Job Rooms, 1865), 189.

51. *OR*, 24(2):177.

52. *OR*, 24(1):57.

53. *OR*, 24(3):350. For Hurlbut, see Jeffrey N. Lash, *A Politician Turned General: The Civil War Career of Stephen Augustus Hurlbut* (Kent, OH: Kent State University Press, 2003).

54. *OR*, 24(3):350–351.

55. *Supplement to the Official Records of the Union and Confederate Armies*, 4:386–388; Special Orders No. 140, May 25, 1863, Special Orders Issued, RG 393, E 4726, NARA.

56. *OR*, 24(3):345–346, 351; *OR*, 24(2):144, 168, 193, 290; Dana, *Recollections of the Civil War*, 67; Jack D. Welsh, *Medical Histories of Union Generals* (Kent, OH: Kent State University Press, 1996), 199; John S. Kountz, *Record of the Organizations Engaged in the Campaign, Siege, and Defense of Vicksburg* (Knoxville: University of Tennessee Press, 2011), 28; Simon, ed., *PUSG*, 8:259, 264; Payson Shumway Diary, May 24 and 25, 1863, Z. Payson Shumway Papers, ALPL; Payson Shumway to cousin, June 13, 1863, Z. Payson Shumway Letters, NL; John L. Harris to Miss Susan, June 8, 1863, John L. Harris Correspondence, ALPL; "United States. Army. Illinois Infantry Regiment, 14th (1861–1863) Company A," May 20 and 24, 1863, ALPL; Balzar Grebe Memoir, undated, Balzar Grebe Papers, ALPL, 19, copy in LOC; William M. Reid Diary, May 24, 1863, ALPL; Charles H. Brush to father, May 19, 1863, Daniel H. Brush Papers, ALPL; Bela T. St. John to father, June 1, 1863, Bela T. St. John Papers, LOC.

57. *OR*, 24(3):345–346, 351; *OR*, 24(2):144, 168, 193, 290; Simon, ed., *PUSG*, 8:259, 264; Payson Shumway Diary, May 24 and 25, 1863, Z. Payson Shumway Papers, ALPL; Payson Shumway to cousin, June 13, 1863, Z. Payson Shumway Letters, NL; John L. Harris to Miss Susan, June 8, 1863, John L. Harris Correspondence, ALPL; "United States. Army. Illinois Infantry Regiment, 14th (1861–1863) Company A," May 20 and 24, 1863, ALPL, Balzar Grebe Memoir, undated, Balzar Grebe Papers, ALPL, 19, copy in LOC; William M. Reid Diary, May 24, 1863, ALPL; Charles H. Brush to father, May 19, 1863, Daniel H. Brush Papers, ALPL; Bela T. St. John to father, June 1, 1863, Bela T. St. John Papers, LOC.

58. *OR*, 24(1):276; *OR*, 24(2):331; Gilbert Denny to father, May 25, 1863, Gilbert H. Denny Letters, IHS.

59. Sherman, *Memoirs*, 1:328; "Telegrams Sent—General J. E. Johnston's Command, June–December 1863," RG 109, Chapter II, Vol. 236 ¾, NARA, 1–17.

60. John H. Reagan, *Memoirs, With Special Reference to Secession and the Civil War*,

Walter Flavius McCaleb, ed. (New York: Neale Publishing Company, 1906), 151–152; Davis, *Jefferson Davis*, 504.

61. For Johnston, see Symonds, *Joseph E. Johnston*.

62. *OR*, 52(2):482.

63. *OR*, 24(3):920; Arthur J. L. Fremantle, *Three Months in the Southern States: April–June, 1863* (Edinburgh: W. Blackwood and Sons, 1863), 59; Joseph E. Johnston, "Jefferson Davis and the Mississippi Campaign," in *Battles and Leaders of the Civil War*, 4 vols. (New York: Century Company, 1884–1887), 3:480; William L. Foster to wife, June 20, 1863, UA. For Gist, see Walter Brian Cisco, *States Rights Gist: A South Carolina General of the Civil War* (Shippensburg, PA: White Man, 1991).

64. *OR*, 24(1):190–191, 215, 224.

65. *OR*, 24(3):911–912, 917, 920; *OR*, 24(1):192; *OR*, 52(2):484; William C. Davis, *Breckinridge: Statesman, Soldier, Symbol* (Baton Rouge: Louisiana State University Press, 1974), 364–365; S. A. J. Clarke to father, May 23, 1863, John Guy Lofton Collection, UM; H. N. Faulkinbury Diary, May 23, 1863, MDAH; George Forney to mother, May 27, 1863, George Hoke Forney Papers, DU; William G. Pirtle Memoirs, 1907, FHS, 182; John S. Jacksman Diary, May 24, 1863, LOC.

66. *OR*, 24(3):911–912, 917, 920; *OR*, 24(1):192; *OR*, 52(2):484; S. A. J. Clarke to father, May 23, 1863, John Guy Lofton Collection, UM; H. N. Faulkinbury Diary, May 23, 1863, MDAH; George Forney to mother, May 27, 1863, George Hoke Forney Papers, DU; William G. Pirtle Memoirs, 1907, FHS, 182; John S. Jacksman Diary, May 24, 1863, LOC; Winfield Featherston to Joseph Johnston, November 10, 1867, Winfield S. Featherston Collection, UM; Albert Theodore Goodloe, *Confederate Echoes: A Voice From the South in the Days of Secession and the Southern Confederacy* (Nashville: Publishing House of the M. E. Church, South, 1907), 279–282; Timothy B. Smith, "Mississippi Nightmare," *Civil War Times* 48, no. 4 (August 2009): 54–58. For Loring, see James W. Raab, *W. W. Loring: Florida's Forgotten General* (Manhattan, KS: Sunflower University Press, 1996).

67. *OR*, 24(1):192–193; Clement Watson to Mary, June 2, 1863, Clement S. Watson Family Papers, TU.

68. *OR*, 24(3):916; W. R. McRory Diary, May 24, 1863, Journals/Letters/Diaries Series, VICK.

69. *OR*, 24(3):346; *OR* 24(1):37–39; Simon, ed., *PUSG*, 8:261.

70. *OR*, 24(3):346; Simon, ed., *PUSG*, 8:255–256, 259–260, 275; Charles F. Craver Diary, May 24, 1863, HL.

71. *OR*, 24(2):21, 209–210, 240; Daniel Buchwalter Memoir, undated, 120th Ohio File, VICK, 19; Alexander Sholl Diary, May 24, 1863, Journals/Letters/Diaries Series, VICK; Soman and Byrne, eds., *A Jewish Colonel*, 282–283; W. L. Rand Diary, May 24, 1863, Rand Family Papers, ALPL; James Keigwin to W. T. Rigby, March 5, 1902, 49th Indiana File, VICK; James B. Taylor Diary, May 23, 1863, 120th Ohio File, VICK.

72. Brian Steel Wills, "A Kentucky Lyon Roars: Hylan B. Lyon in the Civil War," in *Confederate Generals in the Western Theater: Essays on America's Civil War*, 4 vols., Lawrence Lee Hewitt and Arthur W. Bergeron, Jr., eds. (Knoxville: University of

Tennessee Press, 2011), 2:190; Daniel Buchwalter Memoir, undated, 120th Ohio File, VICK, 18; W. L. Rand to brothers, May 26, 1863, Rand Family Papers, ALPL; W. L. Rand Diary, May 25 and 27, and June 3, 15, and 28, 1863, Rand Family Papers, ALPL.

73. *OR*, 24(3):343, 347, 350; Simon, ed., *PUSG*, 8:267.

74. *OR*, 24(3):917.

75. *OR*, 24(3):920.

76. *OR*, 24(3):343.

77. A. S. Abrams, *A Full and Detailed History of the Siege of Vicksburg* (Atlanta: Intelligencer Steam Power Presses, 1863), 36, copy in Journals/Letters/Diaries File, VICK; Richard and Richard, *The Defense of Vicksburg*, 165; Jared Young Sanders II Diary, May 24, 1863, OCM, copy in Journals/Letters/Diaries File, VICK; James J. Ray Diary, May 25, 1863, 19th Kentucky File, VICK. For the originals of the Jared Young Sanders accounts quoted in Richard and Richard, *The Defense of Vicksburg*, see the Jared Young Sanders Family Papers, LSU; and Mary Elizabeth Sanders, ed., *Diary in Gray: Civil War Journal of J. Y. Sanders* (Baton Rouge: Louisiana Genealogical & Historical Society, 1994).

78. Mary Ann Loughborough, *My Cave Life in Vicksburg: With Letters of Trial and Travel* (New York: D. Appleton and Company, 1864), 102; J. W. Cook, "A Reminiscence of the Siege of Vicksburg," *Confederate Veteran* 14, no. 9 (September 1906): 408–409; F. M. Smith to W. T. Rigby, January 28, 1905, 17th Illinois File, VICK; Unknown Diary, May 23, 1863, 9th Iowa File, VICK; J. Q. A. Campbell Diary, May 23, 1863, 5th Iowa File, VICK, copies in WRHS and published as Mark Grimsley and Todd D. Miller, eds., *The Union Must Stand: The Civil War Diary of John Quincy Adams Campbell, Fifth Iowa Volunteer Infantry* (Knoxville: University of Tennessee Press, 2000); Abrams, *A Full and Detailed History*, 37.

79. *OR*, 24(3):915; Anderson, *Memoirs*, 333; James Darsie Heath Diary, May 23, 1863, OCM.

80. Claudius W. Sears Diary, May 19, 1863, MDAH.

81. Theodore D. Fisher Diary, May 25, 1863, Civil War Collection, MHS; William P. Chambers, "My Journal," in *Publications of the Mississippi Historical Society, Centenary Series*, 5 vols. (Jackson: Mississippi Historical Society, 1925), 5: 273; J. H. Jones, "The Rank and File at Vicksburg," in *Publications of the Mississippi Historical Society*, Franklin L. Riley, ed. (Oxford: Mississippi Historical Society, 1903), 7:22; Richard and Richard, *The Defense of Vicksburg*, 229.

82. *OR*, 24(3):914.

83. *OR*, 24(3):918; James L. Power Diary, May 25, 1863, MDAH.

84. Dick Puffer to sister, May 28, 1863, Richard R. Puffer Papers, CHM; Jones, "An Artilleryman's Diary," 64; Simon, ed., *PUSG*, 8:266; *OR*, 24(1):276–277; John Merrilees Diary, May 25, 1863, CHM; J. Q. A. Campbell Diary, May 25, 1863, 5th Iowa File, VICK; Gould D. Molineaux Diary, May 25, 1863, Augustana College; John C. Pemberton to U. S. Grant, May 25, 1863, Letters and Telegrams Sent, Department of Mississippi and East Louisiana, 1863, RG 109, Chapter II, Vol. 60, NARA.

85. Richard and Richard, *The Defense of Vicksburg*, 166; S. H. Stevenson to parents, May 28, 1863, 48th Ohio File, VICK.

86. *OR*, 24(3):348, 918; *OR*, 24(1):276; James McCulloch Diary, May 24, 1863, UGA.

87. Elliott Bush to parents, May 29, 1863, Elliott N. and Henry M. Bush Papers, James S. Schoff Civil War Collection, UMC; Richard Blackstone Diary, May 25, 1863, LMU; General Orders, May 25, 1863, General Orders Issued, 13th Army Corps, RG 393, NARA; John Forney to R. W. Memminger, May 25, 1863, Dabney Maury Order Book, CHM, 288; Lockett, "The Defense of Vicksburg," 489.

88. William L. Foster to wife, June 20, 1863, UA; John A. Griffen Diary, May 25, 1863, ALPL; J. P. Jones to wife, May 27, 1863, John P. Jones Papers, FHS.

89. George Remley to Howard, June 6, 1863, Remley Family Papers, NC; Charles Affeld Diary, May 25, 1863, Journals/Diaries/Letters Series, VICK; William L. Foster to wife, June 20, 1863, UA.

90. F. W. Merrin, "More Vicksburg Reminiscences," *Confederate Veteran* 2, no. 12 (December 1894): 374; Henry J. Reynolds Memoir, 1904, CWTI, USAHEC, 6; J. H. Pepper Diary, May 24 (25), 1863, MDAH; William T. Rigby Diary, May 25, 1863, UIA.

91. *OR*, 24(1):89; Lockett, "The Defense of Vicksburg," 489; *OR*, 24(3):921; John Forney to R. W. Memminger, May 26, 1863, Dabney Maury Order Book, CHM, 288. See the Charles A. Dana Papers, LC for original dispatches.

92. Charles F. Smith Diary, May 25, 1863, NC; James L. Power Diary, May 25, 1863, MDAH; Chambers, "My Journal," 273; Bruce Hoadley to cousin, May 27, 1863, Robert Bruce Hoadley Papers, DU; William L. Faulk Diary, May 25, 1863, OCM, copy in 38th Mississippi File, VICK.

93. Henry J. Reynolds Memoir, 1904, CWTI, USAHEC, 14; Isaac H. Elliott, *History of the Thirty-third Regiment Illinois Veteran Volunteer Infantry in the Civil War, 22nd August 1861, to 7th December, 1865* (Gibson City, IL: The Association, 1902), 45.

94. Joseph Stockton Diary, May 25, 1863, ALPL, copy in Coco Collection, USAHEC; Charles F. Smith Diary, May 25, 1863, NC; *The Story of the Fifty-fifth Regiment Illinois Volunteer Infantry in the Civil War, 1861–1865* (Clinton, MA: W. J. Coulter, 1887), 247; William R. Eddington Memoir, undated, ALPL, 10; George Carrington Diary, May 25, 1863, CHM.

95. *The Story of the Fifty-fifth Regiment*, 247; William L. Foster to wife, June 20, 1863, UA.

96. Nicholas Miller Memoir, undated, OCM, 12; Lee, "The Siege of Vicksburg," 64; John J. Kellogg Memoirs, 1913, Journals/Letters/Diaries Series, VICK, 48.

97. James Slack to Ann, May 28, 1863, James R. Slack Papers, ISL; Chambers, "My Journal," 273.

98. Hander "Excerpts from the Hander Diary," 144; Myron Knight Diary, May 25, 1863, OCM; Isaac O. Shelby Diary, May 26, 1863, UNC; W. R. McRory Diary, May 25, 1863, Journals/Letters/Diaries Series, VICK.

99. Stephen E. Ambrose, ed., "A Wisconsin Boy at Vicksburg: The Letters of James K. Newton," *Journal of Mississippi History* 23, no. 1 (January 1961): 5–6. See also Stephen E. Ambrose, ed., *A Wisconsin Boy in Dixie: The Selected Letters of James K. Newton* (Madison: University of Wisconsin Press, 1961).

100. E. B. Bascom Diary, May 25, 1863, 5th Iowa File, VICK; J. Q. A. Campbell Diary, May 25, 1863, 5th Iowa File, VICK; William L. Foster to wife, June 20, 1863, UA.

101. *OR*, 52(2):485; *OR*, 24(1):89; James Vanderbilt to mother, May 26, 1863, James C. Vanderbilt Papers, ISL; I. H. Elliott to Col. Matthews, May 16, 1902, 33rd Illinois File, VICK.

102. Simon, ed., *PUSG*, 8:267; Hass, ed., "The Vicksburg Diary of Henry Clay Warmouth," 74; Don Pardee to unknown, May 25, 1863, Don A. Pardee Papers, TU.

103. *OR*, 24(2):199; Hickenlooper, "The Vicksburg Mine," 540; Andrew Hickenlooper Reminiscences, undated, Hickenlooper Collection, CHS, 137–138.

104. Lockett, "The Defense of Vicksburg," 490.

105. Lockett, "The Defense of Vicksburg," 490.

106. Lockett, "The Defense of Vicksburg," 490.

107. Richard and Richard, *The Defense of Vicksburg*, 166.

108. W. H. Tunnard, *A Southern Record: The History of the Third Regiment Louisiana Infantry* (Baton Rouge: n.p., 1866), 241; Cyrus Hussey Diary, May 25, 1863, University of Toledo.

109. William L. Faulk Diary, May 25, 1863, OCM; Chambers, "My Journal," 273.

110. L. F. Phillips, *Some Things Our Boy Saw in the War* (Gravity, IA: n.p., 1911), 38, copy in Lewis F. Phillips Papers, CWTI, USAHEC; William L. Foster to wife, June 20, 1863, UA; Martin N. Bertera, *De Golyer's 8th Michigan Black Horse Light Battery* (Wyandotte, MI: TillieAnn Press, 2015), 143.

CHAPTER 4. "MY MEN ARE IN GOOD SPIRITS, AWAITING YOUR ARRIVAL"

1. J. P. Jones to wife, May 27, 1863, John P. Jones Papers, FHS; George Thomas to Minerva, June 10, 1863, Thomas Family Correspondence, ND.

2. Henry Kircher Diary, May 31, 1863, Engelmann-Kircher Family Papers, ALPL.

3. "Later from Vicksburg," May 30, 1863, Natchez *Daily Courier*; Samuel Sherard to Mr. Shelor, May 28, 1863, Samuel W. Sherard Letters, OCM; R. W. Memminger to Major Matthews, May 23, 1863, Letters and Telegrams Sent, Department of Mississippi and East Louisiana, 1863, RG 109, Chapter II, Vol. 60, NARA.

4. *OR*, 24(2):193.

5. *OR*, 24(3):343; *OR*, 24(1):88–89; *OR*, 24(2):181; Joseph Stockton Diary, June 1, 1863, ALPL.

6. *OR*, 24(3):343; *OR*, 24(1):88–89; Lewis T. Hickok Diary, May 24, 1863, James S. Schoff Civil War Collection, UMC.

7. J. P. Jones to wife, May 27, 1863, John P. Jones Papers, FHS.

8. For the navy, see Craig L. Symonds, *Lincoln and His Admirals: Abraham Lincoln, The U.S. Navy, and the Civil War* (New York: Oxford University Press, 2008).

9. For the Grant/Porter relationship, see R. Blake Dunnavent, "'We Had Lively Times Up the Yazoo': Admiral David Dixon Porter," in *Grant's Lieutenants: From Cairo to*

Vicksburg, Steven E. Woodworth, ed. (Lawrence: University Press of Kansas, 2001), 169–181.

    10. *OR*, 24(3):152.

    11. *OR*, 24(3):337–338.

    12. *OR*, 24(3):342.

    13. *OR*, 24(3):361, 368.

    14. *OR*, 24(3):341; John C. Taylor Diary, June 12, 1863, UVA.

    15. *ORN*, 25:38–39; *OR*, 24(1):88, 276–277; Bearss, *The Vicksburg Campaign*, 3:1250; Terrence J. Winschel, *Triumph and Defeat: The Vicksburg Campaign, Volume 2* (New York: Savas Beatie, 2006), 82–83; Abrams, *A Full and Detailed History*, 39; William T. Sherman to David Porter, May 26, 1863, James M. McClintock Papers, LOC; H. C. Tupper to Edward Higgins, May 24, 1863, Letters and Telegrams Sent, Department of Mississippi and East Louisiana, 1863, RG 109, Chapter II, Vol. 60, NARA.

    16. *ORN*, 25:38–39; *OR*, 24(1):88, 276–277; Abrams, *A Full and Detailed History*, 39; John Bannon Diary, May 27, 1863, University of South Carolina; Unidentified Soldier of the 31st Iowa Infantry Diary, May 20, 1863, MHS; William T. Sherman to David Porter, May 26, 1863, James M. McClintock Papers, LOC; Chase Dickinson to friends, May 29, 1863, Chase Hall Dickinson Papers, NL; Paul Dorweiler Diary, May 27, 1863, CWTI, USAHEC.

    17. Tunnard, *A Southern Record*, 241; J. D. Harwell, "In and Around Vicksburg," *Confederate Veteran* 30, no. 9 (September 1922): 334; Richard and Richard, *The Defense of Vicksburg*, 170; Henry Kircher Diary, May 27, 1863, Engelmann-Kircher Family Papers, ALPL; William L. Foster to wife, June 20, 1863, UA; Samuel Addison Whyte Diary, May 27, 1863, UNC.

    18. *ORN*, 25:38–39, 42–43; Tunnard, *A Southern Record*, 241; Winschel, *Triumph and Defeat: The Vicksburg Campaign, Volume 2*, 88–89; R. S. Bevier, *History of the First and Second Missouri Confederate Brigades 1861–1865 and From Wakaruse to Appomattox, A Military Anagraph* (St. Louis: Bryan, Brand and Company, 1879), 207; Isaac O. Shelby Diary, May 27, 1863, UNC.

    19. *ORN*, 25:38–39; *OR*, 24(3):354; Henry Kircher Diary, May 27, 1863, Engelmann-Kircher Family Papers, ALPL.

    20. *OR*, 24(3):926; *OR*, 24(2):340; Winschel, *Triumph and Defeat: The Vicksburg Campaign, Volume 2*, 90; Joseph D. Alison Diary, May 27, 1863, UNC, copies in MDAH.

    21. *OR*, 24(3):933–934, 937; *OR*, 24(2):422–423; R. W. Memminger to Edward Higgins, May 27, 1863, Letters and Telegrams Sent, Department of Mississippi and East Louisiana, 1863, RG 109, Chapter II, Vol. 60, NARA.

    22. *OR*, 24(3):354.

    23. George S. Durfee to mother, May 27, 1863, George S. Durfee Correspondence, UI.

    24. *OR*, 24(3):930.

    25. *OR*, 24(3):364–365, 929; *OR* 24(1):39; Joseph D. Alison Diary, May 30, 1863, MDAH; R. W. Memminger to S. D. Lee, May 28, 1863, Letters and Telegrams Sent, Department of Mississippi and East Louisiana, 1863, RG 109, Chapter II, Vol. 60, NARA.

26. Crummer, *With Grant at Fort Donelson, Shiloh and Vicksburg*, 125; William M. Reid Diary, May 30, 1863, ALPL.

27. *OR*, 24(3):929–930.

28. *OR*, 24(3):930–931; H. C. Tupper to John Bowen, May 29, 1863, Letters and Telegrams Sent, Department of Mississippi and East Louisiana, 1863, RG 109, Chapter II, Vol. 60, NARA.

29. *OR*, 24(2):331; Fritz Hashell, ed., "Col. William Camm War Diary, 1861–1865," *Journal of the Illinois State Historical Society* 18, 4 (January 1926): 952; Anthony B. Burton Diary, May 26, 1863, ALPL; John L. Harris to Miss Susan, June 8, 1863, John L. Harris Correspondence, ALPL; William M. Reid Diary, May 25, 1863, ALPL; "United States. Army. Illinois Infantry Regiment, 14th (1861–1863) Company A," May 25, 1863, ALPL; Balzar Grebe Memoir, undated, Balzar Grebe Papers, ALPL, 19.

30. *OR*, 24(3):922–923.

31. *OR*, 24(3):926–927; Phillip Thomas Tucker, *The Forgotten "Stonewall of the West": Major General John Stevens Bowen* (Macon, GA: Mercer University Press, 1997), 297; R. W. Memminger to Carter Stevenson and R. W. Memminger to John Forney, May 28, 1863, Letters and Telegrams Sent, Department of Mississippi and East Louisiana, 1863, RG 109, Chapter II, Vol. 60, NARA.

32. *OR*, 24(2):412–413; Tucker, *The Forgotten "Stonewall of the West,"* 297–298.

33. *OR*, 24(3):352–353; Simon, ed., *PUSG*, 8:277.

34. *OR*, 24(3):358, 368; Simon, ed., *PUSG*, 8:276, 281.

35. *OR*, 24(2):171; R. L. Howard, *History of the 124th Regiment Illinois Infantry Volunteers, Otherwise Known as the "Hundred and Two Dozen," From August, 1862, to August, 1865* (Springfield, IL: H. W. Rokker, 1880), 110.

36. *OR*, 24(3):171–172; *OR*, 24(2):171–172, 188; Kountz, *Record of the Organizations Engaged in the Campaign, Siege, and Defense of Vicksburg*, 64; Bearss, *The Vicksburg Campaign*, 3:889–890.

37. *OR*, 24(2):172; Kountz, *Record of the Organizations Engaged in the Campaign, Siege, and Defense of Vicksburg*, 65.

38. Solonick, *Engineering Victory*, 19, 173–174.

39. *OR*, 24(3):353–354, 358, 360, 367.

40. *OR*, 24(1):57.

41. *OR*, 24(3):356, 359; *OR*, 24(2):193–194; "United States. Army. Illinois Infantry Regiment, 14th (1861–1863) Company A," June 1, 1863, ALPL.

42. *OR*, 24(3):358, 363–364, 366, 369.

43. *OR*, 24(3):368–369.

44. *OR*, 24(3):359; *OR*, 52(2):485.

45. *OR*, 24(3):365; *OR*, 24(1):42, 193; *OR*, 52(2):487; James Skelton to sister, May 28, 1863, James M. Skelton Letters, UNC.

46. *OR*, 24(1):194.

47. *OR*, 24(3):365.

48. *OR*, 24(3):933–934; James R. Binford Memoir, undated, Patrick Henry Papers, MDAH, 43; William G. Pirtle Memoirs, 1907, FHS, 182.

49. Fremantle, *Three Months in the Southern States*, 54–55, 57–58.

50. Fremantle, *Three Months in the Southern States*, 59, 61, 63–65.

51. Fremantle, *Three Months in the Southern States*, 60–61, 65.

52. Fremantle, *Three Months in the Southern States*, 60, 62, 65.

53. Marszalek et al., eds., *The Personal Memoirs of Ulysses S. Grant*, 375.

54. Ballard, *Grant at Vicksburg*, 33.

55. *OR*, 24(3):355; Simon, ed., *PUSG*, 8:279, 292; Samuel S. Irwin Diary, May 27, 1863, ALPL; James R. Binford Memoir, undated, Patrick Henry Papers, MDAH, 42; Stewart Bruce Terry Diary, May 24, 1863, KHS.

56. *OR*, 24(3):351; *OR*, 24(1):189; *OR*, 24(2):240; Kountz, *Record of the Organizations Engaged in the Campaign, Siege, and Defense of Vicksburg*, 7–8.

57. *OR*, 24(3):351; *OR*, 24(2):211, 220; Samuel Gordon to wife, June 24, 1863, Samuel Gordon Papers, ALPL.

58. Samuel Gordon to wife, June 12 and 24, 1863, Samuel Gordon Papers, ALPL.

59. *OR*, 24(3):351, 356; Samuel Gordon to wife, June 24, 1863, Samuel Gordon Papers, ALPL.

60. *OR*, 24(3):351; Osborn H. Oldroyd, *A Soldier's Story of the Siege of Vicksburg From the Diary of Osborn H. Oldroyd* (Springfield, IL: self-published, 1885), 37, copy in Journals/Diaries/Letters Series, VICK; Special Orders 141, May 26, 1863, Francis J. Herron Papers, RG 94, E 159, NARA; William T. Sherman to David Porter, May 27, 1863, James M. McClintock Papers, LOC; Charles to parents, June 1, 1863, 9th Iowa File, VICK; James McPherson to John Logan, May 26, 1863, James B. McPherson Papers, ALPL.

61. *OR*, 24(3):352; *OR*, 24(1):773; *OR*, 24(2):295, 302, 311; John J. Kellogg Memoirs, 1913, Journals/Letters/Diaries Series, VICK, 60; Kountz, *Record of the Organizations Engaged in the Campaign, Siege, and Defense of Vicksburg*, 20, 23, 25, 31, 35, 38; S. E. Snure to sir, June 21, 1863, S. E. Snure Papers, IHS; William B. Britton to Editors Gazette, June 1, 1863, William B. Britton Letters, OCM; Charles Affeld Diary, May 26, 1863, Journals/Diaries/Letters Series, VICK; Henry Otis Dwight Diary, May 28–June 4, 1863, OHS; Edward Stanfield to father, June 7, 1863, Edward P. Stanfield Papers, IHS; Mahlon Rouch Diary, May 23, 1863, 120th Oho File, VICK; Robert Finley to friend, June 3, 1863, Robert S. Finley Papers, UNC.

62. *OR*, 24(3):352, 354–356; George M. Lucas Diary, May 27 and 28, 1863, ALPL; Charles Affeld Diary, May 27 and 28, 1863, Journals/Diaries/Letters Series, VICK; Edward Wood to wife, June 1, 1863, Edward J. Wood Papers, IHS.

63. *OR*, 24(3):352, 354–356; Simon, ed., *PUSG*, 8:287–288; George M. Lucas Diary, May 27 and 28, 1863, ALPL; Charles Affeld Diary, May 30, 1863, Journals/Diaries/Letters Series, VICK; Curtis P. Lacey Diary, May 29, 1863, NL; John F. Lester Diary, May 26–June 4, 1863, IHS.

64. Oldroyd, *A Soldier's Story*, 38; John W. Chambers Diary, May 31, 1863, ISU; "In the Trenches Before Vicksburg," November 15, 1900, *National Tribune*.

65. *OR*, 24(2):302; George M. Lucas Diary, May 29, 1863, ALPL; Stewart Bruce Terry Diary, May 29, 1863, KHS; Oscar E. Stewart Memoir, undated, OCM, 19.

66. *OR*, 24(3):938–940; *OR*, 24(1):243; *OR*, 24(2):689; L. J. Sanders Diary, May 27 and 31, 1863, WKU; Samuel Eells to unknown, June 9, 1863, Samuel H. Eells Papers, LC; Curtis P. Lacey Diary, May 29, 1863, NL. For Walker, see Russell K. Brown, *To the Manner Born: The Life of William H. T. Walker* (Athens: University of Georgia Press, 1994).

67. *OR*, 24(3):362–363; *OR*, 24(2):200; George M. Lucas Diary, May 30, 1863, ALPL; I. P. Rumsey to parents, June 2, 1863, I. P. Rumsey Papers, NL; Robert S. Martin Diary, May 25–June 6, 1863, SIU; Andrew Hickenlooper Reminiscences, undated, Hickenlooper Collection, CHS, 144.

68. *OR*, 24(3):368.

69. John N. Bell Diary, May 24, 1863, OHS; Samuel S. Irwin Diary, May 30, 1863, ALPL. For the standard treatment of Vicksburg citizens in the war, see Peter F. Walker, *Vicksburg: A People at War, 1860–1865* (Chapel Hill: University of North Carolina Press, 1960).

70. Rowland Chambers Diary, May 24, 1863, LSU; Emma Balfour Diary, May 23, 1863, Journals/Letters/Diaries Series, VICK, copy in MDAH.

71. *OR*, 24(1):277; *OR*, 24(3):31; George W. Cable, ed., "A Woman's Diary of the Siege of Vicksburg," *Century Magazine* 30, no. 5 (September 1885): 771, original draft in George Washington Cable Papers, TU; "Interesting From Vicksburg," August 2, 1863, *New York Herald*, copy in Siege of Vicksburg Accounts Confederate Subject File, MDAH; Rowland Chambers Diary, May 25, 1863, LSU.

72. Loughborough, *My Cave Life in Vicksburg*, 56; "Mrs. M. L. Powell Tells of Cave Life During War," undated, Siege of Vicksburg Cave Life Subject File, MDAH; Theodosia McKinstry Memoirs, undated, Journals/Letters/Diaries File, VICK, 3.

73. "The Caves of Vicksburg," August 15, 1863, *Frank Leslie's Illustrated Newspaper*, copy in Siege of Vicksburg Accounts Confederate Subject File, MDAH; Marszalek et al., eds., *The Personal Memoirs of Ulysses S. Grant*, 391; "Life in Vicksburg," August 3, 1863, Boston *Post*, copy in Siege of Vicksburg Accounts Confederate Subject File, MDAH; "Hough Cave is One of Authentic Caves Used During Siege of City," March 19, 1936, Vicksburg *Evening Post*, copy in Siege of Vicksburg Cave Life Subject File, MDAH; Cable, ed., "A Woman's Diary of the Siege of Vicksburg," 771; "A Child at the Siege of Vicksburg," Vicksburg *Post Herald*, September 27, 1936, copy in Journals/Diaries/Letters, VICK; L. McRae. Bell, "A Girl's Experience in the Siege of Vicksburg," *Harper's Weekly*, June 8, 1912:12.

74. "Mrs. M. L. Powell Tells of Cave Life during War," undated, Siege of Vicksburg Cave Life Subject File, MDAH; Loughborough, *My Cave Life in Vicksburg*, 62–63.

75. Eli W. Thornhill Memoir, undated, OCM, 10; "Hough Cave is One of Authentic Caves Used During Siege of City," March 19, 1936, Vicksburg *Evening Post*, copy in Siege of Vicksburg Cave Life Subject File, MDAH; "Society in Vicksburg," April 16, 1908, Jackson *Clarion Ledger*, copy in Siege of Vicksburg Accounts Civilian Subject File, MDAH.

76. "The Caves of Vicksburg," August 15, 1863, *Frank Leslie's Illustrated Newspaper*, copy in Siege of Vicksburg Accounts Confederate Subject File, MDAH; Richard and Richard, *The Defense of Vicksburg*, 170.

77. Lou Clark, "A Woman in the Siege of Vicksburg," April 16, 1908, Jackson *Clarion Ledger*, copy in Siege of Vicksburg Accounts Civilians Subject File, MDAH.

78. Lou Clark, "A Woman in the Siege of Vicksburg," April 16, 1908, Jackson *Clarion Ledger*, copy in Siege of Vicksburg Accounts Civilians Subject File, MDAH; "A Child at the Siege of Vicksburg," Vicksburg *Post Herald*, September 27, 1936; Emma Balfour Diary, May 24, 1863, Journals/Letters/Diaries Series, VICK; Winschel, *Triumph and Defeat*, 154; L. McRae. Bell, "A Girl's Experience in the Siege of Vicksburg," *Harper's Weekly*, June 8, 1912:13; Jane Bitterman—Cave Life, undated, Journals/Letters/Diaries File, VICK; Virginia Rockwood Memoir, 1904, Journals/Letters/Diaries File, VICK, 6.

79. Emma Balfour Diary, May 30, 1863, Journals/Letters/Diaries Series, VICK; Lida Lord Reed, "A Woman's Experiences During the Siege of Vicksburg," *Century Magazine* 61, no. 6 (April 1901): 926; Loughborough, *My Cave Life in Vicksburg*, 119; Cable, ed., "A Woman's Diary of the Siege of Vicksburg," 771; Theodosia McKinstry Memoirs, undated, Journals/Letters/Diaries File, VICK, 6.

80. Ida Barlow Trotter Memoir, undated, MDAH, 2.

81. "A Vivid Picture of the War and of the Siege of Vicksburg," May 30, 1902, Fredonia (NY) *Freedom Censor* and February 5, 1902, Vicksburg *American*, copy in Siege of Vicksburg Accounts Civilian Subject File, MDAH. For the Shirleys, see Terrence J. Winschel, *Alice Shirley and the Story of Wexford Lodge* (Fort Washington, PA: Eastern National, 2003).

82. Clark, ed., *Downing's Civil War Diary*, 117; Henry J. Seaman Diary, June 1, 1863, CWTI, USAHEC.

83. Ida Barlow Trotter Memoir, undated, MDAH, 4; John A. Higgins to wife, May 28, 1863, John A. Higgins Papers, ALPL.

84. Anne to Emma, June/July 1863, Shannon-Crutcher Family Papers, MDAH; copy in Siege of Vicksburg Accounts Confederate Subject File, MDAH; I. P. Rumsey to parents, June 2, 1863, I. P. Rumsey Papers, NL; Ida Barlow Trotter Memoir, undated, MDAH, 4.

85. Charles F. Craver Diary, May 27, 1863, HL; Caroline Searles, "Lady of 95 Years Tells of the War," Personal Accounts of the Siege of Vicksburg, Journals/Letters/Diaries Series, VICK; Ida Barlow Trotter Memoir, undated, MDAH, 4–5.

86. William Thomson to Ruffin, June 9, 1863, Ruffin Thomson Papers, UNC.

87. Marszalek et al., eds., *The Personal Memoirs of Ulysses S. Grant*, 373.

88. Reed, *Campaigns and Battles of the Twelfth Regiment Iowa Veteran Volunteer Infantry*, 124; John Henry Hammond Diary, June 9, 1863, FHS; Oscar E. Stewart Memoir, undated, OCM, 20; Marszalek et al., eds., *The Personal Memoirs of Ulysses S. Grant*, 373; William W. Belknap, *History of the Fifteenth Regiment, Iowa Veteran Volunteer Infantry, from October, 1861, to August, 1865, When Disbanded at the End of the War* (Keokuk, IA: R. B. Ogden and Son, Print., 1887), 258.

89. Lot Abraham Diary, June 3, 1863, UIA; Henry P. Whipple Diary, June 2, 1863, WHS.

90. Charles Dana Miller Memoir, undated, Journals/Letters/Diaries Series, VICK, 53; William M. Reid Diary, June 15, 1863, ALPL; Henry Kircher Diary, June 8, 1863, Engelmann-Kircher Family Papers, ALPL; Pryce, *Vanishing Footprints*, 135; John G.

Jones to parents, June 9, 1863, John G. Jones Papers, LC; William F. Draper to wife, June 26, 1863, William F. Draper Papers, LC; Thomas Christie to brother, June 5, 1863, James C. Christie and Family Papers, MNHS; Crummer, *With Grant at Fort Donelson, Shiloh and Vicksburg*, 121.

91. Fred Grant Memoir, undated, USGPL, 37–38.

92. Louisa Russell Conner Memoir, 1905, MDAH, 17; John Merrilees Diary, May 24, 1863, CHM; John J. Kellogg Memoirs, 1913, Journals/Letters/Diaries Series, VICK, 55; Cadwallader, *Three Years with Grant*, 96–98.

93. Cadwallader, *Three Years with Grant*, 96–97.

94. Loughborough, *My Cave Life in Vicksburg*, 58.

95. Emma Balfour Diary, May 25, 1863, Journals/Letters/Diaries Series, VICK.

CHAPTER 5. "WE HEAR NOTHING BUT THE CRACK OF GUNS
SMELL NOTHING BUT POWDER"

1. Edwin Obriham to family, June 28, 1863, Edward O. Obriham Letters, Journals/ Letters/Diaries Series, VICK; George Townsend to Ellen, June 26, 1863, George E. Townsend Letters, SHSM.

2. William T. Sherman to W. D. Sanger, June 8, 1863, William T. Sherman Papers, LSU; Arnold Rickard Diary, June 1, 1863, CHM; John Carr Diary, May 27 and June 7, 1863, HCWRT, USAHEC; Joseph Bowker Diary, May 25–26, 1863, 42nd Ohio File, VICK; Edward Wood to wife, June 21, 1863, Edward J. Wood Papers, IHS.

3. Carlos Colby to sister, June 21, 1863, Carlos W. Colby Papers, NL; Bjorn Skaptason, "The Chicago Light Artillery at Vicksburg," *Journal of the Illinois State Historical Society* 106, no. 3–4 (Fall–Winter 2013): 446; George M. Shearer Diary, May 31, 1863, UIA; Henry J. Seaman Diary, June 29, 1863, CWTI, USAHEC.

4. U. G. McAlexander, *History of the Thirteenth Regiment United States Infantry, Compiled from Regimental Records and Other Sources* (N.p.: Regimental Press, Thirteenth Infantry, 1905), 44; Bela T. St. John to father, June 7, 1863, Bela T. St. John Papers, LOC; Special Field Orders, May 20, 1863, John A. Rawlins Papers, CHM; William Taylor to Jane, June 18, 1863, William Taylor Correspondence, WM. For a discussion of Grant's supply efforts, see Smith, *The Union Assaults at Vicksburg*, 138–145.

5. E. L. Chatfield to parents, May 27, 1863, Edward L. Chatfield Papers, HL; Ephraim Shay Diary, May 24, 1863, UMB.

6. William T. Sherman to W. D. Sanger, June 8, 1863, William T. Sherman Papers, LSU; Asa E. Sample Diary, June 4, 1863, ISL; John N. Bell Diary, June 9, 1863, OHS; Charles Affeld Diary, June 22, 1863, Journals/Diaries/Letters Series, VICK; George C. Churcheus Diary, June 23, 1863, OHS; John M. Sullivan to wife, June 12, 1863, John M. Sullivan Papers, OHS.

7. James L. Power Diary, June 9, 1863, MDAH; J. Carroll Harris to Valery, June 13, 1863, Jordan C. Harris Papers, NC; Albert Chipman to wife, June 22, 1863, Albert Chipman Papers, ALPL.

8. Samuel Addison Whyte Diary, May 25, 1863, UNC.

9. *OR*, 24(2):377–378; Lee, "The Siege of Vicksburg," 69.

10. Chambers, "My Journal," 274; *OR*, 24(2):377–378, 398; Lee, "The Siege of Vicksburg," 68.

11. *OR*, 24(2):377–378; *OR*, 24(3):407.

12. *OR*, 24(2):368, 408, 395; Hander "Excerpts from the Hander Diary," 146; Richard and Richard, *The Defense of Vicksburg*, 196, 206.

13. *OR*, 24(2):408; Richard and Richard, *The Defense of Vicksburg*, 196, 206.

14. *OR*, 24(2):331–332, 337–338.

15. Henry Kircher Diary, June 2, 1863, Engelmann-Kircher Family Papers, ALPL; *OR*, 24(1):276–277.

16. John C. Pemberton, *Pemberton: Defender of Vicksburg* (Chapel Hill: University of North Carolina Press, 1942), 194; *OR*, 24(1):278; *SOR*, 4:304; Lockett, "The Defense of Vicksburg," 492; "A Daring Deed," undated, Siege of Vicksburg Accounts Civilian Subject File, MDAH; Richard and Richard, *The Defense of Vicksburg*, 186; George M. Rogers Diary, May 31, 1863, ISL. For specific names of some who went between Pemberton and Johnston, see *OR*, 24(1):294.

17. *OR*, 24(3):943; *OR*, 24(2):367, 376, 419–420; William L. Faulk Diary, June 3, 1863, OCM; Eli W. Thornhill Memoir, undated, OCM, 10; J. H. Jones to W. T. Rigby, May 29, 1863, 38th Mississippi File, VICK.

18. *OR*, 24(2):363; Robert L. Bachman Memoir, undated, OCM, 23–25; J. H. Pepper Diary, June 13, 1863, MDAH; J. Q. A. Campbell Diary, May 30, 1863, 5th Iowa File, VICK.

19. Chambers, "My Journal," 280; Clarke, *Reminiscence and Anecdotes of the War for Southern Independence*, 107.

20. Chambers, "My Journal," 277; Clarke, *Reminiscence and Anecdotes of the War for Southern Independence*, 107.

21. *OR*, 24(2):345, 363.

22. *OR*, 24(2):331, 390–391.

23. Lee, "The Siege of Vicksburg," 68.

24. *OR*, 24(2):331–332; Chambers, "My Journal,"274; Ambrose, ed., "A Wisconsin Boy at Vicksburg," 4.

25. *OR*, 24(2):332–333.

26. *OR*, 24(2):364, 380.

27. *History of the Forty-sixth Regiment Indiana Volunteer Infantry, September, 1861– September, 1865* (Logansport, IN: Press of Wilson, Humphreys and Co., 1888), 65; Cyrus Willford, "Reminiscences of the Civil War," 1899, OHS, 242; Charles Willison to Ellie, May 26, 1863, 76th Ohio Volunteer Infantry Papers, OHS; Dana, *Recollections of the Civil War*, 78; E. H. Ingraham to aunt, June 15, 1863, E. H. and D. G. Ingraham Letters, ALPL; Lee, "The Siege of Vicksburg," 70; Edward E. Schweitzer Diary, June 23, 1863, CWTI, USAHEC.

28. *OR*, 24(1):710; Dana, *Recollections of the Civil War*, 78.

29. Lyman M. Baker Memoir, 1914, ALPL, 14; Albert Chipman to wife, June 3,

1863, Albert Chipman Papers, ALPL; Merrick J. Wald Diary, June 3, 1863, OCM; *OR*, 24(2):321.

30. *OR*, 24(2):320, 322.

31. George O. Cooper to sister, June 9, 1863, George O. Cooper Letters, OCM; Dana, *Recollections of the Civil War*, 93; *OR*, 24(1):111.

32. Charles Willison to Ellie, June 26, 1863, 76th Ohio Volunteer Infantry Papers, OHS.

33. John Merrilees Diary, June 20, 1863, CHM; Tunnard, *A Southern Record*, 264; Charles Affeld Diary, June 23, 1863, Journals/Diaries/Letters Series, VICK; George Carrington Diary, May 30 and June 15, 1863, CHM; Abrams, *A Full and Detailed History*, 39; H. Robinson Report, June 28, 1863, John C. Pemberton Papers, RG 109, E 131, NARA; Theodore D. Fisher Diary, June 15, 1863, Journals/Letters/Diaries Series, VICK; John S. Bell, "The Arkansas Sharpshooters," undated, 12th Arkansas Battalion Sharpshooters File, VICK; Richard and Richard, *The Defense of Vicksburg*, 216.

34. Channing Richards Diary, June 25, 1863, FHS; Byers, *With Fire and Sword*, 94; Hickenlooper, "The Vicksburg Mine," 540; *OR*, 24(2):241; *OR*, 24(1):97.

35. *OR*, 24(1):99; George Carrington Diary, May 25, 1863, CHM; John A. Griffen Diary, June 4 and 21, 1863, ALPL; Albert Chipman to wife, June 19, 1863, Albert Chipman Papers, ALPL; C. P. Alling, "Four Years with the Western Army," undated, 11th Wisconsin File, VICK, 10.

36. Anthony B. Burton Diary, June 29, 1863, ALPL; George Thomas to Minerva, June 16, 1863, Thomas Family Correspondence, ND; Edward Ord to wife, June 27, 1863, E. O. C. Ord Papers, SU; E. H. Ingraham to aunt, May 29, 1863, E. H. and D. G. Ingraham Letters, ALPL; *OR*, 24(1):100; E. B. Bascom Diary, June 1, 1863, 5th Iowa File, VICK.

37. Elliott Morrow to uncle, June 15, 1863, Elliott Morrow Papers, OHS; Abram J. Vanauken Diary, May 23–24, 26–29, and June 2, 4, 15, 21–22, 1863, ALPL.

38. William T. Rigby Diary, June 20–22, 1863, UIA; John W. Griffith Diary, May 27 and 30 and June 20, 1863, OHS.

39. John Ruth to sister, June 11, 1863, John Ruth Letters, OCM.

40. *OR*, 24(1):98; Cyrus W. Randall to mother, June 13, 1863, Cyrus W. Randall Correspondence, ALPL; Samuel Gordon to wife, June 12, 1863, Samuel Gordon Papers, ALPL; *OR*, 24(2):320.

41. Edmund Newsome Diary, June 22, MDAH.

42. Thomas Watson to parents, June 5, 1863, Thomas Watson Correspondence, ALPL; William Harper to wife, June 16, 1863, William Harper Letters, IHS; William A. Harding to Elihu Miller, September 18, 1863, William A. Harding Letter, ALPL; R. W. Burt to Mr. Editor, June 10, 1863, 76th Ohio Volunteer Infantry Papers, OHS; Simon, ed., *PUSG*, 8:377; *OR*, 24(2):107; *SOR*, 4:301.

43. Lucius W. Barber, *Army Memoirs of Lucius W. Barber Company 'D,' 15th Illinois Volunteer Infantry. May 24, 1861, to Sept. 30, 1865* (Chicago: J. M. W. Jones Stationary and Printing Co., 1894), 112; Oliver Boardman to father, June 29, 1863, Oliver Boardman Papers, UIA; Chase Dickinson to friends, May 29, 1863, Chase Hall Dickinson Papers, NL; George Ditto Diary, June 6, 1863, ALPL.

44. S. C. Beck, *A True Sketch of His Army Life* (N.p.: n.p., n.d.), 15, copy in Journals/ Letters/Diaries File, VICK and OCM; William Murray Diary, May 30, 1863, Journals/ Letters/Diaries Series, VICK; Isaac Vanderwarker Diary, June 21, 1863, CWD, USA-HEC; George Carrington Diary, July 1, 1863, CHM.

45. Pryce, *Vanishing Footprints*, 134; Howard Stevens to uncle, July 21, 1863, Howard and Victor H. Stevens Letters, Gregory A. Coco Collection, USAHEC; *OR*, 24(1):720; *OR*, 24(2):403.

46. Jones, "The Rank and File at Vicksburg," 25; Anthony B. Burton Diary, June 9, 1863, ALPL; George Carrington Diary, June 3, 1863, CHM; *OR*, 24(2):353; Charles Scheniman to mother, June 26, 1863, 29th Missouri File, VICK; *OR*, 24(1):100; George Davis to wife, June 17, 1863, George B. Davis Letters, California State University Bakersfield.

47. *OR*, 24(2):351.

48. Donald C. Elder III, ed., *A Damned Iowa Greyhound: The Civil War Letters of William Henry Harrison Clayton* (Iowa City: University of Iowa Press, 1998), 74; Edmund Newsome Diary, June 21, 1863, MDAH; George Carrington Diary, May 27, 1863, CHM.

49. Pryce, *Vanishing Footprints*, 134; George Carrington Diary, May 30, 1863, CHM.

50. Unknown to family, June 10, 1863, Civil War—Campaigns and Battles—Vicksburg, ISL; James Vanderbilt to mother, June 1863, James C. Vanderbilt Papers, ISL; Hoehling, *Vicksburg*, 49; Asa E. Sample Diary, June 6, 1863, ISL; Crooke, *The Twenty-first Regiment of Iowa Volunteer Infantry*, 109.

51. Payson Shumway to cousin, June 13, 1863, Z. Payson Shumway Letters, NL; Reuben H. Falconer Diary, May 26, 1863, OHS; John A. Higgins to wife, June 14, 1863, John A. Higgins Papers, ALPL.

52. Payson Shumway to wife, June 12, 1863, Z. Payson Shumway Papers, ALPL.

53. Carlos Colby to sister, July 3, 1863, Carlos W. Colby Papers, NL; Adoniram Withrow to Lib, June 3, 1863, Adoniram J. Withrow Papers, UNC; Calvin Ainsworth Diary, June 4, 1863, Journals/Letters/Diaries Series, VICK.

OR, 24(3):339.

54. *OR*, 24(2):194–195, 290–291, 318, 321; "United States. Army. Illinois Infantry Regiment, 14th (1861–1863) Company A," June 22, 1863, ALPL; George H. Hynds Diary, June 22–23, 1863, Journals/Letters/Diaries Series, VICK.

55. Charles Dana Miller Diary, May 31, 1863, Journals/Letters/Diaries Series, VICK; Oldroyd, *A Soldier's Story*, 53; George Carrington Diary, July 5, 1863, CHM.

56. *OR*, 24(2):356, 403; Samuel Gordon to wife, June 12, 1863, Samuel Gordon Papers, ALPL.

57. *OR*, 24(2):183, 185.

58. William M. Reid Diary, June 20, 1863, ALPL; Samuel Gordon to wife, May 29, 1863, Samuel Gordon Papers, ALPL; *OR*, 24(2):175; *OR*, 24(1):101; Chambers, "My Journal," 277; Edwin C. Bearss, "The Vicksburg River Defenses and the Enigma of 'Whistling Dick,'" *Journal of Mississippi History* 19, no. 1 (January 1957): 21–30.

59. Job H. Yaggy Diary, June 1, 1863, ALPL; *SOR*, 4:303–304; *OR*, 24(2):409; William L. Foster to wife, June 20, 1863, UA.

60. John Fuller Diary, May 31, 1863, 31st Louisiana File, VICK; James Vanderbilt to mother, June 12, 1863, James C. Vanderbilt Papers, ISL; J. W. Greenman Diary, MDAH, 97.

61. *OR*, 24(2):175; Joseph Stockton Diary, June 6, 1863, ALPL; Daniel Roberts to family, Daniel Roberts Papers, ISL.

62. *OR*, 24(2):318; H. C. Tupper to Carter Stevenson, June 11, 1863, Letters and Telegrams Sent, Department of Mississippi and East Louisiana, 1863, RG 109, Chapter II, Vol. 60, NARA; George Carrington Diary, June 6 and 14, 1863, CHM; William Clemans Memoir, undated, UI, 10.

63. Owen Francis Diary, June 17, 1863, 57th Ohio File, VICK; Edmund Newsome Diary, June 16, 1863, MDAH.

64. William L. Foster to wife, June 20, 1863, UA.

65. Hosea W. Rood, *Story of the Service of Company E, and of the Twelfth Wisconsin Regiment of Veteran Volunteer Infantry in the War of the Rebellion* (N.p.: n.p., n.d.), 193.

66. George Carrington Diary, May 25, June 3, and July 6, 1863, CHM; Anderson, *Memoirs*, 350–351; Jones, "The Rank and File at Vicksburg," 25.

67. Anthony B. Burton Diary, June 12, 1863, ALPL.

68. *OR*, 24(2):403.

69. *OR*, 24(2):694; Tunnard, *A Southern Record*, 242.

70. Ambrose, ed., "A Wisconsin Boy at Vicksburg," 10–11.

71. Joseph Stockton Diary, June 3, 1863, ALPL; "Edwin Dean's Civil War Days," 1906, CWD, USAHEC; George Carrington Diary, June 12, 1863, CHM.

72. George Ditto Diary, June 22, 1863, ALPL; *OR*, 24(2):207; Oldroyd, *A Soldier's Story*, 49; Hickenlooper, "The Vicksburg Mine," 541.

73. George Carrington Diary, June 2, 1863, CHM.

74. Wells, *The Siege of Vicksburg*, 84; Job H. Yaggy Diary, June 9, 1863, ALPL; Beck, *A True Sketch of Army Life*, 11; Cyrus Hussey Diary, May 31, 1863, UTO; Eli W. Thornhill Memoir, undated, OCM, 10; Blanchard, *I Marched with Sherman*, 99; Edmund Newsome Diary, July 1, MDAH; John J. Kellogg Memoirs, 1913, Journals/Letters/Diaries Series, VICK, 60; Winschel, *Triumph and Defeat*, 133.

75. Carlos Colby to sister, June 13, 1863, Carlos W. Colby Papers, NL; Joel Strong Reminiscences, 1910, MHS, 14–15, copy in OCM.

76. Jeffrey L. Patrick, ed., *Three Years with Wallace's Zouaves: The Civil War Memoirs of Thomas Wise Durham* (Macon, GA: Mercer University Press, 2003), 146.

77. Pryce, *Vanishing Footprints*, 133; Crummer, *With Grant at Fort Donelson, Shiloh and Vicksburg*, 156, Tunnard, *A Southern Record*, 255.

78. Jones, "The Rank and File at Vicksburg," 22, 24; Giambrone, *Beneath Torn and Tattered Flags*, 75; Carolyn S. Bridge, ed., *These Men Were Heroes Once: The Sixty-ninth Indiana Volunteer Infantry* (West Lafayette, IN: Twin Publications, 2005), 138; Hugh McIntire to friend, June 4, 1863, Crosier Family Papers, IHS; Howard Stevens to

cousin, May 31, 1863, Howard and Victor Stevens Letters, HCWRT, USAHEC; Benjamin Spooner to Madam, June 7, 1863, Benjamin Spooner Letters, ISL; Joseph Skipworth to wife, June 18, 1863, Joseph Skipworth Papers, SIU.

79. *OR*, 24(2):362–364. For casualties in the 26th Louisiana, see James R. Arnold, *Grant Wins the War: Decision at Vicksburg* (New York: John Wiley & Sons, Inc., 1997), 264–265.

80. George Carrington Diary, June 22, 1863, CHM; Chambers, "My Journal," 275; William L. Faulk Diary, June 25, 1863, OCM.

81. Joseph Waite Diary, June 30, 1863, IHS; Richard and Richard, *The Defense of Vicksburg*, 200; Jones, "The Rank and File at Vicksburg," 24.

82. *OR*, 24(2):692.

CHAPTER 6. "GRANT IS PRESSING, AND MUST BE SUPPLIED"

1. Thomas Watson to parents, June 18, 1863, Thomas Watson Correspondence, ALPL; Samuel S. Irwin Diary, June 6, 1863, ALPL; Thomas B. Beggs to aunt, June 19, 1863, Thomas Benson Beggs Letters, ALPL; Samuel Gordon to wife, June 24, 1863, Samuel Gordon Papers, ALPL; Pryce, *Vanishing Footprints*, 133.

2. *OR* 24(1):40–41; Isaac O. Shelby Diary, May 29, 1863, UNC. For a concise explanation of the approaches, mostly based on the *OR*, see Badeau, *Military History of Ulysses S. Grant*, 342–354.

3. *OR*, 24(1):93; Curtis P. Lacey Diary, June 1, 1863, NL; Gilbert Denny to parents, June 10, 1863, Gilbert H. Denny Papers, IHS; George W. Gordon Diary, June 28, 1863, Gordon Collection, USAHEC; Aurelius L. Voorhis Diary, May 30, 1863, IHS; James Slack to Ann, June 11, 1863, James R. Slack Papers, ISL.

4. Will Patterson to wife, May 28, 1863, William F. Patterson Papers, LC; John F. Lester Diary, June 6, 1863, IHS.

5. *OR*, 24(2):363; Aurelius L. Voorhis Diary, June 28, 1863, IHS; Cyrus E. Dickey to sister, May 29, 1863, Wallace-Dickey Family Papers, ALPL.

6. W. O. Dodd, "Recollections of Vicksburg During the Siege," *The Southern Bivouac* 1, no. 1 (September 1882): 3.

7. J. T. Hogane, "Reminiscences of the Siege of Vicksburg," *Southern Historical Society Papers* 11, no. 7 (July 1883): 294; *OR*, 24(2):691; Bearss, *The Vicksburg Campaign*, 3:810.

8. *OR*, 24(2):408; Lockett, "The Defense of Vicksburg," 491.

9. D. Wintter to Samuel Lockett, May 29, 1863, John C. Pemberton Papers, RG 109, E 131, NARA; P. Rinson Reports, June 1–6, 1863, John C. Pemberton Papers, RG 109, E 131, NARA; R. W. Memminger to Louis Hébert, May 29, 1863, Letters and Telegrams Sent, Department of Mississippi and East Louisiana, 1863, RG 109, Chapter II, Vol. 60, NARA. For a list of the engineers at work, see *OR*, 24(1):293.

10. Unknown to Samuel Lockett, June 2, 1863, 1863, John C. Pemberton Papers, RG

109, E 131, NARA; Samuel Lockett to R. W. Memminger, June 2, 1863, John C. Pemberton Papers, RG 109, E 131, NARA.

11. *OR*, 24(1):278; "Fighting For Vicksburg," August 23, 1894, *National Tribune*; William Sherman to wife, May 25, 1863, William T. Sherman Papers, LOC.

12. *OR*, 24(3):941.

13. *OR*, 24(3):941–942.

14. *OR*, 24(3):942, 945.

15. *OR*, 24(1):56.

16. John B. Sanborn, "Remarks on a Motion to Extend a Vote of Thanks to General Marshall for Above Papers," *Glimpses of the Nation's Struggle, Fourth Series, Papers Read Before the Minnesota Commandery of the Military Order of the Loyal Legion of the United States, 1892–1897* (St. Paul: H. L. Collins Co., 1898), 617–618 (615–622).

17. *OR*, 24(1):93; Special Orders No. 153, June 7, 1863, Special Orders Issued, RG 393, E 4726, NARA.

18. *OR*, 24(2):170–171; Jenney, "Personal Recollections of Vicksburg," 264; Solonick, *Engineering Victory*, 2.

19. Marszalek et al., eds., *The Personal Memoirs of Ulysses S. Grant*, 371–372.

20. *OR*, 24(2):177, 180; James A. Fowler, and Miles M. Miller, *History of the Thirtieth Iowa Infantry Volunteers. Giving a Complete Record of the Movements of the Regiment from Its Organization Until Muster Out* (Mediapolis, IA: T. A. Merrill, Printer, 1908), 30.

21. Mason, *The Forty-second Ohio Infantry*, 227; Scott, *The History of the 67th Regiment*, 39; William M. Reid Diary, June 28, 1863, ALPL; N. M. Baker to C. A. Noble, May 5, 1902, 116th Illinois File, VICK.

22. *OR*, 24(1):90; Wales W. Wood, *A History of the Ninety-fifth Regiment Illinois Infantry Volunteers, From its Organization in the Fall of 1862, Until Its Final Discharge from the United States Service, in 1865* (Chicago: Tribune Company's Book and Job Printing Office, 1865), 80; Grecian, *History of the Eighty-third Regiment*, 89; Joseph Stockton Diary, June 17, 1863, ALPL; Beck, *A True Sketch of His Army Life*, 10, copy in Journals/Letters/Diaries Series, VICK; Theodore F. Davis to W. T. Rigby, March 31, 1902, 83rd Indiana File, VICK.

23. Oscar E. Stewart Memoir, undated, OCM, 19.

24. *OR*, 24(1):92; Dana, *Recollections of the Civil War*, 65.

25. Solonick, *Engineering Victory*, 18–19; Albert Castel, *Tom Taylor's Civil War* (Lawrence: University Press of Kansas, 2000), 64. For Taylor's manuscript letters used in Castel's work, see the Thomas T. Taylor Papers, LSU as well as OHS.

26. *OR*, 24(2):176, 182; John Merrilees Diary, June 4, 1863, CHM.

27. *OR*, 24(2):176, 183; W. S. Morris, *History, 31st Regiment Illinois Volunteers: Organized by John A. Logan* (Herrin, IL: Crossfire Press, 1991), 71; William E. Strong Reminiscences, undated, William E. Strong Papers, ALPL, 44; James Slack to Ann, May 28, 1863, James R. Slack Papers, ISL.

28. P. C. Hains to Walter Scates, June 1, 4, and 8, 1863, John A. McClernand Papers, ALPL.

29. P. C. Hains to Walter Scates, June 5, 1863, John A. McClernand Papers, ALPL; Solonick, *Engineering Victory*, 104.

30. John Merrilees Diary, May 23, 1863, CHM.

31. George O. Cooper to sister, July 8, 1863, George O. Cooper Letters, OCM.

32. Kiper, *Major General John A. McClernand*, 268; George M. Rogers Diary, June 19, 1863, ISL.

33. *OR*, 24(3):375, 378.

34. Simon, ed., *PUSG*, 8:314, 319.

35. *OR*, 24(3):378, 380; *OR*, 24(1):92; Don Pardee to unknown, May 25, 1863, Don A. Pardee Papers, TU.

36. *OR*, 24(3):371; Carlos Colby to sister, June 9, 1863, Carlos W. Colby Papers, NL.

37. *OR*, 24(3):372–373; Milt Shaw to Alf, January 31, 1863, Milton W. Shaw Papers, FHS.

38. *OR*, 24(3):372.

39. *OR*, 24(3):378.

40. *OR*, 24(1):40, 90; Anthony B. Burton Diary, June 1, 1863, ALPL.

41. Curtis P. Lacey Diary, May 26, 1863, NL; Chase Dickinson to friends, June 6, 1863, Chase Hall Dickinson Papers, NL.

42. *OR*, 24(1):40, 90.

43. *OR*, 24(3):360, 366–367, 385–386; *OR*, 24(1):40–41, 90, 92.

44. *OR*, 24(3):377, 381–382, 386; Channing Richards Diary, June 9, 1863, FHS; James H. Goodnow to wife, June 8, 1863, James H. Goodnow Papers, LC.

45. Phillip Roesch Diary, May 31, 1863, OCM; Samuel Eells to unknown, June 2, 1863, Samuel H. Eells Papers, LC; Henry Bechtel to parents, June 5, 1863, Henry Bechtel Letter, UTK.

46. Leander Stillwell, *The Story of a Common Soldier of Army Life in the Civil War, 1861–1865*, 2nd ed. (N.p.: Franklin Hudson Publishing Co., 1920), 135–136; Welsh, *Medical Histories of Union Generals*, 194.

47. *OR*, 24(3):380; OR, 24(1):90; Manning F. Force, "Personal Recollections of the Vicksburg Campaign," in *Sketches of War History 1861–1865 Papers Read Before the Ohio Commandery of the Military Order of the Loyal Legion of the United States 1883–1886, Volume 1* (Cincinnati: Robert Clarke Company, 1888), 293–309; *OR*, 24(2):302, 689; George M. Lucas Diary, May 31, 1863, ALPL; William B. Britton to Editors Gazette, June 1, 1863, William B. Britton Letters, OCM; Charles Affeld Diary, May 31, 1863, Journals/Diaries/Letters Series, VICK; Henry J. Seaman Diary, May 30, 1863, CWTI, USAHEC; Isaac Vanderwarker Diary, May 30 and 31, 1863, CWD, USAHEC, copy in 4th Minnesota File, VICK; Owen Francis Diary, May 30–31, 1863, 57th Ohio File, VICK; Special Orders 150, June 4, 1863, Special Orders Issued, RG 393, E 4726, NARA.

48. *OR*, 24(3):380; OR, 24(1):90; Force, "Personal Recollections of the Vicksburg Campaign," 293–309; *OR*, 24(2):302, 689; George M. Lucas Diary, May 31, 1863, ALPL; William B. Britton to Editors Gazette, June 1, 1863, William B. Britton Letters, OCM; Charles Affeld Diary, May 31, 1863, Journals/Diaries/Letters Series, VICK; Henry J. Seaman Diary, May 30, 1863, CWTI, USAHEC; Isaac Vanderwarker Diary, May 30

and 31, 1863, CWD, USAHEC, copy in 4th Minnesota File, VICK; Owen Francis Diary, May 30–31, 1863, 57th Ohio File, VICK; Special Orders 150, June 4, 1863, Special Orders Issued, RG 393, E 4726, NARA.

49. *OR*, 24(1):93; S. E. Snure to sir, June 21, 1863, S. E. Snure Papers, IHS; Curtis P. Lacey Diary, June 3 and 5, 1863, NL.

50. For Rosecrans, see William M. Lamers, *The Edge of Glory: A Biography of General William S. Rosecrans, U.S.A.* (New York: Harcourt, Brace, and World, 1961).

51. *OR*, 24(3):376, 385; *OR*, 52(2):491.

52. *OR*, 24(3):376, 383–384; Alphonso Crane to father, June 22, 1863, Alphonso Crane Letters, Grace Dunham Collection, AM.

53. *OR*, 24(3):377, 383–384, 387; Harry E. Pratt, ed., "Civil War Letters of Brigadier-General William Ward Orme, 1862–1866," *Journal of the Illinois State Historical Society* 23, no. 2 (July 1930): 271 (246–315); Special Orders No. 148, June 2, 1863, Francis J. Herron Papers, RG 94, E 159, NARA.

54. *OR*, 24(3):386.

55. *OR*, 24(3):380.

56. Johnston, "Jefferson Davis and the Mississippi Campaign," 480; A. D. Kirwan, ed., *Johnny Green of the Orphan Brigade: The Journal of a Confederate Soldier* (Lexington: University Press of Kentucky, 1956), 77–79; John S. Jacksman Diary, May 24, 26–30, and June 3, 1863, LOC; T. B. Roy to John Breckinridge, May 23, 1863, John A. Buckner to Major, June 4, 1863, and John Breckinridge to John Pettus, June 8 and 26, 1863, all in "Letters, Telegrams, and Orders Received and Sent—General Breckinridge's Command, December 1861–November 1863," RG 109, Chapter II, Vol. 311, NARA, 102. For Pettus, see Robert W. Dubay, *John Jones Pettus, Mississippi Fire-eater: His Life and Times, 1813–1867* (Jackson: University Press of Mississippi, 1975).

57. Rufus Cater to cousin, June 3, 1863, Douglas J. and Rufus W. Cater Papers, LOC; M. Jane Johansson, "Daniel Weisiger Adams: Defender of the Confederacy's Heartland," in *Confederate Generals in the Western Theater: Essays on America's Civil War*, 4 vols., Lawrence Lee Hewitt and Arthur W. Bergeron, Jr., eds. (Knoxville: University of Tennessee Press, 2011), 3:102(87–118).

58. *OR*, 24(3):942–943, 946–947, 951–952; J. N. Coleman to Jennie, June 9, 1863, Guthrie Civil War Letters, BU; Johnston, "Jefferson Davis and the Mississippi Campaign," 480; Jack D. Welsh, *Medical Histories of Confederate Generals* (Kent, OH: Kent State University Press, 1995), 227; L. J. Sanders Diary, June 1, 1863, WKU; James Skelton to sister, June 6, 1863, James M. Skelton Letters, UNC; William Jones to Mary, June 3, 1863, William Riley Jones Letters, ADAH.

59. *OR*, 24(1):224; Bearss, *The Vicksburg Campaign*, 3:978, 1008, 1010, 1065, 1071; Terrence J. Winschel, "The Absence of Will: Joseph E. Johnston and the Fall of Vicksburg," in *Confederate Generals in the Western Theater: Essays on America's Civil War*, 4 vols., Lawrence Lee Hewitt and Arthur W. Bergeron, Jr., eds. (Knoxville: University of Tennessee Press, 2010), 2:84, 87(75–92).

60. *OR*, 24(1):193, 224–226; *OR*, 52(2):490; Winschel, *Triumph and Defeat: The Vicksburg Campaign, Volume 2*, 124, 126; L. J. Sanders Diary, June 2, 1863, WKU.

61. *OR*, 24(1):195, 223; Special Orders No. 127, May 28, 1863, Samuel G. French Papers, RG 109, E 120, NARA.

62. Samuel G. French, *Two Wars: An Autobiography of Gen. Samuel G. French* (Nashville: Confederate Veteran, 1901), 178.

63. Simon, ed., *PUSG*, 8:307; Bearss, *The Vicksburg Campaign*, 3:1029, 1084.

64. George M. Lucas Diary, June 1 and 2, 1863, ALPL.

65. *OR*, 24(3):374; Frank Blair to U. S. Grant, June 2, 1863, Blair Family Papers, LOC.

66. *OR*, 24(3):374–376.

67. *OR*, 24(3):375, 379; *OR*, 24(2):213, 215; Robert J. Burdette, *The Drums of the 47th* (Urbana: University of Illinois Press, 2000), 67; Simon, ed., *PUSG*, 8:302–303, 312; George M. Lucas Diary, June 3, 1863, ALPL; J. W. Greenman Diary, MDAH, 97–98; Samuel Eells to unknown, June 9, 1863, Samuel H. Eells Papers, LC; Charles Affeld Diary, June 4, 1863, Journals/Diaries/Letters Series, VICK; Henry A. Robinson to friend, June 18, 1863, Henry A. Robinson Papers, IHS.

68. *OR*, 24(3):379; *OR* 24(1):41; Winschel, *Triumph and Defeat: The Vicksburg Campaign, Volume 2*, 126; Kountz, *Record of the Organizations Engaged in the Campaign, Siege, and Defense of Vicksburg*, 29.

69. *OR*, 24(3):374–376; Stillwell, *The Story of a Common Soldier*, 136; Adolph Engelmann to sister, June 3, 1863, Engelmann-Kircher Family Papers, ALPL.

70. *OR*, 24(2):436; Simon, ed., *PUSG*, 8:309, 311; George M. Lucas Diary, June 4, 1863, ALPL; Adolph Engelmann to wife, June 6, 1863, Engelmann-Kircher Family Papers, ALPL; W. A Rorer to cousin, June 13, 1863, W. A. Rorer Letters, Duke University (copies in MDAH and Lionel Baxter Collection, CWTI, USAHEC); William B. Britton to Editors Gazette, June 13, 1863, William B. Britton Letters, OCM; Charles Affeld Diary, June 4, 1863, Journals/Diaries/Letters Series, VICK; James Lawrence to wife, June 5, 1863, James Lawrence Papers, CHM; Lot Abraham Diary, June 5, 1863, UIA.

71. *OR*, 52(1):65–66; Stewart Bruce Terry Diary, June 4, 1863, KHS; "The Civil War Letters of Carey Campbell Wright," undated, AU, 137.

72. *OR*, 24(3):372, 378–379; *OR* 24(1):41; Kountz, *Record of the Organizations Engaged in the Campaign, Siege, and Defense of Vicksburg*, 25; George M. Lucas Diary, June 6 and 7, 1863, ALPL; J. W. Greenman Diary, MDAH, 98.

73. *OR*, 24(3):384; Simon, ed., *PUSG*, 8:316; Charles Affeld Diary, June 6, 1863, Journals/Diaries/Letters Series, VICK.

74. Simon, ed., *PUSG*, 8:317–318; *OR*, 24(1):94; Bearss, *The Vicksburg Campaign*, 3:1026; Adolph Engelmann to wife, June 6, 1863, Engelmann-Kircher Family Papers, ALPL; Samuel Eells to unknown, June 9, 1863, Samuel H. Eells Papers, LC; Charles Affeld Diary, June 6, 1863, Journals/Diaries/Letters Series, VICK; James Whitehall Memoir, 1879, Journals/Letters/Diaries Series, VICK, copy in CWD, USAHEC; I. P. Rumsey to parents, June 8, 1863, I. P. Rumsey Papers, NL; James Lawrence to wife, June 10 and 11, 1863, James Lawrence Papers, CHM.

75. Simon, ed., *PUSG*, 8:317–318; *OR*, 24(1):94; *OR*, 24(2):438; Bearss, *The Vicksburg Campaign*, 3:1026; Adolph Engelmann to wife, June 6, 1863, Engelmann-Kircher

Family Papers, ALPL; Samuel Eells to unknown, June 9, 1863, Samuel H. Eells Papers, LC; Charles Affeld Diary, June 6, 1863, Journals/Diaries/Letters Series, VICK; James Whitehall Memoir, 1879, Journals/Letters/Diaries Series, VICK, copy in CWD, USA-HEC; I. P. Rumsey to parents, June 8, 1863, I. P. Rumsey Papers, NL; James Lawrence to wife, June 10 and 11, 1863, James Lawrence Papers, CHM; Dana, *Recollections of the Civil War*, 67; Stillwell, *The Story of a Common Soldier*, 137; George M. Lucas Diary, June 7, 1863, ALPL; Channing Richards Diary, June 13, 1863, FHS; John A. Buckner to General, June 5, 1863, "Letters, Telegrams, and Orders Received and Sent—General Breckinridge's Command, December 1861–November 1863," RG 109, Chapter II, Vol. 311, NARA, 103.

76. *OR*, 24(3):387; James Harrison Wilson, "A Staff Officer's Journal of the Vicksburg Campaign, April 30 to July 4, 1863," *Journal of the Military Service Institution of the United States* 43, no. 154 (July–August 1908): 272; Simon, ed., *PUSG*, 8:316; Adolph Engelmann to wife, June 6, 1863, Engelmann-Kircher Family Papers, ALPL.

77. Fred Grant Memoir, undated, USGPL, 36. For a detailed analysis, see Ballard, *Grant at Vicksburg*, 43–63.

78. Catton, *Grant Moves South*, 464; Dana, *Recollections of the Civil War*, 83; Cadwallader, *Three Years with Grant*, 102–110.

79. Simon, ed., *PUSG*, 8:322, 324; Simpson, *Ulysses S. Grant*, 208.

80. Chernow, *Grant*, 272–277; Simpson, *Ulysses S. Grant*, 208; W. T. Sherman to John Tourtelette, February 4, 1887, Civil War Diaries and Letters, UIA; Simon, ed., *PUSG*, 8:323, 325. Wilson's original diaries are in the James H. Wilson Papers, LC.

81. Dana, *Recollections of the Civil War*, 67; Stillwell, *The Story of a Common Soldier*, 137; George M. Lucas Diary, June 7, 1863, ALPL; Channing Richards Diary, June 13, 1863, FHS; Samuel Eells to unknown, June 9, 1863, Samuel H. Eells Papers, LC; Charles Affeld Diary, June 7, 1863, Journals/Diaries/Letters Series, VICK; I. P. Rumsey to parents, June 8, 1863, I. P. Rumsey Papers, NL; John A. Buckner to General, June 5, 1863, "Letters, Telegrams, and Orders Received and Sent—General Breckinridge's Command, December 1861–November 1863," RG 109, Chapter II, Vol. 311, NARA, 103.

82. *OR*, 24(3):950–951.

83. Smith, *Shiloh*, 418. For Albert Sidney Johnston, see Charles P. Roland, *Albert Sidney Johnston: Soldier of Three Republics* (Austin: University of Texas Press, 1964).

CHAPTER 7. "THE MENTAL STRAIN BECAME AWFUL UNDER SUCH CONDITIONS"

1. Richard and Richard, *The Defense of Vicksburg*, 182, 216; Hander "Excerpts from the Hander Diary," 145.

2. E. L. Chatfield to parents, May 27, 1863, Edward L. Chatfield Papers, HL; Town Heaton to Jack, June 21, 1863, Townsend P. Heaton Papers, OHS; John Ritter to Margaret, June 11, 1863, John A. Ritter Papers, NC.

3. Balzar Grebe Memoir, undated, Balzar Grebe Papers, ALPL, 19; Edward McGlynn

to parents, May 22, 1863, Edward McGlynn Letters, UI; James B. McPherson to Isaac F. Quinby, May 26, 1863, Letters Sent, 17th Army Corps, RG 393, NARA; David McKinney to sister, June 21, 1863, David McKinney Papers, FHS.

4. Joseph D. Alison Diary, May 27, 1863, MDAH; Albert C. Lenert Diary, May 25, 1863, UNT, copy in OCM; Levi W. Bennett Diary, June 9, 1863, MDAH.

5. W. R. McRory Diary, May 28, 1863, Journals/Letters/Diaries Series, VICK; Albert C. Lenert Diary, May 30 and June 7, 1863, OCM; William L. Foster to wife, June 20, 1863, UA; J. H. Pepper Diary, May 29, 1863, MDAH.

6. Ira W. Hunt Diary, May 25, 1863, 11th Wisconsin File, VICK; John N. Bell Diary, May 26 and June 3, 1863, OHS; T. G. Larkin to wife, May 24, 1863, Thomas George Larkin Papers, KHS; Eugene McWayne to folks, May 26, 1863, Eugene A. McWayne Papers, Sword Collection, USAHEC.

7. Later from Vicksburg, May 30, 1863, Natchez *Daily Courier*; John N. Bell Diary, June 5, 1863, OHS; W. D. Williams to companion, May 29, 1863, William Williams Letters, OCM; Cotton, ed., *From the Pen of a She-Rebel*, 14; John A. Griffen Diary, May 29, 1863, ALPL.

8. Troy Moore to Clara, June 1, 1863, Troy Moore Letters, ALPL; John G. Jones to parents, June 9, 1863, John G. Jones Papers, LC; I. P. Rumsey to parents, June 2, 1863, I. P. Rumsey Papers, NL; Ballard, *Pemberton*, 173; William Jones to cousin, June 13, 1863, William F. Jones Papers, SHSMC; Andrew Sproul to Fanny, June 9, 1863, Andrew J. Sproul Papers, UNC.

9. John Ramsay. to sir, June 23, 1863, John A. Ramsay Papers, UNC.

10. William R. Clack Diary, June 8, 1863, Journals/Diaries/Letters Series, VICK; Ned to Alice, July 3, 1863, E. H. and D. G. Ingraham Letters, ALPL.

11. William L. Foster to wife, June 20, 1863, UA; Chambers, "My Journal," 273, 277; *OR*, 24(2):382, 398; Richard and Richard, *The Defense of Vicksburg*, 211.

12. Richard and Richard, *The Defense of Vicksburg*, 169.

13. Clarke, *Reminiscence and Anecdotes of the War for Southern Independence*, 109; Jones, "The Rank and File at Vicksburg," 24; Richard and Richard, *The Defense of Vicksburg*, 186.

14. *OR*, 24(2):392, 408–409.

15. Unknown to unknown, June 8, 1863, Henry Ginder Papers, TU; Chambers, "My Journal," 277.

16. Clarke, *Reminiscence and Anecdotes of the War for Southern Independence*, 108.

17. Clarke, *Reminiscence and Anecdotes of the War for Southern Independence*, 109.

18. Richard and Richard, *The Defense of Vicksburg*, 174; Eli W. Thornhill Memoir, undated, OCM, 11; Simeon R. Martin Reminiscences, undated, OCM, 69.

19. Loughborough, *My Cave Life in Vicksburg*, 107; Richard and Richard, *The Defense of Vicksburg*, 184; Chambers, "My Journal," 278; Theodore D. Fisher Diary, June 12, 1863, Journals/Letters/Diaries Series, VICK; Hogane, "Reminiscences of the Siege of Vicksburg—Paper No. 2," 296.

20. Robert L. Bachman Memoir, undated, OCM, 23–24; *OR*, 24(2):356; Richard and Richard, *The Defense of Vicksburg*, 186.

21. Dodd, "Recollections of Vicksburg During the Siege," 8.

22. Richard and Richard, *The Defense of Vicksburg*, 194, 213.

23. Richard and Richard, *The Defense of Vicksburg*, 179; John H. Kelton Diary, June 28, 1863, Journals/Letters/Diaries Series, VICK; William L. Faulk Diary, May 26, 1863, OCM; Eli W. Thornhill Memoir, undated, OCM, 14; J. M. Stafford to Surgeon Bailey, May 30, 1863, Letters and Telegrams Sent, Department of Mississippi and East Louisiana, 1863, RG 109, Chapter II, Vol. 60, NARA.

24. J. H. Pepper Diary, June 19, 1863, MDAH; William L. Faulk Diary, June 1 and 3, 1863, OCM.

25. Eli W. Thornhill Memoir, undated, OCM, 13; Chambers, "My Journal," 278; Richard and Richard, *The Defense of Vicksburg*, 195, 199, 207, 212.

26. Richard and Richard, *The Defense of Vicksburg*, 177; William Milner Kelly, "A History of the Thirtieth Alabama Volunteers (Infantry), Confederate States Army," *Alabama Historical Quarterly* 9, no. 1 (Spring 1947): 142 (115–167), copy in 30th Alabama File, VICK.

27. Richard and Richard, *The Defense of Vicksburg*, 175; William L. Faulk Diary, June 7, 1863, OCM.

28. Charles L. Dubuisson to father, June 26, 1863, Charles L. Dubuisson and Family Papers, MDAH; Jones, "The Rank and File at Vicksburg," 25.

29. Hoehling, *Vicksburg*, 138; William L. Foster to wife, June 20, 1863, UA; Christian W. Hander Diary, May 24, 1863, UTA; William M. Reid Diary, May 27, 1863, ALPL. For the 42nd Georgia, see W. Clifford Roberts, Jr., and Frank E. Clark, *Atlanta's Fighting Forty-Second: Joseph Johnston's "Old Guard"* (Macon, GA: Mercer University Press, 2020).

30. *OR*, 24(2):392; Richard and Richard, *The Defense of Vicksburg*, 218; L. M. Stafford to M. L. Smith, May 24 and J. H. Morrison to Thomas Taylor, May 29, 1863, Letters and Telegrams Sent, Department of Mississippi and East Louisiana, 1863, RG 109, Chapter II, Vol. 60, NARA.

31. Hander "Excerpts from the Hander Diary," 144; Cable, ed., "A Woman's Diary of the Siege of Vicksburg," 772; Robert L. Bachman Memoir, undated, OCM, 21; Clarke, *Reminiscence and Anecdotes of the War for Southern Independence*, 110; J. C. Taylor to M. L. Smith, June 13, 1863, Letters and Telegrams Sent, Department of Mississippi and East Louisiana, 1863, RG 109, Chapter II, Vol. 60, NARA.

32. H. T. Morgan to Ellen, March 28, 1863, Henry T. Morgan Papers, CWD, USA-HEC; George Chatfield to mother, April 15, 1863, George H. Chatfield Papers, CWD, USAHEC; *OR*, 24(1):278–281; Hoehling, *Vicksburg*, 162, 252; Chambers, "My Journal," 280; Richard and Richard, *The Defense of Vicksburg*, 190, 218–219; Lockett, "The Defense of Vicksburg," 492; James L. Power Diary, June 28, 1863, MDAH; Robert L. Bachman Memoir, undated, OCM, 23.

33. Theodore D. Fisher Diary, June 30, 1863, Journals/Letters/Diaries Series, VICK; *OR*, 24(2):359, 392; Richard and Richard, *The Defense of Vicksburg*, 185, 211.

34. Richard and Richard, *The Defense of Vicksburg*, 192, 203, 213, 221; Albert C. Lenert Diary, June 10, 1863, OCM; Hander "Excerpts from the Hander Diary," 146; R. W.

Memminger to Carter Stevenson, June 6, 1863, Letters and Telegrams Sent, Department of Mississippi and East Louisiana, 1863, RG 109, Chapter II, Vol. 60, NARA.

35. Richard and Richard, *The Defense of Vicksburg*, 209; Personal Memoirs of I. V. Smith, 1902, SHSMC, 31; *OR*, 24(3):407; *OR*, 24(1):278.

36. Anderson, *Memoirs*, 337–338; Dodd, "Recollections of Vicksburg During the Siege," 5–6; *OR*, 24(2):392; Richard and Richard, *The Defense of Vicksburg*, 185, 211; Clarke, *Reminiscence and Anecdotes of the War for Southern Independence*, 107; W. H. Rogers, "The Flint Hill Grays," undated, Bible Records, Military Rosters and Reminiscences of Confederate Soldiers, GDAH, 106; Loughborough, *My Cave Life in Vicksburg*, 77.

37. John A. Leavy Diary, June 27, 1863, Journals/Letters/Diaries Series, VICK; Marion B. Richmond, "The Siege of Vicksburg," *Confederate Veteran* 37, no. 4 (April 1929): 140; C. S. O. Rice, "Incidents of the Vicksburg Siege," *Confederate Veteran* 12, no. 2 (February 1904): 77. For more on the camel, see W. Scott Bell, *The Camel Regiment: A History of the Bloody 43rd Mississippi Volunteer Infantry, CSA, 1862–1865* (Gretna, LA: Pelican Publishing Company, 2017).

38. H. Grady Howell, Jr., *Going to Meet the Yankees: A History of the "Bloody Sixth" Mississippi Infantry, C.S.A.* (Jackson: Chickasaw Bayou Press, 1981), 186; Abrams, *A Full and Detailed History*, 55; Clarke, *Reminiscence and Anecdotes of the War for Southern Independence*, 113.

39. Chambers, "My Journal," 280; Thomas Hogan to father, July 5, 1863, Thomas Hogan Letters, MHS.

40. Personal Memoirs of I. V. Smith, 1902, SHSMC, 32; *OR*, 24(2):392; Richard and Richard, *The Defense of Vicksburg*, 185, 211.

41. Richard and Richard, *The Defense of Vicksburg*, 218, 220 Clarke, *Reminiscence and Anecdotes of the War for Southern Independence*, 110.

42. H. T. Morgan to Ellen, March 28, 1863, Henry T. Morgan Papers, CWD, USAHEC; George Chatfield to mother, April 15, 1863, George H. Chatfield Papers, CWD, USAHEC; *OR*, 24(1):278–281; Hoehling, *Vicksburg*, 162, 252; Chambers, "My Journal," 280; Richard and Richard, *The Defense of Vicksburg*, 190, 218–219; Lockett, "The Defense of Vicksburg," 492; James L. Power Diary, June 28, 1863, MDAH; Robert L. Bachman Memoir, undated, OCM, 23; H. C. Tupper to Major Gillespie, R. W. Memminger to John S. Bowen, and J. H. Morrison to Major Gillespie, May 23, and H. C. Tupper o H. C. Bailey, May 30, 1863, Letters and Telegrams Sent, Department of Mississippi and East Louisiana, 1863, RG 109, Chapter II, Vol. 60, NARA.

43. H. T. Morgan to Ellen, March 28, 1863, Henry T. Morgan Papers, CWD, USAHEC; George Chatfield to mother, April 15, 1863, George H. Chatfield Papers, CWD, USAHEC; *OR*, 24(1):278–281; Hoehling, *Vicksburg*, 162, 252; Chambers, "My Journal," 280; Stephen E. Ambrose, *Struggle for Vicksburg: The Battles and Siege That Decided the Civil War* (Harrisburg, PA: Eastern Acorn Press, 1967), 55; Richard and Richard, *The Defense of Vicksburg*, 190, 218–219; Lockett, "The Defense of Vicksburg," 492; James L. Power Diary, June 28, 1863, MDAH; Robert L. Bachman Memoir, undated, OCM, 23; John C. Taylor Diary, June 30, 1863, UVA.

44. Tunnard, *A Southern Record*, 263; Henry Kircher to mother, June 17, 1863, Engelmann-Kircher Family Papers, ALPL.

45. Lynch Perry, "Vicksburg. Some New History in the Experience of Gen. Francis A. Shoup," *Confederate Veteran* 2, no. 6 (June 1894): 174; Winchester Hall, *The Story of the 26th Louisiana Infantry, In the Service of the Confederate States* (N.p.: n.p., 1890), 90; Richard and Richard, *The Defense of Vicksburg*, 195, 201, 217, 219.

46. Jones, "The Rank and File at Vicksburg," 23; Henry Kircher Diary, June 9, 1863, Engelmann-Kircher Family Papers, ALPL; J. Carroll Harriss to Valery, June 4, 1863, Jordan C. Harriss Papers, NC; John G. Jones to parents, June 9, 1863, John G. Jones Papers, LC; Carlos Colby to sister, July 1863, Carlos W. Colby Papers, NL; Andrew Sproul to Fanny, June 9, 1863, Andrew J. Sproul Papers, UNC; James Vanderbilt to mother, May 31, 1863, James C. Vanderbilt Papers, ISL; George Carrington Diary, June 28, 1863, CHM; Henry J. Seaman Diary, June 22, 1863, CWTI, USAHEC; W. Grayum to Harriet, June 13, 1863, 4th West Virginia File, VICK; Joseph Kohout to family, June 4, 1863, Joseph Kohout Papers, UIA; Wells, *The Siege of Vicksburg*, 75.

47. George Carrington Diary, July 6, 1863, CHM.

48. Thomas O. Hall, "The Key to Vicksburg," *The Southern Bivouac* 2, no. 9 (May 1884): 395 (393–396); *OR*, 24(2):368; Lockett, "The Defense of Vicksburg," 492.

49. William L. Foster to wife, June 20, 1863, UA; *OR*, 24(2):392.

50. *OR*, 24(3):383, 393, 407; Lee, "The Siege of Vicksburg," 66; Jones, "The Rank and File at Vicksburg," 24.

51. *OR*, 24(2):693–694, 698; *OR*, 24(3):407; *OR*, 24(2):409; George Ditto Diary, June 22, 1863, ALPL.

52. Bela T. St. John to father, June 1, 1863, Bela T. St. John Papers, LOC; Charles Willison to Ellie, June 8, 1863, 76th Ohio Volunteer Infantry Papers, OHS; John G. Jones to parents, May 29, 1863, John G. Jones Papers, LC.

53. *OR*, 24(3):407; James L. Power Diary, June 8, 1863, MDAH.

54. *OR*, 24(2):393; Richard and Richard, *The Defense of Vicksburg*, 186; Bell Irvin Wiley, *The Life of Johnny Reb: The Common Soldier of the Confederacy* (Indianapolis: Bobbs-Merrill Company, 1943), 200.

55. William L. Faulk Diary, May 26, 1863, OCM; Douglas Maynard, ed., "Vicksburg Diary: The Journal of Gabriel M. Killgore," *Civil War History* 10, no. 1 (March 1964): 49; Richard and Richard, *The Defense of Vicksburg*, 174; Douglas Lee Broadaway, "A Texan Records the Civil War Siege of Vicksburg, Mississippi: The Journal of Maj. Maurice Kavanaugh Simons, 1863," *Southwestern Historical Quarterly* 105, no. 1 (July 2001): 118, 122.

56. *OR*, 24(2):393.

57. *OR*, 24(3):390; William T. Sherman to W. D. Sanger, June 8, 1863, William T. Sherman Papers, LSU.

58. *OR*, 24(3):395.

59. *OR*, 24(3):394.

60. *OR*, 24(3):394–395.

61. *OR*, 24(3):391; *OR*, 24(2):17, 194; *OR*, 24(1):95; Simon, ed., *PUSG*, 8:330–331.

62. *OR*, 24(2):174, 193–195, 197; Bearss, *The Vicksburg Campaign*, 3:945; Hashell, ed., "Col. William Camm War Diary, 1861–1865," 953; William M. Reid Diary, May 31, 1863, ALPL.

63. Simon, ed., *PUSG*, 8:321.

64. *OR*, 24(3):173; *OR*, 24(2):182, 185.

65. *OR*, 24(2):174; P. C. Hains to Walter Scates, June 2, 3, 4, and 5, 1863, John A. McClernand Papers, ALPL; Pryce, *Vanishing Footprints*, 134; Terrence J. Winschel, ed., *The Civil War Diary of a Common Soldier: William Wiley of the 77th Illinois Infantry* (Baton Rouge: Louisiana State University Press, 2001), 55.

66. Bearss, *The Vicksburg Campaign*, 3:808; https://www.nps.gov/vick/learn/history culture/pembertons-headquarters.htm.

67. Winschel, *Triumph and Defeat*, 139; Herman Hattaway, *General Stephen D. Lee* (Jackson: University Press of Mississippi, 1988), 96.

68. Ballard, *Pemberton*, 173; Emma Balfour Diary, May 26 and 29–30, 1863, Journals/Letters/Diaries Series, VICK.

69. *OR*, 24(1):287.

70. Emma Balfour Diary, May 23 and 30, 1863, MDAH; R. W. Memminger to Major Orme, June 17 and J. M. Stafford to Captain Jones, June 26, 1863, Letters and Telegrams Sent, Department of Mississippi and East Louisiana, 1863, RG 109, Chapter II, Vol. 60, NARA.

71. J. S. Smith to John Pemberton, June 19, 1863, John C. Pemberton Papers, RG 109, E 131, NARA; J. C. Taylor to Major Gillespie and also to Surgeon Bryan, June 1, 1863, Letters and Telegrams Sent, Department of Mississippi and East Louisiana, 1863, RG 109, Chapter II, Vol. 60, NARA.

72. George Remley to Howard, June 6, 1863, Remley Family Papers, NC.

73. Grabau, *Ninety-Eight Days*, 426–427; R. W. Memminger to Carter Stevenson and R. W. Memminger to Major Matthews, May 24, 1863, J. C. Taylor to John Forney, May 25, and H. C. Tupper to Carter Stevenson, June 11, 1863, Letters and Telegrams Sent, Department of Mississippi and East Louisiana, 1863, RG 109, Chapter II, Vol. 60, NARA.

74. Edward Higgins to R. W. Memminger, June 27, 1863, John C. Pemberton Papers, RG 109, E 131, NARA; R. W. Memminger to Thomas Taylor, June 24, 1863, Letters and Telegrams Sent, Department of Mississippi and East Louisiana, 1863, RG 109, Chapter II, Vol. 60, NARA.

75. *OR*, 24(1):280–281.

76. *OR*, 24(1):293–294; *OR*, 24(3):919–922; L. M. Montgomery to John Forney, June 20, 1863, John C. Pemberton Papers, RG 109, E 131, NARA; R. W. Memminger to T. H. Taylor, June 7, 1863, Letters and Telegrams Sent, Department of Mississippi and East Louisiana, 1863, RG 109, Chapter II, Vol. 60, NARA; Rice, "Incidents of the Vicksburg Siege," 77; James L. Power Diary, June 11, 1863, MDAH; George H. Hynds Diary, May 28, 1863, Journals/Letters/Diaries Series, VICK; Emma Balfour Diary, May 24, 1863, MDAH. For Taylor, see Ezra J. Warner, *Generals in Gray: Lives of the Confederate Commanders* (Baton Rouge: Louisiana State University Press, 1959), 300–301.

77. John Forney to R. W. Memminger, May 23, 1863, John Forney Endorsement,

June 10, 1863, and John Forney to R. W. Memminger, June 19, 1863, Dabney Maury Order Book, CHM, 282, 299, 301; H. C. Tupper to Major Orme, May 24, W. H. McCardle to S. D. Lee, May 30, W. H. McCardle to John Forney, June 10, R. W. Memminger to John Bowen, June 14, W. H. McCardle to Lt. Col. Beltzhoover, June 16, and R. W. Memminger to Thomas Taylor, June 20, 1863, Letters and Telegrams Sent, Department of Mississippi and East Louisiana, 1863, RG 109, Chapter II, Vol. 60, NARA; John C. Taylor Diary, June 12, 1863, UVA.

78. Winschel, *Triumph and Defeat*, 157–174; Stoker, *The Grand Design*, 269.

79. *OR*, 24(3):403; T. G. Larkin to wife, May 24, 1863, Thomas George Larkin Papers, KHS.

80. *OR*, 24(3):357; *OR*, 24(1):93; Dana, *Recollections of the Civil War*, 71; 30th Illinois Officers to Abraham Lincoln, undated, Elias Dennis File, Journals/Letters/Diaries Series, VICK; George M. Rogers Diary, June 6, 1863, ISL. For Dennis, see the Elias S. Dennis Papers, UNC. For detailed analysis of the racial issues, see Ballard, *Grant at Vicksburg*, 64–85.

81. *OR*, 24(3):378, 388; Thomas R. Hodgson Diary, June 6–7, 1863, OCM, copy in Journals/Letters/Diaries Series, VICK.

82. *OR*, 24(3):935–936, 948; *OR*, 24(2):457–458. For Walker and his division, see Richard G. Lowe, *Walker's Texas Division, C S.A.: Greyhounds of the Trans-Mississippi* (Baton Rouge: Louisiana State University Press, 2004).

83. *OR*, 24(2):447, 458–460, 471–472; *OR*, 24(3):406.

84. *OR*, 24(2):448, 459–460, 467, 469; Anson R. Butler to unknown, June 11, 1863, Anson R. Butler Papers, UIA; Wayne Johnson Jacobs Diary, June 7, 1863, LSU. For Milliken's Bend, see Linda Barnickel, *Milliken's Bend: A Civil War Battle in History and Memory* (Baton Rouge: Louisiana State University Press, 2013).

85. *OR*, 24(2):447, 467; *OR*, 24(1):102; Albert C. Lenert Diary, June 7, 1863, OCM; Unknown Confederate Diary, June 7, 1863, Journals/Letters/Diaries Series, VICK.

86. *OR*, 24(2):446, 453–454; *OR*, 24(1):95; John G. Jones to parents, June 20, 1863, John G. Jones Papers, LC; Samuel Gordon to wife, June 12, 1863, Samuel Gordon Papers, ALPL.

87. *OR*, 24(2):454–455; Henry Kircher Diary, June 7 and 10, 1863, Engelmann-Kircher Family Papers, ALPL; John Henry Hammond Diary, June 8 and 9, 1863, FHS; William E. Lewis to Margaret, June 11 and July 11, 1863, William E. Lewis Letters, SHSMC.

88. Chernow, *Grant*, 280–285; William B. Britton to Editors Gazette, June 13, 1863, William B. Britton Letters, OCM; William F. Draper to wife, June 16, 1863, William F. Draper Papers, LC.

89. *OR*, 24(2):447–448, 458–460, 471–472; *OR*, 24(3):390, 406; George M. Lucas Diary, June 8, 10, 1863, ALPL; Charles Affeld Diary, June 8, 1863, Journals/Diaries/Letters Series, VICK; Hiram Scofield Diary, June 9, 1863, NL.

90. *OR*, 24(3):403–404, 412; F. A. F., *Old Abe, The Eighth Wisconsin War Eagle. A Full Account of His Capture and Enlistment, Exploits in War and Honorable As Well As Useful Career in Peace* (Madison, WI: Curran and Bowen, 1885), 42; John Melvin

Williams, *"The Eagle Regiment," 8th Wis. Inf'ty Vols.: A Sketch of Its Marches, Battles and Campaigns From 1861–1865 With Complete Regimental and Company Roster, and a Few Portraits and Sketches of Its Officers and Commanders* (Belleville, WI: Recorder Print, 1890), 64; Cloyd Bryner, *Bugle Echoes: The Story of the Illinois 47th* (Springfield, IL: Phillips Bros. Printers, 1905), 88–89.

91. *OR*, 24(3):405–406; *OR*, 24(2):450–451, 453; *OR*, 24(1):97; "Notes From the Eagle Regiment," undated, 8th Wisconsin Infantry, Vol. 9, Quiner Scrapbooks, WHS; George M. Lucas Diary, June 14–16, 19, 1863, ALPL; J. W. Greenman Diary, MDAH, 99–101; Charles Affeld Diary, June 14–15, 1863, Journals/Diaries/Letters Series, VICK; M. E. Pattan to friend, June 15, 1863, John Linfor Letters, UMEM.

92. *OR*, 24(3):405–406; *OR*, 24(2):450–451, 453; *OR*, 24(1):97.

CHAPTER 8. "THE MOST MISERABLE PLACE WE HAVE EVER BEEN IN"

1. Louis W. Knobe Diary, June 7, 1863, ISL. For a study into individual motivations, see James M. McPherson, *For Cause and Comrades: Why Men Fought in the Civil War* (New York: Oxford University Press, 1997).

2. Louis W. Knobe Diary, June 7, 1863, ISL.

3. George M. Rogers Diary, June 24, 1863, ISL; James Benson Logan Diary, May 23 and 29 and June 23, 1863, ALPL; Robert Ridge Diary, May 30 and June 23, 1863, ALPL; John A. Griffen Diary, June 21, 1863, ALPL; Charles H. Brush to mother, June 24, 1863, Daniel H. Brush Papers, ALPL.

4. George Ditto Diary, June 10, 1863, ALPL; Richard and Richard, *The Defense of Vicksburg*, 192, 201; A. L. Spencer Diary, June 10, 1863, Journals/Letters/Diaries Series, VICK.

5. Richard and Richard, *The Defense of Vicksburg*, 202.

6. Elbert D. Willett Diary, June 10, 1863, ADAH; William L. Faulk Diary, June 11, 1863, OCM; Hander "Excerpts from the Hander Diary," 145; Aurelius L. Voorhis Diary, June 10, 1863, IHS; Frank Moore, ed., *The Rebellion Record: A Diary of American Events, With Documents, Narratives, Illustrative Incidents, Poetry, Etc.*, 11 vols. (New York: D Van Nostrand, 1861–1868), 7:172.

7. Loughborough, *My Cave Life in Vicksburg*, 113.

8. Crooke, *The Twenty-first Regiment of Iowa Volunteer Infantry*, 109; George M. Rogers Diary, June 10, 1863, ISL; H. H. Bennett Diary, June 11, 1863, WHS.

9. Adnah Eaton Diary, June 10, 1863, NC; Abram J. Vanauken Diary, June 10, 1863, ALPL; Asa E. Sample Diary, June 10, 1863, ISL; Anthony B. Burton Diary, June 10, 1863, ALPL.

10. George Ditto Diary, June 10, 1863, ALPL; James Slack to Ann, June 11, 1863, James R. Slack Papers, ISL; S. E. Snure to sir, June 21, 1863, S. E. Snure Letters, IHS; Samuel S. Irwin Diary, June 10, 1863, ALPL.

11. Henry Kircher Diary, June 11, 1863, Engelmann-Kircher Family Papers, ALPL; James Boardman Diary, June 23, 1863, ND; Lot Abraham Diary, June 10, 1863, UIA;

Charles Affeld Diary, June 10, 1863, Journals/Diaries/Letters Series, VICK; Dempsey Ashford Diary, June 10, 1863, Journals/Diaries/Letters, VICK.

12. *OR*, 24(1):97; Isaac Vanderwarker Diary, June 10, 1863, CWD, USAHEC; Joseph Stockton Diary, June 8–16, 1863, ALPL; William Parrish to family, June 14, 1863, William Parrish Letters, Journals/Letters/Diaries Series, VICK; "United States. Army. Illinois Infantry Regiment, 14th (1861–1863) Company A," June 10–21, 1863, ALPL; John A. Griffen Diary, June 10, 1863, ALPL.

13. George Carrington Diary, June 9, 1863, CHM; John B. Fletcher Diary, June 10, 1863, ALPL.

14. E. H. Ingraham to aunt, May 29, 1863, E. H. and D. G. Ingraham Letters, ALPL; John A. McLaughlin to sister, June 15, 1863, McLaughlin-Jordan Family Papers, IHS.

15. Albert Chipman to wife, June 8, 1863, Albert Chipman Papers, ALPL; William Murphey to brother, June 15, 1863, William Murphey Papers, OHS; George Carrington Diary, June 9, 1863, CHM; John E. Smith to Aimee, June 7, 1863, John E. Smith Letters, Kirby Smith Collection.

16. Chase Dickinson to friends, June 6, 1863, Chase Hall Dickinson Papers, NL; William Murray Diary, June 1, 1863, Journals/Letters/Diaries Series, VICK; R. W. Burt to brother, June 9, 1863, Richard W. Burt Papers, SHSMC; John Merrilees Diary, May 24, 1863, CHM, copy in OCM.

17. Soman and Byrne, eds., *A Jewish Colonel in the Civil War*, 293; *OR*, 24(1):104; Rodney Jeger to sister, July 2, 1863, Rodney Jeger Papers, ISL; J. W. Guthrie to father, July 4, 1863, J. W. Guthrie Letter, LSU.

18. John L. Harris to mother, June 15, 1863, John L. Harris Correspondence, ALPL; *OR*, 24(2):195; E. H. Ingraham to aunt, May 29, 1863, E. H. and D. G. Ingraham Letters, ALPL.

19. *OR*, 24(2):195; E. H. Ingraham to aunt, May 29, 1863, E. H. and D. G. Ingraham Letters, ALPL; Beck, *A True Sketch of Army Life*, 10; Ebenezer Werkheiser to sister, June 8, 1863, Ebenezer Werkheiser Letters, Journals/Letters/Diaries Series, VICK; Thomas N. McLeur Diary, May 24, 1863, OCM; Edward E. Schweitzer Diary, June 7, 1863, CWTI, USAHEC; E. L. Hawk to W. T. Rigby, April 21, 1914, 114th Ohio File, VICK.

20. E. H. Ingraham to aunt, June 15, 1863, E. H. and D. G. Ingraham Letters, ALPL; William M. Reid Diary, May 28–29, 1863, ALPL; Alvin Hovey Memoir, undated, IU, 63–64.

21. Thomas Watson to parents, May 24 and June 5, 1863, Thomas Watson Correspondence, ALPL; William M. Reid Diary, June 2 and 11, 1863, ALPL; Henry Kircher Diary, May 28, 1863, Engelmann-Kircher Family Papers, ALPL; William B. Britton to Editors Gazette, June 1, 1863, William B. Britton Letters, OCM; Isaac Home Diary, May 31, 1863, KHS.

22. Charles Willison to Ellie, June 8, 1863, 76th Ohio Volunteer Infantry Papers, OHS, copy in 76th Ohio File, VICK; Turner S. Bailey Diary, June 19, 1863, UIA; Gilbert Young to mother, May 28, 1863, Gilbert N. Young Letters, Journals/Letters/Diaries Series, VICK; Enoch P. Williams Diary, June 14, 1863, Journals/Letters/Diaries Series, VICK.

23. Isaac Home Diary, May 31, 1863, KHS; John L. Harris to mother, June 15, 1863, John L. Harris Correspondence, ALPL; Unknown to John M. Bucinst, June 28, 1863, John A. Logan Museum.

24. Francis R. Baker Diary, June 8, 1863, ALPL; E. H. Ingraham to aunt, June 15, 1863, E. H. and D. G. Ingraham Letters, ALPL; James K. Danby Diary, June 3, 1863, 8th Indiana File, VICK; Charles Affeld Diary, May 25 and June 8 and 26, 1863, Journals/Diaries/Letters Series, VICK; Calvin Ainsworth Diary, July 1, 1863, Journals/Letters/Diaries Series, VICK; Charles W. Beal to brother, June 10, 1863, Charles W. Beal Papers, ALPL.

25. John G. Jones to parents, July 10, 1863, John G. Jones Papers, LC; Timothy C. Young Diary, June 17 and 21, 1863, Journals/Letters/Diaries Series, VICK; John J. Kellogg Memoirs, 1913, Journals/Letters/Diaries Series, VICK, 56–57.

26. Don Pardee to unknown, May 27 and 31, 1863, Don A. Pardee Papers, TU; Pratt, ed., "Civil War Letters of Brigadier-General William Ward Orme, 1862–1866," 282, 284; George Thomas to Minerva, June 16, 1863, Thomas Family Correspondence, ND.

27. Pratt, ed., "Civil War Letters of Brigadier-General William Ward Orme, 1862–1866," 287; Lyman M. Baker Memoir, 1914, ALPL, 14; John J. Kellogg Memoirs, 1913, Journals/Letters/Diaries Series, VICK, 46–47.

28. Ned to Alice, July 3, 1863, E. H. and D. G. Ingraham Letters, ALPL; John A. Griffen Diary, May 30, 1863, ALPL.

29. Charles H. Brush to mother, June 14, 1863, Daniel H. Brush Papers, ALPL; J. Carroll Harriss to Valery, June 17, 1863, Jordan C. Harriss Papers, NC; John G. Jones to parents, July 1, 1863, John G. Jones Papers, LC; Bela T. St. John Diary, June 21, 1863, LOC; Wells W. Leggett to mother, June 6, 1863, Mortimer Leggett Papers, Lincoln Memorial Shrine; Charles Affeld Diary, June 14 and 23, 1863, Journals/Diaries/Letters Series, VICK; R. W. Burt to Mr. Editor, June 10, 1863, 76th Ohio Volunteer Infantry Papers, OHS; Martin Scoville to friends, July 1, 1863, Martin Scoville Letters, Journals/Letters/Diaries Series, VICK.

30. John A. Botts Poem, June 12, 1863, ISL; George Carrington Diary, June 10, 1863, CHM; R. W. Burt to Lona, July 2, 1863, Richard W. Burt Papers, SHSMC; Charles W. Beal to brother, June 10, 1863, Charles W. Beal Papers, ALPL.

31. Soman and Byrne, eds., *A Jewish Colonel in the Civil War*, 294; Levi W. Bennett Diary, July 4, 1863, MDAH; James S. McHenry Diary, June 12, 1863, ALPL.

32. Grabau, *Ninety-Eight Days*, 442–444; *OR*, 24(2):309; Reed, *Campaigns and Battles of the Twelfth Regiment Iowa*, 124.

33. Albert Chipman to wife, June 30, 1863, Albert Chipman Papers, ALPL; Reed, *Campaigns and Battles of the Twelfth Regiment*, 124; Edmund Newsome Diary, May 31, 1863, MDAH; Hoehling, *Vicksburg*, 162.

34. *OR*, 24(1):89, 101; Clark, ed., *Downing's Civil War Diary*, 120.

35. J. P. Van Nest to wife, June 4, 1863, Joseph P. Van Nest Papers, FHS.

36. Francis R. Baker Diary, May 28, 1863, ALPL; Thomas B. Beggs to aunt, June 19, 1863, Thomas Benson Beggs Letters, ALPL; Charles Henry Snedeker Diary, May 29, 1863, AU; Henry J. Seaman Diary, June 21, 1863, CWTI, USAHEC; William M. Reid Diary, June 18, 1863, ALPL.

37. George C. Churcheus Diary, June 14 and 30, 1863, OHS; James Boardman Diary, June 10–11, 1863, ND; Francis R. Baker Diary, June 11, 1863, ALPL; William J. Pittenger Diary, June 5, 1863, VT; John W. Griffith Diary, June 8, 1863, OHS; Van Bennett Diary, June 1, 1863, WHS; Carlos Colby to sister, June 13 and 19, 1863, Carlos W. Colby Papers, NL; Walter Gresham to wife, June 1, 1863, Walter Q. Gresham Papers, LOC.

38. John B. Fletcher Diary, May 23, 1863, ALPL; John M. Adair, *Historical Sketch of the Forty-fifth Illinois Regiment, With a Complete List of the Officers and Privates and an Individual Record of Each Man in the Regiment* (Lanark, IL: Carroll County Gazette Print, 1869), 12.

39. Asa E. Sample Diary, June 9, 1863, ISL; Carlos Colby to sister, June 9, 1863, Carlos W. Colby Papers, NL; Chase Dickinson to friends, June 11, 1863, Chase Hall Dickinson Papers, NL; Isaac Home Diary, May 31, 1863, KHS.

40. Edmund Newsome Diary, June 14, 1863, MDAH; Joel Strong Reminiscences, 1910, MHS, 14; Francis R. Baker Diary, June 21–24, 1863, ALPL; John W. Griffith Diary, May 28, 1863, OHS; Pryce, *Vanishing Footprints*, 138; Martin N. Bertera, *A Soldier at Dawn: A Remarkable and Heroic Exodus* (N.p.: n.p., n.d.), 64–65, 67; Bertera, *De Golyer's 8th Michigan Black Horse Light Battery*, 146.

41. Calvin Ainsworth Diary, June 17, 1863, Journals/Letters/Diaries Series, VICK.

42. Pratt, ed., "Civil War Letters of Brigadier-General William Ward Orme, 1862–1866," 279–280; Bertera, *De Golyer's 8th Michigan Black Horse Light Battery*, 153; Pryce, *Vanishing Footprints*, 139.

43. Pratt, ed., "Civil War Letters of Brigadier-General William Ward Orme, 1862–1866," 279–280; William M. Reid Diary, June 29, 1863, ALPL; Elder III, ed., *A Damned Iowa Greyhound*, 75.

44. Pryce, *Vanishing Footprints*, 132, 135; John E. Smith to Aimee, May 31, 1863, John E. Smith Letters, Kirby Smith Collection, copy in John E. Smith Letters, Journals/Letters/Diaries Series, VICK; William R. Eddington Memoir, undated, ALPL, 12.

45. John Merrilees Diary, June 15, 1863, CHM.

46. Pryce, *Vanishing Footprints*, 135; Joseph Waite Diary, June 25, 1863, IHS; Richard Hall to parents, July 2, 1863, Richard Hall Letters, Journals/Letters/Diaries Series, VICK; William Barnard to sister, July 2, 1863, William A. Barnard Collection, AM; Charles H. Brush to father, May 28, 1863, Daniel H. Brush Papers, ALPL.

47. Richard Hall to parents, July 2, 1863, Richard A. Hall Letters, LSU.

48. Unknown to unknown, July 3, 1863, Jasper Barker Letters, IHS; Hoehling, *Vicksburg*, 147; Abiel M. Barker Diary, May 25, 1863, OCM; William F. Draper to wife, June 16, 1863, William F. Draper Papers, LC; Samuel Eells to unknown, June 9, 1863, Samuel H. Eells Papers, LC; Stillwell, *The Story of a Common Soldier*, 142.

49. George W. Harwood to friends, June 19, 1863, George W. Harwood Letters, OCM.

50. William P. Hopkins, *The Seventh Regiment Rhode Island Volunteers in the Civil War, 1862–1865* (Providence: Providence Press, 1903), 100–101; Robert Jameson to sister, July 4, 1863, Robert E. Jameson Papers, LC.

51. William Taylor to Jane, June 28, 1863, William Taylor Correspondence, WM.

52. William Taylor to Jane, July 1, 1863, William Taylor Correspondence, WM;

Charles Dana Miller Memoir, undated, Journals/Letters/Diaries Series, VICK, 53, published as Bennett and Tillery, eds., *The Struggle for the Life of the Republic*; Walter Gresham to wife, June 6, 1863, Walter Q. Gresham Papers, LOC, letters also printed in Matilda Gresham, *Life of Walter Quintin Gresham, 1832–1895*, 2 vols. (Chicago: Rand McNally and Company, 1919); Stillwell, *The Story of a Common Soldier*, 137.

53. Edward E. Schweitzer Diary, June 8, 1863, CWTI, USAHEC; William M. Reid Diary, July 2, 1863, ALPL; Stillwell, *The Story of a Common Soldier*, 136–137; *History of the Thirty-sixth Regiment Massachusetts Volunteers, 1862–1865* (Boston: Rockwell and Churchill, 1884), 52.

54. Lyman Jackman, *History of the Sixth New Hampshire Regiment in the War for the Union* (Concord, NH: Republican Press Association, 1891), 169; Bela T. St. John to father, June 1, 1863, Bela T. St. John Papers, LOC; Albert Chipman to wife, July 8, 1863, Albert Chipman Papers, ALPL; Charles H. Brush to father, May 26, 1863, Daniel H. Brush Papers, ALPL; William Jolly to parents, June 12, 1863, William Jolly Letters, Journals/Letters/Diaries Series, VICK; William M. Reid Diary, May 24, 1863, ALPL; Troy Moore to Clara, June 13, 1863, Troy Moore Letters, ALPL.

55. William Taylor to Jane, June 28, 1863, William Taylor Correspondence, WM.

56. Oldroyd, *A Soldier's Story*, 53, 62; William L. Foster to wife, June 20, 1863, UA; John N. Bell Diary, May 24, 1863, OHS; Aurelius L. Voorhis Diary, May 31, 1863, IHS; Henry Kircher Diary, June 21, 1863, Engelmann-Kircher Family Papers, ALPL.

57. Richard and Richard, *The Defense of Vicksburg*, 203; Edward E. Schweitzer Diary, June 1, 1863, CWTI, USAHEC; Clark, ed., *Downing's Civil War Diary*, 121; John M. Sullivan to wife, June 14, 1863, John M. Sullivan Papers, OHS; George C. Churcheus Diary, June 15, 1863, OHS; Carlos Colby to sister, June 21, 1863, Carlos W. Colby Papers, NL; Robert Ridge Diary, May 31 and June 7 and 14, 1863, ALPL; Anson Hemingway Diary, June 24, 1863, Journals/Letters/Diaries Series, VICK.

58. Special Orders No. 93, June 7, 1863, Hugh Ewing Papers, OHS; Thomas Watson to parents, June 8, 1863, Thomas Watson Correspondence, ALPL; Anson Hemingway Diary, June 21 and 28 and July 2, 1863, Journals/Letters/Diaries Series, VICK; John M. Sullivan to wife, June 21, 1863, John M. Sullivan Papers, OHS; George Ditto Diary, June 14, 1863, ALPL.

59. J. Carroll Harriss to Valery, June 4, 1863, Jordan C. Harriss Papers, NC; Henry Oman to wife, June 11, 1863, Henry Oman Papers, UNC; Anson Hemingway Diary, June 17, 1863, Journals/Letters/Diaries Series, VICK; James Newton to mother, May 29, 1863, 14th Wisconsin File, VICK.

60. John Kinsel to friend, June 28, 1863, John Ruckman Letters, Journals/Letters/Diaries Series, VICK; Post, ed., *Soldiers' Letters*, 220.

61. *OR*, 24(1):98, 100; Joseph Stockton Diary, June 21, 1863, ALPL; John A. Griffen Diary, June 30, 1863, ALPL; William Russell to Spencer, June 15, 1863, Russell Family Papers, ALPL.

62. Stillwell, *The Story of a Common Soldier*, 143.

63. Levi W. Bennett Diary, July 2, 1863, MDAH; S. C. Jones, *Reminiscences of the Twenty-second Iowa Volunteer Infantry, Giving Its Organization, Marches, Skirmishes,*

Battles, and Sieges, as Taken from the Diary of Lieutenant S. C. Jones of Company A (Iowa City: n.p., 1907), 40; Samuel to Robert Crouse, May 25, 1863, Robert Crouse Letters, UMB; Francis Bickett to Isabella, May 29, 1863, Francis Bickett Papers, UGA.

64. William Murray Diary, June 24, 1863, Journals/Letters/Diaries Series, VICK; James B. Owen to father, May 27, 1863, James B. Owen Letters, TSLA; Joseph Waite Diary, June 24, 1863, IHS; John A. Griffen Diary, June 30 and July 1, 1863, ALPL; John G. Jones to parents, June 17, 1863, John G. Jones Papers, LC; Samuel Eells to unknown, June 26, 1863, Samuel H. Eells Papers, LC; George C. Churcheus Diary, June 25, 1863, OHS; Post, ed., *Soldiers' Letters*, 221.

65. Ambrose, ed., "A Wisconsin Boy at Vicksburg," 9; John W. Griffith Diary, June 17, 1863, OHS; J. Carroll Harriss to Valery, June 30, 1863, Jordan C. Harriss Papers, NC; "Letters from the Trenches," July 31, 1902, *National Tribune*; James C. Mahan, *Memoirs of James Curtis Mahan* (Lincoln, NE: Franklin Press, 1919), 129; Jones, *Reminiscences of the Twenty-second Iowa*, 41.

66. Nicholas Miller Memoir, undated, OCM, 14; Charles Buckingham to mother, July 1, 1863, Charles H. Buckingham Papers, IHS; Patrick, ed., *Three Years with Wallace's Zouaves*, 145; Cyrus Hussey Diary, June 18, 1863, UTO.

67. Carlos Colby to sister, June 9, 1863, Carlos W. Colby Papers, NL; George C. Churcheus Diary, July 3, 1863, OHS.

68. Cynthia Bush to Edwin Bush, June 1, 1863, Bush Family Collection, AM; "Latest From Vicksburg," May 26, 1863, Alexandria (VA) *Gazette*; "Most Important From Vicksburg," May 26, 1863, Washington (DC) *Evening Star*; George C. Churcheus Diary, June 17, 1863, OHS; Unknown to friends, June 2, 1863, Dixon and Jordan Family Papers, KCPL; George Remley to Howard, June 6, 1863, Remley Family Papers, NC.

69. Henry Schmidt to wife, May 24, 1863, Schmidt Family Papers, FHS; E. H. Ingraham to aunt, May 29, 1863, E. H. and D. G. Ingraham Letters, ALPL; Henry Franks to sister, June 15, 1863, Henry W. Franks Letters, OHS.

70. John McGraw to family, May 28, 1863, John S. McGraw Papers, ISL; Samuel D. Lougheed to wife, June 9, 1863, Samuel D. Lougheed Letters, ALPL; George H. Woodruff, *Fifteen Years Ago, Or The Patriotism of Will County* (Joliet, IL: Joliet Republican Book and Job Steam Printing House, 1876), 126; George M. Shearer Diary, June 21, 1863, UIA.

71. John W. Griffith Diary, June 29, 1863, OHS; Clark, ed., *Downing's Civil War Diary*, 120; J. M. Hobbs Diary, June 9, 1863, 33rd Illinois File, VICK; Will Henderson to friend, July 11, 1863, 17th Illinois File, VICK.

72. "In the Trenches Before Vicksburg," November 15, 1900, *National Tribune*; Don Scott to unknown, June 28, 1863, Scott Family Papers, UNC; Bela T. St. John to father, June 21, 1863, Bela T. St. John Papers, LOC.

73. Henry J. Seaman Diary, June 2, 1863, CWTI, USAHEC; R. W. Burt to wife, June 9, 1863, Richard W. Burt Papers, SHSMC; J. Carroll Harriss to Valery, June 30, 1863, Jordan C. Harriss Papers, NC; George Deal letter fragment, June 1863, George Deal Papers, NL; Burt Scott to Edward Scott, July 10, 1863, Burt Scott Papers, IHS; David Shockley to family, June 5, 1863, David Shockley Papers, IHS.

74. J. Carroll Harriss to Valery, June 4, 1863, Jordan C. Harriss Papers, NC; Samuel Gordon to wife, June 12 and 24, 1863, Samuel Gordon Papers, ALPL; E. L. Chatfield to parents, May 27, 1863, Edward L. Chatfield Papers, HL; S. Wright to brother, June 22, 1863, Allen G. Wright Papers, UMB; Calvin Ainsworth Diary, May 23, 1863, UMB; *History of the 37th Regiment, O. V. V. I., Furnished by Comrades at the Ninth Reunion Held at St. Mary's, Ohio, Tuesday and Wednesday, September 10 and 11, 1889* (Toledo, OH: Montgomery and Vrooman, 1890), 22.

75. Eli Todd to brother, July 19, 1863, Eli J. Todd Papers, OHS; Thomas B. Beggs to aunt, June 19, 1863, Thomas Benson Beggs Letters, ALPL; John Zimmerman to Sarah Dykes, June 28, 1863, Dykes Family Letters, OHS.

76. Matthew Goodrich to father, May 24, 1863, Matthew Goodrich Papers, FHS; David McKinney to sister, June 21, 1863, David McKinney Papers, FHS; Thomas Kirkpatrick Mitchell Diary, July 1, 1863, AU; John A. Higgins to wife, June 18, 1863, John A. Higgins Papers, ALPL; Elliott Morrow to uncle, June 30, 1863, Elliott Morrow Papers, OHS; William Overbey to Anna, July 2, 1863, William Overbey File, Civil War Miscellany, IHS; Henry Oman to wife, June 15, 1863, Henry Oman Papers, UNC.

77. Samuel D. Lougheed to wife, June 23, 1863, Samuel D. Lougheed Letters, ALPL.

78. John A. Higgins to wife, June 10, 1863, John A. Higgins Papers, ALPL; John L. Harris to mother, June 15, 1863, John L. Harris Correspondence, ALPL; Robert Jameson to sister, June 21, 1863, Robert E. Jameson Papers, LC.

79. George Carrington Diary, June 2, 1863, CHM; Charles H. Brush to mother, June 14, 1863, Daniel H. Brush Papers, ALPL; Oldroyd, *A Soldier's Story*, 61; Edwin Loosley to daughters, July 3, 1863, Edwin A. Loosley Papers, SIU.

80. Cable, ed., "A Woman's Diary of the Siege of Vicksburg," 771, copy of Miller Diary in OCM; Ambrose, ed., "A Wisconsin Boy at Vicksburg," 5, 7; "Vicksburg by Moonlight," June 22, 1863, Lowell (MA) *Daily Citizen and News*, copy in Siege of Vicksburg Accounts Confederate Subject File, MDAH.

81. Silas T. Trowbridge, *Autobiography of Silas Thompson Trowbridge, M.D.* (N.p.: n.p., 1872), 148, reprinted by Southern Illinois University Press, 2004; J. H. Pepper Diary, June 25, 1863, MDAH.

82. Loughborough, *My Cave Life in Vicksburg*, 110; Emma Balfour Diary, May 26, 1863, Journals/Letters/Diaries Series, VICK.

83. Hander "Excerpts from the Hander Diary," 146; William L. Foster to wife, June 20, 1863, UA; Claudius W. Sears Diary, May 19, 1863, MDAH.

84. "Mrs. M. L. Powell Tells of Cave Life During War," undated, Siege of Vicksburg Cave Life Subject File, MDAH; Cable, ed., "A Woman's Diary of the Siege of Vicksburg," 771; "A Child at the Siege of Vicksburg," Vicksburg *Post Herald*, September 27, 1936.

85. Hoehling, *Vicksburg*, 158, 252, 262; Abrams, *A Full and Detailed History*, 47; Loughborough, *My Cave Life in Vicksburg*, 79, 92; John C. Taylor Diary, June 22, 1863, UVA.

86. Loughborough, *My Cave Life in Vicksburg*, 92; C. H. Twining to Kate, June 9, 1863, Moody Family Papers, MHS.

87. H. C. Tupper to Bowen, June 9, 1863, Letters and Telegrams Sent, Department

of Mississippi and East Louisiana, 1863, RG 109, Chapter II, Vol. 60, NARA; Charles H. Brush to mother, June 14, 1863, Daniel H. Brush Papers, ALPL; Thomas Taylor to Mjaor Memminger, June 21, 1863, John C. Pemberton Papers, RG 109, E 131, NARA; Hoehling, *Vicksburg*, 223–224; Rowland Chambers Diary, May 25 and June 8–10, 13–14, 16–19, and 23, 1863, LSU.

88. Simon, ed., *PUSG*, 8:371, 384; *OR*, 24(1):96.

89. *OR*, 24(2):332.

90. *OR*, 24(2):338–339; Rowland Chambers Diary, May 26, 1863, LSU.

91. Richard and Richard, *The Defense of Vicksburg*, 178; J. H. Pepper Diary, June 3, 1863, MDAH; Joseph D. Alison Diary, June 2, 1863, MDAH; Anne to Emma, June/July 1863, Shannon-Crutcher Family Papers, MDAH; John C. Taylor Diary, June 1, 1863, UVA; Moore, ed., *The Rebellion Record*, 168; Loughborough, *My Cave Life in Vicksburg*, 69; Rowland Chambers Diary, June 2, 1863, LSU.

92. Chambers, "My Journal," 275; Joseph Stockton Diary, June 2, 1863, ALPL; Ambrose, ed., "A Wisconsin Boy at Vicksburg," 7; Henry Kircher Diary, June 2, 1863, Engelmann-Kircher Family Papers, ALPL; George Ditto Diary, June 2, 1863, ALPL; Aurelius L. Voorhis Diary, June 1, 1863, IHS; Louis W. Knobe Diary, June 2, 1863, ISL.

93. Moore, ed., *The Rebellion Record*, 170; James L. Power Diary, June 21, 1863, MDAH; L. McRae. Bell, "A Girl's Experience in the Siege of Vicksburg," *Harper's Weekly*, June 8, 1912, 13; Reed, "A Woman's Experiences During the Siege of Vicksburg," 925; Charles Affeld Diary, June 25, 1863, Journals/Diaries/Letters Series, VICK; John C. Taylor Diary, June 1, 1863, UVA.

94. John Merrilees Diary, May 29, 1863, CHM; Hoehling, *Vicksburg*, 95; Richard and Richard, *The Defense of Vicksburg*, 201; Emma Balfour Diary, May 24, 1863, Journals/Letters/Diaries Series, VICK; "Mrs. M. L. Powell Tells of Cave Life During War," undated, Siege of Vicksburg Cave Life Subject File, MDAH.

95. Francis R. Baker Diary, June 14–16, 1863, ALPL; William M. Reid Diary, May 29, 1863, ALPL.

96. John Ritter to Margarett, June 8, 1863, John A. Ritter Papers, NC.

97. *OR*, 24(2):216; Anne to Emma, June/July 1863, Shannon-Crutcher Family Papers, MDAH.

98. Sarah F. Bigelow to "Mrs. Woodson," June 16, 1863, Samuel Bassett Hamacker Letters, SHSMC; *OR*, 52(1):65; Simon, ed., *PUSG*, 8:397–398.

99. William Taylor to Jane, June 18, 1863, William Taylor Correspondence, WM; W. A. Rorer to Susan, June 13, 1863, W. A. Rorer Letters, DU; Chase Dickinson to friends, June 6, 1863, Chase Hall Dickinson Papers, NL; Ephraim Dawes to Luce, June 28, 1863, Ephraim C. Dawes Papers, NL.

100. *OR*, 52(1):65. For a Union-focused Vicksburg history with emphasis on the change the campaign wrought on African Americans, see Donald L. Miller, *Vicksburg: Grant's Campaign That Broke the Confederacy* (New York: Simon and Shuster, 2019).

101. Samuel S. Irwin Diary, June 6, 1863, ALPL; John Ritter to Margaret, June 8, 1863, John A. Ritter Papers, NC; Bennett Grigsby to family, May 18, 1863, Bennett Grigsby Papers, IHS.

102. Charles Dana Miller Memoir, undated, Journals/Letters/Diaries Series, VICK, 51.

103. Loughborough, *My Cave Life in Vicksburg*, 63, 91; J. H. Pepper Diary, June 25, 1863, MDAH; William R. Clack Diary, June 4, 1863, TSLA.

104. Joseph Waite Diary, June 21, 1863, IHS; George M. Rogers Diary, June 28–29, 1863, ISL.

105. E. H. Ingraham to aunt, June 15, 1863, E. H. and D. G. Ingraham Letters, ALPL; Thomas Lyons Diary, May 28, 1863, LOC.

106. Force, "Personal Recollections of the Vicksburg Campaign," 307; Charles Dana Miller Memoir, undated, Journals/Letters/Diaries Series, VICK, 52–53.

107. Charles Dana Miller Memoir, undated, Journals/Letters/Diaries Series, VICK, 53–54.

108. C. M. Wildermuth to mother, May 28, 1863, Wildermuth Family Letters, UT; Sarah McLean to son, June 25, 1863, Edgar McLean Papers, NL; Jane Smith to brother, May 25, 1863, David Smith Papers, CWD, USAHEC.

109. J. R. Grassmere to friend, May 27, 1863, Andrew McCornack Letters, Sword Collection, USAHEC.

CHAPTER 9. "CAN'T OUR GOVERNMENT SEND US RELIEF?"

1. Theodore D. Fisher Diary, June 14, 1863, Journals/Letters/Diaries Series, VICK; *OR*, 52(2):493–498; William L. Foster to wife, June 20, 1863, UA; William Brotherton to Levy Brotherton, May 18, 1863, William Brotherton Papers, EU; Hoehling, *Vicksburg*, 246.

2. William L. Foster to wife, June 20, 1863, UA; Richard and Richard, *The Defense of Vicksburg*, 216.

3. William L. Foster to wife, June 20, 1863, UA; Hander "Excerpts from the Hander Diary," 144; William L. Faulk Diary, May 28, 1863, OCM; Anne to Emma, June/July 1863, Shannon-Crutcher Family Papers, MDAH; M. R. Banner to wife, June 22, 1863, Banner Family History, OCM.

4. Chambers, "My Journal," 274, 276; William L. Foster to wife, June 20, 1863, UA.

5. W. R. McRory Diary, June 7, 13, 16, 21, 24, 27, 28, and July 2, 1863, Journals/Letters/Diaries Series, VICK.

6. J. H. Pepper Diary, June 21, 1863, MDAH; Unknown to unknown, June 8, 1863, Henry Ginder Papers, TU; John C. Taylor Diary, May 26 and 29, 1863, UVA.

7. Chambers, "My Journal," 274; Richard and Richard, *The Defense of Vicksburg*, 210; Hander "Excerpts from the Hander Diary," 145–146.

8. Thomas Loudon to father, June 18, 1863, Thomas J. Loudon Letter, OHS; Cotton, ed., *From the Pen of a She-Rebel*, 18; John L. Harris to mother, June 15, 1863, John L. Harris Correspondence, ALPL; Simon, ed., *PUSG*, 8:379.

9. *OR*, 24(3):964; Anne to Emma, June/July 1863, Shannon-Crutcher Family Papers, MDAH.

10. Cadwallader, *Three Years with Grant*, 100; Anne to Emma, June/July 1863, Shannon-Crutcher Family Papers, MDAH.

11. Dana, *Recollections of the Civil War*, 79–80.

12. Jacob B. Wilkin, "Vicksburg," in *Military Essays and Recollections: Papers Read Before the Commandery of the State of Illinois, Military Order of the Loyal Legion of the United States, Volume 4* (Chicago: Cozzens and Beaton Company, 1907), 233–234.

13. Dana, *Recollections of the Civil War*, 61–62; Wilkin, "Vicksburg," 235–237.

14. Simon, ed., *PUSG*, 8:376.

15. W. R. Marshall, "Reminiscences of General U. S. Grant," in *Glimpses of the Nation's Struggle: A Series of Papers Read Before the Minnesota Commandery of the Loyal Legion of the United States* (St. Paul: St. Paul Book and Stationary Company, 1887), 104–105 (89–106); Dana, *Recollections of the Civil War*, 61–62; Wilson, "A Staff Officer's Journal of the Vicksburg Campaign, April 30 to July 4, 1863," 266–273. For Rawlins, see Allen J. Ottens, *General John A. Rawlins: No Ordinary Man* (Bloomington: Indiana University Press, 2021).

16. Albert D. Richardson, *A Personal History of Ulysses S. Grant* (Hartford, CT: American Publishing Company, 1868), 326; *OR*, 24(1):59; Cadwallader, *Three Years with Grant*, 99; Fred Grant Memoir, undated, USGPL, 32; Flood, *Grant and Sherman*, 171; Smith, *The Decision Was Always My Own*, 173.

17. Thomas Taylor to W. T. Rigby, March 19, 1903, 47th Ohio File, VICK; *The Story of the Fifty-fifth Regiment Illinois Volunteer Infantry in the Civil War, 1861–1865*, 249; Gilbert Young to mother, May 28, 1863, Gilbert N. Young Letters, Journals/Letters/Diaries Series, VICK; Timothy C. Young Diary, May 28, 1863, Journals/Letters/Diaries Series, VICK.

18. Wilkin, "Vicksburg," 233.

19. George D. Kellogg to mother, May 25, 1863, 23rd Wisconsin File, VICK; Gilbert Young to mother, May 28, 1863, Gilbert N. Young Letters, Journals/Letters/Diaries Series, VICK; Timothy C. Young Diary, May 28, 1863, Journals/Letters/Diaries Series, VICK.

20. Anthony B. Burton Diary, June 17, 1863, ALPL; Patrick, ed., *Three Years with Wallace's Zouaves*, 141; Crummer, *With Grant at Fort Donelson, Shiloh and Vicksburg*, 128; Thomas Christie to brother, June 5, 1863, James C. Christie and Family Papers, MNHS.

21. James Harrison Wilson, *Under the Old Flag: Recollections of Military Operations in the War for the Union, the Spanish War The Boxer Rebellion, Etc.*, 2 vols. (New York: D. Appleton and Co., 1912), 211–212.

22. Simon, ed., *PUSG*, 8:332, 376–377; Smith, *The Decision Was Always My Own*, 188; Cotton, ed., *From the Pen of a She-Rebel*, 18; Pratt, ed., "Civil War Letters of Brigadier-General William Ward Orme, 1862–1866," 287; Fred Grant Memoir, undated, USGPL, 13, 31, published as Frederick D. Grant, "A Boy's Experience at Vicksburg," *Personal Recollections of the War of the Rebellion: Addresses Delivered before the Commandery of the State of New York, Military Order of the Loyal Legion of the United States*, A. Noel Blakeman, ed. (New York: G. P. Putnam's Sons, 1907), 86–100, and "General

Fred Grant's Scare at Vicksburg," April 27, 1912, *The Literary Digest*; Simon, ed., *PUSG*, 8:439.

23. *OR*, 24(1):131.

24. Stillwell, *The Story of a Common Soldier*, 141; Richard and Richard, *The Defense of Vicksburg*, 199; *OR*, 24(1):136; C. H. Twining to Kate, June 9, 1863, Moody Family Papers, MHS.

25. *OR*, 24(1):131, 133; Stewart Bruce Terry Diary, July 4, 1863, KHS.

26. *OR*, 24(1):131; Marden Sabin Memoirs, undated, ISL, 20–21.

27. *OR*, 24(1):131; Anne to Emma, June/July 1863, Shannon-Crutcher Family Papers, MDAH.

28. *OR*, 24(1):132, 137; Simon, ed., *PUSG*, 8:336, 371; Hoehling, *Vicksburg*, 146; J. P. Van Nest to wife, June 4, 1863, Joseph P. Van Nest Papers, FHS; Edmund Newsome Diary, May 31, 1863, MDAH; Charles Affeld Diary, June 8, 1863, Journals/Diaries/Letters Series, VICK.

29. "In the Trenches Before Vicksburg," November 15, 1900, *National Tribune*; William B. Feis, "The War of Spies and Supplies: Grant and Grenville M. Dodge in the West, 1862–1864," in *Grant's Lieutenants: From Cairo to Vicksburg*, Steven E. Woodworth, ed. (Lawrence: University Press of Kansas, 2001), 197.

30. *OR* 24(1):39–40. For ciphers and military telegrams, see the Thomas T. Eckert Papers, HL.

31. Simon, ed., *PUSG*, 8:332, 376.

32. John Y. Simon, ed., *The Personal Memoirs of Julia Dent Grant [Mrs. Ulysses S. Grant]* (New York: G. P. Putnam's Sons, 1975), 113; Simon, ed., *PUSG*, 8:332, 376–377, 445; Fred Grant Memoir, undated, USGPL, 31.

33. Simon, ed., *PUSG*, 8:377, 445.

34. Simon, *PUSG*, 8:375–376.

35. *OR*, 24(1):94.

36. *OR*, 24(3):952–953.

37. *OR*, 24(3):961, 964.

38. *SOR*, 4:304–305.

39. *OR*, 24(3):959.

40. *OR*, 24(1):199, 227.

41. *OR*, 24(3):953, 961, 963; John C. Taylor Diary, June 13, 1863, UVA.

42. *OR*, 24(3):399, 404; John A. Buckner to John Breckinridge, June 16, 1863, "Letters, Telegrams, and Orders Received and Sent — General Breckinridge's Command, December 1861–November 1863," RG 109, Chapter II, Vol. 311, NARA, 102.

43. *OR*, 24(3):960–961.

44. *OR*, 24(3):953, 955–956, 959–962, 964–965, W. A. Rorer to Susan, June 13, 1863, W. A. Rorer Letters, DU, copy in MDAH.

45. *OR*, 24(3):954; *OR*, 24(1):215, 225–226; *OR*, 52(2):493–494.

46. *OR*, 24(3):963.

47. *OR*, 24(3):958, 961–962; *OR*, 24(1):195; *OR*, 52(2):503.

48. *OR*, 24(3):953, 964.

49. *OR*, 24(1):195, 227.

50. *OR* 24(1):42; Brown, *History of the Fourth Regiment of Minnesota Infantry*, 222; Philip C. Bonney to wife, June 18, 1863, Philip C. Bonney Papers, ALPL; John Wallace to brother, June 26, 1863, John M. Wallace Papers, CHM.

51. *OR*, 24(3):391–392; Simon, ed., *PUSG*, 8:336; Dana, *Recollections of the Civil War*, 67; Cyrus Winters Diary, June 9, 1863, ALPL; Charles Affeld Diary, June 8, 1863, Journals/Diaries/Letters Series, VICK.

52. *OR*, 24(3):391; Special Orders 154, June 8, 1863, Cadwallader C. Washburn Papers, RG 94, E 159, NARA.

53. Ezra J. Warner, *Generals in Blue: Lives of the Union Commanders* (Baton Rouge: Louisiana State University Press), 1964, 542–543; Ephraim Dawes to Kate, June 14, 1863, Ephraim C. Dawes Papers, NL.

54. *OR*, 24(3):392; *OR*, 24(1):94, 100; *OR*, 24(2):222; Simon, ed., *PUSG*, 8:359–360; Levi W. Bennett Diary, July 1, 1863, MDAH; Channing Richards Diary, June 13, 1863, FHS; Charles Affeld Diary, June 9, 1863, Journals/Diaries/Letters Series, VICK.

55. *OR*, 24(3):392; *OR*, 24(1):94, 100; *OR*, 24(2):222; Simon, ed., *PUSG*, 8:359–360; Soman and Byrne, eds., *A Jewish Colonel in the Civil War*, 288, 291, 293; Adolph Engelmann to sister, June 14, 1863, Engelmann-Kircher Family Papers, ALPL; Levi W. Bennett Diary, July 1, 1863, MDAH; Channing Richards Diary, June 13, 1863, FHS; Charles Affeld Diary, June 9, 1863, Journals/Diaries/Letters Series, VICK.

56. *OR*, 24(3):396; Pinckney Skilton Cone Diary, June 7, 1863, ALPL.

57. *OR*, 24(3):398.

58. *OR*, 24(3):392, 401; *OR*, 24(1):98; D. R. Lucas, *New History of the 99th Indiana Infantry Containing Official Reports, Anecdotes, Incidents, Biographies and Complete Rolls* (Rockford, IL: Horner Printing Co., 1900), 62; Cyrus Winters Diary, June 13–19, 1863, ALPL; Adolph Engelmann to wife, June 16, 1863, Engelmann-Kircher Family Papers, ALPL; Phillip Roesch Diary, June 6, 1863, OCM; Samuel Eells to unknown, June 21, 1863, Samuel H. Eells Papers, LC; Andrew Bush to Mary, June 29, 1863, Andrew Bush Letters, Journals/Diaries/Letters Series, VICK; John M. Sullivan to wife, June 10 and 14, 1863, John M. Sullivan Papers, OHS; Marden Sabin Memoirs, undated, ISL, 19.

59. *OR*, 24(3):392, 401; *OR*, 24(1):98; Henry H. Wright, *A History of the Sixth Iowa Infantry* (Iowa City: State Historical Society of Iowa, 1923), 196; Cyrus Winters Diary, June 13–19, 1863, ALPL; Adolph Engelmann to wife, June 16, 1863, Engelmann-Kircher Family Papers, ALPL; Phillip Roesch Diary, June 6, 1863, OCM; Samuel Eells to unknown, June 21, 1863, Samuel H. Eells Papers, LC; Andrew Bush to Mary, June 29, 1863, Andrew Bush Letters, Journals/Diaries/Letters Series, VICK; John M. Sullivan to wife, June 10 and 14, 1863, John M. Sullivan Papers, OHS; Marden Sabin Memoirs, undated, ISL, 19.

60. *OR*, 24(3):392; *OR*, 24(2):318; Elder III, ed., *A Damned Iowa Greyhound*, 69; J. Irvine Dungan, *History of the Nineteenth Regiment Iowa Volunteer Infantry* (Davenport, IA: Luse and Griggs, 1865), 76.

61. *OR*, 24(3):401; *OR*, 24(1):96–97; *OR*, 24(2):318–319, 341; Kenneth P. Williams, *Grant Rises in the West: From Iuka to Vicksburg, 1862–1863* (Lincoln: University of

Nebraska Press, 1997), 407; Anthony B. Burton Diary, June 14, 1863, ALPL; Dana, *Recollections of the Civil War*, 70, 87–88; Pratt, ed., "Civil War Letters of Brigadier-General William Ward Orme, 1862–1866," 276; Charles H. Brush to mother, June 14, 1863, Daniel H. Brush Papers, ALPL; Joseph Waite Diary, June 15, 1863, IHS.

62. *OR*, 24(3):401; *OR*, 24(1):96–97; *OR*, 24(2):318–319, 341; Anthony B. Burton Diary, June 14, 1863, ALPL; Pratt, ed., "Civil War Letters of Brigadier-General William Ward Orme, 1862–1866," 276; Charles H. Brush to mother, June 14, 1863, Daniel H. Brush Papers, ALPL; Joseph Waite Diary, June 15, 1863, IHS.

63. *OR*, 24(2):342, 356; Catton, *Grant Moves South*, 457.

64. *OR*, 24(3):396, 401; Samuel Eells to unknown, June 21, 1863, Samuel H. Eells Papers, LC; John Merrilees Diary, June 5, 1863, CHM.

65. *OR*, 24(3):397; *OR*, 24(1):57.

66. Ephraim Dawes to Kate, June 14, 1863, Ephraim C. Dawes Papers, NL.

67. *OR*, 24(2):222.

68. *OR*, 24(3):389, 397, 399–400.

69. *OR*, 24(3):389, 391, 405.

70. *OR*, 24(3):393–394, 403; *OR*, 52(1):360, *OR*, 52(2):492, 494.

71. *OR*, 24(3):393–394, 403; *OR*, 52(1):360, *OR*, 52(2):492, 494.

72. *OR*, 24(3):402, 405; Bearss, *The Vicksburg Campaign*, 3:1081.

73. *OR*, 24(3):402–403; George M. Lucas Diary, June 21, 1863, ALPL.

74. *OR*, 24(3):409–410.

75. *OR*, 24(3):402–403, 411.

76. *OR*, 24(3):402–403.

77. *OR*, 24(3):409; David Poak to sister, June 12, 1863, David W. Poak Papers, ALPL.

Chapter 10. "I Should Have Relieved Him Long Since"

1. Benjamin Wiley to wife, June 2, 1863, Wiley Collection, John A. Logan Museum; William L. Foster to wife, June 20, 1863, UA. For a medical history of the Vicksburg Campaign, see Lindsay Rae Smith Privette, "'Fightin' Johnnies, Fevers, and Mosquitoes': A Medical History of the Vicksburg Campaign" (PhD diss., University of Alabama, 2018)

2. William L. Foster to wife, June 20, 1863, UA; Theodore D. Fisher Diary, June 10, 1863, Journals/Letters/Diaries Series, VICK; John A. Leavy Diary, June 19, 1863, Journals/Letters/Diaries Series, VICK, copy in OCM; Joseph D. Alison Diary, June 10, 1863, MDAH; *OR*, 24(2):423.

3. Simon, ed., *PUSG*, 8:356–357.

4. Pryce, *Vanishing Footprints*, 136; George Woodard to Gene Burnett, June 11, 1863, George Woodard and Gene Smith Letters, UA; Winschel, ed., *The Civil War Diary of a Common Soldier*, 54.

5. Don Pardee to unknown, May 27, 1863, Don A. Pardee Papers, TU; T. B. Riley to sister, November 22, 1876, T. B. Riley Papers, IHS; *OR*, 24(3):966, 969, 975; General Order 35, n.d., Letters Sent—Medical Department 17th Corps, E 6225, RG 393, NARA;

Simon, ed., *PUSG*, 8:367; William Voglison Memo, June 24, 1864, Frederick Steele Papers, SU; Joseph C. Gordon Diary, June 25, 1863, OCM.

　6. Solomon K. Lynn to father, May 24, 1863, Lynn Family Papers, FHS; Cotton, ed., *From the Pen of a She-Rebel*, 14; Pryce, *Vanishing Footprints*, 140; W. H. Nugen to sister, June 23, 1863, William H. Nugen Letters, DU.

　7. Hoehling, *Vicksburg*, 111.

　8. Hoehling, *Vicksburg*, 113.

　9. "Military History of Captain Thomas Sewell," 1889, DU; Hiram P. Howe to parents, June 8, 1863, Hiram P. Howe Papers, LOC; Andrew McCornack to family, May 24, 1863, NC; John M. Roberts Memoir, undated, IHS, 39; Gilbert Granderson Diary, May 19 and June 16, 1863, HCWRT, USAHEC; Frank McGregor to Susie, June 3, 1863, Frank McGregor Papers, USAHEC; William A. Sypher Diary, June 28, 1863, CHM.

　10. Charles H. Brush to mother, June 24, 1863, Daniel H. Brush Papers, ALPL; For life in the hospitals near Vicksburg, see the George W. Russell Letters, ALPL; William J. Pittenger Diary, June 12, 1863, VT; Gould D. Molineaux Diary, August 2, 1863, Augustana College.

　11. Charles Vanamburg to father, July 4, 1863, Vanamburg Family Papers, Vanamburg Collection, USAHEC; James Palmer Diary, June 17, 1863, MDAH, 10–11.

　12. *OR*, 24(3):419; *OR*, 24(2):210–211.

　13. A. R. Dyson to wife, June 8, 1863, Dyson-Bell-Sans Souci Papers State Historical Society of Missouri–St. Louis; Oldroyd, *A Soldier's Story*, 54; John Sheriff to parents, June 11, 1863, John Sheriff Family Papers, ALPL; William Thomson to Ruffin, June 9, 1863, Ruffin Thomson Papers, UNC; Leonard Loomis to Elizabeth, May 24, 1863, Leonard Loomis Letters, Douwe B. Yntema Collection, AM.

　14. Adolph Engelmann to wife, June 22, 26, and 30, 1863, Engelmann-Kircher Family Papers, ALPL.

　15. James Slack to Ann, June 13, 1863, James R. Slack Papers, ISL; Joseph Lester to family, June 21, 1863, Joseph Lester Papers, LOC; W. Grayum to Harriet, June 5, 1863, 4th West Virginia File, VICK; Adoniram Withrow to Lib, June 3, 1863, Adoniram J. Withrow Papers, UNC; Henry Franks to sister, June 15, 1863, Henry W. Franks Letters, OHS; *History of the Thirty-sixth Regiment Massachusetts Volunteers, 1862–1865*, 55.

　16. Samuel Eells to unknown, June 26, 1863, Samuel H. Eells Papers, LC; Isaac Vanderwarker Diary, June 6, 1863, CWD, USAHEC; William M. Reid Diary, June 4 and 5, 1863, ALPL; E. H. Ingraham to aunt, May 29 and June 4, 1863, E. H. and D. G. Ingraham Letters, ALPL.

　17. Stone, *Memoir of George Boardman Boomer*, 260; Albert Chipman to wife, June 6 and 8, 1863, Albert Chipman Papers, ALPL.

　18. Hoehling, *Vicksburg*, 259; *The Story of the Fifty-fifth Regiment Illinois Volunteer Infantry in the Civil War, 1861–1865*, 247; Edwin Obriham to family, June 14, 1863, Edward O. Obriham Letters, Journals/Letters/Diaries Series, VICK.

　19. William L. Roberts Diary, May 30, 1863, ADAH; William L. Foster to wife, June 20, 1863, UA; Post surgeon to Sir, June 26, 1863, John C. Pemberton Papers, RG 109, E 131, NARA; Rowland Chambers Diary, June 1, 1863, LSU; R. W. Memminger to Surgeon

Bryan, June 3, W. H. McCardle to Captain Jones, June 27, and J. C. Taylor to Samuel Lockett, July 1, 1863, Letters and Telegrams Sent, Department of Mississippi and East Louisiana, 1863, RG 109, Chapter II, Vol. 60, NARA.

20. Tunnard, *A Southern Record*, 273; William L. Foster to wife, June 20, 1863, UA.

21. William L. Foster to wife, June 20, 1863, UA; Theodore D. Fisher Diary, June 10, 1863, Journals/Letters/Diaries Series, VICK; John A. Leavy Diary, June 19, 1863, Journals/Letters/Diaries Series, VICK; Joseph D. Alison Diary, June 10, 1863, MDAH; *OR*, 24(2):423.

22. S. D. Lee to major, June 25, 1863 and H. M. Compton to L. W. Matthews, June 19, 1863, John C. Pemberton Papers, RG 109, E 131, NARA; Terry G. Scriber, *Twenty-seventh Louisiana Volunteer Infantry* (Gretna, LA: Pelican Publishing Company, 2006), 153; W. H. McCardle to E. W. Bryan and to S. D. Lee, June 7, J. C. Taylor to Thomas Taylor, June 10, and W. H. McCardle to Surgeon Bryan, June 26, 1863, Letters and Telegrams Sent, Department of Mississippi and East Louisiana, 1863, RG 109, Chapter II, Vol. 60, NARA.

23. William L. Foster to wife, June 20, 1863, UA.

24. Rowland Chambers Diary, May 23–24, 1863, LSU; Enos Pierson, *Proceedings of Eleven Reunions Held by the 16th Regiment, O. V. I., Including Roll of Honor, Roster of the Survivors of the Regiment, Statistics, &c., &c.* (Millersburg, OH: Republican Steam Press, 1887), 29.

25. John T. Appler Diary, May 24, 1863, MHS; Mupan to family, June 16, 1863, 5th Iowa File, VICK; Rev. Ben E. Bounds Memoirs, 1911, Journals/Letters/Diaries File, VICK.

26. *OR*, 24(3):404; *OR*, 24(2):570; Kenneth P. Williams, *Grant Rises in the West: From Iuka to Vicksburg, 1862–1863* (Lincoln: University of Nebraska Press, 1997), 408; Marszalek et al., eds., *The Personal Memoirs of Ulysses S. Grant*, 378; William H. Osborne, *The History of the Twenty-ninth Regiment of Massachusetts Volunteer Infantry in the Late War of the Rebellion* (Boston: Albert J. Wright, Printer, 1877), 238; George W. Harwood to friends, June 8 and 13, 1863, George W. Harwood Letters, OCM; Alphonso Crane to father, June 15, 1863, and Alphonso Crane to sister, July 3, 1863, Alphonso Crane Letters, Grace Dunham Collection, AM; William F. Draper to wife, June 4, 5, and 10, 1863, William F. Draper Papers, LC.

27. *OR*, 24(3):404; *OR*, 24(2):570; Williams, *Grant Rises in the West*, 408; Marszalek et al., eds., *The Personal Memoirs of Ulysses S. Grant*, 378; Osborne, *The History of the Twenty-ninth Regiment of Massachusetts Volunteer Infantry*, 238; George W. Harwood to friends, June 8 and 13, 1863, George W. Harwood Letters, OCM; Alphonso Crane to father, June 15, 1863, and Alphonso Crane to sister, July 3, 1863, Alphonso Crane Letters, Grace Dunham Collection, AM; William F. Draper to wife, June 4, 5, and 10, 1863, William F. Draper Papers, LC; Robert Jameson to sister, June 17, 1863, Robert E. Jameson Papers, LC.

28. *OR*, 24(3):396–397, 401; *OR*, 52(2):495; *History of the Thirty-sixth Regiment Massachusetts Volunteers*, 49; *History of the Thirty-fifth Regiment Massachusetts*

Volunteers, 1862–1865. With a Roster (Boston: Mills, Knight & Co., 1884), 132; William F. Draper to wife, June 16, 1863, William F. Draper Papers, LC.

29. *OR*, 24(3):403–404, 409–410; *OR*, 24(1):97; Anthony B. Burton Diary, June 18, 1863, ALPL.

30. *OR*, 24(3):409–410; *OR*, 24(1):100; James Wilson to John Rawlins, June 9, 1863, Frank A. Irvin Papers, California State University Northridge.

31. Todd, *The Seventy-ninth Highlanders*, 303; William Taylor to Jane, June 16 and 18 and July 1, 1863, William Taylor Correspondence, WM; Jackman, *History of the Sixth New Hampshire Regiment*, 167; *OR*, 24(3):418; Kountz, *Record of the Organizations*, 5; *History of the Thirty-sixth Regiment Massachusetts Volunteers*, 51; Mary Ellen Hoover, Elin Williams Neiterman, and E. Dianne James, eds., *From Your Loving Son: Civil War Correspondence and Diaries of Private George F. Moore and His Family* (Bloomington, IN: IUniverse, 2011), 197; William Barnard to father, June 19, 1863, William A. Barnard Collection, AM; Orville Babcock Diary, June 19, 1863, USGPL; Brown, *History of the Fourth Regiment of Minnesota*, 226; Lewis Crater, *History of the Fiftieth Regiment Penna. Vet. Vols., 1861–1865* (Reading, PA: Coleman Printing House, 1884), 41; William F. Draper to wife, June 15, 1863, William F. Draper Papers, LC; Robert Jameson to sister, June 17, 1863, Robert E. Jameson Papers, LC; Charles Affeld Diary, June 14, 1863, Journals/Diaries/Letters Series, VICK.

32. *OR*, 24(3):418; Kountz, *Record of the Organizations*, 5; *History of the Thirty-sixth Regiment Massachusetts Volunteers*, 51; Hoover, Neiterman, and James, eds., *From Your Loving Son*, 197; William Barnard to father, June 19, 1863, William A. Barnard Collection, AM; Orville Babcock Diary, June 19, 1863, USGPL; Brown, *History of the Fourth Regiment of Minnesota Infantry*, 226; Crater, *History of the Fiftieth Regiment Penna. Vet. Vols.*, 41; William F. Draper to wife, June 15, 1863, William F. Draper Papers, LC; Robert Jameson to sister, June 17, 1863, Robert E. Jameson Papers, LC; Charles Affeld Diary, June 14, 1863, Journals/Diaries/Letters Series, VICK.

33. *OR*, 52(1):363; George Ditto Diary, July 1, 1863, ALPL; E. B. Bascom Diary, June 21, 1863, 5th Iowa File, VICK.

34. *OR*, 24(3):418; Hopkins, *The Seventh Regiment Rhode Island Volunteers*, 96.

35. *OR*, 52(1):363; William Fish to father, August 15, 1863, William W. Fish Papers, FHS.

36. Edward O. Lord, ed., *History of the Ninth Regiment, New Hampshire Volunteers in the War of the Rebellion* (Concord, NH: Republican Press Association, 1895), 287; William Taylor to Jane, June 19, 1863, William Taylor Correspondence, WM.

37. *OR*, 24(3):415; *OR*, 24(2):508–509; Hugh Ewing to "My Love," June 17, 1863, Hugh Ewing Papers, OHS.

38. *OR*, 24(3):415; *History of the Thirty-fifth Regiment Massachusetts Volunteers*, 135; Orville Babcock Diary, June 17, 1863, USGPL.

39. *OR*, 24(1):102.

40. Charles Affeld Diary, June 22, 1863, Journals/Diaries/Letters Series, VICK.

41. *OR*, 24(3):419–420; *ORN*, 25:66; *OR*, 24(2):172, 188.

42. *OR*, 24(1):99; *OR*, 24(2):172, 189, 192; William R. Eddington Memoir, undated, ALPL, 12.

43. *OR*, 24(2):189, 200.

44. *OR*, 24(2):200; Hickenlooper, "The Vicksburg Mine," 540; Strong, "The Campaign Against Vicksburg," 338; Andrew Hickenlooper Reminiscences, undated, Hickenlooper Collection, CHS, 142.

45. *OR*, 24(1):99, 103; *OR*, 24(2):200, 207; Bearss, *The Vicksburg Campaign*, 3:905. For Powell, see Edward Dolnick, *Down the Great Unknown: John Wesley Powell's 1869 Journey of Discovery and Tragedy Through the Grand Canyon* (New York: HarperCollins, 2001).

46. *OR*, 24(2):200, 332, 371; Tunnard, *A Southern Record*, 248; Francis R. Baker Diary, June 10, 1863, ALPL; Hickenlooper, "The Vicksburg Mine," 540; Lockett, "The Defense of Vicksburg," 491; Cyrus W. Randall to mother, June 13, 1863, Cyrus W. Randall Correspondence, ALPL; Job H. Yaggy Diary, June 9, 1863, ALPL; William L. Faulk Diary, June 9, 1863, OCM; W. A. Lorimer to W. T. Rigby, May 16, 1904, 17th Illinois File, VICK; Thomas Smith Manuscript, undated, MDAH, 5, copy in Columbus Sykes Papers, CWD, USAHEC; Carlos Colby to sister, June 9, 1863, Carlos W. Colby Papers, NL; James Vanderbilt to mother, June 7 and 9, 1863, James C. Vanderbilt Papers, ISL; Wells, *The Siege of Vicksburg*, 75; Jared Lobdell, "A Civil War Tank at Vicksburg," *Journal of Mississippi History* 25, no. 4 (October 1963): 279–283.

47. *OR*, 24(1):99–100–101, 107; *OR*, 24(2):240; Simon, ed., *PUSG*, 8:359, 370–371, 397–398.

48. George Carrington Diary, June 16, 1863, CHM; *OR*, 24(2):184, 410; J. C. Nottingham to W. T. Rigby, December 1, 1901, 8th Indiana File, VICK.

49. *OR*, 24(2):173, 181.

50. *OR*, 24(2):333, 364–365, 391.

51. *OR*, 24(2):185–186; John Forney to R. W. Memminger, July 2, 1863, Dabney Maury Order Book, CHM, 307–308.

52. *OR*, 24(1):102–103; *OR*, 24(2):183; Pratt., ed., "Civil War Letters of Brigadier-General William Ward Orme, 1862–1866," 279–280.

53. *OR*, 24(1):99; *OR*, 24(3):401, 411.

54. *SOR*, 4:304, 306; Bearss, *The Vicksburg Campaign*, 3:941; Ballard, *Vicksburg*, 372; George H. Hynds Diary, June 17, 1863, Journals/Letters/Diaries Series, VICK; William Lowery Diary, June 17, 1863, ADAH.

55. T. Harry Williams, *Lincoln and His Generals* (New York: Alfred A. Knopf, 1952), 230. For detailed analysis of the McClernand issue, see Ballard, *Grant at Vicksburg*, 86–106.

56. Terrence J. Winschel, "Fighting Politician: John A. McClernand," in *Grant's Lieutenants: From Cairo to Vicksburg*, Steven E. Woodworth, ed. (Lawrence: University Press of Kansas, 2001), 129–150.

57. *OR*, 52(1):314.

58. Marszalek et al., eds., *The Personal Memoirs of Ulysses S. Grant*, 294; Ballard, *Grant at Vicksburg*, 91.

59. *OR*, 17(2):420, 502, 528.

60. *OR*, 17(2):420, 502, 528, 562, 567.

61. Marszalek et al., eds., *The Personal Memoirs of Ulysses S. Grant*, 306.

62. *OR*, 24(3):19; Simon, *PUSG*, 7:259.

63. *OR*, 17(2):566–567; Kiper, *Major General John Alexander McClernand*, 207.

64. Simon, *PUSG*, 7:225; Badeau, *Military History of Ulysses S. Grant*, 1:151; James H. Wilson to Adam Badeau, March 9, 1867, James H. Wilson Papers, LC, copy in Vicksburg File, Ulysses S. Grant Presidential Library, hereafter cited as USGPL.

65. *OR*, 24(1):8–9, 11; *ORN*, 24:165, 179; Marszalek et al., eds., *The Personal Memoirs of Ulysses S. Grant*, 305–306.

66. *OR*, 24(3):5; *OR*, 17(2):553, 555, 579; Marszalek et al., eds., *The Personal Memoirs of Ulysses S. Grant*, 304–305; Kiper, *Major General John Alexander McClernand*, 180, 182.

67. Winschel, *Triumph and Defeat: The Vicksburg Campaign, Volume 2*, 69; Winschel, "Fighting Politician," 148.

68. *OR*, 24(3):260, 268–269; *OR*, 24(1):32, 49, 80–81; Simon, *PUSG*, 8: 122–123, 132, 138; Dana, *Recollections of the Civil War*, 41, 45; Richardson, *A Personal History of Ulysses S. Grant*, 306; Badeau, *Military History of Ulysses S. Grant*, 1:209.

69. *OR*, 24(3):270, 279; Simon, *PUSG*, 8:168, 174.

70. *OR*, 24(3):289, 295; Simon, *PUSG*, 8:40.

71. Wilson, *Under the Old Flag*, 182–183, 198; Jenney, "Personal Recollections of Vicksburg," 263.

72. *OR*, 24(3):305–306; *OR*, 24(1):84; Marszalek et al., eds., *The Personal Memoirs of Ulysses S. Grant*, 349–350; Cadwallader, *Three Years with Grant*, 92; Williams, *Lincoln and His Generals*, 230.

73. *OR*, 24(1):37.

74. *OR*, 24(1):87.

75. *OR*, 24(1):105, 165–166.

76. *OR*, 24(1):160–162; William T. Sherman to John Rawlins, June 17, 1863, Blair Family Papers, LOC; James B. McPherson to U. S. Grant, June 18, 1863, Blair Family Papers, LOC; Parrish, *Frank Blair*, 172; "Congratulatory Order of General McClernand," June 13, 1863, Memphis *Evening Bulletin*.

77. *OR*, 24(1):43, 103, 159, 161–162. A Copy of McClernand's order is found in Ohio Knox Papers, OHS.

78. *OR*, 24(1):57; Kiper, *Major General John A. McClernand*, 270; 83rd Indiana Volunteer Regimental History, undated, ISL.

79. John A. McClernand to Henry Halleck, June 28, 1863, John A. McClernand Papers, ALPL; S. G. Burbridge and William Landram Memo, June 9, 1863, John A. McClernand Papers, ALPL; *OR*, 24(3):410.

80. *OR*, 24(3):419; *OR*, 24(1):159, 162, 164–165; Wilson, *Under the Old Flag*, 185–186; Catton, *Grant Moves South*, 466; Jenney, "Personal Recollections of Vicksburg," 263; Steven E. Woodworth, *Nothing but Victory: The Army of the Tennessee, 1861–1865* (New York: Knopf, 2005), 434.

81. *OR*, 24(1):43, 102–103, 105, 158, 165–166; Jenney, "Personal Recollections of Vicksburg," 263.

82. Walter B. Scates to John A. McClernand, June 2, 1863, John A. McClernand Papers, ALPL; Charles Affeld Diary, June 19, 1863, Journals/Diaries/Letters Series, VICK; Carlos Colby to sister, June 19, 1863, Carlos W. Colby Papers, NL; Chase Dickinson to Louise, June 21, 1863, Chase Hall Dickinson Papers, NL; William T. Rigby Diary, June 19, 1863, UIA.

83. Walter B. Scates to John A. McClernand, June 2, 1863, John A. McClernand Papers, ALPL; Charles Affeld Diary, June 19, 1863, Journals/Diaries/Letters Series, VICK; Carlos Colby to sister, June 19, 1863, Carlos W. Colby Papers, NL; Chase Dickinson to Louise, June 21, 1863, Chase Hall Dickinson Papers, NL; William T. Rigby Diary, June 19, 1863, UIA; David McKinney to sister, June 21, 1863, David McKinney Papers, FHS; I. P. Rumsey to parents, June 20, 1863, I. P. Rumsey Papers, NL; Edward Stanfield to father, June 22, 1863, Edward P. Stanfield Papers, IHS; George M. Rogers Diary, June 19, 1863, ISL; Smith, *Life and Letters of Thomas Kilby Smith*, 307.

84. *OR*, 24(3):350–351, 419; *OR*, 24(1):97, 101–102; Solonick, *Engineering Victory*, 102; "Vicksburg Campaign," August 9, 1888, *National Tribune*; W. H. Bentley, *History of the 77th Illinois Volunteer Infantry, Sept. 2, 1862–July 10, 1865* (Peoria, IL: Edward Hine, Printer, 1883), 170; Simon, ed., *PUSG*, 8:386; Soman and Byrne, eds., *A Jewish Colonel in the Civil War*, 297; Chase Dickinson to Louise, June 21, 1863, Chase Hall Dickinson Papers, NL; William B. Feis, "Grant's Relief Man: Edward O. C. Ord," in *Grant's Lieutenants: From Chattanooga to Appomattox*, Steven E. Woodworth, ed. (Lawrence: University Press of Kansas, 2008), 184. For Ord, see Bernarr Cresap, *Appomattox Commander: The Story of General E.O.C. Ord* (San Diego: A. S. Barnes and Company, 1981).

85. William T. Rigby Diary, June 19, 1863, UIA; David McKinney to sister, June 21, 1863, David McKinney Papers, FHS; Walter Scates to Jacob Lauman, June 19, 1862, Jacob G. Lauman Papers, RG 94, E 159, NARA; General Orders No. 1, June 19, 1863, E. O. C. Ord Papers, RG 94, E 159, NARA.

86. *OR*, 24(1):103, 106–107; S. D. Thompson, *Recollections with the Third Iowa Regiment* (Cincinnati: n.p., 1864), 385.

CHAPTER 11. "JOHNSTON WILL ATTACK WITHIN FORTY-EIGHT HOURS"

1. Hoehling, *Vicksburg*, 69; Joseph Lesslie to wife, June 3, 1863, Jospeh Lesslie Letters, Journals/Diaries/Letters Series, VICK.

2. Hoehling, *Vicksburg*, 176.

3. Abrams, *A Full and Detailed History*, 45; John Forney to Martin Smith, May 26, 1863, Dabney Maury Order Book, CHM, 289.

4. Hoehling, *Vicksburg*, 65; Dennis East II, "Wallpaper Journalism," *Timeline* 13, no. 6 (November/December 1996): 26 (22–33); James M. Swords Exhibit, OCM.

5. Vicksburg *Daily Citizen*, June 18, 1863, copy in UVA; Vicksburg *Daily Citizen*,

June 30, 1863, copy in Grand Gulf State Park; "The Price of Our Paper and the News-boys," Vicksburg *Daily Citizen*, June 18, 1863; Cable, ed., "A Woman's Diary of the Siege of Vicksburg," 771.

6. Scriber, *Twenty-seventh Louisiana Volunteer Infantry*, 150; Cable, ed., "A Woman's Diary of the Siege of Vicksburg," 772–773; J. H. Pepper Diary, June 18, 1863, MDAH; Vicksburg *Daily Citizen*, June 18, 1863; James Slack to Ann, June 15, 1863, James R. Slack Papers, ISL.

7. "An Unceremonious Visitor," Vicksburg *Daily Citizen*, June 18, 1863; Hoehling, *Vicksburg*, 177.

8. "Improvement," Vicksburg *Daily Citizen*, June 18, 1863; Elizabeth Bowie Reminiscences, undated, Journals/Letters/Diaries File, VICK.

9. John C. Taylor Diary, June 29, 1863, UVA; Anne to Emma, June/July 1863, Shannon-Crutcher Family Papers, MDAH; Richard and Richard, *The Defense of Vicksburg*, 201; Cable, ed., "A Woman's Diary of the Siege of Vicksburg," 772; June 20 and 27 issues in George H. and Katherine M. Davis Collection, TU; John W. Griffith Diary, June 19, 1863, OHS; James Slack to Ann, June 15, 1863, James R. Slack Papers, ISL; East II, "Wallpaper Journalism," 27, 29; *Daily Citizen* copies in Stephen D. Lee Papers, UNC.

10. Edmund Newsome Diary, May 31, 1863, MDAH.

11. *OR*, 24(3):418–419.

12. William T. Rigby Diary, May 29, 1863, UIA; *SOR*, 4:302; John Merrilees Diary, May 31, 1863, CHM; William Christie to father, May 31, 1863, James C. Christie and Family Papers, MNHS; Louis W. Knobe Diary, May 29, 1863, ISL.

13. *SOR*, 4:302–303, 305; *OR*, 24(2):691–692, 695, 697.

14. *SOR*, 4:302–303; *OR*, 24(2):693; Hoehling, *Vicksburg*, 110.

15. *OR*, 24(1):105; Trowbridge, *Autobiography of Silas Thompson Trowbridge*, 147–148; Anthony B. Burton Diary, June 20, 1863, ALPL; George Ditto Diary, June 20, 1863, ALPL; Cyrus Winters Diary, June 20, 1863, ALPL; Pinckney Skilton Cone Diary, June 20, 1863, ALPL; Curtis P. Lacey Diary, June 21, 1863, NL.

16. Merrick J. Wald Diary, June 20, 1863, OCM; David McKinney to sister, June 21, 1863, David McKinney Papers, FHS; William L. Faulk Diary, June 20, 1863, OCM; *OR*, 24(1):105; Trowbridge, *Autobiography of Silas Thompson Trowbridge*, 147–148; Anthony B. Burton Diary, June 20, 1863, ALPL; Cyrus Winters Diary, June 20, 1863, ALPL; Pinckney Skilton Cone Diary, June 20, 1863, ALPL.

17. *SOR*, 4:305; *OR*, 52(2):499; *OR*, 24(2):396; Richard and Richard, *The Defense of Vicksburg*, 206; Chambers, "My Journal," 278.

18. Jerome Kroll to brother, June 20, 1863, Jerome Kroll Letters, Gordon Smith Collection, AM; Lot Abraham Diary, June 20, 1863, UIA; Asa E. Sample Diary, June 20, 1863, ISL; L. J. Sanders Diary, June 20, 1863, WKU.

19. John C. Taylor Diary, June 12, 1863, UVA.

20. *OR*, 24(1):227, 278–279; Pemberton, *Pemberton*, 208; Symonds, *Joseph E. Johnston*, 212.

21. *OR*, 24(3):965–966; John A. Buckner to Colonel, June 6, 1863, "Letters,

Telegrams, and Orders Received and Sent—General Breckinridge's Command, December 1861–November 1863," RG 109, Chapter II, Vol. 311, NARA, 103; John C. Taylor Diary, June 21, 1863, UVA.

22. *OR*, 24(1):227–228.

23. *OR*, 24(3):967.

24. *OR*, 24(3):967.

25. *OR*, 24(3):966, 971; French, *Two Wars*, 178; Bearss, *The Vicksburg Campaign*, 3:1086.

26. *OR*, 24(3):966–967.

27. *OR*, 24(3):969–970.

28. *OR*, 24(3):970–971.

29. *OR*, 24(3):969; J. H. Pepper Diary, June 23, 1863, MDAH.

30. *OR*, 24(3):971–972.

31. *OR*, 24(3):423–424; Joseph Mower to John Rawlins, June 17, 1863, Frank A. Irvin Papers, CSUN.

32. *OR*, 24(3):426; *SOR*, 4:304.

33. Jeff T. Giambrone, "'One Hour's Hard Fighting': The 4th Iowa Cavalry at the Battle of Hill's Plantation," *North and South Magazine* 9, no. 7 (February 2007): 51–53; Oliver Boardman to father, June 29, 1863, Oliver Boardman Papers, UIA; Lot Abraham Diary, June 11, 1863, UIA.

34. *OR*, 24(1):105–106, 108; *OR*, 52(1):363; *OR*, 24(2):246, 509–512; Bearss, *The Vicksburg Campaign*, 3:1083; Ballard, *Grant at Vicksburg*, 125; Enoch P. Williams Diary, June 25, 1863, OCM; Stewart Bruce Terry Diary, June 22, 1863, KHS; Giambrone, "One Hour's Hard Fighting," 53–59; Charles F. Craver Diary, June 22, 1863, HL; John Mann to father, June 20, 1863, and William Mann to father, June 28, 1863, Mann Family Papers, UIA; Lot Abraham Diary, June 22, 1863, UIA.

35. *OR*, 24(1):105–106, 108; *OR*, 52(1):363; *OR*, 24(2):246, 509–512; Enoch P. Williams Diary, June 25, 1863, OCM; Stewart Bruce Terry Diary, June 22, 1863, KHS; Giambrone, "One Hour's Hard Fighting," 53–59; Charles F. Craver Diary, June 22, 1863, HL; John Mann to father, June 20, 1863, and William Mann to father, June 28, 1863, Mann Family Papers, UIA; Lot Abraham Diary, June 22, 1863, UIA.

36. *OR*, 24(3):427–428.

37. *OR*, 24(3):428; *OR*, 52(1):363–364; E. J. Hart, *History of the Fortieth Illinois Inf., (Volunteers)* (Cincinnati: H. S. Bosworth, 1864), 142; T. W. Connelly, *History of the Seventieth Ohio Regiment From Its Organization to Its Mustering Out* (Cincinnati: Peak Bros., n.d.), 51; John K. Duke, *History of the Fifty-third Regiment Ohio Volunteer Infantry, During the War of the Rebellion 1861 to 1865* (Portsmouth, OH: Blade Printing Co., 1900), 105.

38. Stillwell, *The Story of a Common Soldier*, 139–140.

39. *OR*, 24(3):427–428, 430; *OR*, 24(1):765; *OR*, 52(1):359; *OR*, 24(2):285, 295, 303, 307, 309, 533, 690; Joseph C. Gordon Diary, June 21, 1863, OCM; Henry Otis Dwight Diary, June 22, 1863, OHS.

40. *OR*, 24(3):427–428; *OR*, 24(2):319.

41. *OR*, 24(2):215, 224, 226; Mary Bobbitt Townsend, *Yankee Warhorse: A Biography of Major General Peter Osterhaus* (Columbia: University of Missouri Press, 2010), 115; Samuel Gordon to wife, June 24, 1863, Samuel Gordon Papers, ALPL; Asa E. Sample Diary, June 24, 1863, ISL.

42. Asa E. Sample Diary, June 12–13, 17, 23, 28, and July 2, 1863, ISL.

43. *OR*, 24(3):427, 429; Richard and Richard, *The Defense of Vicksburg*, 222; *OR* 24(1):42; R. W. Memminger to Captain Jones, June 13, 1863, Letters and Telegrams Sent, Department of Mississippi and East Louisiana, 1863, RG 109, Chapter II, Vol. 60, NARA.

44. *OR*, 24(3):428.

45. *OR*, 24(1):106; *OR*, 24(2):245, 533; Timothy C. Young Diary, June 23, 1863, Journals/Letters/Diaries Series, VICK; Oldroyd, *A Soldier's Story*, 64; Sherman, *Memoirs of General William T. Sherman*, 1:329; Isaac Home Diary, June 22, 1863, KHS; Adnah Eaton Diary, June 23, 1863, NC; William Sherman to wife, June 27, 1863, William T. Sherman Papers, LOC; James B. Swan, *Chicago's Irish Legion: The 90th Illinois Volunteers in the Civil War* (Carbondale: Southern Illinois University Press, 2009), 71.

46. *OR*, 24(3):427, 430–431; Swan, *Chicago's Irish Legion*, 72; Ephraim Dawes to Kate, June 28, 1863, Ephraim C. Dawes Papers, NL.

47. *OR*, 24(3):429, 431, 439–440; *OR* 24(1):43–44, 107–108; *OR*, 24(2):246; 533.

48. *OR*, 24(3):429, 431, 439–440; *OR* 24(1):43–44, 107–108; *OR*, 24(2):246; 533.

49. M. D. L. Stephens Recollections, 1899, MDAH, 21–22; William G. Pirtle Memoirs, 1907, FHS, 185; H. N. Faulkinbury Diary, May 28, 1863, MDAH; James to Kate, December 22, 1863, Israel L. Adams Papers, LSU.

50. *OR*, 24(2):245–246.

51. W. L. Rand to father, June 20, 1863, Rand Family Papers, ALPL.

52. Walter Gresham to wife, June 1, 1863, Walter Q. Gresham Papers, LOC; Clarke, *Reminiscence and Anecdotes of the War for Southern Independence*, 105; Job H. Yaggy Diary, June 4, 1863, ALPL; *OR*, 24(2):323, 407, 409.

53. Richard and Richard, *The Defense of Vicksburg*, 174, 178.

54. Richard and Richard, *The Defense of Vicksburg*, 197–198; Claudius W. Sears Diary, May 19, 1863, MDAH; William L. Faulk Diary, June 14, 1863, OCM; *OR*, 24(2):395; Chambers, "My Journal," 276.

55. Chambers, "My Journal," 275; Ike Jackson to Ethan, May 30, 1863, Isaac Jackson Letters, James S. Schoff Civil War Collection, UMC; *SOR*, 4:301; Dana, *Recollections of the Civil War*, 89.

56. Jasper N. Kidwell to mother, June 23, 1863, Ross-Kidwell Papers, IHS; Barber, *Army Memoirs*, 111; Winschel, ed., *The Civil War Diary of a Common Soldier*, 58–59; John C. Taylor Diary, June 21, 1863, UVA.

57. *OR*, 24(1):276; *SOR*, 4:303–304; *OR*, 24(2):690.

58. *OR*, 24(2):420; Chambers, "My Journal," 277.

59. George Carrington Diary, July 2, 1863, CHM; *OR*, 52(2):495.

60. *OR*, 24(2):689; Cadwallader, *Three Years with Grant*, 95; *Sanborn Family in the United States and Brief Sketch of Life of John B. Sanborn* (St. Paul: H. M. Smyth Printing Co., 1887), 62.

61. James Slack to Ann, June 3, 1863, James R. Slack Papers, ISL; *OR*, 24(2):403; Simon, ed., *PUSG*, 8:440; R. W. Memminger to John Bowen, June 11, 1863, Letters and Telegrams Sent, Department of Mississippi and East Louisiana, 1863, RG 109, Chapter II, Vol. 60, NARA.

62. *OR*, 24(2):332; Richard and Richard, *The Defense of Vicksburg*, 184–185; James A. Woodson Diary, May 23–July 4, 1863, ALPL; Clarke, *Reminiscence and Anecdotes of the War for Southern Independence*, 104–105, 108; Payson Shumway to wife, June 12, 1863, Z. Payson Shumway Papers, ALPL.

63. Aurelius L. Voorhis Diary, June 27, 1863, IHS; George M. Rogers Diary, June 9, 1863, ISL; Crooke, *The Twenty-first Regiment of Iowa Volunteer Infantry*, 101.

64. Unknown Diary, June 4, 1863, 9th Iowa File, VICK; *SOR*, 4:305; Chambers, "My Journal," 278–279.

65. Clarke, *Reminiscence and Anecdotes of the War for Southern Independence*, 107–108.

66. Joel Strong Reminiscences, 1910, MHS, 15; *OR*, 24(2):391; Richard and Richard, *The Defense of Vicksburg*, 173, 180.

67. W. R. McRory Diary, June 8, 1863, Journals/Letters/Diaries Series, VICK; E. H. Ingraham to aunt, May 29, 1863, E. H. and D. G. Ingraham Letters, ALPL; *OR*, 24(1):111.

68. Ned to Alice, June 17, 1863, E. H. and D. G. Ingraham Letters, ALPL.

69. *OR*, 24(2):693; Richard and Richard, *The Defense of Vicksburg*, 186, 201–202.

70. *OR*, 24(2):291; *OR*, 24(1):108, 279; Anderson, *Memoirs*, 345; *OR*, 24(2):174; Hashell, ed., "Col. William Camm War Diary, 1861–1865," 955; Simon, ed., *PUSG*, 8:358, 452; James L. Power Diary, June 26, 1863, MDAH; Anthony B. Burton Diary, June 23 and 25, 1863, ALPL; Mortimer Rice Diary, June 23, 1863, ALPL; Bela T. St. John to father, June 30, 1863, Bela T. St. John Papers, LOC; Walter Gresham to wife, June 24, 1863, Walter Q. Gresham Papers, LOC.

71. *OR*, 24(1):111; Anthony B. Burton Diary, June 24, 1863, ALPL.

72. *OR*, 24(2):107.

73. *OR*, 24(2):107, 195, 289, 345; Payson Shumway to wife, July 2, 1863, Z. Payson Shumway Papers, ALPL.

74. *OR*, 24(2):107, 195, 289, 345; Payson Shumway to wife, July 2, 1863, Z. Payson Shumway Papers, ALPL; *OR*, 24(1):108, 279; Anderson, *Memoirs*, 345; *OR*, 24(2):174; William R. Clack Diary, June 22–23, 1863, Journals/Diaries/Letters Series, VICK; Hashell, ed., "Col. William Camm War Diary, 1861–1865," 955; Simon, ed., *PUSG*, 8:358, 452; James L. Power Diary, June 26, 1863, MDAH; Anthony B. Burton Diary, June 23 and 25, 1863, ALPL; Mortimer Rice Diary, June 23, 1863, ALPL; Bela T. St. John to father, June 30, 1863, Bela T. St. John Papers, LOC; Walter Gresham to wife, June 24, 1863, Walter Q. Gresham Papers, LOC; Unnamed Soldier Diary, June 23–24, 1863, UMEM.

75. *OR*, 24(1):108, 279; *OR*, 24(2):174; Simon, ed., *PUSG*, 8:358, 452; James L. Power Diary, June 26, 1863, MDAH; Anthony B. Burton Diary, June 23 and 25, 1863, ALPL; Mortimer Rice Diary, June 23, 1863, ALPL; Bela T. St. John to father, June 30, 1863, Bela T. St. John Papers, LOC.

76. John Ritter to Margarett, June 11, 1863, John A. Ritter Papers, NC; Henry Schmidt to wife, June 21, 1863, Schmidt Family Papers, FHS; Payson Shumway to wife, July 3, 1863, Z. Payson Shumway Papers, ALPL.

77. Hall, *The Story of the 26th Louisiana Infantry*, 88; Richard and Richard, *The Defense of Vicksburg*, 171; Samuel Oviatt to Libby, June 14, 1863, Samuel J. Oviatt Papers, NC.

78. *OR*, 24(2):175–176, 180, 184; Richard and Richard, *The Defense of Vicksburg*, 184; James L. Power Diary, June 22, 1863, MDAH; Unknown to family, June 19, 1863, Anonymous Civil War Letter, LSU.

79. Jones, "The Rank and File at Vicksburg," 23; Ambrose, ed., "A Wisconsin Boy at Vicksburg," 7–8.

80. George Carrington Diary, July 1, 1863, CHM; Richard and Richard, *The Defense of Vicksburg*, 207–208; James L. Power Diary, June 22, 1863, MDAH.

81. Patrick, ed., *Three Years with Wallace's Zouaves*, 144; John J. Kellogg Memoirs, 1913, Journals/Letters/Diaries Series, VICK, 51.

82. *The Story of the Fifty-fifth Regiment Illinois Volunteer Infantry in the Civil War, 1861–1865*, 251.

83. John N. Bell Diary, June 17, 1863, OHS; Jones, "The Rank and File at Vicksburg," 26–27.

84. John C. Taylor Diary, June 15, 1863, UVA; Jones, "The Rank and File at Vicksburg," 23; C. H. Twining to Kate, June 9, 1863, Moody Family Papers, MHS; Richard and Richard, *The Defense of Vicksburg*, 184.

85. Crooke, *The Twenty-first Regiment of Iowa Volunteer Infantry*, 109; Richard and Richard, *The Defense of Vicksburg*, 182; Marszalek et al., eds., *The Personal Memoirs of Ulysses S. Grant*, 388; Samuel Eells to unknown, June 21, 1863, Samuel H. Eells Papers, LC; Will Jolly to Gus, June 12, 1863, William Jolly Letters, Keen Family Papers, SHSI; Beck, *A True Sketch of Army Life*, 13; John J. Kellogg Memoirs, 1913, Journals/Letters/Diaries Series, VICK, 50.

86. Alvin Hovey Memoir, undated, IU, 61–62.

87. *OR*, 24(2):409; Willison, *Reminiscences of a Boy's Service*, 60.

88. R. W. Memminger to Carter Stevenson, June 25, 1863, Letters and Telegrams Sent, Department of Mississippi and East Louisiana, 1863, RG 109, Chapter II, Vol. 60, NARA; Simon, ed., *PUSG*, 8:410; *OR*, 24(2):343; John Merrilees Diary, June 10, 1863, CHM; Fred Grant Memoir, undated, USGPL, 38.

89. Brinkerhoff, *History of the Thirtieth Regiment Ohio*, 78; Samuel Eells to unknown, June 21, 1863, Samuel H. Eells Papers, LC; Calvin Ainsworth Diary, May 28, 1863, Journals/Letters/Diaries Series, VICK; *OR*, 24(3):339; Judson Gill to Soph, June 7, 1863, C. Judson Gill Letters, Journals/Letters/Diaries Series, VICK.

90. William F. Draper to wife, June 26, 1863, William F. Draper Papers, LC; John Merrilees Diary, June 20, 1863, CHM; Carlos Colby to sister, June 19, 1863, Carlos W. Colby Papers, NL; Parrish, *Frank Blair*, 172; Jones, "The Rank and File at Vicksburg," 23; John J. Kellogg Memoirs, 1913, Journals/Letters/Diaries Series, VICK, 49–50; Anderson, *Memoirs*, 347; J. Carroll Harriss to Valery, June 17, 1863, Jordan C. Harriss Papers, NC.

91. Payson Shumway to cousin, June 13, 1863, Z. Payson Shumway Letters, NL; Abrams, *A Full and Detailed History*, 43.

92. Alvin Hovey Memoir, undated, IU, 63; Clarke, *Reminiscence and Anecdotes of the War for Southern Independence*, 105.

Chapter 12. "The Death Hole"

1. William L. Faulk Diary, June 13, 1863, OCM; William Drennan Diary, June 9, 1863, Journals/Letters/Diaries Series, VICK, copy in MDAH; George Ditto Diary, June 27, 1863, ALPL; *OR*, 24(3):430; *OR*, 24(2):246; Fred Grant Memoir, undated, USGPL, 35.

2. William M. Reid Diary, June 30, 1863, ALPL; George Carrington Diary, June 10, 1863, CHM; Simon, ed., *PUSG*, 8:409; *OR*, 24(3):430; Oldroyd, *A Soldier's Story*, 34.

3. W. L. Rand to father, June 20, 1863, Rand Family Papers, ALPL; Samuel Eells to unknown, June 21, 1863, Samuel H. Eells Papers, LC; *OR*, 24(3):435; *OR*, 24(2):208; *OR*, 52(1):362; George D. Ward to sister, June 15, 1863, Ward Family Papers, UIA.

4. William L. Henderson Diary, June 18, 1863, UIA; *OR*, 24(3):422; Cotton, ed., *From the Pen of a She-Rebel*, 14–41; Logan Roots to Edwin Hewett, July 24, 1863, Edwin Crawford Hewett Correspondence, UI; *OR*, 24(3):425–426, 443–444, 469.

5. *OR*, 24(3):966, 969, 975.

6. *OR*, 24(3):435.

7. *OR*, 24(3):435, 437–438.

8. Tucker, *The Forgotten "Stonewall of the West,"* 298–299; Francis Shoup Circular, June 28, 1863, Civil War Documents, SHSM; *OR*, 24(3):976; R. R. Hutchinson to Martin Green, June 24, 1863, "Letter Book, Brig. Gen. J. S. Bowen's Command, August 1862–November 1863," RG 109, Chapter II, Vol. 274, NARA, 60–61.

9. *OR*, 24(3):976; R. W. Memminger to L. W. Oster, May 24, 1863, R. W. Memminger to Alexander Reynolds, and H. C. Tupper to Major Orme, May 25, J. H. Morrison to M. L. Smith, May 29, W. H. McCardle to Carter Stevenson, June 6, J. M. Stafford to John Forney, June 8, R. W. Memminger to M. L. Smith, June 12, J. C. Taylor to M. L. Smith and to John Forney, June 17, W. H. McCardle to Major Orme, June 19, and L. M. Montgomery to Francis Cockrell, June 28, 1863, Letters and Telegrams Sent, Department of Mississippi and East Louisiana, 1863, RG 109, Chapter II, Vol. 60, NARA.

10. R. W. Memminger to Surgeon Bryan, June 3, R. W. Memminger to Captain Wells, June 27, and F. M. Stafford to Thomas Taylor, July 2, 1863, Letters and Telegrams Sent, Department of Mississippi and Eats Louisiana, 1863, RG 109, Chapter II, Vol. 60, NARA.

11. James L. Power Diary, June 24, 1863, MDAH; *OR*, 24(3):975, 978.

12. *OR*, 24(3):974.

13. For the Monterrey surrender, see K. Jack Bauer, *The Mexican War, 1846–1848* (New York: MacMillan, 1974), 99–100.

14. Joseph D. Alison Diary, June 23, 1863, MDAH; James Carlisle Diary, June 1863, Journals/Diaries/Letters Series, VICK, 15; Abrams, *A Full and Detailed History*, 43; Walter Lenoir to brother, July 23, 1863, Lenoir Family Papers, UNC.

15. John C. Taylor Diary, June 1, 1863, UVA; Broadaway, "A Texan Records the Civil War Siege of Vicksburg, Mississippi," 117.

16. *OR*, 24(2):183.

17. *OR*, 24(2):177–178.

18. Solonick, *Engineering Victory*, 232.

19. *OR*, 24(2):174; Thomas Taylor to W. T. Rigby, March 19, 1903, 47th Ohio File, VICK.

20. *OR*, 24(2):174.

21. *OR*, 24(1):108; *OR*, 24(2):185, 196.

22. *SOR*, 4:304.

23. *OR*, 24(2):185.

24. *OR*, 24(2):177; Eli W. Thornhill Memoir, undated, OCM, 10.

25. Solonick, *Engineering Victory*, 178.

26. *OR*, 24(2):172–173.

27. Solonick, *Engineering Victory*, 183–187.

28. *OR*, 24(2):177.

29. *OR*, 24(1):104; *OR*, 24(2):185–186, 202, 396, 409; John S. Bell, "The Arkansas Sharpshooters," undated, 12th Arkansas Battalion Sharpshooters File, VICK; *SOR*, 4:306; Bela T. St. John to father, July 14, 1863, Bela T. St. John Papers, LOC; Edmund W. Pettus to William T. Rigby, March 14, 1903, 30th Alabama File, VICK; John Pemberton to Samuel Lockett, June 13, 1863, Letters and Telegrams Sent, Department of Mississippi and East Louisiana, 1863, RG 109, Chapter II, Vol. 60, NARA.

30. S. McD. Vernon to unknown; Major Smith to John Pemberton, June 17, 1863, John C. Pemberton Papers, RG 109, E 131, NARA; Unknown Memoir, undated, 3rd Louisiana File, VICK, 1.

31. *OR*, 24(1):104, 280; John C. Taylor Diary, June 16, 1863, UVA.

32. *OR*, 24(1):109.

33. *OR*, 24(2):175.

34. Unknown Memoir, undated, 3rd Louisiana File, VICK, 1; *OR*, 24(2):333; Unknown Memoir, undated, 3rd Louisiana File, VICK, 1.

35. *OR*, 24(1):104; *OR*, 24(2):185–186; John S. Bell, "The Arkansas Sharpshooters," undated, 12th Arkansas Battalion Sharpshooters File, VICK.

36. *OR*, 24(2):396, 409; Edmund W. Pettus to William T. Rigby, March 14, 1903, 30th Alabama File, VICK; John Pemberton to Samuel Lockett, June 13, 1863, Letters and Telegrams Sent, Department of Mississippi and East Louisiana, 1863, RG 109, Chapter II, Vol. 60, NARA.

37. Lockett, "The Defense of Vicksburg," 491.

38. "The Charge at Fort Hill," September 29, 1910, *National Tribune*; Solonick, *Engineering Victory*, 180; "More About Vicksburg," September 29, 1910, *National Tribune*.

39. For Hickenlooper, see Andrew Hickenlooper Reminiscences, undated, Hickenlooper Collection, CHS.

40. *OR*, 24(1):87–88; *OR*, 24(2):202.

41. *OR*, 24(1):87–88; *OR*, 24(2):202; Solonick, *Engineering Victory*, 180;

Hickenlooper, "The Vicksburg Mine," 541–542; Andrew Hickenlooper Reminiscences, undated, Hickenlooper Collection, CHS, 145.

42. Hickenlooper, "The Vicksburg Mine," 542.

43. *OR*, 24(2):202; Hickenlooper, "The Vicksburg Mine," 542.

44. *OR*, 24(1):87–88; *OR*, 24(2):202; Solonick, *Engineering Victory*, 183–185; Hickenlooper, "The Vicksburg Mine," 541–542.

45. *OR*, 24(3):439.

46. *OR*, 24(3):438, 441; Winschel, ed., *The Civil War Diary of a Common Soldier*, 58.

47. *OR*, 24(3):438.

48. *OR*, 24(3):440.

49. *OR*, 24(3):440–441; Joseph Stockton Diary, June 25, 1863, ALPL; Ambrose, ed., "A Wisconsin Boy at Vicksburg," 10.

50. *OR*, 24(2):293–295; Martimer D. Leggett to John A. Logan, September 21, 1885, John A. Logan Papers, ALPL.

51. *OR*, 24(2):293–294; Hickenlooper, "The Vicksburg Mine," 542; Adair, *Historical Sketch of the Forty-fifth Illinois Regiment*, 11; Andrew Hickenlooper Reminiscences, undated, Hickenlooper Collection, CHS, 148.

52. William E. Strong Reminiscences, undated, William E. Strong Papers, ALPL.

53. *OR*, 24(2):371; William E. Strong Reminiscences, undated, William E. Strong Papers, ALPL, 46.

54. *OR*, 24(2):372; Unknown Memoir, undated, 3rd Louisiana File, VICK, 2.

55. *OR*, 24(3):440.

56. William E. Strong Reminiscences, undated, William E. Strong Papers, ALPL, 45; Edmund Newsome Diary, June 25, MDAH.

57. Hickenlooper, "The Vicksburg Mine," 542.

58. Solonick, *Engineering Victory*, 189; William E. Strong Reminiscences, undated, William E. Strong Papers, ALPL, 46; John A. Griffen Diary, June 25, 1863, ALPL.

59. Andrew Hickenlooper Reminiscences, undated, Hickenlooper Collection, CHS, 148; William E. Strong Reminiscences, undated, William E. Strong Papers, ALPL, 47.

60. Strong, "The Campaign Against Vicksburg," 340.

61. *OR*, 24(2):202, 294, 372; Hickenlooper, "The Vicksburg Mine," 542; DeBenneville Randolph Keim Notebook, June 25, 1863, UMEM.

62. *OR*, 24(2):202, 294, 372; Trowbridge, *Autobiography of Silas Thompson Trowbridge*, 145; Cadwallader, *Three Years with Grant*, 121; John A. Griffen Diary, June 25, 1863, ALPL.

63. *OR*, 24(2):202, 294, 372; Unknown Memoir, undated, 3rd Louisiana File, VICK, 2.

64. Unknown to John M. Bucinst, June 28, 1863, LM; Anthony B. Burton Diary, June 25, 1863, ALPL; Ned to Alice, June 17, 1863, E. H. and D. G. Ingraham Letters, ALPL; Chambers, "My Journal," 278; Clarke, *Reminiscence and Anecdotes of the War for Southern Independence*, 110; Joseph Lesslie to wife, June 29, 1863, Joseph Lesslie Letters, Journals/Diaries/Letters Series, VICK; George Carrington Diary, June 25, 1863, CHM; Thomas Taylor to W. T. Rigby, March 19, 1903, 47th Ohio File, VICK.

65. *OR*, 24(2):294 *OR*, 24(1):109; Cadwallader, *Three Years with Grant*, 122; Curtis P. Lacey Diary, June 25, 1863, NL; Edwin Howes to Comrade Jennings, March 11, 1902, 20th Illinois File, VICK; John Edmiston to W. T. Rigby, March 8, 1902, 20th Illinois File, VICK.

66. *OR*, 24(2):333, 372; W. T. Ratliff to J. L. Power, November 6, 1900, W. T. Ratliff Letter, Journals/Letters/Diaries Series, VICK.

67. *OR*, 24(2):372; *OR*, 52(2):502; Nicholas Miller Memoir, undated, OCM, 13.

68. Unknown Memoir, undated, 3rd Louisiana File, VICK, 3–4; G. Grimsby to J. A. Calvinston, March 12, 1902, Edwin Howes to Comrade Jennings, March 11, 1902, James F. Cagle to John A. Edmiston, April 11, 1902, R. M. Springer to captain, April 5, 1902, and John Edmiston to W. T. Rigby, March 8, 1902, all in 20th Illinois File, VICK.

69. *OR*, 24(1):109; *OR*, 24(2):207, 333; Solonick, *Engineering Victory*, 190; Adair, *Historical Sketch of the Forty-fifth Illinois Regiment*, 11; Strong, "The Campaign Against Vicksburg," 342; Winschel, *Triumph and Defeat*, 136; William E. Strong Reminiscences, undated, William E. Strong Papers, ALPL, 50; John Wallace to brother, June 26, 1863, John M. Wallace Papers, CHM; Unknown Memoir, undated, 3rd Louisiana File, VICK, 1.

70. *OR*, 24(2):372; *OR*, 24(1):109.

71. Andrew Hickenlooper Reminiscences, undated, Hickenlooper Collection, CHS, 149–150.

72. *OR*, 24(2):207; Grabau, *Ninety-Eight Days*, 432; Crummer, *With Grant at Fort Donelson, Shiloh and Vicksburg*, 140; William E. Strong Reminiscences, undated, William E. Strong Papers, ALPL, 51.

73. Brown, *History of the Fourth Regiment of Minnesota Infantry*, 234; Welsh, *Medical Histories of Union Generals*, 201; "Siege of Vicksburg," November 4, 1897, *National Tribune*.

74. *OR*, 24(2):294, 372; *OR*, 24(1):109; Unknown Memoir, undated, 3rd Louisiana File, VICK, 3; Bertera, *De Golyer's 8th Michigan Black Horse Light Battery*, 156; George Carrington Diary, June 25, 1863, CHM; "Honor Illinois Soldiers," November 11, 1906, Nebraska *State Journal*.

75. *OR*, 24(2):294; "Siege of Vicksburg," November 4, 1897, *National Tribune*.

76. *OR*, 24(2):369, 372, 376, 413, 415; *OR*, 24(1):111; Jones, "The Rank and File at Vicksburg," 27–28; Theodore D. Fisher Diary, June 25, 1863, Journals/Letters/Diaries Series, VICK; William A. Ruyle Memoir, undated, HCWRT, USAHEC, 13; Unknown to W. T. Rigby, April 17, 1903, 3rd Louisiana File, VICK; James E. Payne, "Missouri Troops in the Vicksburg Campaign," *Confederate Veteran* 36, no. 10 (October 1928): 378–379; Unknown Memoir, undated, 3rd Louisiana File, VICK, 3; A. B. Booth to W. T. Rigby, April 25, 1903, 3rd Louisiana File, VICK; John Hampton to J. O. Banks, June 22, 1903, 43rd Mississippi File, VICK, A. C. Riley Report, July 26, 1863, 1st Missouri File, VICK.

77. *OR*, 24(2):294; Crummer, *With Grant at Fort Donelson, Shiloh and Vicksburg*, 142; Hickenlooper, "The Vicksburg Mine," 542.

78. *OR*, 24(2):294; Post, ed., *Soldiers' Letters*, 271; Hickenlooper, "The Vicksburg Mine," 542; Crummer, *With Grant at Fort Donelson, Shiloh and Vicksburg*, 168.

79. *OR*, 24(2):294, 312–313, 372; "Honor Illinois Soldiers," November 11, 1906,

Nebraska *State Journal*; "Siege of Vicksburg," November 4, 1897, *National Tribune*; Morris, *History, 31st Regiment Illinois Volunteers*, 73; Hickenlooper, "The Vicksburg Mine," 542; Edmund Newsome Diary, June 27, MDAH; Unknown to John M. Bucinst, June 28, 1863, LM.

80. Unknown to John M. Bucinst, June 28, 1863, LM; Unknown Memoir, undated, 3rd Louisiana File, VICK, 3.

81. *OR*, 24(2):369, 372, 376, 413, 415; *OR*, 24(1):111; Jones, "The Rank and File at Vicksburg," 27–28; Theodore D. Fisher Diary, June 25, 1863, Journals/Letters/Diaries Series, VICK; William A. Ruyle Memoir, undated, HCWRT, USAHEC, 13; Unknown to W. T. Rigby, April 17, 1903, 3rd Louisiana File, VICK; Payne, "Missouri Troops in the Vicksburg Campaign," 378–379; Unknown Memoir, undated, 3rd Louisiana File, VICK, 3; A. B. Booth to W. T. Rigby, April 25, 1903, 3rd Louisiana File, VICK; John Hampton to J. O. Banks, June 22, 1903, 43rd Mississippi File, VICK, A. C. Riley Report, July 26, 1863, 1st Missouri File, VICK.

82. Marszalek et al., eds., *The Personal Memoirs of Ulysses S. Grant*, 380; Saunier, *A History of the Forty-seventh Regiment Ohio Veteran Volunteer Infantry*, 159.

83. *OR*, 24(3):438, 441; William Van Zandt Diary, June 25–26, 1863, ISU; Unknown to John M. Bucinst, June 28, 1863, LM; Edward Ord to wife, June 1863, E. O. C. Ord Papers, SU.

84. *OR*, 24(2):294, 364, 371; *OR* 24(1):43, 109, 111; Howard, *History of the 124th Regiment Illinois Infantry Volunteers*, 116; Beck, *A True Sketch of Army Life*, 15; Job H. Yaggy Diary, June 25, 1863, ALPL; F. M. Cockrell to Captain Hutchinson, June 27, 1863, John C. Pemberton Papers, RG 109, E 131, NARA; R. W. Memminger to Major Orme, June 9, 1863 and W. H. McCardle to Major Orme, June 10, 1863, Letters and Telegrams Sent, Department of Mississippi and East Louisiana, 1863, RG 109, Chapter II, Vol. 60, NARA.

85. *OR*, 24(2):372; *SOR*, 4:306; *OR*, 52(2):502; William L. Shea and Terrence J. Winschel, *Vicksburg Is the Key: The Struggle for the Mississippi River* (Lincoln,: University of Nebraska Press, 2003), 159; Post, ed., *Soldiers' Letters*, 271; Chase Dickinson to father, June 26, 1863, Chase Hall Dickinson Papers, NL.

86. Broadaway, "A Texan Records the Civil War Siege of Vicksburg, Mississippi," 117.

Chapter 13. "We Are Drawing Nearer Every Day the End of Our Tether"

1. *OR*, 24(3):409, 451; Allen D. Albert, ed., *History of the Forty-fifth Regiment Pennsylvania Veteran Volunteer Infantry, 1861–1865* (Williamsport, PA: Grit Publishing Company, 1912), 69; Samuel Gordon to wife, June 27, 1863, Samuel Gordon Papers, ALPL; Simon, ed., *PUSG*, 8:444–445; Chase Dickinson to friends, May 29, 1863, Chase Hall Dickinson Papers, NL.

2. Simon, ed., *PUSG*, 8:445.

3. Henry Dykes to Sarah Dykes, June 28, 1863, Dykes Family Letters, OHS; Rodney Jeger to sister, July 2, 1863, Rodney Jeger Papers, ISL; James B. Mathews to family, June 28, 1863, James B. Mathews Letters, OCM; Albert Chipman to wife, June 30, 1863, Albert Chipman Papers, ALPL; J. Carroll Harriss to Valery, June 8, 1863, Jordan C. Harriss Papers, NC; Payson Shumway to wife, June 12, 1863, Z. Payson Shumway Papers, ALPL.

4. John C. Taylor Diary, June 27, 1863, UVA; *OR*, 24(3):439, 447; W. R. McRory Diary, June 26, 1863, Journals/Letters/Diaries Series, VICK.

5. L. M. Montgomery to John Bowen, June 26, 1863, Letters and Telegrams Sent, Department of Mississippi and East Louisiana, 1863, RG 109, Chapter II, Vol. 60, NARA; Perry, "Vicksburg," 173; Theodore D. Fisher Diary, July 1, 1863, Journals/Letters/Diaries Series, VICK; Channing Richards Diary, June 25, 1863, FHS; J. H. Pepper Diary, June 27, 1863, MDAH; William L. Roberts Diary, June 21, 1863, ADAH.

6. C. P. Alling, "Four Years with the Western Army," undated, 11th Wisconsin File, VICK, 10; James Slack to Ann, June 13 and 15, 1863, James R. Slack Papers, ISL.

7. *In Memoriam: Charles Ewing* (Philadelphia: J. B. Lippincott, 1888), 53; J. W. Henderson to Sallie, June 7, 1863, J. Watson Henderson Collection, UM; M. E. Thompson to "Most Affectionate Miss," June 7, 1863, Moses E. Thompson Letter, UTK; Larry J. Daniel, *Conquered: Why the Army of Tennessee Failed* (Chapel Hill: University of North Carolina Press, 2019), 140.

8. William Drennan Diary, June 11 and July 3, 1863, Journals/Letters/Diaries Series, VICK; George H. Hynds Diary, June 24, 1863, Journals/Letters/Diaries Series, VICK.

9. *OR*, 24(3):978, 981–982.

10. *OR*, 24(3):423.

11. *OR*, 24(3):439.

12. *OR*, 24(3):447–448, 452, 457; *OR*, 24(1):112; Simon, ed., *PUSG*, 8:439.

13. William Drennan Diary, June 11 and 14, 1863, Journals/Letters/Diaries Series, VICK.

14. Jeff Giambrone, "'Of Men and Measures': The Memoir of Lt. Simeon R. Martin, 46th Mississippi Infantry," *North and South Trader's Civil War* 28, no. 6 (2002): 22 (20–25).

15. *OR*, 24(3):447; *OR*, 24(2):404, 410, 413, 420–421; Abrams, *A Full and Detailed History*, 52, 55–56; Eli W. Thornhill Memoir, undated, OCM, 12; Hogane, "Reminiscences of the Siege of Vicksburg—Paper No. 2," 297; Bruce S. Allardice, *Confederate Colonels: A Biographical Register* (Columbia: University of Missouri Press, 2008), 74–75; James L. Power Diary, June 30, 1863, MDAH; Scriber, *Twenty-seventh Louisiana Volunteer Infantry*, 147.

16. *OR*, 24(2):409; Richard and Richard, *The Defense of Vicksburg*, 207, 209, 216; M. L. Smith to John Pemberton, June 25, and M. L. Smith to Colonel Montgomery, June 26, 1863, John C. Pemberton Papers, RG 109, E 131, NARA.

17. *OR*, 24(2):402; Richard and Richard, *The Defense of Vicksburg*, 216, 218; Welsh, *Medical Histories of Confederate Generals*, 13, 97; Allardice, *Confederate Colonels*, 404.

18. *OR*, 24(3):447; *OR*, 24(2):404, 410, 413, 420–421; Abrams, *A Full and Detailed*

History, 52; Eli W. Thornhill Memoir, undated, OCM, 12; Hogane, "Reminiscences of the Siege of Vicksburg—Paper No. 2," 297; Allardice, *Confederate Colonels*, 74–75; Merrick J. Wald Diary, June 27, 1863, OCM; William B. Britton to Editors Gazette, July 4, 1863, William B. Britton Letters, OCM; John A. Leavy Diary, June 27, 1863, Journals/ Letters/Diaries Series, VICK; Carlos Colby to sister, July 1863, Carlos W. Colby Papers, NL; John S. Bell, "The Arkansas Sharpshooters," undated, 12th Arkansas Battalion Sharpshooters File, VICK. A Federal related what a Confederate told him about Green's death: "Gen Green was shot in front of us, in the act of showing his men how to shoot a Yankee. He called them Cowards, and they dared him to get up and shoot at us, he raised up, but never shot, for a ball passed through his head before he could pull the trigger, this was told me by one of his men."

19. *OR*, 24(3):982–983.

20. Bearss, *The Vicksburg Campaign*, 3:1281; Grabau, *Ninety-Eight Days*, 494; "To Our Friends in Vicksburg," undated, Frederick Steele Papers, SU; Hoehling, *Vicksburg*, 240, 242; "To Our Friends in Vicksburg," June 28, 1863, Rosemonde E. and Emile Kuntz Collection, TU.

21. *OR*, 24(1):112; Simon, ed., *PUSG*, 8:441.

22. *OR*, 24(1):113.

23. Frank Blair to William T. Sherman, July 3, 1863, Blair Family Papers, LOC; Bjorn Skaptason, "The Chicago Light Artillery at Shiloh," *Journal of the Illinois State Historical Society* 104, 1–2 (Spring-Summer 2011): 73–96.

24. *OR*, 24(3):444, 448–449; *OR*, 24(1):113.

25. *OR*, 24(3):451–452.

26. *OR*, 24(3):449, 452; *OR* 24(1):43; Ephraim Dawes to Luce, June 28, 1863, Ephraim C. Dawes Papers, NL.

27. *OR*, 24(3):443–444.

28. *OR*, 24(3):452; *OR*, 24(1):111–112.

29. *OR*, 24(3):444; "Civil War Diary of Henry Salomon," *Wisconsin Magazine of History* 10, no. 2 (December 1926): 208 (205–210), copy in WHS.

30. *OR*, 24(1):111; *OR*, 24(2):190, 333; *SOR*, 4:304.

31. *OR*, 24(2):192; Kountz, *Record of the Organizations*, 65; John Forney to R. W. Memminger, July 2, 1863, Dabney Maury Order Book, CHM, 307–308; Perry, "Vicksburg," 173.

32. Kountz, *Record of the Organizations*, 78.

33. Kountz, *Record of the Organizations*, 63–80.

34. *OR*, 24(1):57–58.

35. *OR*, 24(3):439, 445.

36. *OR*, 24(3):978; Winschel, *Triumph and Defeat: The Vicksburg Campaign, Volume 2*, 126; James Alexander to unknown, June 30, 1863, James S. Alexander Papers, AU; Isaac E. Herring to wife, June 15, 1863, Isaac E. Herring File, OCM; John T. Burgess to brother, June 18, 1863, John T. Burgess File, OCM; S. Ewell to Samuel French, June 28, 1863, Samuel G. French Papers, RG 109, E 120, NARA; John A. Buckner to General, June 24, 1863, "Letters, Telegrams, and Orders Received and Sent—General

Breckinridge's Command, December 1861–November 1863," RG 109, Chapter II, Vol. 311, NARA, 104, 107–108.

37. *OR*, 24(3):450; Lot Abraham Diary, June 25, 1863, UIA; William Standard to Jane, June 28, 1863, William M. Standard Papers, AHC.

38. *OR*, 24(2):247.

39. Asa E. Sample Diary, June 17, 1863, ISL.

40. *OR*, 24(3):443, 449; Soman and Byrne, eds., *A Jewish Colonel in the Civil War*, 296, 298; George B. Marshall Reminiscences, 1912, ISL, 45.

41. *OR*, 24(3):450; Adolph Engelmann to wife, June 30, 1863, Engelmann-Kircher Family Papers, ALPL.

42. *OR*, 24(3):449–450.

43. William Todd, *The Seventy-ninth Highlanders New York Volunteers in the War of Rebellion, 1861–1865* (Albany: Brandow, Barton & Co., 1886), 303.

44. *OR*, 24(1):110–111; *OR*, 24(2):296; Adnah Eaton Diary, June 29, 1863, NC; George W. Modil Diary, June 27, MDAH; John Merrilees Diary, June 27, 1863, CHM; Dud Buck to uncle, June 15, 1863, Dudley E. Buck Letters, IHS; Unknown to brother, August 7, 1863, Ben Price Letters, ISL; Rodney Jeger to sister, July 2, 1863, Rodney Jeger Papers, ISL.

45. *OR*, 24(3):442, 450; Adolph Engelmann to wife, June 30, 1863, Engelmann-Kircher Family Papers, ALPL.

46. *OR*, 24(3):442, 450; Leander W. Cogswell, *A History of the Eleventh New Hampshire Regiment Volunteer Infantry in the Rebellion War, 1861–1865* (Concord, NH: Republican Press Association, 1891), 75; Byron M. Cutcheon, *The Story of the Twentieth Michigan Infantry, July 15th, 1862, to May 30th, 1865, Embracing Official Documents on File in the Records of the State of Michigan and of the United States Referring or Relative to the Regiment* (N.p.: n.p., 1904), 58; Orville Babcock Diary, June 29, 1863, USGPL.

47. William Taylor to Jane, June 30, 1863, William Taylor Correspondence, WM.

48. *OR*, 24(3):449–450.

49. *OR*, 24(3):442; *OR*, 24(2):533, 620; Timothy C. Young Diary, June 26, 1863, Journals/Letters/Diaries Series, VICK.

50. *OR*, 24(3):442, 450.

51. *OR*, 24(3):450; *OR*, 24(2):304–305, 533; Samuel Styre to parents, July 1, 1863, Samuel Styre Papers, DU.

52. *OR*, 24(3):442, 450.

53. *OR*, 24(3):442–443, 450; *OR*, 24(2):246, 248; William T. Sherman to Frederick Steele, June 21, 1863, Frederick Steele Papers, SU.

54. Reed, *Campaigns and Battles of the Twelfth Regiment Iowa Veteran Volunteer Infantry*, 125; J. Q. A. Campbell Diary, June 25–26, 1863, 5th Iowa File, VICK; Adnah Eaton Diary, June 29, 1863, NC; Rodney Jeger to sister, July 2, 1863, Rodney Jeger Papers, ISL; Winifred Keen Armstrong, ed., *The Civil War Letters of Pvt. P. C. Bonney* (Lawrenceville, IL: Lawrence County Historical Society, 1963), n.p., copy in 31st Illinois File, VICK; H. M. Trimble Diary, June 25, 1863, 93rd Illinois File, VICK; Charles F. Craver Diary, June 30, 1863, HL.

55. *OR*, 24(3):449.

56. *OR*, 24(2):247–249.

57. *OR*, 24(3):979.

58. *OR*, 24(3):978, 980, 984.

59. *OR*, 24(3):446, 978; Kountz, *Record of the Organizations*, 65–70; French, *Two Wars*, 178; L. J. Sanders Diary, July 1, 1863, WKU.

60. Douglas Cater to cousin, June 24, 1863, Douglas J. and Rufus W. Cater Papers, LOC.

61. *OR*, 24(3):980; Cipher message, June 26, 1863, Carter L. Stevenson Papers, RG 109, E 134, NARA.

62. Kirwan, ed., *Johnny Green of the Orphan Brigade*, 79; John S. Jacksman Diary, June 3, 7, and 28, 1863, LOC; Welsh, *Medical Histories of Confederate Generals*, 5; Douglas Cater to cousin, June 11, 1863, Douglas J. and Rufus W. Cater Papers, LOC; Timothy B. Smith, *Mississippi in the Civil War: The Home Front* (Jackson: University Press of Mississippi, 2010), 195.

63. *OR*, 24(3):979–980, 986, 1070.

64. *OR*, 24(3):979.

65. *OR*, 24(3):979, 981; *OR*, 24(1):113.

66. Symonds, *Joseph E. Johnston*, 214; *OR*, 24(3):985; *OR*, 24(2):244.

67. Joseph D. Alison Diary, June 10, 1863, MDAH; *OR*, 24(3):448; *ORN*, 25:66; "Letter from Vicksburg," June 30, 1863, Natchez *Daily Courier*, copy in Siege of Vicksburg Cave Life Subject File, MDAH; "From Vicksburg," June 6, 1863, Cincinnati *Daily Gazette*, copy in Siege of Vicksburg Accounts Newspaper Subject File, MDAH.

68. C. Woodward to daughter, June 9, 1863, Siege of Vicksburg Accounts Civilian Subject File, MDAH; *SOR*, 4:305–306; *OR*, 24(1):110; Richard and Richard, *The Defense of Vicksburg*, 218; J. P. Jones to wife, July 12, 1863, John P. Jones Papers, FHS.

69. J. W. Greenman Diary, MDAH, 105–106; Dodd, "Recollections of Vicksburg During the Siege," 5; L. McRae. Bell, "A Girl's Experience in the Siege of Vicksburg," *Harper's Weekly*, June 8, 1912:12–13; Winschel, *Triumph and Defeat: The Vicksburg Campaign, Volume 2*, 105; Loughborough, *My Cave Life in Vicksburg*, 141.

70. C. Woodward to daughter, June 9, 1863, Siege of Vicksburg Accounts Civilian Subject File, MDAH; J. W. Greenman Diary, MDAH, 105–106; Simon, ed., *PUSG*, 8:449; Cable, ed., "A Woman's Diary of the Siege of Vicksburg," 773; Hander "Excerpts from the Hander Diary," 147; Clarke, *Reminiscence and Anecdotes of the War for Southern Independence*, 113; Tunnard, *A Southern Record*, 243; Harwell, "In and Around Vicksburg," 334.

71. Rowland Chambers Diary, June 4, 1863, LSU; Richard and Richard, *The Defense of Vicksburg*, 217; John A. Leavy Diary, June 29, 1863, Journals/Letters/Diaries Series, VICK; C. Woodward to daughter, June 9, 1863, Siege of Vicksburg Accounts Civilian Subject File, MDAH; Lou Clark, "A Woman in the Siege of Vicksburg," April 16, 1908, Jackson *Clarion Ledger*, copy in Siege of Vicksburg Accounts Civilians Subject File, MDAH; Anne to Emma, June/July 1863, Shannon-Crutcher Family Papers, MDAH; Moore, ed., *The Rebellion Record*, 170; Winschel, *Triumph and Defeat*, 153.

72. James L. Power Diary, June 26 and 28, 1863, MDAH; Abrams, *A Full and*

Detailed History, 47; "An Inside View of Vicksburg," July 18, 1863, Washington, DC *Daily National Intelligencer*, copy in Siege of Vicksburg Accounts Confederate Subject File, MDAH; Richard and Richard, *The Defense of Vicksburg*, 217; Abrams, *A Full and Detailed History*, 47; Cotton, ed., *From the Pen of a She-Rebel*, 40–41; C. Woodward to daughter, June 9, 1863, Siege of Vicksburg Accounts Civilian Subject File, MDAH; "Residents Became Hungry Enough to Eat Their Pets," June 12, 1988, Vicksburg *Evening Post*, copy in Siege of Vicksburg Accounts Civilian Subject File, MDAH; Loughborough, *My Cave Life in Vicksburg*, 78–79; Joseph D. Alison Diary, June 10, 1863, MDAH; John C. Taylor Diary, June 24, 1863, UVA.

73. William L. Foster to wife, June 20, 1863, UA; Abrams, *A Full and Detailed History*, 47–48.

74. John C. Taylor Diary, June 26, 1863, UVA; Jones, "The Rank and File at Vicksburg," 28; Pratt, ed., "Civil War Letters of Brigadier-General William Ward Orme, 1862–1866," 289; *OR*, 24(2):698; Calvin Ainsworth Diary, June 30, 1863, Journals/Letters/Diaries Series, VICK; Charles Willison to Ellie, July 1, 1863, 76th Ohio Volunteer Infantry Papers, OHS; Cable, ed., "A Woman's Diary of the Siege of Vicksburg," 773. See John J. Robacher Papers, MDAH, for passes issued by Confederate authorities.

75. Simon, ed., *PUSG*, 8:377; Clarke, *Reminiscence and Anecdotes of the War for Southern Independence*, 111; Herman Hattaway and Archer Jones, *How the North Won: A Military History of the Civil War* (Urbana: University of Illinois Press, 1983), 410.

76. Cable, ed., "A Woman's Diary of the Siege of Vicksburg," 771; Ellen Martin, "The Bombardment of Vicksburg," April 16, 1908, Jackson *Clarion Ledger*, copy in Siege of Vicksburg Accounts Civilian Subject File, MDAH; Loughborough, *My Cave Life in Vicksburg*, 77; Winschel, *Triumph and Defeat: The Vicksburg Campaign, Volume 2*, 111; Loughborough, *My Cave Life in Vicksburg*, 75.

77. Loughborough, *My Cave Life in Vicksburg*, 76, 81, 131; Byers, *With Fire and Sword*, 96.

78. William L. Foster to wife, June 20, 1863, UA.

79. William Thomson to Ruffin, July 2, 1863, Ruffin Thomson Papers, UNC.

80. Pratt, ed., "Civil War Letters of Brigadier-General William Ward Orme, 1862–1866," 291; William Sherman to wife, June 27, 1863, William T. Sherman Papers, LOC; Lot Abraham Diary, June 4, 1863, UIA.

81. Louisa Russell Conner Memoir, 1905, MDAH, 16; Sherman, *Memoirs of General William T. Sherman*, 1:329.

82. *OR*, 24(2):247, 305–306.

83. *OR*, 24(2):311; James G. Fox to father, July 5, 1863, James G. Fox Letter, ALPL; Oldroyd, *A Soldier's Story*, 65, 69; "In the Trenches Before Vicksburg," November 15, 1900, *National Tribune*.

84. *OR*, 24(2):247; Earl J. Hess, "Grant's Ethnic General: Peter J. Osterhaus," in *Grant's Lieutenants: From Cairo to Vicksburg*, Steven E. Woodworth, ed. (Lawrence: University Press of Kansas, 2001), 213.

85. Marszalek, *Sherman*, 228; Sherman, *Memoirs of General William T. Sherman*, 1:329–330.

86. Sherman, *Memoirs of General William T. Sherman*, 1:330.

87. Oldroyd, *A Soldier's Story*, 72–73.

88. French, *Two Wars*, 182; Louisa Russell Conner Memoir, 1905, MDAH, 17; Mary M. Smith to John J. Pettus, June 30, 1863, Pettus Governor Papers, MDAH.

CHAPTER 14. "I ONLY WONDER IT HAS HELD OUT SO LONG"

1. Walter Gresham to wife, July 2, 1863, Walter Q. Gresham Papers, LOC; Pratt, ed., "Civil War Letters of Brigadier-General William Ward Orme, 1862–1866," 284.

2. Walter Gresham to wife, June 24, 1863, Walter Q. Gresham Papers, LOC; J. Carroll Harriss to Valery, June 30, 1863, Jordan C. Harriss Papers, NC; Elder III, ed., *A Damned Iowa Greyhound*, 77; Charles Affeld Diary, July 3, 1863, Journals/Diaries/Letters Series, VICK; Eli Todd to brother, July 19, 1863, Eli J. Todd Papers, OHS.

3. Steven E. Woodworth, *Jefferson Davis and His Generals: The Failure of Confederate Command in the West* (Lawrence: University Press of Kansas, 1990), 214; John A. Leavy Diary, June 28, 1863, Journals/Letters/Diaries Series, VICK.

4. Charles Willison to Ellie, May 26, 1863, 76th Ohio File, VICK; E. Z. Hays, *History of the Thirty-second Regiment Ohio Veteran Volunteer Infantry* (Columbus: Cott & Evans Printers, 1896), 44; W. L. Rand to father, June 1, 1863, Rand Family Papers, ALPL; Charles B. Richards Address, undated, Charles B. Richards Collection, OHS; Chase Dickinson to friends, May 29, 1863, Chase Hall Dickinson Papers, NL; Elliott Morrow to uncle, May 30, 1863, Elliott Morrow Papers, OHS; Jim Giauque to brother, June 24, 1863, Giauque Family Papers, UIA.

5. John Russell to brother, July 14, 1863, John J. Russell Letters, NL; Rodney Jeger to sister, July 2, 1863, Rodney Jeger Papers, ISL.

6. Lafayette McLaws to brother, June 5, 1863, Lafayette McLaws Papers, UNC; Leon Polk to wife, June 17 and 28, 1863, L. L. Polk Papers, UNC; George Gift to Ellen Shackelford, June 6, 1863, George W. Gift Papers, UNC; David Schenck Diary, June 11, 1863, UNC.

7. Richard and Richard, *The Defense of Vicksburg*, 210; Adolph Engelmann to wife, June 26 and July 3, 1863, Engelmann-Kircher Family Papers, ALPL.

8. J. H. Pepper Diary, July 1, 1863, MDAH; William Drennan Diary, July 2 and 3, 1863, Journals/Letters/Diaries Series, VICK.

9. *OR*, 24(3):458.

10. *OR*, 24(1):113; *OR*, 24(2):172, 174–175, 185–186, 333–334; Richard and Richard, *The Defense of Vicksburg*, 204; J. H. Pepper Diary, June 28, 1863, MDAH.

11. *OR*, 24(1):113; *OR*, 24(2):172, 174–175, 185–186, 333–334; Richard and Richard, *The Defense of Vicksburg*, 204; J. H. Pepper Diary, June 28, 1863, MDAH.

12. *OR*, 24(2):190; John Forney to R. W. Memminger, July 1, 1863, Dabney Maury Order Book, CHM, 306.

13. *OR*, 24(2):192.

14. *OR*, 24(3):456; *OR*, 24(2):202–203, 333–334, 365, 368; Lockett, "The Defense of Vicksburg," 491; Edmund Newsome Diary, June 30, MDAH.

15. *OR*, 24(2):173; Solonick, *Engineering Victory*, 197, .

16. *OR*, 24(3):456–457; *OR*, 24(2):317.

17. Solonick, *Engineering Victory*, 199.

18. *OR*, 24(1):113; *OR*, 24(2):173, 334, 368; William R. Eddington Memoir, undated, ALPL, 10; Job H. Yaggy Diary, July 1, 1863, ALPL; James Vanderbilt to mother, July 3, 1863, James C. Vanderbilt Papers, ISL; William R. Eddington Autobiography, undated, 97th Illinois File, VICK, 14.

19. *OR*, 24(2):179; William R. Eddington Memoir, undated, ALPL, 10; Francis R. Baker Diary, June 25, 1863, ALPL; Trowbridge, *Autobiography of Silas Thompson Trowbridge*, 146–147; Clark, ed., *Downing's Civil War Diary*, 122; Joseph Stockton Diary, July 1, 1863, ALPL; J. Carroll Harriss to Valery, July 4, 1863, Jordan C. Harriss Papers, NC; Winschel, *Triumph and Defeat*, 137; J. W. Guthrie to father, July 4, 1863, J. W. Guthrie Letter, LSU.

20. *OR*, 24(2):334, 365, 368, 373, 416; Tunnard, *A Southern Record*, 266; Lockett, "The Defense of Vicksburg," 491; Anderson, *Memoirs*, 351–352, 355; Grabau, *Ninety-Eight Days*, 437.

21. *OR*, 24(2):334, 365, 368, 373, 416; Lockett, "The Defense of Vicksburg," 491; Anderson, *Memoirs*, 355.

22. *OR*, 24(2):334, 365, 368, 373, 416; Philip Thomas Tucker, *Westerners in Gray: The Men of and Missions of the Elite Fifth Missouri Infantry Regiment* (Jefferson, NC: McFarland & Company, 1995), 244–245; Theodore D. Fisher Diary, June 29 and July 2, 1863, Journals/Letters/Diaries Series, VICK.

23. *OR*, 24(3):985; *OR*, 24(2):377; Tunnard, *A Southern Record*, 267.

24. *OR*, 24(1):113; *OR*, 24(2):173, 208, 365, 413, 416; Hickenlooper, "The Vicksburg Mine," 540; Francis R. Baker Diary, June 30, 1863, ALPL; Solonick, *Engineering Victory*, 167. Brigade commander Manning Force gave the idea of the wooden mortars to one of his 20th Ohio soldiers named Friend, and another gave the distinction to a soldier named Hanson Barr. See Force, "Personal Recollections of the Vicksburg Campaign," 307; "In the Trenches Before Vicksburg," November 15, 1900, *National Tribune*.

25. *OR*, 24(2):185–186; Francis R. Baker Diary, July 2, 1863, ALPL; Grecian, *History of the Eighty-third Regiment, Indiana Volunteer Infantry*, 91.

26. *OR*, 24(2):174–175.

27. *OR*, 24(3):458–459; *OR*, 24(1):101, 114; *OR*, 24(2):186; *OR*, 52(1):382–383; Simon, ed., *PUSG*, 8:449; Trowbridge, *Autobiography of Silas Thompson Trowbridge*, 148; Marszalek et al., eds., *The Personal Memoirs of Ulysses S. Grant*, 381; Henry P. Whipple Diary, July 1, 1863, WHS.

28. *OR*, 24(1):114; *OR*, 24(2):175; Rachel Sherman Thorndike, ed., *The Sherman Letters: Correspondence between General and Senator Sherman from 1837 to 1891* (New York: Charles Scribner's Sons, 1894), 206.

29. Kirwan, ed., *Johnny Green of the Orphan Brigade*, 79; William Thomson to

Ruffin, July 2, 1863, Ruffin Thomson Papers, UNC; Thomas M. Gore Memoir, undated, Gore Civil War History Collection, University of Southern Mississippi, 81; Thomas Kirkpatrick Mitchell Diary, July 1, 1863, AU; John S. Jackman Diary, July 1, 1863, LOC; Ben Sibert to mother, July 1, 1863, Mrs. Paul Seehausen Papers, ISL.

30. Kirwan, ed., *Johnny Green of the Orphan Brigade*, 79–80; Henry George, *History of the 3d, 7th, 8th and 12th Kentucky C.S.A.* (Louisville, KY: C. T. Dearing Printing Co., 1911), 65.

31. *OR*, 24(3):986; Bearss, *The Vicksburg Campaign*, 3:1131, 1133; Grabau, *Ninety-Eight Days*, 470; L. J. Sanders Diary, July 1, 1863, WKU; M. D. L. Stephens Recollections, 1899, MDAH, 23; French, *Two Wars*, 182; John S. Jackman Diary, July 2–3, 1863, LOC.

32. *OR*, 24(3):986.

33. *OR*, 24(1):196, 198; *OR*, 52(2):496–497; Symonds, *Joseph E. Johnston*, 213.

34. *OR*, 24(1):244–245; *OR*, 52(2):503; "Our Army," July 3, 1863, Canton *American Citizen*.

35. French, *Two Wars*, 182; Bearss, *The Vicksburg Campaign*, 3:1134.

36. *OR*, 24(1):245; G. B. Lake to Bob, July 5, 1863, Hughes Family Papers, UNC; John Merrilees Diary, June 20, 1863, CHM; Winschel, *Triumph and Defeat: The Vicksburg Campaign, Volume 2*, 127.

37. *OR*, 24(1):244, 279, 287; *OR*, 24(3):964, 974.

38. Uley Burk to family, July 1, 1863, 30th Iowa File, VICK; *OR*, 24(3):458; *OR*, 24(1):113; Simon, ed., *PUSG*, 8:450; W. L. Rand Diary, July 1, 1863, Rand Family Papers, ALPL.

39. *OR*, 24(3):457; *OR*, 24(1):113; *OR*, 24(2):209; Simon, ed., *PUSG*, 8:447, 451.

40. Louis W. Knobe Diary, June 28, 1863, ISL; Crooke, *The Twenty-first Regiment of Iowa Volunteer Infantry*, 111.

41. *OR*, 24(3):458; *OR*, 24(2):246; Albert, ed., *History of the Forty-fifth Regiment Pennsylvania*, 69; Jackman, *History of the Sixth New Hampshire Regiment*, 170; Ephraim Dawes to Luce, July 1, 1863, Ephraim C. Dawes Papers, NL.

42. *OR*, 24(3):459; Robert Jameson to sister, July 4, 1863, Robert E. Jameson Papers, LOC; James Russell Soley, "Naval Operations in the Vicksburg Campaign," in *Battles and Leaders of the Civil War*, 4 vols. (New York: Century Company, 1884–1887), 3:551–570; Belknap, *History of the Fifteenth Regiment*, 261; Samuel S. Irwin Diary, July 3, 1863, ALPL.

43. *ORN*, 25:104.

44. *ORN*, 25:104.

45. *ORN*, 25:47, 146.

46. *ORN*, 25:146–147.

47. *ORN*, 25:36, 47, 51, 53, 66, 80; Samuel Eells to unknown, June 26, 1863, Samuel H. Eells Papers, LC.

48. *ORN*, 25:36, 47, 51, 53, 66, 104.

49. *ORN*, 25:58–59, 61–62.

50. *ORN*, 25:61.

51. *ORN*, 25:89.

52. *ORN*, 25:83–85.

53. *ORN*, 25:37, 98.

54. *ORN*, 25:56–57, 108.

55. *ORN*, 25:73–74, 76–80, 96, 104, 107; *OR*, 24(2):319; Simon, ed., *PUSG*, 8:334; Charles Dana Miller Diary, June 28, 1863, Journals/Letters/Diaries Series, VICK; Robert Blackstone to W. T. Rigby, January 17, 1863, 32nd Ohio File, VICK.

56. *ORN*, 25:73–74, 76–80.

57. Simon, ed., *PUSG*, 8:389–390; William A. Minard to Joe, June 29, 1863, John C. Pemberton Papers, UNC.

58. *ORN*, 25:70–72, 87, 9192.

59. *ORN*, 25:99.

60. *ORN*, 25:93.

61. *ORN*, 25:64, 66, 88; *OR*, 24(2):398; William L. Foster to wife, June 20, 1863, UA.

62. *ORN*, 25:69.

63. *ORN*, 25:48, 68, 71, 82, 84, 94; Simon, ed., *PUSG*, 8:334.

64. Hoehling, *Vicksburg*, 64; *ORN*, 25:48, 70, 94, 96, 101.

65. *ORN*, 25:62, 97.

66. *ORN*, 25:66, 104.

67. *ORN*, 25:104–105; *OR*, 24(1):58; Marszalek et al., eds., *The Personal Memoirs of Ulysses S. Grant*, 396; Dunnavent, "'We Had Lively Times Up the Yazoo': Admiral David Dixon Porter," 178–179.

68. David D. Porter to sir, January 27, 1888, John H. Dorman Papers, OHS.

69. Don Pardee to unknown, May 25 and June 1, 1863, Don A. Pardee Papers, TU; William T. Rigby Diary, June 1 and 14, 1863, UIA.

70. E. B. Bascom Diary, June 14, 1863, 5th Iowa File, VICK; James Pickett Jones, *Black Jack: John A. Logan and Southern Illinois in the Civil War Era* (Carbondale: Southern Illinois University Press, 1995), 172–173; Brown, *History of the Fourth Regiment of Minnesota*, 228–229; Welsh, *Medical Histories of Union Generals*, 203; "In the Trenches Before Vicksburg," November 15, 1900, *National Tribune*.

71. N. M. Baker to C. A. Noble, May 5, 1902, 116th Illinois File, VICK; Robert Oliver to W. T. Rigby, April 6, 1902, and Henry S. Nourse to W. T. Rigby, November 9, 1901, 55th Illinois File, VICK.

72. Henry J. Seaman Diary, June 19, 1863, CWTI, USAHEC; Merrick J. Wald Diary, June 28, 1863, OCM; Welsh, *Medical Histories of Union Generals*, 307; Pratt, ed., "Civil War Letters of Brigadier-General William Ward Orme, 1862–1866," 279; James Slack to Ann, June 3, 1863, James R. Slack Papers, ISL.

73. Welsh, *Medical Histories of Union Generals*, 57; E. H. Ingraham to aunt, June 15, 1863, and Ned to Alice, July 3, 1863, E. H. and D. G. Ingraham Letters, ALPL; W. P. Benton to John A. Rawlins, May 31, 1862, William P. Benton Papers, RG 94, E 159, NARA; William P. Benton Medical Certificate, May 31, 1863, William P. Benton Papers, RG 94, E 159, NARA; Bearss, *The Vicksburg Campaign*, 3:881; William Murray Diary, June 4, 1863, Journals/Letters/Diaries Series, VICK; John A. Bering and Thomas Montgomery,

History of the Forty-Eighth Ohio Vet. Vol. Inf. (Hillsboro, OH: Highland News Office, 1880), 93.

74. Henry J. Seaman Diary, July 4, 1863, CWTI, USAHEC; Bearss, *The Vicksburg Campaign*, 3:882; R. W. Burt to Mr. Editor, June 21, 1863, 76th Ohio Volunteer Infantry Papers, OHS.

75. "Charges and Specifications," undated, Frank P. Blair Papers, RG 94, E 159, NARA; Smith, *Life and Letters of Thomas Kilby Smith*, 65, 68–69, 71, 297–298; James H. St. John Diary, May 24, 1863, ISL; Andrew McCornack to parents, June 30, 1863, Andrew McCormack Letters, Sword Collection, USAHEC; *The Story of the Fifty-fifth Regiment Illinois*, 247; Grecian, *History of the Eighty-third Regiment, Indiana*, 33.

76. *OR*, 24(3):447; *OR*, 24(2):404, 410, 413, 420–421; Bearss, *The Vicksburg Campaign*, 3:882–883; Welsh, *Medical Histories of Union Generals*, 42; George M. Lucas Diary, June 29, 1863, ALPL.

77. I. F. Quinby to William T. Clark, May 31, 1863, Isaac F. Quinby Papers, RG 94, E 159, NARA; Quinby Surgeon's Certificate, May 30, 1863, Isaac F. Quinby Papers, RG 94, E 159, NARA; Henry Cole Quinby, *Genealogical History of the Quinby (Quimby) Family In England and America* (Rutland, VT: Tuttle Company, 1915), 429; George Ditto Diary, June 3, 1863, ALPL; John E. Smith to Aimee, June 7, 1863, John E. Smith Letters, Kirby Smith Collection; *OR*, 24(1):92; Bearss, *The Vicksburg Campaign*, 3:884; "With the Western Army," January 16, 1863, *National Tribune*; Charles H. Matthies Statement, June 2, 1863, C. L. Matthies Papers, RG 94, E 159, NARA.

78. Gilbert Young to mother, May 28, 1863, Gilbert N. Young Letters, Journals/Letters/Diaries Series, VICK; Wells W. Leggett to mother, June 6, 1863, Mortimer Leggett Papers, Lincoln Memorial Shrine, copy in Journals/Letters/Diaries Series, VICK; Mortimer D. Leggett to George W. Childs, November 28, 1863, Mortimer D. Leggett Papers, CHM; M. D. Leggett to Manning Force, June 3, 1863, Manning F. Force Papers, UW, copy in LOC; Edgar Rombauer to Frank Gaiennie, February 17, 1917, 17th Missouri File, VICK; Job H. Yaggy Diary, June 18, 1863, ALPL.

79. *OR*, 24(2):302, 309; Jim Huffstodt, *Hard Dying Men: The Story of General W. H. L. Wallace, General T. E. G. Ransom, and Their "Old Eleventh" Illinois Infantry in the American Civil War (1861–1865)* (Bowie, MD: Heritage Books, 1991), 147; Belcher, *The 11th Missouri*, 132.

80. George Chittenden to wife, June 9, 1863, Chittenden Family Papers, ISL; Uley Burk to family, June 8, 1863, 30th Iowa File, VICK; William M. Reid Diary, June 11, 1863, ALPL.

81. J. T. Hogane, "Reminiscences of the Siege of Vicksburg—Paper No. 3," *Southern Historical Society Papers* 11, no. 11 (November 1883): 487; *OR*, 24(1):281; *OR*, 52(2):503; 207; William L. B. Jenney, "With Sherman and Grant from Memphis to Chattanooga: A Reminisce," in *Military Essays and Recollections: Papers Read Before the Commandery of the State of Illinois, Military Order of the Loyal Legion of the United States, Volume 4* (Chicago: Cozzens and Beaton Company, 1907), 207.

82. *OR*, 24(1):281–282; *OR*, 24(2):346–349, 352; Lockett, "The Defense of Vicksburg," 492; Hattaway, *General Stephen D. Lee*, 97.

83. *OR*, 24(1):282; *OR*, 24(2):374, 383.

84. *OR*, 24(1):282; *OR*, 24(2):405; Lockett, "The Defense of Vicksburg," 492.

85. *OR*, 24(1):282–283.

86. Richard and Richard, *The Defense of Vicksburg*, 220, 222; Chambers, "My Journal," 279.

87. John C. Taylor Diary, July 2, 1863, UVA; *OR*, 24(1):330–331; Bearss, *The Vicksburg Campaign*, 3:1284.

88. *OR*, 24(1):331.

89. *OR*, 24(1):283; *OR*, 24(2):340, 346; Lockett, "The Defense of Vicksburg," 492.

CHAPTER 15. "VICKSBURG HAS SURRENDERED"

1. *OR*, 24(3):459, 467; Simon, ed., *PUSG*, 8:470; Samuel Smith to parents, July 4, 1863, Samuel Smith Letters, OCM, Norman W. Calkins Diary, July 4, 1863, CWD, USA-HEC; James M. McPherson, *Battle Cry of Freedom: The Civil War Era* (New York: Oxford University Press, 1988), 453.

2. *OR*, 27(3):515; Gideon Welles, *Diary of Gideon Welles: Secretary of the Navy under Lincoln and Johnson*, 3 vols. (Boston: Houghton Mifflin Co., 1911), 1:357–358. For Gettysburg, see Stephen W. Sears, *Gettysburg* (Boston: Houghton Mifflin, 2003) and Noah Andre Trudeau, *Gettysburg: A Testing of Courage* (New York: HarperCollins, 2002).

3. For Tullahoma, see David A. Powell and Eric J. Wittenberg, *Tullahoma: The Forgotten Campaign That Changed the Course of the Civil War, June 23–July 4, 1863* (New York: Savas Beatie, 2020).

4. Simon, ed., *PUSG*, 8:389; *OR*, 52(2):504; William Vermilion to Mary, July 6, 1863, Vermilion Family Correspondence, University of California, San Diego; J. P. Jones to wife, July 12, 1863, John P. Jones Papers, FHS.

5. Phillip Roesch Diary, July 4, 1863, OCM; *OR*, 24(2):303, 310; John S. Jacksman Diary, July 4, 1863, LOC; Cater to cousin, July 24, 1863, Douglas J. and Rufus W. Cater Papers, LOC; Sarah Poates Diary, July 4, 1863, Asa Fitch Papers, Cornell University, Ithica, New York.

6. *OR*, 24(2):192; John Ford to father, July 4, 1863, John W. Ford Letters, CWTI, USAHEC; James Vanderbilt to mother, July 3, 1863, James C. Vanderbilt Papers, ISL.

7. William B. Britton to Editors Gazette, July 4, 1863, William B. Britton Letters, OCM; George C. Churcheus Diary, July 4, 1863, OHS.

8. *OR*, 52(2):503; Clarke, *Reminiscence and Anecdotes of the War for Southern Independence*, 104; *OR*, 24(1):58; Simon, ed., *PUSG*, 8:439; Curtis P. Lacey Diary, July 2, 1863, NL.

9. Emore Young to wife, July 4, 1863, Emor Young Papers, FHS; Joseph D. Alison Diary, July 4, 1863, MDAH.

10. "The Terms of Surrender," in *Battles and Leaders of the Civil War*, 4 vols. (New York: Century Company, 1884–1887), 3:543; Louis Hébert Autobiography, 1894, UNC, 13, also in LSU.

11. Lockett, "The Defense of Vicksburg," 492.

12. Moore, ed., *The Rebellion Record*, 173; Marszalek et al., eds., *The Personal Memoirs of Ulysses S. Grant*, 384; *OR*, 24(1):57, 114; *OR*, 52(2):503–504; Jones, "The Rank and File at Vicksburg," 28; William L. Foster to wife, June 20, 1863, UA; Job H. Yaggy Diary, July 3, 1863, ALPL; James L. Power Diary, July 3, 1863, MDAH; John Forney to R. W. Memminger, July 3, 1863, Dabney Maury Order Book, CHM, 308. Captain Robert Buchanan of the 7th Missouri also claimed to have met Bowen. Robert Buchanan to W. T. Rigby, February 21, 1905, 7th Missouri File, VICK; William G. Bek, ed., "The Civil War Diary of John T. Buegel, Union Soldier," *Missouri Historical Review* 40, no. 4 (July 1946): 511.

13. Richard L. Howard, "The Vicksburg Campaign," in *War Papers Read Before the Commandery of the State of Maine, Military Order of the Loyal Legion of the United States, Volume 2* (Portland, ME: Lefavor-Tower Company, 1902), 38; Rood, *Story of the Service of Company E*, 204; Anthony B. Burton Diary, July 3, 1863, ALPL; Hoehling, *Vicksburg*, 270–271; "United States. Army. Illinois Infantry Regiment, 14th (1861–1863) Company A," July 3, 1863, ALPL; William M. Reid Diary, July 4, 1863, ALPL; Balzar Grebe Memoir, undated, Balzar Grebe Papers, ALPL, 21.

14. John J. Kellogg Memoirs, 1913, Journals/Letters/Diaries Series, VICK, 62; George Carrington Diary, July 3, 1863, CHM.

15. Richard and Richard, *The Defense of Vicksburg*, 227; Trowbridge, *Autobiography of Silas Thompson Trowbridge*, 149; Clarke, *Reminiscence and Anecdotes of the War for Southern Independence*, 111; Hander "Excerpts from the Hander Diary," 147; Robert L. Bachman Memoir, undated, OCM, 23; Augustus Lattz Diary, June 3, 1863, LSU.

16. *OR*, 24(1):59; James K. Bigelow, *Abridged History of the Eighth Indiana Volunteer Infantry, from Its Organization, April 21st, 1861, to the Date of Re-enlistment as Veterans, January 1, 1864* (Indianapolis: Ellis Barnes Book and Job Printer, 1864), 21.

17. Brown, *History of the Fourth Regiment of Minnesota Infantry*, 235–236; Fred Grant Memoir, undated, USGPL, 39; Woodworth, *Nothing But Victory*, 448; Tucker, *The Forgotten "Stonewall of the West,"* 305; "More About Vicksburg," September 29, 1910, *National Tribune*.

18. Grecian, *History of the Eighty-third Regiment, Indiana Volunteer Infantry*, 93.

19. *OR*, 24(1):60; Brown, *History of the Fourth Regiment of Minnesota Infantry*, 235–236; William Murray Diary, July 3, 1863, Journals/Letters/Diaries Series, VICK; Chase H. Dickinson Diary, July 3, 1863, NL; Henry Miller to sister, July 13, 1863, Henry H. Miller Papers, CHM.

20. Dana, *Recollections of the Civil War*, 95; Henry Miller to sister, July 13, 1863, Henry H. Miller Papers, CHM; William L. Brown to father, July 4, 1863, William L. Brown Papers, CHM.

21. *OR*, 24(3):460; "The Terms of Surrender," 544; Simpson, *Ulysses S. Grant*, 213; Grabau, *Ninety-Eight Days*, 496; Tucker, *The Forgotten "Stonewall of the West,"* 306; John C. Taylor Diary, July 3, 1863, UVA.

22. *OR*, 24(3):460; "The Terms of Surrender," 544; Simpson, *Ulysses S. Grant*, 213;

Grabau, *Ninety-Eight Days*, 496; Tucker, *The Forgotten "Stonewall of the West*," 306; John C. Taylor Diary, July 3, 1863, UVA; Brown, *History of the Fourth Regiment of Minnesota Infantry*, 235–236.

23. Brown, *History of the Fourth Regiment of Minnesota Infantry*, 235–236; Richard and Richard, *The Defense of Vicksburg*, 223; Chambers, "My Journal," 280.

24. Charles H. Brush to sister, July 7, 1863, Daniel H. Brush Papers, ALPL; Marszalek et al., eds., *The Personal Memoirs of Ulysses S. Grant*, 384.

25. W. H. MCCardle to John Forney, July 3, 1863, Letters and Telegrams Sent, Department of Mississippi and East Louisiana, 1863, RG 109, Chapter II, Vol. 60, NARA; Richard and Richard, *The Defense of Vicksburg*, 223.

26. *OR*, 24(2):319, 410; James L. Power Diary, July 3, 1863, MDAH; Jones, "An Artilleryman's Diary," 76; Wayne Johnson Jacobs Diary, July 3, 1863, LSU.

27. Ballard, *Pemberton*, 179; Fred Grant Memoir, undated, USGPL, 40; Strong, "The Campaign Against Vicksburg," 345; "The Terms of Surrender," 544; Marszalek et al., eds., *The Personal Memoirs of Ulysses S. Grant*, 385; William L. Foster to wife, June 20, 1863, UA.

28. Perry, "Vicksburg," 173–174.

29. "The Terms of Surrender," 544; Ballard, *Pemberton*, 61.

30. *OR*, 24(1):284; "The Terms of Surrender," 544; Marszalek et al., eds., *The Personal Memoirs of Ulysses S. Grant*, 385; Dana, *Recollections of the Civil War*, 97; Thomas Taylor to W. T. Rigby, March 19, 1903, 47th Ohio File, VICK.

31. Marszalek et al., eds., *The Personal Memoirs of Ulysses S. Grant*, 386; "The Terms of Surrender," 544–545; Anderson, *Memoirs*, 357.

32. Jones, "The Rank and File at Vicksburg," 29; William E. Strong Reminiscences, undated, William E. Strong Papers, ALPL, 57; Samuel Joseph Churchill Memoir, undated, OCM.

33. *OR*, 24(1):284; *OR*, 24(3):460; "The Terms of Surrender," 544–545; William L. Faulk Diary, July 4, 1863, OCM; C. H. Bass to mother, July 4, 1863, C. H. Bass Letter, CHM.

34. Dodd, "Recollections of Vicksburg during the Siege," 10; Francis R. Baker Diary, July 3, 1863, ALPL.

35. Marszalek et al., eds., *The Personal Memoirs of Ulysses S. Grant*, 386; "The Terms of Surrender," 545; Fred Grant Memoir, undated, USGPL, 41.

36. *OR*, 24(1):115; *OR*, 24(3):460; Dana, *Recollections of the Civil War*, 97–98; Marszalek et al., eds., *The Personal Memoirs of Ulysses S. Grant*, 386; Grant, "A Boy's Experience at Vicksburg," 98; Catton, *Grant Moves South*, 474–475.

37. *OR*, 24(1):60, 115; Dana, *Recollections of the Civil War*, 97–98; Grant, "A Boy's Experience at Vicksburg," 98; Catton, *Grant Moves South*, 474–475.

38. *OR*, 24(3):460, 467; Anthony B. Burton Diary, July 4, 1863, ALPL; Pinckney Skilton Cone Diary, July 4, 1863, ALPL; James Sinclair Diary, July 4, 1863, CHM.

39. *OR*, 24(2):403; *OR*, 24(1):115; Solonick, *Engineering Victory*, 208; Wilson, *Under the Old Flag*, 221; Perry, "Vicksburg," 173–174; Lockett, "The Defense of Vicksburg,"

492; William E. Strong Reminiscences, undated, William E. Strong Papers, ALPL, 64; Unknown to W. T. Rigby, April 17, 1903, 3rd Louisiana File, VICK; Daniel Roberts to family, July 4, 1863, Daniel Roberts Papers, ISL.

40. *OR*, 24(1):61; *OR*, 24(3):471; Simon, ed., *PUSG*, 8:459.

41. *OR*, 24(1):61; *OR*, 24(3):471; Simon, ed., *PUSG*, 8:459.

42. *OR*, 24(1):61; Fred Grant Memoir, undated, USGPL, 41–42.

43. Trowbridge, *Autobiography of Silas Thompson Trowbridge*, 150; Richard and Richard, *The Defense of Vicksburg*, 226–227; Joseph W. Westbrook Memoir, 1903, Joseph W. Westbrook Papers, CWD, USAHEC.

44. Dana, *Recollections of the Civil War*, 96; Ballard, *Pemberton*, 180; Lockett, "The Defense of Vicksburg," 492, Cornelius Byington Diary, July 4, 1863, AM.

45. John Forney to General, July 4, 1863, Dabney Maury Order Book, CHM, 309; *OR*, 52(2):505; John C. Swift Diary, July 4, 1863, IHS; Abrams, *A Full and Detailed History*, 61.

46. Hall, *The Story of the 26th Louisiana Infantry*, 91; Anderson, *Memoirs*, 337; John S. Bell, "The Arkansas Sharpshooters," undated, 12th Arkansas Battalion Sharpshooters File, VICK; Jones, "The Rank and File at Vicksburg," 29; John J. Kellogg Memoirs, 1913, Journals/Letters/Diaries Series, VICK, 63; Richard and Richard, *The Defense of Vicksburg*, 227; Tunnard, *A Southern Record*, 271; Clarke, *Reminiscence and Anecdotes of the War for Southern Independence*, 113; *OR*, 24(2):403, 410; Chambers, "My Journal," 281; George Ditto Diary, July 4, 1863, ALPL; Alvin Hovey Memoir, undated, IU, 64; George Carrington Diary, July 4, 1863, CHM; John D. Brownley, "History of John D. Browley," undated, Anders Collection, USAHEC; Edward E. Schweitzer Diary, July 4, 1863, CWTI, USAHEC.

47. Thompson, *Recollections with the Third Iowa Regiment*, 387; Henry J. Seaman Diary, July 4, 1863, CWTI, USAHEC; Joel Strong Reminiscences, 1910, MHS, 16; John Hughes Diary, July 4, 1863, LC.

48. Hall, *The Story of the 26th Louisiana Infantry*, 91; Brown, *History of the Fourth Regiment of Minnesota Infantry*, 238–239; William R. Clack Diary, July 4, 1863, TSLA.

49. John J. Kellogg Memoirs, 1913, Journals/Letters/Diaries Series, VICK, 63; George Ditto Diary, July 4, 1863, ALPL; Alvin Hovey Memoir, undated, IU, 64; George Carrington Diary, July 4, 1863, CHM; John D. Brownley, "History of John D. Browley," undated, Andres Collection, USAHEC; Edward E. Schweitzer Diary, July 4, 1863, CWTI, USAHEC.

50. Jones, "The Rank and File at Vicksburg," 29; John J. Kellogg Memoirs, 1913, Journals/Letters/Diaries Series, VICK, 63; Richard and Richard, *The Defense of Vicksburg*, 227; Tunnard, *A Southern Record*, 271; Clarke, *Reminiscence and Anecdotes of the War for Southern Independence*, 113; *OR*, 24(2):403, 410; Chambers, "My Journal," 281; George Ditto Diary, July 4, 1863, ALPL; George Carrington Diary, July 4, 1863, CHM; John D. Brownley, "History of John D. Browley," undated, Andres Collection, USAHEC; Edward E. Schweitzer Diary, July 4, 1863, CWTI, USAHEC.

51. *OR*, 24(2):334, 358, 368; Tom J. Foster, "Reminiscences of Vicksburg,"

Confederate Veteran 2, no. 8 (August 1894): 244; Richard and Richard, *The Defense of Vicksburg*, 226; Lockett, "The Defense of Vicksburg," 492.

52. Patrick, ed., *Three Years with Wallace's Zouaves*, 147; Anderson, *Memoirs*, 357; Andrew Hickenlooper Reminiscences, undated, Hickenlooper Collection, CHS, 152.

53. Jones, "The Rank and File at Vicksburg," 30; Eli W. Thornhill Memoir, undated, OCM, 14; Claudius W. Sears Diary, July 4, 1863, MDAH; Charles Affeld Diary, July 4, 1863, Journals/Diaries/Letters Series, VICK.

54. *OR*, 24(3):466–467; Richard and Richard, *The Defense of Vicksburg*, 227; Clarke, *Reminiscence and Anecdotes of the War for Southern Independence*, 113; Castel, *Tom Taylor's Civil War*, 65; Hoehling, *Vicksburg*, 278; Charles Dana Miller Diary, July 4, 1863, Journals/Letters/Diaries Series, VICK; Unknown to Miss, July 28, 1863, Henry County File, Civil War Miscellany, IHS.

55. James G. Fox to father, July 5, 1863, James G. Fox Letter, ALPL; William M. Reid Diary, July 4, 1863, ALPL; Adolph Engelmann to wife, July 7, 1863, Engelmann-Kircher Family Papers, ALPL; *OR*, 24(2):294, 319, 323; *OR*, 24(3):476; Tamara A. Smith, "A Matter of Trust: Grant and James B. McPherson," in *Grant's Lieutenants: From Cairo to Vicksburg*, Steven E. Woodworth, ed. (Lawrence: University Press of Kansas, 2001), 160; Brown, *History of the Fourth Regiment of Minnesota Infantry*, 234, 244; J. Carroll Harriss to Valery, July 4, 1863, Jordan C. Harriss Papers, NC; John A. Griffen Diary, July 4, 1863, ALPL; Hander "Excerpts from the Hander Diary," 147; Dana, *Recollections of the Civil War*, 100; Anthony B. Burton Diary, July 4, 1863, ALPL; Marszalek et al., eds., *The Personal Memoirs of Ulysses S. Grant*, 382; George O. Smith, "Brief History of the 17th Regiment of the Illinois Volunteer Infantry," 1913, ALPL, 6; James L. Power Diary, July 4, 1863, MDAH; J. P. Jones to wife, July 4, 1863, 45th Illinois File, VICK.

56. James G. Fox to father, July 5, 1863, James G. Fox Letter, ALPL; William M. Reid Diary, July 4, 1863, ALPL; Adolph Engelmann to wife, July 7, 1863, Engelmann-Kircher Family Papers, ALPL; *OR*, 24(2):294, 319, 323; *OR*, 24(3):476; Brown, *History of the Fourth Regiment of Minnesota Infantry*, 234, 244; J. Carroll Harriss to Valery, July 4, 1863, Jordan C. Harriss Papers, NC; John A. Griffen Diary, July 4, 1863, ALPL; Hander "Excerpts from the Hander Diary," 147; Dana, *Recollections of the Civil War*, 100; Anthony B. Burton Diary, July 4, 1863, ALPL; Marszalek et al., eds., *The Personal Memoirs of Ulysses S. Grant*, 382; George O. Smith, "Brief History of the 17th Regiment of the Illinois Volunteer Infantry," 1913, ALPL, 6; James L. Power Diary, July 4, 1863, MDAH; J. P. Jones to wife, July 4, 1863, 45th Illinois File, VICK.

57. Patrick, ed., *Three Years with Wallace's Zouaves*, 147; Thomas Taylor to W. T. Rigby, March 19, 1903, 47th Ohio File, VICK; Joel Strong Reminiscences, 1910, MHS, 16; J. Carroll Harriss to Valery, July 4, 1863, Jordan C. Harriss Papers, NC; Edmund Newsome Diary, July 4, MDAH; Henry H. Bennett Diary, July 4, 1863, Journals/Diaries/Letters Series, VICK; Walter Gresham to wife, July 4, 1863, Walter Q. Gresham Papers, LOC.

58. John J. Kellogg Memoirs, 1913, Journals/Letters/Diaries Series, VICK, 63.

59. Louis Hébert Autobiography, 1894, UNC, 13–14; Unknown to comrades,

October 28, 1902, 77th Illinois File, VICK; Smith, "A Matter of Trust: Grant and James B. McPherson," 160.

60. "The Surrender of Vicksburg," November 22, 1900, *National Tribune*; William E. Strong Reminiscences, undated, William E. Strong Papers, ALPL, 67–72; Henry Kircher Diary, July 4, 1863, Engelmann-Kircher Family Papers, ALPL.

61. *OR*, 24(3):474, 476–477; Ballard, *Pemberton*, 180; James S. McHenry Diary, July 4 and 5, 1863, ALPL; John E. Smith to Aimee, July 4, 1863, John E. Smith Letters, Kirby Smith Collection; Ambrose, ed., "A Wisconsin Boy at Vicksburg," 12; J. W. Greenman Diary, MDAH, 103; William E. Strong Reminiscences, undated, William E. Strong Papers, ALPL, 65–66; William L. Foster to wife, June 20, 1863, UA.

62. *OR*, 24(3):474, 476–477; John C. Taylor Diary, July 4, 1863, UVA; Ballard, *Pemberton*, 180; Dana, *Recollections of the Civil War*, 99–100; Fred Grant Memoir, undated, USGPL, 42–44; James S. McHenry Diary, July 4 and 5, 1863, ALPL; John E. Smith to Aimee, July 4, 1863, John E. Smith Letters, Kirby Smith Collection; Ambrose, ed., "A Wisconsin Boy at Vicksburg," 12; J. W. Greenman Diary, MDAH, 103; William E. Strong Reminiscences, undated, William E. Strong Papers, ALPL, 65–66; William L. Foster to wife, June 20, 1863, UA.

63. Porter, *Incidents and Anecdotes*, 200–201.

64. Broadaway, "A Texan Records the Civil War Siege of Vicksburg, Mississippi," 124; Abrams, *A Full and Detailed History*, 63; Richard and Richard, *The Defense of Vicksburg*, 227–228, 232; *OR*, 24(3):471; Simon, ed., *PUSG*, 8:474; William L. Foster to wife, June 20, 1863, UA; William Van Zandt Diary, July 4, 1863, ISU.

65. Saunier, *A History of the Forty-seventh Regiment Ohio Veteran Volunteer Infantry*, 162; Anderson, *Memoirs*, 362.

66. Fred Grant Memoir, undated, USGPL, 42–43; Marszalek et al., eds., *The Personal Memoirs of Ulysses S. Grant*, 389; William M. Reid Diary, July 4, 1863, ALPL; Richard and Richard, *The Defense of Vicksburg*, 227, 229; Lockett, "The Defense of Vicksburg," 492; "The Terms of Surrender," 545; George Bradley Memoir, 1896, OCM, 11; J. W. Greenman Diary, MDAH, 102; Oscar E. Stewart Memoir, undated, OCM, 22.

67. Marszalek et al., eds., *The Personal Memoirs of Ulysses S. Grant*, 393; Clarke, *Reminiscence and Anecdotes of the War for Southern Independence*, 113; Richard and Richard, *The Defense of Vicksburg*, 233–234; Oscar E. Stewart Memoir, undated, OCM, 22.

68. Lockett, "The Defense of Vicksburg," 492; Jones, "The Rank and File at Vicksburg," 30.

69. Clarke, *Reminiscence and Anecdotes of the War for Southern Independence*, 113; Marszalek et al., eds., *The Personal Memoirs of Ulysses S. Grant*, 389; Richard and Richard, *The Defense of Vicksburg*, 234.

70. Jones, "The Rank and File at Vicksburg," 30.

71. Marszalek et al., eds., *The Personal Memoirs of Ulysses S. Grant*, 393; Simon, ed., *PUSG*, 8:482–483.

72. *ORN*, 25:105; *OR*, 24(3):459, 470; Simon, ed., *PUSG*, 8:470, 472.

73. *OR*, 24(3):470.

74. *OR*, 24(3):460–461.

75. *OR*, 24(2):525, 534; *OR*, 24(3):461.

76. *OR*, 24(2):249; *OR*, 52(1):387, 391; *OR*, 24(3):463, 475.

77. *OR*, 24(3):461–462.

78. *OR*, 24(3):462.

79. *OR*, 24(3):463, 469; Thomas Watson to parents, July 4, 1863, Thomas Watson Correspondence, ALPL.

80. *ORN*, 25:106; *OR*, 24(3):471, 474; J. Q. A. Campbell Diary, July 4, 1863, 5th Iowa File, VICK.

81. *OR*, 24(3):463; Adnah Eaton Diary, July 4, 1863, NC; Ambrose, ed., "A Wisconsin Boy at Vicksburg," 11; Soman and Byrne, eds., *A Jewish Colonel in the Civil War*, 300; Levi W. Bennett Diary, July 4, 1863, MDAH; Lyman M. Baker Memoir, 1914, ALPL, 15; "Triumphal March of General Grant's Army into Vicksburg, July 4, 1863, Fourth of July Address," July 4, 1863, Robert M. Woodruff July 4 Oration, ALPL; Isaac Home Diary, July 4, 1863, KHS.

82. Henry J. Seaman Diary, July 5, 1863, CWTI, USAHEC; Payson Shumway to cousin, July 25, 1863, Z. Payson Shumway Letters, NL; Curtis P. Lacey Diary, July 5, 1863, NL; Chase Dickinson to father, July 5, 1863, Chase Hall Dickinson Papers, NL; Henry Miller to sister, July 13, 1863, Henry H. Miller Papers, CHM; John Merrilees Diary, July 4, 1863, CHM; Josiah W. Underhill Diary, July 4, 1863, IHS; Darius Dodd to sister, July 28, 1863, Darius H. Dodd Papers, IHS; Winschel, ed., *The Civil War Diary of a Common Soldier*, 60; Wayne Johnson Jacobs Diary, July 4, 1863, LSU; Aurelius L. Voorhis Diary, July 5, 1863, IHS; Reed, *Campaigns and Battles of the Twelfth Regiment Iowa Veteran Volunteer Infantry*, 125–126; Soman and Byrne, eds., *A Jewish Colonel in the Civil War*, 300; Alvin Hovey Memoir, undated, IU, 65; Charles Willison to Ellie, July 4, 1863, 76th Ohio Volunteer Infantry Papers, OHS; Unknown to parents, July 4, 1863, Helm Family Papers, FHS.

83. *OR*, 24(3):463, 466, 470–471, 474–475; J. P. Van Nest to wife, July 12, 1863, Joseph P. Van Nest Papers, FHS; Simon, ed., *PUSG*, 8:474, 479; Samuel Gordon to wife, July 5, 1863, Samuel Gordon Papers, ALPL, Richard Markle to mother, July 19, 1863, Richard Markle Letters, ALPL; Levi W. Bennett Diary, June 9, 1863, MDAH; Adolph Engelmann to wife, July 4, 1863, Engelmann-Kircher Family Papers, ALPL; Alvin Hovey Memoir, undated, IU, 65; Edward Ord to wife, July 5, 1863, E. O. C. Ord Papers, SU.

84. *OR*, 24(3):987, 989, 992; Thomas Watson to parents, July 4, 1863, Thomas Watson Correspondence, ALPL; William G. Pirtle Memoirs, 1907, FHS, 189; William Jones to Mary, July 5, 1863, William Riley Jones Letters, ADAH.

85. French, *Two Wars*, 182.

86. *OR*, 24(3):987, 989, 992–993; Kirwan, ed., *Johnny Green of the Orphan Brigade*, 80; Thomas M. Gore Memoir, undated, Gore Civil War History Collection, University of Southern Mississippi, 81; Jerry Smith to brother, July 18, 1863, Jerry Smith Letters, NYSL; M. D. L. Stephens Recollections, 1899, MDAH, 23.

87. *OR*, 24(3):475, 987–988; Samuel S. Irwin Diary, July 5, 1863, ALPL.

88. *OR*, 24(1):199, 229–230; *OR*, 24(3):475; John A. Higgins to wife, May 28, 1863, John A. Higgins Papers, ALPL.

89. Young, *Around the World with General Grant*, 213; William Barnard to sister, July 2, 1863, William A. Barnard Collection, AM.

CHAPTER 16. "GEN. GRANT HAS 'CAUGHT THE RABBIT'"

1. Adolph Engelmann to wife, July 4, 1863, Engelmann-Kircher Family Papers, ALPL; "Glorious News," 1863, Ohio *State Journal*, copy in OHS; Anthony B. Burton Diary, July 4, 1863, ALPL; Charles Willison to Ellie, July 4, 1863, 76th Ohio Volunteer Infantry Papers, OHS; Elder III, ed., *A Damned Iowa Greyhound*, 78.
2. Matilda Champion to Sidney S. Champion, July 10, 1863, Sidney S. Champion Papers, DU; Sarah Poates Diary, July 6, 1863, Asa Fitch Papers, Cornell University.
3. Colin McRae to sister, August 30, 1863, Colin J. McRae Papers, ADAH; Simon, ed., *The Personal Memoirs of Julia Dent Grant*, 113. See *Harper's Weekly* editions for June 6, 13, 20, and 27, 1863.
4. William Vermilion to Mary, July 6, 1863, Vermilion Family Correspondence, UCSD; Albert Chipman to wife, July 4, 1863, Albert Chipman Papers, ALPL; John Whitten Diary, July 4, 1863, LOC; Myron Underwood to wife, July 5, 1863, Myron Underwood Papers, UIA; Thomas Sterns to wife, July 4, 1863, Sterns Family Papers, UIA; William Brown to father, July 4, 1863, William L. Brown Papers, CHM; Judson Gill to Soph, July 4, 1863, C. Judson Gill Letters, Journals/Letters/Diaries Series, VICK; Charles Vanamburg to father, July 4, 1863, Charles Vanamburg Papers, USAHEC; George Brinsmaid to father, July 5, 1863, George B. Brinsmaid Papers, KHS; Lyman Humphrey to parents, July 31, 1863, Lyman Underwood Humphrey Correspondence, KHS; Edward Ord to wife, July 5, 1863, E. O. C. Ord Papers, SU; George M. Lucas Diary, July 5, 1863, ALPL.
5. Charles Calvin Enslow Diary, July 6, 1863, LC; John A. Logan to wife, July 5, 1863, John A. Logan Papers, LC; James Lee McDonough, *William Tecumseh Sherman: In the Service of My Country: A Life* (New York: W. W. Norton & Company, 2016), 414; Arthur W. Utter to Helen, July 30, 1863, Arthur W. Utter Papers, FHS.
6. Frank Willey Diary, July 7, 1863, OHS; "Vicksburg," July 25, 1863, Portland *Daily Advertiser*, copy in Siege of Vicksburg Accounts Confederate Subject File, MDAH; George Stratton to sister, July 7, 1863, George D. Stratton Papers, ISL; Williams, *Grant Rises in the West*, 420–421; *OR* 24(1):44, 62; John F. Marszalek, *Lincoln and the Military* (Carbondale: Southern Illinois University Press, 2014), 58; *Diary of Gideon Welles*, 1:320, 364.
7. W. L. Park Journal, July 1863, NL; Marszalek et al., eds., *The Personal Memoirs of Ulysses S. Grant*, 392; Hiram P. Howe to parents, July 14, 1863, Hiram P. Howe Papers, LOC; Thorndike, ed., *The Sherman Letters*, 208; "Army of the Gulf," December 4, 1886, *National Tribune*; T. K. White to mother, July 7, 1863, Thomas K. White Papers, OHS; Henry Schmidt to wife, July 4, 1863, Schmidt Family Papers, FHS. For Port Hudson, see Lawrence Lee Hewitt, *Port Hudson: Confederate Bastion on the Mississippi* (Baton Rouge: Louisiana State University Press, 1987) and Edward Cunningham, *The Port Hudson Campaign, 1862–1863* (Baton Rouge: Louisiana State University Press, 1963).

8. *OR*, 24(1):199, 201; "The Late General Pemberton," New York *Herald*, August 17, 1881, copy in John C. Pemberton Papers, LOC; *OR*, 52(2):506–507; John J. Pettus to Jefferson Davis, July 9, 1863, Pettus Governor Papers, MDAH.

9. Hoehling, *Vicksburg*, 275; East II, "Wallpaper Journalism," 29; "On Dit," and "Note," Vicksburg *Daily Citizen*, July 2 and 4, 1863, copy in LOC, William G. Richards Jr. Collection, University of Louisiana Lafayette, and Cyrus T. Cochran Papers, ALPL; Marszalek et al., eds., *The Personal Memoirs of Ulysses S. Grant*, 389.

10. J. P. Jones to wife, July 12, 1863, John P. Jones Papers, FHS; J. Carroll Harriss to Valery, July 4, 1863, Jordan C. Harriss Papers, NC; Abner J. Wilkes Memoir, undated, OCM, 6; Hoehling, *Vicksburg*, 279; J. B. Childs Reminiscences, undated, GDAH, 1; Richard Bridges to sister, July 22, 1863, Richard C. Bridges Collection, UM.

11. *OR*, 24(2):324–325, 328; "Vicksburg," July 25, 1863, Portland *Daily Advertiser*, copy in Siege of Vicksburg Accounts Confederate Subject File, MDAH; *OR*, 24(3):474; Lee, "The Siege of Vicksburg," 57; Bertera, *De Golyer's 8th Michigan Black Horse Light Battery*, 140; James G. Fox to father, July 5, 1863, James G. Fox Letter, ALPL.

12. Adolph Engelmann to wife, July 7, 1863, Engelmann-Kirçher Family Papers, ALPL; *OR*, 24(2):178, 336; *OR*, 24(3):474; Leo M. Kaiser, ed., "The Civil War Diary of Florison D. Pitts," *Mid-America: An Historical Review* 40, no. 1 (January 1958): 39; "Report of Field and Siege Guns and Ammunition on Rear Line of Defense, Vicksburg," July 4, 1863, Frederick M. Dearborn Collection, Houghton Library, HU; *OR*, 24(1):62.

13. Grabau, *Ninety-Eight Days*, 410; Jason Niles Diary, July 15, 1863, UNC; "Effective Strength of Gen. Grant's Command at Vicksburg, Miss.," June 30, 1863, Samuel W. Richey Collection, Miami University; *OR*, 24(2):328; Hattaway and Jones, *How The North Won*, 411; Hashell, ed., "Col. William Camm War Diary, 1861–1865," 955; J. W. McElnary to W. T. Rigby, April 16, 1904, 30th Ohio File, VICK; George Boyd Smith Memoir, undated, LOC, 7–8.

14. *OR*, 24(3):476–477; Aaron Dunbar and Harvey M. Trimble, *History of the Ninety-third Regiment Volunteer Infantry From Organization to Muster Out* (Chicago: Blakely Printing Co., 1898), 41–42; General Order No. 20, July 4, 1863, William T. Clark Papers, CHM; William Sherman to wife, July 5, 1863, William T. Sherman Papers, LOC; *ORN*, 25:105–111; William T. Sherman to 15th Corps, July 27, 1863, William T. Sherman Letter, Journals/Letters/Diaries Series, VICK.

15. *ORN*, 25:105–107, 109.

16. Charles W. Beal to brother, June 10, 1863, Charles W. Beal Papers, ALPL; "Dusty Foot" to "Mr. Editor," July 4, 1863, Russell Family Papers, ALPL; *OR*, 24(3):472; *OR* 24(1):6, 62–63; *ORN*, 25:111; John F. Marszalek, "'A Full Share of All the Credit': Sherman and Grant to the Fall of Vicksburg," in *Grant's Lieutenants: From Cairo to Vicksburg*, Steven E. Woodworth, ed. (Lawrence: University Press of Kansas, 2001), 19; Smith, *The Decision Was Always My Own*, 203.

17. Ida Corbin, "Biography of Nathan Albert Corbin," 1891, Nathan Albert Corbin Unpublished Biography, ALPL; John L. Harris to Miss Susan, July 24, 1863, John L. Harris Correspondence, ALPL; Unknown to parents, July 4, 1863, Helm Family Papers, FHS; Logan Roots to Edwin Hewett, July 24, 1863, Edwin Crawford Hewett Correspondence,

UI; John H. Wickizer to "My Dear Judge," May 24, 1863, John H. Wickizer Letters, ALPL; Thomas Watson to parents, July 10, 1863, Thomas Watson Correspondence, ALPL.

18. Richard Hall to parent, July 2, 1863, Richard A. Hall Letters, LSU; Albert Chipman to wife, July 10, 1863, Albert Chipman Papers, ALPL; Chambers, "My Journal," 281; Clarke, *Reminiscence and Anecdotes of the War for Southern Independence*, 115; *OR*, 24(3):478.

19. R. C. Lipsey to Jeremiah Gage, June 10, 1863, Gage Family Collection, UM; Michael B. Ballard, "Misused Merit: The Tragedy of John C. Pemberton," in *Civil War Generals in Defeat*, Steven E. Woodworth, ed. (Lawrence: University Press of Kansas, 1999), 160, also published as "Misused Merit: The Tragedy of John C. Pemberton," in *Confederate Generals in the Western Theater*, 4 vols., Lawrence Lee Hewitt and Arthur W. Bergeron, Jr., eds. (Knoxville: University of Tennessee Press, 2010), 103–121.

20. Perry, "Vicksburg" 174; Lettie Downs Diary, July 8, 1863, MDAH; William Brown to father, July 4, 1863, William L. Brown Papers, CHM; Cable, ed., "A Woman's Diary of the Siege of Vicksburg," 774.

21. Richard and Richard, *The Defense of Vicksburg*, 223; Chambers, "My Journal," 281.

22. John C. Pemberton Letter, 1877 or 1878, John C. Pemberton Papers, MDAH and LOC; Jefferson Davis to Braxton Bragg, June 29, 1872, Samuel W. Richey Collection, Miami University; Reagan, *Memoirs*, 233.

23. Jones, *Civil War Command & Strategy*, 162; George R. Agassiz, ed., *Meade's Headquarters, 1863–1865: Letters of Colonel Theodore Lyman From the Wilderness to Appomattox* (Boston: Atlantic Monthly Press, 1922), 102.

24. Sidney S. Champion to wife, June 25, 1863, Sidney S. Champion Papers, DU; George H. Hynds Diary, July 4 and 5, 1863, Journals/Letters/Diaries Series, VICK; John C. Taylor Diary, June 17, 1863, UVA.

25. James Skelton to sister, July 9, 1863, James M. Skelton Letters, UNC; *OR*, 24(1):199, 248; Stoker, *The Grand Design*, 273; Winschel, "The Absence of Will," 88–89.

26. Robert K. Krick, "'Snarl and Sneer and Quarrel': General Joseph E. Johnston and an Obsession with Rank," in *Leaders of the Lost Cause: New Perspectives on the Confederate High Command*, Gary W. Gallagher and Joseph T. Glatthaar, eds. (Mechanicsburg, PA: Stackpole Books, 2004), 188; Williams, *Grant Rises in the West*, 455; Winschel, *Triumph and Defeat: The Vicksburg Campaign, Volume 2*, 128.

27. *OR*, 24(1):157; Simon, ed., *PUSG*, 8:480.

28. *OR*, 24(1):165, 167; John A. McClernand to Edwin M. Stanton, June 27, 1863, John A. McClernand Papers, ALPL; George W. Childs Circular Questionnaire, July 20, 1863, John A. McClernand Papers, ALPL.

29. *OR*, 24(1):167–168; Richard Yates et al. to Abraham Lincoln, August 6, 1863, and Abraham Lincoln to John A. McClernand, August 12, 1863, John A. McClernand Papers, RG 94, E 159, NARA.

30. *OR*, 24(1):167–169, 186.

31. General Orders No. 214, July 10, 1863, E. O. C. Ord Papers, RG 94, E 159,

NARA. For the Red River Campaign, see Gary D. Joiner, *Through the Howling Wilderness: The 1864 Red River Campaign and Union Failure in the West* (Knoxville: University of Tennessee Press, 2006).

32. J. T. R. to mother, July 5, 1863, John Todd Roberts Papers, FHS; Richard and Richard, *The Defense of Vicksburg*, 226; J. B. Sanders to family, July 11, 1863, J. B. Sanders Papers, MDAH; John J. Kellogg Memoirs, 1913, Journals/Letters/Diaries Series, VICK, 53.

33. Untitled, undated newspaper, copy in Siege of Vicksburg Accounts Confederate Subject File, MDAH; *OR*, 24(1):62, 292; *OR*, 24(3):987.

34. Francis R. Baker Diary, June 19 and 20, 1863, ALPL; *OR*, 24(2):175, 178, 392.

35. *OR*, 24(1):286, 292.

36. Charles Swift Northen III, ed., *All Right Let Them Come: The Civil War Diary of an East Tennessee Confederate* (Knoxville: University of Tennessee Press, 2003), 95; *OR*, 24(2):369, 382, 417; *OR*, 24(1):285–286.

37. *OR*, 24(2):177.

38. John Henry Hammond Diary, July 4, 1863, FHS; Solonick, *Engineering Victory*, 4, 214.

39. Edwin Obriham to family, July 8, 1863, Edward O. Obriham Letters, Journals/Letters/Diaries Series, VICK; "Dusty Foot" to "Mr. Editor," July 4, 1863, Russell Family Papers, ALPL; "An Inside View of Vicksburg," July 18, 1863, Washington *Daily National Intelligencer*, copy in Siege of Vicksburg Accounts Confederate Subject File, MDAH; Carlos Colby, "Memoirs of Military Service," undated, Bilby Collection, USAHEC; Edward E. Howe to Mattie, October 27, 1863, Edward E. Howe Letter, ALPL.

40. "Scenes in Vicksburg," July 28, 1863, Richmond *Whig*, copy in Siege of Vicksburg Accounts Confederate Subject File, MDAH; Daniel Roberts to family, July 6, 1863, Daniel Roberts Correspondence, ISL.

41. "Life in Vicksburg," August 3, 1863, Boston *Post*, copy in Siege of Vicksburg Accounts Confederate Subject File, MDAH; L. McRae Bell, "A Girl's Experience in the Siege of Vicksburg," *Harper's Weekly*, June 8, 1912, 13.

42. Abrams, *A Full and Detailed History*, 64; "Vicksburg," July 25, 1863, Portland *Daily Advertiser*, copy in Siege of Vicksburg Accounts Confederate Subject File, MDAH; Edgar L. Erickson, ed., "With Grant at Vicksburg: From the Civil War Diary of Captain Charles E. Wilcox," *Journal of the Illinois State Historical Society* 30, no. 4 (January 1938): 496; Annie Laura Harris Broidrick, "A Recollection of Thirty Years Ago, 1893, UNC, 18; Edwin Obriham to family, July 8, 1863, Edward O. Obriham Letters, Journals/Letters/Diaries Series, VICK; Reed, "A Woman's Experiences During the Siege of Vicksburg," 928.

43. *OR*, 24(3):474; W. J. Brigham to father, July 31, 1863, Brigham Family Letters, TSLA; Elizabeth Parkman to Mrs. McGahey, undated, Alexander F. McGahey File, OCM.

44. Hoehling, *Vicksburg*, 281–282; Stewart Bruce Terry Diary, July 4, 1863, KHS; Albert Chipman to wife, June 30, 1863, Albert Chipman Papers, ALPL; Anita Dwyer Withers Diary, August 15, 1863, UNC.

45. L. McRae. Bell, "A Girl's Experience in the Siege of Vicksburg," *Harper's Weekly*, June 8, 1912, 13; Abrams, *A Full and Detailed History*, 64.

46. Anne to Emma, June/July 1863, Shannon-Crutcher Family Papers, MDAH.

47. Richard and Richard, *The Defense of Vicksburg*, 232; Francis R. Baker Diary, July 13, 1863, ALPL.

48. Richard and Richard, *The Defense of Vicksburg*, 231–232; *OR*, 24(3):477, 479. For USCT troops, see David H. Slay, "Abraham Lincoln and the Mississippi Colored Troops," *Journal of Mississippi History* 70, no. 1 (Spring 2008): 65–84.

49. Samuel Styre to parents, July 5, 1863, Samuel Styre Papers, DU; Henry Franks to sister, June 15, 1863, Henry W. Franks Letters, OHS; Unknown to family, August 1, 1863, Kays Family Correspondence, ALPL; Henry Schmidt to wife, July 18, 1863, Schmidt Family Papers, FHS; Albert Hiffman Memoirs, undated, Hiffman Family Papers, MHS; "Charges and Specifications," July 1863, Jacob G. Lauman Papers, RG 94, E 159, NARA; William Lewis to wife, July 20, 1863, William Lewis (Lenis) Letters, Journals/Diaries/Letters Series, VICK; Hugh Ewing to wife, July 14, 1863, Hugh B. Ewing Letter, USM; Wayne Johnson Jacobs Diary, July 7, 1863, LSU. For Joseph Davis, see the Joseph E. Davis Collection, UM; and Janet Sharp Hermann, *Joseph E. Davis: Pioneer Patriarch* (Jackson: University Press of Mississippi, 1991). For more on Jackson, see Jim Woodrick, *The Civil War Siege of Jackson, Mississippi* (Charleston: History Press, 2016).

50. J. S. Clark, *The Thirty-fourth Iowa Regiment: Brief History* (Des Moines: Watters-Talbott Printing Co., 1895), 15; Charles Lutz to brother, July 20, 1863, Charles Lutz Papers, CWD, USAHEC; U. S. Grant to Judson Bingham, July 25, 1863, Ulysses S. Grant Order, ND; William Fish to father, August 15, 1863, William W. Fish Papers, FHS; William F. Draper to wife, June 9, 1863, William F. Draper Papers, LC.

51. Howard Stevens to uncle, July 21, 1863, Howard and Victor Stevens Letters, HCWRT, USAHEC; Dana, *Recollections of the Civil War*, 102; George C. Churcheus Diary, July 5, 1863, OHS.

52. M. K. Lawler to John A. Rawlins, July 4, 1863, Michael K. Lawler Surgeon Certificate, July 4, 1863, Michael K. Lawler Papers, RG 94, E 159, NARA; John McArthur to John A. Rawlins, July 26, 1863, John McArthur Papers, RG 94, E 159, NARA; "Military History of Eugene A. Carr," undated, Eugene A. Carr Papers, RG 94, E 159, NARA; James Tuttle Medical Certificate, July 30, 1863, James M. Tuttle Papers, RG 94, E 159, NARA; Thorndike, ed., *The Sherman Letters*, 209; Dick Puffer to sister, July 22, 1863, Richard R. Puffer Papers, CHM; Townsend, *Yankee Warhorse*, 119.

53. General Orders No. 1, July 5, 1863, John A. Logan Papers, RG 94, E 159, NARA; Abrams, *A Full and Detailed History*, 69; Dodd, "Recollections of Vicksburg During the Siege," 10; Thomas Christie to brother, June 5, 1863, James C. Christie and Family Papers, MNHS; Reed, "A Woman's Experiences During the Siege of Vicksburg," 927; Virginia Rockwood Memoir, 1904, Journals/Letters/Diaries File, VICK, 2–3, copy in OCM.

54. Hall, *The Story of the 26th Louisiana Infantry*, 92.

55. "Scenes in Vicksburg," July 28, 1863, Richmond *Whig*, copy in Siege of Vicksburg Accounts Confederate Subject File, MDAH; Asa Wilson to brother, July 6, 1863, Asa Wilson Letter, Journals/Letters/Diaries Series, VICK.

56. Richmond, "The Siege of Vicksburg," 141; Eli W. Thornhill Memoir, undated, OCM, 14; Clarke, *Reminiscence and Anecdotes of the War for Southern Independence*, 114–115.

57. Robert L. Bachman Memoir, undated, OCM, 25; Beck, *A True Sketch of Army Life*, 17.

58. Clarke, *Reminiscence and Anecdotes of the War for Southern Independence*, 115; Abrams, *A Full and Detailed History*, 67; Claudius W. Sears Diary, July 14, 1863, MDAH.

59. Chambers, "My Journal," 281; Rex Miller, "Dowdell's Volunteers," undated, 37th Alabama File, VICK, 12; *OR*, 24(3):478.

60. Richard and Richard, *The Defense of Vicksburg*, 228, 233; Hander "Excerpts from the Hander Diary," 148.

61. Abrams, *A Full and Detailed History*, 68.

62. Howell, Jr., *Going to Meet the Yankees*, 187–188; John Forney to General, July 10, 1863, Dabney Maury Order Book, CHM, 310; *OR*, 24(1):202, 207, 231; Marszalek et al., eds., *The Personal Memoirs of Ulysses S. Grant*, 392–393.

63. *OR*, 24(3):478–483; Richard and Richard, *The Defense of Vicksburg*, 233; Rice, "Incidents of the Vicksburg Siege," 77.

64. Chambers, "My Journal," 281–282; Philip Sartorius Autobiography, undated, Center for Jewish History, 41; Clark Wright to Daniel Hixon, October 10, 1863, Gail and Stephen Rudin Slavery Collection, CU.

65. Anderson, *Memoirs*, 364; J. B. Sanders to family, July 11, 1863, J. B. Sanders Papers, MDAH; James B. McPherson to George W. Cullum, December 25, 1863, James B. McPherson Papers, RG 94, E 159, NARA; Personal Memoirs of I. V. Smith, 1902, SHSMC, 33; William A. Ruyle Memoir, undated, HCWRT, USAHEC, 13; Purchase Order, July 10, 1863, M. W. Boyd Collection, UM; Arthur W. Bergeron, Jr., "Martin Luther Smith and the defense of the Lower Mississippi River Valley, 1861–1863," in *Confederate Generals in the Western Theater: Essays on America's Civil War*, 4 vols., Lawrence Lee Hewitt and Arthur W. Bergeron, Jr., eds. (Knoxville: University of Tennessee Press, 2011), 3:79(61–85); M. L. Smith to U. S. Grant, July 15, 1863, John G. Devereux Papers, UNC.

66. John Pemberton to Joseph Johnston, July 12, 1863, John C. Pemberton Papers, RG 109, E 131, NARA.

67. J. P. Van Nest to wife, July 12, 1863, Joseph P. Van Nest Papers, FHS; Scriber, *Twenty-seventh Louisiana Volunteer Infantry*, 162; Richard and Richard, *The Defense of Vicksburg*, 243, 245, 249; William R. Clack Diary, July 21, 1863, Journals/Diaries/Letters Series, VICK.

68. Scriber, *Twenty-seventh Louisiana Volunteer Infantry*, 162; Richard and Richard, *The Defense of Vicksburg*, 243, 245, 249; William R. Clack Diary, July 21, 1863, Journals/Diaries/Letters Series, VICK; Chambers, "My Journal," 282; Hander "Excerpts from the Hander Diary," 148.

69. C. S. O. Rice Memoir, 1903, TSLA, 32–33, copy in UTK; Lorenzo A. Barker Diary, July 27, 1863, AM.

70. Chambers, "My Journal," 282–283; Unknown to unknown, undated, Daniel Williams Papers, MSU.

71. Clarke, *Reminiscence and Anecdotes of the War for Southern Independence*, 116–119.

72. Clarke, *Reminiscence and Anecdotes of the War for Southern Independence*, 116–119.

73. Clarke, *Reminiscence and Anecdotes of the War for Southern Independence*, 116–119.

74. Joseph B. Lightsey Recollections, 1908, OCM, 1; J. C. Mitchell to Mrs. McGahey, August 7, 1863, and Elizabeth Parkman to Mrs. McGahey, undated, Alexander F. McGahey File, OCM.

75. Anderson, *Memoirs*, 365–366; Tucker, *The Forgotten "Stonewall of the West,"* 313; Payne, "Missouri Troops in the Vicksburg Campaign," 379.

76. Terry Whittington, "In the Shadow of Defeat: Tracking the Vicksburg Parolees," *Journal of Mississippi History* 64, no. 4 (Winter 2002): 307–330; Ballard, *Pemberton*, 182; Winschel, *Triumph and Defeat: The Vicksburg Campaign, Volume 2*, 128.

Epilogue

1. *OR*, 24(3):464; *ORN*, 25:104; Marszalek et al., eds., *The Personal Memoirs of Ulysses S. Grant*, 391, 397.

2. James Skelton to sister, July 9, 1863, James M. Skelton Letters, UNC; Henry Walke to William Hoel, July 13, 1863, William R. Hoel Papers, CHS; Evan to family, June 11, 1863, Rosemonde E. and Emile Kuntz Collection, TU; Winschel, *Triumph and Defeat: The Vicksburg Campaign, Volume 2*, 141–158; Eli Todd to brother, July 19, 1863, Eli J. Todd Papers, OHS; Henry A. Robinson to wife, August 17, 1863, Henry A. Robinson Papers, IHS; "Perry Tells Story of the Siege of Vicksburg," Vicksburg *Evening Post*, June 16, 1926. See also Michael Wright, "Vicksburg and the Trans-Mississippi Supply Line (1861–1863)," *Journal of Mississippi History* 43, no. 3 (August 1981): 210–225.

3. Wells, *The Siege of Vicksburg*, 87; Lorenzo A. Barker Diary, July 7, 1863, AM; Zadoc Rhodes to William Terwilliger, December 12, 1863, Zadoc Rhodes Letters, NYSL; Simon, ed., *PUSG*, 8:445; Badeau, *Military History of Ulysses S. Grant*, 375; *OR*, 24(1):63.

4. Badeau, *Military History of Ulysses S. Grant*, 1:399–400; Richardson, *A Personal History of Ulysses S. Grant*, 337.

5. Catton, *U. S. Grant and the American Military Tradition*, 104.

6. J. B. Jones, *A Rebel War Clerk's Diary: At the Confederate States Capital, Volume 1: April 1861–July 1863*, 2 vols., James I. Robertson, Jr., ed. (Lawrence: University Press of Kansas, 2015), 1:295, 299, 301, 307–308, 332–333; Sarah Woolfolk Wiggins, ed., *The Journals of Josiah Gorgas, 1857–1878* (Tuscaloosa: University of Alabama Press, 1995), 75.

7. Robert Ould Statement, July 13, 1863, John G. Devereux Papers, UNC; Chambers, "My Journal," 284–287; Joseph B. Lightsey Recollections, 1908, OCM, 1; "Special Order No. 123," September 16, 1863, UM. For occupied Vicksburg, see Bradley R.

Clampitt, *Occupied Vicksburg* (Baton Rouge: Louisiana State University Press, 2016). For the fate of the parolees, see Whittington, "In the Shadow of Defeat: Tracking the Vicksburg Parolees," 307–330.

8. Charles Affeld Diary, June 22, 1863, Journals/Diaries/Letters Series, VICK; Post, ed., *Soldiers' Letters*, 321; Crummer, *With Grant at Fort Donelson, Shiloh and Vicksburg*, 137.

9. Richard and Richard, *The Defense of Vicksburg*, 201; Brown, *History of the Fourth Regiment of Minnesota Infantry*, 247–248; James Vanderbilt to mother, July 4, 1863, James C. Vanderbilt Papers, ISL; Timothy B. Smith, *The Golden Age of Battlefield Preservation: The Decade of the 1890s and the Establishment of America's First Five Military Parks* (Knoxville: University of Tennessee Press, 2008), 14–15.

10. George Hildt to parents, June 19, 1863, George H. Hildt Papers, OHS; Thorndike, ed., *The Sherman Letters*, 209; E. B. Bascom to W. T. Rigby, February 25, 1907, 5th Iowa File, VICK; "Historical Vicksburg," 1901, and C. A. Hobbs, "Vicksburg," 1880, Mississippi Broadside Collection, DU; "Arrivée des Prisonniers de Vicksburg et de Port-Hudson," July 1863, Rosemonde E. and Emile Kuntz Collection, TU; Smith, *The Golden Age of Battlefield Preservation*, 179. For Vicksburg National Cemetery, see Richard Myers, *The Vicksburg National Cemetery: An Administrative History* (Washington, DC: National Park Service, 1968).

11. The literature on Vicksburg National Military Park is large despite there not being as yet a volume dedicated to the history of the park. See Christopher Waldrep, *Vicksburg's Long Shadow: The Civil War Legacy of Race and Remembrance* (New York: Rowman and Littlefield Publishers, 2005); Michael W. Panhorst, "'The First of Our Hundred Battle Monuments': Civil War Battlefield Monuments Built by Active-Duty Soldiers During the Civil War," *Southern Cultures* 20, no. 4 (Winter 2014): 22–43; Michael W. Panhorst, *The Memorial Art and Architecture of Vicksburg National Military Park* (Kent, OH: Kent State University Press, 2015); Terrence J. Winschel, "Stephen D. Lee and the Making of an American Shrine," *Journal of Mississippi History* 63, no. 1 (2001): 17–32; Terrence J. Winschel, "A Soldier's Legacy: William T. Rigby and the Establishment of Vicksburg National Military Park," *Journal of Mississippi History* 75, no. 4 (Winter 2013): 93–110; Timothy B. Smith, *"Altogether Fitting and Proper": Civil War Battlefield Preservation in History, Memory, and Policy, 1861–2015* (Knoxville: University of Tennessee Press, 2017); Smith, *The Golden Age of Battlefield Preservation*; J. Parker Hills, *Vicksburg National Military Park—Art of Commemoration*. (Washington, DC: National Park Service, 2011).

12. "Scrapbook of Photographs, Newspaper Clippings, etc., with Reference to Vicksburg Reunion, May 21st and 22nd, 1937," John C. Pemberton III Papers, MDAH; Theodore F. Davis to W. T. Rigby, March 31, 1902, 83rd Indiana File, VICK; G. P. Clarke to friend, July 22, 1899, William M. Cleaveland Papers, CWD, USAHEC; "Confederate Soldier Shot," undated, Ligonier (IN) *Banner*, copy in 37th Alabama File, VICK; Smith, *The Golden Age of Battlefield Preservation*, 206–207.

13. Unknown Memoir, undated, 3rd Louisiana File, VICK, 4.

14. "Honor Illinois Soldiers," November 11, 1906, Nebraska *State Journal*.

BIBLIOGRAPHY

Manuscripts

Abraham Lincoln Presidential Library, Springfield, Illinois
  Francis R. Baker Diary
  Lyman Baker Memoirs
  Charles W. Beal Papers
  Thomas B. Beggs Papers
  Albert C. Boals Diary
  Philip C. Bonney Papers
  Daniel H. Brush Papers
  Anthony Burton Diary
  Albert Chipman Papers
  Cyrus T. Cochran Papers
  Pinckney Skilton Cone Diary
  Nathan Albert Corbin Unpublished Biography
  George Ditto Diary
  William R. Eddington Memoir
  Engelmann-Kircher Family Papers
  John B. Fletcher Diary
  James G. Fox Letter
  Samuel Gordon Papers
  Balzar Grebe Papers
  John A. Griffen Diary
  William A. Harding Letter
  John L. Harris Correspondence
  John A. Higgins Papers
  Edward E. Howe Letter
  E. H. and D. G. Ingraham Letters
  Edward F. Ingraham Papers
  Samuel S. Irwin Diary
  Kays Family Correspondence

William J. Kennedy Letters
James Benson Logan Diary
John A. Logan Papers
Samuel D. Lougheed Letters
George M. Lucas Diary
Richard Markle Letters
John A. McClernand Papers
James S. McHenry Diary
James B. McPherson Papers
Troy Moore Letters
David W. Poak Papers
Rand Family Papers
Cyrus W. Randall Papers
William M. Reid Diary
Mortimer Rice Diary
Robert Ridge Diary
Russell Family Papers
George W. Russell Papers
John Sheriff Papers
Z. Payson Shumway Papers
George O. Smith, "Brief History of the 17th Regiment of the Illinois Volunteer Infan-
    try, U.S.A."
Joseph Stockton Diary
William E. Strong Papers
"United States. Army. Illinois Infantry Regiment, 14th (1861–1863) Company A"
Abram J. Vanauken Diary
Wallace-Dickey Family Papers
Thomas Watson Papers
John H. Wickizer Papers
Cyrus Winters Diary
Robert M. Woodruff July 4 Oration
James A. Woodson Diary
Job H. Yaggy Diary
Alabama Department of Archives and History, Montgomery, Alabama
    William Riley Jones Letters
    William Lowery Diary
    Colin J. McRae Papers
    William Roberts Diary
    Elbert Willett Diary
Archives of Michigan
    Lorenzo A. Barker Diary
    William A. Barnard Collection
    Bush Family Collection
    Cornelius Byington Diary

Grace Dunham Collection
    Alphonso Crane Letters
Gordon Smith Collection
    Jerome Kroll Letters
Douwe B. Yntema Collection
    Leonard Loomis Letters
Atlanta History Center, Atlanta, Georgia
    George H. Daniel Correspondence
    William M. Standard Papers
Auburn University, Auburn, Alabama
    James S. Alexander Papers
    Thomas Kirkpatrick Mitchell Diary
    Aaron S. Oberly Papers
    Charles Henry Snedeker Diary
    Southern Railroad Records
    Wright Family Papers
    "The Civil War Letters of Carey Campbell Wright"
Augustana College, Rock Island, Illinois
    Gould D. Molineaux Diary
Baylor University, Waco, Texas
    Guthrie Civil War Letters
    War of the Rebellion Collection
        Map of the Siege of Vicksburg
California State University Bakersfield, Bakersfield, California
    George B. Davis Letters
California State University Northridge, Northridge, California
    Frank A. Irvin Papers
Center for Jewish History, New York, New York
    Philip Sartorius Autobiography
Chicago History Museum, Chicago, Illinois
    A. Achen Letter
    C. H. Bass Letter
    William L. Brown Papers
    George Carrington Diary
    William T. Clark Papers
    John L. Hancock Papers
    James Lawrence Papers
    Mortimer Leggett Papers
    General Maury's Order Book, 1863
    John Merrilees Diary
    Henry H. Miller Papers
    William Puffer Papers
    John A. Rawlins Papers
    Arnold Rickard Diary

Frederick W. Russell Letters
James C. Sinclair Diary
William A. Sypher Diary
John M. Wallace Papers
Cincinnati Historical Society, Cincinnati, Ohio
Hickenlooper Collection
William R. Hoel Papers
Sobieski Jolly Papers
Cornell University, Ithaca, New York
Asa Fitch Papers
Gail and Stephen Rudin Slavery Collection
Duke University, Durham, North Carolina
Sidney S. Champion Papers
George Hoke Forney Papers
Robert B. Hoadley Papers
"Military History of Captain Thomas Sewell"
Mississippi Broadside Collection
William H. Nugen Letters
W. A. Rorer Letters
Samuel Styre Papers
Emory University, Atlanta, Georgia
William Brotherton Papers
Filson Historical Society, Louisville, Kentucky
William W. Fish Papers
Matthew Goodrich Papers
Ezra Greene Papers
Helm Family Papers
John Henry Hammond Diary
John P. Jones Papers
Lynn Family Papers
David McKinney Papers
William G. Pirtle Memoirs
Channing Richards Diary
John Todd Roberts Papers
Schmidt Family Papers
Milton W. Shaw Papers
Arthur W. Utter Papers
Joseph P. Van Nest Papers
Emor Young Papers
Georgia Department of Archives and History, Atlanta, Georgia
Bible Records, Military Rosters and Reminiscences of Confederate Soldiers
W. H. Rogers, "The Flint Hill Grays"
J. B. Childs Reminiscences

Georgia Historical Society, Savannah, Georgia
    Robert H. Harris Letters
Grand Gulf State Park, Port Gibson, Mississippi
    Vicksburg *Daily Citizen*, June 30, 1863
Harvard University, Cambridge, Massachusetts
    Baker Library
        Southern Railroad Currency, 1861
    Houghton Library
        Frederick M. Dearborn Collection
            "Report of Field and Siege Guns and Ammunition on Rear Line of Defense,
                Vicksburg"
Huntington Library, San Marino, California
    Edward L. Chatfield Papers
    Charles F. Craver Diary
    Thomas T. Eckert Papers
Indiana Historical Society, Indianapolis, Indiana
    Jasper Barker Letters
    Richard Emerson Blair Letters
    Dudley E. Buck Letters
    Charles H. Buckingham Papers
    Civil War Miscellany
        Henry County File
        William Overbey File
    Crosier Family Papers
    Gilbert H. Denny Letters
    Darius H. Dodd Papers
    James F. Elliott Diary
    Bennett Grigsby Papers
    William Harper Letters
    James Leeper Papers
    John F. Lester Diary
    McLaughlin-Jordan Family Papers
    T. B. Riley Papers
    John M. Roberts Reminiscences
    Henry A. Robinson Papers
    Ross-Kidwell Papers
    Burt Scott Papers
    David S. Scott Papers
    David Shockley Papers
    S. E. Snure Papers
    Edward P. Stanfield Papers
    John C. Swift Diary
    Hubbard T. Thomas Papers

Josiah W. Underhill Diary
Aurelius L. Voorhis Diary
Joseph Waite Diary
Edward J. Wood Papers
Indiana State Library, Indianapolis, Indiana
"83rd Indiana Volunteers Regimental History"
John A. Botts Poem
Chittenden Family Papers
Civil War: Campaigns and Battles: Vicksburg
Rodney Jeger Papers
Louis W. Knobe Diary
Leeson Family Papers
George B. Marshall Reminiscences
John S. McGraw Papers
James McLaughlin Papers
Ben Price Letters
Daniel Roberts Correspondence
Henry A. Robinson Papers
George M. Rogers Diary
Marden Sabin Memoirs
Asa E. Sample Diary
Mrs. Paul Seehausen Papers
James R. Slack Letters
Benjamin Spooner Letters
James H. St. John Diary
George D. Stratton Papers
James C. Vanderbilt Letters
Indiana University, Bloomington, Indiana
Alvin P. Hovey Memoir
Iowa State University, Ames, Iowa
John W. Chambers Diary
William Van Zandt Diary
Kansas City Public Library, Kansas City, Missouri
Dixon and Jordan Family Papers
Kansas Historical Society, Topeka, Kansas
George B. Brinsmaid Papers
Isaac Home Diary
Lyman Underwood Humphrey Correspondence
Thomas George Larkin Papers
Stewart Bruce Terry Diary
Kirby Smith Collection, Wisconsin
John E. Smith Letters

Library of Congress, Washington, DC
  Wimer Bedford Papers
  Blair Family Papers
  Douglas J. and Rufus W. Cater Papers
  Cyrus B. Comstock Papers
  Charles A. Dana Papers
  William F. Draper Papers
  Samuel H. Eells Papers
  Charles Calvin Enslow Diary
  Manning F. Force Papers
  James H. Goodnow Papers
  Balzar Grebe Papers
  Walter Q. Gresham Papers
  Hiram P. Howe Papers
  John Hughes Diary
  John S. Jackman Diary
  Robert E. Jameson Papers
  John G. Jones Correspondence
  Joseph Lester Papers
  John A. Logan Papers
  Thomas Lyons Diary
  James M. McClintock Papers
  William F. Patterson Papers
  John C. Pemberton Papers
  William T. Sherman Papers
  George Boyd Smith Memoir
  Bela T. St. John Papers
  John Whitten Diary
  James H. Wilson Papers
Lincoln Memorial Shrine, Redlands, California
  Wells W. Leggett Letter
  Mortimer Leggett Papers
John A. Logan Museum, Murphysboro, Illinois
  Unknown Soldier Letter
  Wiley Collection
Louisiana State University, Baton Rouge, Louisiana
  Israel L. Adams Papers
  Anonymous Civil War Letter
  Rowland Chambers Diary
  Louis Guion Diary
  J. W. Guthrie Letter
  Richard A. Hall Letters

Louis Hébert Autobiography
Wayne Johnson Jacobs Diary
Augustus Lattz Diary
Jared Young Sanders Family Papers
William T. Sherman Papers
Thomas T. Taylor Papers
Loyola Marymount University, Los Angeles, California
Richard Blackstone Diary
Miami University, Oxford, Ohio
Samuel W. Richey Collection
Minnesota Historical Society, St. Paul, Minnesota
James C. Christie and Family Papers
Mississippi Department of Archives and History, Jackson, Mississippi
Joseph Dill Alison Diary
Emma Balfour Diary
Levi W. Bennett Diary
Louisa Russell Conner Memoir
Lettie Downs Diary
William A. Drennan Papers
Charles L. Dubuisson and Family Papers
H. N. Faulkinbury Diary
J. W. Greenman Diary
Patrick Henry Papers
Mississippi Governor, John J. Pettus, Correspondence and Papers, 1859–1863
George W. Modil Diary
Edmund Newsome Diary
James Palmer Diary
John C. Pemberton Papers
John C. Pemberton III Papers
J. H. Pepper Diary
J. L. Power Diary
John J. Robacher Papers
W. A. Rorer Letters
J. B. Sanders Papers
Claudius W. Sears Diary
Shannon-Crutcher Family Papers
Siege of Vicksburg Accounts Civilian Subject File
Siege of Vicksburg Accounts Confederate Subject File
Siege of Vicksburg Accounts Newspaper Subject File
Siege of Vicksburg Cave Life Subject File
Thomas Smith Manuscript
M. D. L. Stephens Recollections
William M. Stone Manuscript

Columbus Sykes Papers
Ida Barlow Trotter Memoir
Vicksburg Accounts Confederate Subject File
Mississippi State University, Starkville, Mississippi
Daniel Williams Papers
Missouri Historical Society, St. Louis, Missouri
John T. Appler Diary
Civil War Collection
Theodore D. Fisher Diary
David P. Grier Papers
Hiffman Family Papers
Thomas Hogan Letters
Emilie R. McKinley Diary
Moody Family Papers
Joel Strong Reminiscences
Unidentified Soldier of the 31st Iowa Infantry Diary
National Archives and Records Administration, Washington, DC
RG 94—Records of the Adjutant General's Office
E 159—General's Papers
William P. Benton Papers
Frank P. Blair Papers
Eugene A. Carr Papers
Francis J. Herron Papers
Jacob G. Lauman Papers
Michael K. Lawler Papers
John A. Logan Papers
C. L. Matthies Papers
John McArthur Papers
John A. McClernand Papers
James B. McPherson Papers
E. O. C. Ord Papers
Isaac F. Quinby Papers
James M. Tuttle Papers
Cadwallader C. Washburn Papers
RG 109—War Department Collection of Confederate Records
E 120—Samuel G. French Papers
E 131—John C. Pemberton Papers
E 134—Carter L. Stevenson Papers
Chapter II, Vol. 60—Letters and Telegrams Sent, Department of Mississippi and East Louisiana, 1863
Chapter II, Vol. 236 ¾—"Telegrams Sent: General J. E. Johnston's Command, June: December 1863"

Chapter II, Vol. 274—"Letter Book, Brig. Gen. J. S. Bowen's Command, August 1862–November 1863"
Chapter II, Vol. 311—"Letters, Telegrams, and Orders Received and Sent: General Breckinridge's Command, December 1861–November 1863"
RG 393—Records of United States Army Continental Commands
E 4726—Special Orders Issued
E 5541—General Orders Issued, 13th Army Corps
E 6294—Letters Sent, 17th Army Corps
E 6225—Letters Sent: Medical Department 17th Corps
Navarro College, Corsicana, Texas
Adnah Eaton Diary
Jordan C. Harris Papers
Andrew McCornack Papers
Samuel J. Oviatt Papers
Remley Family Papers
John Ritter Papers
Charles F. Smith Diary
Newberry Library, Chicago, Illinois
Carlos Colby Papers
Ephraim C. Dawes Papers
George Deal Papers
Chase Hall Dickinson Papers
Curtis P. Lacey Diary
Edgar McLean Papers
W. L. Park Journal
I. P. Rumsey Papers
John J. Russell Letters
Hiram Scofield Diary
Z. Payson Shumway Papers
L. S. Willard Letters
New York State Library, Albany, New York
Zadoc Rhodes Letters
Jerry Smith Letters
Notre Dame University, South Bend, Indiana
James Boardman Diary
Ulysses S. Grant Order
Thomas Family Correspondence
Ohio Historical Society, Columbus, Ohio
76th Ohio Volunteer Infantry Papers
John N. Bell Diary
George C. Churcheus Diary
John H. Dorman Papers
Henry Otis Dwight Diary

Dykes Family Letters
Hugh Ewing Papers
Reuben H. Falconer Diary
Carlos Forbes and Mary Jane Pond Collection
Henry W. Franks Letters
"Glorious News," 1863, Ohio *State Journal*
John W. Griffith Diary
Townsend P. Heaton Papers
George H. Hildt Papers
Ohio Knox Papers
Thomas J. Loudon Letter
Elliott Morrow Papers
William Murphey Papers
Charles B. Richards Collection
John M. Sullivan Papers
Thomas T. Taylor Papers
Flavius J. Thackary Diary
Eli J. Todd Papers
Thomas K. White Papers
Frank Willey Diary
Cyrus Willford, "Reminiscences of the Civil War"
Old Courthouse Museum, Vicksburg, Mississippi
Robert L. Bachman Memoir
Banner Family History
Abiel M. Barker Diary
Stephen C. Beck, "A True Sketch of His Army Life"
George Bradley Memoir
W. B. Britton Letters
John T. Buegel Diary
John T. Burgess File
Samuel Joseph Churchill Memoir
George O. Cooper Letters
W. L. Faulk Diary
Theodore D. Fisher Diary
Joseph C. Gordon Diary
George W. Harwood Letters
James Darsie Heath Diary
Isaac E. Herring File
Thomas R. Hodgson Diary
Myron Knight Diary
John A. Leavy Diary
A. C. Lenert Diary
Joseph B. Lightsey Memoir

James F. Mallinckrodt Diary
Simeon R. Martin, "Facts About Company 'I' of the 46th Mississippi Infantry"
James B. Mathews Letters
Thomas W. McCluer Diary
Alexander F. McGahey File
John Merrilees Diary
Dora Richards Miller Diary
Nicholas Miller Memoir
Edmund Newsome Diary
Virginia Rockwood Memoir
Phillip Roesch Diary
John Ruth Letter
Jared Young Sanders II Diary
Samuel W. Sherard Letters
Samuel Smith Letters
Oscar E. Stewart Memoir
James M. Swords Exhibit
Eli W. Thornhill Memoir
Merrick J. Wald Diary
Thomas B. White Letters
Abner J. Wilkes Memoir
Elbert Willett Diary
Enoch P. Williams Diary
William Williams Letters
Southern Illinois University, Carbondale, Illinois
Edwin A. Loosley Papers
Robert S. Martin Diary
Joseph Skipworth Papers
Stanford University, Stanford, California
Samuel Fowler Diary
E. O. C. Ord Papers
Frederick Steele Papers
State Historical Society of Iowa, Iowa City, Iowa
Keen Family Papers
William H. Jolly Letters
State Historical Society of Missouri: Columbia, Missouri
John T. Buegel Diary
Richard W. Burt Papers
Civil War Documents
Francis Shoup Circular
Samuel Bassett Hamacker Letters
William F. Jones Papers
William E. Lewis Letters

Personal Memoirs of I. V. Smith
George E. Townsend Letters
State Historical Society of Missouri, St. Louis, Missouri
Dyson-Bell-Sans Souci Papers
Tennessee State Library and Archives, Nashville, Tennessee
Brigham Family Letters
William R. Clack Diary
James B. Owen Letters
C. S. O. Rice Memoir
Tulane University, New Orleans, Louisiana
George Washington Cable Papers
George H. and Katherine M. Davis Collection
Vicksburg *Daily Citizen,* June 20 and 27, 1863
Henry Ginder Papers
Rosemonde E. and Emile Kuntz Collection
"Arrivée des Prisonniers de Vicksburg et de Port-Hudson"
Evan Letter
"To Our Friends in Vicksburg"
Don A. Pardee Papers
Clement S. Watson Family Papers
Ulysses S. Grant Presidential Library, Starkville, Mississippi
Orville Babcock Diary
Fred Grant, "A Boy's Experience at Vicksburg"
Vicksburg File
United States Army Historical Education Center, Carlisle, Pennsylvania
Anders Collection
John D. Brownley, "History of John D. Brownley, Company D, 57th Ohio, Veteran
Volunteer Infantry"
Bilby Collection
Carlos W. Colby, "Memoirs of Military Service"
Tim Brookes Collection
Isaac T. Williams Papers
Civil War Documents
Norman W. Calkins Diary
George H. Chatfield Papers
William M. Cleveland Papers
"Edwin Dean's Civil War Days"
Charles Lutz Papers
George S. Marks Papers
Henry T. Morgan Papers
David Smith Papers
Columbus Sykes Papers
Isaac Vanderwarker Diary

        Joseph W. Westbrook Papers
        James Whitehall Memoir
    Civil War Times Illustrated Collection
        Lionel Baxter Collection
            W. A. Rorer Letters
        L. B. Claiborne Memoirs
        Paul Dorweiler Diary
        John W. Ford Letters
        Lewis F. Phillips Papers
        Henry Johnson Reynolds Memoir
        Edward Schweitzer Diary
        Henry Seaman Diary
    Gordon Collection
        George W. Gordon Diary
    Harrisburg Civil War Roundt Table Collection
        John Carr Diary
        Coco Collection
            Howard and Victor H. Stevens Letters
            "War Diary of Brevet Brigadier General Joseph Stockton"
        Gilbert Granderson Diary
        William A. Ruyle Memoir
        Howard and Victor Stevens Letters
    Latimer Collection
        Thomas P. Latimer Letters
    Frank McGregor Papers
    Sword Collection
        Andrew McCornack Letters
        Eugene A. McWayne Papers
    Vanamburg Collection
        Vanamburg Family Papers
University of Alabama, Tuscaloosa, Alabama
    William L. Foster Letter
    George Woodard and Gene Smith Letters
University of California, San Diego, San Diego, California
    Vermilion Family Correspondence
University of Chicago, Chicago, Illinois
    Jenkin Lloyd Jones Papers
University of Georgia, Athens, Georgia
    Francis Bickett Letters
    James McCulloch Diary
University of Illinois, Urbana, Illinois
    William Clemans Papers
    George S. Durfee Correspondence

Edwin Crawford Hewett Correspondence
Edward McGlynn Letters
University of Iowa, Iowa City, Iowa
　Lot Abraham Diary
　Turner S. Bailey Diary
　Oliver Boardman Papers
　Anson R. Butler Papers
　Joseph Child Diary
　Civil War Diaries and Letters
　Giauque Family Papers
　William L. Henderson Diary
　Edwin C. Hewett Correspondence
　Joseph Kohout Letters
　Mann Family Papers
　George M. Shearer Diary
　Sterns Family Papers
　Myron Underwood Papers
　Ward Family Papers
University of Louisiana Lafayette, Lafayette, Louisiana
　William G. Richards Jr. Collection
　　Vicksburg *Daily Citizen*
University of Memphis, Memphis, Tennessee
　John Linfor Letters
　DeBenneville Randolph Keim Notebook
　Unnamed Soldier Diary
University of Michigan, Ann Arbor, Michigan
　Bentley Library
　　Calvin Ainsworth Diary
　　Robert Crouse Letters
　　Ephraim Shay Diary
　　Allen G. Wright Papers
　Clements Library
　　James S. Schoff Civil War Collection
　　　Elliott N. and Henry M. Bush Papers
　　　Lewis T. Hickok Diary
　　　Isaac Jackson Letters
University of Mississippi, Oxford, Mississippi
　M. W. Boyd Collection
　Richard C. Bridges Collection
　Joseph E. Davis Collection
　Winfield S. Featherston Collection
　Gage Family Collection
　J. Watson Henderson Collection

John Guy Lofton Collection
"Special Order No. 123"
University of North Carolina, Chapel Hill, North Carolina
Joseph Dill Alison Diary
Annie Laurie Broidrick, "A Recollection of Thirty Years Ago"
J. F. H. Claiborne Papers
Elias S. Dennis Papers
John G. Devereux Papers
Robert S. Finley Papers
George W. Gift Papers
Louis Hébert Autobiography
Hughes Family Papers
Stephen D. Lee Papers
Lenoir Family Papers
Samuel H. Lockett Papers
Lafayette McLaws Papers
Jason Niles Diary
Henry Oman Papers
John C. Pemberton Papers
L. L. Polk Papers
John A. Ramsay Papers
David Schenck Diary
Scott Family Papers
Isaac O. Shelby Diary
James M. Skelton Letters
Andrew J. Sproul Papers
Ruffin Thomson Papers
Samuel Addison Whyte Diary
Anita Dwyer Withers Diary
Adoniram Judson Withrow Papers
University of North Texas, Denton, Texas
A. C. Lenert Diary
University of South Carolina
John Bannon Diary
University of Southern Mississippi, Hattiesburg, Mississippi
Hugh B. Ewing Letter
Thomas M. Gore Memoir
University of Tennessee, Knoxville, Tennessee
Henry Bechtel Letter
Robert T. Jones Letters
Moses E. Thompson Letter
Wildermuth Family Letters

University of Texas, Austin, Texas
  Christian Wilhelm Hander Diary
University of Toledo, Toledo, Ohio
  Cyrus Hussey Diary
University of Virginia, Charlottesville, Virginia
  John C. Taylor Diary
  Vicksburg *Daily Citizen,* June 18, 1863
University of Washington, Seattle, Washington
  Manning F. Force Papers
Vicksburg National Military Park Journals/Letters/Diaries File
  A. S. Abrams, *A Full and Detailed History of the Siege of Vicksburg*
  G. C. Adams Letter
  Charles E. Affeld Diary
  Calvin Ainsworth Diary
  Dempsey Ashford Diary
  Emma Balfour Diary
  S. C. Beck, "A True Sketch of His Army Life"
  Henry H. Bennett Diary
  Jane Bitterman: Cave Life
  Rev. Ben E. Bounds Memoirs
  Elizabeth Bowie Reminiscences
  Anthony Burton Diary
  Andrew Bush Letters
  James Carlisle Diary
  "A Child at the Siege of Vicksburg"
  William R. Clack Diary
  Elias Dennis File
  William Drennan Diary
  Theodore D. Fisher Diary
  Clarkson Fogg File
  William L. Foster Letter
  C. Judson Gill Letters
  Richard A. Hall Letters
  Anson Hemingway Diary
  Thomas R. Hodgson Diary
  George H. Hynds Diary
  Will Jolly Letter
  J. J. Kellogg Reminiscences
  John H. Kelton Diary
  John Kinsel Letters
  John A. Leavy Diary
  Mortimer Leggett Papers

Jospeh Lesslie Letters
William Lewis (Lenis) Letters
W. R. McCrory Diary
Theodosia McKinstry Memoirs
Charles Dana Miller Memoir
Charlie Moore Letter
William Murray Diary
"A Narrative of the Services of Brevet Major Charles Dana Miller, 76th Ohio, in the
    War of the Great Rebellion, 1861–1865"
Edwin C. Obriham Letter
Osborn Oldroyd Diary
William Parrish Letters
J. H. Pepper Diary
Personal Accounts of the Siege of Vicksburg
    "Lady of 95 Years Tells of the War"
W. T. Ratliff Letter
John P. Reese Letter
William M. Reid Diary
Virginia Rockwood Memoir
John Ruckman Letters
Jared Young Sanders II Diary
Martin Scoville Letters
William T. Sherman Letter
Alexander Sholl Diary
A. L. Slack Diary
John E. Smith Letters
A. L. Spencer Diary
Unknown Confederate Diary
Ebenezer Werkheiser Letter
James Whitehall Memoir
Enoch P. Williams Diary
Asa Wilson Letter
G. N. Young Letters
Timothy C. Young Diary
Vicksburg National Military Park Regimental Files, Vicksburg, Mississippi
    C. P. Alling, "Four Years With the Western Army," 11th Wisconsin File
    N. M. Baker Letter, 116th Illinois File
    E. B. Bascom Letter, 5th Iowa File
    John S. Bell, "The Arkansas Sharp Shooters," 12th Arkansas File
    John A. Bering Letter, 48th Ohio File
    Richard Blackstone Letter, 32nd Ohio File
    A. B. Booth Letter, 3rd Louisiana File
    Joseph Bowker Diary, 42nd Ohio File

Robert Buchanan Letter, 7th Missouri File
Daniel Buchwalter Memoirs, 120th Ohio File
Uley Burk Letter, 30th Iowa File
James F. Cagle Letter, 20th Illinois File
J. Q. A. Campbell Diary, 5th Iowa File
John W. Carroll Letter, 77th Illinois File
Charles Letter, 9th Iowa File
"The Civil War Letters of Pvt. P. C. Bonney," 31st Illinois File
"Confederate Soldier Shot," 37th Alabama File
A. E. Cook Statement, 21st Iowa File
John Crane Letter, 17th Wisconsin File
James K. Danby Diary, 8th Indiana File
Theodore F. Davis Letter, 83rd Indiana File
William R. Eddington Autobiography, 97th Illinois File
John Edmiston Letter, 20th Illinois File
I. H. Elliott Letter, 33rd Illinois File
W. L. Faulk Diary, 38th Mississippi File
Theodore D. Fisher Diary, 1st Missouri File
Owen Francis Diary, 57th Ohio File
John Frist Letter, 113th Illinois File
John Fuller Diary, 31st Louisiana File
"George Theodore Hyatt," 127th Illinois File
W. Grayum Letter, 4th West Virginia File
John F. Hampton Letter, 43rd Mississippi File
E. L. Hawk Letter, 114th Ohio File
Will Henderson Letter, 17th Illinois File
J. M. Hobbs Diary, 33rd Illinois File
Edwin Howes Letter, 20th Illinois File
Ira W. Hunt Diary, 11th Wisconsin File
Johnse Letter, 17th Louisiana File
J. L. Jones Letter, 38th Mississippi File
J. P. Jones Letter, 45th Illinois File
James Keigwin Letter, 49th Indiana File
George D. Kellogg Letter, 23rd Wisconsin File
William Milner Kelly, "A History of the Thirtieth Alabama Volunteers (Infantry),
     Confederate States Army," 30th Alabama File
Jesse M. Lee Diary, 59th Indiana File
S. D. Lee Letter, 27th Louisiana File
Edward J. Lewis Diary, 33rd Illinois File
William A. Lorimer Letter, 17th Illinois File
Simeon R. Martin, "Facts About Company 'I' of the 46th Mississippi Infantry,"
     46th Mississippi File
J. W. McElnary Letter, 30th Ohio File

Rex Miller, *Dowdell's Volunteers: 37th Alabama Infantry*
Mupan Letter, 5th Iowa File
James K. Newton Letter, 14th Wisconsin File
T. Northrop Letter, 23rd Wisconsin File
J. A. Nottingham Letter, 8th Indiana File
Henry S. Nourse Letter, 55th Illinois File
Robert Oliver Letter, 55th Illinois File
Joseph F. Parker Letter, 130th Illinois File
J. M. Pearson Letters, 30th Alabama File
E. W. Pettus Letter, 30th Alabama File
S. N. Pickens Letter, 27th Louisiana File
James J. Ray Diary, 19th Kentucky File
A. C. Riley Report, 1st Missouri File
Edgar Rombauer Letter, 17th Missouri File
Mahlon Rouch Diary, 120th Ohio File
Jesse Sawyer Letter, 77th Illinois File
Charles Scheniman Letter, 29th Missouri File
Henry Seaman Diary, 13th Illinois File
John G. Sever Letter, 99th Illinois File
C. M. Shelley Letter, 30th Alabama File
F. M. Smith Letter, 17th Illinois File
F. M. Smith Letter, 81st Illinois File
R. M. Springer Letter, 20th Illinois File
S. H. Stevenson Letter, 48th Ohio File
James B. Taylor Diary, 120th Ohio File
Thomas J. Taylor Letter, 47th Ohio File
H. M. Trimble Diary, 93rd Illinois File
Unknown Diary, 9th Iowa File
Unknown Letter, 3rd Louisiana File
Unknown Letter, 77th Illinois File
Unknown Memoir, 3rd Louisiana File
Isaac Vanderwarker Diary, 4th Minnesota File
Charles Willison Letter, 76th Ohio File
Virginia Tech University, Blacksburg, Virginia
    William J. Pittenger Diary
Western Kentucky, University, Bowling Green, Kentucky
    George Messer Papers
    L. J. Sanders Diary
Western Reserve Historical Society, Cleveland, Ohio
    John Quincy Adams Campbell Diaries
William and Mary College, Williamsburg, Virginia
    William Taylor Correspondence
Wisconsin Historical Society, Madison, Wisconsin

H. H. Bennett Diary
Van Bennett Diary
"Civil War Diary of Henry Salomon"
Jenkin Lloyd Jones, "An Artilleryman's Diary"
E. B. Quiner Scrapbooks
Henry P. Whipple Diary

NEWSPAPERS

Alexandria (Virginia) *Gazette*
Boston *Post*
Canton *American Citizen*
Cincinnati *Daily Gazette*
Frank Leslie's Illustrated Newspaper
Fredonia (NY) *Freedom Censor*
Harper's Weekly
Jackson *Clarion Ledger*
Ligonier (IN) *Banner*
Lowell (MA) *Daily Citizen and News*
Memphis *Evening Bulletin*
Natchez *Daily Courier*
Nebraska *State Journal*
New York *Herald*
Ohio *State Journal*
Portland (ME) *Daily Advertiser*
Richmond *Whig*
Vicksburg *Evening Post*
Vicksburg *Post Herald*
Washington, DC *Daily National Intelligencer*
Washington, DC *Evening Star*

PRIMARY AND SECONDARY SOURCES

Abrams, A. S. *A Full and Detailed History of the Siege of Vicksburg*. Atlanta: Intelligencer Steam Power Presses, 1863.
Adair, John M. *Historical Sketch of the Forty-fifth Illinois Regiment, With a Complete List of the Officers and Privates and an Individual Record of Each Man in the Regiment.* Lanark, IL: Carroll County Gazette Print, 1869.
Agassiz, George R., ed. *Meade's Headquarters, 1863–1865: Letters of Colonel Theodore Lyman from the Wilderness to Appomattox.* Boston: Atlantic Monthly Press, 1922.

Albert, Allen D., ed. *History of the Forty-fifth Regiment Pennsylvania Veteran Volunteer Infantry, 1861–1865*. Williamsport, PA: Grit Publishing Company, 1912.

Allardice, Bruce S. *Confederate Colonels: A Biographical Register*. Columbia: University of Missouri Press, 2008.

Ambrose, Stephen E. *Struggle for Vicksburg: The Battles and Siege That Decided the Civil War*. Harrisburg, PA: Eastern Acorn Press, 1967.

_____, ed. "A Wisconsin Boy at Vicksburg: The Letters of James K. Newton." *Journal of Mississippi History* 23, no. 1 (January 1961): 1–14.

_____, ed. *A Wisconsin Boy in Dixie: The Selected Letters of James K. Newton*. Madison: University of Wisconsin Press, 1961.

Anderson, Ephraim McD. *Memoirs: Historical and Personal Including the Campaigns of the First Missouri Confederate Brigade*. St. Louis: Times Publishing Co., 1868.

Armstrong, Winifred Keen, ed. "The Civil War Letters of Pvt. P. C. Bonney." Lawrence County Historical Society, 1963.

"Army of the Gulf," December 4, 1886, *National Tribune*.

Arnold, James R. *Grant Wins the War: Decision at Vicksburg*. New York: John Wiley & Sons, Inc., 1997.

Badeau, Adam. *Military History of Ulysses S. Grant, From April, 1861, to April, 1865*. 2 vols. New York: D. Appleton & Co., 1881.

Ballard, Michael B. *Grant at Vicksburg: The General and the Siege*. Carbondale: Southern Illinois University Press, 2013.

_____. "Misused Merit: The Tragedy of John C. Pemberton." In *Civil War Generals in Defeat*, Steven E. Woodworth, ed. Lawrence: University Press of Kansas, 1999, 141–160.

_____. "Misused Merit: The Tragedy of John C. Pemberton." In *Confederate Generals in the Western Theater*. 4 vols. Lawrence Lee Hewitt and Arthur W. Bergeron, Jr., eds. Knoxville: University of Tennessee Press, 2010, 103–121.

_____. *Pemberton: The General Who Lost Vicksburg*. Jackson: University Press of Mississippi, 1991.

_____. *Vicksburg: The Campaign That Opened the Mississippi*. Chapel Hill: University of North Carolina Press, 2004.

Barber, Lucius W. *Army Memoirs of Lucius W. Barber Company 'D,' 15th Illinois Volunteer Infantry. May 24, 1861, to Sept. 30, 1865*. Chicago: J. M. W. Jones Stationary and Printing Co., 1894.

Barney, C. *Recollections of Field Service with the Twentieth Iowa Infantry Volunteers; Or, What I Saw in the Army*. Davenport, IA: Gazette Job Rooms, 1865.

Barnickel, Linda. *Milliken's Bend: A Civil War Battle in History and Memory*. Baton Rouge: Louisiana State University Press, 2013.

Barton, Thomas H. *Autobiography of Dr. Thomas H. Barton, The Self-made Physician of Syracuse, Ohio: Including a History of the Fourth Regt. West Va. Vol. Inf'y, with an Account of Col. Lightburn's Retreat Down the Kanawha Valley, Gen. Grant's Vicksburg and Chattanooga Campaigns, Together with the Several Battles in Which The*

Fourth Regiment Was Engaged, and Its Losses by Disease, Desertion and in Battle. Charleston: West Virginia Printing Co., 1890.

Bauer, K. Jack. *The Mexican War, 1846–1848.* New York: MacMillan, 1974.

Bearss, Edwin C. *Hardluck Ironclad: The Sinking and Salvage of the Cairo.* Rev. ed. Baton Rouge: Louisiana State University Press, 1980.

_____. *Rebel Victory at Vicksburg.* Vicksburg: Vicksburg Centennial Commission, 1963.

_____. *The Vicksburg Campaign.* 3 vols. Dayton, OH: Morningside, 1985.

_____. "The Vicksburg River Defenses and the Enigma of 'Whistling Dick.'" *Journal of Mississippi History* 19, no. 1 (January 1957): 21–30.

_____, ed. *A Southern Record: The History of the Third Regiment Louisiana Infantry.* Dayton, OH: Morningside, 1970.

_____, and J. Parker Hills. *Receding Tide: Vicksburg and Gettysburg, The Campaigns That Changed the Civil War.* Washington, DC: National Geographic, 2010.

Beck, S. C. *A True Sketch of His Army Life.* N.p.: n.p., n.d.

Bek, William G., ed. "The Civil War Diary of John T. Buegel, Union Soldier." *Missouri Historical Review* 40, no. 4 (July 1946): 503–530.

Belcher, Dennis W. *The 11th Missouri Volunteer Infantry in the Civil War: A History and Roster.* Jefferson, NC: McFarland & Company, Inc., 2011.

Belknap, William W. *History of the Fifteenth Regiment, Iowa Veteran Volunteer Infantry, from October, 1861, to August, 1865, When Disbanded at the End of the War.* Keokuk, IA: R. B. Ogden and Son, Print., 1887.

Bell, L. McRae. "A Girl's Experience in the Siege of Vicksburg." *Harper's Weekly,* June 8, 1912: 12–13.

Bell, W. Scott. *The Camel Regiment: A History of the Bloody 43rd Mississippi Volunteer Infantry, CSA, 1862–1865.* Gretna, LA: Pelican Publishing Company, 2017.

Bennett, Stuart, and Barbara Tillery, eds. *The Struggle for the Life of the Republic: A Civil War Narrative by Brevet Major Charles Dana Miller, 76th Ohio Volunteer Infantry.* Kent, OH: Kent State University Press, 2004.

Bentley, W. H. *History of the 77th Illinois Volunteer Infantry, Sept. 2, 1862–July 10, 1865.* Peoria, IL: Edward Hine, Printer, 1883.

Bergeron, Arthur W. "Martin Luther Smith and the defense of the Lower Mississippi River Valley, 1861–1863." In *Confederate Generals in the Western Theater: Essays on America's Civil War.* 4 vols. Lawrence Lee Hewitt and Arthur W. Bergeron, Jr., eds. Knoxville: University of Tennessee Press, 2011, 3:61–85.

Bering, John A., and Thomas Montgomery. *History of the Forty-Eighth Ohio Vet. Vol. Inf.* Hillsboro, OH: Highland News Office, 1880.

Bertera, Martin N. *De Golyer's 8th Michigan Black Horse Light Battery.* Wyandotte, MI: TillieAnn Press, 2015.

_____. *A Soldier at Dawn: A Remarkable and Heroic Exodus.* N.p.: n.p., n.d.

Bevier, R. S. *History of the First and Second Missouri Confederate Brigades, 1861–1865 and From Wakaruse to Appomattox, A Military Anagraph.* St. Louis: Bryan, Brand and Company, 1879.

Bigelow, James K. *Abridged History of the Eighth Indiana Volunteer Infantry, from Its Organization, April 21st, 1861, to the Date of Re-enlistment as Veterans, January 1, 1864*. Indianapolis: Ellis Barnes Book and Job Printer, 1864.

Black, Robert C. III. *The Railroads of the Confederacy*. Chapel Hill: University of North Carolina Press, 1952.

Blanchard, Ira. *I Marched with Sherman: Civil War Memoirs of the 20th Illinois Volunteer Infantry*, Nancy Ann Mattingly, ed. New York: toExcel, 1992.

Bradley, Mark L. *This Astounding Close: The Road to Bennett Place*. Chapel Hill: University of North Carolina Press, 2000.

Bridge, Carolyn S., ed. *These Men Were Heroes Once: The Sixty-ninth Indiana Volunteer Infantry*. West Lafayette, IN: Twin Publications, 2005.

Brinkerhoff, Henry R. *History of the Thirtieth Regiment Ohio Volunteer Infantry, From Its Organization, To the Fall of Vicksburg, Miss*. Columbus: James W. Osgood, Printer, 1863.

Broadaway, Douglas Lee. "A Texan Records the Civil War Siege of Vicksburg, Mississippi: The Journal of Maj. Maurice Kavanaugh Simons, 1863." *Southwestern Historical Quarterly* 105, no. 1 (July 2001): 93–131.

Brockett, L. P. *The Camp, The Battle Field, and the Hospital; Or, Lights and Shadows of the Great Rebellion*. Philadelphia: National Publishing Company, 1866.

Brown, Alonzo L. *History of the Fourth Regiment of Minnesota Infantry Volunteers During the Great Rebellion, 1861–1865*. St. Paul: Pioneer Press Company, 1892.

Brown, Russell K. *To the Manner Born: The Life of William H. T. Walker*. Athens: University of Georgia Press, 1994.

Bryner, Cloyd. *Bugle Echoes: The Story of the Illinois 47th*. Springfield, IL: Phillips Bros. Printers, 1905.

Buckles, Stanley D. *Not Afraid to Go Any Whare: A History of the 114th Regiment Illinois Volunteer Infantry*. Bend, OR: Maverick Publications, 2019.

Burdette, Robert J. *The Drums of the 47th*. Urbana: University of Illinois Press, 2000.

Burnham, John H. *The Thirty-third Regiment Illinois Infantry in the Civil War, 1861–1865; Prepared by Capt. J. H. Burnham at the Request of the Directors of the Illinois Historical Society for the 1912 Annual Meeting of That Society*. N.p.: n.p., 1912.

Byers, S. H. M. *With Fire and Sword*. New York: Neale Publishing Company, 1911.

Cable, George W., ed. "A Woman's Diary of the Siege of Vicksburg." *Century Magazine* 30, no. 5 (September 1885): 767–775.

Cadwallader, Sylvanus. *Three Years with Grant*, Benjamin P. Thomas, ed. Lincoln: University of Nebraska Press, 1996.

Castel, Albert. *Tom Taylor's Civil War*. Lawrence: University Press of Kansas, 2000.

Catton, Bruce. *Grant Moves South*. Boston: Little, Brown and Co., 1960.

———. *U. S. Grant and the American Military Tradition*. Boston: Little, Brown and Co., 1954.

———. "Vicksburg: Myths and Realities." *North and South Magazine* 6, no. 7 (November 2003): 62–69.

Chambers, William P. "My Journal." In *Publications of the Mississippi Historical Society, Centenary Series*. 5 vols. Jackson: Mississippi Historical Society, 1925.

"The Charge at Fort Hill." September 29, 1910, *National Tribune*.

Chernow, Ron. *Grant*. New York: Penguin Press, 2017.

Cisco, Walter Brian. *States Rights Gist: A South Carolina General of the Civil War*. Shippensburg, PA: White Man, 1991.

"Civil War Diary of Henry Salomon." *Wisconsin Magazine of History* 10, no. 2 (December 1926): 205–210.

Clampitt, Bradley R. *Occupied Vicksburg*. Baton Rouge: Louisiana State University Press, 2016.

Clarke, George Powell. *Reminiscence and Anecdotes of the War for Southern Independence*. N.p.: n.p., n.d.

Clark, J. S. *The Thirty-fourth Iowa Regimen: Brief History*. Des Moines: Watters-Talbott Printing Co., 1895.

Clark, Olynthus B., ed. *Downing's Civil War Diary*. Des Moines: Historical Department of Iowa, 1916.

Cobb, James C. *The Most Southern Place on Earth: The Mississippi Delta and the Roots of Regional Identity*. New York: Oxford University Press, 1994.

Cogswell, Leander W. *A History of the Eleventh New Hampshire Regiment Volunteer Infantry in the Rebellion War, 1861–1865*. Concord, NH: Republican Press Association, 1891.

"Concerning the Siege at Vicksburg." *Confederate Veteran* 2, no. 10 (October 1894): 295.

Connelly, Thomas L. *Army of the Heartland: The Army of Tennessee, 1861–1862*. Baton Rouge: Louisiana State University Press, 1967.

Connelly, T. W. *History of the Seventieth Ohio Regiment From Its Organization to Its Mustering Out*. Cincinnati: Peak Bros., n.d.

Cook, J. W. "A Reminiscence of the Siege of Vicksburg." *Confederate Veteran* 14, no. 9 (September 1906): 408–409.

Cotton, Gordon A., ed., *From the Pen of a She-Rebel: The Civil War Diary of Emilie Riley McKinley*. Columbia: University of South Carolina Press, 2001.

Crater, Lewis. *History of the Fiftieth Regiment Penna. Vet. Vols., 1861–1865*. Reading, PA: Coleman Printing House, 1884.

Cresap, Bernarr. *Appomattox Commander: The Story of General E. O. C. Ord*. San Diego: A. S. Barnes and Company, 1981.

Crooke, George. *The Twenty-first Regiment of Iowa Volunteer Infantry: A Narrative of Its Experience in Active Service, Including a Military Record of Each Officer, Non-Commissioned Officer, and Private Soldier of the Organization*. Milwaukee: King, Fowle & Co., 1891.

Crouch, Jerry Evan. *Silencing the Vicksburg Guns: The Story of the 7th Missouri Infantry Regiment as Experienced by John Davis Evans Union Private and Mormon Pioneer*. Victoria, BC: Trafford Publishing, 2005.

Crummer, Wilbur F. *With Grant at Fort Donelson, Shiloh and Vicksburg, and an Appreciation of General U. S. Grant*. Oak Park, IL: E. C. Crummer and Co., 1915.

Cunningham, Edward. *The Port Hudson Campaign, 1862–1863*. Baton Rouge: Louisiana State University Press, 1963.

Cutcheon, Byron M. *The Story of the Twentieth Michigan Infantry, July 15th, 1862, to May 30th, 1865, Embracing Official Documents on File in the Records of the State of Michigan and of the United States Referring or Relative to the Regiment.* N.p.: n.p., 1904.

Dana, Charles A. *Recollections of the Civil War.* New York: D. Appleton and Co., 1898.

Daniel, Larry J. *Conquered: Why the Army of Tennessee Failed.* Chapel Hill: University of North Carolina Press, 2019.

Davis, George B., Leslie J. Perry, and Joseph W. Kirkley. *Atlas to Accompany the Official Records of the Union and Confederate Armies.* Washington, DC: US Government Printing Office, 1891–1895.

Davis, William C. *Breckinridge: Statesman, Soldier, Symbol.* Baton Rouge: Louisiana State University Press, 1974.

_____. *Jefferson Davis: The Man and His Hour, A Biography.* New York: HarperCollins, 1991.

Dodd, W. O. "Recollections of Vicksburg During the Siege." *The Southern Bivouac* 1, no. 1 (September 1882): 2–11.

Dolnick, Edward. *Down the Great Unknown: John Wesley Powell's 1869 Journey of Discovery and Tragedy Through the Grand Canyon.* New York: HarperCollins, 2001.

Donald, David Herbert. *Lincoln.* New York: Simon and Shuster, 1995.

Dubay, Robert W. *John Jones Pettus, Mississippi Fire-eater: His Life and Times, 1813–1867.* Jackson: University Press of Mississippi, 1975.

Duke, John K. *History of the Fifty-third Regiment Ohio Volunteer Infantry, During the War of the Rebellion 1861 to 1865.* Portsmouth, OH: Blade Printing Co., 1900.

Dunbar, Aaron, and Harvey M. Trimble. *History of the Ninety-third Regiment Volunteer Infantry from Organization to Muster Out.* Chicago: Blakely Printing Co., 1898.

Dungan, J. Irvine. *History of the Nineteenth Regiment Iowa Volunteer Infantry.* Davenport, IA: Luse and Griggs, 1865.

Dunnavent, R. Blake. "'We Had Lively Times Up The Yazoo': Admiral David Dixon Porter." In *Grant's Lieutenants: From Cairo to Vicksburg.* Steven E. Woodworth, ed. Lawrence: University Press of Kansas, 2001, 169–181.

East, Dennis, II. "Wallpaper Journalism." *Timeline* 13, no. 6 (November/December 1996): 22–33.

Elder, Donald C. III, ed. *A Damned Iowa Greyhound: The Civil War Letters of William Henry Harrison Clayton.* Iowa City: University of Iowa Press, 1998.

Elliott, Isaac H. *History of the Thirty-third Regiment Illinois Veteran Volunteer Infantry in the Civil War, 22nd August 1861, to 7th December, 1865.* Gibson City, IL: The Association, 1902.

Erickson, Edgar L., ed. "With Grant at Vicksburg: From the Civil War Diary of Captain Charles E. Wilcox." *Journal of the Illinois State Historical Society* 30, no. 4 (January 1938): 441–503.

F., F. A. *Old Abe, The Eighth Wisconsin War Eagle. A Full Account of His Capture and Enlistment, Exploits in War and Honorable As Well As Useful Career in Peace.* Madison, WI: Curran and Bowen, 1885.

Feis, William B. "Grant's Relief Man: Edward O. C. Ord" In *Grant's Lieutenants: From Chattanooga to Appomattox*, Steven E. Woodworth, ed. Lawrence: University Press of Kansas, 2008, 173–194.

_____. "The War of Spies and Supplies: Grant and Grenville M. Dodge in the West, 1862–1864." In *Grant's Lieutenants: From Cairo to Vicksburg*. Steven E. Woodworth, ed. Lawrence: University Press of Kansas, 2001, 183–198.

"Fighting For Vicksburg." August 23, 1894, *National Tribune*.

Flood, Charles Bracelen. *Grant and Sherman: The Friendship That Won the Civil War*. New York: Farrar, Straus and Giroux, 2005.

Force, Manning F. "Personal Recollections of the Vicksburg Campaign." In *Sketches of War History, 1861–1865, Papers Read Before the Ohio Commandery of the Military Order of the Loyal Legion of the United States, 1883–1886, Volume 1*. Cincinnati: Robert Clarke Company, 1888, 293–309.

Foster, Tom J. "Reminiscences of Vicksburg." *Confederate Veteran* 2, no. 8 (August 1894): 244.

Fowler, James A., and Miles M. Miller. *History of the Thirtieth Iowa Infantry Volunteers. Giving a Complete Record of the Movements of the Regiment from Its Organization Until Muster Out*. Mediapolis, IA: T. A. Merrill, Printer, 1908.

Fremantle, Arthur J. L. *Three Months in the Southern States: April–June, 1863*. Edinburgh: W. Blackwood and Sons, 1863.

French, Samuel G. *Two Wars: An Autobiography of Gen. Samuel G. French*. Nashville: Confederate Veteran, 1901.

Fuller, J. F. C. *The Generalship of Ulysses S. Grant*. Bloomington: Indiana University Press, 1958.

Gage, M. D. *From Vicksburg to Raleigh; Or, A Complete History of the Twelfth Regiment Indian Volunteer Infantry, and the Campaigns of Grant and Sherman, with an Outline of the Great Rebellion*. Chicago: Clarke & Co., 1865.

"General Fred Grant's Scare at Vicksburg." April 27, 1912, *The Literary Digest*.

George, Henry. *History of the 3d, 7th, 8th and 12th Kentucky C.S.A.* Louisville, KY: C. T. Dearing Printing Co., 1911.

Giambrone, Jeff T. *Beneath Torn and Tattered Flags: A History of the 38th Mississippi Infantry, C.S.A.* Bolton, MS: Smokey Row Press, 1998.

_____. "'Of Men and Measures': The Memoir of Lt. Simeon R. Martin, 46th Mississippi Infantry." *North and South Trader's Civil War* 28, no. 6 (2002): 20–25.

_____. "'One Hour's Hard Fighting': The 4th Iowa Cavalry at the Battle of Hill's Plantation." *North and South Magazine* 9, no. 7 (February 2007): 48–60.

Goodloe, Albert Theodore. *Confederate Echoes: A Voice From the South in the Days of Secession and the Southern Confederacy*. Nashville: Publishing House of the M. E. Church, South, 1907.

Grabau, Warren E. *Ninety-Eight Days: A Geographer's View of the Vicksburg Campaign*. Knoxville: University of Tennessee Press, 2000.

Grant, Frederick D. "A Boy's Experience at Vicksburg." *Personal Recollections of the War of the Rebellion: Addresses Delivered before the Commandery of the State of New*

York, Military Order of the Loyal Legion of the United States. A. Noel Blakeman, ed. New York: G. P. Putnam's Sons, 1907, 86–100.

Grant, Ulysses S. *Personal Memoirs of U. S. Grant*. 2 vols. New York: Charles L. Webster & Co., 1892.

Grecian, J. *History of the Eighty-third Regiment, Indiana Volunteer Infantry. For Three Years With Sherman*. Cincinnati: John F. Uhlhorn, Printer, 1865.

Gresham, Matilda. *Life of Walter Quintin Gresham, 1832–1895*. 2 vols. Chicago: Rand McNally and Company, 1919.

Grimsley, Mark, and Todd D. Miller, eds. *The Union Must Stand: The Civil War Diary of John Quincy Adams Campbell, Fifth Iowa Volunteer Infantry*. Knoxville: University of Tennessee Press, 2000.

Guarneri, Carl J. *Lincoln's Informer: Charles A. Dana and the Inside Story of the Union War*. Lawrence: University Press of Kansas, 2019.

Hains, Peter C. "An Incident of the Battle of Vicksburg." In *Military Order of the Loyal Legion of the United States, Commandery of the District of Columbia, War Papers* 1. N.p.: n.p., 1887, 63–72.

Hall, Thomas O. "The Key to Vicksburg." *The Southern Bivouac* 2, no. 9 (May 1884): 393–396.

Hall, Winchester. *The Story of the 26th Louisiana Infantry, In the Service of the Confederate States*. N.p.: n.p., 1890.

Halleck, Henry W. *Elements of Military Art and Science: Or, Course of Instruction in Strategy, Fortification, Tactics of Battles, &c.; Embracing the Duties of Staff, Infantry, Cavalry, Artillery, and Engineers. Adapted to the Use of Volunteers and Militia*. New York: D. Appleton and Company, 1846.

Hart, E. J. *History of the Fortieth Illinois Inf., (Volunteers)*. Cincinnati: H. S. Bosworth, 1864.

Harwell, J. D. "In and Around Vicksburg." *Confederate Veteran* 30, no. 9 (September 1922): 333–334.

Hashell, Fritz, ed. "Col. William Camm War Diary, 1861–1865." *Journal of the Illinois State Historical Society* 18, 4 (January 1926): 793–969.

Hass, Paul H., ed. "The Vicksburg Diary of Henry Clay Warmoth: Part II (April 28, 1863–May 26, 1863)." *Journal of Mississippi History* 32, no. 1 (February 1970): 60–74.

Hattaway, Herman. *General Stephen D. Lee*. Jackson: University Press of Mississippi, 1988.

_____, and Archer Jones. *How the North Won: A Military History of the Civil War*. Urbana: University of Illinois Press, 1983.

Hays, E. Z. *History of the Thirty-second Regiment Ohio Veteran Volunteer Infantry*. Columbus: Cott & Evans Printers, 1896.

Hearn, Chester G. *Admiral David Dixon Porter: The Civil War Years*. Annapolis: Naval Institute Press, 1996.

_____. *The Capture of New Orleans 1862*. Baton Rouge: Louisiana State University Press, 1995.

Heinman, Kenneth J. *Civil War Dynasty: The Ewing Family of Ohio*. New York: New York University Press, 2012.

Hermann, Janet Sharp. *Joseph E. Davis: Pioneer Patriarch*. Jackson: University Press of Mississippi, 1991.

Hess, Earl J. *Civil War Infantry Tactics: Training, Combat, and Small-Unit Effectiveness*. Baton Rouge: Louisiana State University Press, 2015.

_____. "Grant's Ethnic General: Peter J. Osterhaus." In *Grant's Lieutenants: From Cairo to Vicksburg*. Steven E. Woodworth, ed. Lawrence: University Press of Kansas, 2001, 199–216.

Hewitt, Lawrence Lee. *Port Hudson: Confederate Bastion on the Mississippi*. Baton Rouge: Louisiana State University Press, 1987.

Hickenlooper, Andrew. "The Vicksburg Mine." In *Battles and Leaders of the Civil War*. 4 vols. New York: Century Company, 1884–1887, 3:539–542.

Hills, J. Parker. "Failure and Scapegoat: May 22." In *The Vicksburg Assaults: May 19–22, 1863*. Ed. Steven E. Woodworth and Charles D. Grear. Carbondale: Southern Illinois University Press, 2019, 27–56.

_____. "Haste and Underestimation: May 19." In *The Vicksburg Assaults: May 19–22, 1863*. Ed. Steven E. Woodworth and Charles D. Grear. Carbondale: Southern Illinois University Press, 2019, 7–26.

_____. *Vicksburg National Military Park—Art of Commemoration*. Washington, DC: National Park Service, 2011.

History of the 37th Regiment, O. V. V. I., Furnished by Comrades at the Ninth Reunion Held at St. Mary's, Ohio, Tuesday and Wednesday, September 10 and 11, 1889. Toledo, OH: Montgomery and Vrooman, 1890.

"History of the Corps." February 16, 1893, *National Tribune*.

History of the Forty-sixth Regiment Indiana Volunteer Infantry, September, 1861–September, 1865. Logansport, IN: Press of Wilson, Humphreys and Co., 1888.

History of the Thirty-fifth Regiment Massachusetts Volunteers, 1862–1865. With a Roster. Boston: Mills, Knight & Co., 1884.

History of the Thirty-sixth Regiment Massachusetts Volunteers, 1862: 1865. Boston: Rockwell and Churchill, 1884.

Hoehling, A. A. *Vicksburg: 47 Days of Siege*. Upper Saddle River, NJ: Prentice Hall, 1969.

Hogane, J. T. "Reminiscences of the Siege of Vicksburg." *Southern Historical Society Papers* 11, no. 7 (July 1883): 291–297.

_____. "Reminiscences of the Siege of Vicksburg: Paper No. 3." *Southern Historical Society Papers* 11, no. 11 (November 1883): 484–489.

Hoover, Mary Ellen, Elin Williams Neiterman, and E. Dianne James, eds. *From Your Loving Son: Civil War Correspondence and Diaries of Private George F. Moore and His Family*. Bloomington, IN: IUniverse, 2011.

Hopkins, William P. *The Seventh Regiment Rhode Island Volunteers in the Civil War, 1862–1865*. Providence: Providence Press, 1903.

Howard, R. L. *History of the 124th Regiment Illinois Infantry Volunteers, Otherwise Known as the "Hundred and Two Dozen," From August, 1862, to August, 1865*. Springfield, IL: H. W. Rokker, 1880.

Howard, Richard L. "The Vicksburg Campaign." In *War Papers Read Before the Commandery of the State of Maine, Military Order of the Loyal Legion of the United States, Volume 2*. Portland, ME: Lefavor-Tower Company, 1902, 28–40.

Howe, M. A. DeWolfe, ed. *Home Letters of General Sherman*. New York: Charles Scribner's Sons, 1909.

Howell, H. Grady, Jr. *Going to Meet the Yankees: A History of the "Bloody Sixth" Mississippi Infantry, C.S.A.* Jackson: Chickasaw Bayou Press, 1981.

Huffstodt, Jim. *Hard Dying Men: The Story of General W. H. L. Wallace, General T. E. G. Ransom, and Their "Old Eleventh" Illinois Infantry in the American Civil War (1861–1865)*. Bowie, MD: Heritage Books, 1991.

In Memoriam: Charles Ewing. Philadelphia: J. B. Lippincott, 1888.

"In the Trenches Before Vicksburg." November 15, 1900, *National Tribune*.

Jackman, Lyman. *History of the Sixth New Hampshire Regiment in the War for the Union*. Concord, NH: Republican Press Association, 1891.

Jenney, William L. B. "Personal Recollections of Vicksburg." In *Military Essays and Recollections: Papers Read Before the Commandery of the State of Illinois, Military Order of the Loyal Legion of the United States, Volume 3*. Chicago: Dial Press, 1899, 247–265.

_____. "With Sherman and Grant from Memphis to Chattanooga: A Reminisce." In *Military Essays and Recollections: Papers Read Before the Commandery of the State of Illinois, Military Order of the Loyal Legion of the United States, Volume 4*. Chicago: Cozzens and Beaton Company, 1907, 193–214.

Johansson, M. Jane. "Daniel Weisiger Adams: Defender of the Confederacy's Heartland." In *Confederate Generals in the Western Theater: Essays on America's Civil War*. 4 vols. Lawrence Lee Hewitt and Arthur W. Bergeron, Jr., eds. Knoxville: University of Tennessee Press, 2011, 3:87–118.

Johnson, Timothy D. *A Gallant Little Army: The Mexico City Campaign*. Lawrence: University Press of Kansas, 2007.

Johnston, Joseph E. "Jefferson Davis and the Mississippi Campaign." In *Battles and Leaders of the Civil War*. 4 vols. New York: Century Company, 1884–1887, 3:472–482.

Joiner, Gary D. *Mr. Lincoln's Brown Water Navy: The Mississippi Squadron*. New York: Rowman and Littlefield, 2007.

_____. *Through the Howling Wilderness: The 1864 Red River Campaign and Union Failure in the West*. Knoxville: University of Tennessee Press, 2006.

Jones, Archer. *Civil War Command and Strategy: The Process of Victory and Defeat*. New York: The Free Press, 1992.

Jones, J. B. *A Rebel War Clerk's Diary: At the Confederate States Capital, Volume 1: April 1861–July 1863*. 2 vols. James I. Robertson, Jr., ed. Lawrence: University Press of Kansas, 2015.

Jones, J. H. "The Rank and File at Vicksburg." In *Publications of the Mississippi Historical Society*, Franklin L. Riley, ed. Oxford: Mississippi Historical Society, 1903, 7:17–31.

Jones, James Pickett. *Black Jack: John A. Logan and Southern Illinois in the Civil War Era*. Carbondale: Southern Illinois University Press, 1995.

Jones, Jenkin Lloyd. "An Artilleryman's Diary." *Wisconsin History Commission: Original Papers, No. 8* (February 1914): 1–368.

Jones, S. C. *Reminiscences of the Twenty-second Iowa Volunteer Infantry, Giving Its Organization, Marches, Skirmishes, Battles, and Sieges, as Taken from the Diary of Lieutenant S. C. Jones of Company A*. Iowa City: np, 1907.

Kaiser, Leo M., ed. "The Civil War Diary of Florison D. Pitts." *Mid-America: An Historical Review* 40, no. 1 (January 1958): 22–63.

Kellogg, J. J. *The Vicksburg Campaign and Reminiscences, "Milliken's Bend" to July 4, 1863*. Washington, IA: Evening Journal, 1913.

Kelly, William M. "A History of the 30th Alabama Volunteers (Infantry), Confederate States Army." *Alabama Historical Quarterly* 9, no. 1 (Spring 1947): 115–167.

Kiper, Richard L. *Major General John A. McClernand: Politician in Uniform*. Kent, OH: Kent State University Press, 1999.

Kirwan, A. D., ed. *Johnny Green of the Orphan Brigade: The Journal of a Confederate Soldier*. Lexington: University Press of Kentucky, 1956.

Kountz, John S. *Record of the Organizations Engaged in the Campaign, Siege, and Defense of Vicksburg*. Knoxville: University of Tennessee Press, 2011.

Krick, Robert K. "'Snarl and Sneer and Quarrel': General Joseph E. Johnston and an Obsession with Rank." In *Leaders of the Lost Cause: New Perspectives on the Confederate High Command*, Gary W. Gallagher and Joseph T. Glatthaar, eds. Mechanicsburg, PA: Stackpole Books, 2004, 165–203.

Lamers, William M. *The Edge of Glory: A Biography of General William S. Rosecrans, U.S.A.* New York: Harcourt, Brace, and World, 1961.

Lash, Jeffrey N. *A Politician Turned General: The Civil War Career of Stephen Augustus Hurlbut*. Kent, OH: Kent State University Press, 2003.

Lee, Stephen D. "The Siege of Vicksburg." *Publications of the Mississippi Historical Society*. Oxford: Mississippi Historical Society, 1900, 3: 55–71.

"Letters from the Trenches." July 31, 1902, *National Tribune*.

Lobdell, Jared. "A Civil War Tank at Vicksburg." *Journal of Mississippi History* 25, no. 4 (October 1963): 279–283.

Lockett, S. H. "The Defense of Vicksburg." In *Battles and Leaders of the Civil War*. 4 vols. New York: Century Company, 1884–1887, 3:482–492.

Lord, Edward O., ed. *History of the Ninth Regiment, New Hampshire Volunteers in the War of the Rebellion*. Concord, NH: Republican Press Association, 1895.

Loughborough, Mary Ann. *My Cave Life in Vicksburg: With Letters of Trial and Travel*. New York: D. Appleton and Company, 1864.

Lowe, Richard G. *Walker's Texas Division, C S.A.: Greyhounds of the Trans-Mississippi*. Baton Rouge: Louisiana State University Press, 2004.

Lucas, D. R. *New History of the 99th Indiana Infantry Containing Official Reports, Anecdotes, Incidents, Biographies and Complete Rolls*. Rockford, IL: Horner Printing Co., 1900.

Luraghi, Raimondo. *A History of the Confederate Navy*. Annapolis: Naval Institute Press, 1996.

Mahan, D. H. *A Complete Treatise on Field Fortifications, with the General Outlines of the Principles Regulating the Arrangement, the Attack, and the Defense of Permanent Works*. New York: Wiley and Long, 1836.

_____. *A Treatise on Field Fortification, Containing Instructions on the Methods of Laying Out, Constructing, Defending, and Attacking Intrenchments, with the General Outlines Also of the Arrangement, the Attack and Defence of Permanent Fortifications*. New York: John Wiley, 1861.

Mahan, James C. *Memoirs of James Curtis Mahan*. Lincoln, NE: Franklin Press, 1919.

Marshall, W. R. "Reminiscences of General U. S. Grant." In *Glimpses of the Nation's Struggle: A Series of Papers Read Before the Minnesota Commandery of the Loyal Legion of the United States*. St. Paul: St. Paul Book and Stationary Company, 1887, 89–106.

Marszalek, John F. *Commander of All Lincoln's Armies: A Life of General Henry W. Halleck*. Cambridge: Harvard University Press, 2004.

_____. "'A Full Share of All the Credit': Sherman and Grant to the Fall of Vicksburg." In *Grant's Lieutenants: From Cairo to Vicksburg*. Steven E. Woodworth, ed. Lawrence: University Press of Kansas, 2001, 5–20.

_____. *Lincoln and the Military*. Carbondale: Southern Illinois University Press, 2014.

_____. *Sherman: A Soldier's Passion for Order*. New York: The Free Press, 1993.

_____, David F. Nolen, and Louie P. Gallo. *The Personal Memoirs of Ulysses S. Grant: The Complete Annotated Edition*. Cambridge: Harvard University Press, 2017.

Mason, F. H. *The Forty-second Ohio Infantry: A History of the Organization and Services of That Regiment in the War of the Rebellion; With Biographical Sketches of Its Field Officers and a Full Roster of the Regiment*. Cleveland, OH: Cobb, Andrews and Co., Publishers, 1876.

Maynard, Douglas, ed. "Vicksburg Diary: The Journal of Gabriel M. Killgore." *Civil War History* 10, no. 1 (March 1964): 33–53.

McAlexander, U. G. *History of the Thirteenth Regiment United States Infantry, Compiled from Regimental Records and Other Sources*. N.p.: Regimental Press, Thirteenth Infantry, 1905.

McCaul, Edward B., Jr. *To Retain Command of the Mississippi: The Civil War Naval Campaign for Memphis*. Knoxville: University of Tennessee Press, 2014.

McDonough, James Lee. *William Tecumseh Sherman: In the Service of My Country: A Life*. New York: W. W. Norton & Company, 2016.

McPherson, James M. *Battle Cry of Freedom: The Civil War Era*. New York: Oxford University Press, 1988.

_____. *For Cause and Comrades: Why Men Fought in the Civil War*. New York: Oxford University Press, 1997.

Memminger, R. W. "The Surrender of Vicksburg: A Defense of General Pemberton," *Southern Historical Society Papers* 12, no. 7–9 (July–September 1884): 352–360.

Merrin, F. W. "More Vicksburg Reminiscences." *Confederate Veteran* 2, no. 12 (December 1894): 374.

Miller, Donald L. *Vicksburg: Grant's Campaign That Broke the Confederacy*. New York: Simon and Shuster, 2019.

Moore, Frank, ed. *The Rebellion Record: A Diary of American Events, With Documents,*

Narratives, Illustrative Incidents, Poetry, Etc. 11 vols. New York: D. Van Nostrand, 1861–1868.

"More About Vicksburg." September 29, 1910, *National Tribune*.

Morris, W. S. *History, 31st Regiment Illinois Volunteers: Organized by John A. Logan.* Herrin, IL: Crossfire Press, 1991.

Myers, Richard. *The Vicksburg National Cemetery: An Administrative History*. Washington, DC: National Park Service, 1968.

Northen, Charles Swift III, ed. *All Right Let Them Come: The Civil War Diary of an East Tennessee Confederate*. Knoxville: University of Tennessee Press, 2003.

The Official Records of the Union and Confederate Navies in the War of the Rebellion. 30 vols. Washington, DC: US Government Printing Office, 1894–1922.

Oldroyd, Osborn H. *A Soldier's Story of the Siege of Vicksburg from the Diary of Osborn H. Oldroyd*. Springfield: self-published, 1885.

"Opening of the Mississippi." November 2, 1905, *National Tribune*.

Osborne, William H. *The History of the Twenty-ninth Regiment of Massachusetts Volunteer Infantry in the Late War of the Rebellion*. Boston: Albert J. Wright, Printer, 1877.

Ottens, Allen J. *General John A. Rawlins: No Ordinary Man*. Bloomington: Indiana University Press, 2021.

Panhorst, Michael W. "'The First of Our Hundred Battle Monuments': Civil War Battlefield Monuments Built by Active-Duty Soldiers During the Civil War." *Southern Cultures* 20, no. 4 (Winter 2014): 22–43.

_____. *The Memorial Art and Architecture of Vicksburg National Military Park*. Kent, OH: Kent State University Press, 2015.

Parrish, William E. *Frank Blair: Lincoln's Conservative*. Columbia: University of Missouri Press, 1998.

Patrick, Jeffrey L., ed. *Three Years with Wallace's Zouaves: The Civil War Memoirs of Thomas Wise Durham*. Macon, GA: Mercer University Press, 2003.

Payne, James E. "Missouri Troops in the Vicksburg Campaign." *Confederate Veteran* 36, no. 10 (October 1928): 377–379.

Pemberton, John C. *Pemberton: Defender of Vicksburg*. Chapel Hill: University of North Carolina Press, 1942.

Perry, Lynch. "Vicksburg. Some New History in the Experience of Gen. Francis A. Shoup." *Confederate Veteran* 2, no. 6 (June 1894): 172–174.

Phillips, L. F. *Some Things Our Boy Saw in the War*. Gravity, IA: n.p., 1911.

Pierson, Enos. *Proceedings of Eleven Reunions Held by the 16th Regiment, O. V. I., Including Roll of Honor, Roster of the Survivors of the Regiment, Statistics, &c., &c.* Millersburg, OH: Republican Steam Press, 1887.

Plummer, Leonard B., ed. "Excerpts from the Hander Diary." *Journal of Mississippi History* 26, no. 2 (May 1964): 141–149.

Porter, David Dixon. *Incidents and Anecdotes of the Civil War*. New York: D. Appleton and Company, 1885.

Post, Lydia Minturn, ed. *Soldiers' Letters. From Camp, Battle-field and Prison*. New York: Bunce and Huntington, Publishers, 1865.

Powell, David A., and Eric J. Wittenberg. *Tullahoma: The Forgotten Campaign That*

Changed the Course of the Civil War, June 23–July 4, 1863. New York: Savas Beatie, 2020.

Pratt, Harry E., ed. "Civil War Letters of Brigadier-General William Ward Orme, 1862–1866." *Journal of the Illinois State Historical Society* 23, no. 2 (July 1930): 246–315.

Privette, Lindsay Rae Smith. "'Fightin' Johnnies, Fevers, and Mosquitoes': A Medical History of the Vicksburg Campaign." PhD diss., University of Alabama, 2018.

Pryce, Samuel D. *Vanishing Footprints: The Twenty-Second Iowa Volunteer Infantry in the Civil War*, Jeffry C. Burden, ed. Iowa City: Camp Pope Bookshop, 2008.

Quinby, Henry Cole. *Genealogical History of the Quinby (Quimby) Family In England and America*. Rutland, VT: Tuttle Company, 1915.

Raab, James W. *W. W. Loring: Florida's Forgotten General*. Manhattan, KS: Sunflower University Press, 1996.

Reagan, John H. *Memoirs, With Special Reference to Secession and the Civil War*, Walter Flavius McCaleb, ed. New York: Neale Publishing Company, 1906.

Reed, David W. *Campaigns and Battles of the Twelfth Regiment Iowa Veteran Volunteer Infantry From Its Organization, September, 1861, to Muster Out, January 20, 1866*. N.p.: n.p., 1903.

Reed, Lida Lord. "A Woman's Experiences During the Siege of Vicksburg." *Century Magazine* 61, no. 6 (April 1901): 922–928.

Rice, C. S. O. "Incidents of the Vicksburg Siege." *Confederate Veteran* 12, no. 2 (February 1904): 77–78.

Richard, Allen C., Jr., and Mary Margaret Higginbotham Richard. *The Defense of Vicksburg: A Louisiana Chronicle*. College Station: Texas A&M University Press, 2004.

Richardson, Albert D. *A Personal History of Ulysses S. Grant*. Hartford, CT: American Publishing Company, 1868.

Richmond, Marion B. "The Siege of Vicksburg." *Confederate Veteran* 37, no. 4 (April 1929): 139–141.

Roberts, W. Clifford, Jr., and Frank E. Clark. *Atlanta's Fighting Forty-Second: Joseph Johnston's "Old Guard."* Macon, GA: Mercer University Press, 2020.

Roland, Charles P. *Albert Sidney Johnston: Soldier of Three Republics*. Austin: University of Texas Press, 1964.

Rood, Hosea W. *Story of the Service of Company E, and of the Twelfth Wisconsin Regiment of Veteran Volunteer Infantry in the War of the Rebellion*. N.p.: n.p., n.d.

Sanborn, John B. "Remarks on a Motion to Extend a Vote of Thanks to General Marshall for Above Papers." *Glimpses of the Nation's Struggle, Fourth Series, Papers Read Before the Minnesota Commandery of the Military Order of the Loyal Legion of the United States, 1892–1897*. St. Paul: H. L. Collins Co., 1898, 615–622.

Sanborn Family in the United States and Brief Sketch of Life of John B. Sanborn. St. Paul: H. M. Smyth Printing Co., 1887.

Sanders, Mary Elizabeth, ed. *Diary in Gray: Civil War Journal of J. Y. Sanders*. Baton Rouge, LA: Louisiana Genealogical & Historical Society, 1994.

Saunier, Joseph A. *A History of the Forty-seventh Regiment Ohio Veteran Volunteer*

Infantry, Second Brigade, Second Division, Fifteenth Army Corps, Army of the Ten-nessee. Hillsboro, OH: Lyle Printing Company, 1903.

Scott, R. B. *The History of the 67th Regiment Indiana Infantry Volunteers, War of the Rebellion*. Bedford, IN: Herald Book and Job Print, 1892.

Scriber, Terry G. *Twenty-seventh Louisiana Volunteer Infantry*. Gretna, LA: Pelican Publishing Company, 2006.

Sears, Stephen W. *Gettysburg*. Boston: Houghton Mifflin, 2003.

Shea, William L., and Terrence J. Winschel, *Vicksburg is the Key: The Struggle for the Mississippi River*. Lincoln: University of Nebraska Press, 2003.

Sherman, William T. *Memoirs of General William T. Sherman: Written by Himself*. 2 vols. New York: D. Appleton and Co., 1875.

"Siege of Vicksburg." November 4, 1897, *National Tribune*.

Simon, John Y., ed. *The Personal Memoirs of Julia Dent Grant [Mrs. Ulysses S. Grant]*. New York: G. P. Putnam's Sons, 1975.

_____, and John F. Marszalek, eds. *The Papers of Ulysses S. Grant*. 32 vols. Carbondale: Southern Illinois University Press, 1967–2014.

Simpson, Brooks D. *Ulysses S. Grant: Triumph Over Adversity, 1822–1865*. Boston: Houghton Mifflin Company, 2000.

Skaptason, Bjorn. "The Chicago Light Artillery at Shiloh." *Journal of the Illinois State Historical Society* 104, 1–2 (Spring-Summer 2011): 73–96.

_____. "The Chicago Light Artillery at Vicksburg." *Journal of the Illinois State Historical Society* 106, no. 3–4 (Fall/Winter 2013): 422–462.

Slay, David H. "Abraham Lincoln and the Mississippi Colored Troops." *Journal of Mississippi History* 70, no. 1 (Spring 2008): 65–84.

Smith, Tamara A. "A Matter of Trust: Grant and James B. McPherson." In *Grant's Lieutenants: From Cairo to Vicksburg*. Steven E. Woodworth, ed. Lawrence: University Press of Kansas, 2001, 151–167.

Smith, Timothy B. *"Altogether Fitting and Proper": Civil War Battlefield Preservation in History, Memory, and Policy, 1861–2015*. Knoxville: University of Tennessee Press, 2017.

_____. *Champion Hill: Decisive Battle for Vicksburg*. New York: Savas Beatie, 2004.

_____. *Corinth 1862: Siege, Battle, Occupation*. Lawrence: University Press of Kansas, 2012.

_____. *The Decision Was Always My Own: Ulysses S. Grant and the Vicksburg Campaign*. Carbondale: Southern Illinois University Press, 2018.

_____. *The Golden Age of Battlefield Preservation: The Decade of the 1890s and the Establishment of America's First Five Military Parks*. Knoxville: University of Tennessee Press, 2008.

_____. *Grant Invades Tennessee: The 1862 Battles for Forts Henry and Donelson*. Lawrence: University Press of Kansas, 2016.

_____. *Mississippi in the Civil War: The Home Front* (Mississippi Heritage Series). Jackson: University Press of Mississippi, 2010.

_____. "Mississippi Nightmare." *Civil War Times* 48, no. 4 (August 2009): 54–58.

_____. *The Real Horse Soldiers: Benjamin Grierson's Epic 1863 Civil War Raid Through Mississippi*. New York: Savas Beatie, 2018.

_____. *Shiloh: Conquer or Perish*. Lawrence: University Press of Kansas, 2014.

_____. *The Union Assaults at Vicksburg: Grant Attacks Pemberton, May 17–22, 1863*. Lawrence: University Press of Kansas, 2020.

_____. "Victory at Any Cost: The Yazoo Pass Expedition." *Journal of Mississippi History* 67, no. 2 (Summer 2007): 147–166.

_____. "'A Victory Could Hardly Have Been More Complete': The Battle of Big Black River Bridge." In *The Vicksburg Campaign: March 29–May 18, 1863*. Steven E. Woodworth and Charles D. Grear, eds. Carbondale: Southern Illinois University Press, 2013, 173–193.

Smith, Walter George. *Life and Letters of Thomas Kilby Smith, Brevet Major-General United States Volunteers, 1820–1877*. New York: G. P. Putnam's Sons, 1898.

Soley, James Russell. "Naval Operations in the Vicksburg Campaign." In *Battles and Leaders of the Civil War*. 4 vols. New York: Century Company, 1884–1887, 3:551–570.

Solonick, Justin S. *Engineering Victory: The Union Siege of Vicksburg*. Carbondale: Southern Illinois University Press, 2015.

Soman, Jean Powers, and Frank L. Byrne, eds., *A Jewish Colonel in the Civil War: Marcus M. Spiegel of the Ohio Volunteers*. Kent, OH: Kent State University Press, 1985.

Stillwell, Leander. *The Story of a Common Soldier of Army Life in the Civil War, 1861–1865*. 2nd ed. N.p.: Franklin Hudson Publishing Co., 1920.

Stoker, Donald. *The Grand Design: Strategy and the U.S. Civil War*. New York: Oxford University Press, 2010.

Stone, Mary Amelia (Boomer). *Memoir of George Boardman Boomer*. Boston: Press of Geo. C. Rand & Avery, 1864.

The Story of the Fifty-fifth Regiment Illinois Volunteer Infantry in the Civil War, 1861–1865. Clinton, MA: W. J. Coulter, 1887.

Strong, William E. "The Campaign Against Vicksburg." In *Military Essays and Recollections: Papers Read Before the Commandery of the State of Illinois, Military Order of the Loyal Legion of the United States, Volume 2*. Chicago: A. C. McClurg and Company, 1894, 313–354.

Supplement to the Official Records of the Union and Confederate Armies. 100 vols. Wilmington, NC: Broadfoot Publishing Company, 1994.

"The Surrender of Vicksburg." November 22, 1900, *National Tribune*.

Swan, James B. *Chicago's Irish Legion: The 90th Illinois Volunteers in the Civil War*. Carbondale: Southern Illinois University Press, 2009.

Symonds, Craig L. *Joseph E. Johnston: A Civil War Biography*. New York: Norton, 1992.

_____. *Lincoln and His Admirals: Abraham Lincoln, The U.S. Navy, and the Civil War*. New York: Oxford University Press, 2008.

"The Terms of Surrender." In *Battles and Leaders of the Civil War*. 4 vols. New York: Century Company, 1884–1887, 3: 543–546.

Thompson, S. D. *Recollections with the Third Iowa Regiment*. Cincinnati: n.p., 1864.

Thorndike, Rachel Sherman, ed. *The Sherman Letters: Correspondence Between General and Senator Sherman from 1837 to 1891*. New York: Charles Scribner's Sons, 1894.

Throne, Mildred, ed. *The Civil War Diary of Cyrus F. Boyd Fifteenth Iowa Infantry, 1861–1863*. Baton Rouge: Louisiana State University Press, 1998.

Todd, William. *The Seventy-ninth Highlanders New York Volunteers in the War of Rebellion, 1861–1865*. Albany: Brandow, Barton & Co., 1886.

Tomblin, Barbara Brooks. *The Civil War on the Mississippi: Union Sailors, Gunboat Captains, and the Campaign to Control the River*. Lexington: University Press of Kentucky, 2016.

Townsend, Mary Bobbitt. *Yankee Warhorse: A Biography of Major General Peter Osterhaus*. Columbia: University of Missouri Press, 2010.

Trowbridge, Silas T. *Autobiography of S. T. Trowbridge, M.D.* N.p.: n.p., 1872.

_____. *Autobiography of Silas Thompson Trowbridge, M.D.* Carbondale: Southern Illinois University Press, 2004.

Trudeau, Noah Andre. *Gettysburg: A Testing of Courage*. New York: HarperCollins, 2002.

Tucker, Philip Thomas. *The Forgotten Stonewall of the West: Major General John Stevens Bowen*. Macon, GA: Mercer University Press, 1997.

_____. *Westerners in Gray: The Men and Missions of the Elite Fifth Missouri Infantry Regiment*. Jefferson, NC: McFarland & Company, 1995.

Tunnard, W. H. *A Southern Record: The History of the Third Regiment Louisiana Infantry*. Baton Rouge: n.p., 1866.

"Vicksburg Campaign." August 9, 1888, *National Tribune*.

Waldrep, Christopher. *Vicksburg's Long Shadow: The Civil War Legacy of Race and Remembrance*. New York: Rowman and Littlefield Publishers, 2005.

Walker, Peter F. *Vicksburg: A People at War, 1860–1865*. Chapel Hill: University of North Carolina Press, 1960.

Warner, Ezra J. *Generals in Blue: Lives of the Union Commanders*. Baton Rouge: Louisiana State University Press, 1964.

_____. *Generals in Gray: Lives of the Confederate Commanders*. Baton Rouge: Louisiana State University Press, 1959.

War of the Rebellion: A Compilation of the Official Records of the Union and Confederate Armies. Washington, DC: US Government Printing Office, 1880–1901.

Welles, Gideon. *Diary of Gideon Welles: Secretary of the Navy under Lincoln and Johnson*. 3 vols. Boston: Houghton Mifflin Co., 1911.

Wells, Seth J. *The Siege of Vicksburg from the Diary of Seth J. Wells, Including Weeks of Preparation and of Occupation After the Surrender*. Detroit: William H. Rowe, Publisher, 1915.

Welsh, Jack D. *Medical Histories of Confederate Generals*. Kent, OH: Kent State University Press, 1995.

_____. *Medical Histories of Union Generals*. Kent, OH: Kent State University Press, 1996.

Whaley, Elizabeth J. *Forgotten Hero: General James B. McPherson*. New York: Exposition Press, 1955.

White, Ronald C. *American Ulysses: A Life of Ulysses S. Grant*. New York: Random House, 2016.

Whittington, Terry. "In the Shadow of Defeat: Tracking the Vicksburg Parolees." *Journal of Mississippi History* 64, no. 4 (Winter 2002): 307–330.

Wiggins, Sarah Woolfolk, ed. *The Journals of Josiah Gorgas, 1857–1878*. Tuscaloosa: University of Alabama Press, 1995.

Wiley, Bell Irvin. *The Life of Johnny Reb: The Common Soldier of the Confederacy*. Indianapolis: Bobbs-Merrill Company, 1943.

Wilkin, Jacob B. "Vicksburg." In *Military Essays and Recollections: Papers Read Before the Commandery of the State of Illinois, Military Order of the Loyal Legion of the United States, Volume 4*. Chicago: Cozzens and Beaton Company, 1907, 215–237.

Williams, John Melvin. *"The Eagle Regiment," 8th Wis. Inf'ty Vols.: A Sketch of Its Marches, Battles and Campaigns From 1861–1865 With Complete Regimental and Company Roster, and a Few Portraits and Sketches of Its Officers and Commanders*. Belleville, WI: Recorder Print, 1890.

Williams, Kenneth P. *Grant Rises in the West: From Iuka to Vicksburg, 1862–1863*. Lincoln: University of Nebraska Press, 1997.

Williams, T. Harry. *Lincoln and His Generals*. New York: Alfred A. Knopf, 1952.

Willison, Charles A. *Reminiscences of a Boy's Service with the 76th Ohio, In the Fifteenth Army Corps, Under General Sherman, During the Civil War, By That "Boy" at Three Score*. Menasha, WI: George Banta Publishing Company, 1908.

Wills, Brian Steel. "A Kentucky Lyon Roars: Hylan B. Lyon in the Civil War." In *Confederate Generals in the Western Theater: Essays on America's Civil War*. 4 vols. Lawrence Lee Hewitt and Arthur W. Bergeron, Jr., eds. Knoxville: University of Tennessee Press, 2011, 2:187–214.

Wilson, James Harrison. "A Staff Officer's Journal of the Vicksburg Campaign, April 30 to July 4, 1863." *Journal of the Military Service Institution of the United States* 43, no. 154 (July–August 1908): 93–109.

_____. "A Staff Officer's Journal of the Vicksburg Campaign, April 30 to July 4, 1863." *Journal of the Military Service Institution of the United States* 43, no. 155 (September–October 1908): 261–275.

_____. *Under the Old Flag: Recollections of Military Operations in the War for the Union, the Spanish War, the Boxer Rebellion, Etc.* 2 vols. New York: D. Appleton and Co., 1912.

Winschel, Terrence J. "The Absence of Will: Joseph E. Johnston and the Fall of Vicksburg." In *Confederate Generals in the Western Theater: Essays on America's Civil War*. 4 vols. Lawrence Lee Hewitt and Arthur W. Bergeron, Jr., eds. Knoxville: University of Tennessee Press, 2010, 2:75–92.

_____. *Alice Shirley and the Story of Wexford Lodge*. Fort Washington, PA: Eastern National, 2003.

_____. "Applicability in the Modern Age: Ulysses S. Grant's Vicksburg Campaign." *Journal of Mississippi History* 80, nos. 1 and 2 (Spring/Summer 2018): 35–47.

_____. "Fighting Politician: John A. McClernand." In *Grant's Lieutenants: From Cairo to Vicksburg*. Steven E. Woodworth, ed. Lawrence: University Press of Kansas, 2001, 129–150.

_____. "A Soldier's Legacy: William T. Rigby and the Establishment of Vicksburg National Military Park." *Journal of Mississippi History* 75, no. 4 (Winter 2013): 93–110.

_____. "Stephen D. Lee and the Making of an American Shrine." *Journal of Mississippi History* 63, no. 1 (2001): 17–32.

_____. *Triumph and Defeat: The Vicksburg Campaign*. Mason City, IA: Savas Publishing Company, 1999.

_____. *Triumph and Defeat: The Vicksburg Campaign, Volume 2*. New York: Savas Beatie, 2006.

_____. "The Vicksburg Campaign." In *The Cambridge History of the American Civil War*. 3 vols. Aaron Sheehad-Dean, ed. Cambridge: Cambridge University Press, 2019, 1:246–268.

_____, ed. *The Civil War Diary of a Common Soldier: William Wiley of the 77th Illinois Infantry*. Baton Rouge: Louisiana State University Press, 2001.

"With the Western Army." January 16, 1863, *National Tribune*.

Wood, D. W. *History of the 20th O. V. V. I. Regiment, and Proceedings of the First Reunion at Mt. Vernon, Ohio, April 6, 1876*. Columbus: Paul and Thrall, Book and Job Printers, 1876.

Wood, Wales W. *A History of the Ninety-fifth Regiment Illinois Infantry Volunteers, From its Organization in the Fall of 1862, Until Its Final Discharge from the United States Service, in 1865*. Chicago: Tribune Company's Book and Job Printing Office, 1865.

Woodrick, Jim. *The Civil War Siege of Jackson, Mississippi*. Charleston: History Press, 2016.

Woodruff, George H. *Fifteen Years Ago, Or the Patriotism of Will County*. Joliet, IL: Joliet Republican Book and Job Steam Printing House, 1876.

Woodworth, Steven E. *Jefferson Davis and His Generals: The Failure of Confederate Command in the West*. Lawrence: University Press of Kansas, 1990.

_____. *Nothing but Victory: The Army of the Tennessee, 1861–1865*. New York: Knopf, 2005.

_____, and Charles D. Grear, eds. *Vicksburg Besieged*. Carbondale: Southern Illinois University Press, 2020.

Work, David. *Lincoln's Political Generals*. Urbana: University of Illinois Press, 2009.

Wright, Henry H. *A History of the Sixth Iowa Infantry*. Iowa City: State Historical Society of Iowa, 1923.

Wright, Michael. "Vicksburg and the Trans-Mississippi Supply Line (1861–1863)." *Journal of Mississippi History* 43, no. 3 (August 1981): 210, 225.

Young, John Russell. *Around the World With General Grant: A Narrative of the Visit of General U. S. Grant, Ex-President of the United States, to Various Countries in Europe, Asia, and Africa, in 1877, 1878, 1879. To which are Added Certain Conversations with General Grant on Questions Connected with American Politics and History*. New York: American News Company, 1879.

INDEX

714   INDEX

Lum House, 495
Lyford, Stephen C., 70
Lynd, Solomon, 299
Lyon, Hylan B., 76
Lyons, J. D., 151

MacFeely, Robert, 162
Mack, Eugene, 455, 460
Macon's Ford, Mississippi, 277
Mahan, Dennis Hart, xviii, xxv, xxvii, 372, 383
Malmborg, Oscar, 411, 473
Maltby, Jasper A., 393
Manter, Francis H., 100–101, 111, 164, 210, 412, 464–465, 544
Manter's Approach, 100–101, 164, 210, 311, 412
Marks, Leon D., 404
Markum's Plantation, 419
Marlborough, Duke of, 108
Martin, Simeon, 193
Martin, William W., 405
Maryland, 11
Maryland Troops (CS)
  3rd Battery, 554
Massachusetts, 219, 234–235, 304–305, 307, 453, 523
Massachusetts Troops
  29th Infantry, 541
  35th Infantry, 540
  36th Infantry, 304, 540
Mathews, James B., 401
Matthies, Charles L., 346, 465–466, 502, 546, 551
Maurice, Thomas D., 550
Maxey, Samuel B., 73, 558
McAlester, Miles D., 372, 410, 447
McArthur, John, 37, 58, 65, 69, 71, 111–112, 115, 163, 346–347, 384–385, 415, 419–420, 432, 453–454, 466, 503, 524, 550
McCall's Plantation, 344
McCardle, William H., 214
McClellan, George B., xvii, 516
McClernand, John A., xiv, 71, 86, 104, 109, 111, 146, 171, 179, 190, 269, 277–281, 306, 341, 446–447, 457–458, 463–464, 503, 511, 515–517, 541

and preliminary activities, 12, 15–17, 22
removal of, 317–329
and siege operations, 58–61, 67, 69, 91, 100, 127, 163–167, 207, 209–210, 228, 262, 275, 315–317, 334, 372–373, 376
and Vicksburg assaults, 27–28, 39–42, 44–45
McClernand, Minerva, 321, 463
McClintok, J. M., 261
McCown, James, 397
McCullough, Henry E., 217
McGahey, Alexander F., 530
McKinley, Emilie, 260
McKinstry, Theodosia, 120
McLaurin, Laurin L., 405
McLaws, Lafayette, 437
McMillen, William L., 465, 546
McNair, Evander, 73, 557
McNulta, John, 136, 145
McPherson, James B., 111, 115, 121, 124, 139–140, 189, 277–278, 283, 306, 321, 323–325, 329, 346, 380, 383–385, 387, 397, 399, 423, 458, 465–466, 478, 481–482, 484, 486, 491–495, 503, 549
and preliminary activities, 22
and results of siege, 511, 524–526
and siege operations, 58–63, 65–67, 69, 90, 156, 163, 166–167, 206–207, 210, 262, 313, 316, 367, 376, 407, 409–410, 437, 440, 442–443, 446
and Vicksburg assaults, 27–29, 37, 39, 41–43
McRae, Lucy, 428, 520
McRory, W. R., 254
Mechanicsburg, Mississippi, 114–115, 121, 179–181, 183–185, 187, 219, 270–271, 277, 350
Medal of Honor, 95, 392
Memminger, Robert W., 3, 214
Memphis, Tennessee, 5–6, 12, 15–16, 21, 25, 69–70, 77, 93, 100, 104–105, 171, 175, 178, 232, 237, 263, 268–270, 272–273, 275–276, 284, 305, 319, 408, 448, 454–455, 499, 508, 533, 546
  Battle of, 5
Memphis and Charleston Railroad, 70, 105
Memphis *Evening Bulletin*, 324